R
KB
15
Call
2014
c.6
2w

Canadian Guide to Uniform Legal Citation
8th Edition

D0617355

Manuel canadien de référence juridique
8e édition

CARSWELL®

DALHOUSIE LAW LIBRARY   LIBRARY USE ONLY

© 2014 Dean of the Faculty of Law at McGill University as Trustee of the McGill Law Journal Endowment Fund /
Le Doyen, Faculté de droit, Université McGill Fiduciare du fonds en fiducie de la Revue de droit de McGill

NOTICE AND DISCLAIMER: All rights reserved. No part of this publication may be reproduced, stored in a
retrieval system, or transmitted, in any form or by any means, electronic, mechanical, photocopying, recording or
otherwise, without the prior written consent of the publisher (Carswell).

Carswell and all persons involved in the preparation and sale of this publication disclaim any warranty as to accuracy
or currency of the publication. This publication is provided on the understanding and basis that none of Carswell, the
author's or other persons involved in the creation of this publication shall be responsible for the accuracy or currency
of the contents, or for the results of any action taken on the basis of the information contained in this publication, or
for any errors or omissions contained herein.

No one involved in this publication is attempting herein to render legal, accounting or other professional advice. If
legal advice or other expert assistance is required, the services of a competent professional should be sought. The
analysis contained herein should in no way be construed as being either official or unofficial policy of any govern-
mental body.

ISBN 978-0-7798-6076-0 (bound) – 978-0-7798-6075-3 (pbk)

A cataloguing record for this publication is available from Library and Archives Canada.

CARSWELL, A DIVISION OF THOMSON REUTERS CANADA LIMITED

	Customer Relations
One Corporate Plaza	Toronto 1-416-609-3800
2075 Kennedy Road	Elsewhere in Canada/U.S. 1-800-387-5164
Toronto, Ontario	Fax 1-416-298-5082
M1T 3V4	E-mail www.carswell.com/contact
www.carswell.com	

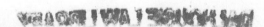

Editions adopted by ~ Éditions adoptées par
Alberta Law Review
Annals of Air and Space Law
Appeal: Review of Current Law and Law Reform
Asian Journal of International Law
Canadian Bar Review ~ Revue du Barreau canadien
Canadian Class Action Review
Canadian Journal of Comparative and Contemporary Law
Canadian Journal of Criminology and Criminal Justice
Canadian Journal of Family Law ~ Revue canadienne de droit familial
Canadian Journal of Human Rights
Canadian Journal of Law and Jurisprudence
Canadian Journal of Law Library Review
Canadian Journal of Law and Technology
Canadian Labour & Employment Law Journal
Constitutional Forum Constitutionnel
Dalhousie Journal of Legal Studies
Dalhousie Law Journal
Health Law Journal
Health Law Review (Alberta)
Indigenous Law Journal
Journal of Arbitration and Mediation ~ Revue d'arbitrage et de médiation
Journal of International Law and International Relations
Journal of Law and Equality
Journal of Law and Social Policy
Manitoba Law Journal
McGill International Journal of Sustainable Development Law and Policy ~ Revue
internationale de droit et politique du développement durable
McGill Journal of Law and Health ~ Revue de droit et santé de McGill
McGill Law Journal ~ Revue de droit de McGill
Osgoode Hall Law Journal
Ottawa Law Review ~ Revue de droit d'Ottawa
Queen's Law Journal
Refuge: Canada's Journal on Refugees
Review of Constitutional Studies ~ Revue d'études constitutionnelles
Revue de droit de l'Université de Sherbrooke
Revue québécoise de droit international
Saskatchewan Law Review
Singapore Journal of Legal Studies
Singapore Law Review
University of British Columbia Law Review
University of New Brunswick Law Journal
University of Toronto Faculty of Law Review
University of Toronto Law Journal
Windsor Review of Legal and Social Issues
Windsor Yearbook of Access to Justice

As of first printing (April 2014), the courts listed below have adopted particular editions of the Guide, or have adopted the Guide with exceptions, as indicated. Please consult with the appropriate court directly in order to determine current practice.

~

Au moment de la première impression (avril 2014), les cours énumérées ci-dessous ont adopté une édition particulière du Manuel, ou ont adopté le Manuel en y apportant quelques exceptions, comme indiqué. S'il vous plaît, consulter directement le tribunal compétent afin de déterminer les pratiques actuelles.

Court of Appeal for British Columbia[‡]
Court of Appeal for New Brunswick ~ Cour d'appel du Nouveau-Brunswick[†]
Supreme Court of Newfoundland and Labrador, Trial Division[††]
Court of Appeal for Ontario[††]
Ontario Superior Court of Justice[††]
Supreme Court of Yukon[‡]
Territorial Court of Yukon[‡]

—

[†] *Seventh Edition ~ septième édition*
[‡] *Seventh Edition with exceptions ~ septième édition avec exceptions*
[††]*Sixth Edition ~ sixième édition*

SUMMARY TABLE OF CONTENTS / TABLE DES MATIÈRES ABRÉGÉE

English

A Word from the Editor .... E-vii
Foreword by the Honourable John I. Laskin .... E-ix
Foreword by the Honourable Nicholas Kasirer .... E-xi

Table of Contents
    1.   General Rules E-3
    2.   Legislation E-23
    3.   Jurisprudence E-49
    4.   Government Documents E-77
    5.   International Materials E-89
    6.   Secondary Sources and Other Materials E-119
    7.   Foreign Sources E-163

Index E-231

French

Mot de le rédacteur .... F-i
Préface par l'honorable Nicholas Kasirer .... F-iii
Préface par l'honorable John I. Laskin .... F-vii

Table des matières
    1.   Règles fondamenales F-3
    2.   Législation F-23
    3.   Jurisprudence F-49
    4.   Documents gouvernementaux F-77
    5.   Documentation internationale F-89
    6.   Doctrine et autres documents F-127
    7.   Sources étrangères F-175

Index F-237

Appendices / Annexes

Table of contents / Table des matières
    A.   Jurisdiction Abbreviations ~ Abréviations des juridictions A-5
    B.   Courts and Tribunals ~ Cours et tribunaux A-13
    C.   Caselaw Reporters ~ Recueils de jurisprudence A-31
    D.   Periodicals and Yearbooks ~ Périodiques et annuaires A-75
    E.   Online Databases ~ Bases de données en ligne A-115

A WORD FROM THE EDITOR

The eighth edition of the *Canadian Guide to Uniform Legal Citation* aims, as did its predecessors, to facilitate effective communication between authors and readers. In order to serve this purpose, every edition of the *Guide* has structured and organized its rules in accordance with the principles of logic, clarity, and accessibility.

This purpose and these principles, however, have always been considered in context. Although it may be among the most prosaic aspects of legal writing, citation form touches every constituency in the legal profession and as such has the widest possible range of stakeholders. What users of this *Guide* will find in its pages is the result of balancing its governing purpose and principles with professional conventions, evolution in legal writing practices, and feedback from users and advisors.

That spirit of balance infuses the whole of the *Guide* from its first page onwards. Even the uniformity that its title declares is tempered: readers will note that some of the adopting courts have specific directives prevailing over the corresponding rules of the *Guide*. Not all legal communities whose citation requirements are addressed by the *Guide*'s rules have—or could ever be expected to have—precisely identical needs. As Justice Laskin's foreword makes clear, each audience has distinct interests. Whether writing articles, briefs of argument, or judgments, legal citation communicates different information to different readers, and the *Guide* aims to provide flexible rules that may be modulated accordingly.

Providing a single, uniform standard in legal citation for the *Guide*'s multilayered multiplicities of stakeholders, communities and audiences is a complex task. In giving context to the circumstances of the *Guide*'s inception, Justice Kasirer's foreword makes mention of both *droit commun* and legal pluralism. We might usefully relate the project of the *Guide* to these ideas. The *Guide*'s editors have worked to address the needs of a plurality of participant voices; but despite differences in perspective, all aim at the common goal of finding a clear and accurate method for communicating the information that legal citation seeks to provide. In such circumstances, the rules collectively settled upon should be approached not as a rigid statute, but rather—as this work's title indicates—a guide.

No shortage of hard work went into this edition. A great debt is owed to Mtre Daniel Boyer (Associate Dean of User Services of the McGill Library and Head Librarian, Nahum Gelber Law Library, McGill University), without whose advice and assistance the *Guide* would not be the institution it has become. Many thanks are also due to both the Honourable Nicholas Kasirer (Judge of the Court of Appeal for Quebec and Researcher at the Paul-André Crépeau Centre for Private and Comparative Law), and the Honourable John I. Laskin (Judge of the Court of Appeal for Ontario), for kindly having taken the time to share their thoughts on legal citation and the *Guide*.

We would also like to thank the Citations Advisory Subcommittee members, Neil Campbell, Mtre Anne-Marie Lizotte, Ilana Ludwin (2012–2013) and Mtre Svetlana Samochkine (2013–2014), for their invaluable counsel on the changes and additions proposed, and for guidance on the publication process; the editors who made up the Citations Committees for volume 58 and 59, Lawrence David, Caitlin Morin, Thang Nguyen, Mark Phillips, Isabelle Rémillard, Michael Shortt, Sara Shearmur, William Stephenson, Nicholas Torti, Aaron Wenner, and Nancy Zagbayou, for their input on the *Guide* and their diligent proofreading of the drafts; and all the law librarians and court officers who provided valuable feedback and excellent suggestions. In addition, my sincere thanks go to the Editor in Chief, the Executive Editors, and the Managing Editor of volume 59 of the *McGill Law Journal*, for their much-appreciated constant support.

I would like to extend a special thank you to my predecessor, Montano Cabezas, for his enormous overall contribution and commitment to the improvement of the *Guide*, and his rigorous attention to detail in the editing process.

Most of all, I would like to thank my wife, Nancy, for her strength, grace, and support throughout the process of bringing this *Guide* to completion.

A. Max Jarvie
Citations Editor
McGill Law Journal, volume 59

If you have any comments or suggestions, please contact us at:

> McGill Law Journal
> 3644 Peel Street
> Montreal (Qc), H3A 1W9
> Canada
>
> Telephone: 514.398.7397
> Fax: 514.398.7360
> **http://lawjournal.mcgill.ca**
> journal.law@mcgill.ca

Foreword by the Honourable John I. Laskin

Every four years, beginning in 1986, the *McGill Law Journal* has published a new edition of the *Canadian Guide to Uniform Legal Citation*. I am delighted to write a foreword to this, the eighth edition of the *Guide*.

The *Guide's* purpose was to establish a uniform standard for legal citation in Canada and a nationally accepted reference. This purpose has largely been achieved. Most Canadian law journals, practitioners and universities, and many courts, have endorsed the *Guide* as the authoritative Canadian reference on legal citation.

As one of many judges who routinely delegate the task of checking the accuracy of citations to their law clerks, I have perhaps been guilty of underestimating the importance of legal citation. But I have come to appreciate its critical importance in the work of the courts—both for readers and writers.

For readers, legal citation serves two significant functions. First, it enables readers to find, quickly and easily, a reliable version of the source cited, be it a court decision or a journal article, and, where appropriate or necessary, to verify and trace the roots of the source. Second, the citation conveys important information about the source. For cases, for example, the citation shows the year the case was decided, the jurisdiction in which it was decided, and the level of the court that made the decision. This information is often needed to assess the importance of the case.

This second function of legal citation has influenced my own judicial writing. Several years ago, I experimented with relegating the legal citations in my judgments to footnotes. The experiment was short-lived. I soon realized that the information conveyed by a legal citation was too important to be left to a footnote; it deserved to be in the body of my reasons.

Thus, legal citation in the courts is not just important for readers; it is important for writers: for judges when they write reasons, and especially for advocates when they write briefs of argument for the court.

By writing briefs that contain thorough and accurate citations, advocates demonstrate that their work is well researched. And by doing so, they enhance their credibility with the courts. On the other hand, most judges take a dim view of the credibility of advocates who, too often, either fail to acknowledge a source, or acknowledge the source but cite it incorrectly.

So far I have written about the general importance of legal citation. I also want to say a few words about this eighth edition of the *Guide* itself. The two qualities of the *Guide* I most appreciate are its clarity and its accessibility. The *Guide* sets out its citation rules in detail, yet does so in a way that makes them easy to locate. It gives clear explanations for its rules, and it provides numerous examples to make the rules easier to apply.

I also appreciate the flexibility that the *Guide* provides for applying many of its rules. The writer often has the option of giving additional information where it would be helpful to the reader. Where practical, the eighth edition expands on this flexibility for some of the rules, and thus increases their general utility.

The authors of the *Guide*—the past and current editors of the *McGill Law Journal*—have given all of us who work in the law—judges, practitioners, academics, and legal publishers—a superb and invaluable resource. For producing and updating the *Guide*, we owe them an irredeemable debt of gratitude.

John Laskin
Court of Appeal for Ontario
January 2014

Foreword by the Honourable Nicholas Kasirer

The title of this important book gives the reader only a gentle hint as to the ambitions of its editors: in point of fact, this *Guide* is no mere guide; it rightly has the aspiration to set a standard—a "référence" to cite the French title, and one that is "Uniform" at that—for all legal citations in Canada.[1] It is fair to see standard-setting as the unstated goal upon which this great adventure in legal methodology rests. Now in its eighth edition, the McGill Red Book is best understood not just as a "cite guide" but as something of a "site of normativity" for Canadian law as well.

"Adopted"[2] by numerous learned journals, courts and tribunals, students, practitioners, and scholars, there seems little doubt that the *Guide* has earned its place in the legal order. To what extent, then, does "ordering" play a part in this success? Certainly the *Guide* has brought a measure of order to the law's chaos—at the very least in the secondary sense spoken to by Jean Carbonnier who saw in the legal order "une simple nécessité d'hygiène sociale".[3] But in taming some of the confusion with which Canadian jurists marshalled legal authorities prior to its first edition, the *Guide* has also self-consciously imposed a discipline on its readers. In this sense, the McGill Red Book would seem to have a plainly normative ambition.[4] To what extent should this book on sources of the law be considered a source of law itself?

It is hard to imagine that the editors of the first edition that appeared in 1986 did not harbour ambitions beyond indicating the proper etiquette for deploying square brackets and commas in legal texts. When one recalls that they were all students in the Faculty at a time when their professors were deeply engaged in a critical inquiry as to the nature of law and its proper sources, it would be right to surmise that the editors of the day hoped to shape the path of the law in their own way too. Certainly, the idea that law found expression outside the statute books and the law reports was voiced in the Faculty's finest scholarship of the day: concerns about what constitutes "persuasive authority" in law;[5] about the recognition of law's "normativité implicite et 'inférentielle';"[6] about the wide range

---

1   Are the normative ambitions of the work alluded to differently in the French and English titles of the McGill Red Book? A "guide" is primarily a directing principle or a person who leads the way by example (generally something more than a guidebook); a *manuel* is merely a book of instructions, as in the *Chicago Manual of Style*. While there is room for shared meaning between guide and *manuel*, where is the word "uniform" in the French title? Is it implied in the word "référence"? On the happy idea that French and English should be read together to form one text in Canadian law, see Roderick Macdonald, "Legal Bilingualism" (1997) 42:1 McGill LJ 119.

2   The editors use this soft term as if to suggest that the choice to adhere to the *Guide* was not imposed by some norm—an emerging custom?—other than free will. See the impressive list of journals and tribunals having adopted the *Guide*, above at E-iii–E-iv.

3   Jean Carbonnier, *Droit civil I : Introduction, Les personnes, La famille*, (Paris: Presses Universitaires de France & Quadrige, 2004) No 105.

4   There are examples on every page of this new edition of the *Guide*. See e.g. the distinctions drawn (and the rules to follow) in differentiating "See e.g." from "See", "See also", "See especially", "See generally", "But see" and the all-seeing "*Contra*": below at E-8.

5   H Patrick Glenn, "Persuasive Authority" (1987) 32:2 McGill LJ 261.

6   Roderick Macdonald, "Pour la reconnaissance d'une normativité juridique implicite et « inférentielle »" (1986) 18 Sociologie et sociétés 47.

of legal artifacts relevant to discovering the sources of obligations;[7] about ideas of the *droit commun* lying outside of enactment;[8] about the far flung sources that must be canvassed to account for a legal culture,[9] and more. Echoing through that first edition of the *Guide* is the not so crazy idea that a group of students in the Faculty basement could have a hand in law-in-the-making. Today's editors are modest about their role and even take care not to prescribe a "hierarchy of sources" on unsuspecting readers.[10] But the *Guide* is without question a leading example of what civilians consider to be "doctrine as a source of law."[11]

And the *Guide* seeks to shape behaviour for Canadian jurists mindful that it does so from the trans-systemic vantage point that McGill offers on the law. The editors' superbly sophisticated perspective on language is a prime example. It matters not, they counsel, whether one is writing in Lyons or Lyon, Londres or London but whether one writes in English or French.[12] There are principled exceptions—the title to the *Civil Code of Québec*, trans-systemic Latin, one aspect of the style of cause before bilingual courts[13]—all explained in lucid prose in both languages. The editors write of their extraordinary linguistic achievement with great humility: "The *Guide* is a Canadian work and applies to texts written in the country's two official languages."[14] Few in Canada are as well placed as McGill student editors to do so with as much *savoir-vivre*.

Elsewhere, there are small hints of the influence of McGill's unique legal episte-mology: abbreviations for the Institutes of Justinian, the Digest and the Codex stand only a few pages from *Halsbury's Laws of England*; no confusion here between the status of the Civil Code and the Criminal Code in the list of enact-ments;[15] and there is a catalogue of "foreign sources" that nomadically straddles, seemingly without effort, the common law–civil law divide. This new edition of the *Guide* has appeared in the heady air and infinite space of a faculty of law domi-nated by an ever more ambitious approach to law's disparate sources, resolutely comparative and pluralist in its assumptions. At the very least, the *Guide* has expanded the compass of what can and should be cited as law in Canada, whether those sources are styled as international, foreign or even micro-systemic. As others

---

[7] Paul-André Crépeau, *Théorie générale de l'obligation juridique : Éléments d'une introduction* (Montreal: McGill University & Quebec Research Centre of Private and Comparative Law, 1987).

[8] John EC Brierley, "Quebec's 'Common Laws' (droits communs): How Many Are There?" in Ernest Caparros, ed, *Mélanges Louis-Philippe Pigeon* (Montreal: Wilson Lafleur, 1989) at 109.

[9] G Blaine Baker et al, *Sources in the Law Library of McGill University for a Reconstruction of the Legal Culture of Quebec, 1760-1890* (Montreal: McGill University & Montreal Business History Project, 1987).

[10] When the editors direct that in citing cases, one must always follow the "hierarchy of sources", their concern is not for Kelsen's pyramid but for distinguishing more "authoritative" sources of case citation, such as neutral cites, from unofficial case reporting: see below at E-49.

[11] See John EC Brierley and Roderick Macdonald, eds, *Quebec Civil Law* (Toronto: Emond Montgomery, 1993) No 102.

[12] The editors explain the "rule" as follows: "[w]hen writing in English, use the English citation rules regardless of the language of the source," and vice versa: see below at E-7.

[13] This latter exception is particularly nuanced: when does one use "*v*" (for "versus") as opposed to "*c*" (for "contre") in recording the style of cause of decided cases? The editors explain: "The use of *v* and *c* in the style of cause indicates the language of the decision. If the decision is in English, use *v*. If the decision is in French, use *c*. If the decision is bilingual, use *v* if you are writing in English" [and *c* if you are writing in French] (E-51, below).

[14] E-18, below.

[15] See E-23, E-34, below.

rightly celebrate McGill's focus on legal pluralism as "a description of what law is like,"[16] the *Guide* reflects in concrete form the fact that the Faculty of Law has been "navigating the trans-systemic"[17] for well over a decade.

The *Guide* is not a manual for a new legal order or some imagined polyjural place, but the expression of a way of knowing law that embodies—to the enduring credit of the editors—the highest aspirations for trans-systemic scholarship, thereby honouring the Faculty of Law at McGill University.

Nicholas Kasirer
Judge of the Court of Appeal for Quebec
Researcher at the Paul-André Crépeau Centre
for Private and Comparative Law
January 2014

---

[16] Sally Engle Merry, "McGill Convocation Address: Legal Pluralism in Practice" (2013) 59:1 McGill LJ 1 at 2.
[17] Shauna Van Praagh, "Navigating the Transsystemic: A Course Syllabus" (2005) 50:4 McGill LJ 701.

TABLE OF CONTENTS

E — A WORD FROM THE EDITOR..E-vii

E — FOREWORD BY THE HONOURABLE JOHN I. LASKIN .... E-ix

E — FOREWORD BY THE HONOURABLE NICHOLAS KASIRER......... E-xi

E — 1 GENERAL RULES..E-3

E -1.1 Bibliographies / Tables of Authorities E-3

E -1.2 In-text References — Memorandum and Factum E-4
    E -1.2.1 Memorandum...E-5
    E -1.2.2 Factum...E-5

E -1.3 Footnotes: Rules E-6
    E -1.3.1 When to Footnote E-6
    E -1.3.2 How to Indicate a Footnote in the Text................E-6
    E -1.3.3 Where Footnotes Appear............................E-7
    E -1.3.4 When to Combine Footnotes E-7
    E -1.3.5 Citation of Non-English Sources E-7
    E -1.3.6 Introductory Signals E-7
    E -1.3.7 Parenthetical Information Within Footnotes...........E-9

E -1.4 Prior and Subsequent References to a Citation............ E-9
    E -1.4.1 Establishing a Short Form E-9
      E -1.4.1.1 General Rules...........................E-9
      E -1.4.1.2 Legislation................................ E-10
      E -1.4.1.3 Cases E-10
      E -1.4.1.4 Secondary Materials E-11
    E -1.4.2 *Ibid.*... E-12
    E -1.4.3 *Supra*... E-12
    E -1.4.4 *Infra* E-13
    E -1.4.5 Above and Below................................ E-13

E -1.5 Pinpoints E-13

E -1.6 Online Resources.. E-14

E -1.7 Citing Sources that Quote or Reprint the Original Source E-15
    E -1.7.1 Obscure Original Source E-15
    E -1.7.2 Emphasis on the Citing Source E-16

E -1.8 General Rules for Quotations................................... E-17
    E -1.8.1 Positioning of Quotations................................ E-17
    E -1.8.2 Format of Quotations E-17
    E -1.8.3 Quoting a Source in Another Language............. E-18

E -1.9 Writing in a Foreign Language E-18

E — 2 LEGISLATION E-23

E -2.1 Statutes E-23

E -2.1.1 General Form... E-23
E -2.1.2 Point in Time Citations.. E-24
E -2.1.3 Sources... E-24
E -2.1.4 Title.. E-27
E -2.1.5 Revised Statutes and Annual Volumes................................. E-28
E -2.1.6 Loose-leafs.. E-28
E -2.1.7 Jurisdiction E-29
E -2.1.8 Year, Session, and Supplement E-30
E -2.1.9 Chapter E-31
E -2.1.10 Pinpoint E-31
E -2.1.11 Amendments, Repeals, and Re-enactments E-32
E -2.1.12 Appendices E-32
E -2.1.13 Statutes Within Statutes... E-33

E -2.2   Constitutional Statutes E-33
E -2.2.1 Pinpoint E-34

E -2.3   Codes E-34

E -2.4   Bills E-35

E -2.5   Regulations E-36
E -2.5.1 Federal Regulations.. E-36
        E -2.5.1.1 Revised Regulations E-36
        E -2.5.1.2 Unrevised Regulations.. E-37
E -2.5.2 Provincial and Territorial Regulations................................... E-37
        E -2.5.2.1 Alberta, British Columbia E-37
        E -2.5.2.2 Manitoba... E-37
        E -2.5.2.3 New Brunswick... E-38
        E -2.5.2.4 Newfoundland and Labrador.................................. E-38
                E -2.5.2.4.1 Unrevised E-38
                E -2.5.2.4.2 Revised... E-38
        E -2.5.2.5 Northwest Territories... E-38
                E -2.5.2.5.1 Unrevised E-38
                E -2.5.2.5.2 Revised... E-39
        E -2.5.2.6 Nova Scotia... E-39
        E -2.5.2.7 Nunavut.. E-39
        E -2.5.2.8 Ontario.. E-39
                E -2.5.2.8.1 Unrevised E-39
                E -2.5.2.8.2 Revised... E-39
        E -2.5.2.9 Prince Edward Island E-40
        E -2.5.2.10 Quebec E-40
                E -2.5.2.10.1 Historical Versions.................................. E-40
                E -2.5.2.10.2 Current Version (Cited to the Compilation
                            of Quebec Laws and Regulations) E-40
        E -2.5.2.11 Saskatchewan.. E-40
                E -2.5.2.11.1 Unrevised E-40
                E -2.5.2.11.2 Revised... E-40
        E -2.5.2.12 Yukon E-41

E -2.6   Other Information Published in Gazettes E-41
E -2.6.1 General Form.. E-41

E -2.6.2 Orders in Council E-42
      E -2.6.2.1 Federal.. E-43
      E -2.6.2.2 Provincial and Territorial.................................. E-43
E -2.6.3 Proclamations and Royal Instructions E-44

E -2.7 Municipal By-laws.. E-44

E -2.8 Rules of Practice... E-45

E -2.9 Securities Commissions E-46

E — 3 JURISPRUDENCE E-49

E -3.1 Sources E-49

E -3.2 General Form E-50
E -3.2.1 Neutral Citation Available E-50
E -3.2.2 Neutral Citation Not Available E-50

E -3.3 Style of Cause E-51
E -3.3.1 Names of Parties E-51
E -3.3.2 Person Represented by Guardian or Tutor E-52
E -3.3.3 Names of Companies and Partnerships................................. E-52
E -3.3.4 Countries, Federal Units, Provinces, and Municipalities............ E-52
E -3.3.5 Wills and Estates E-53
E -3.3.6 Bankruptcies and Receiverships.. E-53
E -3.3.7 Statute Titles.. E-53
E -3.3.8 The Crown E-53
E -3.3.9 Government Entities... E-54
E -3.3.10 Crown Corporations E-54
E -3.3.11 Municipal Boards and Bodies E-55
E -3.3.12 School Boards E-55
E -3.3.13 Unions E-55
E -3.3.14 Social Welfare Agencies E-55
E -3.3.15 Parties' Names that are Undisclosed E-55
E -3.3.16 If The Case Is Known Under Two Names—The Sub Nom Rule... E-56
E -3.3.17 One Party Acting for Someone Else—The Ex Rel Rule............ E-56
E -3.3.18 Procedural Phrases and Constitutional References................. E-56

E -3.4 Year of Decision... E-57

E -3.5 Neutral Citation E-57
E -3.5.1 Year E-58
E -3.5.2 Tribunal Identifier E-58
E -3.5.3 Decision Number E-59

E -3.6 Pinpoint... E-60
E -3.6.1 General Form.. E-60
E -3.6.2 Cited Reporter.. E-60

E -3.7 Printed Reporter... E-61
E -3.7.1 Year of Reporter E-61
E -3.7.2 Reporter E-62
      E -3.7.2.1 Official Reporters E-62
      E -3.7.2.2 Semi-Official Reporters.................................. E-62

E -3.7.2.3 Unofficial Reporters E-63

E -3.7.3 Series E-63

E -3.7.4 First Page E-64

E -3.8 Online Databases.. E-64

E -3.8.1 Published Judgments and Judgments with a Neutral Citation E-64

E -3.8.2 Unpublished Judgments With No Neutral Citation.................. E-65

E -3.8.2.1 CanLII.. E-65

E -3.8.2.2 Quicklaw.. E-65

E -3.8.2.3 Westlaw Canada.. E-65

E -3.8.2.4 Azimut E-66

E -3.8.2.5 Other Services E-66

E -3.9 Jurisdiction and Court E-66

E -3.10 Judge E-67

E -3.11 History of Case E-68

E -3.11.1 Prior History.. E-68

E -3.11.2 Subsequent History... E-68

E -3.11.3 Prior and Subsequent History E-69

E -3.11.4 Leave to Appeal... E-69

E -3.12 Unreported Decisions Without a Neutral Citation E-71

E -3.13 Interlocutory Judgments and Motions.. E-72

E -3.14 Administrative Bodies and Tribunals E-72

E -3.14.1 Decisions in Printed Reporters................................ E-72

E -3.14.1 Online Decisions E-73

E -3.15 Arguments and Evidentiary Documents............................. E-73

E — 4 GOVERNMENT DOCUMENTS E-77

E -4.1 Parliamentary Papers.. E-77

E -4.1.1 Debates... E-77

E -4.1.2 Journals... E-78

E -4.1.3 Order Papers E-78

E -4.1.4 Sessional Papers E-79

E -4.1.5 Votes and Proceedings... E-79

E -4.1.6 Reports Published in Debates................................... E-80

E -4.1.7 Reports Published Separately................................... E-80

E -4.2 Non-parliamentary Documents E-80

E -4.2.1 General Form.. E-81

E -4.2.1.1 Reports, Manuals, and Other Book-length
Publications E-81

E -4.2.1.2 Articles, Bulletins, and Other Short Publications....... E-82

E -4.2.2 Tax Interpretation Bulletins (ITs) and Information Circulars (ICs)... E-83

E -4.2.3 Reports of Inquiries and Commissions E-84

E -4.2.3.1 Reports Published Under a Single Title E-84

E -4.2.3.2 Reports Published Under Multiple Titles E-84

E -4.2.4 Public Papers of Intergovernmental Conferences E-85

E — 5 INTERNATIONAL MATERIALS..E-89

E -5.1 International Documents.. E-89
 E -5.1.1 Treaties, UN Documents, and Other International Agreements ... E-89
  E -5.1.1.1 Australian Treaty Neutral Citation E-92
 E -5.1.2 United Nations Documents.. E-92
  E -5.1.2.1 Charter of the United Nations E-92
  E -5.1.2.2 Official Records E-92
   E -5.1.2.2.1 Meetings...................................... E-93
   E -5.1.2.2.2 Supplements................................. E-94
   E -5.1.2.2.3 Annexes E-95
  E -5.1.2.3 UN Masthead Documents (Mimeographs) E-95
  E -5.1.2.4 Periodicals E-96
  E -5.1.2.5 Yearbooks.. E-96
  E -5.1.2.6 Sales Publications E-96
 E -5.1.3 European Union Documents.. E-96
  E -5.1.3.1 Regulations, Directives, and Decisions.................. E-96
  E -5.1.3.2 Debates of the European Parliament E-97
  E -5.1.3.3 Other Documents E-98
 E -5.1.4 Council of Europe Documents E-98
 E -5.1.5 Organization of American States Documents E-99
 E -5.1.6 World Trade Organization (WTO) and the General Agreement
  on Tariffs and Trade (GATT) Documents E-100
 E -5.1.7 Organisation for Economic Co-operation and Development
  (OECD) Documents E-101
 E -5.1.8 First Nations Treaties E-102

E -5.2 Cases E-102
 E -5.2.1 Permanent Court of International Justice (1922–1946)............E-102
  E -5.2.1.1 Judgments, Orders, and Advisory Opinions E-102
  E -5.2.1.2 Pleadings, Oral Arguments, and Documents..........E-103
 E -5.2.2 International Court of Justice (1946–present) E-103
  E -5.2.2.1 Judgments, Orders, and Advisory Opinions E-104
  E -5.2.2.2 Pleadings, Oral Arguments, and Documents..........E-104
 E -5.2.3 Court of Justice of the European Communities and European
  Court of First Instance E-105
 E -5.2.4 European Court of Human Rights and European Commission
  of Human Rights...E-105
  E -5.2.4.1 Before 1999...E-105
  E -5.2.4.2 1999 and Later..E-106
 E -5.2.5 Inter-American Court of Human Rights...............................E-107
  E -5.2.5.1 Judgments, Orders, and Advisory Opinions E-107
  E -5.2.5.2 Pleadings, Oral Arguments, and Documents..........E-107
 E -5.2.6 Inter-American Commission on Human Rights.....................E-108
 E -5.2.7 International Criminal Tribunals E-108
 E -5.2.8 General Agreement on Tariffs and Trade (GATT) 1947 Panel
  Reports E-109
 E -5.2.9 World Trade Organization (WTO) Panel and Appellate Body
  Reports E-110

E -5.2.10 Canada-United States Free Trade Agreement Panels E-111
E -5.2.11 North American Free Trade Agreement (NAFTA)
            Binational Panels E-111
E -5.2.12 International Arbitration Cases E-112
E -5.2.13 World Intellectual Property Organization (WIPO)
            Arbitration Cases E-112
        E -5.2.13.1 Uniform Domain Name Dispute Resolution
                     Policy (UDRP)...E-112
E -5.2.14 International Law Cases Decided Before National Courts E-113

E -5.3   Websites E-113

E — 6 SECONDARY SOURCES AND OTHER MATERIALS......E-119

E -6.1   Periodicals..E-119
        E -6.1.1 General Form..E-119
        E -6.1.2 Author..E-119
                 E -6.1.2.1 Single Author E-119
                 E -6.1.2.2 Joint Authors.......................................E-119
        E -6.1.3 Title of Article...E-120
        E -6.1.4 Year of Publication E-120
        E -6.1.5 Volume, Issue, and Series....................................E-120
        E -6.1.6 Title of Journal E-121
                 E -6.1.6.1 France E-122
        E -6.1.7 First Page of Article E-122
                 E -6.1.7.1 Article Published in Parts......................E-122
        E -6.1.8 Pinpoint..E-123

E -6.2   Books E-124
        E -6.2.1 General Form..E-124
        E -6.2.2 Author..E-125
                 E -6.2.2.1 Single Author E-125
                 E -6.2.2.2 Joint Authors.......................................E-125
                 E -6.2.2.3 Editor of a Collection............................E-125
                 E -6.2.2.4 Editor or Reviser of the Text of Another E-126
                           E -6.2.2.4.1 Author's Name is Part of the Title E-126
                           E -6.2.2.4.2 Author's Name is Not Part of the
                                        Title...E-126
                 E -6.2.2.5 Translator E-126
                           E -6.2.2.5.1 Published Translation E-126
                           E -6.2.2.5.2 Providing a Translation E-127
        E -6.2.3 Title..E-127
                 E -6.2.3.1 Published Proceedings of Conferences or
                             Symposia...E-128
        E -6.2.4 Volume Number...E-128
                 E -6.2.4.1 Books in English E-128
                           E -6.2.4.1.1 Volumes Published Under Separate
                                        Titles E-128
                           E -6.2.4.1.2 Volumes Published Under a Single
                                        Title...E-128

E -6.2.4.2 Books in French...E-129
E -6.2.5 Edition..E-129
E -6.2.6 Books in Loose-leaf Form.................................E-129
E -6.2.7 Place of Publication E-130
E -6.2.8 Publisher E-130
E -6.2.9 Year of Publication E-131
E -6.2.10 Pinpoint..E-132

E -6.3 Collections of Essays...E-132

E -6.4 Dictionaries & Encyclopedias E-133
E -6.4.1 General Dictionaries.......................................E-133
E -6.4.2 Specialized Dictionaries E-133
E -6.4.3 Encyclopedias E-134

E -6.5 Encyclopedic Digests...E-134
E -6.5.1 Canadian Encyclopedic Digest..........................E-134
E -6.5.1.1 CED Print Edition E-134
E -6.5.1.2 CED Online Edition...........................E-135
E -6.5.2 Halsbury's Laws of Canada...............................E-135
E -6.5.2.1 Halsbury's Laws of Canada Print Edition E-135
E -6.5.2.2 Halsbury's Laws of Canada Online Edition E-136
E -6.5.3 Common Law...E-136
E -6.5.4 France E-136
E -6.5.4.1 General Form...................................E-136
E -6.5.4.2 Subject Headings E-137

E -6.6 Codes of Professional Conduct E-138

E -6.7 Arbitration Cases..E-138
E -6.7.1 Published Arbitration Cases E-138
E -6.7.2 Unpublished Arbitration Cases E-139

E -6.8 Book Reviews E-139

E -6.9 Case Comments and Comments on Legislation E-140
E -6.9.1 France E-140
E -6.9.1.1 Annotation......................................E-140
E -6.9.1.2 Comments Published in General Reporters E-141

E -6.10 Comments, Remarks, and Notes...................................E-141

E -6.11 Historical Legal Materials...E-142
E -6.11.1 Roman Law...E-142
E -6.11.2 Canon Law..E-143
E -6.11.3 Talmudic Law...E-143

E -6.12 Unpublished Manuscripts...E-144
E -6.12.1 General Form...E-144
E -6.12.2 Forthcoming Manuscripts..................................E-144
E -6.12.3 Theses and Dissertations E-145

E -6.13 Addresses and Papers Delivered at Conferences.....................E-146

E -6.14 Course Materials E-146

E -6.15 Magazines...E-147

E -6.16 Newspapers, Newswires, and Other News Sources..................E-148
    E -6.16.1 Editorials and Letters to the Editor E-149

E -6.17 News Releases E-149

E -6.18 Letters, Memoranda, and Interviews E-150

E -6.19 Archival Materials E-150

E -6.20 Intellectual property E-151
    E -6.20.1 Patents...E-151
    E -6.20.2 Trade-marks E-151
    E -6.20.3 Copyright E-152

E -6.21 Working Papers E-152

E -6.22 Electronic Sources..E-153
    E -6.22.1 Online Databases...E-153
    E -6.22.2 Online Journals (eJournals)..E-154
    E -6.22.3 Websites...E-154
        E -6.22.3.1 Web Logs (Blogs)......................................E-154
            E -6.22.3.1.1 Posts E-154
            E -6.22.3.1.2 Comments...................................E-155
        E -6.22.3.2 Social Media...E-155
            E -6.22.3.2.1 Twitter Posts (Tweets)..................E-155
            E -6.22.3.2.2 Facebook Posts..........................E-155
            E -6.22.3.2.3 Reddit Posts E-156
        E -6.22.3.3 Online Video & Video Aggregators E-156
    E -6.22.4 Other Digital Media...E-156
    E -6.22.5 Digital Object Identifiers E-157

E — 7 FOREIGN SOURCES E-163

E -7.1 Common Law Jurisdictions E-163
    E -7.1.1 General Form..E-163
    E -7.1.2 Style of Cause, Pinpoint, Short Form, and Case History E-163
    E -7.1.3 Year E-163
    E -7.1.4 Neutral Citation, Printed Reporter, Online Database, or
          Unreported Decision E-164
    E -7.1.5 Jurisdiction and Court...E-164
    E -7.1.6 Judge E-165

E -7.2 Civil Law Jurisdictions E-165

E -7.3 United Kingdom E-166
    E -7.3.1 Legislation..E-166
        E -7.3.1.1 Statutes...E-166
            E -7.3.1.1.1 Northern Ireland...........................E-166
                E -7.3.1.1.1.1 Legislation Passed by
                        the United Kingdom E-166
                E -7.3.1.1.1.2 Legislation Passed by
                        Northern Ireland..........E-166
            E -7.3.1.1.2 Scotland E-167
            E -7.3.1.1.3 Wales E-167

E -7.3.1.2 Bills E-168
    E -7.3.1.2.1 United Kingdom E-168
    E -7.3.1.2.2 Northern Ireland...........................E-168
    E -7.3.1.2.3 Scotland E-168
E -7.3.1.3 Regulations E-169
    E -7.3.1.3.1 United Kingdom E-169
    E -7.3.1.3.2 Northern Ireland Regulations and
                  Orders E-169
    E -7.3.1.3.3 Scotland E-170
        E -7.3.1.3.3.1 Regulations Passed by the
                     United Kingdom...........E-170
        E -7.3.1.3.3.2 Regulations Passed by the
                     Scottish Parliament E-170
    E -7.3.1.3.4 Wales E-170
E -7.3.2 Jurisprudence...E-171
    E -7.3.2.1 General Form....................................E-171
    E -7.3.2.2 Neutral Citation.................................E-171
    E -7.3.2.3 Appeal Courts E-171
    E -7.3.2.4 High Court.......................................E-172
    E -7.3.2.5 Reporter E-172
        E -7.3.2.5.1 Law Reports E-172
            E -7.3.2.5.1.1 From 1875–1890.........E-173
            E -7.3.2.5.1.2 From 1865–1875.........E-173
            E -7.3.2.5.1.3 From 1537–1865.........E-173
            E -7.3.2.5.1.4 Retroactive Neutral
                     Citation.....................E-174
    E -7.3.2.6 Yearbooks......................................E-174
    E -7.3.2.7 Reprints..E-174
    E -7.3.2.8 Scotland, Ireland, and Northern Ireland E-175
        E -7.3.2.8.1 Neutral Citation............................E-175
            E -7.3.2.8.1.1 Scotland E-175
            E -7.3.2.8.1.2 Ireland......................E-176
            E -7.3.2.8.1.3 Northern Ireland..........E-176
    E -7.3.2.9 Judge E-176
    E -7.3.2.10 Online Databases E-177
        E -7.3.2.10.1 BAILII E-177
        E -7.3.2.10.2 Service with No Identifier (Justis).......E-177
E -7.3.3 Government Documents...................................E-177
    E -7.3.3.1 Debates..E-177
        E -7.3.3.1.1 Before 1803................................E-177
        E -7.3.3.1.2 1803 and After E-178
    E -7.3.3.2 Journals...E-179
    E -7.3.3.3 Parliamentary Papers E-179
    E -7.3.3.4 Non-parliamentary Papers E-180
E -7.4 United States E-181
  E -7.4.1 Legislation...E-181
    E -7.4.1.1 Federal and State Constitutions E-181
    E -7.4.1.2 Federal and State Statutes E-182

E -7.4.1.2.1 Codes E-182
E -7.4.1.2.2 Session Laws E-184
E -7.4.1.2.3 Unofficial Reporters of Session Laws ... E-185
E -7.4.1.3 Uniform Codes, Uniform Acts, and Restatements E-185
E -7.4.1.4 Bills and Resolutions E-186
E -7.4.1.4.1 Federal Bills E-186
E -7.4.1.4.2 Federal Resolutions E-186
E -7.4.1.4.3 State Bills and Resolutions E-187
E -7.4.1.5 Regulations E-188
E -7.4.1.5.1 The Code of Federal Regulations E-188
E -7.4.1.5.2 Administrative Registers E-188
E -7.4.2 Jurisprudence E-189
E -7.4.2.1 General Form E-189
E -7.4.2.2 Style of Cause E-189
E -7.4.2.3 Neutral Citation E-189
E -7.4.2.4 Reporter and Series E-190
E -7.4.2.5 Pinpoint E-191
E -7.4.2.6 Court E-192
E -7.4.2.6.1 Federal Courts E-192
E -7.4.2.6.2 State Courts E-192
E -7.4.2.7 Year of Decision E-192
E -7.4.2.8 Online Databases E-193
E -7.4.2.8.1 Westlaw E-193
E -7.4.2.8.2 Lexis E-193
E -7.4.3 Government Documents E-193
E -7.4.3.1 Debates E-193
E -7.4.3.2 Committee Hearings E-194
E -7.4.3.2.1 Federal E-194
E -7.4.3.2.2 State E-194
E -7.4.3.3 Reports and Documents E-195
E -7.4.3.3.1 Federal E-195
E -7.4.3.3.1.1 Numbered Documents
and Reports E-195
E -7.4.3.3.1.2 Unnumbered Documents
and Committee Prints ... E-196
E -7.4.3.3.2 State E-196

E -7.5 France E-197
E -7.5.1 Legislation E-197
E -7.5.1.1 Statutes and Other Legislative Instruments E-197
E -7.5.1.2 Codes E-197
E -7.5.2 Jurisprudence E-198
E -7.5.2.1 General Form E-198
E -7.5.2.2 Court E-198
E -7.5.2.2.1 Courts of First Instance E-198
E -7.5.2.2.2 Court of Appeal E-199
E -7.5.2.2.3 Cour de cassation E-199
E -7.5.2.2.4 Conseil d'État E-200
E -7.5.2.2.5 Conseil constitutionnel E-200

E -7.5.2.3 Style of Cause...E-201
E -7.5.2.4 Year...E-201
E -7.5.2.5 Session...E-201
E -7.5.2.6 Reporter...E-201
E -7.5.2.7 Section...E-202
E -7.5.2.8 Page and Decision Number............................E-203
E -7.5.2.9 Pinpoint...E-203
E -7.5.2.10 Parallel Citation...E-203
E -7.5.2.11 Annotations, Reports, and Conclusions...........E-203
E -7.5.3 Government Documents.....................................E-203
    E -7.5.3.1 Debates...E-204
        E -7.5.3.1.1 From 1787 to 1860.......................E-204
        E -7.5.3.1.2 1871 to the Present.......................E-204
    E -7.5.3.2 Earlier Versions of the Journal officiel...........E-205
    E -7.5.3.3 Parliamentary Documents................................E-206
        E -7.5.3.3.1 Travaux et réunions parlementaires....E-206
        E -7.5.3.3.2 Rapports d'information (Reports).......E-207
    E -7.5.3.4 Non-parliamentary Documents.........................E-208

E -7.6 Australia...E-208
  E -7.6.1 Legislation...E-208
    E -7.6.1.1 Statutes...E-208
    E -7.6.1.2 Delegated Legislation (Regulations)...................E-209
  E -7.6.2 Jurisprudence...E-210
    E -7.6.2.1 General Form..E-210
    E -7.6.2.2 Neutral Citation..E-210
    E -7.6.2.3 Reporter..E-211
        E -7.6.2.3.1 Law Reports...............................E-211
    E -7.6.2.4 Jurisdiction and Court....................................E-212
  E -7.6.3 Government Documents.....................................E-212
    E -7.6.3.1 Debates...E-213
    E -7.6.3.2 Parliamentary Papers......................................E-213
    E -7.6.3.3 Non-Parliamentary Papers................................E-214
    E -7.6.3.4 Ministerial Documents....................................E-214

E -7.7 New Zealand...E-215
  E -7.7.1 Legislation...E-215
    E -7.7.1.1 Statutes...E-215
    E -7.7.1.2 Delegated Legislation (Regulations)...................E-215
  E -7.7.2 Jurisprudence...E-216
    E -7.7.2.1 General Form..E-216
    E -7.7.2.2 Neutral Citation..E-216
    E -7.7.2.3 Reporter..E-216
        E -7.7.2.3.1 Law Reports...............................E-216
    E -7.7.2.4 Court...E-218
  E -7.7.3 Government Documents.....................................E-218
    E -7.7.3.1 Debates...E-218
    E -7.7.3.2 Parliamentary Papers......................................E-219

E -7.8 Singapore..E-220

E -7.8.1 Legislation...E-220
        E -7.8.1.1 Constitutional Documents E-220
        E -7.8.1.2 Statutes..E-220
        E -7.8.1.3 Amendments and Repeals..................................E-221
        E -7.8.1.4 English Statutes Applicable in Singapore E-221
        E -7.8.1.5 Subsidiary Legislation (Rules, Regulations,
                    Notifications, Orders).......................................E-221
                 E -7.8.1.5.1 Revised...E-221
                 E -7.8.1.5.2 Unrevised E-222
        E -7.8.2 Jurisprudence..E-222
        E -7.8.2.1 General Form...E-222
        E -7.8.2.2 Neutral Citation...E-223
        E -7.8.2.3 Reporters...E-223
        E -7.8.2.4 Court E-223
        E -7.8.2.5 Unreported Decisions without Neutral Citation........E-224
        E -7.8.2.6 Online Databases...E-224
    E -7.8.3 Government Documents...E-224
        E -7.8.3.1 Parliamentary Debates E-224
        E -7.8.3.2 Supreme Court Practice Directions.......................E-224
                 E -7.8.3.2.1 Consolidated Practice Directions E-225
                 E -7.8.3.2.2 Amendments to Practice Directions....E-225

E -7.9 South Africa..E-225
    E -7.9.1 Legislation...E-225
        E -7.9.1.1 Statutes...E-225
        E -7.9.1.2 Amendments and Repeals..................................E-225
        E -7.9.1.2 Bills E-226
    E -7.9.2 Jurisprudence..E-226
        E -7.9.2.1 General Form...E-226
        E -7.9.2.2 Neutral Citation...E-226
        E -7.9.2.3 Reporters...E-227
        E -7.9.2.4 Court E-228
    E -7.9.3 Government Documents...E-228
        E -7.9.3.1 Debates...E-228
        E -7.9.3.2 Reports, Discussion Papers, and Issue Papers E-229

Index E-231

General Rules

1   General Rules E-3

E -1.1 Bibliographies / Tables of Authorities E-3

E -1.2 In-text References — Memorandum and Factum E-4
    E -1.2.1 Memorandum E-5
    E -1.2.2 Factum E-5

E -1.3 Footnotes: Rules E-6
    E -1.3.1 When to Footnote E-6
    E -1.3.2 How to Indicate a Footnote in the Text E-6
    E -1.3.3 Where Footnotes Appear E-7
    E -1.3.4 When to Combine Footnotes E-7
    E -1.3.5 Citation of Non-English Sources E-7
    E -1.3.6 Introductory Signals E-7
    E -1.3.7 Parenthetical Information Within Footnotes E-9

E -1.4 Prior and Subsequent References to a Citation E-9
    E -1.4.1 Establishing a Short Form E-9
        E -1.4.1.1 General Rules E-9
        E -1.4.1.2 Legislation E-10
        E -1.4.1.3 Cases E-10
        E -1.4.1.4 Secondary Materials E-11
    E -1.4.2 *Ibid.* E-12
    E -1.4.3 *Supra* E-12
    E -1.4.4 *Infra* E-13
    E -1.4.5 Above and Below E-13

E -1.5 Pinpoints E-13

E -1.6 Online Resources E-14

E -1.7 Citing Sources that Quote or Reprint the Original Source E-15
    E -1.7.1 Obscure Original Source E-15
    E -1.7.2 Emphasis on the Citing Source E-16

E -1.8 General Rules for Quotations E-17
    E -1.8.1 Positioning of Quotations E-17
    E -1.8.2 Format of Quotations E-17
    E -1.8.3 Quoting a Source in Another Language E-18

E -1.9 Writing in a Foreign Language E-18

Demise = Issue 3

1   GENERAL RULES

- The rules in this *Guide* apply only to **footnote citations**, **in-text citations**, and **bibliographies**. They do not apply to the main text or textual footnotes (i.e., sentences and clauses that exist outside the confines of the citation); a style guide, such as the *Chicago Manual of Style*, should be used for issues arising in these areas.

- Use the rules from the English section when writing in English, even if the source being referred to is in another language. Use the French rules only when writing in French.

- If a rule states that parentheses ( ) must be used, do not replace them with brackets [ ] and vice versa.

- The **bold, coloured font** has been used to make some examples in this *Guide* explicit.

1.1 BIBLIOGRAPHIES / TABLES OF AUTHORITIES

LEGISLATION

Anti-terrorism Act, SC 2001, c 41.
Aggregate Resources Act, RSO 1990, c A.8.
National Arts Council Act (Cap 193A, 1992 Rev Ed Sing).
Tobacco Product Control Act, RSC 1985, c 14 (4th Supp).

JURISPRUDENCE

Delgamuukw v British Columbia, [1997] 3 SCR 1010, 153 DLR (4th) 193.
Kendle v Melsom, [1998] HCA 13.
Létourneau c Laflèche Auto Ltée, [1986] RJQ 1956 (Sup Ct).
Nova Scotia (Workers' Compensation Board) v Martin, 2003 SCC 54, [2003] 2 SCR 504.

SECONDARY MATERIAL: MONOGRAPHS

Bakan, Joel *et al*, *Canadian Constitutional Law*, 3rd ed (Toronto: Edmont Montgomery, 2003).
Baudouin, Jean-Louis & Pierre-Gabriel Jobin. *Les obligations*, 5th ed (Cowansville, Que: Yvon Blais, 1998).
Christians, Allison; Samuel A. Donaldson & Philip F. Postlewaite. *United States International Taxation*, 2nd ed (New Providence, NJ: LexisNexis, 2011).
Macklem, Patrick. *Indigenous Difference and the Constitution of Canada* (Toronto: University of Toronto Press, 2001).
Nadeau, Alain-Robert. *Vie privée et droits fondamentaux* (Cowansville, Qc: Yvon Blais, 2000).
Smith, Graham JH. *Internet Law and Regulation*, 3rd ed (London, UK: Sweet & Maxwell, 2002).

SECONDARY MATERIAL: ARTICLES

Borrows, John. "With or Without You: First Nations Law (in Canada)" (1996) 41 McGill LJ 629.
———. "Wampum at Niagara: The Royal Proclamation, Canadian Legal History, and Self-Government" in Michael Asch, ed, *Aboriginal and Treaty Rights in Canada: Essays on Law, Equity,*

> *and Respect for Difference* (Vancouver: UBC Press, 1997) 155.
> Deleury, E. "Naissance et mort de la personne ou les confrontations de la médecine et du droit" (1976) 17 C de D 265.
> Wang Sheng Chang. "Combination of Arbitration with Conciliation and Remittance of Awards: With Special Reference to the Asia-Oceana Region" (2002) 19 J Int Arb 51.

Divide bibliographies and tables of authorities into the following sections: **Legislation**, **Jurisprudence**, and **Secondary Materials**. If a source does not fit into a defined section, a residual section entitled **Other Materials** may be used. When appropriate, divide the Legislation and Jurisprudence sections into subsections (e.g., **Legislation: Canada**; **Legislation: France**; **Jurisprudence: Foreign**; etc.). It may also be useful to divide the **Secondary Material** section into subsections (e.g., **Secondary Material: Articles**; **Secondary Material: Monographs**).

Within each section, **list the entries in alphabetical order**. Sort legislation by title, jurisprudence by style of cause, and secondary materials by the author's family name.

If a citation directly follows a citation to another work by the same author, replace the author's names with a 3-em dash (i.e., three em dashes in a row, see the "Wampum at Niagara" example, above).

For secondary material included in a bibliography, **the author's family name appears first** to facilitate the classification in alphabetical order. Depending on cultural conventions, a family name may appear before, after, or in-between given names. If the family name normally appears first (e.g., **Wang Sheng Chang**), do not place a comma after it. If the given name normally appears first, place a comma after the surname (e.g., **Smith, Graham JH**). In the service of accuracy and respect for the source, present the author's name as it appears in the source publication, including any initials, even if this leads to different versions of his or her name in a subsequent reference to that author's work.

If there is more than one author for a reference, write the given name before the surname for every author except the first one (e.g., **Baudouin, Jean-Louis & Pierre-Gabriel Jobin**).

If there is a work by a single author and a work by that same author and others (e.g., **Baudouin** and **Baudouin & Jobin**), cite the one with a single author first.

Insert a **hanging indent** of 0.63 cm ($^1/4$ inch) before each citation. Indent all the lines except for the first one.

1.2   IN-TEXT REFERENCES: MEMORANDUM AND FACTUM

In legal writing, the standard rule is to use footnotes; however, in memoranda and facta, citations should be included **in the main text**.

1.2.1 Memorandum

In addition to the requirement of an "actionable wrong" independent of the breach sued upon, punitive damages will only be awarded "where the defendant's misconduct is so malicious, oppressive, and high-handed that it offends the court's sense of decency" (*Hill v Church of Scientology of Toronto*, **[1995] 2 SCR 1130 at para 196, 184 NR 1, Cory J [*Hill*]**). Such behaviour has included defamation (*ibid*), failure to provide medical care (*Robitaille v Vancouver Hockey Club*, **[1981] 3 WWR 481, 124 DLR (3d) 228 (BCCA)**), and exceptionally abusive behaviour by an insurance company (*Whiten v Pilot Insurance*, **2002 SCC 18, [2002] 1 SCR 595 [*Whiten*]**). Since the primary vehicle of punishment is the criminal law, punitive damages should be scarcely used (*ibid* **at para 69**). It is also important to underline that there cannot be joint and several responsibility for punitive damages because they arise from the misconduct of the particular defendant against whom they are awarded (*Hill* **at para 195**).

- Include the reference immediately after the text, in parentheses.
- The first time a reference is used, follow the usual rules for footnotes. If a reference is repeated later in the text, include a short form after the first citation (see *Hill*). If a reference is not repeated, do not include a short form (see *Robitaille*).
- After the first time a reference is used, use only the short form and include a pinpoint reference if appropriate (e.g., *Hill* **at para 195**).
- Use *ibid* (section 1.4.2) to refer to the immediately preceding reference. Use *supra* (section 1.4.3) when a reference has been mentioned before. Do not use *infra* (section 1.4.4) in a memorandum.

1.2.2 Factum

5.   In addition to the requirement of an "actionable wrong" independent of the breach sued upon, punitive damages will only be awarded "where the defendant's misconduct is so malicious, oppressive and high-handed that it offends the court's sense of decency" (*Hill*). Such behaviour has included defamation (*Hill*), failing to provide medical care (*Robitaille*), and exceptionally abusive behaviour by an insurance company (*Whiten*).

> *Hill v Church of Scientology of Toronto*, **[1995] 2 SCR 1130 at paras 196, 62–64, 184 NR 1, Cory J [*Hill*].**
> *Robitaille v Vancouver Hockey Club*, **124 DLR (3d) 228, [1981] 3 WWR 481(BCCA) [*Robitaille* cited to DLR].**
> *Whiten v Pilot Insurance*, **2002 SCC 18, [2002] 1 SCR 595 [*Whiten*].**

6.   Since the primary vehicle of punishment is the criminal law, punitive damages should be scarcely used (*Whiten*). It is also important to underline that there cannot be joint and several responsibility for punitive damages because they arise from the misconduct of the particular defendant against whom they are awarded (*Hill*).

> *Whiten, supra* **para 5 at para 69.**
> *Hill, supra* **para 5 at para 195.**

- Paragraphs must be numbered. These numbers normally begin at the "Facts" section.

General Rules

- Provide a short form for every source cited.

- Place the short form in parentheses immediately after the relevant text.

- Write the complete reference **at the end of each paragraph**. Indent from both margins and use a smaller font size.

- Organize the references **in the order in which they appear in the paragraph text**. Start a new line after each reference. Do not use a semicolon.

- Write the short form, used in the paragraph text, in brackets after the **first** citation of each source.

- Subsequent references need only use the short form with *supra* (1.4.3), which guides the reader to the appropriate paragraph (e.g., **Whiten, *supra* para 5 at para 69**). Do not use either *ibid* (section 1.4.2) or *infra* (section 1.4.4) in a factum.

- Include relevant pinpoints in the order that they are referenced in the paragraph text (e.g., **Whiten v Pilot Insurance, 2002 SCC 18 at paras 69, 101, 110, [2002] 1 SCR 595**).

1.3 FOOTNOTES: RULES

In legal writing, the two most common forms of footnotes are textual footnotes and citation footnotes. **Textual footnotes** contain peripheral information that is relevant but would detract from the thrust of the argument if placed in the main text. **Citation footnotes** are used to indicate the source from which an argument or quotation has been drawn. Both textual and citation information can occur within a single footnote.

1.3.1 When to Footnote

- Footnotes are required under the following circumstances: (1) at the first reference to the source; (2) at every subsequent quotation from the source; and (3) at every subsequent reference or allusion to a particular passage in the source. The full citation should be provided in the first footnote referring to a source.

1.3.2 How to Indicate a Footnote in the Text

- In legal writing, footnotes are indicated by superscripted numbers. Roman numerals and special characters such as *, †, and ‡ are not normally used (the traditional exception being the use of * to indicate the author's biographical information at the beginning of an article).

  - Generally, place the footnote number at the end of the sentence, after the punctuation.[1]

  - When referring to a word, place the footnote number[2] directly after the word, wherever it occurs in the sentence.

  - When quoting a source, place the footnote number "after the quotation marks"[2] and, "where applicable, the punctuation."[3] Note the contrast with the applicable rule for French footnote indications, where the footnote number precedes the punctuation.

1.3.3 Where Footnotes Appear

Place footnotes on the same page as the text to which they refer (if possible). Set footnotes in a **smaller font** with a **horizontal line** separating them from the body of the text.

1.3.4 When to Combine Footnotes

> [3] Martin Loughlin, "The Functionalist Style in Public Law" (2005) 55 UTLJ 361; Martin Loughlin, *Public Law and Political Theory* (Oxford: Clarendon Press, 1992).

Never place more than one footnote number at any given point in the main text. Instead, combine the supporting citations into one footnote. **Separate different citations in a footnote with a semicolon,** and end the entire footnote with a period.

Where the result is not confusing, citations to multiple sources may be combined into a single footnote at the end of a sentence or paragraph. Avoid combining footnotes that cite quotations from different sources.

1.3.5 Citation of Non-English Sources

> [1] Sylvio Normand, *Introduction au droit des biens* (Montreal: Wilson & Lafleur, 2000) at 40.
> [2] *Loi n° 94-653 du 29 juillet 1994*, JO, 30 July 1994, (1994 2e sem) Gaz Pal Lég 576.

When writing in English, use the English citation rules regardless of the language of the source, with the exception of the **title of the source**: keep the title in its original language and follow that language's rules for capitalization and punctuation. For all other elements of the citation, follow the English rules.

1.3.6 Introductory Signals

> **See** *Chaoulli v Quebec (AG)*, 2005 SCC 35, [2005] 1 SCR 791 [*Chaoulli*]; *HN c Québec (Ministre de l'Éducation)*, 2007 QCCA 1111, [2007] RJQ 2097. **But see** *Flora v Ontario Health Insurance Plan*, 2008 ONCA 538, 91 OR (3d) 412 [*Flora*].

Where appropriate, use an introductory signal to indicate the logical relationship between the cited source and the proposition stated in the main text.

An introductory signal relates to **every citation included in the sentence**. In the example above, the signal **see** relates to both *Chaoulli* and *HN*.

Italicize *cf* and ***contra*** only; **e.g.** remains in Roman font. While not exhaustive, the following list presents the standard introductory signals:

Chaoulli	There is no introductory signal when the source cited is being **quoted or explicitly referred to in the main text**.
See *Chaoulli*	The source cited **directly supports** the proposition.
See especially *Chaoulli*	The source cited is **the strongest** of several that support the proposition. Use only when listing the best of many possible sources.
See e.g. *Chaoulli*	*Exempli gratia*, literally "**for example**". The source cited is one of several that support the proposition given, but the other supporting sources are not cited. When used as an introductory signal, do not follow **e.g.** with a comma or a colon (main text and textual footnotes require either a comma or a colon following this abbreviation).
See generally *Chaoulli* (for the debate over arbitrariness as a principle of fundamental justice)	The source cited **supports and provides background information** relevant to the proposition. Explanatory parenthetical remarks are recommended (See section 1.3.7).
See also *Chaoulli*	The source cited provides **added support** for the proposition, but is **not the most authoritative or is not directly on point**.
Accord *Chaoulli*	As with "see also", the source cited provides **added support** for the proposition; in this instance, however, the source cited **directly supports the proposition and is as authoritative as the source with which it accords. Accord** is also used to indicate that the law of one jurisdiction accords with the law of another.
Cf Chaoulli	*Confer*, literally "compare". The source cited supports a different proposition, but one that is **sufficiently analogous so as to lend support** to the proposition. Explanatory parenthetical remarks are recommended (See section 1.3.7).
Compare *Chaoulli*	The source cited provides a useful contrast to illustrate the proposition being discussed. **The *contrast* lends support rather than the cited authority itself**.
But see *Chaoulli*	The source cited is in **partial disagreement** with the proposition, but does not directly contradict it.
Contra Chaoulli	The source cited directly **contradicts** the proposition.

1.3.7 Parenthetical Information Within Footnotes

> ¹ *Roncarelli v Duplessis*, [1959] SCR 121, 16 DLR (2d) 689, Rand J **(discretionary decisions must be based on "considerations pertinent to the object of the administration" at 140)**; *Oakwood Development Ltd v St François Xavier (Municipality)*, [1985] 2 SCR 164, 20 DLR (4th) 641, Wilson J [*Oakwood* cited to SCR] **("[t]he failure of an administrative decision-maker to take into account a highly relevant consideration is just as erroneous as the improper importation of an extraneous consideration" at 174)**.

> ² See *Lawson v Wellesley Hospital* (1975), 9 OR (2d) 677, 61 DLR (3d) 445, aff'd [1978] 1 SCR 893, 76 DLR (3d) 688 [*Lawson*] **(duty of hospital to protect patient)**; *Stewart v Extendicare*, [1986] 4 WWR 559, 38 CCLT 67 (Sask QB) [*Stewart*] **(duty of nursing home to protect resident)**.

▨ Where it is helpful to clarify how the cited source supports the in-text proposition, provide a **brief description or quotation of not more than one sentence** in parentheses following the citation. A pinpoint reference must follow any quotation in parentheses (see *Oakwood*).

▨ Begin the parenthetical information with a lower case letter. If the citation begins with a capital letter, change it to lower case in brackets (see *Oakwood*).

▨ Parenthetical information refers to the source immediately preceding it. Therefore, in the *Lawson* example, the parenthetical information would be placed immediately before **aff'd** if it were meant to refer only to the court of appeal decision.

1.4 PRIOR AND SUBSEQUENT REFERENCES TO A CITATION

Indicate the full citation only the first time a source appears. Subsequent references refer back to this initial citation.

1.4.1 Establishing a Short Form

1.4.1.1 General Rules

▨ Do not create a short title if there is no further reference to the source in the work.

▨ If the title of a source is short (around three words or less), the full title may be used in all subsequent references (see note 10). If the title of a source is longer, create a short title for subsequent references.

> ¹ *Kadlak v Nunavut (Minister of Sustainable Development)*, 2001 NUCJ 1, [2001] 6 WWR 276 **[Kadlak]**.
> ⁵ *Kadlak*, *supra* note 1 at para 15.
> ⁷ *R v W (R)*, [1992] 2 SCR 122 at para 1, 74 CCC (3d) 134.
> ¹⁰ *R v W (R)*, *supra* note 7 at para 3.
> ¹⁴ James E Ryan, "The Supreme Court and Voluntary Integration" (2007) 121 Harv L Rev 131.
> ⁴⁰ **Ryan**, *supra* note 14 at 132.

General Rules

Place the short title in brackets directly after the citation but before any parenthetical information (see *Stewart* in section 1.3.7) and case history (see section 3.11). Do not italicize the brackets.

Always italicize the short title for cases or legislation (e.g., *Charter*). Abbreviations of codes such as **CCQ** are not considered short forms, and thus should not be italicized.

In subsequent footnotes, use the appropriate cross-referencing signals (*supra*, *ibid*) and, where appropriate, the short title to direct the reader back to the footnote containing the full citation (see note 5).

1.4.1.2 Legislation

If a statute has an **official short title**, use only this short title in the initial citation. If the short title is brief, it may also be used in subsequent references (e.g., *Museums Act*).

If a statute has **no official short title**, or if the official short title is too long for subsequent references, create a distinctive short title and indicate it in brackets at the end of the citation.

[1] *Museums Act*, SC 1990, c 3.
[2] *Nordion and Theratronics Divestiture Authorization Act*, SC 1990, c 4 **[*Nordion Act*]**.
[3] *Canadian Charter of Rights and Freedoms*, Part I of the *Constitution Act, 1982*, being Schedule B to the *Canada Act 1982* (UK), 1982, c 11 **[*Charter*]**.
[4] *Charter of the French language*, CQLR c C-11 **[*Bill 101*]**.
[5] *Canada Business Corporations Act*, RSC 1985, c C-44) **[*CBCA*]**.

Well-recognized abbreviations may also be used (e.g., *CBCA*).

1.4.1.3 Cases

[1] *PPL Corp v Commissioner*, 569 US ___, 133 S Ct 1897 (2013) **[*PPL*]**.
[2] *R v Van der Peet*, [1996] 2 SCR 507, 137 DLR (4th) 289 **[*Van der Peet* cited to SCR]**.
[5] *Quebec (AG) v A*, 2013 SCC 5 **[*Eric v Lola*]**.
[7] *Van der Peet, supra* note 1 at 510.
[8] *Overseas Tankship (UK) Ltd v Miller Steamship Co* (1966), [1967] 1 AC 617 at 625, [1966] 2 All ER 709 **[*Wagon Mound No 2*]**.
[10] *R v Ruzic*, 2001 SCC 24 at para 2, [2001] 1 SCR 687 [*Ruzic*].
[11] *Apotex v Pfizer*, 2009 FCA 8 **[*Viagra*]**.
[12] *R v Morgentaler*, [1993] 3 SCR 463, 107 DLR (4th) 537 **[*Morgentaler* 1993]**.
[13] *Pappajohn v R*, [1980] 2 SCR 120, 111 DLR (3d) 1 **[*Pappajohn* SCC]**.
[14] *R v Pappajohn*, (1979) 45 CCC (2d) 67, [1979] 1 WWR 562 (BCCA) **[*Pappajohn* CA]**.
[15] *Ruzic, supra* note 10 at para 18.

Create a short form by choosing **one of the parties' surnames or a distinctive part of the style of cause** (e.g., *PPL*). If appropriate, you may use other elements to identify the case, for example: a more widely known style of cause from a lower court (e.g., *Eric v Lola*); the name of a ship in admiralty cases (e.g., *Wagon Mound No 2*); or the name of the drug in pharmaceutical patent litigation (e.g., *Viagra*). To eliminate confusion when there are multiple cases with the same name, use the date of the decision for clarity (e.g., *Morgentaler* 1993 [note that the date is in Roman type]). To distinguish decisions from the same case at different court levels, use the abbreviations found in **Appendix B-2** (e.g., *Pappajohn* **SCC**; *Pappajohn* **CA** [note that the court abbreviation is in Roman type]).

If the initial citation includes more than one source, but contains no pinpoint reference, indicate the reporter to which subsequent pinpoint references will be made by including **cited to** followed by the abbreviation of the reporter (e.g., ***Van der Peet* cited to SCR**).

If there is a pinpoint reference in the initial citation, do not include **cited to** (see note 10).

Make all further pinpoint references to the same source (e.g., ***Van der Peet*** in the example above cannot be cited to the DLR for subsequent pinpoints).

For cases with a neutral citation, do not indicate the reporter to which subsequent references are directed. Paragraph numbers are determined by the court and are uniform across all reporters.

1.4.1.4 Secondary Materials

Use the author's surname in subsequent references to the source (e.g., **Humphrey**).

If citing two or more authors with the same last name, include an initial for each (e.g., **S Smith & L Smith**), or several if appropriate.

If **more than one work by a particular author is cited**, create a short form consisting of the author's name and a shortened form of the title of the work, separated by a comma (e.g., **Baker, "Post-Confederation Rights"**). In the short form of the title, maintain the same formatting as the full title—italics for books and quotation marks for articles.

[1] G Blaine Baker, "The Reconstitution of Upper Canadian Legal Thought in the Late Victorian Empire" (1985) 3 Law & History Rev 219 **[Baker, "Reconstitution"]**.
[2] John Humphrey, *No Distant Millennium: The International Law of Human Rights* (Paris: UNESCO, 1989).
[3] G Blaine Baker, "The Province of Post-Confederation Rights" (1995) 45 UTLJ 77 **[Baker, "Post-Confederation Rights"]**.
[7] Stephen A Smith, "Duties, Liabilities, and Damages" (2012) 125:7 Harv L Rev 1727.
[9] Lionel Smith, "The Province of the Law of Restitution" (1992) 71:4 Can Bar Rev 672.
[12] **Humphrey**, *supra* note 2 at 25.
[13] Rebecca Veinott, "Child Custody and Divorce: A Nova Scotia Study, 1866-1910" in Philip Girard & Jim Phillips, eds, *Essays in the History of Canadian Law,* vol 3 (Toronto: University of Toronto Press, 1990) 273.
[14] **Baker, "Post-Confederation Rights"**, *supra* note 3 at 86.
[20] **S Smith**, *supra* note 7 at 1731.
[27] **L Smith**, *supra* note 9 at 675.
[86] Kimberley Smith Maynard, "Divorce in Nova Scotia, 1750-1890" in **Girard & Phillips**, *supra* note 13, 232 at 239.
[91] Maynard, *supra* note 86 at 243.

If there are **two or more essays from the same collection**, apply these rules to create a short form for the collection, and then use that form in the first citation of each additional essay (e.g., **Girard & Phillips**, see notes 13 & 86). The short form rules found in this section (section 1.4.1.4) should be applied normally to the subsequent references of any essay from that collection (see note 91).

General Rules

1.4.2   *Ibid*

> [1] See *Canada Labour Relations Board v Halifax Longshoremen's Association, Local 269*, [1983] 1 SCR 245, 144 DLR (3d) 1 [*HLA* cited to SCR].
> [2] *Ibid* at 260. See also *Fraser v Canada (Public Service Staff Relations Board)*, [1985] 2 SCR 455 at 463, 23 DLR (4th) 122 [*Fraser*]; *Heustis v New Brunswick Electric Power Commission*, [1979] 2 SCR 768, 98 DLR (3d) 622 [*Heustis* cited to SCR].
> [3] *Heustis, supra* note 2 at 775.
> [6] *Ibid* at 780–82.
> [7] *Ibid*.
> [8] *Heustis, supra* note 2.
> [98] For a more detailed analysis, see *Union des employés de service, Local 298 v Bibeault*, [1988] 2 SCR 1048, 95 NR 161 [*Bibeault* cited to SCR]. The Court cited a "patently unreasonable" standard of review (*ibid* at 1084–85).
> [99] But see *Business Corporations Act*, RSS 1978, c B-10, s 18 [*BCA*].
> [100] See *BCA, ibid*, s 22.

▢ *Ibid* is an abbreviation of the Latin word *ibidem*, meaning "in the same place".

▢ Use *ibid* to direct the reader to the **immediately preceding reference**. Do not provide the number of the footnote in which the preceding reference appears.

▢ *Ibid* may be used **after a full citation** (see note 2), **after a** *supra* (see note 6) or even **after another** *ibid* (see note 7). For clarity, if there is more than one reference in the previous footnote, use *supra* rather than *ibid* (see note 3).

▢ An *ibid* used without a pinpoint reference refers to the same pinpoint as in the previous footnote (see note 7).

▢ To cite the source as a whole, where the previous reference includes a pinpoint, use *supra* (see note 8).

▢ To refer to the previous source within the same footnote, use *ibid* in parentheses (see note 98).

1.4.3   *Supra*

> [1] *MacMillan Bloedel Ltd v British Columbia (AG)* (1996), 22 BCLR (3d) 137 at 147, 30 WCB (2d) 446 (CA) [*MacMillan*]; *Towne Cinema Theatres Ltd v R*, [1985] 1 SCR 494 at 501, 18 DLR (4th) 1 [*Towne Cinema*].
> [2] *MacMillan, supra* note 1.
> [57] *Ibid* at 150. *Cf Towne Cinema, supra* note 1 at 501.
> [58] *Supra* note 1 at 140.
> [59] *Ibid*.
> [60] See also *Faraggi, supra* note 24 **and accompanying text**.

▢ *Supra* is the Latin word for "above".

▢ Use the short form in combination with *supra* to refer to the **footnote containing the original, full citation**. Do not use *supra* to refer to either an *ibid* or another *supra*.

▢ Unlike *ibid*, *supra* always refers to the source alone and never implies reference to a pinpoint. Accordingly, reiterate the pinpoint even if the *supra* cites to the same passage as the original reference (see note 57 *Towne Cinema*).

▢ If the source is clearly identified in the main text (e.g., "***MacMillan* juxtaposes restitution with**

disgorgement for wrongdoing[58]"), it is unnecessary to re-identify that source in the footnote (see note 58).

▪ To refer to both a previous footnote and the main text to which that footnote relates, use *supra* note # **and accompanying text** (see note 60).

▪ To refer only to the main text (rather than a footnote), use **above** rather than *supra* (section 1.4.5).

1.4.4   *Infra*

▪ *Infra* is a Latin word meaning "below".

▪ Use *infra* to refer a reader to a **subsequent footnote**.

▪ *Infra* is **rarely appropriate and its use is strongly discouraged**. Provide the full citation the first time the source is mentioned.

▪ Do not use *infra* merely to refer the reader to a subsequent reference that contains a full citation. It exists to direct the reader to a general comment or a large group of references appearing in a later footnote that would not be convenient to reproduce (e.g. "For further discussion and general references on this matter, see *infra* note 58").

▪ To refer only to the main text and not to the footnote, use **below** instead of *infra* (section 1.4.5).

1.4.5   Above and Below

▪ Use the words **above** and **below** to direct the reader to **a portion of the main text** and not to the footnotes.

▪ If there are no easily identifiable section or paragraph markers, or if the final pagination of the text is unclear at the time of writing, use the formulation **see the text accompanying note** #.

[1] See Part III-A, **above**, for more on this topic.
[2] Further discussion of this case will be found at 164–70, **below**.
[3] For further analysis of the holding in *Oakes*, **see the text accompanying note 41**.

1.5   PINPOINTS

	page	paragraph	section	article	footnote
singular	*Ibid* at 512.	*Ibid* at **para** 6.	*Ibid*, **s** 4(1).	*Ibid*, **art** 1457.	*Ibid* at 512, **n** 139.
plural	*Ibid* at 512–14.	*Ibid* at **paras** 6, 12.	*Ibid*, **ss** 4(1), 6(2)(*b*)(i)–(ii).	*Ibid*, **arts** 1457–69.	*Ibid* at 512, **nn** 139, 142–46.

▪ This section contains general guidelines for pinpoints. For more specific instructions, see the "Pinpoint" sections relating to the various sources (i.e., Legislation, Jurisprudence, Secondary Sources, etc.).

- Use a pinpoint to cite to a specific portion of the text.

- Separate **non-consecutive pinpoints** by a **comma**, and **consecutive pinpoints** by an **en dash** (–), not a **hyphen** (-).

- Retain at least the two last digits following the en dash (e.g., **159–60**).

- If the page indexing system contains hyphens (e.g., **70.1-3, 70.1-4** etc.) or any other system that would otherwise be confusing to the reader when coupled with en dashes, prefer "**to**" when citing to a range of pages (e.g., **70.1-3 to 70.1-5**).

- It is generally preferable to cite to a specific number or range, but to indicate a **general area**, place **ff** (the abbreviation of the Latin word "*folio*" or "*folium*", used to indicate "and following") immediately after the number (e.g., see paras **69ff**).

- Do not abbreviate unnumbered elements (e.g., **Preamble**, **Schedule**, **Appendix**, **Preliminary Provision**, etc.) in a pinpoint.

1.6   ONLINE RESOURCES

Traditional citation,	online: <URL>.
Steven M Davidoff, "Choices Ahead for the Dell Board, but Not Much Time" *The New York Times* (24 July 2013) at "**update**",	online: <dealbook.nytimes.com/2013/07/24/choices-ahead-for-the-dell-board-but-not-much-time/> .
Theodore de Bruyn, *A Plan of Action for Canada to Reduce HIV/AIDS-related Stigma and Discrimination*, at 66,	online: **Canadian HIV/AIDS Legal Network** <www.aidslaw.ca/publications/interfaces/downloadFile.php?ref=48> .
"Defamation in the Internet Age" (1 June 2008) **(podcast) at 00h:03m:30s,**	online: **Osler, Hoskin & Harcourt LLP** <www.osler.com/outlook/fall2008en/linkit_001.html> .
Ardavani v Minister of Citizenship and Immigration (30 May 2005), VA4-01907,	online: **Immigration and Refugee Board** <www.canlii.org/en/ca/irb/doc/2005/2005canlii56963/2005canlii56963.html> .
The Commissioner of Competition v Canfor Corporation (30 March 2004), CT-2004-002,	online: **Competition Tribunal** <www.ct-tc.gc.ca/CMFiles/CT-2004-002_0001b_38LMA-4272004-3987.pdf> .

- With the exception of purely online sources (e.g., blogs, podcasts, webpages, etc.), the inclusion of a URL should only be a supplement to traditional citation.

- On balance, online source citations are at present not as stable as print. Notable exceptions include the official online sources for provincial and federal statutes. Accordingly, prefer traditional citations supplemented with online sources, and cite to online sources only if you believe that the source will provide an archive of material for a reasonable period of time, preferably several years.

- When citing to online resources, provide the full traditional citation, followed by a comma. Add **online:** followed by the URL enclosed in angle brackets (i.e., < >).

- The pinpoint should be placed before the URL. Where appropriate, pinpoint to elements other than page numbers (e.g., **(podcast) at 00h:03m:30s**).

▨ Add any additional information necessary to situate the reader vis-a-vis the website before the URL (e.g., **Immigration and Refugee Board**, **Competition Tribunal**).

▨ Cite the full URL of the source, but exclude the **http://** protocol. Include the protocol if it is anything else (for example **https://**).

    ☐ Include **www where the source itself includes it**; omission may lead to retrieval of a different document.

    ☐ If the source URL begins with something other than www, cite to that instead (e.g. **ftp.sccwrp.org**; **ilreports.blogspot.ca**).

▨ Eliminate any superfluous part of the URL, such as parameters or arguments, which are not necessary to bring you to the referenced website. Testing of the unembellished URL in a browser, to ensure its functionality, is recommended.

✓	online: <dealbook.nytimes.com/2013/07/15/citigroup-profit-climbs-42-percent/>
✗	online: <dealbook.nytimes.com/2013/07/15/citigroup-profit-climbs-42-percent/?partner = rss&emc = rss>

▨ Some websites may not include the names of authors or formal titles for written work. In these cases, exercise judgment and include basic, critical information in place of the traditional citation (see **Osler** example).

▨ When citing **podcasts,** add (**podcast**) after the traditional citation and before the pinpoint (see the **Osler** example, above). If provided, write the name of the speaker instead of the author.

▨ If provided, include the paragraph number in the pinpoint. When the printed pagination is reproduced in the electronic source, refer to this page numbering.

1.7 CITING SOURCES THAT QUOTE OR REPRINT THE ORIGINAL SOURCE

It is always preferable to cite directly to an original source. If an original source is quoted in another work (the citing source), consult the original work in order to verify the context and accuracy of the reference.

1.7.1 Obscure Original Source

Cited in	*Papers Relating to the Commission appointed to enquire into the state and condition of the Indians of the North-West Coast of British Columbia*, British Columbia Sessional Papers, 1888 at 432–33, **cited in** Hamar Foster, "Honouring the Queen's Flag: A Legal and Historical Perspective on the Nisga'a Treaty" (1998) 120 BC Studies 11 at 13.

The original source may sometimes be **difficult to find** or may have been **destroyed**. In such exceptional circumstances, it may be necessary to cite to the original source as presented in a citing source. Provide as much information on the original work as possible, followed by **cited in** and the citation to the citing source.

Reprinted in	George R to Governor Arthur Phillip, Royal Instruction, 25 April 1787 (27 Geo III), **reprinted in** *Historical Documents of New South Wales*, vol 1, part 2 (Sydney: Government Printer, 1892–1901) 67.

In certain cases, the original version of a document fully reprinted in a collection (e.g., collections reprinting debates, letters, treaties or manuscripts) is **only available in archives**. Provide a complete citation to the original work, followed by **reprinted in** and the citation to the citing source.

Do not refer to books reprinting excerpts from original sources that are readily available (e.g., textbooks).

	International Covenant on Civil and Political Rights, (19 December 1966), 999 UNTS 171, 1976 Can TS No 47.
	International Covenant on Civil and Political Rights, (19 December 1966), 999 UNTS 171, 1976 Can TS No 47, reprinted in Hugh M Kindred et al, eds, *International Law Chiefly as Interpreted and Applied in Canada: Documentary Supplement* (Toronto: Emond Montgomery, 2000) 87.

1.7.2 Emphasis on the Citing Source

Citing	*Canada (Citizenship and Immigration) v Khosa*, 2009 SCC 12 at para 38, [2009] 1 SCR 339, **citing** Pierre-André Côté, *Interprétation des lois,* 3rd ed (Cowansville, Que: Yvon Blais, 1999) at 91, n 123.

To highlight the fact that a work is referring to the original material (e.g., when the secondary work is more eminent or trustworthy) include the citation to the citing source, followed by **citing** and the citation to the original source.

1.8 GENERAL RULES FOR QUOTATIONS

These rules apply to both main text and footnotes.

1.8.1 Positioning of Quotations

This principle, which has existed since 1929, is based on a dynamic conception of the constitution as **"a living tree capable of growth and expansion."** [1]

Justice LeBel, writing for the Court, invoked the scenario that Justice Dickson (as he then was) used in *Perka* to explain the concept:

> **By way of illustration in *Perka*, Dickson J. evoked the situation of a lost alpinist who, on the point of freezing to death, breaks into a remote mountain cabin. The alpinist confronts a painful dilemma: freeze to death or commit a criminal offence. Yet as Dickson J pointed out at p 249, the alpinist's choice to break the law "is no true choice at all; it is remorselessly compelled by normal human instincts", here of self-preservation.** [2]

The *Civil Code of Quebec* begins in a peculiar way, introducing two legal concepts that are meaningless to the common citizen. Article 1 reads as following:

> **Every human being possesses juridical personality and has the full enjoyment of civil rights.** [3]

Place short quotations of **four lines or fewer** in quotation marks and incorporate them directly into the text.

Indent from both margins and single space quotations of **more than four lines**. Do not use quotation marks. Legislative provisions may be indented even if they are fewer than four lines long.

1.8.2 Format of Quotations

Spelling, capitalization, and internal punctuation in a quotation must be **exactly the same as in the original source**; any changes and additions must be clearly indicated in brackets.

If the sentence becomes grammatically incorrect, make the proper adjustments in brackets (for example, change a lower case letter to an upper case letter).

In-text
It was clear from this moment that "[t]he centre . . . of American jurisprudence had changed." [32]
"[A] mixed question of fact and law" must be appealable. [42]

Use an ellipsis (. . .) to indicate the omission of a passage from the quoted material. An ellipsis at the beginning or the end of the quoted material is usually unnecessary. Use an ellipsis at the extremities of a quotation only where the sentence is deliberately left grammatically incomplete.

General Rules

✓	The petitioner must prove that '[c]onsidering the circumstances, the opposing party will not be able to shift the burden of proof."
✗	The petitioner must prove that '[...] considering the circumstances, the opposing party will not be able to shift the burden of proof."

  Where the original source contains an error, **enclose the correction in square brackets, replacing the erroneous word or phrase**. Refrain from using [*sic*], unless drawing attention to the original error.

  Text may be emphasized by using italics and placing **[emphasis added]** at the end of the citation. If the text was emphasized in the original copy, place **[emphasis in original]** at the end of the citation. If there are footnotes in the original text that are not reproduced in the quotation, place **[footnotes omitted]** at the end of the citation. (Note that the placement of such expressions after the citation in the footnote is contrary to the rule applicable in French.)

> **Footnotes**
> [31] *Norris, supra* note 21 **[emphasis added]**.
> [32] *Kadlak v Nunavut (Minister of Sustainable Development)*, 2001 NUCJ 1 at para 32, [2001] 6 WWR 276 [*Kadlak*] **[emphasis in original]**.
> [77] Lamontagne, *supra* note 65 at 109 **[footnotes omitted]**.

Place these expressions after the establishment of a short form (see note 32).

1.8.3   Quoting a Source in Another Language

> [1] Jacques Ghestin & Gilles Goubeaux, *Traité de droit civil: Introduction générale*, 4th ed (Paris: Librairie générale de droit et de jurisprudence, 1994) at para 669 **[translated by author]**.

If at all possible, use an English version of a source when writing in English and a French version when writing in French. Every Canadian jurisdiction passes statutes in English.

If quoting in another language, a translation may be provided, but is not required. Clearly indicate any translation in the footnote and identify the translator. If the work is translated by a professional, indicate the translator's name (see section 6.2.2.5.1). If you, the author, translated the work, include **[translated by author]**.

1.9   WRITING IN A FOREIGN LANGUAGE

The *Guide* is a Canadian work and applies to texts written in the country's two official languages. However, it is possible to adapt these rules to any other language, inspired by the English **or** the French section. The guidelines are **uniformity**, **clarity** and **facility of retracing a source** for the reader. The following guidelines are examples of adaptation rules.

- **Translate expressions** such as "see", "cited in", "reprinted in", "emphasis added", and "with reference to", but keep the Latin expressions as they are.

- Follow the **form** rules, such as the order of elements and the structure of the document.

- Follow the **punctuation** rules of the language in which the text is written. If needed, consult grammar and usage guides. Make sure that the form of the punctuation marks remains consistent throughout the text.

- For **legislation and jurisprudence**, follow the Canadian general forms, or adapt the forms presented in Foreign Sources (section 7). Use the statute volume and jurisdiction abbreviations as presented in the legislation's official document. Include the court and jurisdiction.

- For **jurisprudential sources**, follow the hierarchy of sources. Always keep the audience in mind and verify that the information is accessible to the reader. Use the abbreviation of the reporter as presented in the source, and always include the court and jurisdiction.

2   Legislation..E-23

E -2.1 Statutes E-23
    E -2.1.1 General Form... E-23
    E -2.1.2 Point in Time Citations................................. E-24
    E -2.1.3 Sources... E-24
    E -2.1.4 Title.. E-27
    E -2.1.5 Revised Statutes and Annual Volumes...................... E-28
    E -2.1.6 Loose-leafs.. E-28
    E -2.1.7 Jurisdiction E-29
    E -2.1.8 Year, Session, and Supplement E-30
    E -2.1.9 Chapter E-31
    E -2.1.10 Pinpoint E-32
    E -2.1.11 Amendments, Repeals, and Re-enactments E-32
    E -2.1.12 Appendices E-32
    E -2.1.13 Statutes Within Statutes................................... E-33

E -2.2 Constitutional Statutes E-33
    E -2.2.1 Pinpoint.. E-34

E -2.3 Codes E-34

E -2.4 Bills E-35

E -2.5 Regulations E-36
    E -2.5.1 Federal Regulations... E-36
        E -2.5.1.1 Revised Regulations E-36
        E -2.5.1.2 Unrevised Regulations........................... E-37
    E -2.5.2 Provincial and Territorial Regulations E-37
        E -2.5.2.1 Alberta, British Columbia E-37
        E -2.5.2.2 Manitoba... E-37
        E -2.5.2.3 New Brunswick................................... E-38
        E -2.5.2.4 Newfoundland and Labrador..................... E-38
            E -2.5.2.4.1 Unrevised........................... E-38
            E -2.5.2.4.2 Revised E-38
        E -2.5.2.5 Northwest Territories............................ E-38
            E -2.5.2.5.1 Unrevised........................... E-38
            E -2.5.2.5.2 Revised E-39
        E -2.5.2.6 Nova Scotia...................................... E-39
        E -2.5.2.7 Nunavut.. E-39
        E -2.5.2.8 Ontario... E-39
            E -2.5.2.8.1 Unrevised........................... E-39
            E -2.5.2.8.2 Revised E-39
        E -2.5.2.9 Prince Edward Island E-40
        E -2.5.2.10 Quebec E-40
            E -2.5.2.10.1 Historical Versions E-40
            E -2.5.2.10.2 Current Version (Cited to the Compilation of
                              Quebec Laws and Regulations) E-40
        E -2.5.2.11 Saskatchewan................................. E-40
            E -2.5.2.11.1 Unrevised........................... E-40
            E -2.5.2.11.2 Revised E-40
        E -2.5.2.12 Yukon E-41

E -2.6   Other Information Published in Gazettes E-41
     E -2.6.1 General Form.. E-41
     E -2.6.2 Orders in Council E-42
          E -2.6.2.1 Federal... E-43
          E -2.6.2.2 Provincial and Territorial............................ E-43
     E -2.6.3 Proclamations and Royal Instructions E-44

E -2.7   Municipal By-laws... E-44

E -2.8   Rules of Practice.. E-45

E -2.9   Securities Commissions E-46

Legislation

2   LEGISLATION

2.1 STATUTES

2.1.1 General Form

Title,	statute volume	Juris-diction	year,	chapter,	other indexing element,	(session or supplement),	pinpoint.
Criminal Code,	RS	C	1985,	c C-46,			s 745.
Income Tax Act,	RS	C	1985,	c 1		(5th Supp),	s 18(1)(m) (iv)(c).
Charter of human rights and freedoms,	C	QLR		c C-12,			s 10.
SkyDome Act (Bus Parking),	S	O	2002,	c 8,	Schedule K,		s 2.
Securities Act,	C	QLR		c V-1.1,			s 9.
An Act Respecting the caisses d'entraide économique,	RS	Q		c C-3,			s 1.

- Do not include a space between the statute volume and the jurisdiction (e.g., *Income Tax Act*, **RSC** 1985; *SkyDome Act (Bus Parking)*, **SO** 2002).

- If the statute reference includes session or supplement information, omit the comma that normally follows the immediately preceding element; see *Income Tax Act*.

- To cite the version of Quebec legislation that is currently in force use the **CQLR** designation (Compilation of Quebec Laws and Regulations). Reserve **RSQ** and **SQ** for citing historical versions.

- For Constitutional statutes, see section 2.2.

- For Bills, see section 2.4.

2.1.2   Point in Time Citations

When citing to a particular point in time, and the standard citation form is inadequate, use **as it appeared on [day month year]** or **as it appeared on [month year]** to clarify the point in time cited to.

> *Income Tax Act*, RSC 1985, c 1 (5th Supp), s 20(1)(c) **as it appeared on 12 October 2012**.
> *Oil and Gas Conservations Act*, RSA 2000, c O-6, s 4 **as it appeared on December 2007**.

2.1.3   Sources

Find legislation in the appropriate jurisdiction's **official electronic versions**. If unavailable, refer to the printed **revised** or **re-enacted statutes**, **annual volumes**, and **loose-leaf consolidations**. Official electronic versions are cited in the same manner as print sources; a URL reference is not required.

Jurisdiction	Order of the sources to cite from

Canada	Refer to the **official electronic version** at <www.laws-lois.justice.gc.ca/eng/> . This website includes historical versions of legislation dating back to 2001.
	If the official version is unavailable online:
	Refer to latest printed version of the **revised statutes** whenever possible (last revision: 1985).
	Refer to the printed **annual volumes** if:
	  ☐ referring to a statute that was enacted since the last revision was published; or,
	  ☐ referring to a section that has been added or amended since the revision date.

Alberta	Refer to the **official electronic version** at <www.qp.alberta.ca/Laws_Online.cfm> .
	If the official version is unavailable online:
	Refer to latest printed version of the **revised statutes** whenever possible (last revision: 2000).
	Refer to the printed **annual volumes** if:
	  ☐ referring to a statute that was enacted since the last revision was published; or,
	  ☐ referring to a section that has been added or amended since the revision date.

British Columbia	British Columbia **does not** currently have an official electronic version (an unofficial database is maintained at <www.bclaws.ca>). Refer to the latest printed **revised statutes** whenever possible (last revision: 1996). Refer to the printed **annual volumes** if: ☐ referring to a statute that was enacted since the last revision was

Legislation

	published; or,
	☐ referring to a section that has been added or amended since the revision date.
Manitoba	Manitoba **does not** currently have an official electronic version (an unofficial database is maintained at <www.gov.mb.ca/laws>). Refer to the latest printed **revised statutes** whenever possible (last revision: 1987). Refer to the printed **annual volumes** if:
	☐ referring to a statute that was enacted since the last revision was published; or,
	☐ referring to a section that has been added or amended since the revision date.
	Optional: provide a parallel citation to the **Continuing Consolidation of the Statutes of Manitoba** (CCSM), a loose-leaf publication, after the reference to the annual volumes (section 2.1.5).
New Brunswick	Refer to the **official electronic version** at <www2.gnb.ca/content/ gnb/en/departments/attorney_general/acts_regulations.html> . This website contains the latest revision (2011), laws currently in force, and annual volumes dating back to 2000. *If the official version is unavailable online (i.e., before 2000):* Refer to the printed **annual volumes**.
Newfoundland & Labrador	Refer to the **official electronic version** at <www.assembly.nl.ca/ legislation/> . This website contains the latest revision (1990), laws currently in force, and annual volumes dating back to 1990. *If the official version is unavailable online (i.e., before 1990):* Refer to the printed **annual volumes**.
Northwest Territories	The Northwest Territories **do not** currently have an official electronic version. Note, however, that the website <www.justice.gov.nt.ca/Legislation/ AlphaSearch.shtml> does contain updated PDFs of the latest legislation, which are printed by the Territorial Printer. Refer to the latest printed **revised statutes** whenever possible (last revision: 1988). Refer to the printed **annual volumes** if:
	☐ referring to a statute that was enacted since the last revision was published; or,
	☐ referring to a section that has been added or amended since the revision date.
Nova Scotia	Refer to the **official electronic version** at <www.assembly.nl.ca/ legislation/> for statutes assented to in the second session of 2003 or later. *If the official version is unavailable online (i.e., before 2003):* Refer to the latest printed **revised statutes** or **loose-leaf consolidation** whenever possible (last revision: 1989).

	Refer to the printed **annual volumes** if: ☐ referring to a statute that was enacted since the last revision was published; or, ☐ referring to a section that has been added or amended since the revision date.
Nunavut	Refer to the **official electronic version** at <www.justice.gov.nu.ca/> for statutes assented to in the second session of 2003 or later. The website contains pdfs of all Territorial Printer publications. ☐ For statutes enacted specifically for Nunavut by the Northwest Territories prior to 1 April 1999, provide the standard citation followed by: "as enacted for Nunavut, pursuant to the *Nunavut Act*, SC 1993, c 28" (e.g., *Nunavut Judicial System Implementation Act*, SNWT 1998, c 34, **as enacted for Nunavut, pursuant to the *Nunavut Act*, SC 1993, c 28**). ☐ Many Northwest Territories statutes are applied, *mutatis mutandis,* to Nunavut via section 29 of the federal *Nunavut Act*, SC 1993, c 28. When applicable, provide the standard citation followed by: "as duplicated for Nunavut by s 29 of the *Nunavut Act*, SC 1993, c 28" (e.g., *Official Languages Act*, RSNWT 1998, c O-1, **as duplicated for Nunavut by s 29 of the *Nunavut Act*, SC 1993, c 28**).
Ontario	Refer to the **official electronic version** at <www.e-laws.gov.on.ca>. This website includes historical versions of legislation dating back to 1990 (the date of the latest revision). *If the official version is unavailable online (i.e., before 1990):* Refer to the printed **annual volumes**.
Prince Edward Island	Prince Edward Island **does not** currently have an official electronic version (an unofficial database is maintained at <www.gov.pe.ca/law/regulations/index.php3>). Refer to the latest printed **revised statutes** whenever possible (last revision: 1988). Refer to the printed **annual volumes** if: ☐ referring to a statute that was enacted since the last revision was published; or, ☐ referring to a section that has been added or amended since the revision date.
Quebec	Quebec maintains the *Compilation of Quebec Laws and Regulations* (CQLR), an **official, updated compilation** of its laws in force, at <www2.publicationsduquebec.gouv.qc.ca/home.php>. Statutes cited to this database use CQLR instead of the usual SQ or RSQ designation. The database is constantly updated and is undated; accordingly, do provide a date when citing to the CQLR. A Point in Time citation may be appropriate in some cases (see section 2.1.2). Official **historical versions of legislation,** dating back until 1969,

	are available online at <www3.publicationsduquebec.gouv.qc.ca/loisreglements/loisannuelles.fr.html> . When citing historical versions, use the RSQ or SQ designation (and not CQLR). At present, the years 1977–1995 are only available in French. *If the official version is unavailable online:* Refer to the latest printed **revised statutes** whenever possible (the last revision was in 2009). Refer to the printed **annual volumes/compilations** if: ☐ referring to a statute that was enacted since the last revision was published; or, ☐ referring to a section that has been added or amended since the revision date.
Saskatchewan	Saskatchewan **does not** currently have an official electronic version (an unofficial database is maintained at <www.qp.gov.sk.ca/>). Refer to the latest printed **revised statutes** whenever possible (last revision: 1978). Refer to the printed **annual volumes** if: ☐ referring to a statute that was enacted since the last revision was published; or, ☐ referring to a section that has been added or amended since the revision date.
Yukon	The Yukon **does not** currently have an official electronic version (an unofficial database is maintained at <www.gov.yk.ca/legislation/>). Refer to the latest printed **revised statutes** whenever possible (last revision: 2002). Refer to the printed **annual volumes** if: ☐ referring to a statute that was enacted since the last revision was published; or, ☐ referring to a section that has been added or amended since the revision date.

2.1.4 Title

■ Italicize the title of the statute and place a non-italicized comma after the title.

> *Civil Marriage Act*, SC 2005, c 41.
> *Reciprocal Enforcement of Maintenance Orders Act*, SY 1980, c 25, s 5(2).
> *Income War Tax Act, 1917*, SC 1917, c 28.

■ Provide the **official short title**, which is usually found in the first section of the statute. If no official short title is provided, use the title found at the head of the statute. Include **The** only if it forms part of the title (as indicated in the official short title or at the head of the statute).

■ If the title of the statute is provided in the main text, do not repeat it in the citation.

Follow the capitalization of words in the title as set out in the statute. Many English titles of Quebec statutes follow French capitalization rules. Do *not* capitalize letters in these titles to conform to English language capitalization rules.

If the year is included as part of the title of the statute, ensure that it appears in italics (e.g., *Income War Tax Act, 1917*). Add the year after the jurisdiction even if the year is part of the title.

NB: The statutes of the following jurisdictions are adopted in both English and French: Canada, Manitoba, New Brunswick, Ontario, Quebec, Nunavut, the Northwest Territories, and the Yukon. However, statutes adopted prior to a certain date may exist only in English.

2.1.5   Revised Statutes and Annual Volumes

Revised statutes	*Children's Law Reform Act,* **RS** O 1990, c C.12.
Annual volumes	*Agricultural Land Commission Act,* **S** BC 2002, c 36.

Both **Revised Statutes** and **Re-enacted Statutes** are abbreviated to **RS**. For citations to annual volumes, abbreviate **Statutes** to **S**.

Use **S** for Statutes (and not **O** for Ordinances) when referring to any volume, past or present, of Northwest Territories or Yukon legislation.

NB: If a statute cannot be found in the current Revised Statutes, do not assume that it does not exist or that it is no longer relevant. For example, the *York University Act, 1965*, SO 1965, c 143, is still in force, despite not being included in a revision. Some jurisdictions, such as Ontario, list these statutes in a Table of Unconsolidated Statutes.

2.1.6   Loose-leafs

Manitoba	*Retirement Plan Beneficiaries Act*, SM 1992, c 31, **CCSM c R138**, s 14.

Do not place a comma between the name of the volume and the chapter number.

Loose-leafs are consolidations of legislation that are continually updated; accordingly, a citation to a loose-leaf service does not contain a date as it is assumed to be to the most recent version of the referenced statute (if greater clarity with respect to the date of the legislation is needed, use Point in Time Citation, section 2.1.2). With the advent of online consolidations, loose-leafs are generally falling out of use.

Only the provinces of Manitoba and Nova Scotia publish an official loose-leaf compilation. (Some jurisdictions, like Alberta, publish an unofficial consolidation.)

The Nova Scotia loose-leafs do not have any special catalogue identifiers and should accordingly be cited in the same manner as revised statutes and annual volumes (see section 2.1.5).

▨ The contents of Nova Scotia's loose-leafs may also be found via the province's online official consolidation.

▨ Manitoba, which does not have an official online legislative database, maintains a loose-leaf service entitled the *Continuing Consolidation of the Statutes of Manitoba* (CCSM); this publication, however, should be used only as an optional parallel source, with the main citation being to either the revised statutes or the annual volumes.

▨ Quebec discontinued its loose-leaf updates to the RSQ in 2010 when the service was superseded by the Compilation of Quebec Laws and Regulations.

2.1.7   Jurisdiction

▨ Place the jurisdiction immediately after the statute volume.

> *Proceeds of Crime (Money Laundering) and Terrorist Financing Act*, **SC** 2000, c 17.
> *Workers Compensation Act*, **SPEI** 1994, c 67.

Jurisdiction abbreviations for legislation:

Canada	C
Alberta	A
British Columbia	BC
Lower Canada	LC
Manitoba	M
New Brunswick	NB
Newfoundland (Statutes and Regulations repealed before 6 December 2001 / *Gazette* published before 21 December 2001)	N
Newfoundland and Labrador (Statutes and Regulations in force on or after 6 December 2001 / *Gazette* published 21 December 2001 and after)	NL
Northwest Territories	NWT
Nova Scotia	NS
Nunavut (1 April 1999 and after)	Nu
Ontario	O
Prince Edward Island	PEI
Province of Canada	Prov C
Quebec	Q
Saskatchewan	S

Upper Canada	UC
Yukon	Y

See **Appendix A-1** for other Jurisdiction abbreviations (e.g., Regulations, Courts, Reporters, etc.)

2.1.8   Year, Session, and Supplement

Year	*Animal Protection Act*, RSA **2000**, c A-41.
Session spanning more than one year	*Government Organization Act, 1983*, SC **1980–81–82–83**, c 167.
More than one session in a year	*An Act to amend the Business Licence Act*, SNWT **1985 (3rd Sess)**, c 1.
Supplement	*Customs Act*, RSC 1985, c 1 **(2nd Supp)**.
Regnal year	*An Act respecting the Civilization and Enfranchisement of certain Indians*, S Prov C 1859 **(22 Vict)**, c 9.

Place the year after the jurisdiction, followed by a comma. If a session or regnal year follows the year, place the comma after the session or regnal year.

Omit the year when citing the Compilation of Quebec Laws and Regulations (CQLR), or the loose-leaf edition of the statutes of Manitoba (CCSM), as these sources are continually updated and do not contain a date of publication. If greater accuracy with respect to the date is needed, use Point in Time citation (section 2.1.2).

When a **session spans more than one year**, write the full date span of the volume (e.g., **1980–81**).

If a **statute volume is divided into several sessions** with independent chapter numbering, place the number of the session (**1st**, **2nd**, **3rd** or **4th**) and the abbreviation **Sess** in parentheses following the year.

Refer to the **supplement** for acts and amendments that were passed during the year in which the *Revised Statutes* were issued, but that were not included in the revision. For example, the 1985 RSC was not proclaimed in force until late 1988; accordingly the statutes from 1985–1988 were reprinted to bring them within the ambit of the newly revised statutes (First Supplement = 1985 Acts; Second Supplement = 1986 Acts; Third Supplement = 1987 Acts; Fourth Supplement = 1988 Acts; Fifth Supplement = *Income Tax Act*). Place the supplement number and the abbreviation **Supp** in parentheses after the chapter.

Anne	Ann		George	Geo
Edward	Edw		Victoria	Vict
Elizabeth	Eliz		William	Will

For federal statutes enacted before 1867, and for provincial statutes enacted before the province entered Confederation, give the **regnal year** in parentheses following the calendar year. Otherwise give the calendar year and not the regnal year.

2.1.9   Chapter

Abbreviate chapter to **c**.

Write the numeric or alphanumeric chapter designation exactly as shown in the statute volume, **including dashes and periods**.

Holocaust Memorial Day Act, SBC 2000, **c 3**.
Law Reform Act, SNB 1993, **c L-1.2**.
An Act respecting acupuncture, CQLR c A-5.1.
Child Welfare Act, 1972, SN 1972, **No 37**.

NB: Between 1934 and 1975–76, statutes in Newfoundland's annual volumes are designated by number. Abbreviate **Number** to **No**.

2.1.10   Pinpoint

To cite a specific section of a statute, place a comma after the chapter and then indicate the section or sections.

Abbreviate **section** to **s** and **sections** to **ss** in the footnotes, but always write the full word in the text. Do not insert **at**.

Separate **consecutive** sections by an **en-dash** and **non-consecutive** sections by a **comma** (see note 1).

[1] *Environmental Protection and Enhancement Act*, RSA 2000, c E-12, **ss 2, 38–42, 84**.
[2] *Legal Profession Act, 1990*, SS 1990, c L-10.1, **ss 4(1), 6(2)(b)(i)–(ii), 9**.
[3] *Charter of the French language*, CQLR c C-11, **Preamble, para 3**.
[4] *Access to Information Act*, RSC 1985, c A-1, **Schedule II**.

It is generally preferable to cite to specific sections, but to indicate a **general area**, place **ff** immediately after the number (e.g., ss **69ff**).

Indicate further subdivisions (e.g., subsections, paragraphs, subparagraphs) as they appear in the legislation (see note 2). Cite an unnumbered or unlettered subdivision like a paragraph, abbreviated as **para** in the singular and **paras** in the plural (see note 3). Do not use parentheses.

Do not abbreviate **Preamble** (see note 3) or **Schedule** (see note 4).

The **provisions of Quebec codes are articles, not sections**. Abbreviate article and articles to **art** and **arts** respectively (section 2.3).

Legislation

2.1.11   Amendments, Repeals, and Re-enactments

Presumed to be amended	*Crown Liability and Proceedings Act*, RSC 1985, c C-50.
Indicating amended status	*Emergency Measures Act*, SM 1987, c 11, **as amended by SM 1997, c 28**. *Municipal Government Act*, RSA 2000, c M-26, s 694(4), **as amended by Municipal Government Amendment Act, SA 2003, c 43, s 4**.
Indicating repealed status	*Family Benefits Act*, RSO 1990, c F.2, **as repealed by** *Social Assistance Reform Act, 1997*, **SO 1997, c 25, s 4(1)**.
Act amending an earlier act	*An Act to Amend the Labour Standards Act*, SNWT 1999, c 18, **amending RSNWT 1988, c L-1**.
Act repealing an earlier act	*An Act respecting the James Bay Native Development Corporation*, CQLR c S-9.1, **repealing** *An Act to incorporate the James Bay Native Development Corporation*, **SQ 1978, c 96**.

▦ Citations are presumed to be to the statute **as amended on the date of publication** of the author's text.

▦ Indicate that the statute has been amended only if it is relevant to the point being discussed in the text. When indicating an amendment, cite the original statute first, followed by **as amended by** and the citation for the amending statute.

▦ When an act has been **repealed**, always indicate the repeal in the citation (**as repealed by**).

▦ Use **amending** when referring specifically to a statute that amends an earlier statute, and use **repealing** when citing a statute that repeals an earlier statute.

▦ Indicate the title of the second statute only if it is different from the title of the first statute, or if it is not included in the title of the first statute cited (see *Emergency Measures Act* and *Labour Standards Act* examples, above).

▦ If a statute or part of a statute was repealed and another substituted, cite the original statute first, followed by **as re-enacted by** and the citation for the new replacement section. Use this term only if the repeal and substitute provision are found in the same section.

2.1.12   Appendices

▦ For statutes that appear in an appendix, always provide the official citation first, followed by the citation to the appendix.

> *Canadian Bill of Rights*, SC 1960, c 44, **reprinted in** RSC 1985, **Appendix III**.

▦ Introduce the appendix reference with the phrase **reprinted in**.

▦ Indicate the statute revision or volume to which the appendix is attached (e.g., **RSC 1985**), followed by a comma and the appendix number.

▨ Write the appendix number in Roman numerals.

2.1.13 Statutes Within Statutes

▨ Refer first to the title of the statute within the statute. Indicate the relevant part of the containing act and its full citation, introduced by a comma and **being**.

> *Enterprise Cape Breton Corporation Act*, s 25, **being** Part II of the *Government Organization Act, Atlantic Canada, 1987*, RSC 1985, c 41 (4th Supp).

▨ Place pinpoint references to section numbers before the citation to the containing act.

2.2 CONSTITUTIONAL STATUTES

Constitution Act, 1867	*Constitution Act, 1867* (UK), 30 & 31 Vict, c 3, reprinted in RSC 1985, Appendix II, No 5.
Canada Act 1982	*Canada Act 1982* (UK), 1982, c 11.
Constitution Act, 1982	*Constitution Act, 1982*, being Schedule B to the *Canada Act 1982* (UK), 1982, c 11.
Charter	*Canadian Charter of Rights and Freedoms*, Part I of the *Constitution Act, 1982*, being Schedule B to the *Canada Act 1982* (UK), 1982, c 11.
Other constitutional statutes	*Saskatchewan Act*, SC 1905, c 42.

▨ Many constitutional statutes were enacted under different names than those used today; use the **new title**. Consult the Schedule to the *Constitution Act, 1982* to determine the new title for the statute. If appropriate, provide the old title in parentheses at the end of the citation.

▨ Since the *Canada Act 1982* is a British statute, use the rules for the United Kingdom (section 7.3.1).

▨ Since the *Charter* is not an independent enactment, cite it as Part I of the *Constitution Act, 1982*.

▨ If necessary, include a citation to **Appendix II of RSC 1985** after the official citation. Most Canadian constitutional statutes are reprinted in Appendix II.

2.2.1 Pinpoint

Constitution Act, 1867	*Constitution Act, 1867* (UK), 30 & 31 Vict, c 3, **s 91**, reprinted in RSC 1985, Appendix II, No 5.
Canada Act 1982	*Canada Act 1982* (UK), 1982, c 11, **s 1**.
Constitution Act, 1982	*Constitution Act, 1982*, **s 35**, being Schedule B to the *Canada Act 1982* (UK), 1982, c 11.
Charter	*Canadian Charter of Rights and Freedoms*, **s 7**, Part I of the *Constitution Act, 1982*, being Schedule B to the *Canada Act 1982* (UK), 1982, c 11.
Other constitutional statutes	*Saskatchewan Act*, SC 1905, c 42, **s 2**.

▨ Place pinpoint references to the *Charter* and the *Constitution Act, 1982* immediately after the title (section 2.1.10).

▨ For any other constitutional statutes, place pinpoint references after the chapter number.

2.3 CODES

Civil Code of Québec	art 1260 **CCQ**
Civil Code of Québec (1980)	art 435 **CCQ (1980)**
Civil Code of Lower Canada	art 1131 **CCLC**
Code of Civil Procedure	art 477 **CCP**
Code of Penal Procedure	art 104 **CPP**

▨ **Do not use full citation form when referring to codes.** To cite one of the codes illustrated here, use the abbreviated name.

▨ To cite another Canadian code, write the full title of the code at the first reference, and create a short form if needed. If the title does not indicate the jurisdiction, include that information in Roman type before the short form (e.g., **art 1** *Professional Code* **[QC Prof C]**).

▨ For foreign codes, see the appropriate rules in section 7 of this Guide.

▨ The provisions of Quebec codes are **articles, not sections**. Abbreviate article to **art** and **articles** to **arts**.

▨ Cite an unnumbered or unlettered subdivision like a **paragraph**, abbreviated as **para** in the singular and **paras** in the plural (e.g., **art 1457, para 2 CCQ**).

Legislation

▨ To cite a Preliminary Provision (or other similarly discrete sections), follow the same principle as that applying to articles (e.g., **Preliminary Provision, para 2 CCQ**).

▨ To cite the **Minister's Comments** on the Civil Code of Quebec, see section 4.2.1.

NB: The **CCQ (1980)** is a series of family law enactments implemented in 1980: *An Act to establish a new Civil Code and to reform family law*, SQ 1980, c 39. Do not confuse this with the *Civil Code of Quebec*, CQLR c C-1991 (CCQ), which came into force on 1 January 1994, replacing the *Civil Code of Lower Canada* of 1866 (CCLC).

2.4 BILLS

	Number,	*title*,	session,	legislature,	jurisdiction,	year,	pinpoint	(additional information) (optional).
Canada	Bill C-26,	*An Act to establish the Canada Border Services Agency,*	1st Sess,	38th Parl,		2005,	cl 5(1)(e)	(as passed by the House of Commons 13 June 2005).
	Bill S-3,	*An Act to amend the Energy Efficiency Act,*	2nd Sess,	40th Parl,		2009,	cl 5	(first reading 29 January 2009).
Provinces and territories	Bill 59,	*An Act to amend the Civil Code as regards marriage,*	1st Sess,	37th Leg,	Quebec,	2004		(assented to 10 November 2004), SQ 2004, c 23.

▨ Add **C-** before bills originating in the House of Commons and **S-** before bills originating in the Senate.

▨ **Use the long title of the bill**. Italicize the title and follow the bill's capitalization.

▨ If referring to a provincial bill, include the jurisdiction.

▨ Do not provide the regnal year.

▨ The subdivisions of a bill are **clauses**, abbreviated to **cl** and **cls** for plural.

▨ Include additional information as needed (e.g., the date of first reading or the state that the bill has reached at the time of writing). Place the information in parentheses at the end of the citation.

▨ If the chapter number of the bill is known, include the **future statute citation** after the date of assent as additional information (e.g., **(assented to 10 November 2004), SQ 2004, c 23**).

2.5 REGULATIONS

Jurisdiction	Unrevised	Consolidated, Revised, or Re-enacted
Canada	SOR/2000-111, s 4.	CRC, c 1035, s 4.
Alberta	Alta Reg 184/2001, s 2.	–
British Columbia	BC Reg 362/2000, s 4.	–
Manitoba	Man Reg 155/2001, s 3.	Man Reg 368/97R, s 2.
New Brunswick	NB Reg 2000-8, s 11.	–
Newfoundland	Nfld Reg 78/99, s 4.	–
Newfoundland and Labrador	NLR 08/02, s 2.	CNLR 1151/96, s 6.
Northwest Territories	NWT Reg 253-77, s 3.	RRNWT 1990, c E-27, s 16.
Nova Scotia	NS Reg 24/2000, s 8.	–
Nunavut	Nu Reg 045-99, s 2.	–
Ontario	O Reg 426/00, s 2.	RRO 1990, Reg 1015, s 3.
Prince Edward Island	PEI Reg EC1999-598, s 3.	–
Quebec	OC 868-97, 2 July 1997, (1997) GOQ II 3692, s 2.	CQLR c A-2.1, r 2.
Saskatchewan	Sask Reg 67/2001, s 3.	RRS, c C-50-2, Reg 21, s 6.
Yukon	YOIC 2000/130, s 9.	–

2.5.1 Federal Regulations

2.5.1.1 Revised Regulations

▨ Abbreviate **Consolidated Regulations of Canada** to **CRC**.

▨ Indicate the year of revision of the revised regulations (optional). Citations are assumed

Title,	CRC,	chapter,	pinpoint	(year) (optional).
Migratory Birds Regulations,	CRC,	c 1035,	s 4	(1978).

to be to the latest revision. For greater clarity with respect to the date of the revision, Point in Time citation may be used (section 2.1.2).

2.5.1.2 Unrevised Regulations

Title (optional),	SOR/	year-regulation number,	pinpoint.
Offset of Taxes by a Refund or a Rebate (GST/HST) Regulations,	SOR/	91-49,	s 4.
Canadian Aviation Security Regulations,	SOR/	2000-111,	s 4.

- Find federal regulations promulgated after the Consolidation **in Part II of the *Canada Gazette***. Do not include a direct citation to the *Gazette*.
- Abbreviate **Statutory Orders and Regulations** to **SOR**.
- Indicate the title (optional).
- For regulations starting with the year 2000, include the four digits of the year. For years up until 1999, use only the last two digits (e.g., write **98** and not **1998**).

2.5.2 Provincial and Territorial Regulations

- Include the title of the regulations (optional) in italics at the beginning of the citation, followed by a comma.
- Some jurisdictions use all four digits to indicate the year starting with the year 2000.

NB: Alberta, British Columbia, New Brunswick, Nova Scotia, Nunavut, Prince Edward Island, and the Yukon do not publish revised versions of their regulations.

2.5.2.1 Alberta, British Columbia

- Cite the Alberta and British Columbia consolidations in the same manner as unrevised regulations (section 2.5.1.2).

Jurisdiction	Reg	number/year,	pinpoint.
Alta	Reg	184/2001,	s 2.
BC	Reg	362/2000,	s 6.

2.5.2.2 Manitoba

	Jurisdiction	Reg	number/year,	pinpoint.
Not re-enacted	Man	Reg	155/2001,	s 3.
Re-enacted	Man	Reg	468/88R,	s 2.

Most of Manitoba's regulations were re-enacted in English and in French in **1987** and **1988**. To indicate a re-enacted regulation, insert **R** immediately following the year.

2.5.2.3 New Brunswick

Jurisdiction	Reg	year-number,	pinpoint.
NB	Reg	2000-8,	s 11.

The New Brunswick regulations were last revised in **1963**.

2.5.2.4 Newfoundland and Labrador

All references to Newfoundland were retroactively amended to Newfoundland and Labrador. Indicate **Newfoundland** only for regulations repealed before 6 December 2001.

2.5.2.4.1 Unrevised

Write **Nfld Reg** to indicate regulations repealed before 6 December 2001. Use **NL** for other regulations.

Jurisdiction	R	number/last two digits of year,	pinpoint.
NL	R	8/02,	s 2.

2.5.2.4.2 Revised

Newfoundland and Labrador regulations were revised and consolidated in 1996. Use **CNLR** to indicate a **Consolidated Newfoundland and Labrador Regulation**.

CNLR	number/year of consolidation,	pinpoint.
CNLR	1151/96,	s 6.

Use **CNR** for **Consolidated Newfoundland Regulation** to indicate regulations repealed before 6 December 2001.

2.5.2.5 Northwest Territories

2.5.2.5.1 Unrevised

Jurisdiction	Reg	number-last two digits of year,	pinpoint.
NWT	Reg	253-77,	s 3.

2.5.2.5.2 Revised

RRNWT	year of revision,	chapter,	pinpoint.
RRNWT	1990,	c E-27,	s 16.

2.5.2.6 Nova Scotia

Jurisdiction	Reg	number/year,	pinpoint.
NS	Reg	24/2000,	s 8.

2.5.2.7 Nunavut

Jurisdiction	Reg	number-last two digits of year,	pinpoint.
Nu	Reg	045-99,	s 2.

▨ Consult the *Nunavut Gazette* for all regulations since 1 April 1999.

▨ Consult the *Revised Regulations of the Northwest Territories* (1990) and *The Northwest Territories Gazette*, Part II, for all regulations made prior to 1 April 1999.

▨ No official revised version of the Nunavut Regulations has been issued.

2.5.2.8 Ontario

2.5.2.8.1 Unrevised

Jurisdiction	Reg	number/last two digits of year,	pinpoint.
O	Reg	426/00,	s 2.

2.5.2.8.2 Revised

RRO	year of revision,	Reg	number,	pinpoint.
RRO	1990,	Reg	1015,	s 3.

Legislation

2.5.2.9 Prince Edward Island

Jurisdiction	Reg	ECyear-number	pinpoint.
PEI	Reg	EC1999-598,	s 3.

▓ EC is the abbreviation for **Executive Council**. There is no space between **EC** and **year-number**.

2.5.2.10 Quebec

2.5.2.10.1 Historical Versions

OC	number-year,	date,	*Gazette* citation,	pinpoint.
OC	1240-2000,	25 October 2000,	(2000) GOQ II, 6817,	s 2.

▓ To cite the *Gazette officielle du Québec*, see section 2.6.1.

2.5.2.10.2 Current Version (Cited to the Compilation of Quebec Laws and Regulations)

CQLR	number,	rule number,	pinpoint.
CQLR	c C-11,	r 9,	s 10.

2.5.2.11 Saskatchewan

2.5.2.11.1 Unrevised

Jurisdiction	Reg	number/year,	pinpoint.
Sask	Reg	67/2001,	s 3.

2.5.2.11.2 Revised

RRS	chapter,	number,	pinpoint.
RRS,	c C-502,	Reg 21,	s 6.

2.5.2.12 Yukon

Jurisdiction	OIC	year/number,	pinpoint.
Y	OIC	2000/130,	s 9.

▪ Abbreviate **Order in Council** to **OIC**.

2.6   OTHER INFORMATION PUBLISHED IN *GAZETTES*

2.6.1   General Form

Title (additional information),	(year)	*Gazette* abbreviation	part of *Gazette*,	page	(additional information) (optional).
Ministerial Order 36/91,	(1991)	A Gaz	I,	1609.	
Notice (City of Abbotsford),	(2004)	C Gaz	I,	2520.	
OC 309/2001,	(2001)	A Gaz	I,	1752	(*Provincial Parks Act*).

▪ Include a space between the *Gazette* abbreviation and the part of the *Gazette* (e.g., **C Gaz I**).

▪ Indicate the title of the item if appropriate. If the item is numbered in some way, include the number with the title, as it appears in the *Gazette*. Include the statutory instrument number (**SI**) if there is one. Include the name of the person or body concerned by a notice in parentheses after the title (optional).

▪ Indicate the part of the *Gazette* following the abbreviation. If the *Gazette* is **not published in parts**, add a comma after the abbreviation and cite the page number (e.g., **GOQ, 74**).

▪ Include additional information, such as the name of the statute under which an order in council is made (see *Provincial Parks Act*).

Abbreviations of *Gazettes*:

The Alberta Gazette	A Gaz
The British Columbia Gazette	BC Gaz
Canada Gazette	C Gaz
Gazette officielle du Québec	GOQ
The Manitoba Gazette	M Gaz
New Brunswick: *The Royal Gazette*	NB Gaz
Northwest Territories Gazette	NWT Gaz
The Newfoundland Gazette (before 21 December 2001)	N Gaz
The Newfoundland and Labrador Gazette (21 December 2001 and after)	NL Gaz
Nova Scotia: *Royal Gazette*	NS Gaz
Nunavut Gazette	Nu Gaz
The Ontario Gazette	O Gaz
Prince Edward Island: *Royal Gazette*	PEI Gaz
The Saskatchewan Gazette	S Gaz
The Yukon Gazette	Y Gaz

NB: The PDF of the *Canada Gazette* has been official since 1 April 2003 at <www.canadagazette.gc.ca>.

2.6.2   Orders in Council

An Order in Council is an instrument issued by the executive, which implements a government decision (such as the creation of a regulation).

2.6.2.1 Federal

Title (if available),	PC year-number or SI/year-number,	Gazette citation	(additional information) (optional).
	PC 1997-627,	(1997) C Gaz II, 1381.	
Withdrawal from Disposal Order (North Slave Region NWT),	SI/97-42,	(1997) C Gaz II, 1338.	

▓ Include the title in italics, if applicable.

▓ Abbreviate **Privy Council** to **PC**.

▓ Include the statutory instrument (**SI**) number, if there is one.

▓ Provide additional information (e.g., the title of the act under which the order in council is made) if necessary.

2.6.2.2 Provincial and Territorial

Title (if available),	Order in Council number,	Gazette citation	(additional information) (optional).
	OIC 1989/19,	(1989) Y Gaz II, 57.	
Town of Paradise Order,	OC 99-529,	(1999) N Gaz II, 451	(Municipalities Act).
Regulation respecting the lifting of the suspension and the application of section 41.1 of the Act respecting labour standards for certain employees,	OIC 570-93,	(1993) GOQ II, 2607.	

▓ Include the title of the instrument if available.

▓ Use the abbreviation for **Order in Council** as it appears in the relevant *Gazette*.

▓ Use the Order in Council number as it appears in the *Gazette*; this may include the year or the last two digits of the year.

▓ Provide additional information, such as the title of the act under which the order in council is made.

2.6.3   Proclamations and Royal Instructions

Citation of law that entered into force or issuer of proclamation or instruction,	type of document,	date,	SI/year-number,	*Gazette* or other citation.
Sex Offender Information Registration Act, SC 2004, c 10,		proclaimed in force 15 December 2004,	SI/2004-157,	(2004) C Gaz II, 2021.
	Proclamation,	1 April 1991,		(1991) S Gaz I, 1174.
George R,	Proclamation,	7 October 1763 (3 Geo III),		reprinted in RSC 1985, App II, No 1.
George R to Governor Arthur Phillip,	Royal Instruction,	25 April 1787 (27 Geo III),		reprinted in *Historical Documents of New South Wales*, vol 1, part 2 (Sydney: Government Printer, 1892-1901) 67.

▢ Use the words **Proclamation** or **Royal Instruction** if it is appropriate in the context.

▢ Include the date, followed by the *Gazette* or other citation.

▢ To cite the federal proclamations dating from 1972, include the statutory instrument (**SI**) number.

2.7   MUNICIPAL BY-LAWS

	Municipality,	by-law or revised by-law	number,	*title*	(date),	pin-point.
Unrevised	City of Whitehorse,	by-law	No 97-42,	*Zoning By-law*	(11 May 1998),	s 1.
Revised	City of Montreal,	revised by-law	C S-0.1.1,	*By-law Concerning Collection Services*,		s 5.

▢ Include the by-law number. Provide the full title if no short title is available.

2.8   RULES OF PRACTICE

Jurisdiction (if applicable),	issuing body (if applicable),	*title,*	indexing number, (if applicable)	additional indexing information, (if applicable)	pinpoint.
		Federal Court Immigration Rules,			r 18.
Manitoba,		*Court of Queen's Bench Rules,*			r 275.2.
	Commission québécoise des libérations condition- nelles,	*Règles de pratique,*			r 10(4).
Alberta,		*Rules of Court,*	AR 124/2010,	vol 1,	r 10.50.

- Rules of practice (or rules of court) are procedural regulations governing judiciary and administrative bodies.

- Include the jurisdiction and issuing body unless it is part of the title of the rules.

- Do not indicate **Canada** for the rules of the Supreme Court of Canada or the Federal Court.

- Abbreviate **rule** as **r**.

- To cite to the Quebec *Code of Civil Procedure* or *Code of Penal Procedure*, see section 2.3.

2.9 SECURITIES COMMISSIONS

Title,	commission	document	bulletin (if applicable)	(date),	pinpoint.
Mutual Reliance Review System for Exemptive Relief Applications,	OSC	NP 12-201		(26 August 2005).	
Proposed Amendments to Multilateral Instrument 52-109 Certification of Disclosure in Issuers' Annual and Interim Filings and Companion Policy 52-109CP,	MSC	Notice 2005-19		(1 April 2005).	
CSA Notice — Amendments to NI 31-101 National Registration System and NP 31-201 National Registration System,	OSC6	CSA Notice,	(2006) 29 OSCB 3955		at 3956.

▦ Cite securities national instruments, national policies and other documents to **provincial securities commissions**.

▦ Abbreviate **National Policy** as **NP** and **National Instrument** as **NI**.

▦ For amendments, proposed rules, staff notices, requests for comments, and other commission documents, cite to the **securities commission bulletin** or similar publication, if available.

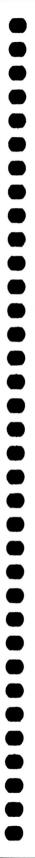

Jurisprudence

3   Jurisprudence **E-49**

E -3.1   Sources E-49

E -3.2   General Form E-50
    E -3.2.1   Neutral Citation Available E-50
    E -3.2.2   Neutral Citation Not Available E-50

E -3.3   Style of Cause E-51
    E -3.3.1   Names of Parties E-51
    E -3.3.2   Person Represented by Guardian or Tutor E-52
    E -3.3.3   Names of Companies and Partnerships........................... E-52
    E -3.3.4   Countries, Federal Units, Provinces, and Municipalities.................. E-52
    E -3.3.5   Wills and Estates E-53
    E -3.3.6   Bankruptcies and Receiverships...................................... E-53
    E -3.3.7   Statute Titles.. E-53
    E -3.3.8   The Crown E-53
    E -3.3.9   Government Entities.. E-54
    E -3.3.10 Crown Corporations E-54
    E -3.3.11 Municipal Boards and Bodies E-55
    E -3.3.12 School Boards E-55
    E -3.3.13 Unions E-55
    E -3.3.14 Social Welfare Agencies E-55
    E -3.3.15 Parties' Names that are Undisclosed E-55
    E -3.3.16 If The Case Is Known Under Two Names—The Sub Nom Rule E-56
    E -3.3.17 One Party Acting for Someone Else—The Ex Rel Rule................. E-56
    E -3.3.18 Procedural Phrases and Constitutional References...................... E-56

E -3.4   Year of Decision.. E-57

E -3.5   Neutral Citation E-57
    E -3.5.1   Year E-58
    E -3.5.2   Tribunal Identifier E-58
    E -3.5.3   Decision Number E-59

E -3.6   Pinpoint... E-60
    E -3.6.1   General Form.. E-60
    E -3.6.2   Cited Reporter.. E-60

E -3.7   Printed Reporter.. E-61
    E -3.7.1   Year of Reporter E-61
    E -3.7.2   Reporter E-62
        E -3.7.2.1   Official Reporters E-62
        E -3.7.2.2   Semi-Official Reporters E-62
        E -3.7.2.3   Unofficial Reporters E-63
    E -3.7.3   Series E-63
    E -3.7.4   First Page E-64

E -3.8   Online Databases.. E-64
    E -3.8.1   Published Judgments and Judgments with a Neutral Citation E-64
    E -3.8.2   Unpublished Judgments With No Neutral Citation...................... E-65
        E -3.8.2.1   CanLII.. E-65
        E -3.8.2.2   Quicklaw.. E-65

E -3.8.2.3 Westlaw Canada E-65
E -3.8.2.4 Azimut E-66
E -3.8.2.5 Other Services E-66

E -3.9 Jurisdiction and Court E-66

E -3.10 Judge E-67

E -3.11 History of Case E-68
E -3.11.1 Prior History... E-68
E -3.11.2 Subsequent History.. E-68
E -3.11.3 Prior and Subsequent History E-69
E -3.11.4 Leave to Appeal... E-69

E -3.12 Unreported Decisions Without a Neutral Citation E-71

E -3.13 Interlocutory Judgments and Motions E-72

E -3.14 Administrative Bodies and Tribunals E-72
E -3.14.1 Decisions in Printed Reporters E-72
E -3.14.1 Online Decisions E-73

E -3.15 Arguments and Evidentiary Documents E-73

Jurisprudence

3 JURISPRUDENCE

3.1 SOURCES

Hierarchy of sources:

```
┌─────────────────────────────┐
│       Neutral citation      │
└─────────────────────────────┘
               ⇩
┌─────────────────────────────┐
│  Official reporter for national│
│  jurisdictions (e.g., SCR, FCR, or Ex│
│  CR); semi-official reporters for│
│  provincial jurisdictions (e.g., OR,│
│              RJQ)            │
└─────────────────────────────┘
               ⇩
┌─────────────────────────────────────────────────┐
│  Other sources (unofficial reporters, online databases, etc.)  │
└─────────────────────────────────────────────────┘
```

 Providing the reader with at least two sources ("parallel citation") is strongly recommended.

- ☐ Citing to several sources provides greater ease of access to the referenced decision.

- ☐ In conjunction with the hierarchy of sources, parallel citation allows for the communication of added relevance that a decision's appearance in a highly regarded or practice-specific reporter (e.g., DLR, CCC, Admin LR, etc.) may provide.

 Before citing less authoritative sources, make sure that more authoritative sources are not available (e.g., do not cite to an unofficial reporter before citing to an official reporter).

- ☐ Always provide the neutral citation if it is available.

- ☐ After the neutral citation, provide the official reporters (SCR, FCR, or Ex CR) for national jurisdictions or semi-official reporters for provincial jurisdictions (e.g., OR, RJQ).

- ☐ Lastly, provide other sources (unofficial reporters, online databases, etc.).

Choose the **other sources** carefully and keep in mind their accessibility to readers.

- ☐ For printed reporters, prefer general reporters that cover a **large geographic area** and that are more **readily available** (section 3.7.2).

- ☐ For online databases, prefer research databases that are freely accessible (e.g., CanLII) over commercial subscription services.

Consult the following table to determine which sources to cite depending on what is available.

Sources available	Rule	Example
Neutral citation only	Cite to neutral citation only. Do not cite to an online database.	*Adoption — 091*, **2009 QCCQ 628**.
Neutral citation and printed reporter(s)	Include neutral citation and then cite to the most authoritative printed reporter available.	*R v Latimer*, **2001 SCC 1, [2001] 1 SCR 3**.
Official reporter and other reporter(s)	Cite to official reporter, including the most authoritative reporter as a parallel citation.	*Baker v Canada (Minister of Citizenship and Immigration)*, **[1999] 2 SCR 817, 174 DLR (4th) 193**.
Unofficial reporter(s) and/or online database(s)	Cite to the two most accessible sources.	*Coldmatic Refrigeration of Canada Ltd v Leveltek Processing LLC* (2004), **70 OR (3d) 758, 2004 CanLII 14550** (CA).
No source available	Follow rules for unreported decisions in section 3.12.	*Commission des droits de la personne du Québec c Brasserie O'Keefe* (**13 September 1990**), Montreal **500-05-005826-878** (Qc Sup Ct).

3.2   GENERAL FORM

3.2.1   Neutral Citation Available

Style of cause,	neutral citation	pinpoint,	reporter	judge (if applicable)	[short form].
Fisher v Fisher,	2008 ONCA 11	at paras 52–59,	88 OR (3d) 241	Lang JA	[*Fisher*].
Stewart v Berezan,	2007 BCCA 150	at paras 11, 15,	64 BCLR (4th) 152	Donald J	[*Stewart*].

3.2.2   Neutral Citation Not Available

Style of cause	(year of the decision) (if necessary),	reporter	pinpoint	parallel citation	(jurisdiction) (if necessary)	judge (if applicable)	[short form].
Gordon v Goertz		[1996] 2 SCR 27	at para 13,	134 DLR (4th) 321,		McLachlin J	[*Gordon*].
R v Dimic	(1998),	54 CRR (2d) 290,		1998 CanLII 3153	(Ont CA)		[*Dimic*].

Jurisprudence

3.3   STYLE OF CAUSE

The style of cause is a shorter version of the title, referring to a decision informally.

When the style of cause is provided by the reporter, keep it as is. If the decision does not indicate the style of cause, follow the supplementary rules indicated in sections 3.3.1 to 3.3.18, below.

If the style of cause is indicated in the text, do not repeat it in the footnote.

Italicize both the names of the parties and the *v* or *c* that separates their names.

The use of *v* and *c* in the style of cause indicates the language of the decision. If the decision of the tribunal is in English, use *v*. If the decision of the tribunal is in French, use *c*. If the decision is bilingual, use *v* if you are writing in English.

When the style of cause includes terms normally appearing italicized, they should appear in roman type (reverse italics). This applies, for example, to a ship sued *in rem* (e.g., *Porter v The* **Pinafore**). As indicated above, this rule does not apply to *v* and *c*.

Decision in English	*Pacific Developments Ltd v Calgary (City of)*
Decision in French	*Traverse Trois-Pistoles Escoumins Ltée c Quebec (Commission des Transports)*
Bilingual decision	*Committee for the Equal Treatment of Asbestos Minority Share-holders v Ontario (Securities Commission)*

3.3.1   Names of Parties

✔	*Toneguzzo-Norvell v Savein* *Best v Best*
✗	*Jessica Teresa Toneguzzo-Norvell v Nelson Savein* *T Best v M Best*

Use **surnames**; omit given names or first initials.

Where more than one person is on either side of the action, use only the first person's name.

Refrain from using **et al** to indicate multiple parties.

Capitalize the first letter of a party name and the first letter of all words, other than prepositions, conjunctions, and words in procedural phrases (e.g., *in re, ex rel*).

Translate into English descriptions such as **city** but do not translate words forming part of the name of a party, such as **University**, and abbreviations such as **Ltd** or **LLP**.

Do not include **The, Le, La, L', or Les** as the first word of a party name, even if it is part of a company name. Include these words if they are part of the name of an object proceeded against *in rem* (such as aircraft or ships: *The Mihalis Angelos*).

Jurisprudence

3.3.2   Person Represented by Guardian or Tutor

> *Williams **(Guardian ad litem of)** v Canadian National Railway*
> *Dobson **(Litigation guardian of)** v Dobson*

3.3.3   Names of Companies and Partnerships

- It is important to identify business entities as such. Accordingly, always include **Co, Corp, Inc, Ltd, ltée, Limited, srl, LLP**. Do not translate these identifying words or abbreviations.

- Include given names and initials that form part of a company or firm name. Also include the names of all partners in a partnership.

✓	*Sloan v **Union Oil Co of Canada Ltd*** *Metson v **RW de Wolfe Ltd*** *Prowse Chowne **LLP** v Northey* *National Party of Canada v Canadian Broadcasting **Corp*** ***Shell Canada Ltd** v Canada* *Wickberg v **Shatsky & Shatsky***
✗	*Sloan v Union Oil* *Metson v de Wolfe* *Shell Canada v Canada*

- When a company has a bilingual name, use the name of the company in the language of the decision. If the decision is bilingual, use the name of the company in the language in which you are writing.

3.3.4   Countries, Federal Units, Provinces, and Municipalities

Country	✓	*United States v Burns*
	✗	*The United States of America v Burns*
Province, State		*Mercier v **Alberta** (AG)*
Municipality		*Bay Colony Ltd v Wasaga Beach **(Town of)*** *Markle v Toronto **(City of)*** *Toronto Dominion Bank v **Alfred** **(Township of)***

- Use the **common name of a country**, not its formal name or abbreviation.

- Omit **Province of**, **State of**, **People of**, or any other similar identifiers.

- Include identifiers such as **City of**, **County of**, **District of**, or **Township of** in parentheses.

3.3.5   Wills and Estates

Name of estate	*Kipling v **Kohinsky Estate***
Name of estate if no plaintiff or defendant is included in the style of cause	***Re Eurig Estate***

▢ Do not use the names of executors.

▢ The term **Re** should precede the name of the estate. However, always follow the style of cause provided by a reporter, even if the **Re** is placed differently (e.g., ***Lipton Estate (Re)***).

3.3.6   Bankruptcies and Receiverships

*Chablis Textiles **(Trustee of)** v London Life Insurance* *Confederation Trust Co **(Liquidator of)** v Donovan*	▢ Use the name of the bankruptcy or company in receivership followed by **Trustee of**, **Receiver of**, or **Liquidator of** in parentheses.

3.3.7   Statute Titles

Jurisdiction is obvious from the name of the statute	*Re Canadian Labour Code*
Jurisdiction cannot be discerned from the name of the statute	*Reference Re Fisheries Act (Canada)*

3.3.8   The Crown

▢ Use **R** to refer to the Crown. It should also replace expressions such as **The Queen**, **Regina**, **The Crown**, or **The Queen in Right of**.

***R** v Blondin*

3.3.9 Government Entities

Attorney General (AG)		*Schreiber v Canada* **(AG)**
Minister of National Revenue (MNR)		*Buckman v* **MNR**
Other government bodies		*Susan Shoe Industries Ltd v Ontario* **(Employment Standards Officer)**
Do not repeat the name of the jurisdiction	✓	*Laurentian Bank of Canada v Canada* **(Human Rights Commission)**
	✗	*Laurentian Bank of Canada v Canada* **(Canadian Human Rights Commission)**
Do not include the name of an individual representing a government body	✓	*Canada* **(Combines Investigation Branch, Director of Investigation and Research)** *v Southam*
	✗	*Lawson AW Hunter (Director of Investigation and Research of the Combines Investigation Branch) v Southam*

- **Include the name of the jurisdiction** that the government entity represents.
- Place the name of the government body (such as an agency, commission, or department) in parentheses after the name of the jurisdiction.
- Abbreviate the **Minister of National Revenue** to **MNR**, the **Deputy Minister of National Revenue** to **Deputy MNR**, and **Attorney General** to **AG**.
- To cite a federal or provincial **administrative tribunal**, see section 3.14.
- Do not include the name of an individual representing a government body.

3.3.10 Crown Corporations

Westaim Corp v **Royal Canadian Mint**

Do not include the name of the jurisdiction before the name of the Crown corporation.

3.3.11   Municipal Boards and Bodies

> *Johnson v Sarnia (City of)* **Commissioners of Police**

▨ Indicate the name of the municipal board or body after the jurisdiction (e.g., ***Sarnia (City of)***).

3.3.12   School Boards

✓	*Prince Albert **Rural School Division No 56** v Teachers of Saskatchewan*
✗	*Board of Education of Prince Albert Rural School Division No 56 v Teachers of Saskatchewan*

▨ Omit such terms as **Board of Education**, **Board of Trustees**, or **Governors of**. Include only the name of the institution.

3.3.13   Unions

▨ Do not abbreviate union names, as such abbreviations vary widely.

✓	***Canadian Autoworkers Union, Local 576** v Bradco Construction Ltd*
✗	*CAU, Local 576 v Bradco Construction Ltd*

3.3.14   Social Welfare Agencies

> *Doe v **Metropolitan Toronto Child and Family Services***
> *EP v **Winnipeg (Director of Child and Family Services)***

▨ Include the name of the community where the aid agency is based unless it forms part of the name of the agency.

3.3.15   Parties' Names that are Undisclosed

▨ If the names of the parties are not disclosed in the case, use initials where available, or the title and numerical description provided by the reporter.

> ***Droit de la famille - 1544***
> ***M v H***

3.3.16   If The Case Is Known Under Two Names—The *Sub Nom* Rule

> *Reference Re Resolution to Amend the Constitution*, [1981] 1 SCR 753, **(sub nom *Reference Re Amendment of the Constitution of Canada (Nos 1, 2 and 3)*)** 125 DLR (3d) 1.

- *Sub nom* is the abbreviated version of *sub nomine*, which is Latin for "under the name of".

- Use the style of cause **provided in the most** authoritative **source** (i.e., official reporter over unofficial reporter; see the hierarchy of sources at section 3.1).

- If a **parallel citation refers to the parties by different names**, enclose this style of cause in parentheses introduced by the phrase *sub nom*. Place the parentheses immediately before the citation for the reporter using those names.

3.3.17   One Party Acting for Someone Else—The *Ex Rel* Rule

- *Ex rel* is the abbreviated version of *ex relatione*, which is Latin for "upon relation or information".

> *Ryel v Quebec (AG)* **ex rel** *Société immobilière du Québec*

- Where a third party enters the suit to act on behalf of one of the parties, note this by using the phrase *ex rel*.

3.3.18   Procedural Phrases and Constitutional References

Constitutional	*Reference Re* *Firearms Act*
Other	*Re* Gray *Ex parte* James: *Re* Condon

- Use *Reference Re* for constitutional cases only; in all other cases, use *Re* alone before the subject.

- Shorten *In re*, **In the matter of**, and *Dans l'affaire de* to *Re*.

- Write *Ex parte* in full. The expression indicates that the named party is the one that has brought the action.

Jurisprudence

3.4   YEAR OF DECISION

When a decision has a neutral citation, do not write the year in parentheses after the style of cause. **Apply the following rules if there is no neutral citation**:

Year of reporter is not indi-cated	Provide the year of decision in parentheses	*R v Borden* **(1993),** 24 CR (4th) 184 (NSCA).
Year of reporter and year of decision different	Provide both years	*Joyal c Hôpital du Christ-Roi* **(1996), [1997]** RJQ 38 (CA).
Year of reporter and year of decision are the same	Provide the year of the reporter	*Cadbury Schweppes v FBI Foods Ltd,* **[1999]** 1 SCR 142. ✗ *Cadbury Schweppes v FBI Foods Ltd* (1999), [1999] 1 SCR 142.

▨   Provide the year of the decision in parentheses after the style of cause and followed by a comma.

▨   **Use parentheses** for the **year of the decision**. Follow the parentheses by a comma.

▨   **Use brackets** for the **year of the reporter**. Precede the brackets by a comma.

3.5   NEUTRAL CITATION

The number of the neutral citation emanates from the court itself; **never create a neutral citation** when an official one is unavailable. Each Canadian court and a growing number of administrative tribunals have adopted the neutral citation. The date of its implementation for each entity is available at **Appendix B-3**.

The neutral citation can be used to identify a particular case independently from the reporter or electronic database in which it is published. For more information, see section 3.2.2 ("Neutral Citation") of the Canadian Citation Committee's *The Preparation Citation and Distribution of Canadian Decisions* at <lexum.org/ccc-ccr/preparation/en/>.

Style of cause,	neutral citation			optional elements		traditional citation.
	year	tribunal identifier	decision number	paragraph pinpoint	footnote pinpoint	
R v Law,	2002	SCC	10,			[2002] 1 SCR 227.
R v Senko,	2004	ABQB	60	at para 12,		352 AR 235.
Ordre des arpenteurs-géomètres du Québec c Tremblay,	2001	QCTP	24	at para 18,	n 14.	
Effigi Inc v Canada (AG),	2004	FC	1000	at paras 34–35, 40.		

▪ The neutral citation is assigned by the court and cannot be changed.

▪ The jurisdiction and level of court are indicated in a neutral citation. It is not necessary to include supplementary abbreviations of jurisdictions and courts. Some databases provide citations that resemble neutral citations (e.g., Quicklaw's SCJ or OJ). Use these identifiers only when citing to that database's source, and not in lieu of an official neutral citation.

▪ When writing for foreign audiences or when citing foreign jurisprudence, it may be appropriate to include the country's neutral three letter **ISO-3166-1 alpha-3** reference code before the neutral citation (e.g., *R v Law*, **CAN 2002 SCC 10**). Other codes include **GBR** for the United Kingdom, **FRA** for France, **AUS** for Australia, **NZL** for New Zealand, **SGP** for Singapore and **ZAF** for South Africa.

3.5.1   Year

The neutral citation begins with the year in which the decision was rendered by the court.

3.5.2   Tribunal Identifier

The tribunal identifier is assigned by the court and can be up to eight characters in length. It is composed of two elements. With the exception of the Northwest Territories, the provincial and territorial identifiers begin with a prefix of **two characters**.

Alberta	AB
British Columbia	BC
Manitoba	MB
New Brunswick	NB
Newfoundland and Labrador	NL (NF — before 2002)
Northwest Territories	NWT
Nova Scotia	NS
Nunavut	NU
Ontario	ON
Prince Edward Island	PE
Quebec	QC
Saskatchewan	SK
Yukon	YK

▨ The usual acronym of the tribunal or court follows this prefix. Omit the reintroduction of any letters representing the jurisdiction (e.g., the "Tribunal des professions du Québec" is **QCTP** and not **QCTPQ**).

▨ Federal tribunals and courts do not follow the prefix rule described above (e.g., Supreme Court of Canada = **SCC**, Federal Court of Appeal = **FCA**, Federal Court = **FC**, Tax Court of Canada = **TCC**). Note that the Federal Court went by the **FCT** abbreviation from 2001–2003. See **Appendix B-3** for a complete list of Neutral Citation Abbreviations.

3.5.3 Decision Number

▨ The sequence number is assigned by the court. This number reverts to "1" on 1 January of every year.

Jurisprudence

3.6   PINPOINT

3.6.1   General Form

Place the pinpoint reference **after the neutral citation**. If there is no neutral citation, place it after the first page of the reporter.

Always refer to **paragraphs** if there is a neutral citation or official paragraph number (i.e., determined by the court and uniform across all reporters). If there is no neutral citation or official paragraph number, refer to a page number or

> *R v Proulx*, 2000 SCC 5 **at para 27**, [2000] 1 SCR 61.
> *Bousquet v Barmish Inc* (1991), 37 CPR (3d) 516 **at 527** (FCTD).
> *Schofield v Smith* (2003), 119 NBR (2d) 130 **at 135ff**.
> *Vriend v Alberta (AG)*, [1998] 1 SCR 493 **at 532–34**, 156 DLR (4th) 385.
> *R c Kouri*, [2004] RJQ 2061 **at 2368, 2370** (CA).
> *Ordre des arpenteurs-géomètres du Québec c Tremblay*, 2001 QCTP 24 at para 18, n 14.

a paragraph and indicate the cited reporter (section 3.6.2). Begin a page or paragraph pinpoint with **at**. Do not place a comma before **at** and do not use **p** to indicate the page number. Cite paragraphs by using **para** or **paras**.

To indicate a **general area** rather than a specific set of pages or paragraphs, place **ff** (used to indicate "and following") immediately after the number (see *Schofield*). It is preferable, however, to cite a specific set of pages or paragraphs.

Separate **consecutive page or paragraph numbers** by an en-dash, retaining at least the two last digits (e.g. **32–35**, not **32–5**).

Non-sequential page or paragraph numbers are separated by a comma (e.g., **160, 172**).

Cite to footnotes using **n** (see *Ordre des arpenteurs-géomètres*). Include the corresponding paragraph number for ease of reference, and separate the paragraph and footnote indications by a comma.

3.6.2   Cited Reporter

> *R v Gimson*, [1991] 3 SCR 692, 62 OAC 282 [*Gimson* **cited to SCR**].
> *Delgamuukw v British Columbia*, 79 DLR (4th) 185, [1991] 3 WWR 97 (BCSC) [*Delgamuukw* **cited to DLR**].
> *Université du Québec à Trois-Rivières v Larocque*, [1993] 1 SCR 471 **at 473**, 101 DLR (4th) 494 [*Larocque*].
> *R v Sharpe*, **2007 BCCA 191**, 219 CCC (3d) 187 [*Sharpe*].

The page and paragraph numbering often differ from one reporter to the other. The reader must know to which reporter the pinpoint references cite.

Cite the pinpoint reference to the **most official reporter, mentioned first**. For every subsequent pinpoint, cite to the same reporter.

Jurisprudence

If subsequently citing to pinpoints, add **cited to** after the short title, followed by the abbreviation of the reporter (see *Delgamuukw*). No **cited to** is necessary when not subsequently referring to pinpoints or if the first citation contains a pinpoint.

Do not specify the source of the pinpoint in the subsequent references if there is a pinpoint reference the first time a case is mentioned (see *Laroque*). It is implied that the subsequent references will follow the same model and cite to the same reporter.

Do not specify the source of the pinpoint when there is a neutral citation with numbered paragraphs (see *Sharpe*). In this case, the paragraph numbers are set by the court and not by the individual publishers.

3.7   PRINTED REPORTER

3.7.1   Year of Reporter

Reporter organized by year	one volume published per year	*Hébert c Giguère* **(2002)**, **[2003]** RJQ 89.
	several volumes published per year	*Reference re Secession of Quebec*, **[1998] 2** SCR 217.
Reporter published in volumes numbered in series		*R v Innocente*, 2003 NSCA 50, **214** NSR (2d) 295.
		Elliott v Parksville (City) (1990), 66 DLR (4th) 107 (BCCA).

Reporters are published either in volumes organized by year of publication (e.g., SCR, RJQ) or in volumes numbered in series (e.g., DLR, CCC).

☐ If the reporter volumes are numbered by **year of publication**, enclose the year in brackets.

☐ Some reporters organized by year of publication publish **several volumes per year** (e.g., SCR). Indicate the year in brackets followed by the volume number.

☐ If the reporter volumes are numbered in **series**, no year is needed to identify the reporter volume (but remember to include the year in the style of cause if not otherwise indicated in the citation; see section 3.4). Note that, by convention, reporters use **2d** and **3d** for "second" and "third" respectively.

Note that **some reporters have changed their mode of organization**.

☐ The *Supreme Court Reports* were organized by volume from 1877–1923 (e.g., **27** SCR). Then, from 1923–1974, they were organized by year (e.g., **[1950] SCR**). Since 1975, they have been organized by year with several volumes per year (e.g., **[1982] 2 SCR**).

☐   Prior to 1974, the *Ontario Reports* were organized by year of publication (e.g., **[1973] OR**). Since 1974, they have been published in a numbered series (e.g., **20 OR**).

3.7.2   Reporter

Bakken v Harris (2005), 261 **Sask R** 46 (QB).

▨ Abbreviate the name of the reporter according to the list in **Appendix C**.

3.7.2.1 Official Reporters

▨ Official reporters apply to federal jurisdictions and are published by the Queen's Printer.

▨ Whenever there is a discrepancy between two versions of the same case, the version in the official reporter takes precedence.

List of official reporters:

Canada Supreme Court Reports (1970–present) *Canada Law Reports: Supreme Court of Canada* (1923–1969) *Canada Supreme Court Reports* (1876–1922)	SCR
Federal Court Reports (2003–present) *Canada Federal Court Reports* (1971–2002)	FCR FC
Exchequer Court of Canada Reports (1923–1970) *Exchequer Court of Canada Reports* (1875–1922)	Ex CR

3.7.2.2 Semi-Official Reporters

▨ Semi-official reporters are published under the auspices of a provincial or territorial bar association. Currently, only the bar associations of New Brunswick, Newfoundland & Prince Edward Island, Nova Scotia, Ontario, and Quebec maintain semi-official reporters.

▨ Many unofficial reporters have adopted names that may be mistaken for a semi-official reporter (e.g., *British Columbia Law Reports* (Carswell), *Manitoba Law Reports* (Maritime Law Book)). Despite their names, these publications remain unofficial as they are not associated with a governing body like the Queen's Printer or a bar association.

List of current semi-official reporters:

New Brunswick	*New Brunswick Reports* (2d) (1969–present)	NBR (2d)
Newfoundland & Prince Edward Island	*Newfoundland & Prince Edward Island Reports* (1971–present)	Nfld & PEIR
Nova Scotia	*Nova Scotia Reports* (2d) (1969–present)	NSR (2d)
Ontario	*Ontario Reports* (3d) (1991–present)	OR (3d)
Quebec	*Recueils de jurisprudence du Québec* (1975–present)	RJQ

For a complete listing of semi-official reporters, current and historical, see **Appendix C-2**.

3.7.2.3 Unofficial Reporters

▨ To choose the appropriate reporter, follow these general guidelines:

    ☐ **General reporters** (e.g. *Western Weekly Reports*) are preferred to specific reporters (e.g. *Canadian Criminal Cases*). However, if writing for a specialized audience, citing to a practice specific reporter (e.g., *Administrative Law Reports*, *Canadian Labour Law Reporter*) may be more appropriate.

    ☐ Reporters covering a **large geographic area** (e.g. Dominion Law Reports) are preferred to reporters covering a smaller geographic area (e.g. Saskatchewan Reports).

    ☐ Reporters that are **most readily available** (e.g. Dominion Law Reports) are preferred to more obscure reporters.

▨ See **Appendix C-3** for a list of unofficial reporters.

3.7.3 Series

Series number	✓	*R v Innocente*, 2003 NSCA 50, 214 NSR **(2d)** 295. *Rohani v Rohani* (2004), 34 BCLR **(4th)** 62 (CA).
	✗	*Rohani v Rohani* (2004), 34 BCLR (4th) 62 (CA).
New series		*Citizen's Mining Council of Newfoundland and Labrador Inc v Canada (Minister of the Environment)* (1999), 29 CELR **(NS)** 117 (FCTD).

▨ If the reporter has been published in more than one series, indicate the series in parentheses, between the reporter abbreviation and the first page of the judgment.

Jurisprudence

- Do not put the series number in superscript (e.g. (**4th**) and not (**4th**)).
- Note that, by tradition, reporters use **2d** and **3d** for "second" and "third" respectively.
- Abbreviate **New Series** or *Nouvelle série* to **NS**.

3.7.4   First Page

> *Reference re Secession of Quebec*, [1998] 2 SCR **217**.

- Indicate the number of the first page of the decision after the reporter.

3.8   ONLINE DATABASES

- Before citing to an online database, make sure it is the most appropriate source (section 3.1).
- Do not cite to an online database to which the majority of readers will not have access. For example, avoid Azimut if writing for an audience outside of Quebec.
- Include the paragraph number for the pinpoint reference. **Do not cite the page numbers** reproduced in the online source, as these are specific to the service used and can vary in different forms (e.g., PDF, txt, html).
- Abbreviations for online databases can be found in **Appendix E**.

3.8.1   Published Judgments and Judgments with a Neutral Citation

Reference to a printed reporter or neutral citation,	online database identifier	(abbreviation for online database if not obvious from database citation).
Desputeaux c Éditions Chouette (1987) Inc, [2001] RJQ 945,	AZ-50085400	(Azimut).
R v Wilkening, 2009 ABCA 9,	2009 CarswellAlta 11	(WL Can).
Caisse populaire de Maniwaki v Giroux, [1993] 1 SCR 282,	1993 CanLII 151.	

- When a judgment **has been published in a printed reporter or has a neutral citation**, write the neutral citation or the printed reporter, then the online database identifier. If the service provides no identifier for the judgment, simply write the name of the online database in parentheses (using the abbreviations found in **Appendix E**).

3.8.2   Unpublished Judgments with No Neutral Citation

3.8.2.1 *CanLII*

Style of cause,	online database identifier	pinpoint	(jurisdiction and/or court) (if applicable).
Kellogg v Black Ridge Gold Ltd,	1993 CanLII 2848	at para 15	(NWTSC).

■ The Canadian Legal Information Institute (CanLII) is freely accessible on <canlii.org>. To ensure accessibility by all readers, CanLII should be preferred over commercial services.

3.8.2.2 *Quicklaw*

Style of cause,	online database identifier	(Quick-law)	pinpoint	(jurisdiction and/or court) (if applicable).
Fuentes v Canada (Minister of Citizenship and Immigration),	[1995] FCJ No 206	(QL)	at para 10	(TD).

■ Find the Quicklaw identifier below the style of cause. Do not confuse it with printed reporters (e.g., **AJ** for Alberta Judgments, **BCJ** for British Columbia Judgments, **OJ** for Ontario Judgments).

■ Make sure that the judgment was not reported elsewhere by checking QuickCITE, which lists most sources for a particular decision.

3.8.2.3 *Westlaw Canada*

Style of cause,	online database identifier	(WL Can)	pin-point	(jurisdiction and/or court) (if applicable).
Underwood v Underwood,	1995 Carswell-Ont 88	(WL Can)		(Gen Div).

■ If the only identifier is the one provided by Westlaw Canada, the judgment is otherwise unreported.

3.8.2.4 Azimut

Style of cause,	(year),	online database identifier	(Azimut)	pinpoint	(jurisdiction and/or court) (if applicable).
Desputeaux c Éditions Chouette	(2001),	AZ-50085400	(Azimut)	at para 19	(QCCA).

▧ Azimut is a service created by the Société québécoise d'information juridique (SOQUIJ). If the prospective readers are not from Quebec, do not cite Azimut.

3.8.2.5 Other Services

▧ Refer to online databases that have comprehensive indexes, search tools, and professional editors.

Style of cause,	(year) (if applicable),	online database identifier	(online database name) (if applicable)	pinpoint	(jurisdiction and/or court)
Abitibi-Consolidated Inc v Doughan,		EYB 2008-139174	(REJB)	at para 23	(Qc Sup Ct).

▧ Add the year and the name of the online database only if the information is not already included in the database identifier.

▧ If the abbreviation of the online database is not included in **Appendix E** of the *Guide*, use the most commonly used name. For example, write **REJB** and not **Répertoire électronique de jurisprudence du Barreau**.

▧ If the online database has no identifier, follow the model found in section 7.3.2.10.2.

3.9   JURISDICTION AND COURT

Taylor v Law Society of Prince Edward Island (1992), 97 DLR (4th) 427 **(PEISC (AD))**.
Ballard v Ballard (2001), 201 Nfld & PEIR 352 **(Nfld SC (TD))**.
O'Brien v Centre de location Simplex ltée (1993), 132 NBR (2d) 179 **(CA)**.
Boisjoli c Goebel (1981), [1982] **CS** 1 **(Qc)**.
Dobson (Litigation Guardian of) v Dobson, [1999] 2 **SCR** 753.

▧ The jurisdiction and court should be indicated if:

☐ there is **no neutral citation** (which indicates both jurisdiction and court level); **and,**

☐ this **information is not evident** from the title of the reporter (see *Ballard* and *O'Brien*).

- Indicate the jurisdiction and court in parentheses, following all parallel citations.

- If the court is bilingual, use English abbreviations. If the court renders judgments only in French, use the French abbreviations.

- There is no space in an abbreviation consisting solely of upper case letters. Leave a space when an abbreviation consists of both upper case letters and lower case letters (e.g. **BCCA**; **Ont Div Ct**; **NS Co Ct**; **Alta QB**).

- Use the abbreviations for the jurisdictions found in **Appendix A-1** and the court abbreviations in **Appendix B**.

3.10   JUDGE

- If relevant, a reference to the name of the judge may be included. Add **dissenting** if it's a dissenting opinion.

- Do not insert a comma between the name of the judge and the office.

- Where the entire bench (and not a select panel) heard the case, the term **en banc** may be used.

> *R v Sharpe*, 2001 SCC 2 at para 24, [2001] 1 SCR 45, **McLachlin CJC**.
> *Gosselin c Québec (PG)*, [1999] RJQ 1033 (CA), **Robert JA, dissenting**.
> *R v Wholesale Travel Group Inc*, [1991] 3 SCR 154, 84 DLR (4th) 161, **en banc**.

Office abbreviations:

CJC	Chief Justice of Canada
CJA	Chief Justice of Appeal
CJ	Chief Justice, Chief Judge
JA	Justice of Appeal, Judge of Appeals Court
JJA	Justices of Appeal, Judges of Appeals Court
J	Justice, Judge
JJ	Justices, Judges
LJ	Lord Justice
LJJ	Lord Justices
Mag	Magistrate

3.11   HISTORY OF CASE

3.11.1   Prior History

Affirming	*Law v Canada (Minister of Employment and Immigration)*, [1999] 1 SCR 497, **aff'g** (1996), 135 DLR (4th) 293 (FCA).
Reversing	*Wilson & Lafleur ltée c Société québécoise d'information juridique*, [2000] RJQ 1086 (CA), **rev'g** [1998] RJQ 2489 (Sup Ct).

▪ Cite the prior history of the case as the last element of the citation if it is relevant to the argument.

▪ Separate different decisions with a comma.

▪ Abbreviate affirming to **aff'g**. Abbreviate reversing to **rev'g**.

▪ Both **aff'g** and **rev'g** refer to the first citation. In *Tsiaprailis*, the Supreme Court affirmed the Court

> *Tsiaprailis v Canada*, 2005 SCC 8, 248 DLR (4th) 385, **aff'g** 2003 FCA 136, [2003] 4 FC 112, **rev'g** [2012] 1 CTC 2858, 2002 DTC 1563 (TCC [General Procedure]).

of Appeal, and upheld the reversal of the Tax Court of Canada decision by the Court of Appeal.

▪ If the decision is affirming or reversing the prior decision on grounds other than those being discussed, use **aff'g on other grounds** or **rev'g on other grounds**.

▪ If the decision is affirming or reversing the prior decision only in part, use **aff'g in part** or **rev'g in part.**

3.11.2   Subsequent History

Affirmed	*R v Paice* **(2003)**, [2004] 5 WWR 621 (CA), **aff'd** 2005 SCC 22, [2005] 1 SCR 339.
Reversed	*Ontario English Catholic Teachers' Association v Ontario (AG)* (1998), 162 DLR (4th) 257 (Ont Gen Div), **rev'd in part** (1999), 172 DLR (4th) 193 (Ont CA), **rev'd** 2001 SCC 15, [2001] 1 SCR 470.

▪ Cite the subsequent history of the case if it was subsequently appealed to other courts.

▪ Place the subsequent history of the case as the last element of the citation.

▪ Separate different decisions with a comma.

▪ Abbreviate affirmed to **aff'd** and reversed to **rev'd**.

▪ If the decision was affirmed or reversed on grounds other than those being discussed, use **aff'd on other grounds** or **rev'd on other grounds**.

▪ If the decision was affirmed or reversed only in part, use **aff'd in part** or **rev'd in part**.

Both **aff'd** and **rev'd** refer to the first citation. In *Ontario English Catholic Teachers' Association*, the Supreme Court agreed with the Court of Appeal that the judgment of the Ontario Court of Justice, General Division, should be reversed; the Supreme Court did not reverse the decision of the Ontario Court of Appeal.

3.11.3   Prior and Subsequent History

Affirmed	*Ardoch Algonquin First Nation v Ontario* (1997), 148 DLR (4th) 126 (Ont CA), **rev'g** [1997] 1 CNLR 66 (Ont Gen Div), **aff'd** 2000 SCC 37, [2000] 1 SCR 950.
Reversed	*Canada v Canderel Ltd*, [1995] 2 FC 232 (CA), **rev'g** [1994] 1 CTC 2336 (TCC), **rev'd** [1998] 1 SCR 147.

Apply the rules for prior and subsequent history listed above.

All affirming and reversing decisions refer back to the first citation.

☐ In *Ardoch*, the Ontario Court of Appeal reversed a decision by the lower court; the reversal was later affirmed by the Supreme Court of Canada.

☐ In *Canderel Ltd*, the Federal Court of Appeal reversed the decision of the Tax Court of Canada, but the Federal Court of Appeal was in turn reversed by the Supreme Court of Canada (i.e., the Supreme Court of Canada upheld the Tax Court's decision).

Place prior history before subsequent history.

3.11.4   Leave to Appeal

	Citation of the decision for which leave to appeal is requested,	court,	citation of the decision as to the appeal.
Requested	*White Resource Management Ltd v Durish* (1992), 131 AR 273 (CA),	leave to appeal to SCC **requested**.	
Granted	*Westec Aerospace v Raytheon Aircraft* (1999), 173 DLR (4th) 498 (BCCA),	leave to appeal to SCC **granted**,	[2000] 1 SCR xxii.
Refused	*Procter & Gamble Pharmaceuticals Canada Inc v Canada (Minister of Health)*, 2004 FCA 393,	leave to appeal to SCC **refused**,	30714 (21 April 2005).
As of Right	*Whiten v Pilot Insurance* (1996), 132 DLR (4th) 568 (Ont Gen Div),	**appeal as of right** to the CA.	

The **Supreme Court of Canada** decisions on leave to appeal are available on CanLII, Lexum, Westlaw Canada, and Quicklaw, as well as at the beginning of the SCR. Pre-2005 decisions are only listed at the beginning of the SCR.

Jurisprudence

- Decisions on leave to appeal to a **court of appeal** are sometimes available in printed reporters and online databases.
- Include the citation of the decision for which leave to appeal is requested.
- Indicate the court to which the appeal is requested. If available, indicate whether leave was granted or refused and include the citation for that decision.
- Provide either the printed reporter reference (see *Westec Aerospace*) or the docket number (followed by the date in parentheses; see *Procter & Gamble*).
- Certain applications for leave are published. In this case, cite using the normal rules for decisions, and include the result (i.e., **leave to appeal to [court] granted, or leave to appeal to [court] refused**; see *Gallagher*).

> *R v Gallagher*, 2013 ABCA 269, leave to appeal to Alta CA refused.

Leave Decision Availability by Jurisdiction		
Supreme Court	Leave decisions are available on CanLII, Lexum, Westlaw Canada and Quicklaw, as well as at the beginning of the SCR.	
Federal Court of Appeal	Leave decisions are not currently listed online.	
Alberta	Certain leave decisions are given a standard neutral citation and are available via the court's website.	www.albertacourts.ab.ca
British Columbia	Certain leave decisions are given a standard neutral citation and are available via the court's website.	www.courts.gov.bc.ca
Manitoba	Certain leave decisions are given a standard neutral citation and are available via CanLII.	
New Brunswick	Certain leave decisions dating back until 2010 are listed in the Rulings on Motions.	www.gnb.ca/cour/03COA1/motions-e.asp
Newfoundland and Labrador	Leave decisions are not currently listed online.	
Northwest Territories	Certain leave decisions are available on the Department of Justice's website.	www.justice.gov.nt.ca/CourtLibrary/library_decisions.shtml

Jurisprudence

Nova Scotia	Certain leave decisions are given a standard neutral citation and are available via the court's website.	decisions.courts.ns.ca/site/nsc/en/nav.do
Nunavut	Certain leave decisions are available on the Department of Justice's website.	www.justice.gov.nt.ca/CourtLibrary/library_decisions.shtml
Ontario	Motions for leave to appeal dating back to 2002 are listed with their docket number.	www.ontariocourts.ca/coa/en/leave/
Prince Edward Island	Certain leave decisions are given a standard neutral citation and are available via the court's website.	www.gov.pe.ca/courts/supreme/reasons.php3
Quebec	Certain leave decisions are given a standard neutral citation and are available via a provincial database.	www.jugements.qc.ca/
Saskatchewan	Certain leave decisions are given a standard neutral citation and are available via CanLII or a provincial database (which links to CanLII) .	www.lawsociety.sk.ca/library/public-resources/court-of-appeal-judgments.aspx
Yukon	Leave decisions are not currently listed online.	

▦ NB: the information given on court websites is also usually available via CanLII or other online databases.

3.12 UNREPORTED DECISIONS WITHOUT A NEUTRAL CITATION

Style of cause	(date),	judicial district	docket number	JE number (Quebec only) (if available)	(jurisdiction and court).
R v Crête	(18 April 1991),	Ottawa	97/03674		(Ont Prov Ct).
Lalancette c Gagnon	(18 April 1995),	Montreal	500-02-019902-944,	JE 95-1255	(CQ).

▢ Indicate the style of cause, the full date of the decision in parentheses followed by a comma, the judicial district, and the docket number. Place the jurisdiction and court in parentheses at the end of the citation.

▢ **For Quebec cases**, include the *Jurisprudence Express* (**JE**) number (if available) preceded by a comma after the docket number.

3.13 INTERLOCUTORY JUDGMENTS AND MOTIONS

Style of cause or names of parties	(date),	judicial district,	court identifier	docket number	type of document (e.g. motion to dismiss).
Marris Handold v Tyson Blair	(23 April 2011),	Montreal,	Que CA	500-02-019902-944	(interlocutory judgment).

3.14 ADMINISTRATIVE BODIES AND TRIBUNALS

3.14.1 Decisions in Printed Reporters

Adversarial	*Clarke Institute of Psychiatry v Ontario Nurses' Assn (Adusei Grievance)* (2001), 95 LAC (4th) 154 (OLRB).
Non-adversarial	*Re Writers' Union of Canada Certification Application (Certification)* (1998), 84 CPR (3d) 329 (Canadian Artists and Professional Relations Tribunal).

▢ Include the style of cause and indicate whether the case is adversarial (separate the parties with *v*) or non-adversarial (prefix the style of cause with *Re*). Where there is no style of cause, use the decision number instead.

▢ Include the abbreviation as provided by the administrative body or tribunal in parentheses at the end of the citation if it is not evident from the title of the cited reporter (if an abbreviation cannot be found, use the full name).

▢ Abbreviate provinces and territories to the shortest provincial abbreviations (the Ontario Securities Commission is abbreviated **OSC**, and the Newfoundland and Labrador Human Rights Commission is abbreviated **NLHRC**). Note that abbreviations of a printed reporter (e.g., **OSC Bull**) may be different from the abbreviation of the agency (e.g., **OSC**).

Jurisprudence

3.14.2   Online Decisions

Style of cause	(date),	decision number (if applicable),	online:	administra- tive body or tribunal	<address>.
Acuity Funds Ltd	(13 March 2009),		online:	OSC	<www.osc.gov.on.ca/en/ SecuritiesLaw_ord_20110218_ 217_acuity.htm> .
13th Street – a new specialty channel	(14 December 2000),	2000-449,	online:	CRTC	<www.crtc.gc.ca> .
The Commissioner of Competition v Elkhorn Ranch & Resort Ltd	(23 November 2009),	CT-2009-018,	online:	Competition Tribunal	<www.ct-tc.gc.ca/CMFiles/CT- 2009-018_Registered%20Con- sent%20Agreement_1_45_ 11-23-2009_6123.pdf> .

▨ Enclose the date of the decision in parentheses after the style of cause. Place a comma after the date.

▨ If applicable, include the decision number followed by **online**: and the abbreviation used by the administrative body or tribunal. These abbreviations usually do not contain periods. Note that most abbreviations consist of single letters for each important word in the name. Abbreviate provinces and territories to the shortest provincial abbreviations (e.g., the Ontario Securities Commission is abbreviated **OSC** and the Newfoundland and Labrador Human Rights Commission is abbreviated **NLHRC**).

▨ If possible, give a URL that leads directly to the cited source. However, if the stability of the full URL is in question, provide the address of the home page in order to avoid a dead link (see *13th Street*).

3.15   ARGUMENTS AND EVIDENTIARY DOCUMENTS

Factum	*Reference re Secession of Quebec*, [1998] 2 SCR 217 (**Factum of the Appellant at para 16**).
Oral pleading	*Vriend v Alberta*, [1998] 1 SCR 493 (**Oral argument, Appellant**).
Public Settlement Agreement	*Mulroney v Canada (AG)* [**Settlement Agreement**], [1997] QJ No 45 (Sup Ct) (QL).
Evidence	*R v Swain*, [1991] 1 SCR 933 (**Evidence, Dr Fleming's recommendation that the appellant be released in the community**).

▨ When referring to a **factum**, provide the full citation of the case. Then, indicate in parentheses **Factum of**, the party (**Appellant** or **Respondent**), and the page number or paragraph number. A short form can be established following the first reference to the document (e.g., **Factum of the Appellant at para 16 [FOA]**).

- When referring to an **oral argument**, provide the full citation of the case, then place **Oral argument** and the party in parentheses.

- When referring to a **public settlement agreement**, provide the style of cause, followed by **Settlement Agreement** in brackets before the other elements of the citation. If the agreement was announced through a news release, see section 6.17.

- When referring to **evidence**, provide the full citation of the case, followed by **Evidence** in parentheses with a brief statement identifying the item.

- Adapt the general form provided above for other types of documents, including **testimonies, depositions, affidavits, subpoenas, memoranda, transcripts,** etc.

4 Government Documents E-77

E -4.1 Parliamentary Papers.. E-77
    E -4.1.1 Debates... E-77
    E -4.1.2 Journals.. E-78
    E -4.1.3 Order Papers E-78
    E -4.1.4 Sessional Papers E-79
    E -4.1.5 Votes and Proceedings................................... E-79
    E -4.1.6 Reports Published in Debates........................... E-80
    E -4.1.7 Reports Published Separately........................... E-80

E -4.2 Non-parliamentary Documents E-80
    E -4.2.1 General Form... E-81
        E -4.2.1.1 Reports, Manuals, and Other Book-length Publications.... E-81
        E -4.2.1.2 Articles, Bulletins, and Other Short Publications............. E-82
    E -4.2.2 Tax Interpretation Bulletins (ITs) and Information Circulars (ICs) E-83
    E -4.2.3 Reports of Inquiries and Commissions E-84
        E -4.2.3.1 Reports Published Under a Single Title E-84
        E -4.2.3.2 Reports Published Under Multiple Titles E-84
    E -4.2.4 Public Papers of Intergovernmental Conferences E-85

Government Documents

4   GOVERNMENT DOCUMENTS

4.1 PARLIAMENTARY PAPERS

This section applies to documents directly published by a parliamentary body. For every federal government document, indicate the jurisdiction (**Canada**) only when other citations to international materials may confuse the reader.

4.1.1 Debates

Jurisdiction,	legislature,	*title*,	legislative session,	volume and/or number	(date)	pinpoint	(speaker) (if any).
		House of Commons Debates,	37th Parl, 1st Sess,	No 64	(17 May 2001)	at 4175	(Hon Elinor Caplan).
		Debates of the Senate,	39th Parl, 2nd Sess,	No 44	(1 April 2008)	at 1017	(Noël A Kinsella).
Ontario,	Legislative Assembly,	*Official Report of Debates (Hansard),*	37th Parl, 2nd Sess,	No 53	(18 October 2001)	at 2819	(Julia Munro).
Yukon,	Legislative Assembly,	*Hansard,*	30th Leg, 2nd Sess,	No 18	(22 November 2000)	at 552	(Peter Jenkins).

- Indicate the jurisdiction (if a province) and the legislature, unless this information is mentioned in the title of the debates. Do not superscript **st, nd** and **th**.

- Write the title, in italics, as it appears on the title page of the document.

- Place the volume and/or document number, if any, after the title, preceded by a non-italicized comma.

- Include the full date in parentheses followed by the pinpoint.

- Include the name of the speaker, if any, in parentheses at the end of the citation.

- Where relevant, indicate the title of the bill being debated in quotation marks, followed by a comma and the reading, before the jurisdiction, legislature and title (e.g., **"Bill C-8, An Act to amend the Copyright Act and the Trade-marks Act and to make consequential amendments to other Acts", 2nd reading,** *House of Commons Debates*, 41st Parl, 2nd Sess, No 9 (28 October 2013) at 1504 (Hon Steven Blaney)).

4.1.2   Journals

Jurisdiction,	legislature,	*title,*	legislative session,	volume and/or number	(date)	pinpoint	(speaker) (if applicable).
	Senate,	*Journals of the Senate,*	39th Parl, 1st Sess,	No 108	(14 June 2007).		
	House of Commons,	*Journals,*	40th Leg, 2nd Sess,	No 36	(30 March 2009)	at 588.	
Saskatchewan,		*Journals of the Legislative Assembly,*	23rd Leg, 3rd Sess,	vol 105	(9 March 1998)	at 7.	
		Journals of the House of Assembly of Lower-Canada,	8th Parl, 2nd Sess,	vol 25	(26 January 1816)	at 15	(Thomas Douglass).

- Indicate the jurisdiction (if a province) and the legislature, unless this information is mentioned in the title of the journals.
- Cite the title, in italics, as it appears on the title page.
- Place the volume and/or document number after the title, preceded by a non-italicized comma.
- Include the full date in parentheses followed by the pinpoint.
- Include the name of the speaker, if any, in parentheses at the end of the citation.

4.1.3   Order Papers

Jurisdiction,	legislature,	*title,*	legislative session,	number	(date)	pinpoint.
	House of Commons,	*Order Paper,*	39th Leg, 1st Sess,	No 175	(20 June 2007).	
Québec,	National Assembly,	*Feuilleton et préavis,*	38th Leg, 1st Sess,	No 79	(6 May 2008).	

- Indicate the jurisdiction if a province.
- At the federal level, the *Order Paper* and the *Notice Paper* are two parts of a single publication. Only cite the relevant part in the title.

4.1.4   Sessional Papers

Jurisdiction,	legislature,	"title of report"	by	author	in	*title,*	number	(year)	pinpoint.
	Parliament,	"Report of the Chief Inspector of Dominion Lands Agencies"	by	HG Cuttle	in	*Sessional Papers,*	No 25	(1920)	at 3.
Ontario,	Legislative Assembly,	"Report on Workmen's Compensation for Injuries"	by	James Mavor	in	*Sessional Papers,*	No 40	(1900)	at 6–7.

▦ Indicate the jurisdiction (if a province) and the legislature, unless this information is mentioned in the title of the report.

▦ Indicate the title of the report in quotation marks after the legislature.

▦ If an author is given, place **by** and the name after the title of report.

▦ If the sessional paper is numbered, cite the number after the title, preceded by a comma.

▦ Indicate the year only, not the full date, in parentheses.

4.1.5   Votes and Proceedings

Jurisdiction,	legislature,	*title,*	legislative session,	volume and/or document number	(date)	pinpoint.
Quebec,	National Assembly,	*Votes and Proceedings,*	39th Leg, 1st Sess,	No 48	(18 June 2009)	at 517.
Ontario,	Legislative Assembly,	*Votes and Proceedings,*	38th Leg, 2nd Sess,	No 34	(14 December 2005).	

▦ Indicate the jurisdiction (if a province) and the legislature, unless this information is mentioned in the title.

▦ Cite the title, in italics, as it appears on the title page of the document.

▦ Indicate the number of the legislative session.

▦ Place the volume and/or document number, if any, after the number of the legislature, preceded by a comma.

4.1.6   Reports Published in Debates

Jurisdic-tion,	legislature,	issuing body,	"title of report"	in	title,	number	(date)	pinpoint.
Ontario,	Legislative Assembly,	Standing Committee on Regulations and Private Bills,	"Election of Chair"	in	*Official Report of Debates (Hansard),*	No T-6	(26 September 2001)	at 41.

▨   Indicate the jurisdiction if a province.

▨   For debates, follow the rules from section 4.1.1. After the name of the legislature, add the name of issuing body and the title of the report. Place the title of the report in quotation marks.

▨   Place the number of the paper, if any, after the title, preceded by a comma.

4.1.7   Reports Published Separately

Jurisdic-tion,	legislature,	Issuing body,	Title	(date)	pinpoint	(Chair) (if applicable).
	House of Commons,	Standing Committee on Agriculture and Agri-Food,	*Labelling of Genetically Modified Food and its Impact on Farmers: Report of the Standing Committee on Agriculture and Agri-Food*	(June 2002)		(Chair: Charles Hubbard).

▨   Indicate the jurisdiction if a province.

▨   After the name of the legislature, add the name of issuing body, followed by the title of the report in italics.

▨   Provide the complete date as provided by the report in parentheses.

▨   If the Chair is indicated on the cover page, add the information in parentheses.

▨   This section applies to reports directly published by a parliamentary body. If the report is published by any other body, see section 4.2 on non-parliamentary documents.

4.2   NON-PARLIAMENTARY DOCUMENTS

This section applies to all government-published documents that do not emanate directly from a legislative body. Apply the general rules of section 4.2.1, unless the document falls into one of the specific categories covered by sections 4.2.2–4.2.4.

Government Documents

4.2.1 General Form

For the purposes of citation, *most* government documents are divided into the two sub-categories described in 4.2.1.1 and 4.2.1.2. Choose the document category that best fits the nature of the source (4.2.1.1 or 4.2.1.2), bearing in mind that the category into which a given document is placed is less important than ensuring that readers are provided with complete and accurate information about a source.

4.2.1.1 Reports, Manuals, and Other Book-length Publications

Jurisdiction,	issuing body,	*title,*	other information (if applicable)	(publication information)	pinpoint.
Canada,	Royal Commission on Electoral Reform and Party Financing,	*Reforming Electoral Democracy,*	vol 4	(Ottawa: Communication Group, 1991)	at 99.
	Canadian Intellectual Property Office,	*Manual of Patent Office Practice,*	December 2010 update	(Ottawa: Industry Canada, 1998)	at 12.
	Statistics Canada,	*Police-Reported Crime Statistics in Canada, 2011,*	by Shannon Brennan, Catalogue No 82-002-X	(Ottawa: Statistics Canada, 11 October 2012).	
Quebec,	Ministère de la justice,	*Commentaires du ministre de la justice,*	vol 1	(Quebec: Publications du Québec, 1993)	at 705.
Quebec,	Office de revision du Code civil,	*Rapport sur les obligations,*	by the Comité du droit des obligations	(Montréal: ORCC, 1975).	

Include the jurisdiction unless it is mentioned in another element of the citation.

Include the issuing body unless it is mentioned in the title of the report.

If there is an individual author, or an institutional author that differs from the issuing body, provide the author's name after the title, separated from the title with a comma and preceded by the word "by." In all other respects, follow the rules of section 6.2.2.

After the document title, and following the name of an individual or institutional author if included, provide all other information that would help readers to locate a source (e.g. catalogue information), or to assess a source's authority (e.g. the date on which a source was updated, or whether the source is currently under review or cancelled). Separate each element by a comma. If the document is divided into multiple volumes, follow the rules at section 6.2.4.

▦ The name of the president or commissioner associated with the issuing body may also be placed in parentheses after the title.

▦ Where the issuing body is also the publisher of the document, its name may be shortened or replaced by an acronym in the publication information section (see Office de révision du Code civil example). In all other respects, provide publication information according to the rules of sections 6.2.5–6.2.9.

▦ If the type of document (e.g., **Study**; **Working Document**; or **Guide**) is indicated on the title page, provide this information between parentheses after the title of the document (e.g., Commission de la santé et de la sécurité du travail du Québec, "Planification des mesures d'urgence pour assurer la sécurité des travailleurs" **(Guide)** (Quebec: CSST, 1999) at 53).

▦ Unless another location appears in the document itself, presume that federal documents are published in Ottawa, and that provincial/territorial documents are published in the provincial/territorial capital.

4.2.1.2 Articles, Bulletins, and Other Short Publications

Jurisdiction,	issuing body,	"title",	other information (if applicable)	(publication information)	pinpoint
	Correctional Service of Canada,	"Leisure Activities",	Commissioner's Directive No 760	(Ottawa: CSC, 25 September 2008)	at para 7.
	Canadian Agency for Drugs and Technology in Health,	"CEDAC Final Recommendation: Abacavir/ Lamivudine",	by Canadian Expert Drug Advisory Committee	(Ottawa: CADTH, 16 November 2005)	at paras 2–4.
Nova Scotia,	Workers' Compensation Board,	"Chronic Pain",		(Halifax: WCB, April 2008).	
Canada,	Department of National Defence,	"Defence Terminology Programme",	Defence Administrative Orders and Directives No 6110-1, under review	(Ottawa: DND, 29 January 2010).	
	Statistics Canada,	"Mixed Unions",	by Anne Milan & Brian Hamm, in *Canadian Social Trends*, Catalogue No 11-008-X	(Ottawa: Statistics Canada, 2004).	

▦ Include the jurisdiction unless it is mentioned in another element of the citation.

▦ Include the issuing body unless it is mentioned in the title of the report.

▦ If there is an individual author, or an institutional author that differs from the issuing body, provide the author's name after the title, separated from the title with a comma and preceded by the word "by." In all other respects, follow the rules of section 6.2.2.

▦ After the title and the author (if any), provide the document type unless it would be obvious from the title of the document (see CEDAC Final Recommendation example), or unless the document type would not help readers to locate or understand the source (e.g., the chronic pain document was labelled a "fact sheet" but this information does not add to a reader's appreciation of the source).

▢ Following the document type, provide all other information that would help readers to locate a source (e.g., catalogue information), or to assess a source's authority (e.g., the date on which a source was updated, or whether the source is currently under review or cancelled). Separate each element by a comma.

▢ Where the issuing body is also the publisher of the document, its name may be shortened or replaced by an acronym in the publication information section (see Correctional Service Canada example). In all other respects, provide publication information according to the rules of sections 6.2.5–6.2.9.

▢ Unless another location appears in the document itself, presume that federal documents are published in Ottawa, and that provincial/territorial documents are published in the provincial/territorial capital.

▢ Provide the most complete publication date available based on information contained in the source document.

▢ The name of the president or commissioner associated with the issuing body may also be placed in parentheses after the title.

4.2.2 Tax Interpretation Bulletins (ITs) and Information Circulars (ICs)

Department,	Document Type	Document number,	"title"	(date)	pinpoint.
Canada Revenue Agency,	Interpretation Bulletin	IT-459,	"Income Tax Act Adventure or Concern in the Nature of Trade"	(8 September 1980).	
Canada Revenue Agency,	Information Circular	IC-70-6R5,	"Advance Income Tax Rulings"	(17 May 2002).	
Revenu Québec,	Interpretation Bulletin	IMP 1131-1/R3,	"Capital Tax Liability"	(30 June 2011)	at para 4.

▢ **ITs** are income tax interpretation bulletins published by the Canada Revenue Agency. **ICs** are information circulars, also published by the Canada Revenue Agency. Analogous documents exist at the provincial level.

▢ If the bulletin has been revised insert **R** after the document number. The number of revisions is indicated by the number following the R (e.g., **R3**).

▢ When tax documents are divided into paragraphs, pinpoint to a paragraph.

4.2.3   Reports of Inquiries and Commissions

4.2.3.1 Reports Published Under a Single Title

Jurisdiction,	issuing body,	Title	(publication information)	volume	(Chair) (if applicable)	pinpoint.
		Commission of Inquiry on the Blood System in Canada: Final Report	(Ottawa: Public Works and Government Services Canada, 1997)	vol 1		at 100.
Canada,	Commission of Inquiry into the Sponsorship Program and Advertising Activities,	Who is Responsible? Fact Finding Report	(Ottawa: Public Works and Government Services Canada, 2005)			at 33.

▨ Include the jurisdiction unless it is mentioned in another element of the citation.

▨ Include the issuing body unless it is mentioned in the title of the report.

▨ To distinguish the volumes, indicate **vol** or any other appellation used in the report (such as "book").

▨ Do not repeat the volume number in subsequent references unless there is a citation to a different volume anywhere else in the citing document (e.g., *Blood System Report*, **vol 2**, *supra* note 5 at 64).

4.2.3.2 Reports Published Under Multiple Titles

Citation for volume 1	;	citation for volume 2
Report of the Royal Commission on Aboriginal Peoples: Looking Forward, Looking Back, **vol 1** (Ottawa: Supply and Services Canada, 1996).	;	*Report of the Royal Commission on Aboriginal Peoples: Restructuring the Relationship*, **vol 2** (Ottawa: Supply and Services Canada, 1996) at 14.

☐ To cite a report published in multiple volumes with different titles, include a full citation for each volume separated by a semicolon. Treat the title of the volume as a subtitle of the entire work.

☐ Subsequent references must include the volume number following the short title (e.g. *Aboriginal Peoples Report*, **vol 2**, *supra* note 4 at 32).

☐ In all other respects, follow the rules in section 4.2.3.1.

4.2.4   Public Papers of Intergovernmental Conferences

Name of conference or committee,	*title,*	document number	(location of conference:	date of conference).
Meeting of the Continuing Committee of Ministers on the Constitution,	*The Canadian Charter of Rights and Freedoms: Discussion Draft, July 4, 1980,*	Doc 830-81/027	(Ottawa:	8–12 September 1980).
Federal-Provincial-Territorial Meeting of Ministers Responsible for Justice,	*Dealing with Impaired Driving in Prince Edward Island: A Summary 1986-1997,*	Doc 830-600/021	(Montreal:	4–5 December 1997).

░ Indicate the name of the conference or committee in full, followed by the title of the paper and the document number.

░ Provide the location and full date of the conference in parentheses.

5 International Materials E-89

E -5.1 International Documents E-89
    E -5.1.1 Treaties, UN Documents, and Other International Agreements E-89
        E -5.1.1.1 Australian Treaty Neutral Citation E-92
    E -5.1.2 United Nations Documents E-92
        E -5.1.2.1 Charter of the United Nations E-92
        E -5.1.2.2 Official Records E-92
                E -5.1.2.2.1 Meetings E-93
                E -5.1.2.2.2 Supplements E-94
                E -5.1.2.2.3 Annexes E-95
        E -5.1.2.3 UN Masthead Documents (Mimeographs) E-95
        E -5.1.2.4 Periodicals E-96
        E -5.1.2.5 Yearbooks E-96
        E -5.1.2.6 Sales Publications E-96
    E -5.1.3 European Union Documents E-96
        E -5.1.3.1 Regulations, Directives, and Decisions E-96
        E -5.1.3.2 Debates of the European Parliament E-97
        E -5.1.3.3 Other Documents E-98
    E -5.1.4 Council of Europe Documents E-98
    E -5.1.5 Organization of American States Documents E-99
    E -5.1.6 World Trade Organization (WTO) and the General Agreement
                on Tariffs and Trade (GATT) Documents E-100
    E -5.1.7 Organisation for Economic Co-operation and Development
                (OECD) Documents E-101
    E -5.1.8 First Nations Treaties E-102

E -5.2 Cases E-102
    E -5.2.1 Permanent Court of International Justice (1922–1946) E-102
        E -5.2.1.1 Judgments, Orders, and Advisory Opinions E-102
        E -5.2.1.2 Pleadings, Oral Arguments, and Documents E-103
    E -5.2.2 International Court of Justice (1946–present) E-103
        E -5.2.2.1 Judgments, Orders, and Advisory Opinions E-104
        E -5.2.2.2 Pleadings, Oral Arguments, and Documents E-104
    E -5.2.3 Court of Justice of the European Communities and European
                Court of First Instance E-105
    E -5.2.4 European Court of Human Rights and European Commission
                of Human Rights E-105
        E -5.2.4.1 Before 1999 .... E-105
        E -5.2.4.2 1999 and Later E-106
    E -5.2.5 Inter-American Court of Human Rights E-107
        E -5.2.5.1 Judgments, Orders, and Advisory Opinions E-107
        E -5.2.5.2 Pleadings, Oral Arguments, and Documents E-107
    E -5.2.6 Inter-American Commission on Human Rights E-108
    E -5.2.7 International Criminal Tribunals E-108
    E -5.2.8 General Agreement on Tariffs and Trade (GATT) 1947 Panel
                Reports E-109
    E -5.2.9 World Trade Organization (WTO) Panel and Appellate Body
                Reports E-110
    E -5.2.10 Canada-United States Free Trade Agreement Panels E-111

International Materials

E -5.2.11 North American Free Trade Agreement (NAFTA) Binational
Panels..E-111
E -5.2.12 International Arbitration Cases E-112
E -5.2.13 World Intellectual Property Organization (WIPO) Arbitration
Cases E-112
E -5.2.13.1 Uniform Domain Name Dispute Resolution Policy
(UDRP) E-112
E -5.2.14 International Law Cases Decided Before National Courts E-113

E -5.3 Websites E-113

5   INTERNATIONAL MATERIALS

5.1   INTERNATIONAL DOCUMENTS

5.1.1   Treaties, UN Documents, and Other International Agreements

Treaty Name,	parties, if applicable,	date of signature,	treaty series reference	pinpoint	(date of entry into force and optional additional information) .
Treaty Relating to Boundary Waters and Questions Arising with Canada,	United States and United Kingdom,	11 January 1909,	36 US Stat 2448		(entered into force 5 May 1910).
Convention for the Protection of Human Rights and Fundamental Freedoms,		4 November 1950,	213 UNTS 221	at 223	(entered into force 3 September 1953) [*ECHR*].
International Covenant on Civil and Political Rights,		19 December 1966,	999 UNTS 171	arts 9–14	(entered into force 23 March 1976, accession by Canada 19 May 1976) [*ICCPR*].
North American Free Trade Agreement Between the Government of Canada, the Government of Mexico and the Government of the United States,		17 December 1992,	Can TS 1994 No 2		(entered into force 1 January 1994) [*NAFTA*].
General Agreement on Tariffs and Trade,		30 October 1947,	58 UNTS 187		(entered into force 1 January 1948) [*GATT 1947*].

> Write the complete title of the treaty. When the names of the signatories appear in the title of a treaty, shorten them to reflect common usage (e.g., **United Kingdom**, not **United Kingdom of Great Britain and Northern Ireland**) but do not abbreviate them (e.g., **UK**).

> If the names of the parties to a bilateral treaty are not mentioned in the title, include the shortened (but not abbreviated) names of the parties after the title, between commas. The names of the parties to a multilateral treaty may be included in parentheses at the end of the citation.

> Provide the date when the treaty was first signed or opened for signature.

> Provide the date of entry into force at the end of the citation, in parentheses.

> Provide the treaty series citation after the date.

> Following the treaty series citation, optionally provide a parallel citation to other treaty series, referring to treaty series in the following order of preference: (1) *United Nations*

Treaty Series [**UNTS**] or *League of Nations Treaty Series* [**LNTS**]; (2) official treaty series of a state involved (e.g., *Canada Treaty Series* [**Can TS**], *United Kingdom Treaty Series* [**UKTS**]); (3) other series of international treaties.

▪ If available, provide a parallel citation to *International Legal Materials* [**ILM**].

▪ Provide any additional information at the end of the citation, following the date of entry into force (e.g., the names of the parties to a multilateral treaty, the number of ratifications, and the status of particular countries).

Treaty series and their abbreviations:

Air and Aviation Treaties of the World	AATW
Australian Treaty Series	ATS
British and Foreign State Papers	UKFS
Canada Treaty Series	Can TS
Consolidated Treaty Series	Cons TS
Documents juridiques internationaux	DJI
European Treaty Series	Eur TS
International Legal Materials	ILM
Journal officiel	JO
League of Nations Treaty Series	LNTS
Organization of American States Treaty Series	OASTS
Recueil des traités d'alliance, de paix, de trêve, de neutralité, de commerce, de limites, d'échange, et plusieurs autres actes à la connaissance des relations étrangères des puissances et États de l'Europe	Rec TA
Recueil des traités de la Société des Nations	RTSN
Recueil des traités des Nations Unies	RTNU
Recueil des traités du Canada	RT Can
Recueil des traités et accords de la France	RTAF
Recueil général des traités de la France	Rec GTF
Série des traités et conventions européennes	STE
Treaties and other International Agreements of the United States of America 1776-1949	TI Agree (formerly USBS)
United Kingdom Treaty Series	UKTS
United Nations Treaty Series	UNTS
United States Statutes at Large	US Stat
United States Treaties and Other International Acts Series	TIAS
United States Treaties and Other International Agreements	UST

5.1.1.1 Australian Treaty Neutral Citation

The Australian Commonwealth government has adopted a method of neutral citation for treaties that should precede citation to a printed source. The form consists of the publication year in brackets, the identifier, and the document number. This citation should follow the treaty name and the year of signing.

Identifiers for neutral citation:

Australian Treaty Series	ATS	*Agreement on the Conservation of Albatrosses and Petrels*, 19 June 2001, [2004] ATS 5.
Australian Treaty National Interest Analysis	ATNIA	
Australian Treaty not yet in force	ATNIF	

5.1.2   United Nations Documents

Not all UN documents contain every element found in the examples below. Adapt the citation and provide the information necessary to identify the document clearly.

Abbreviations of commonly used words and phrases:

Decision	Dec	Plenary	Plen
Document	Doc	Recommendation	Rec
Emergency	Emer	Regulation	Reg
Meeting	Mtg	Resolution	Res
Mimeograph(ed)	Mimeo	Session	Sess
Number	No	Special	Spec
Official Records	OR	Supplement	Supp

5.1.2.1 Charter of the United Nations

The *Charter of the United Nations* does not require a full citation. Cite it as: ***Charter of the United Nations*, 26 June 1945, Can TS 1945 No 7**.

5.1.2.2 Official Records

Official records published by UN organizations contain three parts: **Meetings**, **Supplements**, and **Annexes**. The official records are identified by the particular body's acronym followed by **OR**. Provide the full names of UN bodies that have no official acronym.

International Materials

Official acronyms of the principal United Nations bodies:

Economic and Social Council	ESC
First Committee, Second Committee, etc.	C1, C2, etc.
General Assembly	GA
Security Council	SC
Trade and Development Board	TDB
Trusteeship Council	TC
United Nations Conference on Trade and Development	UNCTAD

5.1.2.2.1 Meetings

UN body's acronym and OR,	session number or number of years since the body's inception,	meeting,	UN doc number (and sales number if applicable)	(year of document) (if applicable)	pin-point	[provisional].
UNCTAD TDBOR,	23rd Sess,	565th Mtg,	UN Doc TD/B/SR.565	(1981).		
UNSCOR,	53rd Year,	3849th Mtg,	UN Doc S/PV.3849	(1998)		[provisional].
UNES-COR,	1984,	23rd Plen Mtg,	UN Doc E/1984/SR.23.			

- Indicate **UN** (unless **UN** is part of the body's acronym) followed by the **UN body's acronym** and **OR** (**Official Records**). Do not add a space between **UN** and the acronym.

- Provide the **session number** after the name of the body. If the session number is not available, give the year of the body since its inception. If neither the session number nor the year of the body are available, provide the calendar year.

- Provide the **meeting number** after the sessional information.

- Provide the **UN document number** after the meeting number. If a document has more than one document number, indicate all the numbers, separated by a hyphen. Give the **sales document number** after the document number in parentheses (e.g., **Sales No #**) (if applicable).

- Provide the **calendar year** in parentheses after the UN document number, unless previously indicated.

- Indicate **provisional documents** by placing **[provisional]** at the end of the citation.

5.1.2.2.2 Supplements

UN resolutions, decisions, and reports appear as supplements to documents published in the Official Records.

	Author (if applicable),	title,	UN body Res or Dec number,	UN body's acronym and OR,	session number or calendar year,	Supp No,	UN Doc number	(calendar year)	1st page and pinpoint.
Resolutions		Universal Declaration of Human Rights,	GA Res 217A (III),	UNGAOR,	3rd Sess,	Supp No 13,	UN Doc A/810	(1948)	71.
Decisions		Protection of the heritage of indigenous people,	ESC Dec 1998/ 277,	UNESCOR,	1998,	Supp No 1,	UN Doc E/1998/ 98,		113 at 115.
Reports	Commission on Crime Prevention and Criminal Justice,	Report on the Ninth Session,		UNESCOR,	2000,	Supp No 10,	UN Doc E/2000/ 30.		
		Report of the UN Commissioner for Refugees,		UNGAOR,	15th Sess,	Supp No 11,	UN Doc A/4378/ Rev.1	(1960).	

- For reports, provide the name of the author if not mentioned in the title.
- Provide the title in italics.
- For decisions and resolutions, provide the **decision or resolution number** after the title.
- Indicate **UN** (unless UN is part of the body's acronym) followed by the **UN body's acronym** and **OR (Official Records)**. Do not add a space between UN and the acronym. For resolutions and decisions, provide this information after the resolution or decision number. For reports, provide this information immediately after the report's title.
- Provide the **session number** after the UN body's official records acronym. If the session number is not available, give the **year of the body since its inception**. If neither the session number nor the year of the body is available, provide the **calendar year**.
- Provide the **supplement number** and the UN document number after the sessional information.
- Provide the **calendar year** in parentheses after the UN document number, unless it has been indicated previously.
- If possible, conclude the citation with the first page number and pinpoint. Add a comma when there is no information provided between the UN document number and the first page.

5.1.2.2.3 Annexes

Title,	UN body's acronym and OR,	session number or number of years since the body's inception,	annex, agenda item no,	UN Doc number	(year) (if applicable)	1st page (if applicable) and pinpoint.
Protectionism and structural adjustment,	UNCTAD TDBOR,	32nd Sess,	Annex, Agenda Item 6,	UN Doc TD/B/1081	(1986)	at 23.
USSR: Draft Resolution,	UNESCOR,	3rd year, 7th Sess,	Annex, Agenda Item 7,	UN Doc E/884/Rev.1	(1948)	at para 3.

- Provide the title of the document in italics.
- Provide the UN body's acronym and **OR (Official Records)** after the title. Do not add a space between **UN** and the acronym.
- Provide the **session number** after the UN body's acronym. If the session number is not available, give the **year of the body since its inception**. If neither the session number nor the year of the body is available, provide the **calendar year**.
- Indicate **Annex** and the agenda item number, followed by the UN document number.
- Provide the calendar year in parentheses after the UN document number, unless it has been indicated previously.
- Conclude the citation with the first page number if the document is part of a bound collection of documents. Add a comma when there is no information provided between the UN document number and the first page.

5.1.2.3 UN Masthead Documents (Mimeographs)

Name of body,	name of sub-body or commission	author (if applicable),	title,	session, Meeting, Supplement,	UN Doc number,	date	pin-point	[short form].
UNSC,	Disarmament Commission,		*Questions about Arms Manufacturing in Eastern Iraq,*		UN Doc S/CN.10/L.666,	July 1993.		

- A mimeograph is an official document of the UN. Refer to one only when the document has not been reproduced in the Official Reports. Mimeographs are available at <documents.un.org>.
- Not every document will indicate all of the elements listed above.
- The most important element is the **UN Doc number**, as that is the easiest way to find the document online, followed by the name of the body, the title, and the date. The other elements are less essential, but should be included if they are on the title page.

5.1.2.4 Periodicals

When referring to periodical articles published by the UN, follow the rules for citing articles (see section 6.1). If it is unclear from the title of the periodical that the UN is the publisher, include **UN** and

> CP Romulo, "External Debt in Central America" (1987) CEPAL Review No 32 (UN, Economic Commission for Latin America and the Caribbean).

the particular body responsible for the publication in parentheses at the end of the citation.

5.1.2.5 Yearbooks

Cite UN yearbooks using the same rules as those provided for collections of essays, at section 6.3. Give the UN document number of the article cited and of the yearbook, if available.

> "Report of the Commission to the General Assembly on the work of its thirty-ninth Session" (UN Doc A/42/10) in *Yearbook of the International Law Commission 1987*, vol 2, part 2 (New York: UN, 1989) at 50 (UNDOC. A/CN 4/SER.A/1987/Add. 1).

5.1.2.6 Sales Publications

> UN, *Recommendations on the Transport of Dangerous Goods*, 9th ed (New York: UN, 1995) at 18.

Cite sales publications using the rules for books, at section 6.2.

5.1.3   European Union Documents

European Union regulations, directives, decisions, debates, and other documents are published in the ***Official Journal of the European Union*** (OJ). The OJ is published every working day in every official language. It consists of two related series (**the L series for legislation** and **the C series for information and notices**) and a supplement (**the S series for public tenders,** which is available only in electronic format as of 1 July 1998). The title replaced the *Official Journal of the European Communities* as of 1 February 2003.

5.1.3.1 Regulations, Directives, and Decisions

Legislation from the European Communities includes instruments referred to as regulations, directives, and decisions. They are published in the legislation (**L**) series of the *Official Journal of the European Union.*

	EC,	title,	[year of journal]	OJ,	series and issue number/ 1st page	pin-point.
Regulations	EC,	*Commission Regulation (EC) 218/2005 of 10 February 2005 opening and providing for the administration of an autonomous tariff quota for garlic from 1 January 2005,*	[2005]	OJ,	L 39/5	at 6.
Directives	EC,	*Commission Directive 2004/29/EC of 4 March 2004 on determining the characteristics and minimum conditions for inspecting vine varieties,*	[2004]	OJ,	L 71/22.	
Decisions	EC,	*Commission Decision 98/85/EC of 16 January 1998 concerning certain protective measures with regard to live birds coming from, or originating in Hong Kong and China,*	[1998]	OJ,	L 15/45	at 46.

▦ Write **EC** for **European Community** and provide the full title of the instrument in italics.

▦ The **instrument number** is included in the title. The number in **directives and decisions** consists of the year and a sequential number (e.g., **98/85** or **2004/29**). Note that only the last two digits of the year are used until 1998. Beginning with 1999, all four digits are used.

▦ To cite **regulations**, write the sequential number first, followed by the last two digits of the year until 1998 and the full year starting in 1999 (e.g., **2514/98**).

▦ Indicate the **OJ series**, then the issue number and the first page of the instrument, separated by a slash (e.g., **L 15/45**). Cite EC legislation to the **L** series of the *Official Journal of the European Union.*

5.1.3.2 Debates of the European Parliament

EC,	date of sitting or title,	[year]	OJ	Annex issue number/first page	pinpoint.
EC,	*Sitting of Wednesday, 5 May 1999,*	[1999]	OJ	Annex 4-539/144	at 152.

▦ The debates of the European Parliament can be found in the Annex to the *Official Journal of the European Union* (**OJ**).

▦ Write **EC** and provide the title of the document or the date of the sitting.

▦ Provide the year the sitting was reported in brackets, followed by **OJ**, then **Annex** and the **issue number**. A slash (/) separates the issue number from the first page (e.g., **4-539/144**).

5.1.3.3 *Other Documents*

Information and notices	EC, *Explanatory note concerning Annex III of the EU-Mexico Agreement (Decision 2/2000 of the EU-Mexico Joint Council)*, [2004] OJ C 40/2.
General publications	EC, Commission, *Report from the Commission to the Council and the European Parliament* (Luxembourg: EC, 1995).
Periodicals	EC, *External Trade: Monthly Statistics* (1994) No 1 at 16.

▓ Write **EC** as the author of all EC documents. If available, provide a more precise authoring body.

▓ Cite the *Official Journal of the European Union: Information and Notices* (**C series**) in the same manner as other sections of the official journal.

▓ For **general publications**, see Chapter 6 of this *Guide*.

▓ For **periodicals**, italicize the title of the periodical and indicate the issue number after the year.

5.1.4   Council of Europe Documents

Documents from the Council of Europe can be found in the following official publications.

Official publication	Abbreviation
Documents: Working Papers	Documents
Information Bulletin on Legal Affairs	Inf Bull
Official Report of Debates	Debates
Orders of the Day and Minutes of Proceedings	Orders
Texts Adopted by the Assembly	Texts Adopted

	Council of Europe,	body,	sessional information,	*title* (if applicable),	official publication	(year)	pinpoint.
Debates	Council of Europe,	PA,	2001 Ordinary Sess (First Part),		Debates, vol 1	(2001)	at 67.
Texts Adopted	Council of Europe,	CA,	21st Sess, Part 3,		Texts Adopted, Rec 585	(1970)	at 1.
Orders and minutes	Council of Europe,	CA,	21st Sess, Part 2,		Orders, 10th Sitting	(1969)	at 20.
Working Papers	Council of Europe,	PA,	2000 Ordinary Sess (Third Part),	*Situation of lesbians and gays in Council of Europe member states,*	Documents, vol 5, Doc 8755	(2000)	at 1.
Series	Council of Europe,	Committee of Ministers,		*Recommendation R(82)1,*	(1980) 12 Inf Bull 58.		

▪ Write **Council of Europe,** followed by the particular body responsible for the instrument. Abbreviate **Parliamentary Assembly** to **PA**, and **Consultative Assembly** to **CA**.

▪ Provide the sessional information followed by the title of the document, if applicable.

▪ Indicate the official publication in abbreviated form.

▪ Indicate the year of publication in parentheses after the official publication.

▪ To cite periodicals (**Inf Bull**), see section 6.1.

5.1.5 Organization of American States Documents

OAS,	issuing body,	session number (if applicable),	*title,*	OAS document number	(year)	pin-point.
OAS,	General Assembly,	2d Sess,	*Draft Standards Regarding the Formulation of Reservations to Multilateral Treaties,*	OR OEA/Ser.P/AG/ Doc.202	(1972).	
OAS,	Inter-American Commission on Human Rights,		*Draft of the Inter-American Declaration on the Rights of Indigenous Peoples,*	OR OEA/Ser.L/V/II. 90/Doc.14, rev. 1	(1995)	at 1.

▪ **OAS documents do not have an author**. Include the particular issuing body, if one exists, unless it is clear from the title of the report.

International Materials

▓ Where applicable, put the session or meeting number after the name of the issuing body.

▓ Use the official title of the document.

▓ Place **OR** before the OAS document number. The document number begins with the letters **OEA** (Organización de los Estados Americanos) and not OAS.

▓ Conclude the citation with the year of the document in parentheses.

5.1.6 World Trade Organization (WTO) and the General Agreement on Tariffs and Trade (GATT) Documents

	GATT or WTO,	*title,*	Decision, Recommendation, or **Document number,**	session number,	BISD	online information (if applicable).
Decisions and recommen-dations		*Accession of Guatemala,*	GATT CP Decision L/6824,	47th Sess,	38th Supp BISD (1991) 16.	
		Freedom of Contract in Transport Insurance,	GATT CP Recommendation of 27 May 1959,	15th Sess,	8th Supp BISD (1960) 26.	
Reports	GATT,	*Report of the Panel adopted by the Committee on Anti-Dumping Practices on 30 October 1995,*	GATT Doc ADP/137,		42nd Supp BISD (1995) 17.	
	WTO,	*Report of the Working Party on the Accession of Bulgaria,*	WTO Doc WT/ACC/BGR/5 (1996),			online: WTO <docsonline. wto.org> .
Meetings	WTO, General Council,	*Minutes of Meeting* (held on 22 November 2000),	WTO Doc WT/GC/M/60,			online: WTO <docsonline. wto.org> .

▓ **Decisions and recommendations do not have an author**. GATT and WTO are the authors of all reports. Include the particular issuing body, if one exists, unless it is clear from the title of the report.

▓ Give the decision, recommendation, or document number. If none, give the full date of the decision or recommendation. Abbreviate **Contracting Parties** to **CP**, **Decision** to **Dec** and **Recommendation** to **Rec**.

▦ Where possible, cite GATT documents to the *Basic Instruments and Selected Documents* (**BISD**), followed by the year in parentheses and the first page of the document.

▦ If a report is printed independently with no document number, use the rules for books, at section 6.2 (e.g., **GATT,** *The International Markets for Meat: 1990/91* (**Geneva: GATT, 1991**)).

5.1.7 Organisation for Economic Co-operation and Development (OECD) Documents

	OECD, authoring body (if applicable),	*title,*	series title,	working paper number or other publication information,	Doc No	(publication information or year).
Series	OECD, Development Assistance Committee,	*Japan (No 34),*	Development Cooperation Review Series,			(Paris: OECD, 1999).
Working Papers	OECD, Economics Department,	*Encouraging Environmentally Sustainable Growth in Australia,*		Working Paper No 309,	Doc No ECO/WKP (2001) 35	(2001).
Periodical	OECD,	*OECD Economic Surveys: China,*		Economic Surveys, vol 2005, No 13,		(2005).

▦ Indicate **OECD** and the authoring body, followed by the title in italics.

▦ If the document is a work in a series, provide the series title.

▦ If the document is a working paper, provide the working paper number, if applicable, and the OECD document number. Note that some document numbers begin with **OCDE**, in French or English.

▦ Include other information such as the volume number for a periodical or series.

▦ Provide the publication information in parentheses at the end of the citation. For periodicals, provide the month of publication, if applicable.

DALHOUSIE LAW LIBRARY

5.1.8   First Nations Treaties

Title,	date (if not in title),	online: <www.aadnc-aandc.gc.ca/full path>	[short form].
Treaty 3 between Her Majesty the Queen and the Saulteaux Tribe of the Ojibbeway Indians at the Northwest Angle on the Lake of the Woods with Adhesions,	3 October 1873,	online: <www.aadnc-aandc.gc.ca/eng/ 1100100028667/ 1100100028669>	[Treaty 3].
Treaty No 8 Made June 21, 1899,		online: <www.aadnc-aandc.gc.ca/eng/ 1100100028805/ 1100100028807>	[Treaty 8].

▨   Indicate the full title of the treaty.

5.2   CASES

See **Appendix A-5** for a list of abbreviations of international organizations and their reporters.

5.2.1   Permanent Court of International Justice (1922–1946)

To cite acts and rules of the PCIJ, write the title, volume number, and name of publication, followed by the first page or document number (e.g., ***Revised Rules of the Court* (1926), PCIJ 33 (Ser D) No 1**).

5.2.1.1 Judgments, Orders, and Advisory Opinions

	Style of cause (names of parties)	(year),	type of decision,	reporter	case No	pinpoint.
Judgments	Panevezys-Saldutiskis Railway Case (Estonia v Lithuania)	(1939),		PCIJ (Ser A/B)	No 76	at 16.
Orders	Panevezys-Saldutiskis Railway Case (Estonia v Lithuania),		Order of 30 June 1938,	PCIJ (Ser A/B)	No 75	at 8.
Advisory Opinions	Case of the Customs Régime Between Germany and Austria	(1931),	Advisory Opinion,	PCIJ (Ser A/B)	No 41	at 3.

▨   Indicate the style of cause and, for judgments and orders, the names of the parties involved.

▨   For judgments and advisory opinions, provide the year of the decision in parentheses after the style of cause.

- Specify if the document is an order or an advisory opinion. If referring to an order, provide the full date. In such a case, no indication of the year in parentheses is required after the style of cause.

- Provide the PCIJ series followed by the case number. **Judgments of the PCIJ** are published in *Series A: Collection of Judgments* (**PCIJ (Ser A)**) and in *Series A/B: Judgments, Orders and Advisory Opinions* (**PCIJ (Ser A/B)**). **Orders** and **advisory opinions** are published in *Series B: Collection of Advisory Opinions* (**PCIJ (Ser B)**) and in *Series A/B: Judgments, Orders and Advisory Opinions* (**PCIJ (Ser A/B)**).

5.2.1.2 Pleadings, Oral Arguments, and Documents

Style of cause (names of parties),	"title of document"	(date),	reporter	case No,	first page	pinpoint.
Lighthouses Case Between France and Greece (France v Greece),	"Oral argument of Professor Basdevant"	(5 February 1934),	PCIJ (Series C)	No 74,	222	at 227.
Pajzs, Csáky, Esterházy Case (Hungary v Yugoslavia),	"Application Instituting Proceedings"	(1 December 1935),	PCIJ (Series C)	No 79,	10	at 12.

- Indicate the style of cause and, in parentheses, the names of the parties involved.

- Provide the official title of the document, followed by the full date in parentheses.

- Indicate the PCIJ Series and the case number. Pleadings, oral arguments, and other documents from **before 1931** are published in *Series C: Acts and Documents Relating to Judgments and Advisory Opinions Given by the Court* (**PCIJ (Series C)**), and **after 1931** in *Series C: Pleadings, Oral Statements and Documents* (**PCIJ (Series C)**). **Basic Documents**, **Annual Reports** and **Indices** are published in series D through series F.

- Place a comma between the case number and the first page of the document.

5.2.2 International Court of Justice (1946–present)

To cite acts and rules of the ICJ, write the title, volume number, and name of publication, followed by the first page or document number (e.g., *Travel and Subsistence Regulations of the International Court of Justice*, **[1947] ICJ Acts & Doc 94**).

International Materials

5.2.2.1 Judgments, Orders, and Advisory Opinions

Refer to the ICJ website <www.icj-cij.org> (see section 5.3) for ICJ judgments, opinions, or orders not yet printed. Follow the online citation rules for jurisprudence (see section 5.3).

	Style of cause (names of parties),	type of decision,	[year of reporter]	reporter	first page	pinpoint.
Judgments	Case concerning East Timor (Portugal v Australia),		[1995]	ICJ Rep	90	at 103.
Orders	Certain Activities Carried Out by Nicaragua in the Border Area (Costa Rica v Nicara-gua),	Order of 8 March 2011,	[2011]	ICJ Rep	6.	
Advisory Opinions	Legality of the Threat or Use of Nuclear Weapons Case,	Advisory Opinion,	[1996]	ICJ Rep	226	at 230.

▨ Begin with the style of cause and the names of the parties involved. Although the ICJ Reports sometimes separates the parties' names with a slash (*El Salvador/Honduras*), always separate them with a *v* (***Portugal v Australia***). Names of the parties are not provided for advisory opinions.

▨ Specify if the document is an order or an advisory opinion. If referring to an order, provide the full date.

▨ Provide the year of the reporter in brackets, followed by the reporter and the first page. Judgments, orders, and advisory opinions of the ICJ are published in the court's official reporter: ***Reports of Judgments, Advisory Opinions and Orders*** (ICJ Rep).

5.2.2.2 Pleadings, Oral Arguments, and Documents

Style of cause (names of parties),	"title of document"	(date),	[year of reporter]	reporter (vol)	first page	pin-point.
Case concerning Right of Passage over Indian Territory (Portugal v India),	"Oral argument of Shri MC Setalvad"	(23 September 1957),	[1960]	ICJ Pleadings (vol 4)	14	at 23.
Fisheries Jurisdiction Case (Spain v Canada),	"Application Instituting Proceedings Submitted by Spain"	(28 March 1995),		ICJ Pleadings	3.	

▨ Indicate the style of cause and, in parentheses, the names of the parties.

▨ After the style of cause, provide the title of the document as indicated in the reporter, followed by the date in parentheses.

▨ Indicate the reporter and the first page of the document. The ICJ publishes pleadings and other documents in ***Pleadings, Oral Arguments and Documents*** (ICJ Pleadings). If there is a volume number, cite it in Arabic numerals (e.g., **1, 2, 3**) and in parentheses (e.g., **ICJ Pleadings (vol 4)**) before the number of the first page.

▨ After 1981, ICJ Pleadings do not indicate the date of publication of the reporter. Pleadings are available on the ICJ website: <www.icj-cij.org>.

5.2.3 Court of Justice of the European Communities and European Court of First Instance

	Style of cause,	case number,	[year of reporter]	reporter	first page	pinpoint,	parallel citation.
ECJ	Commission v Luxembourg,	C-26/99,	[1999]	ECR	I-8987	at I-8995.	
CFI	Kesko v Commission,	T-22/97,	[1999]	ECR	II-3775	at II-3822.	

▨ Write the style of cause. Abbreviate the names of institutions (e.g., **Council** rather than **Council of the European Communities**).

▨ Write the case number. **C-** indicates a decision of the Court of Justice of the European Communities, also known as the **European Court of Justice** (ECJ). **T-** indicates a decision of the **European Court of First Instance** (CFI).

▨ Cite the reporter and indicate the first page of the case. Decisions of the ECJ and the CFI are published in the Courts' official reporter *Reports of Cases before the Court of Justice and the Court of First Instance*. Cite it as the **European Court Reports** (**ECR**).

▨ Precede page numbers by **I** for **ECJ decisions** and by **II** for **CFI decisions**.

▨ If possible, provide a parallel citation to the *Common Market Law Reports* (**CMLR**) or to the *Common Market Reporter* (**CMR**).

5.2.4 European Court of Human Rights and European Commission of Human Rights

5.2.4.1 Before 1999

Style of cause	(year of judgment),	volume number	reporter	first page,	parallel citation.
Kurt v Turkey	(1998),	74	ECHR (Ser A)	1152,	27 EHRR 373.
Spencer v United Kingdom	(1998),	92A	Eur Comm'n HR DR	56,	41 YB Eur Conv HR 72.

▨ Indicate the style of cause followed by the year of the decision in parentheses.

International Materials

■ Provide the volume number of the official reporter before the name of the reporter, followed by the name of the reporter and the first page of the judgment. Cite the official reporters of the Court and Commission: *European Court of Human Rights, Series A: Judgments and Decisions* (**ECHR (Ser A)**); *Collection of Decisions of the European Commission of Human Rights* (**Eur Comm'n HR CD** (1960-1974)); *Decisions and Reports of the European Commission of Human Rights* (**Eur Comm'n HR DR** (1975-1999)).

■ Provide a parallel citation to the *Yearbook of the European Convention on Human Rights* (**YB Eur Conv HR**) or to the *European Human Rights Reports* (**EHRR**).

5.2.4.2 1999 and Later

Protocol No 11 to the Convention for the Protection of Human Rights and Fundamental Freedoms came into force on 1 November 1998, replacing the old court and commission with a new full-time court.

Style of cause,	application No,	[year]	vol number	reporter	first page,	parallel citation.
Allard v Sweden,	No 35179/97,	[2003]	VII	ECHR	207,	39 EHRR 321.
Cyprus v Turkey,	No 25781/94,	[2001]	IV	ECHR	1,	35 EHRR 731.

■ Add **[GC]** at the end of the style of cause, before the comma, if the judgment was given by the Grand Chamber of the Court.

■ Other information may also be added in parentheses after the style of cause, before the comma: **(dec)** for a **decision on admissibility**, **(preliminary objections)** for a judgment concerning only **preliminary objections**, **(just satisfaction)** for a judgment concerning only **just satisfaction**, **(revision)** for a judgment concerning **revision**, **(interpretation)** for a judgment concerning **interpretation**, **(striking out)** for a judgment **striking the case out**, or **(friendly settlement)** for a judgment concerning a **friendly settlement**.

■ If there is more than one application number, include only the first number.

■ For unreported decisions, give the application number followed by the date the judgment was rendered (e.g., *Roche v United Kingdom*, **No 32555/96 (19 October 2005)**).

5.2.5   Inter-American Court of Human Rights

5.2.5.1 Judgments, Orders, and Advisory Opinions

	Style of cause (name of state concerned)	(year of judgment),	type of decision and number,	reporter	case or report No,	pinpoint,	parallel citation.
Judgments	Neira Alegría Case (Peru)	(1996),		Inter-Am Ct HR (Ser C)	No 29,	at para 55,	Annual Report of the Inter-American Court of Human Rights: 1996, OEA/Ser.L/V/III.19/doc.4 (1997) 179.
Advisory Opinions	Reports of the Inter-American Commission on Human Rights (Art 51 of the American Convention on Human Rights) (Chile)	(1997),	Advisory Opinion OC-15/97,	Inter-Am Ct HR (Ser A)	No 15,	at para 53,	Annual Report of the Inter-American Commission on Human Rights: 1997, OEA/Ser.L/V/III.39/doc.5 (1998) 307.

- Indicate the style of cause. If the case involves an individual state, include the name of that state in parentheses.

- Provide the year of the decision in parentheses.

- Specify if the document is an **advisory opinion** and provide the advisory opinion number.

- Provide the reporter and case number. The Inter-American Court of Human Rights publishes **judgments** in *Inter-American Court of Human Rights, Series C: Decisions and Judgments* (**Inter-Am Ct HR (Ser C)**) and **advisory opinions** in *Inter-American Court of Human Rights, Series A: Judgments and Opinions* (**Inter-Am Ct HR (Ser A)**).

- Provide a parallel citation to the **annual report of the court**, to *International Legal Materials* (**ILM**) or to the *Inter-American Yearbook on Human Rights*.

5.2.5.2 Pleadings, Oral Arguments, and Documents

Style of cause (name of the state concerned),	type of decision and number,	"title of document"	(date of document),	reporter and (series)	first page	pin-point.
Proposed Amendments to the Naturalization Provisions of the Constitution of Costa Rica,	Advisory Opinion OC-4/84,	"Verbatim Record of Public Hearing"	(7 September 1983),	Inter-Am Ct HR (Ser B)	23.	

- Indicate the style of cause. If the name of the state concerned is not already included in the style of cause, write the name in parentheses.

- Specify if it is an **advisory opinion** and give the advisory opinion number.

- Include the title of the document in quotation marks, followed by the full date in parentheses.

- Provide the reporter and first page. The Inter-American Court of Human Rights publishes pleadings, oral arguments, and other documents in *Inter-American Court of Human Rights, Series B: Pleadings, Oral Arguments and Documents* (**Inter-Am Ct HR (Ser B)**).

5.2.6   Inter-American Commission on Human Rights

Style of cause	*(year of judgment),*	*Inter-Am Comm HR,*	*case or report No,*	*pinpoint,*	*annual report,*	*document number.*
Sánchez v Mexico	(1992),	Inter-Am Comm HR,	No 27/92,		Annual Report of the Inter-American Commission on Human Rights: 1992-93,	OEA/Ser.L/V/II.83/ doc.14 104.

- Indicate the style of cause followed by the year of decision in parentheses.

- Indicate **Inter-Am Comm HR** followed by the case or report number.

- Decisions of the Inter-American Commission on Human Rights are published in the commission's annual reports. Cite the commission's annual report and the document number. The document number starts with the letters **OEA** (Organización de les Estados Americanos) and not OAS, no matter the language of the document.

5.2.7   International Criminal Tribunals

- This section provides guidelines for citing documents created by:

  - ☐ the International Criminal Court;
  - ☐ the International Criminal Tribunal for the former Yugoslavia;
  - ☐ the International Criminal Tribunal for Rwanda;
  - ☐ the Special Court for Sierra Leone; and
  - ☐ the Special Panels for Serious Crimes (East Timor).

Style of cause,	case number,	title of document (version)	(date of document)	pinpoint	(tribunal),	source.
Prosecutor v Zdravko Mucic (Celebici Camp Case),	IT- 96- 21-*Abis*,	Judgment on Sentence Appeal	(8 April 2003)	at para 8	(International Criminal Tribunal for the former Yugoslavia, Appeals Chamber),	(WL).
Prosecutor v Théoneste Bagosora,	ICTR-98- 41-I,	Minutes of Proceedings	(2 April 2002)		(International Criminal Tribunal for Rwanda, Trial Chamber),	online: ICTR <www.ictr.org>.
Deputy General Prosecutor for Serious Crimes v Sito Barros,	01/2004,	Final Judgment	(12 May 2005)	at para 12	(Special Panels for Serious Crimes (East Timor)),	online: Judicial System Monitoring Program <www.jsmp. minihub.org>.

▨ Include the **given name** of the accused where available in the style of cause.

▨ If there are **multiple accused** in the style of cause, use only the name of the first accused in the style of cause.

▨ Include **informal designation** in parentheses, after the title, if necessary (e.g., *Celebici Camp Case*).

▨ The title reflects the nature of the document, which can vary considerably. Indicate whether the document cited is the **public version** (designated **Public** or **Public redacted**) or the **confidential version** to which public access is limited.

▨ For Internet citations, see section 5.3. The official Internet sites of the adjudicative bodies report only a limited portion of available documents. Some commercial online databases provide wider coverage.

▨ If the name of the website is the same as that of the tribunal, use only the initials when identifying the website (e.g., **ICTR**).

5.2.8 General Agreement on Tariffs and Trade (GATT) 1947 Panel Reports

Style of cause (complainant)	(year of decision),	GATT Doc number,	BISD volume and (year)	first page and pinpoint,	parallel citation.
Republic of Korea—Restrictions on Imports of Beef (Complaint by New Zealand)	(1989),	GATT Doc L/ 6505,	36th Supp BISD (1990)	234 at 237.	
United States—Countervailing Duties on Fresh, Chilled and Frozen Pork from Canada (Complaint by Canada)	(1991),	GATT Doc DS7/R,	38th Supp BISD (1990- 91)	30.	

- Indicate the style of cause followed by the name of the complainant(s) in parentheses.
- Provide the year of the decision in parentheses followed by a comma and the GATT document number.
- Cite the GATT's **BISD** (*Basic Instruments and Selected Documents*) by providing the supplement number, followed by **BISD**, the year in parentheses, and the initial page of the document.
- Include pinpoint references to paragraphs immediately after the document reference.
- For Internet citations, see section 5.3.

5.2.9   World Trade Organization (WTO) Panel and Appellate Body Reports

	Style of cause (complainant)	(year of decision),	WTO Doc number	pin-point	(type of report),	parallel citation.
Panel Report	United States—Sections 301-310 of The Trade Act of 1974 (Complaint by the European Communities)	(1999),	WTO Doc WT/DS152/R	at para 3.1	(Panel Report),	online: WTO <docsonline.wto.org> .
Appellate Body Report	India—Patent Protection for Pharmaceutical and Agricultural Chemical Pro-ducts (Complaint by the United States)	(1997),	WTO Doc WT/DS50/AB/R		(Appellate Body Report),	online: WTO <docsonline.wto.org> .

- Provide the style of cause, followed by the names of the complainants. If the **complaints are treated as one** in the report, provide the names of all complainants after the style of cause. If there are **many complainants** and each complaint is treated separately, provide only the name of the complainant to which the report is destined. If there are more than three complainants, provide the name of one complainant followed by **et al**.
- Provide the year of the decision in parentheses, followed by the WTO document number. A report can have more than one document number (e.g., **WT/DS 8, 10, 11/ AB/R**). In the document number, **WT/DS** indicates **World Trade Dispute Settlement**, **AB** indicates an **Appellate Body**, and R indicates **report**. If the case involves more than one complainant, different reports may be addressed to particular complainants. In such cases, the last element of the document number will indicate the name of the particular complainant to which the report is destined (e.g., **WT/DS27/R/USA**).
- Following the WTO document number, specify in parentheses whether it is a Panel Report or an Appellate Body Report.
- For Internet citations, see section 5.3.

5.2.10   Canada-United States Free Trade Agreement Panels

	Style of cause	(year of decision),	file number,	reporter	(type of panel),	parallel citation.
Published	Re Red Raspberries from Canada	(1990),	USA-89-1904-01,	3 TCT 8175	(Ch 19 Panel),	online: NAFTA Secretariat <www.nafta-sec-alena.org>.
Unpublished	Re Fresh, Chilled or Frozen Pork from Canada	(1991),	ECC-91-1904-01USA		(ECC),	online: NAFTA Secretariat <www.nafta-sec-alena.org>.

▪ After the style of cause, provide the date of the decision in parentheses, followed by the file number. Indicate a reporter reference, if the panel is published.

▪ Provide the chapter under which the complaint was brought. Abbreviate the various panels as follows: **Ch 18 Panel (Canada-United States Trade Commission Panel under Chapter 18)**, **Ch 19 Panel (Canada-United States Binational Panel under Chapter 19)**, and **ECC (Extraordinary Challenge Committee)**.

▪ For Internet citations, see section 5.3.

5.2.11   North American Free Trade Agreement (NAFTA) Binational Panels

	Style of cause (names of parties)	(year of decision),	file number	(type of panel),	parallel citation.
Review of US Agency Final Determination	Re Certain Softwood Lumber from Canada (United States v Canada)	(2005),	ECC-2004-1904-01USA	(ECC),	online: NAFTA Secretariat <www.nafta-sec-alena.org>.
Review of Mexican Agency Final Determination	Re Polystyrene and Impact Crystal from the United States of America (United States v Mexico)	(1995),	MEX-94-1904-03	(Ch 19 Panel),	online: NAFTA Secretariat <www.nafta-sec-alena.org>.
Review of Canadian Measures	Re Tariffs Applied by Canada to Certain US-Origin Agricultural Products (United States v Canada)	(1996),	CDA-95-2008-01	(Ch 20 Panel),	online: NAFTA Secretariat <www.nafta-sec-alena.org>.

▪ Indicate the style of cause, followed by the names of the parties involved in parentheses.

▪ Provide the year of the decision in parentheses. Include the file number and refer to a reporter if possible.

▪ Provide the chapter under which the complaint was brought. Abbreviate the various panels as follows: **Chapter 19 Binational Panel** to **Ch 19 Panel**, **Chapter 20: Arbitral Panel** to **Ch 20 Panel**, and **Chapter 19 Extraordinary Challenge Committee** to **ECC**.

███ Internet parallel citation should follow the rules set out in section 5.3.

5.2.12   International Arbitration Cases

	Style of cause or Case No	(year of decision),	reporter and pinpoint	(framework)	(names of arbitrators) (optional).
Names of parties available	Southern Pacific Properties v Egypt	(1992),	32 ILM 933 at 1008	(International Centre for Settlement of Investment Disputes)	(Arbitrators: Dr Eduardo Jiménez de Aréchaga, Mohamed Amin El Mahdi, Robert F Pietrowski Jr).
Names of parties not revealed	Case No 6248	(1990),	19 YB Comm Arb 124 at 129	(International Chamber of Commerce).	

███ Indicate the style of cause including the parties' names, if available. If parties are reported anonymously, indicate the case number.

███ Indicate the year of the decision in parentheses, followed by the citation to a reporter.

███ Specify the organization responsible for providing the arbitration framework or mechanism in parentheses at the end of the citation.

███ Provide names of arbitrators in parentheses at the end of the citation (optional).

5.2.13   World Intellectual Property Organization (WIPO) Arbitration Cases

5.2.13.1 Uniform Domain Name Dispute Resolution Policy (UDRP)

Style of cause,	case number	<domain name>	(WIPO Arbitration and Mediation Center (UDRP)).
CareerBuilder, LLC v Names for sale,	D2005-0186	<careersbuilder.com>	(WIPO Arbitration and Mediation Center (UDRP)).

███ After the style of cause, include the case number and the domain name that is the subject of the arbitration.

5.2.14   International Law Cases Decided Before National Courts

Style of cause,	domestic reporter,	international reporter	(country and court).
Re Noble and Wolf,	[1949] 4 DLR 375,	[1948] Ann Dig ILC 302	(Can, Ont CA).
Lindon v Commonwealth of Australia (No 2)	(1996), 136 ALR 251,	118 ILR 338	(Austl, HC).
Institute of Chartered Accountants in England and Wales v Commissioners of Customs and Excise,	[1999] 2 All ER 449,	[1999] 2 CMLR 1333	(UK, HL).

▨ Cite a national reporter if a national court decides an international case. Provide a second citation to an internationally available reporter, e.g., the *Annual Digest and Reports of Public International Law Cases* (**Ann Dig ILC**), the *International Law Reports* (**ILR**), the *Common Market Law Reports* (**CMLR**), or the *Common Market Reporter* (**CMR**). After 1950, the Ann Dig ILC became the ILR.

▨ Indicate the country and the jurisdiction where the case was held, and specify the court that made the decision.

5.3   WEBSITES

Traditional citation,	online:	name of website	<URL>.
US, Commission on Security and Cooperation in Europe, *Presidential Elections and Independence Referendums in the Baltic States, the Soviet Union and Successor States* (Washington, DC: The Commission, 1992) at 53,	online:	Commission on Security and Cooperation in Europe	<www.csce.gov>.
Convention on the Rights of the Child, 20 November 1989, 1577 UNTS 3,	online:	United Nations Treaty Collection	<treaties.un.org>.

▨ Provide the full traditional citation, followed by a comma. Add **online:** and the name of the website, followed by the URL.

▨ Cite the URL of the **home page of the website**.

▨ Many online articles expire after a short period of time. Cite to online sources only if the source provides an archive of material for a reasonable period of time, preferably several years.

▨ Include a paragraph number as a pinpoint reference, if available. If the page numbering of a printed source is reproduced in the electronic source, reference may be made to those page numbers.

6   Secondary Sources and Other Materials E-119

E -6.1   Periodicals...E-119
   E -6.1.1 General Form..E-119
   E -6.1.2 Author...E-119
       E -6.1.2.1 Single Author E-119
       E -6.1.2.2 Joint Authors.....................................E-119
   E -6.1.3 Title of Article..E-120
   E -6.1.4 Year of Publication E-120
   E -6.1.5 Volume, Issue, and Series E-120
   E -6.1.6 Title of Journal E-121
       E -6.1.6.1 France E-122
   E -6.1.7 First Page of Article E-122
       E -6.1.7.1 Article Published in Parts.....................E-122
   E -6.1.8 Pinpoint E-123

E -6.2   Books E-124
   E -6.2.1 General Form..E-124
   E -6.2.2 Author...E-125
       E -6.2.2.1 Single Author E-125
       E -6.2.2.2 Joint Authors.....................................E-125
       E -6.2.2.3 Editor of a Collection..........................E-125
       E -6.2.2.4 Editor or Reviser of the Text of Another E-126
           E -6.2.2.4.1 Author's Name is Part of the Title...........E-126
           E -6.2.2.4.2 Author's Name is Not Part of the Title E-126
       E -6.2.2.5 Translator E-126
           E -6.2.2.5.1 Published Translation.........................E-126
           E -6.2.2.5.2 Providing a Translation.......................E-127
   E -6.2.3 Title...E-127
       E -6.2.3.1 Published Proceedings of Conferences or Symposia.....E-128
   E -6.2.4 Volume Number..E-128
       E -6.2.4.1 Books in English E-128
           E -6.2.4.1.1 Volumes Published Under Separate Titles .E-128
           E -6.2.4.1.2 Volumes Published Under a Single Title....E-128
       E -6.2.4.2 Books in French..................................E-129
   E -6.2.5 Edition..E-129
   E -6.2.6 Books in Loose-leaf Form................................E-129
   E -6.2.7 Place of Publication E-130
   E -6.2.8 Publisher E-130
   E -6.2.9 Year of Publication E-131
   E -6.2.10 Pinpoint E-132

E -6.3   Collections of Essays...E-132

E -6.4   Dictionaries & Encyclopedias E-133
   E -6.4.1 General Dictionaries......................................E-133
   E -6.4.2 Specialized Dictionaries E-133
   E -6.4.3 Encyclopedias E-134

E -6.5   Encyclopedic Digests E-134
   E -6.5.1 Canadian Encyclopedic Digest..........................E-134
       E -6.5.1.1 CED Print Edition E-134

E -6.5.1.2 CED Online Edition..E-135
E -6.5.2 Halsbury's Laws of Canada..E-135
E -6.5.2.1 Halsbury's Laws of Canada Print Edition E-135
E -6.5.2.2 Halsbury's Laws of Canada Online Edition E-136
E -6.5.3 Common Law...E-136
E -6.5.4 France...E-136
E -6.5.4.1 General Form..E-136
E -6.5.4.2 Subject Headings E-137

E -6.6 Codes of Professional Conduct E-137

E -6.7 Arbitration Cases..E-138
E -6.7.1 Published arbitration cases E-138
E -6.7.2 Unpublished arbitration cases E-139

E -6.8 Book Reviews...E-139

E -6.9 Case Comments and Comments on Legislation E-140
E -6.9.1 France E-140
E -6.9.1.1 Annotation..E-140
E -6.9.1.2 Comments Published in General Reporters E-141

E -6.10 Comments, Remarks, and Notes......................................E-141

E -6.11 Historical Legal Materials..E-142
E -6.11.1 Roman Law E-142
E -6.11.2 Canon Law..E-143
E -6.11.3 Talmudic Law...E-143

E -6.12 Unpublished Manuscripts..E-144
E -6.12.1 General Form..E-144
E -6.12.2 Forthcoming Manuscripts...E-144
E -6.12.3 Theses and Dissertations E-145

E -6.13 Addresses and Papers Delivered at Conferences.......................E-146

E -6.14 Course Materials E-146

E -6.15 Magazines...E-147

E -6.16 Newspapers, Newswires, and Other News Sources.......................E-148
E -6.16.1 Editorials and Letters to the Editor E-149

E -6.17 News Releases E-149

E -6.18 Letters, Memoranda, and Interviews E-150

E -6.19 Archival Materials E-150

E -6.20 Intellectual property E-151
E -6.20.1 Patents..E-151
E -6.20.2 Trade-marks E-151
E -6.20.3 Copyright E-152

E -6.21 Working Papers E-152

E -6.22 Electronic Sources..E-153
    E -6.22.1 Online Databases..E-153
    E -6.22.2 Online Journals (eJournals)..E-154
    E -6.22.3 Websites..E-154
        E -6.22.3.1 Web Logs (Blogs)..E-154
            E -6.22.3.1.1 Posts..E-154
            E -6.22.3.1.2 Comments E-155
        E -6.22.3.2 Social Media..E-155
            E -6.22.3.2.1 Twitter Posts (Tweets) E-155
            E -6.22.3.2.2 Facebook Posts E-155
            E -6.22.3.2.3 Reddit Posts.....................................E-156
        E -6.22.3.3 Online Video & Video Aggregators...........................E-156
    E -6.22.4 Other Digital Media...E-156
    E -6.22.5 Digital Object Identifiers E-157

6   SECONDARY SOURCES AND OTHER MATERIALS

6.1   PERIODICALS

6.1.1   General Form

Author,	"title of article"	(year)	vo-lume	:	issue (if applic-able)	abbreviation of journal	page	pin-point	(electronic service) (if applicable).
John Borrows,	"Creating an Indigenous Legal Community"	(2005)	50	:	1	McGill LJ	153	at 155	(QL).

6.1.2   Author

6.1.2.1 Single Author

■ Indicate the author's name **as it is presented on the title page of the article**. Include all names and initials used, but do not add a space between two initials. Do not substitute names when initials are used, and do not substitute initials when names are used.

> **Lynn A Iding**, "In a Poor State: The Long Road to Human Rights Protection on the Basis of Social Condition" (2003) 41:2 Alta LR 513.
> **HW Arthurs**, "The Political Economy of Canadian Legal Education" (1998) 25:1 JL & Soc'y 14.

■ Include **titles** such as **The Honourable**, **Madam Justice**, **Rabbi**, **Professor**, or **Lord** if they appear on the title page. Include **name suffixes** such as **Jr** or **IV**. Do not include authors' degrees or other credentials.

6.1.2.2 Joint Authors

> **David Weissbrodt & Muria Kruger**, "Norms on the Responsibilities of Transnational Corporations and Other Business Enterprises with Regard to Human Rights" (2003) 97:4 AJIL 901.
> **Rafael La Porta et al**, "Law and Finance" (1998) 106:6 Journal of Political Economy 1113 at 1152.

■ Include up to three authors.

   ☐ If there are **two authors**, separate the authors' names with an ampersand (**&**).

   ☐ If there are **three authors**, separate the first two authors with a comma and place an ampersand (**&**) before the last one.

   ☐ If there are **more than three authors**, include only the first author's name and **et al**.

For **collaborations** other than full joint authorship, follow the usage on the title page.

6.1.3   Title of Article

Place the title of the article **in quotation marks**.

Do not put a comma after the title.

> Suzanne A Kim, "'Yellow' Skin, 'White' Masks: Asian American 'Impersonations' of Whiteness and the Feminist Critique of Liberal Equality" (2001) 8:1 Asian LJ 89.
>
> Darcy L MacPherson, **"Extending Corporate Criminal Liability?: Some Thoughts on Bill C-45"** (2005) 30:3 Man LJ 253.

Separate a title from a subtitle with a colon. Do not use an em-dash (—) or an en-dash (–).

Capitalize the title according to the conventions of the language of the title.

Follow the punctuation rules of the language of the title. Always use double quotation marks (e.g., **"Title"**) around the title if you are writing in English.

For further rules on language and punctuation of titles, see section 6.2.3.

6.1.4   Year of Publication

Journal organized by volume	David M. Brown, "Freedom From or Freedom For?: Religion As a Case Study in Defining the Content of Charter Rights" **(2000)** 33:3 UBC L Rev 551.
Journal organized by year	Frédéric Pollaud-Dulian, "À propos de la sécurité juridique" **[2001]** RTD civ 487.

If a journal is **organized by volume number**, indicate the year of publication **in parentheses**.

If a journal is **not organized by volume number, but by year**, provide the year **in brackets**.

6.1.5   Volume, Issue, and Series

Author, "title of article" (year of publication)	volume	:	issue	title of journal	series (if applicable)	first page of article.
David Lametti, "Publish *and* Profit?: Justifying the Ownership of Copyright in the Academic Setting" (2001)	26	:	2	Queen's LJ		497.
Peter Hanford, "Edward John Eyre and the Conflict of Laws" (2008)	32	:	3	Melbourne UL Rev		822.
RRA Walker, "The English Property Legislation of 1922–6" (1928)	10	:	1	J Comp Legis & Intl L	(3rd)	1.

Place the volume number after the year of publication, followed by a colon and the issue number. **Always indicate the issue number**, whether or not the issues of a volume are consecutively paginated.

◾ Provide the volume and issue number in Arabic numerals (e.g., **1, 2, 3**), even if the journal itself uses Roman numerals.

◾ Indicate the **series number** (if applicable) in parentheses after the title of the journal.

6.1.6 Title of Journal

> Janet Conway, "Civil Resistance and the 'Diversity of Tactics' in the Anti-Globalization Movement: Problems of Violence, Silence, and Solidarity in Activist Politics" (2003) 41:2–3 **Osgoode Hall LJ** 505.
> Meaghan Sunderland, "Criminal Law Reform in the People's Republic of China: Any Hope for Those Facing the Death Penalty?" (2002) 8 **Appeal** 18.

◾ Abbreviate the title of the periodical according to the list of abbreviations in **Appendix D**.

◾ Where the abbreviation provided in **Appendix D** is likely to be recognized only by members of a narrowly specialized area of practice, prefer writing out the title of the periodical in full.

◾ If the journal does not appear in **Appendix D**, apply the following abbreviation rules. Write out in full any word that does not appear on the list.

- ☐ And = &
- ☐ Association = Assoc
- ☐ Bulletin = Bull
- ☐ Canada or Canadian = Can
- ☐ Gazette = Gaz
- ☐ International = Intl
- ☐ Law = L
- ☐ Legal = Leg
- ☐ Journal = J
- ☐ Review = Rev
- ☐ Quarterly = Q
- ☐ University = U
- ☐ Yearbook = YB

◾ Omit the words "of" and "the" from the abbreviated title.

◾ Place a space between any two words that have lower-case letters, and between an ampersand and the words or letters on each side of it (e.g., **Criminal Rev** or **Can J Tax & Bankruptcy**. Do not place a space between adjacent capital letters (e.g., **JL Policy & Freedom**).

◾ Apply the jurisdiction abbreviations of **Appendix A** to place names. If there is no such abbreviation, write the place name out in full.

◾ Where a journal has a subtitle, omit the subtitle and abbreviate only the main title.

▨ The titles of French-language journals that do not appear in **Appendix D** should be abbreviated following the rules in the French section of this Guide.

▨ Do not italicize the title or the abbreviation.

6.1.6.1 France

Author,	"title of article"	publication information.
Fabrice Leduc,	"La détermination du prix, une exigence exceptionnelle ?"	(1992) JCP I 3631.

▨ Refer to sections 6.1.2 and 6.1.3 to cite the author and title of articles published in French general reporters. See also the list of reporters in **Appendix C-3**.

▨ Cite the reporter as set out in section 3.7.

Reporter abbreviations:

Actualité juridique de droit administratif	AJDA
Bulletin des arrêts de la Cour de cassation, chambre civile	Bull civ
Gazette du Palais	Gaz Pal
Recueil Dalloz and *Recueil Dalloz Sirey* (1945–present)	D
Recueil des décisions du Conseil d'État or *Recueil Lebon*	Rec
Semaine juridique (1937–present)	JCP

6.1.7   First Page of Article

▨ Indicate the first page of the article after the title of the journal. **Do not** include "at".

Joseph Eliot Magnet, "National Minorities and the Multinational State" (2001) 26:2 Queen's LJ **397**.

6.1.7.1 Article Published in Parts

Publication in two separate volumes	RA Macdonald, "Enforcing Rights in Corporeal Moveables: Revendication and Its Surrogates" (1986) 31:4 McGill LJ 573 **&** (1986) 32:1 McGill LJ 1.
Publication in two separate parts of the same volume	Edward W Keyserlingk, "The Unborn Child's Right to Prenatal Care" (1982) 3:1 Health L Can **10 & 31**.

▦ If parts of the article are published in **different volumes**, provide the author and the title as usual. Include both full citations, separated by an ampersand (**&**).

▦ If the article is published in parts of **one volume**, include both first page numbers, separated by an ampersand (**&**).

6.1.8   Pinpoint

Bradley J Freedman & Robert JC Deane, "Trade-marks and the Internet: A Canadian Perspective" (2001) 34:2 UBC L Rev 345 **at 399**.

Louise Arbour & Fannie Lafontaine, "Beyond Self-Congratulation: The *Charter* at 25 in an International Perspective" (2007) 47:2 Osgoode Hall LJ 239 **at 259, n 63**.

SM Waddams, *The Law of Contracts*, 5th ed (Toronto: Canada Law Book, 2005) **at para 292**.

▦ Place the pinpoint reference after the publication information.

▦ Prefer paragraph pinpoints to page pinpoints. Begin a page or paragraph pinpoint with **at**. Cite paragraphs by using **para** or **paras**. Do not include **p** to indicate the page number.

▦ Separate **consecutive** page or paragraph references by an en-dash. For multiple-digit numbers, retain at least the last two digits at all times (e.g., **159–60** or **32–35**, but not **32–5**).

▦ Separate **non-consecutive** page numbers or paragraphs by a comma (e.g., **at 35, 38**).

▦ To indicate a **general section** of the text without referring to specific pages or paragraphs, use **ff** following the page or paragraph number(s). It is preferable, however, to cite a specific set of pages or paragraphs.

▦ To pinpoint to a specific footnote, abbreviate **footnote** to **n** (e.g., **at 99, n 140**) and **footnotes** to **nn** (e.g., **at 142, nn 73–75**). If page numbers are not available because the article is online, simply cite to the footnote number (e.g., **at n 140**).

▦ Use the same number format as the text (e.g., **5–6; v–vi**).

6.2 BOOKS

6.2.1 General Form

Author,	*title,*	edition	other elements	(place of publication:	publisher,	year of publication)	pin-point	(electronic service) (if applicable).
Philip Girard,	*Bora Laskin: Bringing Law to Life*			(Toronto:	University of Toronto Press for the Osgoode Society for Canadian Legal History,	2005)	at 20.	
Margaret Somerville,	*Death Talk: The Case against Euthanasia and Physician-Assisted Suicide*			(Montreal:	McGill-Queen's University Press,	2001)	at 78.	
Martha Derthick,	*Up in Smoke: From Legislation to Litigation in Tobacco Politics,*	2nd ed		(Washington, DC:	CQ Press,	2005).		

Provide any other element in the "other elements" section between the edition and the place of publication. Their order of presentation is the following: **name of editor or compiler** (section 6.2.2.3), **name of translator** (section 6.2.2.5), **total number of volumes or number of cited volume** (section 6.2.4), **volume title**, **series title and volume number within series**, **loose-leaf** (section 6.2.6).

Secondary Sources and Other Materials

6.2.2   Author

6.2.2.1 Single Author

▨ Indicate the author's name **as it is presented on the title page of the book**. Include all names and initials used, but note that there is no space between two initials. Do not substitute names when initials are used, and do not substitute initials when names are used.

> **Ellen Anderson**, *Judging Bertha Wilson: Law as Large as Life* (Toronto: University of Toronto Press for The Osgoode Society for Canadian Legal History, 2001).
> **Rt Hon Lord Denning**, *What Next in the Law* (London, UK: Butterworths, 1982).
> **H Patrick Glenn**, *Legal Traditions of the World* (Oxford: Oxford University Press, 2000).
> **David Fraser**, *Cricket and the Law: the Man in White is Always Right* (London, UK: Routledge, 2005).

▨ Include **titles** such as **The Honourable**, **Madam Justice**, **Rabbi**, **Professor**, or **Lord** if they appear on the title page. Include **name suffixes** such as **Jr** or **IV**. Do not include authors' degrees or other credentials.

6.2.2.2 Joint Authors

> [1] **Monique Mattei Ferraro & Eoghan Casey**, *Investigating Child Exploitation and Pornography: The Internet, the Law and Forensic Science* (Boston: Elsevier/Academic Press, 2005).
> [9] **Joel Bakan** et al, *Canadian Constitutional Law*, 3rd ed (Toronto: Emond Montgomery, 2003).
> [10] **Pierre-Gabriel Jobin with the collaboration of Nathalie Vézina**, *Baudouin et Jobin : Les obligations*, 6th ed (Cowansville, Que: Yvon Blais, 2005).

▨ Include **up to three authors**, separating the first two authors' names with a comma, and the last two with an ampersand (**&**).

▨ If there are **more than three authors**, include only the first author's name followed by et al.

▨ For **collaborations** other than full joint authorship, follow the usage on the title page of the book (see note 10).

6.2.2.3 Editor of a Collection

▨ Indicate the name of the editor before the title of the collection.

▨ Include **up to three editors**, separating the first two editors' names with a comma, and the last two with an ampersand (**&**).

> **David Dyzenhaus & Mayo Moran**, **eds**, *Calling Power to Account: Law, Reparations and the Chinese Canadian Head Tax Case* (Toronto: University of Toronto Press, 2005).

▨ If there are **more than three editors**, include only the first editor's name followed by et al.

▨ Abbreviate **editor** to ed and **editors** to eds, preceded and followed by a comma.

▨ To cite an **essay in particular**, and not the collection in general, include the name of the author and the title of the essay before the name of the editor (see section 6.3).

6.2.2.4 Editor or Reviser of the Text of Another

6.2.2.4.1 Author's Name is Part of the Title

Editor,	ed,	title,	edition (if applicable)	(publication information).
HG Beale,	ed,	Chitty on Contracts,	29th ed	(London, UK: Sweet & Maxwell, 2004).

▪ If the author's name is part of the title, treat the editor as the author, followed by **ed**.

6.2.2.4.2 Author's Name is Not Part of the Title

Au-thor,	title,	edition (if applicable)	ed by	editor	(publication information).
SA De Smith,	Judicial Review of Administrative Action,	5th	ed by	Lord Woolf & Jeffrey Jowell	(London, UK: Sweet & Maxwell, 1995).

▪ If the author's name is not part of the title, indicate the editor after the edition.

▪ Precede the name(s) of editor(s) name with **ed by**. If there is a numbered edition, mention it (e.g., **5th ed by**).

▪ Provide the names of both the author(s) and the editor(s) as they appear in the publication.

6.2.2.5 Translator

Translate languages likely to be unfamiliar to readers. The original language of a quotation may be provided in the footnote.

6.2.2.5.1 Published Translation

Author,	title,	translated by	name of translator	(publication information)	[modified by author] (if applicable).
Averroës,	The Book of the Decisive Treatise Determining the Connection Between the Law and Wisdom,	translated by	Charles E Butterworth	(Provo: Brigham Young University Press, 2001).	

▪ For published translations, include the translator's name, preceded by **translated by**, before the publication information.

■ If it is necessary to modify the translation, indicate this with **[modified by author]** after the publication information, but before the final period.

■ If providing both the editor or reviser's information (section 6.2.2.4) and the translator's information (section 6.2.2.5), always provide the editor's information first.

6.2.2.5.2 Providing a Translation

Author,	*title*	(publication information)	pinpoint	[translated by author].
María José Falcón y Tella,	*La desobediencia civil*	(Madrid: Marcial Pons, 2000)	at 28	[translated by author].

■ When writing and providing a translation for ease of understanding, cite to the work and insert **[translated by author] in the footnote** (and not after the translated text, as required in the French rule). The expression refers to you, the author, and not to the author of the work being cited.

6.2.3   Title

[1] Petri Mäntysaari, *Comparative Corporate Governance: Shareholders as a Rule-maker* (New York: Springer, 2005).

[2] Janet Dine, *Companies, International Trade and Human Rights* (New York: Cambridge University Press, 2005).

[3] WR Cornish & G de M Clark, *Law and Society in England, 1750–1950* (London, UK: Sweet & Maxwell, 1989).

[4] Cesare Beccaria, *Dei delliti e delle pene* **[On Crimes and Punishment]**, 5th ed (London, UK: Transaction Publishers, 2009).

[5] Waldo Ansaldi, ed, *Democracy in Latin America: A Boat Adrift* **(in Spanish)** (Buenos Aires: Fondo de Cultura Económica, 2007).

■ Indicate the title in full, in italics. Use the spelling and punctuation of the published title, with the following exceptions:

☐ precede subtitles by a colon (notes 1 and 5); and

☐ place a comma before dates included at the end of the title (note 3).

■ Capitalize the title according to the conventions of the language of the title.

■ If the title of a work is in a language other than English, French, or a language that will be familiar to readers, use **either** of the following rules:

☐ Provide the title in the original language, followed by a translation of the title into English (note 4). Place the translation in non-italic font, in brackets with no punctuation between the original title and translation. Transliterate titles in languages that are not written in Latin characters, such as Chinese and Hebrew (e.g., **Menachem Elon, *Ha-Mishpat Ha-Ivri* [Jewish Law]**).

☐ Provide a translation of the title in English in italics, followed by the name of the original language of the text in parentheses (note 5). Do not include any punctuation between the translation of the title and the parentheses.

6.2.3.1 Published Proceedings of Conferences or Symposia

▨ Treat information about the conference or symposium as part of the title. Place this information in italics after a comma.

> Paul Brand, Kevin Costello & WN Osborough, eds, *Adventures of the Law: Proceedings of the Sixteenth British Legal History Conference, Dublin, 2003* (Dublin: Four Courts Press in association with The Irish Legal History Society, 2005).

6.2.4   Volume Number

6.2.4.1 Books in English

6.2.4.1.1 Volumes Published Under Separate Titles

▨ Place the volume before the publication information.

> David Gillies, *Telecommunications Law*, **vol 1** (London, UK: Butterworths, 2003).

▨ Provide the volume number in Arabic numerals (e.g., **1, 2, 3**), even if the book itself uses Roman numerals.

▨ Insert a comma between the title and the volume number.

▨ Do not repeat the volume number in subsequent references unless there is a citation to a different volume elsewhere in the citing document (e.g., **Gillies, vol 2,** *supra* **note 57 at 101**).

6.2.4.1.2 Volumes Published Under a Single Title

▨ If the volumes are subdivisions of a single title, insert the volume after the publication information.

> Karl Marx, *Capital: A Critical Analysis of Capitalist Production*, ed by Friedrich Engels, translated by Samuel Moore & Edward B Aveling (London, UK: Swan Sonnenschein, 1908) **vol 1** at 15.

▨ Do not put a comma between the publication information and the volume.

▨ Provide the volume number in Arabic numerals (e.g., **1, 2, 3**) even if the book itself uses Roman numerals.

▨ Do not repeat the volume number in subsequent references unless there is a citation to a different volume elsewhere in the citing document (e.g., **Marx, vol 2,** *supra* **note 99**).

6.2.4.2 Books in French

Author,	title,	tome and/or volume,	edition	editor (if applicable)	(publication information).
Jean Carbonnier,	Droit civil : les obligations,	t 4,	22nd ed		(Paris: Presses Universitaires de France, 2000).
Henri Mazeaud et al,	Leçons de droit civil,	t 3, vol 1,	7th ed	by Yves Picod	(Paris: Montchrestien, 1999).

▨ French legal writing may be divided into **tomes** (**t**), with each tome further subdivided into **volumes** (**v**).

▨ Use only Arabic numerals (e.g., **1, 2, 3**) for tome and volume numbers.

▨ Tome and volume information appears after the title.

▨ Do not repeat the tome or volume number in subsequent references unless there is a citation to a different tome or volume elsewhere in the citing document (e.g., **Mazeaud et al, t 3, vol 2,** *supra* note 4).

6.2.5   Edition

▨ If the work has appeared in several editions, place the number of the edition (e.g., **8th ed**) after the title. Do not superscript the **st, nd, rd** or **th** following the number.

> Richard Clayton & Hugh Tomlinson, eds, *Civil Actions Against the Police*, **3rd ed** (London, UK: Sweet & Maxwell, 2004).
> Carlos L Israels & Egon Guttman, *Modern Securities Transfer*, **revised ed** (Boston: Warren, Gorham & Lamont, 1971).

▨ Abbreviate **edition** to **ed**.

▨ If the work has been revised but no edition number is given, insert **revised ed** after the title.

6.2.6   Books in Loose-leaf Form

Author,	title	(publication information)	(loose-leaf revision / supplement number or date),	pinpoint.
Georges Audet et al,	Le congédiement en droit québécois en matière de contrat individuel de travail	(Cowansville, Que: Yvon Blais, 1991)	(loose-leaf revision 18:1),	ch 5 at 71.
Madeleine Lemieux,	Tribunaux administratifs du Québec : Règles et législation annotées	(Cowansville, Que: Yvon Blais, 2002)	(loose-leaf revision 15),	ch R9 at 85.
Robert W Hillman,	Hillman on Lawyer Mobility: The Law and Ethics of Partner Withdrawals and Law Firm Breakups, 2nd ed	(Austin: Wolters Kluwer, 1998)	(loose-leaf 2009 supplement),	ch 2 at 85.

Secondary Sources and Other Materials

- This section applies to **books that are continually updated**. For legislation in loose-leaf format, see section 2.1.6.

- After the publication information, place in parentheses the phrase **loose-leaf** followed by the revision or supplement number.

- Optionally include the year of the revision if it is not already indicated as part of the revision or supplement number (e.g., JD Green, *The Law of Tort* (Toronto: Thomson Reuters, 2011) (loose-leaf **updated 2013**, release 20), ch 5 at 71).

- Use the publication date that appears on the copyright page, even if it differs from a date that appears elsewhere in the loose-leaf manual.

- Use the chapter and the page number to pinpoint if available.

6.2.7   Place of Publication

- Include place of publication where it is available. Place of publication may signal to the reader the jurisdiction relevant to the cited material.

  > Bruce MacDougall, *Queer Judgments: Homosexuality, Expression, and the Courts in Canada* (**Toronto**: University of Toronto Press, 2000).
  > Lee Edwards, ed, *Bringing Justice to the People: the Story of the Freedom-Based Public Interest Law Movement* (**Washington, DC**: Heritage Books, 2004).

- Indicate the place of publication as it appears on the title page or on the verso of the title page. Use an **English form** of a name if it exists (e.g., **Munich** and not München; **Prague** and not Praha).

- If **more than one place of publication** is listed, include the first place only.

- If **no place of publication** is listed, omit the place and the trailing colon.

- If additional information is required to identify the place of publication (e.g., the province, state, or country) include that information, in abbreviated form, after the place of publication. If a location could be confused with another, provide additional information (e.g., **London, Ont** and **London, UK**).

- See the commonly used Canadian province abbreviations of **Appendix A-1** and the American state abbreviations of **Appendix A-2**.

6.2.8   Publisher

✓	Martha M Ertman & Joan C Williams, *Rethinking Commodification: Cases and Readings in Law and Culture* (New York: **New York University Press**, 2005). Ellen Anderson, *Judging Bertha Wilson: Law as Large as Life* (Toronto: **University of Toronto Press for The Osgoode Society for Canadian Legal History**, 2001).
✓	Gaëlle Breton-LeGoff, *L'influence des organisations non gouvernementales (ONG) sur la négociation de quelques instruments internationaux* (Cowansville, Que: **Yvon Blais**, 2001).
✗	Gaëlle Breton-LeGoff, *L'influence des organisations non gouvernementales (ONG) sur la négociation de quelques instruments internationaux* (Cowansville, Que: **Les Éditions Yvon Blais inc**, 2001).

▓ Write the publisher's name **as it appears on the title page**.

▓ Do not abbreviate the publisher's name (e.g., **University Press** and not **UP**).

▓ Omit the definite article (**the**) if it is the first word of the publisher's name.

▓ Omit terms that identify corporate status (e.g., **Ltd**, **Inc**).

▓ Omit the words "Publishing" or "Publishers" and "éditions" unless it is part of an indivisible whole (e.g., **Éditions de l'Homme**). Follow the same rule for other languages (e.g., **Verlag**).

▓ Write **Press** in English and **Presses** in French if included in the publisher's name on the title page.

▓ For references to **copublishers**, provide the places of publication first, followed by the names of the publishers and the year. Separate the places of publication from each other by an ampersand (&). Similarly, separate the names of the publishers from each other by an ampersand. Separate the places and names by a colon. See the example below.

(First place of publication &	second place of publication	:	first publisher &	second publisher,	year).
(Latzville, BC &	Montreal	:	Oolichan Books &	Institute for Research on Public Policy,	1992).

▓ If a publisher is **working for an organization** write **for** immediately before the organization's name (e.g., **Janet E Gans Epner for The Commission on Women in the Profession**).

▓ If **no publisher** is listed, write **publisher unknown**.

6.2.9 Year of Publication

▓ Indicate the year of the **current edition**, not of the first edition. Generally, use the most recent copyright date, unless a year of publication is given explicitly.

> Michael Hames-García, *Fugitive Thought: Prison Movements, Race and the Meaning of Justice* (Minneapolis: University of Minnesota Press, **2004**).

▓ Do not cite the year of printing.

▓ If **no year is listed**, omit the year.

6.2.10   Pinpoint

Secondary Sources and Other Materials

▨ Place the pinpoint after the publication information.

▨ **Prefer paragraph pinpoints** to page pinpoints. Begin a paragraph pinpoint with **at para** or **at paras**. Do not include **p** to indicate the page number.

▨ Separate **consecutive** page or paragraph references by an en-dash, and retain at least the last two digits at all times (e.g., **159–60** or **32–35**, but not **32–5**).

▨ **Non-consecutive** page numbers are separated by a comma (e.g., **35, 38**).

> Ronald Joseph Delisle & Don Stuart, eds, *Evidence: Principles and Problems*, 6th ed (Toronto: Carswell, 2001) **ch 4 at 450ff**.
> Kent Roach, *Constitutional Remedies in Canada* (Aurora, Ont: Canada Law Book, 1994) **at para 12.30**.
> Donald Bloxham, *Genocide on Trial: War Crimes Trials and the Formation of Holocaust History and Memory* (Oxford: Oxford University Press, 2001) **at 43, n 139**.
> Beth Harris, *Defending the Right to a Home: The Power of Anti-Poverty Lawyers* (Aldershot, UK: Ashgate, 2004) **at 45–47**.

▨ To indicate a **general section** of the text use **ff** following the page or paragraph number(s). It is preferable, however, to cite a specific set of pages or paragraphs.

▨ Abbreviate **chapter** and **chapters** to **ch**.

▨ To pinpoint to a specific footnote, abbreviate **footnote** to **n** (e.g., **at 43, n 139**) and **footnotes** to **nn** (e.g., **at 43, nn 139–41**). If page numbers are not available, refer to the footnote number (e.g., **at n 140**).

▨ Write numbers (page, paragraph, or other) as they appear in the text (e.g., **5–6**; **v–vi**).

6.3   COLLECTIONS OF ESSAYS

Author of essay,	"title of essay"	in	editor (if applicable),	ed,	title of book	(publication information)	first page of essay	pin-point.
Gabriel J Chin,	"Race, the War on Drugs and Collateral Consequences of Criminal Conviction"	in	Christopher Mele & Teresa A Miller,	eds,	*Civil Penalties, Social Consequences*	(New York: Routledge, 2005)	43	at 45.
Adelle Blackett,	"Promoting Domestic Workers' Human Dignity through Specific Regulation"	in	Antoinette Fauve-Chamoux,	ed,	*Domestic Service and the Formation of European Identity: Understanding the Globalization of Domestic Work, 16th-21st Centuries*	(Bern: Peter Lang SA, Éditions scientifiques européennes, 2005)	211	at 215.
Guénaël Mettraux,	"Preface"	in	Guénaël Mettraux,	ed,	*Perspectives on the Nuremberg Trial*	(New York: Oxford University Press, 2008)	xi.	

- Place the name of the author and the title of the essay before the collection.

- Introduce the collection with **in**.

- Follow the name(s) of the editor(s) of the collection by **ed** or **eds**, placed between commas. Some collections have no named editor. Do not provide any editor in such cases.

- Provide the title of the collection in italics, followed by the publication information.

- Where there are other elements to be added (see section 6.2.1), insert these between the title of the collection and the publication information.

- Indicate the first page of the essay and any applicable pinpoint references after the publication information.

- If referring to the **foreword, preface, introduction, or conclusion** of a book, indicate it as if it were an entry in a collection of essays. Use **Foreword**, **Preface**, etc. or the title of that section in lieu of the title of the essay (see the Guénaël Mettraux example).

- If citing two or more essays from the same source, refer to the second and any subsequent essays using the applicable Secondary Materials short form (see section 1.4.1.4).

6.4   DICTIONARIES & ENCYCLOPEDIAS

6.4.1   General Dictionaries

Title,	edition,	*sub verbo*	"keyword".
The Oxford English Dictionary,	2nd ed,	*sub verbo*	"law".
Black's Law Dictionary,	7th ed,	*sub verbo*	"promissory estoppel".

- Provide the title of the dictionary in italics.

- Indicate the edition or year.

- *Sub verbo* is Latin for "under the word".

6.4.2   Specialized Dictionaries

Editor or author,	ed (if applicable),	*title,*	edition (if applicable)	(publication information)	*sub verbo*	"keyword".
F Allard et al,	eds,	*Private Law Dictionary of Obligations and Bilingual Lexicons,*		(Cowansville, Que: Yvon Blais, 2003)	*sub verbo*	"code".
Hubert Reid,		*Dictionnaire de droit québécois et canadien*		(Montreal: Wilson & Lafleur, 1994)	*sub verbo*	"hypothèque".

- Cite the specialized dictionary as if it were a book. See section 6.2.

- *Sub verbo* is Latin for "under the word".

6.4.3 Encyclopedias

Author (if applicable),	"title of entry"	in	title of encyclopedia,	edition (if applicable)	by	editor	(publication information).
Rev Edward Mewburn Walker,	"Constitution of Athens"	in	*Encyclopaedia Britannica,*	11th ed	by	Hugh Chisholm	(New York: Encyclopaedia Britannica, 1911).

- Some encyclopedias explicitly credit contributors. Cite the contributing author's name where available.

- Prefer replacement of the ligature æ, even where one appears in the published title, with the digraph ae.

6.5 ENCYCLOPEDIC DIGESTS

6.5.1 Canadian Encyclopedic Digest

- The *Canadian Encyclopedic Digest* (CED) is published in loose-leaf format and provides a broad narrative of the law. Each volume is organized by subject matter (e.g., criminal law, family law).

6.5.1.1 CED Print Edition

CED	(series	edition),	volume,	title	section.
CED	(Ont	4th),	vol 1,	title 2	at § 10.

- Write **CED**, not the name of the digest in full.

- Indicate the series: **Ontario CED (Ont)** or **Western CED (West)**.

6.5.1.2 CED Online Edition

CED	edition	(online),	subject matter	(series), (if applicable)	"detailed subject heading & sub-headings" (optional)	(CED subheading code) (optional)	section.
CED	4th	(online),	Actions	(Ont),	"Forms and Classes of Action: Penal Actions: General"	(II.5.(a))	at § 3.
CED	4th	(online),	Securities and Stock Exchanges,		"Securites Offences Under the Criminal Code: Fraudulent Manipulation of Stock Exchange Transactions"	(II.1)	at § 191-195.

▨ CED editions are cited by number only (**4th**, not **4th ed**).

▨ Separate the detailed subject headings and subheadings by colons.

▨ Indicate the numerical subheading code as it appears in the CED online.

▨ Prefer citing to the online version. If you wish to cite to a print version, cite according to the rule in section 6.5.1.1 above, including the series. Westlaw provides a link to print citation information for all subjects through the online version of the CED.

6.5.2 Halsbury's Laws of Canada

▨ *Halsbury's Laws of Canada* provides summary statements of a broad range of legal subjects. Each volume is organized by subject matter (e.g., criminal procedure, insurance).

▨ Updates are made through cumulative supplements, issued annually.

6.5.2.1 Halsbury's Laws of Canada Print Edition

Halsbury's Laws of Canada,	volume,	subject matter	(publication information)	section	update (if applicable).
Halsbury's Laws of Canada,	vol 2,	Business Corporations	(Markham, Ont: LexisNexis Canada, 2008)	at HBC-298 "Focus on Interests"	(Cum Supp Release 4).

▨ If the cited section has been updated in a cumulative supplement, cite the supplement and its release number in parentheses following the section, using an abbreviated form (**Cum Supp Release** x).

Secondary Sources and Other Materials

6.5.2.2 Halsbury's Laws of Canada Online Edition

Halsbury's Laws of Canada (online),	subject matter,	"detailed subject heading & subheadings" (optional)	(subheading code) (optional)	section	update (if applicable).
Halsbury's Laws of Canada (online),	*Business Corporations,*	"Shareholder Remedies: The Oppression Remedy: Meaning of Oppression"	(XIII.2.(2))	at HBC-298 "Focus on Interests"	(Cum Supp Release 4).

▨ If the cited section has been updated in a cumulative supplement, cite the supplement and its release number in parentheses following the section, using an abbreviated form (**Cum Supp Release** x).

6.5.3   Common Law

Halsbury's Laws of England, vol 34, 4th ed (London, UK: Butterworths, 1980) at 60, para 71. *American Jurisprudence*, vol 17A, 2nd ed (Rochester, NY: Lawyer's Cooperative, 1991) "Contracts", § 97.

▨ Follow the rules for books in section 6.2, but **do not include the author's name**.

▨ Where available, **use the paragraph or section numbers** instead of page numbers. Use the section sign (**§**, plural **§§**) for American digests.

▨ If the section in question has a title, include it in quotation marks, after the publication information (see *American Jurisprudence* example).

6.5.4   France

6.5.4.1 General Form

Title of collection,	edition (if applicable),	subject heading	by	author of the section of the encyclopedia,	pin-point.
Juris-classeur civil,		art 3, fasc N	by	Phillipe Malaurie,	No 38.
Encyclopédie juridique Dalloz : Répertoire de droit civil,	2nd ed,	"Publicité foncière"	by	Marc Donnier,	No 528.

▨ Whenever possible, refer to the *Juris-classeur civil*.

▨ Provide the full title of the collection in italics.

▨ If **more than one edition** of the encyclopedia has been published, include the number of the edition.

Secondary Sources and Other Materials

▓ Do not introduce the pinpoint with "at".

▓ Establish a short form (see section 1.4.1) by using the abbreviated title of the encyclopedia.

Abbreviations of the principal encyclopedias:

Encyclopédie juridique Dalloz : Répertoire de droit administratif	*Rép admin*
Encyclopédie juridique Dalloz : Répertoire de droit civil	*Rép civ*
Encyclopédie juridique Dalloz : Répertoire de droit commercial	*Rép com*
Juris-classeur administratif	*J-cl admin*
Juris-classeur civil	*J-cl civ*
Juris-classeur civil annexe	*J-cl civ annexe*
Juris-classeur commercial	*J-cl com*
Juris-classeur commercial : Banque et crédit	*J-cl com BC*
Juris-classeur répertoire notarial	*J-cl rép not*
Juris-classeur responsabilité civile	*J-cl resp civ*

6.5.4.2 Subject Headings

Organized alphabetically	*Encyclopédie juridique Dalloz : Répertoire de droit civil*, **"Parenté-alliance"** by Janine Revel. *Juris-classeur civil annexes*, **"Associations", fasc 1-A**, by Robert Brichet.
Organized by articles of a code	*Juris-classeur civil*, **art 3, fasc 4** by Yves Luchaire. *Juris-classeur civil*, **art 1354 to 1356, fasc 20** by Daniel Veaux.
Organized by volume	*Juris-classeur commercial : Concurrence consommation*, **vol 1, fasc 360** by Véronique Sélinsky.

▓ **Organized alphabetically**: Include the keyword indicating the section in quotation marks. If there is a fascicle number corresponding to the section, insert **fasc** followed by the number.

▓ **Organized by articles of a code**: Provide the article number under which the section is classified. Use the same form as is used in the collection. If applicable, indicate **fasc** followed by the number.

▓ **Organized by volume**: Provide the number of the volume in which the section is found. If applicable, indicate **fasc** followed by the number.

Secondary Sources and Other Materials

░ Regardless of the system of classification of the subject headings, indicate the number of the fascicle after the volume number, separated by a comma.

░ Do not cite the date of the revision of the fascicle.

6.6 CODES OF PROFESSIONAL CONDUCT

Issuing body,	title of the code,	publication information,	pinpoint.
The Canadian Bar Association,	CBA Code of Professional Conduct,	Ottawa: CBA, 2006,	ch III, commentary 1.
The Law Society of Manitoba,	Code of Professional Coduct,	Winnipeg: Law Society of Manitoba, 2007,	ch 6.1(1)(f).

░ If the issuing body and the editor is the same entity, use the official abbreviation in the publication information (e.g., **CBA** for The Canadian Bar Association).

░ Some codes of professional conduct are enacted by legislation. Cite them like regular laws (see section 2.1) (e.g., *Professional Code*, **CQLR c C-26**).

6.7 ARBITRATION CASES

For **international arbitration** cases, see section 5.2.12. For **WIPO** cases, see section 5.2.13.

6.7.1   Published Arbitration Cases

Style of cause or case number	(year of decision),	reporter	pinpoint	(names of arbitrators) (optional).
California State University v State Employers Trade Council — United	(2009),	126 Lab Arb (BNA) 613		(Arbitrator: Bonnie G Bogue).

░ Indicate the style of cause or the case number, followed by the year of the decision in parentheses.

░ If the case is published in a printed reporter, cite the arbitration reporter in the same manner as a jurisprudence reporter (see section 3.7).

░ Add the **name of the arbitrator** in parentheses (optional).

6.7.2   Unpublished Arbitration Cases

Style of cause or **case number**	**(year of deci-sion),**	**identifier given by service**	**(service)** (if applicable)	**pin-point**	**(names of arbitrators)** (optional).
Winona School District ISD 861 Winona v Winona Education Association	(2006),	2006 WL 3876585	(WL Can)		(Arbitrator: Daniel J Jacobowski).

▨ Indicate the style of cause or the case number, followed by the year of the decision in parentheses.

▨ If the case is published on an online database, write the identifier given by the service. Add the abbreviation of the service in parentheses if it's not already included in the identifier.

▨ Add the **name of the arbitrator** in parentheses (optional).

6.8   BOOK REVIEWS

Author of book review,	**"title of book review",** (if applicable)	**Book Review of**	*title of book being reviewed*	**by**	**author or editor of book reviewed,**	**citation information.**
Heather Jensen,		Book Review of	*Girl Trouble: Female Delinquency in English Canada*	by	Joan Sangster,	(2004) 67:2 Sask L Rev 658.
Christopher Heer, Michael Hong & Jason J Kee,		Book Review of	*Intellectual Property Disputes: Resolution and Remedies*	by	Ronald E Dimock, ed,	(2004) 62:1 UT Fac L Rev 93.
Larry Lee,	"Reading the Seattle Manifesto: In Search of a Theory",	Book Review of	*Whose Trade Organization? Corporate Globalization and the Erosion of Democracy: An Assessment of the World Trade Organization*	by	Lori Wallach & Michelle Sforza,	(2003) 78:6 NYUL Rev 2305.

▨ If the review has a title, include it after the author of the review, followed by a comma.

▨ Insert **Book Review of** before the title of the book reviewed. Change the expression to Book Note of if that terminology is used in the publication.

▨ After the title of the book being reviewed, indicate the name of the author of the book introduced with **by**.

☐ If the title of the review includes **both the title of the book reviewed and its author**, do not repeat this information. Instead, just write **Book Review**, leaving out "of".

□   If the title of the review includes *either* **the author or the title**, but not both, then all the information should be indicated after **Book Review of**, even if some of it will be repeated.

▨ If the book being reviewed has an editor instead of an author, write **ed** after the name of the editor of the book reviewed and a comma (e.g., **Ronald E Dimock, ed**).

6.9   CASE COMMENTS AND COMMENTS ON LEGISLATION

	Author,	"title" (if applicable),	type of comment	on	style of cause or title of law or bill (if applicable),	(citation).
Case Comment	Jessie L Givener,	"*Lavoie v Canada*: Reconciling Equality Rights and Citizenship-based Law",	Case Comment,			(2003-2004) 35:2 Ottawa L Rev 277.
Legislative Comment	John Boston,	"The *Prison Litigation Reform Act*: The New Face of Court Stripping",	Legislative Comment	on	Pub L No 104-134, 110 Stat 1321-66 (1996),	(2001) 67:2 Brook L Rev 429.

▨ Indicate the title of the comment (if available) in quotation marks.

▨ For **case comments**, indicate **Case Comment**. Also include the style of cause preceded by **on**, unless it is in the title.

▨ For **legislative comments**, indicate **Legislative Comment**. Also include the title of the law or bill preceded by **on**, unless it is in the title.

6.9.1   France

6.9.1.1 *Annotation*

Author,	Annotation of	court,	date of decision,	(year of publication)	reporter	section	first page.
Christophe Caron,	Annotation of	Cass com,	28 avril 2004,	(2004)	JCP	II	2045.

▨ Add a space between each item of information (e.g., **(2004) JCP II 2045**).

▨ Introduce the case citation with **Annotation of**.

▨ See section 7.5.2 for the rules on citing French jurisprudence.

6.9.1.2 Comments Published in General Reporters

Author,	"title"	(year of publication)	reporter	section	first page	pinpoint.
Dominique Karsenty,	"La réparation des détentions"	(2003)	JCP	I	225	at 227.
Florence Bussy,	"Nul ne peut être juge et partie"	(2004)	D	Chron	1745	at 1750.

▨ Add a space between each item of information (e.g., **(2004) D Chron 1745 at 1750**).

▨ After the title, indicate the reporter information according to the rules at section 7.5.2.6.

6.10 COMMENTS, REMARKS, AND NOTES

Author (if applicable),	"title" (if applicable),	type of document,	citation.
Thomas M Franck,	"Criminals, Combatants, or What — An Examination of the Role of Law in Responding to the Threat of Terrorism",	Editorial Comment,	(2004) 98:4 AJIL 686.
Eric J Feigin,	"Architecture of Consent: Internet Protocols and Their Legal Implications",	Note,	(2004) 56:4 Stan L Rev 901.

▨ Include the type of document (**Note, Comment** or **Remark**) before the citation information. Do not enclose it in quotation marks. If the document has a title, place the title in quotation marks.

6.11   HISTORICAL LEGAL MATERIALS

6.11.1   Roman Law

Collection	Abbreviation	Example
Laws of the Twelve Tables	XII Tab	XII Tab 8.2
Institutes of Gaius	G	G 3.220
Code of Theodosius	Cod Th	Cod Th 8.14.1
Institutes of Justinian	Inst	Inst 4.4 pr (translated by Birks & McLeod)
Digest of Justinian	Dig	Dig 47.10.1 (Ulpian)
Codex of Justinian	Cod	Cod 6.42.16
Novels	Nov	Nov 22.3

▪ Refer to the **traditional divisions of the work** (generally book, title, section), not to the page number of the particular edition or translation. There are no spaces between the numbers of the different divisions.

▪ Use Arabic numerals separated by periods to indicate the divisions, regardless of the usage of the edition or translation used.

▪ The abbreviation **pr** means "*principium*" or "beginning" and refers to the unnumbered material before the first section of a title. It is preceded by a space.

▪ For **Justinian's** *Digest*, indicate the author of the passage in question parenthetically after the citation.

▪ Indicate the particular edition or translation used in parentheses at the end of the citation (e.g., **(translated by Birks & McLeod)**).

Secondary Sources and Other Materials

6.11.2   Canon Law

Collection	Abbreviation	Example
Decretum of Gratian	Decr (optional)	**Part 1**: D 50 c 11 **Part 2**: C 30 q 4 c 5 **Part 2, De poenitentia**: De poen D 1 c 75 **Part 3**: De cons D 1 c 5
Decretals of Gregory IX (*Liber extra*)	X	X 5.38.12
Decretals of Boniface VIII (*Liber sextus*)	VI	VI 5.2.16
Constitutions of Clement V (*Clementinae*)	Clem	Clem 3.7.2
Extravagants of John XXII (*Extravagantes Johannis XXII*)	Extrav Jo XII	Extrav Jo XII 14.2
Common Extravagants (*Extravagantes communes*)	Extrav Com	Extrav Com 3.2.9
Codex Iuris Canonici (1917)	1917 Code	1917 Code c 88, § 2
Codex Iuris Canonici (1983)	1983 Code	1983 Code c 221, § 1

Secondary Sources and Other Materials

- Refer to the traditional divisions of the work, not the page number of the particular edition or translation.

- Use Arabic numerals (e.g., **1, 2, 3**) to indicate the divisions, regardless of the usage of the edition or translation.

- Indicate the particular edition or translation used in parentheses at the end of the citation.

6.11.3   Talmudic Law

- Indicate Babylonian or Jerusalem Talmud.

- Italicize the tractate.

- When using the Babylonian Talmud, refer to the **traditional pagination** (Vilna edition) and not to the page number given by the publisher or translator. It is always assumed that the cited text is the Vilna edition. When using a different edition (e.g. Warsaw), indicate the edition in parentheses following the pinpoint.

Talmud,	*tractate,*	pinpoint.
Babylonian Talmud,	*Bava Metzia,*	11b.
Jerusalem Talmud,	*Sanhedrin,*	Mish 1 Hal 5.

- Use Arabic numerals (e.g., **1, 2, 3**) to indicate the leaf number and **a** or **b** to indicate the page.

- When referring to a **particular edition or translation**, indicate the publication information in parentheses following the pinpoint (see sections 6.2.2.5.1 and 6.2.7 to 6.2.9).

- When providing a translation, insert **[translated by author]** after the initial citation and pinpoint (see section 6.2.2.5.2).

- Pinpoint the **Jerusalem Talmud** to the Mishna (**Mish**) and the Halacha (**Hal**) and not to the page, as there are various editions with different pagination. Pinpoint to a page if the full publication information in parentheses can be provided, as set out in sections 6.2.7 to 6.2.9.

6.12   UNPUBLISHED MANUSCRIPTS

6.12.1   General Form

Author,	*title* or "title"	(date of creation)	[unpublished,	archived at	location].
Irwin Cotler,	*Canadian Charter of Rights and Freedoms*	(1998)	[unpublished,	archived at	McGill University Faculty of Law Library].

- Include the title according to the genre. If it is an article, place the title in quotation marks. If it is a book, place the title in italics.

- Include the date of creation in parentheses after the title.

- Indicate that the manuscript is unpublished by enclosing **unpublished, archived at** and the location of the manuscript in brackets.

6.12.2   Forthcoming Manuscripts

Author,	*title*, or "title",	publication information	[forthcoming in	projected date of publication].
Joshua AT Fairfield,	"Anti-Social Contracts: The Contractual Governance of Virtual Worlds",	53:3 McGill LJ	[forthcoming in	2008].
Alain Supiot,	*Le Nouvel âge du droit social*,	Seuil	[forthcoming in	October 2009].

- Indicate the title according to the type of manuscript. If the manuscript is an article, place the title in quotation marks. If the manuscript is a book, place the title in italics.

Secondary Sources and Other Materials

■ Include the publication information according to the classification of the document, but do not indicate the year of publication.

　□ If the publication is a journal and the forthcoming issue number is known, include the issue number.

■ Indicate that the manuscript has not yet been published by enclosing **forthcoming in** and with the projected date of publication in brackets, if available.

6.12.3 Theses and Dissertations

Author,	title	(degree,	institution,	year)	publication information or [unpublished].
Julie Desrosiers,	L'isolement, le retrait et l'arrêt d'agir dans les centres de réadaptation pour jeunes	(DCL Thesis,	McGill University Institute of Comparative Law,	2005)	[unpublished].
Rachel Kiddell-Monroe,	Global Governance for Health: A Proposal	(LLM Thesis,	McGill University Faculty of Law,	2013)	[unpublished].

■ After the author's name and the title of the thesis or dissertation, indicate the degree for which it was written, the institution, and the year in parentheses. If the degree or institution is unknown, include the **field of study** (e.g., law, political science, economics).

■ At the end of the citation include **unpublished** in brackets.

■ If the thesis has been published, cite the published source. Follow the corresponding rules of the *Guide* for that publication.

■ Cite theses issued by microform services (e.g., **University Microfilms International**) in the same manner as published books, with the service in lieu of publisher.

6.13   ADDRESSES AND PAPERS DELIVERED AT CONFERENCES

Speaker,	"title" (if available) or Address	(lecture series, paper, or other information	delivered at the	conference or venue,	date),	publication information or [unpublished].
Chris Tollefson,	"The Implications of *Okanagan Indian Band* for Public Interest Litigants: A Strategic Discussion Paper"	(Paper	delivered at the	AGM of the Court Challenges Program of Canada, Winnipeg,	19 November 2005)	[unpublished].
John Borrows,	"Creating an Indigenous Legal Community"	(John C Tait Memorial Lecture in Law and Public Policy	delivered at the	Faculty of Law, McGill University,	14 October 2004),	(2005) 50 McGill LJ 153.

▨ If the address has a title, provide the title. If it has **no title**, indicate **Address**.

▨ Include the lecture series in which the address was delivered, if available.

▨ Indicate the **location** or institution where the address was delivered or the paper presented.

▨ Provide the publication information, preceded by a comma, if the address has been published.

▨ If the address is **unpublished**, insert **[unpublished]** at the end of the citation. Indicate, if available, where a transcript of the unpublished address is available (see section 6.12.1).

  ☐ If the unpublished address is available online, indicate its location in lieu of publication information (see section 6.22).

▨ If the address is **published as a collection**, cite it in the same manner as a collection of essays (see section 6.3).

6.14   COURSE MATERIALS

Professor,	title	type of document (if applicable)	(faculty,	date or year)	pinpoint.
Shauna Van Praagh,	*Coursepack: Extra-contractual Obligations/Torts*		(Faculty of Law, McGill University,	2011)	at 20.
Jean-Sébastien Brière,	*Droit des brevets,*	Coursepack	(Faculté de droit, Université de Sherbrooke,	Fall 2008)	at 331.

Indicate the type of document if it is not already included in the title. Insert a comma between the title and the type of document.

☐ **Coursepacks** are booklets of material put together by professors for a particular class. Although it is always preferable to cite to the original material, if the citation or pinpoint is unavailable, one may cite to the coursepack.

☐ **Lecture notes** are notes written by the professor for use in a particular class.

6.15 MAGAZINES

Author (if available),	"title of article",	title of magazine	volume number: issue number	(date)	first page of article,	pin-point,	electronic source (if applicable).
	"The Case Against Clones",	The Economist		(2 February 2013),			online: <www.economist.com>.
Luiza Ch Savage,	"Judges Are Like Umpires",	Maclean's		(26 September 2005)	36,		online: <www.macleans.ca>.
Benjamin Phelan,	"Buried Truths",	Harper's Magazine	309:1855	(December 2004)	70.		

Include the name of the author of the article, if available, followed by the title of the article in quotation marks.

Provide the name of the magazine in italics. Enclose any other optional identifying information, such as the place of publication, in brackets and italics immediately following the name of the magazine.

Include the **volume number** and **issue number**, separated by a colon. Add no spaces between the numbers and the colon.

Insert the **full date** in parentheses. If the date is a timespan rather than a precise date, indicate the **first day of coverage** (e.g., **22 November** not **22–28 November**).

6.16 NEWSPAPERS, NEWSWIRES, AND OTHER NEWS SOURCES

Author	"title of article",	newspaper	(date)	page	electronic source (if applicable).
Naomi Wolf,	"Take the Shame Out of Rape",	The Guardian	(25 November 2005),		online: <www.guardian.co.uk>.
	"Ottawa Eyes Six Candidates in Search of New Supreme Court Judge",	Canadian Press	(17 October 2005)		(QL).
	"Ruling on Baby with Three Mothers",	BBC News	(10 November 2005),		online: <news.bbc. co.uk>.
Bill Curry,	"PM, Premiers Work Out Deal on Aboriginal Health Care",	The Globe and Mail	(26 November 2005)	A4.	
Karen Montheith	"CIPO Contemplating Changes — Extensions of Time in Examinations"		(30 September 2009),		online: Canadian Trademark Blog <www.trademarkblog. ca>.

▨ Provide the name of the author, if available, followed by the title of the article in quotation marks.

▨ Provide the name of the newspaper, newswire, or other source in italics.

▨ If geographic information is required to identify the source, indicate it within brackets in the title (e.g., *Business Times [of Singapore]* or *The [Montreal] Gazette*).

▨ **Newspapers:**

　□ If pages are numbered by section, provide the section identifier (e.g., **A4**).

　□ If the article is contained on a single page, do not repeat that page for a pinpoint.

▨ **Newswires:**

　□ A newswire is a service transmitting the latest news via satellite and various other electronic media.

　□ Replace the newspaper name in italics with the newswire name in italics.

▨ For further information on citing to online sources, see section 6.22.

Secondary Sources and Other Materials

6.16.1   Editorials and Letters to the Editor

Author (if applicable),	"title of the editorial" (if applicable),	style of document,	*newspaper*	(date)	page	electronic source (if applicable).
	"More Independence for the FISA Court",	Editorial,	*The New York Times*	(28 July 2013),		online: <www.nytimes.com> .
Harold von Cramon,		Letter to the Editor,	*The [Montreal] Gazette*	(26 September 2005)	A26.	
Ken Lum,		Letter to the Editor,	*The Vancouver Sun*	(6 December 2004)	A10.	

▨ Indicate **Letter to the Editor** after the author of a letter to the editor.

▨ Indicate **Editorial** after the title of an editorial.

▨ Italicize the name of the newspaper, magazine, or other source. Enclose any other optional identifying information, such as the place of publication, in brackets and italics (e.g., ***Business Times [of Singapore]*** or ***The [Montreal] Gazette***).

6.17   NEWS RELEASES

Issuing body,	type of document,	document number,	"title" (optional)	(date)	electronic source (if applicable).
Indian and Northern Affairs,	News Release,	2-02688,	"Inuit Firms Secure Three Contaminated Sites Contracts"	(6 July 2005).	
Canadian Council for Refugees,	Media Release,		"CCR decries security policy's impact on refugees"	(28 April 2004),	online: CCR <www.ccrweb.ca> .
United Nations,	Press Release,	SG/SM/ 12548-OBV/ 820-WOM/ 1764	"Secretary-General, Marking International Day of Rural Women, Calls for Scaling Up Investments in Resources, Infrastructure, Services to Improve Rural Women's Lives"	(15 October 2009),	online: UN Meetings Coverage & Press Releases <www.un.org/en/ unpress> .

▨ Indicate the type of document as it appears at the top of the page (e.g., **News Release**).

▨ If the document is **numbered**, provide the number immediately after the type of document.

▨ Include the **date** at the end of the citation, before the electronic source.

Secondary Sources and Other Materials

6.18   LETTERS, MEMORANDA, AND INTERVIEWS

Letter or Interview	persons involved	(date)	further information.
Letter from	Sir Robert Wilmot to Lord George Sackville	(16 November 1753)	in James Walton, ed, "*The King's Business": Letters on the Administration of Ireland 1740-1761, from the Papers of Sir Robert Wilmot* (New York: AMS Press, 1996).
Interview of	Edward Beauvais by Douglas Sanderson	(29 May 1948)	on *This Week*, CBC Radio, Toronto, CBC Radio Archives.
	PE Moore, Acting Superintendent of Medical Services, Indian Affairs Branch, to EL Fairclough, Minister of Citizenship	[nd]	Hull, Indian and Northern Affairs Canada (6-24-3, vol 2).

- Include the parties' names, followed by the date the letter was written. If there is **no date available**, place **[nd]**.

- Indicate an **interview** or **memorandum** by writing **Interview of** or **Memorandum from** and the parties' names at the beginning of the citation.

- If the position of a person involved is not obvious or is not mentioned in the text, include as much detail on the position as necessary, preceded by a comma (e.g., **PE Moore, Acting Superintendent of Medical Services, Indian Affairs Branch**).

- If the author is not the interviewer, include the name of the interviewer. If the author (you) is the interviewer, it is not necessary to do so.

- If the letter, memorandum, or interview is published, appears online, or is held in an archive, include the appropriate citation for such sources.

6.19   ARCHIVAL MATERIALS

Title of document **and** (other information),	location of archive,	name of archive	(classification number).
Daniel Tracey v Jean Baptiste Bourtron dit Larochelle (23 December 1830),	Montreal,	Archives Nationales du Québec	(files of the Court of Quarter Sessions).
Chief Andrew Paull to TA Crerar (22 June 1944),	Ottawa,	National Archives of Canada	(RG 10, vol 6826, file 496-3-2, pt 1).

- If a document is located in an archive, provide as much information on the document as possible using the traditional citation rules, followed by the archival information.

6.20 INTELLECTUAL PROPERTY

6.20.1 Patents

"Title of Invention",	country	Patent No	PCT patent No	(filing date),	pinpoint.
"Violin Shoulder Cradle",	Can	Patent No 2414383,	PCT Patent No PCT/US2001/021243	(29 June 2001),	clm 10.
"Parallel network processor array",	US	Patent No 6854117		(31 October 2000),	fig 9.

- Indicate the **title of the invention** in quotation marks.
- Indicate the abbreviation of the **country where the patent was granted** and the **patent number**.
- If a patent was granted through the **Patent Cooperation Treaty** (PCT), use the same form for citation (**PCT Patent No**).
- Indicate the **filing date**.
- If necessary, include both the country and the PCT patent numbers, separated by a comma.
- Pinpoint to the abstract (**abstract**), a claim number (**clm**) or a figure (**fig**).
- For **patent applications**, write **application filed on** before the **filing date** (e.g. **application filed on 30 August 2008**).

6.20.2 Trade-marks

"Trade-mark",	registrant,	country	registration number	(registration date)	status.
"Kellogg's Cinnamon Mini Buns à la Cannelle",	Kellogg Company,	Can	No TMA424258	(4 March 1994)	expunged.
"Lego",	Lego Juris A/S,	USA	78882203	(3 June 2008)	live.

- Indicate the **trade-mark** in quotation marks.
- Indicate the abbreviation of the **country where the trade-mark was registered**.
- Write the **registration number**. The format of the number varies for every jurisdiction.
- Indicate the registration date in parentheses.
- Write the **status** of the trade-mark in the register. Write **dead** or **live** for United States trade-marks, and **registered** or **expunged** for Canada.

6.20.3   Copyright

"Title of the protected work"	(type of work)	owner of the copyright,	country	registration number	(registration date)	status.
"Twilight"	(music)	Mary Chapin Carpenter,	USA	Pau002997899	(20 December 2005).	
"Feel Happy"	(sound recording)	Warner Music Canada,	Can	1035760	(24 January 2006)	registered.
"Agrippa : Le livre noir"	(literary)	Éditions Michel Quintin,	Can	1056747	(11 March 2003)	registered.

- Indicate the **title of the protected work** in quotation marks.

- In Canada, the type of work includes original **literary, artistic, dramatic** and **musical** works, **performer's performances, sound recordings** and **communication signals**, as well as **mechanical contrivance**.

- Indicate the **owner of the copyright** and the **abbreviation of the country** where the copyright was issued.

- Write the **registration number**. The format of the number varies for each jurisdiction.

- Indicate the **registration date** in parentheses.

- If provided, indicate the status (**registered** or **expunged**) of the copyright in the register.

6.21   WORKING PAPERS

Author,	"title"	(year)	institution	Working Paper	series number.
Suzanne Scotchmer,	"Patents in the University: Priming the Pump and Crowding Out"	(2013)	National Bureau of Economic Research	Working Paper	No 19252.
Bram Akkermans & Eveline Ramaekers,	"Lex rei sitae in Perspective: National Developments of a Common Rule?"	(2012)	Maastricht European Law Institute	Working Paper	No 2012/14.

- If the working paper is available online, indicate the location after the series number (see section 1.6).

Secondary Sources and Other Materials

6.22 ELECTRONIC SOURCES

With the exception of online databases (section 6.22.1), this section provides guidance for sources found solely or primarily online. For general guidance in citing to online sources that supplement access to print publications, see section 1.6. For specific guidance with respect to certain sources available both online and in print, see the relevant section (e.g., jurisprudence (3.8), encyclopedic digests (6.5), newspapers (6.16)).

Where a source is only available online, exercise prudence in citing to potentially ephemeral content (e.g., personal webpages hosted by employing institutions, Facebook posts, Reddit threads).

6.22.1 Online Databases

Traditional citation	(electronic service and database).
Kristin Savell, "Human Rights in the Age of Technology: Can Law Rein in the Medical Juggernaut?" (2001) 23:3 Sydney L Rev 423	(Lexis).
Alan D Gold, *Expert Evidence in Criminal Law: The Scientific Approach* (Toronto: Irwin Law, 2003)	(QL).

Online databases aggregate diverse sources of information, including jurisprudence, legislation, and journal articles. When citing to an electronically-aggregated source where there is an authoritative printed version, provide the full traditional citation, followed by the electronic service in parentheses.

If a publisher is not listed, or if the text is not published anywhere other than in the electronic service, cite the online service as the publisher (e.g., **(Kingston, Ont: QL, 2001)**).

Do not cite to an electronic service that the majority of readers will not be able to access. For example, do not cite to Lawnet (Singapore) when writing for a Canadian audience.

For a list of online databases and their abbreviations, see **Appendix E**.

6.22.2   Online Journals (eJournals)

Traditional citation,	online:	(year)	volume: issue (if applicable)	journal	article number	pinpoint	\<URL\>.
Grant Yang, "Stop the Abuse of Gmail!",	online:	(2005)		Duke L & Tech Rev	14	at para 5	\<www.law. duke.edu/ journals/dltr/\> .
Kahikino Noa Dettweiler, "Racial Classification or Cultural Identification?: The Gathering Rights Jurisprudence of Two Twentieth Century Hawaiian Supreme Court Justices",	online:	(2005)	6:1	Asian Pac L & Pol'y J	5		\<www. hawaii.edu/ aplpj\> .

▨ Some journals are published exclusively online with their own system of citation.

▨ Cite the journal according to this internal system. Include the URL of the home page of the journal at the end of the citation.

6.22.3   Websites

6.22.3.1 Web Logs (Blogs)

6.22.3.1.1 Posts

Author,	"title"	(date),	blog name (blog),	online: \<URL\>.
Michael Geist,	"Posner on Copyright: Restrictive Fair Use a Risk to Creativity"	(2 October 2012),	Michael Geist (blog),	online: \<www.michaelgeist. ca /content/view/6645/125/\> .
Randall Munroe,	"Beliefs",		xkcd (blog),	online: \<xkcd.com/154\> .

Secondary Sources and Other Materials

6.22.3.1.2 Comments

Name or Handle	(date and time),	online: <URL> (if available),	comment on	full blog post reference (as above).
Gary P Rodriguez	(16 Feb 2011 at 11:14am),		comment on	Daniel Poulin & Frédéric Pelletier, "Are We to Live with Useless Periods Forever?" (15 February 2011) *Slaw* (blog), online: <www.slaw.ca/2011/ 02/15/are-we-to-live-with-useless-periods-forever> .
petes_PoV	(6 Oct 2012 at 12:09pm),	online: <news.slash dot.org/comments. pl?sid = 3167773& cid = 41568655 > ,	comment on	Timothy, "Gas Prices Jump: California Hardest Hit" (6 Oct 2012) *Slashdot* (blog).

▨ For sites which allow linking directly to an individual comment, provide that URL rather than the one to the main blog entry.

6.22.3.2 Social Media

6.22.3.2.1 Twitter Posts (Tweets)

Name,	"full content of tweet"	(date and time),	online: <twitter.com/full_path>.
The White House,	"Detailed, thorough timeline from Day 1: The Ongoing Administration-Wide Response to the BP Oil Spill http://bit.ly/aYOIA3"	(5 May 2010 at 9:00am),	online: Twitter <twitter.com/white-house/status/13433979066> .

6.22.3.2.2 Facebook Posts

Author,	"first sentence of post"	(date posted),	posted on *group or individual profile page*,	online: <URL>.
Ryan Lamarche,	"Should we Reform or Abolish the Senate?"	(14 February 2013),	posted on *Canadian Senate Reform*,	online: Facebook <www. facebook.com/groups/ 129971927176063/perma link/ 129972520509337/> .

▨ If the length of the first sentence is excessive, truncate appropriately and add an ellipsis before the closing quotation mark (e.g., "**Again our mighty Senators are blowing our tax money . . .**").

▨ If citing a group page or an individual profile page rather than a specific post, replace the **first sentence of post** with the name of the group or individual profile, followed by the date of creation of the group or profile if available.

6.22.3.2.3 Reddit Posts

Author,	"first sentence of post"	(date posted),	posted in *thread title*,	online: <URL>.
Lawrence Lessig,	"I spend as little time with lawmakers as possible"	(2 July 2013),	posted in *I am Lawrence Lessig (academic, activist, now collaborator with DEMAND PRO-GRESS) AMA,*	online: Reddit <www.reddit.com/r/IAmA/comments/1hibzy/ i_am_lawrence_lessig_academic_activist_now/caum9w2> .

▨   If the length of the first sentence is excessive, truncate appropriately and add an ellipsis before the closing quotation mark (e.g., "**You advocate in your book . . .**").

6.22.3.3 Online Video & Video Aggregators

Website title/ Account name,	"video title"	(date uploaded),	online: <URL>	pinpoint hh:mm:ss.
CPAC,	"Supreme Court Hearings: Supreme Court Reference Case on the Appointment of Justice Marc Nadon"	(January 15, 2014),	online: CPAC <www.cpac.ca/en/programs/supreme-court-hearings/episodes/29928389/>	at 02h:29m:30s.
UCTelevision,	"Russ Feingold – Legally Speaking"	(27 June 2013),	online: YouTube <www.youtube.com/watch?v = CkljtxRD5zM>	at 00h:12m:15s.
C-SPAN,	"Justice Kagan on Chief Justice Roberts"	(10 December 2010),	online: YouTube <www.youtube.com/watch?v = Rylr0_ia030> .	

▨   Online videos are frequently reposted without permission or attribution. Always cite to the website of origin, or the original account that uploaded the video, if available.

6.22.4   Other Digital Media

Traditional citation,	type of digital media:	*title of the media if different*	(publication information).
Peter W Hogg & Mary Ellen Turpel, "Implementing Aboriginal Self-Government: Constitutional and Jurisdictional Issues,"	CD-ROM:	*For Seven Generations: An Information Legacy of the Royal Commission on Aboriginal Peoples*	(Ottawa: Libraxus, 1997).
The Paper Chase, 1973,	DVD		(Beverly Hills, Cal: 20th Century Fox Home Entertainment, 2003).

▦ Provide the traditional citation for the document being cited, followed by a comma.

▦ Indicate the type of digital media (e.g., **CD-ROM**, **DVD, BluRay, MiniDisc**) after the comma. If the title of the media is different from the title in the traditional citation, add a colon.

▦ Indicate the title of the disc in italics, followed by a comma and the update, if applicable.

▦ In parentheses, provide the publication information for the digital medium. Include the place of publication, the publisher, and the year of publication.

6.22.5   Digital Object Identifiers

Traditional citation,	DOI: <digital object identifier>.
Sir Daniel Bethlehem, "The Secret Life of International Law" (2012) 1:1 Cambridge J of Intl & Comp L 23,	DOI: <10.7574/cjicl.01.01.1>.

▦ A digital object identifier (DOI) is a permanent, unique resource locator used to identify documents online, independent of their online location(s) at any given time. Documents assigned a DOI can be retrieved by entering the identifier into a search tool that recognizes and/or resolves them.

▦ Where a DOI is available for a given document, optionally append the DOI to the end of the traditional citation.

▦ Some periodicals have created DOIs for issues and volumes. Prefer individual article DOIs where available.

▦ Where individual DOIs are not available, cite to the volume or issue DOI by prefixing **volume** or **issue** to the DOI: indicator as appropriate (e.g., **issue DOI: <10.7574/ cjicl.01.01.11>**).

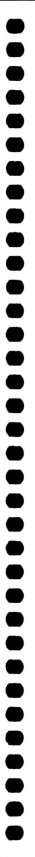

Foreign Sources

7 Foreign Sources E-163

E -7.1   Common Law Jurisdictions E-163
    E -7.1.1   General Form..E-163
    E -7.1.2   Style of Cause, Pinpoint, Short Form, and Case History E-163
    E -7.1.3   Year E-163
    E -7.1.4   Neutral Citation, Printed Reporter, Online Database, or
              Unreported Decision E-164
    E -7.1.5   Jurisdiction and Court...E-164
    E -7.1.6   Judge E-165

E -7.2   Civil Law Jurisdictions E-165

E -7.3   United Kingdom E-166
    E -7.3.1   Legislation..E-166
        E -7.3.1.1   Statutes...E-166
            E -7.3.1.1.1   Northern Ireland E-166
                E -7.3.1.1.1.1   Legislation Passed by the
                            United Kingdom.................E-166
                E -7.3.1.1.1.2   Legislation Passed by
                            Northern Ireland E-166
            E -7.3.1.1.2   Scotland..E-167
            E -7.3.1.1.3   Wales...E-167
        E -7.3.1.2   Bills..E-168
            E -7.3.1.2.1   United Kingdom.....................................E-168
            E -7.3.1.2.2   Northern Ireland E-168
            E -7.3.1.2.3   Scotland..E-168
        E -7.3.1.3   Regulations E-169
            E -7.3.1.3.1   United Kingdom.....................................E-169
            E -7.3.1.3.2   Northern Ireland Regulations and Orders ...E-169
            E -7.3.1.3.3   Scotland..E-170
                E -7.3.1.3.3.1   Regulations Passed by the
                            United Kingdom.................E-170
                E -7.3.1.3.3.2   Regulations Passed by the
                            Scottish Parliament E-170
            E -7.3.1.3.4   Wales...E-170
    E -7.3.2   Jurisprudence..E-171
        E -7.3.2.1   General Form..E-171
        E -7.3.2.2   Neutral Citation......................................E-171
        E -7.3.2.3   Appeal Courts...E-171
        E -7.3.2.4   High Court..E-172
        E -7.3.2.5   Reporter E-172
            E -7.3.2.5.1   Law Reports..E-172
                E -7.3.2.5.1.1   From 1875–1890 ....E-173
                E -7.3.2.5.1.2   From 1865–1875 ....E-173
                E -7.3.2.5.1.3   From 1537–1865 ....E-173
                E -7.3.2.5.1.4   Retroactive Neutral Citation...E-174
        E -7.3.2.6   Yearbooks..E-174
        E -7.3.2.7   Reprints...E-174
        E -7.3.2.8   Scotland, Ireland, and Northern Ireland E-175
            E -7.3.2.8.1   Neutral Citation E-175

E -7.3.2.8.1.1 Scotland...........................E-175
E -7.3.2.8.1.2 Ireland E-176
E -7.3.2.8.1.3 Northern Ireland E-176
E -7.3.2.9 Judge E-176
E -7.3.2.10 Online Databases.........................E-177
E -7.3.2.10.1 BAILII...............................E-177
E -7.3.2.10.2 Service with No Identifier (Justis) E-177
E -7.3.3 Government Documents........................E-177
E -7.3.3.1 Debates.................................E-177
E -7.3.3.1.1 Before 1803 ....E-177
E -7.3.3.1.2 1803 and After....................E-178
E -7.3.3.2 Journals.................................E-179
E -7.3.3.3 Parliamentary Papers E-179
E -7.3.3.4 Non-parliamentary Papers E-180

E -7.4 United States E-181
E -7.4.1 Legislation.....................................E-181
E -7.4.1.1 Federal and State Constitutions E-181
E -7.4.1.2 Federal and State Statutes E-182
E -7.4.1.2.1 Codes E-182
E -7.4.1.2.2 Session Laws E-184
E -7.4.1.2.3 Unofficial Reporters of Session Laws E-185
E -7.4.1.3 Uniform Codes, Uniform Acts, and Restatements.........E-185
E -7.4.1.4 Bills and Resolutions.....................E-186
E -7.4.1.4.1 Federal Bills E-186
E -7.4.1.4.2 Federal Resolutions...............E-186
E -7.4.1.4.3 State Bills and Resolutions....................E-187
E -7.4.1.5 Regulations E-188
E -7.4.1.5.1 The Code of Federal Regulations.............E-188
E -7.4.1.5.2 Administrative Registers E-188
E -7.4.2 Jurisprudence...................................E-189
E -7.4.2.1 General Form...........................E-189
E -7.4.2.2 Style of Cause..........................E-189
E -7.4.2.3 Neutral Citation........................E-189
E -7.4.2.4 Reporter and Series....................E-190
E -7.4.2.5 Pinpoint...............................E-191
E -7.4.2.6 Court E-192
E -7.4.2.6.1 Federal Courts E-192
E -7.4.2.6.2 State Courts......................E-192
E -7.4.2.7 Year of Decision E-192
E -7.4.2.8 Online Databases.......................E-193
E -7.4.2.8.1 Westlaw..........................E-193
E -7.4.2.8.2 Lexis E-193
E -7.4.3 Government Documents........................E-193
E -7.4.3.1 Debates................................E-193
E -7.4.3.2 Committee Hearings E-194
E -7.4.3.2.1 Federal E-194
E -7.4.3.2.2 State............................E-194
E -7.4.3.3 Reports and Documents.....................E-195
E -7.4.3.3.1 Federal E-195

Foreign Sources

        E -7.4.3.3.1.1 Numbered Documents and
                Reports............................E-195
        E -7.4.3.3.1.2 Unnumbered Documents and
                Committee Prints...............E-196
    E -7.4.3.3.2 State...E-196

E -7.5 France E-197
    E -7.5.1 Legislation..E-197
        E -7.5.1.1 Statutes and Other Legislative Instruments.................E-197
        E -7.5.1.2 Codes E-197
    E -7.5.2 Jurisprudence...E-198
        E -7.5.2.1 General Form..E-198
        E -7.5.2.2 Court E-198
            E -7.5.2.2.1 Courts of First Instance E-198
            E -7.5.2.2.2 Court of Appeal...................................E-199
            E -7.5.2.2.3 Cour de cassation................................E-199
            E -7.5.2.2.4 Conseil d'État E-200
            E -7.5.2.2.5 Conseil constitutionnel E-200
        E -7.5.2.3 Style of Cause.......................................E-201
        E -7.5.2.4 Year E-201
        E -7.5.2.5 Session E-201
        E -7.5.2.6 Reporter E-201
        E -7.5.2.7 Section...E-202
        E -7.5.2.8 Page and Decision Number E-203
        E -7.5.2.9 Pinpoint E-203
        E -7.5.2.10 Parallel Citation E-203
        E -7.5.2.11 Annotations, Reports, and Conclusions E-203
    E -7.5.3 Government Documents...................................E-203
        E -7.5.3.1 Debates..E-204
            E -7.5.3.1.1 From 1787 to 1860 ....E-204
            E -7.5.3.1.2 1871 to the Present............................E-204
        E -7.5.3.2 Earlier Versions of the Journal officiel E-205
        E -7.5.3.3 Parliamentary Documents..............................E-206
            E -7.5.3.3.1 Travaux et réunions parlementaires E-206
            E -7.5.3.3.2 Rapports d'information (Reports)..............E-207
        E -7.5.3.4 Non-parliamentary Documents E-208

E -7.6 Australia...E-208
    E -7.6.1 Legislation..E-208
        E -7.6.1.1 Statutes..E-208
        E -7.6.1.2 Delegated Legislation (Regulations)............................E-209
    E -7.6.2 Jurisprudence...E-210
        E -7.6.2.1 General Form..E-210
        E -7.6.2.2 Neutral Citation......................................E-210
        E -7.6.2.3 Reporter E-211
            E -7.6.2.3.1 Law Reports....................................E-211
        E -7.6.2.4 Jurisdiction and Court................................E-212
    E -7.6.3 Government Documents...................................E-212
        E -7.6.3.1 Debates..E-213
        E -7.6.3.2 Parliamentary Papers E-213
        E -7.6.3.3 Non-Parliamentary Papers E-214

E -7.6.3.4 Ministerial Documents E-214

E -7.7 New Zealand E-215
   E -7.7.1 Legislation...E-215
      E -7.7.1.1 Statutes...E-215
      E -7.7.1.2 Delegated Legislation (Regulations)...........................E-215
   E -7.7.2 Jurisprudence..E-216
      E -7.7.2.1 General Form...E-216
      E -7.7.2.2 Neutral Citation...E-216
      E -7.7.2.3 Reporter E-216
         E -7.7.2.3.1 Law Reports.....................................E-216
      E -7.7.2.4 Court E-218
   E -7.7.3 Government Documents...E-218
      E -7.7.3.1 Debates..E-218
      E -7.7.3.2 Parliamentary Papers E-219

E -7.8 Singapore..E-220
   E -7.8.1 Legislation...E-220
      E -7.8.1.1 Constitutional Documents E-220
      E -7.8.1.2 Statutes...E-220
      E -7.8.1.3 Amendments and Repeals...................................E-221
      E -7.8.1.4 English Statutes Applicable in Singapore E-221
      E -7.8.1.5 Subsidiary Legislation (Rules, Regulations,
             Notifications, Orders)..E-221
         E -7.8.1.5.1 Revised E-221
         E -7.8.1.5.2 Unrevised E-222
   E -7.8.2 Jurisprudence..E-222
      E -7.8.2.1 General Form...E-222
      E -7.8.2.2 Neutral Citation...E-223
      E -7.8.2.3 Reporters..E-223
      E -7.8.2.4 Court E-223
      E -7.8.2.5 Unreported Decisions without Neutral Citation E-224
      E -7.8.2.6 Online Databases...E-224
   E -7.8.3 Government Documents...E-224
      E -7.8.3.1 Parliamentary Debates E-224
      E -7.8.3.2 Supreme Court Practice Directions.........................E-224
         E -7.8.3.2.1 Consolidated Practice Directions..............E-225
         E -7.8.3.2.2 Amendments to Practice Directions E-225

E -7.9 South Africa...E-225
   E -7.9.1 Legislation...E-225
      E -7.9.1.1 Statutes...E-225
      E -7.9.1.2 Amendments and Repeals...................................E-225
      E -7.9.1.2 Bills E-226
   E -7.9.2 Jurisprudence..E-226
      E -7.9.2.1 General Form...E-226
      E -7.9.2.2 Neutral Citation...E-226
      E -7.9.2.3 Reporters..E-227
      E -7.9.2.4 Court E-228
   E -7.9.3 Government Documents...E-228
      E -7.9.3.1 Debates..E-228
      E -7.9.3.2 Reports, Discussion Papers, and Issue Papers E-229

7   FOREIGN SOURCES

7.1   COMMON LAW JURISDICTIONS

7.1.1   General Form

To cite a source from a common law jurisdiction that is not listed in this chapter, use the following model as a guide.

Style of cause	(year of the decision) (if necessary),	neutral citation, printed reporter, etc.	pinpoint	parallel citation	(court, if neces-sary	jurisdiction)	[short title].
Singh v Punjab,		[1980] 2 Supreme Court Journal 475	at 524		(	India)	*[Singh]*.
Hong Kong v Chan Hing Hung,		[1998] 4 Hong Kong Court 487	at 488C		(CFI	Hong Kong)	*[Chan]*.
Alla Rahka v Mohamed Ahmed	(1956),	29 LRK 6			(	Kenya)	*[Alla Rahka]*.
Campbell v MGN Ltd,		[2004] UKHL 22,		[2004] 2 AC 457	(	UK)	*[MGN]*.

7.1.2   Style of Cause, Pinpoint, Short Form, and Case History

▨   Use the rules for Canadian jurisprudence for the style of cause (section 3.3), pinpoints (section 3.6), printed reporters (section 3.7), and case history (section 3.11).

▨   For guidance on short forms, see section 1.4.1.

7.1.3   Year

▨   Generally, provide the year of the decision or omit it following the rules in section 3.4.

▨   When necessary to avoid ambiguity (e.g., when citing an unreported decision) indicate the full date rather than the year alone.

7.1.4   Neutral Citation, Printed Reporter, Online Database, or Unreported Decision

	year and/ or volume	reporter or tribunal identifier	(series)	first page or decision number	(online database)	pinpoint.
neutral citation	[2004]	UKHL		22.		
printed reporter	11	F Supp	(2d)	858		at 860.
online database	[1995]	FCJ		no 206	(QL).	

▨ Prefer neutral citation to a printed reporter. Follow the conventions for the neutral citation adopted by the country (e.g., the UK uses square brackets around the year), but otherwise follow the advice given in the section on Canada (year, volume, reporter, series, page).

▨ Prefer a printed reporter to an online database. Follow section 3.7 for printed reporters.

▨ For online databases, use the citation provided. Unless the database is likely to be known to the reader, append its name in parentheses.

▨ For unreported judgments for which none of the above exist, follow the convention adopted by the jurisdiction, if one exists, or provide clear identifying information such as the judicial district followed by docket number (as in section 3.12). Indicate the full date in parentheses following the style of cause, rather than simply the year of the decision.

▨ Among printed reporters, the order of preference from highest to lowest is

☐ official reporters;

☐ semi-official reporters; and

☐ reporters with the broadest possible geographic scope.

7.1.5   Jurisdiction and Court

Write the name of the country and the court in full, with the following exceptions:

▨ Abbreviations that are very likely to be familiar to the reader (e.g., US or UK).

▨ A distinctive name that is commonly used in place of a country's official name (e.g., Netherlands rather than "Kingdom of the Netherlands").

▨ Clear indication of the name of the court and/or its jurisdiction elsewhere in the citation.

7.1.6 Judge

▨ Use abbreviations for their titles only if they are likely to be familiar to the reader (e.g. CJ can usually be assumed to mean Chief Justice).

7.2 CIVIL LAW JURISDICTIONS

To cite a source from a civil law jurisdiction that is not listed in this chapter, use the following as a guide.

Court and chamber,	city,	date,	style of cause (if applicable)	(year of publi- cation),	reporter or journal	sec- tion	page and/or decision number	(annota- ted by author)	(coun- try).
Tribunal de Com- merce,	Ostende,	12 October 1987		(1988),	Revue de Droit Commerci al Belge		268	(annota- ted by Veroug- straete)	(Bel- gium).
Corte Suprema de Justicia [Supreme Court],		15 Novem- ber 1954,	Suàrez, Alfredo c Perez Estella,		190 Revista Gaceta Jurídica		145, No 124-2008		(Chile).
Interm People's Court,	Shang- hai,	11 May 1988,	China National Technical Importer/ Exporter v Industry Res	(22 August 1988),	China Law & Practice		26		(China).
Mahkamat al-Tamiez [Court of Cassation	Tamiez],	6 March 1974,			year 5, 1 Al-Nashra al- Qadaiah		161, No 1428		(Iraq).

▨ Include all elements that are applicable.

▨ Include an English translation of the name of the court or chamber, in brackets, if it would help the reader.

7.3   UNITED KINGDOM

For general rules, see *Oxford Standard for Citation of Legal Authorities*.

7.3.1   Legislation

7.3.1.1 Statutes

| Before 1963 | *Statute of Westminster, 1931* (UK), 22 & 23 Geo V, c 4, s 2. |
| 1 January 1963 and after | *Terrorism Act 2000* (UK), c 11, s 129. |

▪ Include **(UK)** after the title of the statute to indicate its origin.

▪ **Before 1963**: When the title includes a year, place a comma before the year. Cite the regnal year in Arabic numerals (e.g., **1, 2, 3**) and the number following the abbreviation for the monarch in Roman numerals (**Geo V**).

▪ **1 January 1963 and after**: When the title includes a year, do not place a comma before the year. When the title does not include a year, indicate the calendar year after the comma following **(UK)**, followed by a comma.

7.3.1.1.1 Northern Ireland

7.3.1.1.1.1 Legislation Passed by the United Kingdom

| Before 1963 | *Public Health (Ireland) Act, 1878* (UK), 41 & 42 Vict, c 52. |
| 1 January 1963 and after | *Northern Ireland Act 1998* (UK), c 47, s 5. |

▪ Cite legislation applying to Northern Ireland passed by the United Kingdom in the same manner as United Kingdom legislation.

7.3.1.1.1.2 Legislation Passed by Northern Ireland

1921-1972	*Criminal Law Amendment (Northern Ireland) Act*, RSNI 1923, c 8.
	National Insurance Act, NI Pub Gen Acts 1946, c 23, s 7.
1999-present	*Family Law Act (Northern Ireland) 2001* (NI), c 12.

▪ Abbreviate **Northern Ireland Public General Acts** to **NI Pub Gen Acts**.

▪ Abbreviate **Statutes Revised, Northern Ireland** to **RSNI**.

Foreign Sources

The United Kingdom passed legislation for Northern Ireland from 1972—1999. On 19 November 1998, the Northern Ireland Assembly was created and empowered to pass legislation as of 2 December 1999. For legislation passed by the Assembly after 1999, include **(NI)** after the title of the statute to indicate its origin. Note that after 2 December 1999, the United Kingdom can still pass legislation affecting Northern Ireland.

NB: The Northern Ireland Assembly and the Executive have been periodically suspended. During such periods, responsibility and control of Northern Ireland Departments have been assumed by the *Secretary of State for Northern Ireland* and the *Northern Ireland Office*.

7.3.1.1.2 Scotland

Before 1998	*Contract (Scotland) Act 1997* (UK), 1997, c 34.
	Scotland Act 1998 (UK), c 46, s 4.
1998–present	*Standards in Scotland's Schools etc Act*, ASP 2000, c 6, s 2.

Cite legislation from before 1998 in the same manner as United Kingdom legislation.

Note that Acts passed by the United Kingdom still apply to Scotland if the legislation pertains to a reserved or non-devolved matter.

From 19 November 1998, abbreviate **Acts of Scottish Parliament** to **ASP**.

7.3.1.1.3 Wales

Government of Wales Act 1998 (UK), c 38, s 3.
Public Audit (Wales) Act 2013, ANAW, c 3, s 4.

Cite legislation passed before 25 July 2006 in the same manner as United Kingdom legislation.

In 2006, the National Assembly for Wales acquired limited legislative powers concerning devolved matters. Each measure passed between 25 July 2006 and 5 May 2011 required approval from the United Kingdom before passage. Cite this legislation in the same manner as United Kingdom legislation.

From 5 May 2011, the Assembly gained direct lawmaking powers for the twenty Subjects outlined in the *Government of Wales Act 2006* (UK), c 32 s 7. Abbreviate **Acts of the National Assembly for Wales** to **ANAW**.

7.3.1.2 Bills

7.3.1.2.1 United Kingdom

Bill no,	title,	session,	year,	pinpoint	(additional information) (optional).
Bill 45,	London Olympics Bill,	2005–2006 sess,	2005		(1st reading 14 July 2005).
Bill 40,	Harbours Bill [HL],	2005–2006 sess,	2005,	s 2.	

◼ For bills that originate in the House of Lords, indicate **[HL]** (not italicized) in the title.

7.3.1.2.2 Northern Ireland

Number,	title,	session,	year,	pinpoint	(additional information) (optional).
NIA Bill 15/00,	A Bill to amend the Game Preservation (Northern Ireland) Act 1928,	2001–2002 sess,	2001,	s 2	(Committee Stage Extension 29 October 2001).
NIA Bill 17/07,	Child Maintenance Bill,	2007–2008 sess,	2008,	s 12.	

7.3.1.2.3 Scotland

Number,	title,	session,	year,	pinpoint	(additional information) (optional).
SP Bill 42,	Human Tissue (Scotland) Bill,	sess 2,	2005,	s 6	(1st reading 3 June 2005).
SP Bill 17,	Climate Change (Scotland) Bill,	sess 3,	2008,	s 3(2)(b)	(State 1 debate 6-7 May 2009).

7.3.1.3 Regulations

7.3.1.3.1 United Kingdom

	Title (optional),	SR & O or SI	year/number.
Before 1948	*Public Health (Prevention of Tuberculosis) Regulations 1925,*	SR & O	1927/757.
1948 and after	*The Welfare Food (Amendment) Regulations 2005,*	SI	2005/688.

▦ Including the title of the regulation is optional.

▦ For regulations before 1948, abbreviate *Statutory Rules & Orders* to **SR & O**. For regulations after 1948, abbreviate *Statutory Instruments* to **SI**.

7.3.1.3.2 Northern Ireland Regulations and Orders

Title (optional),	SR & O or SI	year/number	(NI number).
The Proceeds of Crime (Northern Ireland) Order 1996,	SI	1996/1299	(NI 9).
The Tax Credits 2001 (Miscellaneous Amendments No. 8) (Northern Ireland) Regulations,	SI	2001/3086.	
Cheese Regulations (NI) 1970,	SR & O	1970/14.	
Dangerous Substances in Harbour Areas Regulations (Northern Ireland) 1991,	SR	1991/509.	

▦ Including the title of the regulation is optional.

▦ A regulation or order passed by the UK is contained in the *Statutory Instruments* (**SI**).

▦ A regulation passed by the Northern Ireland Assembly is called a *Statutory Rule* (**SR**).

▨ Northern Ireland regulations are also included in *Statutory Regulations and Orders* (abbreviated **SR & O**) beginning in 1922.

▨ If there is a **Northern Ireland Order number**, include it after the year/number to indicate that the order was passed by the Northern Ireland Assembly.

7.3.1.3.3 Scotland

Cite Scottish regulations in the same manner as United Kingdom regulations (see section 7.3.1.3.1).

7.3.1.3.3.1 Regulations Passed by the United Kingdom

Title (optional),	SR & O or SI	year/number.
Employment Tribunals (Constitution and Rules of Procedure) (Scotland) Regulations 2001,	SI	2001/1170.
Local Government Pension Scheme Amendment (Scotland) Regulations 2009,	SI	2009/93.

7.3.1.3.3.2 Regulations Passed by the Scottish Parliament

Title (optional),	Scot SI	year/number.
National Health Service (General Ophthalmic Services) (Scotland) Amendment Regulations 2001,	Scot SI	2001/62.
Plastic Materials and Articles in Contact with Food (Scotland) Regulations 2009,	Scot SI	2009/30.

▨ Abbreviate *Scottish Statutory Instruments* to Scot SI.

7.3.1.3.4 Wales

Title (optional),	SR & O or SI	year/number	(W number).
Children's Homes Amendment (Wales) Regulations 2001,	SI	2001/140	(W 6).

▨ After the **year/number**, include the Welsh regulation number to indicate that the regulation was passed by the National Assembly for Wales.

Foreign Sources

7.3.2 Jurisprudence

7.3.2.1 General Form

Style of cause	(year of deci-sion),	neutral citation,	[year of reporter]	vol	reporter	page	(court).
R v Woollin	(1998),		[1999]	1	AC	82	(HL (Eng)).
Campbell v MGN Ltd,		[2004] UKHL 22,	[2004]	2	AC	457.	

▨ Cite the *Law Reports* (see section 7.3.2.5.1) in preference to the *Weekly Law Reports* (**WLR**) or the *All England Law Reports* (**All ER**).

▨ See **Appendix B-2** for a list of courts and their abbreviations, and **Appendix C-3** for a list of United Kingdom reporters and their abbreviations.

7.3.2.2 Neutral Citation

▨ Many courts in the United Kingdom have officially adopted a system of neutral citation. The form is the same as that of Canadian neutral citation (section 3.5), with the exception that the year is placed in brackets.

▨ For retroactive neutral citation, see section 7.3.2.5.1.4.

7.3.2.3 Appeal Courts

> [1] *Campbell v MGN Limited*, [2004] UKHL 22.
> [2] *Fraser v HM Advocate*, [2011] UKSC 24.
> [3] *Copping v Surrey County Council*, [2005] EWCA Civ 1604 at para 15.

Supreme Court of The United Kingdom	[year] UKSC number
House of Lords	[year] UKHL number
Privy Council	[year] UKPC number
England and Wales Court of Appeal (Civil Division)	[year] EWCA Civ number
England and Wales Court of Appeal (Criminal Division)	[year] EWCA Crim number

Foreign Sources

■ The neutral citations for the Appeal Courts and the Administrative Court of the High Court became **official on 11 January 2001**.

■ The Supreme Court of the United Kingdom assumed the judicial functions of the House of Lords on 1 October 2009.

■ Place the year of the decision in brackets followed by the court identifier and the case number.

7.3.2.4 High Court

[Year]	court	number	(division)	pinpoint.
[2005]	EWHC	1974	(Admlty)	at para 10.
[2005]	EWHC	2995	(Comm).	

■ Neutral citations to the High Court were **officially adopted on 14 January 2002**.

■ For cases heard in the High Court, the division of the Court is placed in parentheses *after* the case number.

■ NB: Cases heard by the Administrative Court in 2001 should follow the form **year EWHC Admin number**, similar to the Court of Appeal (section 7.3.2.3).

■ Pinpoint to paragraphs and use **at para**.

■ The High Court has three principal divisions and several specialist courts.

High Court Divisions and Abbreviations:

Queen's Bench Division	QB
Administrative Court	Admin
Commercial Court	Comm
Admiralty Court	Admlty
Technology & Construction Court	TCC

Chancery Division	Ch
Patents Court	Pat
Companies Court	Comp

Family Division	Fam

7.3.2.5 Reporter

7.3.2.5.1 Law Reports

■ *Law Reports* are **divided into series**. Do not refer to the *Law Reports*, but rather to the series.

- Since there is no separate reporter for the Court of Appeal, include **CA** (the abbreviation of Court of Appeal) at the end of each citation to a case heard in that court.

Law Reports **and abbreviations:**

Appeal Cases (House of Lords and Judicial Committee of the Privy Council)	AC
Chancery (Chancery Division and appeals therefrom in the Court of Appeal)	Ch
Common Pleas	CP
Family (1972–present)	Fam
Industrial Courts Reports (1972–1974) and *Industrial Cases Reports* (1975–present)	ICR
Probate (1891–1971) (Family Division, Probate, Divorce, and Admiralty Division, appeals therefrom, and Ecclesiastical Courts)	P
Queen's (King's) Bench (Queen's (King's) Bench Division and appeals therefrom in the Court of Appeal)	QB (KB)
Law Reports Restrictive Practices (1957–1972) (National Industrial Relations Court and Restrictive Practices Court, appeals therefrom, and decisions of the High Court relevant to industrial relations)	LR RP

7.3.2.5.1.1 From 1875–1890

Akerblom v Price, Potter, Walker & Co (1881), 7 **QBD** 129 (CA) [*Akerblom*].

- Include **D** for **Division** after the reporter to distinguish the 1875–1890 series of reporters from the later series with the same name.

7.3.2.5.1.2 From 1865–1875

Rylands v Fletcher (1868), **LR** 3 HL 330.

- Include **LR** for **Law Reports** before the volume number to distinguish the 1865–1875 series of reporters from the later series with the same name.

7.3.2.5.1.3 From 1537–1865

Lord Byron v Johnston (1816), 2 Mer 28, 35 ER 851 (Ch).

Foreign Sources

Prior to 1865, there were neither official nor comprehensive law reports. Instead, individual lawyers and judges published private law reports under their own names. Few readers will have access to these historical "nominate" reporters. Whenever possible, cite to *English Reports* (**ER**) in preference to a nominate reporter, or at least provide a parallel citation.

The *English Reports* and *All England Reports Reprints* are reprints. The complete *English Reports* are publicly accessible on the CommonLII website.

7.3.2.5.1.4 Retroactive Neutral Citation

Thomas v Sorrell, **[1673] EWHC KB J85**, 124 ER 1098, Vaughan 330.

Many older cases, especially those of the House of Lords and the Privy Council, have been assigned retroactive neutral citations. Treat these retroactive neutral citations as court-assigned neutral citation. Retroactive neutral citations are available on BAILII.

7.3.2.6 *Yearbooks*

Style of cause	(year),	year-book	term	regnal year	mon-arch,	plea number,	folio number.
Waldon v Marshall	(1370),	YB	Mich	43	Edw III,	pl 38,	fol 33.

Abbreviate Michaelmas to **Mich**, Hilary to **Hil**, Easter to **Pach**, and Trinity to **Trin**.

Indicate the regnal year in Arabic numerals (e.g., **1, 2, 3**).

Cite the monarch using Roman numerals.

Abbreviate plea to **pl**.

Abbreviate folio to **fol**.

7.3.2.7 *Reprints*

Yearbook citation,	reprinted in,	translated by (if applicable)	translator / editor,	citation.
Randolph v Abbot of Hailes (1313-14), YB 6&7 Edw II (Eyre of Kent),	reprinted in *Yearbooks of 6 Edward II* (1926),	translated by	William Craddock, ed,	27 Selden Soc 32 at 33.

■ When citing to a reprint, provide as much information about the original yearbook entry as possible. Cite to the location where the reprint is found.

7.3.2.8 Scotland, Ireland, and Northern Ireland

Scotland	*M'Courtney v HM Advocate*, [1977] JC 68 (HCJ **Scot**).
Ireland	*Johnson v Egan*, [1894] 2 **IR** 480 (QBD).
Northern Ireland	*R v Crooks*, [1999] **NI** 226 (CA).

■ Where the jurisdiction is not obvious from the title of the reporter, and there is no neutral citation, abbreviate Scotland to **Scot**, Ireland to **Ir**, and Northern Ireland to **NI**. Enclose the abbreviation in parentheses at the end of the citation.

■ As each volume is divided according to the court reported and each section is paginated separately, include the name of the court.

■ See **Appendix B** for court abbreviations and **Appendix C** for reporter abbreviations.

7.3.2.8.1 Neutral Citation

■ The rules for neutral citation are the same for Scotland, Ireland, and Northern Ireland. The rules are similar to those of Canadian neutral citation (section 3.5), with the exception that the year is placed in square brackets.

7.3.2.8.1.1 Scotland

■ As the neutral citation does not indicate the jurisdiction, add **Scot** for Scotland in parentheses at the end of the entire citation (following all parallel citations).

Smith v Brown, [2005] HCJT 2 (Scot).

Kinross v Dunsmuir, [2005] HCJAC 3 at para 12 (Scot).

McBride v MacDuff, [2005] CSOH 4 (Scot).

High Court of Justiciary	[year] HCJT number
Court of Criminal Appeal	[year] HCJAC number
Court of Session, Outer House	[year] CSOH number
Court of Session, Inner House	[year] CSIH number

7.3.2.8.1.2 Ireland

Finnigan v O'Dair, [2006] IEHC 4. *Mackey v Mackey*, [2005] IESC 2 at para 4.	

High Court	[year] IEHC number
Supreme Court	[year] IESC number
Court of Criminal Appeal	[year] IECCA number

7.3.2.8.1.3 Northern Ireland

McDonnell v Henry, [2005] NICA 17. *Barkley v Whiteside*, [2004] NIQB 12 at para 12.	

Court of Appeal	[year] NICA number
Crown Court	[year] NICC number
County Court	[year] NICty number
Magistrates Court	[year] NIMag number

High Court:

Queen's Bench Division	[year] NIQB number
Family Division	[year] NIFam number
Chancery Division	[year] NICh number

7.3.2.9 *Judge*

Lord Justice	LJ
Lord Justices	LJJ
Master of the Rolls	MR
Lord Chancellor	LC
Vice Chancellor	VC
Baron	B
Chief Baron	CB

7.3.2.10 Online Databases

7.3.2.10.1 BAILII

Style of cause,	identifier given by service	(BAILII)	pinpoint	(jurisdiction and/or court) (if applicable).
London Borough of Harrow v Johnstone,	[1997] UKHL 9	(BAILII)	at para 6.	

- Do not confuse BAILII's identifier with a neutral citation. Add **(BAILII)** after the identifier to avoid confusion.

7.3.2.10.2 Service with No Identifier (Justis)

Style of cause	(year),	pinpoint	(jurisdiction and/or court)	(available on	name of the online database).
R v Woollin	(1998),	at para 23	(HL)	(available on	Justis).

7.3.3 Government Documents

Indicate **UK** at the beginning of the citation.

7.3.3.1 Debates

7.3.3.1.1 Before 1803

UK,	house,	Parliamentary History of England,	volume,	column	(date)	(speaker) (optional).
UK,	HC,	Parliamentary History of England,	vol 17,	col 1357	(27 May 1774).	
UK,	HL,	Parliamentary History of England,	vol 2,	col 791	(24 May 1641).	

░ For debates prior to 1803, cite to the *Parliamentary History of England*.

░ Abbreviate **House of Commons** to HC and **House of Lords** to HL.

░ Indicate the speaker (if provided) in parentheses at the end of the citation.

7.3.3.1.2 1803 and After

UK,	house,	*title,*	series or **session** (if applicable),	volume,	column	pinpoint	(date)	(speaker) (optional).
UK,	HL,	*Parliamentary Debates,*	5th ser,	vol 442,	col 6		(3 May 1983)	(Baroness Masham of Ilton).
UK,	SP,	*Official Report,*	sess 1 (2000),	vol 7, No 6,	col 634		(22 June 2000)	(Peter Peacock).
UK,	NIA,	*Official Report,*				at 500	(24 October 2000).	
UK,	NAW,	*Official Record,*				at 27	(19 July 2001).	

░ Indicate the speaker (if provided) in parentheses at the end of the citation.

░ After UK, indicate the house.

Houses' abbreviations:

House of Commons	HC
House of Lords	HL
National Assembly for Wales	NAW
Northern Ireland Assembly	NIA
Scottish Parliament	SP

7.3.3.2 Journals

UK,	journal,	volume	(date)	pinpoint.
UK,	Journal of the House of Commons,	vol 234	(9 December 1977)	at 95.
UK,	Journal of the House of Lords,	vol 22	(10 January 1995)	at 89.

▨ Do not repeat the house, since it is already included in the title of the journal.

7.3.3.3 Parliamentary Papers

UK,	house,	"title",	sessional or command paper number	in Sessional Papers,	vol	(year)	first page	pinpoint	(president) (if any).
UK,	HC,	"Report of the Committee on the Law Relating to Rights of Light",	Cmnd 473	in Sessional Papers,	vol 17	(1957–58)	955		(President: CE Harman).
UK,	HC,	"Monopolies and Mergers Commission Report on the Supply in the U.K. of the Services of Administering Performing Rights and Film Synchronisation Rights",	Cm 3147	in Sessional Papers		(1995–96)	1.		

▨ Indicate the title as it appears on the title page of the report.

▨ Place the sessional number or command paper number after the title of the paper.

▨ Cite to the **House of Commons' bound** *Sessional Papers* unless the paper only appears in the House of Lords' *Sessional Papers*.

▨ Place the volume number, if specified, after *Sessional Papers*, preceded by a comma.

▨ Include the name of the president (if provided) in parentheses at the end of the citation.

▓ **The proper abbreviation of Command is essential for identifying the document**. It is indicated on the title page of each *Command Paper*:

1833–1869	1st series (1–4222)	c
1870–1899	2nd series (1–9550)	C
1900–1918	3rd series (1–9239)	Cd
1919–1956	4th series (1–9889)	Cmd
1957–1986	5th series (1–9927)	Cmnd
1986–present	6th series (1–)	Cm

▓ Indicate the first page of the paper after the date.

▓ Pinpoint to the internal pagination of the paper.

7.3.3.4 Non-parliamentary Papers

UK,	issuing body,	*title*	(nature of paper) (if applicable)	authors (if applicable)	(publication information).
UK,	Royal Commission on Criminal Procedure,	*Police Interrogation: The Psychological Approach*			(London: Her Majesty's Stationery Office, 1980).
UK,	Royal Commission on the Press,	*Studies on the Press*	(Working Paper No 3)	by Oliver Boyd-Barrett, Dr Colin Seymour-Ure & Professor Jeremy Turnstall	(London: Her Majesty's Stationery Office, 1978).
UK,	Law Commission,	*Contempt of Court*	(Consultation Paper No 209)		(London: The Stationery Office, 2012).
UK,		*Report of the Committee on Homosexual Offences and Prostitution*			(London: Her Majesty's Stationery Office, 1957).

Foreign Sources

◾ Cite non-parliamentary papers in the same manner as Canadian non-parliamentary papers, according to the rules at section 4.2.

◾ Do not write the issuing body if it is already in the title (see the *Report of the Committee on Homosexual Offences and Prostitution* example).

◾ Many of the official publishing functions of Her Majesty's Stationery Office were assumed by The Stationery Office (TSO), a private corporation, in 1996.

7.4 UNITED STATES

See the latest edition of ***The Bluebook: A Uniform System of Citation.***

7.4.1 Legislation

7.4.1.1 Federal and State Constitutions

> US Const art III, § 2, cl 3.
> US Const amend XIV, § 1.
> NM Const art IV, § 7.

◾ Abbreviate **article** to **art**, **section** to **§**, and **sections** to **§§**.

◾ A paragraph within a section is labeled a **clause**, and is abbreviated to **cl** or **cls** in the plural.

◾ Abbreviate **amendment** to **amend**.

◾ Abbreviate **preamble** to **pmbl**.

◾ Indicate article and amendment numbers in capital Roman numerals. Indicate section and clause numbers in Arabic numerals (e.g., **1, 2, 3**).

See **Appendix A-2** for a list of state abbreviations.

7.4.1.2 Federal and State Statutes

Order of preference of sources:

```
┌─────────────────┐
│  Official code  │
└─────────────────┘
         ⇩
┌─────────────────┐
│ Unofficial code │
└─────────────────┘
         ⇩
┌───────────────────────────────┐
│ Official reporter of session laws │
└───────────────────────────────┘
         ⇩
┌────────────────────────────────┐
│ Unofficial reporter of session laws │
└────────────────────────────────┘
         ⇩
┌──────────────────┐
│ Loose-leaf service │
└──────────────────┘
```

7.4.1.2.1 Codes

- A code in the United States is a consolidation and codification by subject matter of the general and permanent federal or state laws.

- An **official code** is a code of the laws of the United States organized under fifty subject titles, prepared under the supervision of an appropriate government authority (e.g., federal Department of Justice).

- The official federal code is the *United States Code* (**USC**).

- To determine whether a state code is official or unofficial consult the *Bluebook*, or the list of state codes available at Findlaw (http://statelaws.findlaw.com/state-codes/).

- An **unofficial code** is a code of the laws of the United States prepared by a private publisher. Unofficial federal codes include:

  ☐ the *United States Code Service* (**USCS**) and
  ☐ the *United States Code Annotated* (**USCA**).

	Title (exceptionally),	division of code (if applicable)	abbreviated code name	title number (if applicable)	section	(publisher (if applicable)	supplement (if applicable)	year).
Official codes	*Patient Protection and Affordable Care Act,*	42	USC		§ 18001			(2010).
			Minn Stat		§ 169.94			(2004).
			IRC		§ 61			(2000).
Unofficial codes		8	USCA		§ 1182	(West		1997).
			Pa Stat Ann	tit 63	§ 425.3	(West	Supp	1986).
			Wis Stat Ann		§ 939.645	(West	Supp	1992).

- Once a statute has been codified, its original title is not usually cited. **Include the title only for a special reason** (e.g., because it is commonly known by that name). Italicize the title.

- If the code is **divided** into separate numbered titles, chapters, or volumes, include the number of that division. When citing federal codes, indicate the division before the code abbreviation.

- Do not italicize the abbreviated name of the code. For citations to the Internal Revenue Code, it is possible to replace **26 USC** with **IRC**.

- When citing to an unofficial code, include the name of the publisher before the year, or before **Supp** where applicable.

- When citing a supplement found in a pocket insert, place **Supp** before the year.

- Include the year of publication of the code in parentheses at the end of the citation. When citing a **bound volume**, provide the year that appears on the spine of the volume. When citing a **supplement**, provide the year that appears on the title page of the supplement.

Foreign Sources

7.4.1.2.2 Session Laws

Session laws are the statutes passed by a session of Congress, bound and indexed chronologically. Session laws track the historical development of a law.

Title or date of enact-ment,	public law num-ber or chapter number,	section (option-al),	session laws re-porter	first page of act	pinpoint to repor-ter	(year) (if not in ti-tle)	(codifi-cation informa-tion) (option-al).
The In-dian Child Welfare Act of 1978,	Pub L No 95-608,		92 Stat	3069			(codified as amended at 25 USC § 1901–1963 (1988)).
Antiter-rorism and Ef-fective Death Penalty Act of 1996,	Pub L No 104–132,	§ 327,	110 Stat	1214	at 1257	(1997).	
Act of 25 April 1978,	c 515,	§ 3,	1978 Ala Acts	569	at 570.		

▪ Provide the name of the statute in italics. If it has no name, identify it by the date of its enactment in Roman type, not italics (**Act of 25 April 1978**). If no date of enactment is available, identify it by the date on which the act came into effect (**Act effective [date]**).

▪ Provide the public law number, introduced by the abbreviation **Pub L No**, or the chapter number of the statute, introduced by **c**. The number before the hyphen in the public law number is the session. The number following the hyphen is the identifier.

▪ To cite a **particular section**, indicate the section number directly after the public law number or the chapter number. Include a pinpoint to the reporter.

▪ For federal statutes, the **official reporter** is the *Statutes at Large*, abbreviated to **Stat**. The abbreviation of the reporter is preceded by the volume number, followed by the first page of the act. To determine whether a reporter of state session laws is official or unofficial, consult the *Bluebook*.

- Indicate a **pinpoint** following the citation to the first page of the act. Include a pinpoint to the particular section after the public law number or the chapter number.

- Indicate the **year the statute was enacted** in parentheses at the end of the citation, unless the year is part of the name of the statute. The year in the title might not coincide with the year in which the statute was published, in which case you must provide both. See the *Antiterrorism and Effective Death Penalty Act of 1996* example.

- **Codification information** for the law should be provided if it is available. If a single statute is divided and codified under many subject-headings of the code, indicate this with parenthetical information at the end of the citation (**(codified as amended in scattered sections of 26 USC)**).

7.4.1.2.3 Unofficial Reporters of Session Laws

Title,	public law number,	[volume]	unofficial reporter	pinpoint,	session law citation.
Veteran's Benefits Improvements Act of 1996,	Pub L No 104-275,	[1996]	USCCAN	3762,	110 Stat 3322.

- The most important unofficial reporter of session laws is the *United States Code Congressional and Administrative News*, abbreviated to **USCCAN**.

- When citing to the USCCAN, indicate the volume and page number of the *Statutes at Large* (**Stat**) in which the law will subsequently appear.

7.4.1.3 Uniform Codes, Uniform Acts, and Restatements

Title	section	(year of adoption).
UCC	§ 2-012	(1995).
Uniform Partnership Act	§ 23	(1969).
Restatements of Security	§ 51	(1941).
Restatement (Second) of the Law of Property	§ 15	(1977).

- **Uniform Codes** and **Uniform Acts** are proposed legislation, published by the National Conference of Commissioners of Uniform State Laws, to be adopted in all state legislatures, districts, and protectorates. **Restatements** are reports of the state of US common law on given topics and interpretation of statutes, published by the American Law Institute.

Foreign Sources

- Italicize the title, unless it is a code.
- Do not place a comma after the title of a code or a restatement.
- When more than one restatement has been produced, indicate the number in parentheses.
- At the end of the citation, in parentheses, indicate the year of adoption, promulgation, or latest amendment, which often appears on the title page.

7.4.1.4 Bills and Resolutions

7.4.1.4.1 Federal Bills

US,	Bill	house	number,	title,	Congress number,	year,	pinpoint	(status, if enacted).
US,	Bill	HR	1,	*No Child Left Behind Act of 2001,*	107th Cong,	2001		(enacted).
US,	Bill	S	7,	*Prescription Drug Benefit and Cost Containment Act of 2003,*	108th Cong,	2003,	s 107.	

- Abbreviate **House of Representatives** as **HR** and **Senate** as S.

7.4.1.4.2 Federal Resolutions

US,	type of resolution	number,	title,	Congress number,	year	(status, if enacted).
US,	HR Con Res	6,	*Expressing the Sense of the Congress Regarding the Need to Pass Legislation to Increase Penalties on Perpetrators of Hate Crimes,*	107th Cong,	2001.	
US,	HR Res	387,	*Providing for consideration of the bill (HR 3283) to enhance resources to enforce United States trade rights,*	109th Cong,	2005	(enacted).

Abbreviations of the type of resolution:

House Concurrent Resolutions	HR Con Res
House Resolutions	HR Res
House Joint Resolutions	HRJ Res
Senate Concurrent Resolutions	S Con Res
Senate Resolutions	S Res
Senate Joint Resolutions	SJ Res

7.4.1.4.3 State Bills and Resolutions

US,	type of bill or resolution	number,	*title,*	year or legislature number,	number or designation of legislative session,	state,	year,	pinpoint	(status, if enacted).
US,	AB	31,	*An Act to Add Section 51885 to the Education Code, Relating to Educational Technology,*	1997-98,	Reg Sess,	Cal,	1996,	s 1.	
US,	SR	10,	*Calling for the Establishment of a Delaware State Police Community Relations Task Force,*	141st Gen Assem,	Reg Sess,	Del,	2001		(enacted).

▨ In addition to Regular Sessions, state legislatures may hold **First, Second, and Third Extraordinary Sessions**. Abbreviate these as **1st Extra Sess**, **2d Extra Sess**, and **3d Extra Sess**, respectively. **Special Sessions** may be abbreviated **Spec Sess**.

▨ Abbreviate the state according to the list in **Appendix A-2**.

Foreign Sources

7.4.1.5 Regulations

7.4.1.5.1 The Code of Federal Regulations

The *Code of Federal Regulations* is the codification of the regulations of the United States, organized under the same 50 subject titles as the United States Code.

Title (exceptionally),	volume	reporter	section	(year).
EPA Effluent Limitations Guidelines,	40	CFR	§ 405.53	(1980).
	47	CFR	§ 73.609	(1994).

- Indicate the title of the rule or regulation when it is commonly known under that name.
- When possible, cite federal rules and regulations to the *Code of Federal Regulations*.
- The *Code of Federal Regulations* (**CFR**) is the official compilation of the federal government.

NB: For a list of official state administrative compilations, consult the *Bluebook*.

7.4.1.5.2 Administrative Registers

Administrative registers report, among other things, administrative regulations enacted by government authorities.

Title (if applicable)	volume	Fed Reg	first page	(year)	(codification information	pinpoint).
	44	Fed Reg	12437221	(1979)	(to be codified at 29 CFR	§ 552).
Outer Continental Shelf Air Regulations Consistency Update for California,	70	Fed Reg	19472	(2009)	(to be codified at 40 CFR	§ 55).

- When rules and regulations have not been codified, cite them to an administrative register.
- For federal rules and regulations, cite the *Federal Register* (**Fed Reg**).
- Include the number of the volume, the abbreviation of the register, the page number, and the year.
- When possible, at the end of the citation indicate where the rule or regulation will appear in the official compilation.

Foreign Sources

NB: To identify state administrative registers, and for more information on citing American legislation, consult the *Bluebook*.

7.4.2   Jurisprudence

7.4.2.1 *General Form*

Style of cause,	vol	reporter	(series)	first page	pinpoint	(jurisdiction and/ or court	year of decision)	(other information) (if applicable).
Texas Beef Group v Winfrey,	11	F Supp	(2d)	858		(ND Tex	1998).	
Dell Computer Corp,	121	FTC		616	at 619		(1996).	
Distribution Center of Columbus,	83	Lab Arb Rep (BNA)		163			(1984)	(Seidman, Arb).

▨ Administrative adjudications and arbitrations are cited in the same manner as other cases.

▨ For arbitrations, place the name of the arbitrator followed by a comma and **Arb** in parentheses at the end of the citation.

7.4.2.2 *Style of Cause*

▨ Indicate the style of cause according to the rules in section 3.3.

▨ For a state or country, use the common name, not the full formal name or abbreviation.

✓	*California v United States* *Larez v Los Angeles (City of)*
✗	*State of California v United States of America* *Larez v LA*

▨ If the case involves a city whose name could be mistaken for a state, enclose the relevant identifying information in parentheses: **New York (City of)** or **Washington (DC)**.

7.4.2.3 *Neutral Citation*

There is currently **no one uniform standard for neutral citation** in the United States, although some jurisdictions have adopted such citations. Consult the *Bluebook* for details.

7.4.2.4 *Reporter and Series*

▨ After the style of cause, provide the volume number, the reporter abbreviation, the series number, and the first page of the case. **There is always a space between the reporter abbreviation and the series number.**

> *Murray v Earle*, 405 **F (3d)** 278 (5th Cir 2005).
> *Scott v Sanford*, 60 **US** (19 How) 393 (1857).

▨ *US Reports* **prior to 1875** are also numbered consecutively for each editor. Place this number and the editor's name in parentheses after **US**.

Abbreviations of editors:

Wallace	Wall
Black	Black
Howard	How
Peters	Pet
Wheaton	Wheat
Cranch	Cranch
Dallas	Dall

Abbreviations of principal reporters:

Atlantic Reporter	A
California Reporter	Cal
Federal Reporter	F
Federal Supplement	F Supp
Lawyers' Edition	L Ed (2d)
New York Supplement	NYS
North Eastern Reporter	NE
North Western Reporter	NW
Pacific Reporter	P
South Eastern Reporter	SE
South Western Reporter	SW
Southern Reporter	So
Supreme Court Reporter	S Ct
United States Reports	US
United States Law Week	USLW

▓ For the United States Supreme Court, cite reporters in the following order of preference: **US → S Ct → L Ed (2d) → USLW**.

▓ For federal courts, cite to **F** or **F Supp**.

▓ For state courts, cite to a regional reporter in preference to a state reporter.

▓ See **Appendix C-3** for a list of common reporters and their abbreviations.

7.4.2.5 Pinpoint

United States v McVeigh, 153 F (3d) 1166 **at 1170** (10th Cir 1998).
McVeigh, *supra* note 1 **at 1173**.

▓ Place **at** before a pinpoint reference.

Foreign Sources

7.4.2.6 Court

7.4.2.6.1 Federal Courts

United States Supreme Court	*Bush v Gore*, 531 US 98 (2000). *Boy Scouts of America v Dale*, 68 USLW 4625 (**US** 28 June 2000).
Courts of Appeal	*United States v Kaczynski*, 154 F (3d) 930 (**9th Cir** 1998).
District Courts	*A&M Records v Napster*, 114 F Supp (2d) 896 (**ND Cal** 2000).

- The **United States Supreme Court** does not require an abbreviation unless the citation is to the *United States Law Week* (**USLW**). When citing to the USLW, place **US** and the full date in parentheses at the end of the citation.

- For Courts of Appeal cite the numbered circuit.

- Abbreviate the **District of Columbia Circuit Court** to **DC Cir** and the **Federal Circuit Court** to **Fed Cir**.

- For district courts provide the abbreviated name of the district.

7.4.2.6.2 State Courts

Peevyhouse v Garland Coal & Mining, 382 P (2d) 109 (**Okla Sup Ct** 1963).
Truman v Thomas, 165 **Cal** Rptr 308 (1980).
Hinterlong v Baldwin, 308 **Ill App** (3d) 441 (App Ct 1999).

- Provide the court and the jurisdiction in parentheses, using the abbreviations from **Appendices A-2 and B.**

- Omit the jurisdiction if it is obvious from the name of the reporter.

- Omit the court if it is the highest court in its jurisdiction.

7.4.2.7 Year of Decision

- Place the year of decision in parentheses at the end of the citation. If there is also a court abbreviation, combine the two within the same parentheses: (**App Ct 1999**).

Foreign Sources

7.4.2.8 Online Databases

7.4.2.8.1 Westlaw

Style of cause,	identifier given by service	pinpoint	(jurisdiction and/or court) (if applicable).
Fincher v Baker,	1997 WL 675447	at 2	(Ala Civ App).

If the only identifier is the one provided by Westlaw, the judgment is otherwise unreported.

7.4.2.8.2 Lexis

Style of cause,	identifier given by service	pinpoint	(jurisdiction and/or court) (if applicable).
Association for Molecular Pathology v Myriad Genetics,	2013 US Lexis 4540	at 5	(USSC).

If the only identifier is the one reported by Lexis, the judgment is otherwise unreported.

7.4.3 Government Documents

Indicate **US** at the beginning of the citation.

7.4.3.1 Debates

US,	Cong Rec,	edition,	volume,	part,	pinpoint	(date)	(speaker) (optional).
US,	Cong Rec,		vol 125,	15,	at 18691	(1979).	
US,	Cong Rec,	daily ed,	vol 143,	69,	at H3176	(22 May 1977)	(Rep Portman).

Cite congressional debates after 1873 to the *Congressional Record* (**Cong Rec**).

For information on how to cite earlier congressional debates, consult the *Bluebook*.

Use the **daily edition** only if the debate is not yet in the bound edition.

7.4.3.2 Committee Hearings

7.4.3.2.1 Federal

US,	title,	Congress number	(publication information)	pinpoint	(speaker) (optional).
US,	*Federal Property Campaign Fundraising Reform Act of 2000: Hearing on HR 4845 Before the House Committee of the Judiciary*,	106th Cong	(2000)	at 2–3.	
US,	*Assisted Suicide: Legal, Medical, Ethical and Social Issues: Hearing Before the Subcommittee on Health and Environment of the House Committee on Commerce*,	105th Cong	(Washington, DC: United States Government Printing Office, 1997)	at 2	(Dr C Everett Koop).

▨ Always cite the year of publication, and provide further publication information if available.

7.4.3.2.2 State

US,	title,	number of the legislative body or, if not numbered, the year,	legislature number or designation,	state	(publication information)	pinpoint	(speaker) (optional).
US,	*Rico Litigation: Hearing on S 1197 Before the Senate Comm On Commerce and Econ Dev*,	41st Legis,	1st Reg Sess 5,	Ariz	(1993)		(Barry Wong, policy analyst).

▨ Abbreviate the state according to the list in **Appendix A-2**.

▨ Always cite the year of publication, and provide further publication information if available.

Foreign Sources

7.4.3.3 Reports and Documents

7.4.3.3.1 Federal

7.4.3.3.1.1 Numbered Documents and Reports

US,	issuing body,	title	(number)	(publication information)	pinpoint.
US,		*Secrecy: Report of the Commission on Protecting and Reducing Government Secrecy: Pursuant to Public Law 236, 103rd Congress*	(S Doc No 105-2)	(Washington, DC: US Government Printing Office, 1997)	at 3.
US,	Senate Committee on the Budget, 111th Cong,	*Concurrent Resolution on the Budget FY 2010*		(Washington, DC: US Government Printing Office, 2009)	at 213.

▪ Indicate the issuing body unless it is named in the title of the report.

▪ Always cite the year of publication, and provide further publication information if available.

Abbreviations of numbers:

Documents	Reports
HR Doc No	HR Rep No
HR Misc Doc No	HR Conf Rep No
S Doc No	S Rep No
S Exec Doc No	

Foreign Sources

7.4.3.3.1.2 Unnumbered Documents and Committee Prints

US,	issuing body,	*title*	Committee Print (if relevant)	(publication information)	pinpoint.
US,	Staff of House Committee on Veterans' Affairs, 105th Cong,	*Persian Gulf Illnesses: An Overview,*	Committee Print	(1998)	at 15.
US,	National Commission on Children,	*Beyond Rhetoric: A New American Agenda for Children and Families*		(Washington, DC: The Commission, 1991)	at 41.

▨ Include the Congress number with the issuing body, if relevant.

▨ Always cite the year of publication, and provide further publication information if available.

7.4.3.3.2 State

	US,	issuing body,	*title*	(number) (if applicable)	(publication information)	pinpoint.
Numbered Documents and Reports	US,	California Energy Commission,	*Existing Renewable Resources Account, vol 1*	(500-01-014V1)	(2001).	
Unnumbered Documents	US,	Washington State Transport Commission,	*Washington's Transportation Plan 2003-2022*		(Washington State Department of Transportation, 2002).	

▨ Provide the document number, if available.

▨ Always cite the year of publication, and provide further publication information if available.

7.5   FRANCE

7.5.1   Legislation

7.5.1.1 Statutes and Other Legislative Instruments

Title,	JO,	publication date	(NC) (if applicable),	page,	parallel citation.
Loi n° 99-493 du 15 juin 1999,	JO,	16 June 1999,		8759,	(1999) D Lég 3.7.
Ordonnance n° 2001-766 du 29 août 2001,	JO,	31 August 2001,		13946,	(2001) D Lég 2564.
Décret du 5 décembre 1978 portant classement d'un site pittoresque,	JO,	6 December 1978	(NC),	9250.	

▦ Cite the title of the statute in French, but provide the date of publication and all related information in English.

▦ If the legislation has a number, then the descriptive title is optional. If the legislation does not have a number, include its descriptive title in full.

▦ Always cite first to the *Journal officiel de la République française*, abbreviated to **JO**, followed by the publication date and the page number. For JO supplements, place **(NC)** for *numéro complémentaire* after the publication date. For a list of earlier versions of the *Journal officiel*, consult section 4.4.2.

▦ When possible, provide a parallel citation to a French reporter, according to the rules at section 7.5.2.10.

7.5.1.2 Codes

Code civil des Français (1804–1807)	art 85 **CcF**
Code Napoléon (1807–1814)	art 85 **CN**
Code civil (1815–)	art 1536 **C civ**
Code pénal	art 113-10 **C pén**
Nouveau Code de procédure civile	art 1439 **NC proc civ**
Code de propriété intellectuelle	art 123(8) **CPI**
Code de procédure pénale	art 144(2) **C proc pén**

▨ Full citations are never used when referring to codes.

▨ To cite to one of the codes illustrated here, use the abbreviated name.

▨ To cite to another code, write the full title of the code at the first reference, and create a short form if needed (e.g., **art 1** *Code de la consommation* **[C cons]**).

7.5.2 Jurisprudence

▨ Always use the **page numbers at the top** of the pages of *La semaine juridique* and not the numbers at the bottom.

7.5.2.1 General Form

	Court (if applicable)	city (if applicable),	date,	*style of cause* (if applicable),	(year of publication)	repor-ter	section (if applicable),	page and/or deci-sion number	(Annotation) (if applicable).
Cour de Cassation	Cass civ 2ᵉ,		14 June 2001,		(2001)	D	Jur,	3075	(Annotation Didier Cholet).
Court of Appeal	CA	Paris,	12 January 2000,		(2000)	JCP	II,	10433	(Annotation Philippe Pierre).
Court of First Instance	Trib gr inst	Mans,	7 September 1999,		(2000)	JCP	II,	10258	(Annotation Colette Saujot).

7.5.2.2 Court

7.5.2.2.1 Courts of First Instance

Court	city,	date,	*style of cause* (if applicable),	(year of publication	session) (if applicable)	reporter	section (if applicable)	page	(Annotation) (if applicable).
Trib admin	Nantes,	27 November 1981,	*Mme Robin,*	(1981)		Rec		544.	
Trib gr inst	Paris,	10 September 1998,		(1999	1ʳᵉ sem)	Gaz Pal	Jur	37.	

▨ Indicate the city where the court sits after the name of the court.

Abbreviations of the names of the courts:

Tribunal administratif	Trib admin
Tribunal civil or Tribunal de première instance (Civil court of original general jurisdiction, prior to 1958)	Trib civ
Tribunal commercial	Trib com
Tribunal correctionnel	Trib corr
Tribunal de grande instance (Civil court of original general jurisdiction, after 1958)	Trib gr inst
Tribunal d'instance (Small claims court, after 1958)	Trib inst

For a more complete list, see **Appendix B-2**.

7.5.2.2.2 Court of Appeal

CA	city,	date,	style of cause (if applicable)	(year of publi-cation	session) (if applic-able)	reporter	sec-tion	page,	decision number	(Annota-tion).
CA	Or-léans,	23 Oc-tober 1997,		(1999	1re sem)	Gaz Pal	Jur	217,		(Annotation Benoît de Roque-feuil).
CA	Paris,	21 mai 2008,	K c E et Sté nationale de télévision France 2	(2008)		JCP	Jur	390,	No 06/07678.	

7.5.2.2.3 Cour de cassation

Chamber,	date,	(year of publica-tion)	reporter	section	page,	decision number (if applicable).
Cass civ 1re,	30 March 1999,	(1999)	Bull civ	I	77,	No 118.
Cass crim,	24 February 2009,	(2009)	D Jur		951,	No 08-87.409.

Abbreviations of chambers:

Chambre civile	Cass civ 1re Cass civ 2e Cass civ 3^{e}
Chambre commerciale	Cass com
Chambre sociale	Cass soc
Chambre criminelle	Cass crim
Chambre des requêtes	Cass req
Chambres réunies (before 1967)	Cass Ch réun
Assemblée plénière (after 1967)	Cass Ass plén
Chambre mixte	Cass mixte

7.5.2.2.4 Conseil d'État

Court,	date,	*style of cause,*	(year of publication)	reporter	page.
CE,	27 January 1984,	*Ordre des avocats de la Polynésie française,*	(1984)	Rec	20.

▢ Abbreviate *Conseil d'État* to **CE**.

7.5.2.2.5 Conseil constitutionnel

Court,	date,	*style of cause,*	(year of publication)	reporter	page,	decision number.
Cons const,	25 June 1986,	*Privatisations,*	(1986)	Rec	61,	86-207 DC.

▢ Abbreviate **Conseil constitutionnel** to **Cons const**.

▢ Indicate the decision number at the end of the citation.

Foreign Sources

7.5.2.3 *Style of Cause*

> Cass civ 1re, 5 February 1968, *Ligny-Luxembourg*, (1968 1re sem) Gaz Pal Jur 264.

▨ **Omit the style of cause except in the following circumstances**:

☐ when citing a decision from an administrative tribunal or the Conseil d'État (but not in every case);

☐ when citing an unpublished decision or one that is summarized in the *Sommaire* section of a reporter;

☐ to avoid confusion (e.g. where two decisions were rendered on the same day by the same court);

☐ when the case is better known by the names of the parties than by the usual information.

▨ When the style of cause is included, italicize it and place it after the date, set off by commas.

7.5.2.4 *Year*

> Paris, 5 February 1999, (**1999** 2^e sem) Gaz Pal Jur 452.

▨ Include the year of publication in parentheses, before the abbreviation of the reporter.

7.5.2.5 *Session*

▨ When citing the *Gazette du Palais* (**Gaz Pal**), indicate the session number in the parentheses, after the year of publication.

7.5.2.6 *Reporter*

Court	date,	year of publication of reporter	session number) (if applicable)	reporter	section	page and/ or decision number.
Cass civ 3e,	23 June 1999,	(2000)		JCP	II	10333.
Cass soc,	3 February 1998,	(1998	1re sem)	Gaz Pal	Jur	176.

▨ Place a single space between each informational element: **(1998 1re sem) Gaz Pal Jur 176.**

Common French reporters:

Actualité juridique de droit administratif	AJDA
Bulletin de la Cour de cassation, section civile	Bull civ
Gazette du Palais	Gaz Pal
Recueil Dalloz and *Recueil Dalloz et Sirey* (1945-present)	D
Recueil des décisions du Conseil d'État or *Recueil Lebon*	RCE or Rec
Semaine Juridique (1937-present)	JCP

See **Appendix C-3** for more French reporter abbreviations.

7.5.2.7 Section

▢ When the sections in the volume are numbered, indicate the section number in Roman numerals after the year of publication.

▢ When the sections are not numbered, provide the abbreviation of the section title.

▢ Do not include the section when citing the *Recueil Lebon* (**Rec**) or the *Actualité juridique de droit administratif* (**AJDA**).

Abbreviation of section titles:

Assemblée plénière	Ass plén
Chambre mixte	Ch Mixte
Chambres des requêtes	Req
Chambres réunies	Ch réun
Chroniques	Chron
Doctrine	Doctr
Informations rapides	Inf
Jurisprudence	Jur
Législation, Lois et décrets, Textes de lois, etc.	Lég
Panorama de jurisprudence	Pan
Sommaire	Somm

Foreign Sources

7.5.2.8 Page and Decision Number

Semaine juridique	Ass plén, 6 November 1998, (1999) JCP II **10000 bis**.
Bulletin de la Cour de cassation	Cass civ 2e, 7 June 2001, (2001) Bull civ II **75, No 110**.

- Indicate the page number after the section or the year of publication.

- For the *Semaine Juridique*, provide the decision number (e.g., **10000 bis**).

- For the *Bulletin de la Cour de cassation* cite both the page and decision number separated by a comma and a space.

7.5.2.9 Pinpoint

Trib gr inst Narbonne, 12 March 1999, (1999 1re sem) Gaz Pal Jur 405 **at 406**.

- Pinpoint citations are rarely used, given the brevity of most decisions. If required, it is always placed after the page number and introduced by **at**.

7.5.2.10 Parallel Citation

First citation,	parallel citation.
Cass civ 1re, 26 May 1999, (1999) Bull civ I 115, No 175,	**(1999) JCP II 10112**.
Cass crim, 21 janvier 2009, (2009) Bull crim 74, n° 08-83.492,	**(2009) D Jur 374.**

7.5.2.11 Annotations, Reports, and Conclusions

Cass civ 1re, 6 juillet 1999, (1999) JCP II 10217 **(Annotation Thierry Garé)**.

- Any annotation or other writing appended to or included with a case must be indicated at the end of the citation, in parentheses.

- Write **Annotation**, **Report**, or **Conclusion** followed by the author's name.

7.5.3 Government Documents

Indicate **France** at the beginning of the citation of every government document.

7.5.3.1 Debates

7.5.3.1.1 From 1787 to 1860

France,	*Archives parlemen- taires,*	series,	tome,	date,	pinpoint	(speaker) (optional).
France,	*Archives parlemen- taires,*	1st series,	t 83,	5 January 1794,	s 3.	

Cite to *Archives parlementaires: Recueil complet des débats législatifs et politiques des chambres françaises*, using the short title ***Archives parlementaires***.

Indicate the series after the title. The first series covers 1787–1799, the second 1800–1860.

Pinpoint to **sections**, not to articles.

Add the name of the speaker (if provided) in parentheses at the end of the citation.

7.5.3.1.2 1871 to the Present

France,	*journal,*	house,	Débats parle- men- taires,	division,	number and date,	pin- point,	(speak- er) (op- tional).
France,	JO,	Assem- blée nationale,	Débats parle- men- taires,	Compte rendu intégral,	2nd ses- sion of 10 February 2004,	at 1570,	(Pascal Clément).
France,	JO,	Sénat,	Débats parle- men- taires,	Compte rendu intégral,	Session of 20 No- vember 2003.		

From 1871 to the present, parliamentary debates are published in the ***Journal officiel de la République française***, abbreviated ***JO***.

☐ Indicate the house, followed by **Débats parlementaires**.

☐ 1871–1880: omit both the house and **Débats parlementaires**.

☐ 1943–1945; 1945–1946; 1947–1958: indicate only **Débats de [name of house]**.

Names of houses according to the period:

1881–1940	Chambre des députés	1880–1940	Sénat
1943–1945	Assemblée consultative provisoire		
1945–1946	Assemblée constituante		
1947–1958	Assemblée de l'Union française	1946–1958	Conseil de la République
1958–	Assemblée nationale	1958–	Sénat

■ Indicate the division only from 1980 to the present for the Assemblée nationale, and from 1983 to the present for the Sénat. The divisions are **Compte rendu intégral** and **Questions écrites remises à la Présidence de l'Assemblée nationale et réponses des ministres** for the Assemblée nationale, and **Compte rendu intégral** and **Questions remises à la Présidence du Sénat et réponses des ministres aux questions écrites** for the Sénat.

■ Indicate the number (if provided) and the date of the session followed by the pinpoint.

■ The name of the speaker may be added in parentheses at the end of the citation.

7.5.3.2 Earlier Versions of the Journal officiel

France,	*title,*	**year** or **date of publication,**	**tome** or volume	**pinpoint.**
France,	*Journal officiel de l'Empire français,*	1868,	t 1	at 14.
France,	*Gazette nationale, ou le Moniteur universel,*	1 July 1791,	t 9	at 3.

■ **Before 1871,** parliamentary debates, parliamentary documents, and non-parliamentary documents were generally published in the various precursors to the *Journal officiel de la République française*:

1789–1810	*Gazette nationale, ou le Moniteur universel*
1811–1848	*Moniteur universel*
1848–1852	*Moniteur universel, Journal officiel de la République*
1852–1870	*Journal officiel de l'Empire français*

▨   The citation form varies according to the organization of the journal. In general, the citation should include at least the title, the year in question or the date of publication, the tome or volume (if any), and the pinpoint.

7.5.3.3 Parliamentary Documents

7.5.3.3.1 Travaux et réunions parlementaires

France,	house,	issuing body,	"title",	Compte rendu or Bulletin	(date)	(President) (optional).
France,	Assemblée nationale,	Délégation aux droits des femmes,	"Auditions sur le suivi de l'application des lois relatives à l'IVG et à la contraception",	Compte rendu No 4	(6 November 2001)	(President: Martine Lignières-Cassou).
France,	Sénat,	Commission des affaires étrangères,	"Auditions de M. Dominique de Villepin, Ministre des affaires étrangères",	Bulletin de la semaine du 27 janvier 2003	(28 January 2003)	(President: André Dulait).

▨   Indicate the title of the *travaux*, then the number of the corresponding **Compte rendu** (for *travaux* of the Assemblée nationale) or the date of the **Bulletin** (for *travaux* of the Sénat). Unlike **Compte rendu**, *Bulletin* should be in italics.

▨   Add the name of the president (if provided) in parentheses at the end of the citation.

7.5.3.3.2 Rapports d'information (Reports)

France,	house,	issuing body (if applicable),	*title,*	by author(s),	report number	(date)	pin-point.
France,	Sénat,	Déléga-tion pour l'Union europé-enne,	*Le projet de traité établis-sant une Constitu-tion pour l'Europe,*	by Hubert Haenel,	Report No 3	(1 Octo-ber 2003)	at 4.
France,	Assem-blée na-tionale,		*Rapport d'infor-mation déposé en appli-cation de l'article 145 du Règle-ment par la mission d'infor-mation commune sur le prix des car-burants dans les départe-ments d'outre-mer,*	by Jac-ques Le Guen & Jérôme Cahuzac,	Report No 1885	(23 July 2009)	at 63.

7.5.3.4 Non-parliamentary Documents

France,	issuing body,	*title*,	report number or volume,	publica- tion infor- mation	pinpoint	(addition- al infor- mation) (optional).
France,		*Commis- sion d'en- quête sur la sécurité du transport maritime des pro- duits dan- gereux ou polluants*,	Report No 2535, vol 1,			(5 July 2000; Pre- sident: Da- niel Paul).
France,	Conseil économi- que et so- cial,	*La conjonc- ture écono- mique et sociale en 2005*,		Avis et rap- ports du Conseil économi- que et so- cial, *JO*, No 2005-09	at I-8	(1 June 2005; re- port by Luc Guyau).
France,	Ministère de la jus- tice,	*Bulletin of- ficiel*,	No 82		at 3	(1 April–30 June 2001).

Follow the rules for Canadian non-parliamentary documents in section 4.2.

7.6   AUSTRALIA

7.6.1   Legislation

7.6.1.1 Statutes

Title	(jurisdiction),	pinpoint.
Corporations Act 2001	(Cth).	
Electricity Reform Act 2001	(NT).	
Marine Pollution Act 1987	(NSW),	s 53(1)(d).

Cite the act's official short title in italics. Include the year of act as part of the title.

▨   Place the abbreviation of the jurisdiction after the title.

Abbreviations of jurisdictions:

Commonwealth	Cth
Australian Capital Territory	ACT
New South Wales	NSW
Northern Territory	NT
Queensland	Qld
South Australia	SA
Tasmania	Tas
Victoria	Vic
Western Australia	WA

Statutory compilations:

Acts of Parliament of the Commonwealth of Australia		Queensland Statutes
Laws of the Australian Capital Territory, Acts		South Australia Statutes
Statutes of New South Wales		Tasmanian Statutes
Northern Territory of Australia Laws		Acts of the Victorian Parliament
Laws of the Northern Territory of Australia		Victorian Statutes
Queensland Acts		Statutes of Western Australia

7.6.1.2 Delegated Legislation (Regulations)

Title	(regulatory compilations or session laws),	pinpoint.
Admiralty Rules 2002	(Cth),	r 5(b).
Income Tax Regulations (Amendment) 1996	(Cth).	
Education Regulation 2005	(ACT),	s 5.

Foreign Sources

Regulations and Rules generally follow the same style as statutes (section 7.6.1.1).

Compilations of regulations:

Commonwealth Statutory Rules
Laws of the Australian Capital Territory, Subordinate Legislation
New South Wales Rules, Regulations, and By-Laws
Queensland Subordinate Legislation
Tasmanian Statutory Rules
Victorian Statutory Rules, Regulations, and By-Laws
Western Australia Subsidiary Legislation

7.6.2   Jurisprudence

7.6.2.1 General Form

Style of cause	(year),	neutral citation	[year of reporter]	vol	reporter	page	(court) (if required).
Neilson v Overseas Projects Corporation of Victoria Ltd,		[2005] HCA 54.					
Macleod v Australian Securities and Investment Commission,		[2002] HCA 37,		211	CLR	287.	
Standard Portland Cement Company Pty Ltd v Good	(1983),			57	ALJR	151	(PC).
Thwaites v Ryan	(1983),		[1984]		VR	65	(SC).

Provide the year of reporter only if it differs from the year of judgment.

7.6.2.2 Neutral Citation

[year]	court	number	pinpoint.
[2005]	HCA	54	at para 15.

Many Australian courts have adopted neutral citation. Neutral citation in Australia follows the same format as Canadian neutral citation (see section 3.5) except that the year is placed in square brackets.

7.6.2.3 Reporter

7.6.2.3.1 Law Reports

Abbreviations of the series for the *Law Reports*:

Commonwealth Law Reports (1903–present)—Official	CLR
Australian Law Reports (1973–present)	ALR
Federal Court Reports (1984–present)—Official	FCR
Federal Law Reports (1956–present)	FLR
Australian Law Journal Reports (1958–present)	ALJR
New South Wales Law Reports (1971–present)—Official	NSWLR
Queensland State Reports (1902–1957)—Official	Qd SR
Queensland Reports (1958–present)—Official	Qd R
South Australia State Reports (1922–present)—Official	SASR
Tasmanian Law Reports (1896–1940)—Official	Tas LR
Tasmanian State Reports (1941–1978)	Tas SR
Tasmanian Reports (1979–present)—Official	Tas R
Victorian Law Reports (1875–1956)	VLR
Victorian Reports (1957–present)—Official	VR
Western Australia Law Reports (1899–1959)	WALR
Western Australia Law Reports (1960–present)—Official	WAR
Australian Capital Territory Reports (1973–present)	ACTR
Northern Territory Reports (1978–present)	NTR
Northern Territory Law Reports (1992–present)	NTLR

For **Privy Council** (PC) and **High Court of Australia** (HCA) decisions, cite to (in order of preference): **CLR**, **ALR**.

▨ For other federal court decisions, cite to the official **FCR** before **FLR**.

▨ For Australian States and Territories, cite to the official state or territorial court reporter when possible.

7.6.2.4 Jurisdiction and Court

Abbreviations of the courts:

Court	Abbreviation and identifiers
Privy Council (Australia)	PC
High Court of Australia	HCA
Federal Court of Australia	FCA
Supreme Court of Queensland—Court of Appeal	QCA
Supreme Court of Queensland	QSC
Supreme Court of the Australian Capital Territory	ACTSC
Supreme Court of New South Wales	NSWSC
Supreme Court of New South Wales—Court of Appeal	NSWCA
Supreme Court of Tasmania	TASSC
Supreme Court of Victoria—Court of Appeal	VSCA
Supreme Court of Victoria	VSC
Supreme Court of Southern Australia	SASC
District Court of Southern Australia	SADC
Supreme Court of Western Australia	WASC
Supreme Court of Western Australia—Court of Appeal	WASCA
Supreme Court of the Northern Territory	NTSC

▨ For state and territorial courts, if the jurisdiction is evident from the reporter cited, only indicate the level of court.

7.6.3   Government Documents

Place **Austl** at the beginning of the citation.

7.6.3.1 Debates

Austl,	jurisdic-tion,	house,	*Parliamentary Debates*	(date)	pinpoint	(speaker) (optional).
Austl,	Common-wealth,	House of Represen-tatives,	*Parliamentary Debates*	(17 September 2001)	at 30739	(Mr Howard, Prime Minister).
Austl,	Victoria,	Legislative Assembly,	*Parliamentary Debates*	(23 October 1968)	at 1197.	

▨ After **Austl**, indicate the jurisdiction. See **Appendix A-3** for Australian abbreviations.

▨ Always indicate the reporter as **Parliamentary Debates**.

7.6.3.2 Parliamentary Papers

Austl,	jurisdiction,	*title,*	number	(year)	pinpoint.
Austl,	Common-wealth,	*Department of Foreign Affairs Annual Report 1975,*	Parl Paper No 142	(1976)	at 5.
Austl,	Common-wealth,	*Community Affairs Legislation Committee — Senate Standing — Compliance Audits on Medicare Benefits,*	Parl Paper No 118.		

▨ The number is preceded by **Parl Paper No**.

7.6.3.3 Non-Parliamentary Papers

Austl,	juris-diction,	issuing body,	*title*	(nature of pa-per)	by author(s) (if applic-able)	(publication information)	pin-point.
Austl,	Com-mon-wealth,	Royal Com-mission into Aboriginal Deaths in Custody,	*Report of the Inquiry into the Death of Stanley John Gollan*		by Com-missioner Elliott Johnston	(Canberra: Australian Government Publishing Service, 1990)	at 31.
Austl,	Com-mon-wealth,	Law Reform Commis-sion,	*Annual Re-port 1998*	(Report No 49)		(Canberra: Australian Government Publishing Service, 1988).	

7.6.3.4 Ministerial Documents

Author,	jurisdic-tion,	*title*,	document service,	number	(date)	pinpoint.
Paul Keat-ing,	Common-wealth (Austl),	*Opening of the Global Cultural Di-versity Confer-ence,*	Ministerial Document Service,	No 172/94-95	(27 April 1995)	at 5977.

If additional information is required to identify the jurisdiction as within Australia, include **Austl** in parentheses following the jurisdiction named and before the comma preceding the title.

7.7   NEW ZEALAND

7.7.1   Legislation

7.7.1.1 Statutes

Title	(NZ),	year/number,	volume RS	first page.
Abolition of the Death Penalty Act 1989	(NZ),	1989/119,	41 RS	1.
Kiwifruit Industry Restructuring Act 1999	(NZ),	1999/95.		

▓ Provide the volume number followed by **RS** (for Reprint Series).

7.7.1.2 Delegated Legislation (Regulations)

Title	(NZ),	year/number or *Gazette* year,	*Gazette* page	vol RS	page.
Kiwifruit Export Regulations 1999	(NZ),	1999/310.			
Ticketing of Meat Notice 1979	(NZ),	*Gazette* 1979,	2030.		
High Court Amendment Rules (No 2) 1987	(NZ),	1987/169,		40 RS	904.

▓ Provide the volume number followed by **RS** (for Reprint Series).

Foreign Sources

7.7.2   Jurisprudence

7.7.2.1 General Form

Style of cause	(year of deci-sion),	neutral citation	[year of reporter]	volume	reporter	page	(jurisdic-tion and/or court) (if ap-plic-able).
R v Clarke,		[2005] NZSC 60.					
Pfizer v Commis-sioner of Patents,			[2005]	1	NZLR	362	(HC).

7.7.2.2 Neutral Citation

▨ The Supreme Court of New Zealand officially adopted the use of neutral citation for judgments rendered in 2005 and after. Neutral citation in New Zealand follows the same format as Canadian neutral citation (see section 3.5) except that the year is placed in square brackets.

[Year]	court	number of decision	pinpoint.
[2005]	NZSC	46	at para 4.

7.7.2.3 Reporter

7.7.2.3.1 Law Reports

▨ *Law Reports* are divided into series. **Reference is not made to the *Law Reports* but rather to the series**.

▨ There is no separate reporter for the **Judicial Committee of the Privy Council** (post-1932), the **Court of Appeal**, or the **High Court**. Include abbreviations **PC**, **CA**, or **HC** at the end of each citation to a case heard in that court.

Abbreviations of the series for the *Law Reports*:

New Zealand Law Reports (1883–present) (Privy Council, Supreme Court of New Zealand, Court of Appeal, High Court)	NZLR
New Zealand Privy Council Cases (1840–1932)	NZPCC
Gazette Law Reports (1898–1953) (Court of Appeal, Supreme Court (High Court), Court of Arbitration)	GLR
District Court Reports (1980–present)	NZDCR
Magistrates' Court Decisions (1939–1979)	MCD
Magistrates' Court Reports (1906–1953)	MCR
Book of Awards (1894–1991) (Arbitration Court, Court of Appeal)	BA
Employment Reports of New Zealand (1991–present) (Court of Appeal, Labour Court, Aircrew Industrial Tribunal)	ERNZ
New Zealand Industrial Law Reports (1987–1990) (Labour Court, Court of Appeal, Aircrew Industrial Tribunal)	NZILR
Judgments of the Arbitration Court of New Zealand (1979–1986) (Arbitration Court, Court of Appeal)	NZAC
New Zealand Family Law Reports (1981–present) (Privy Council, Court of Appeal, High Court, Family Court, Youth Court, District Court)	NZFLR
Criminal Reports of New Zealand (1993–present) (Court of Appeal, High Court)	CRNZ

7.7.2.4 Court

Privy Council (New Zealand)	PC
New Zealand Supreme Court — established in 2004	NZSC
New Zealand Court of Appeal	NZCA
New Zealand High Court	NZHC
District Court of New Zealand	DCNZ
Magistrates' Court of New Zealand	Mag Ct NZ
Coroners Court	Cor Ct
New Zealand Employment Court	NZ Empl Ct
Environment Court	Env Ct
Family Court of New Zealand	Fam Ct NZ
Maori Land Court / *Te Kooti Whenua Maori*	Maori Land Ct
Maori Appellate Court	Maori AC
New Zealand Youth Court	NZYC
Waitangi Tribunal / *Te Rōpū Whakamana i te Tiriti o Waitangi*	Waitangi Trib

NB: The **Supreme Court Act 2003** established the Supreme Court of New Zealand and abolished appeals from New Zealand to the Privy Council.

7.7.3   Government Documents

Indicate **NZ** at the beginning of the citation.

7.7.3.1 Debates

NZ,	*Hansard,*	stage: sub-ject	(question number)	date	(speaker) (optional).
NZ,	*Hansard,*	Questions To Ministers: Biosecurity Risk-Motor Vehicle and Equipment Imports	(No 3)	1 March 2000	(Ian Ewen-Street).

- *Hansard* provides the type of stage: **Questions to Ministers, Debate-General, Report of [a named] Committee** or **Miscellaneous**.

- Indicate the title of the debate as the subject (e.g., **Labour, Associate Minister-Accountability**). If the stage and the subject are the same, do not repeat the information.

7.7.3.2 Parliamentary Papers

NZ,	"title",	date,	session	(chair) (optional)	shoulder number.
NZ,	"Report of the Government Administration Committee, Inquiry into New Zealand's Adoption Laws",	August 2001,	46th Parliament	(Dianne Yates, Chair).	
NZ,	"Report of the Game Bird Habitat Trust Board for the year ended 31 August 1999",	February 2000,			C22.

- Do not add a space between the prefix of the shoulder and the actual number. The prefix of the shoulder number indicates the subject group, as follows:

Subject groups	Prefix
Political and Foreign Affairs	A
Finance and Revenue	B
Environment and Primary Production	C
Energy and Works	D
Welfare and Justice	E
Communications	F
General	G
Commissions, Royal Commissions	H

7.8 SINGAPORE

7.8.1 Legislation

NB: If there is no other indication that the legislative document is from Singapore, write **Rev Ed Sing** instead of **Rev Ed.**

7.8.1.1 Constitutional Documents

> *Constitution of the Republic of Singapore* (1999 Rev Ed), art 12(1).
> *Independence of Singapore Agreement 1965* (1985 Rev Ed).
> *Republic of Singapore Independence Act* (1985 Rev Ed), No 9 of 1965, s 2.

- Cite constitutional amendments in the same manner as ordinary legislation.
- Revised Edition is abbreviated to **Rev Ed**.

7.8.1.2 Statutes

Statutes from the Revised Edition	*Penal Code* (Cap 224, 1985 Rev Ed Sing), s 34.
Statutes not yet assigned a *Revised Edition* chapter number	*United Nations Act 2001* (No 44 of 2001, Sing), s 2.

- ***Revised Edition of the Statutes of the Republic of Singapore*** is abbreviated to **Rev Ed Sing**.

- **Cap** refers to Chapter. For recent acts that have not yet been assigned a chapter number in a revised edition, use the act number as in the example above. The act number is not to be confused with the **Acts Supplement** number, which is a number given to each supplement of the Government *Gazette* publishing subsequent amendments to the act.

- For legislation **prior to 15 August 1945**, the following abbreviations should be inserted after the title of the statute:

  ☐ For legislation enacted during the **Straits Settlements period** (1 April 1867 to 15 February 1942) use **(SS)**.

  ☐ For legislation enacted by the **Japanese Military Administration** during the occupation of Singapore (15 February 1942 to 15 August 1945) use **(JMA)**.

- For legislation enacted **after 15 August 1945**, write **(Sing)** to cite legislation passed during the following periods:

  ☐ British Military Administration;

  ☐ Colony of Singapore;

☐ State of Singapore, both before and during federation with Malaysia; and

☐ Republic of Singapore.

7.8.1.3 Amendments and Repeals

> *Penal Code* (Cap 224, 1985 Rev Ed Sing), s 73, **as amended by** *Penal Code (Amendment) Act*, No 18 of 1998, s 2.
> *Control of Imports and Exports Act* (Cap 56, 1985 Rev Ed Sing), **as amended by** *Regulation of Imports and Exports Act 1995* (No 24 of 1995, Sing).

▨ For further information, see section 2.1.11.

7.8.1.4 English Statutes Applicable in Singapore

> *Misrepresentation Act* (Cap 390, 1994 Rev Ed Sing), s 2.
> *Hire-Purchase Act* (Cap 125, 1999 Rev Ed Sing), s 5.

▨ English statutes now applicable in Singapore under the *Application of English Law Act* (Cap 7A, 1994 Rev Ed Sing) may be cited to their Singapore revised edition in the same manner as Singapore statutes.

7.8.1.5 Subsidiary Legislation (Rules, Regulations, Notifications, Orders)

7.8.1.5.1 Revised

Title	(Chapter number, legislation type and number, year Rev Ed Sing),	pinpoint.
Housing and Development Conveyancing Fees Rules	(Cap 129, R 2, 1999 Rev Ed Sing),	r 2.
Telecommunications (Class Licenses) Regulations	(Cap 323, Reg 3, 2000 Rev Ed Sing),	reg 10.

▨ When citing to revised subsidiary legislation, the chapter (**Cap**) refers to the chapter number of the parent legislation.

▨ For legislation type, use **Reg** for **regulation**, **R** for **rule**, **N** for **notification** or **O** for **order**, followed by the number.

▨ The year indicated should refer to the Revised Edition where the subsidiary legislation is found.

▨ **Revised Edition** is abbreviated to **Rev Ed**.

▦ Pinpoint using **reg** for **regulation**, **r** for **rule**, **o** for **order** or **n** for **notification**. Note that the type of pinpoint may differ from the type of instrument (e.g. a rule may contain orders).

7.8.1.5.2 Unrevised

Title	(S number/year Sing),	pinpoint.
United Nations (Anti-Terrorism Measures) Regulations 2001	(S 561/2001 Sing),	reg 3.
Monetary Authority of Singapore (Merchant Banks — Annual Fees) Notification 2005	(S 405/2005 Sing),	n 2(2).
Payment and Settlement Systems (finality and Netting) (Designated System) Order 2002	(S 620/2002 Sing),	o 3(a).

7.8.2   Jurisprudence

7.8.2.1 General Form

Style of cause	(year of decision),	neutral citation,	[year of reporter]	volume	reporter	page	(court) (if applic- able).
Er Joo Nguang v Public Prose- cutor,			[2000]	2	SLR	645	(HC).
Firstlink En- ergy Pte Ltd v Creanovate Pte Ltd,		[2006] SGHC 19.					
Re Ong Yew Teck	(1960),			26	MLJ	67	(Sing HC).

▦ Owing to the plurality of cultural practices governing names in Singapore, **always provide the full name of individuals**.

▦ Include the abbreviation **Sing** in parentheses at the end of the citation unless the citation is from the *Singapore Law Reports* or its reissue.

7.8.2.2 Neutral Citation

[year]	court	decision number	pinpoint.
[2005]	SGCA	55	[11].

- Singapore courts have officially adopted neutral citation. The form is the same as that of Canadian neutral citation, with the exception that the year is placed in brackets (see section 3.5).

- Provide the paragraph number in brackets (e.g., **[11]**).

- The Supreme Court established that citation to the Singapore Law Reports prevails over the neutral citation.

7.8.2.3 Reporters

Abbreviations of the principal reporters:

Singapore Law Reports	SLR
Singapore Law Reports (Reissue) (1965–2002)	SLR (R)
Malayan Law Journal	MLJ
Criminal Law Aid Scheme News	CLASN
Straits Settlements Law Reports	SSLR

- ***Singapore Law Reports (Reissue)*** for the years 1965–2002 changed the headnotes and numbered the paragraphs. The reissued volumes are as authoritative as the original *Singapore Law Reports.*

7.8.2.4 Court

Court abbreviations:

Court	abbrev	identifier
Court of Appeal	CA	SGCA
High Court	HC	SGHC
District Court	Dist Ct	SGDC
Magistrates' Court	Mag Ct	SGMC

- District Courts have no subdivisions.

Foreign Sources

7.8.2.5 Unreported Decisions without Neutral Citation

Style of cause	(date),	case number	(jurisdiction and/or court) (if applicable).
Public Prosecutor v Loh Chai Huat	(31 May 2001),	DAC No 36923 of 2000	(Sing Dist Ct).

7.8.2.6 Online Databases

Style of cause	(year),	database identifier given by service	(Lawnet)	pinpoint	(jurisdiction and/or court).
Beryl Claire Clarke and Others v Silkair (Singapore) Pte Ltd	(2001),	Suit Nos 1746, 1748–1752 of 1999	(Lawnet)	at para 10	(Sing HC).

7.8.3   Government Documents

7.8.3.1 Parliamentary Debates

Parliamentary Debates Singapore: Official Report,	volume	column	(date)	(speaker) (optional).
Parliamentary Debates Singapore: Official Report,	vol 73	at col 2436	(15 October 2001)	(Professor S Jayakumar).
Parliamentary Debates Singapore: Official Report,	vol 80	at col 2293	(13 February 2006)	(Professor Ivan Png Paak Liang).

7.8.3.2 Supreme Court Practice Directions

Practice directions are issued by the courts to regulate litigation. Until 1994, they were issued as discrete documents. Since then, they have been consolidated into a publication known as the *Supreme Court Practice Directions*.

7.8.3.2.1 Consolidated Practice Directions

Sing,	*The Supreme Court Practice Directions*	(year)	part	section.
Sing,	*The Supreme Court Practice Directions*	(2007)	part XV	s 123(1).

7.8.3.2.2 Amendments to Practice Directions

Sing,	Supreme Court PD	number	of year,	section.
Sing,	Supreme Court PD	No 1	of 2008,	s 7.

▨ Abbreviate **Practice Directions** to **PD**.

7.9 SOUTH AFRICA

7.9.1 Legislation

7.9.1.1 Statutes

Title	(S Afr),	number	of year,	pinpoint.
Constitution of the Republic of South Africa, 1996,		No 108	of 1996.	
Consumer Protection Act	(S Afr),	No 68	of 2008,	s 33.

7.9.1.2 Amendments and Repeals

Constitution of the Republic of South Africa, n° 108 of 1996 **as amended by** *Constitution of the Republic of South Africa Amendment Act*, n° 3 of 1999.

▨ For further information, see section 2.1.11.

Foreign Sources

7.9.1.2 Bills

Number,	title	(S Afr),	session,	parlia-ment,	year,	pinpoint.
B30-2005,	Precious Metals Bill	(S Afr),	3d sess,	3d Parl,	2005.	
B26-2005,	Nursing Bill	(S Afr),	3d sess,	3d Parl,	2005,	s 17.

7.9.2   Jurisprudence

7.9.2.1 General Form

Style of cause	(year of deci-sion),	[year of reporter]	volume	reporter	page	pinpoint	(jurisdic-tion and/or court) (if ap-plic-able).
Oosthui-zen v Stanley,		[1938]		AD	322		(S Afr SC).
Messina Associ-ated Car-riers v Klein-haus,		[2001]	3	S Afr LR	868		(SCA).

Cite to the **South African Law Reports** or to the **Butterworths Constitutional Law Reports** if possible.

7.9.2.2 Neutral Citation

[year]	court	number	paragraph.
[2006]	ZACC	25	at para 1.

Foreign Sources

▒ Some South African courts have officially adopted neutral citation. The form is the same as that of Canadian neutral citation (section 3.5), with the exception that the year is placed in brackets.

7.9.2.3 Reporters

Abbreviations of the principal reporters:

All South African Law Reports	All SA
Butterworths Constitutional Law Reports	B Const LR
South African Law Reports, Appellate Division (1910–1946)	S Afr LR, AD
South African Law Reports (1947–present)	S Afr LR

▒ For a more complete listing of reporters, see **Appendix C-3**.

7.9.2.4 Court

Abbreviations of the courts:

Bophuthatswana High Court	Boph HC
Cape Provincial Division	Cape Prov Div
Ciskei High Court	Ciskei HC
Constitutional Court of South Africa	S Afr Const Ct
Durban and Coast Local Division	D&C Local Div
Eastern Cape Division	E Cape Div
Labour Court of South Africa	S Afr Labour Ct
Labour Court of Appeal of South Africa	S Afr Labour CA
Land Claims Court of South Africa	S Afr Land Claims Ct
Natal Provincial Division	Natal Prov Div
Northern Cape Division	N Cape Div
Orange Free State Provincial Division	OFS Prov Div
South-Eastern Cape Division	SE Cape Div
Supreme Court of Appeal of South Africa	S Afr SC
Transkei High Court	Transkei HC
Transvaal Provincial Division	Transv Prov Div
Venda High Court	Venda HC
Witwatersrand Local Division	Wit Local Div

7.9.3   Government Documents

7.9.3.1 Debates

S Afr,	*Hansard,*	House,	date	pinpoint	(speaker) (optional).
S Afr,	*Hansard,*	National Assembly,	9 February 2009	at 1	(MJ Ellis).

Foreign Sources

7.9.3.2 Reports, Discussion Papers, and Issue Papers

Title,	Commission (if applicable),	Project number (if applicable)	(date)	pinpoint.
Truth and Re-conciliation Commission of South Africa Report			(29 October 1998)	at ch 1, para 91.
Report on Trafficking in Persons,	South African Law Reform Commission,	Project No 131	(August 2008)	at 23.
Domestic Violence,	South African Law Reform Commission,	Project No 100	(30 May 1997)	at 14.

▨ Write the name of the commission if it is not included in the title of the report.

INDEX

Arbitration Cases, E-138
published cases, E-138
unpublished cases, E-139

Archival Material, E-150

Australia, *see also* **Common Law Jurisdiction Sources**
debates, E-212
delegated legislation, E-209–10
jurisprudence, E-208–12
   courts, abbreviations of, E-212
   general form, E-210
   jurisdiction, E-212
   Law Reports, abbreviations,
      E-211–12
   neutral citation, E-210–11
   reporter, E-211–12
ministerial documents, E-214
non-parliamentary papers, E-214
parliamentary papers, E-213
regulations, E-209–10
   compilations of regulations,
      E-210
   general form, E-210
statutes, E-208–09
   abbreviations of jurisdictions, E-209
   general form, E-208
   statutory compilations, E-209
treaty neutral citation, E-92

Author. *See* **Books**

Authorities, Tables Of, E-3-4

Bibliographies, E-3–4

Bills, E-35

Book Reviews, E-139

Books, E-124
author, E-125
   editor of collection, E-125
   editor/reviser of text of another, E-126
      author's name part of title, E-126
      author's name not part of title, E-126

joint authors, E-125
single author, E-125
translator, E-126–27
   providing a translation,
      E-127
   published translation,
      E-126–27
edition, E-129
editor. *See* author
general form, E-124
loose-leaf format books, E-129–30
pinpoint, E-132
place of publication, E-130
publisher, E-130–31
title, E-127–28
   books, E-127–28
   published proceedings of conferences/
      symposia, E-128
translator. *See* author
volume number, E-128–29
   books in English, E-128
      volumes published under separate
         titles, E-128
      volumes published under single title,
         E-128
   books in French, E-129
year of publication, E-131

Brackets, E-3, E-6, E-9–10,
quotations, format of, E-17–18

By-Laws, Municipal, E-44

Canon Law, E-143

Case/Legislation Comments. E-140–41
France, E-140
   annotation, E-140
   general reporters, comments in, E-141
general form, E-140

Cases. *See* **Jurisprudence**

Civil Law Jurisdiction Sources, E-165

Codes, Generally, E-34–35

Codes of Professional Conduct, E-138

Comments, E-141

Common Law Jurisdiction Sources
Australia. *See* Australia
case history, E-163
electronic service, E-164
general form, E-163
judge, E-165
jurisdiction and court, E-164–65
neutral citation, E-164
New Zealand. *See* New Zealand
pinpoint, E-163
printed reporter, E-164
short form, E-163
Singapore. *See* Singapore
South Africa. *See* South Africa
style of cause, E-163
United Kingdom. *See* United Kingdom
United States. *See* United States
unreported decision, E-164
year, E-163

Conference Address and Papers, E-146

Constitutional Statutes,
  E-33
pinpoint, E-34
sources of, E-33

Course Materials, E-146–47

Dictionaries, E-133
encyclopaedias, E-134
general dictionaries, E-133
specialized dictionaries, E-133–34

Documents. *See* **Government Documents;**
  International Documents

Electronic Sources, *see also* **Internet Sites**
digital media (DVD, CD-ROM),
  E-156–57
digital object identifiers, E-157
online databases, E-153
online journals, E-154
online video and video aggregators, E-156
social media, E-155–56
  Facebook posts, E-155

  Reddit posts, E-156
  Twitter posts (tweets), E-155
web logs (blogs), E-154
  comments, E-155
  posts, E-154

Encyclopedias, E-134

Encyclopedic Digests, E-134
Canadian Encyclopedic Digest, E-134
  online edition, E-135
  print edition, E-134
common law, E-136
France, E-136–37
  abbreviations, E-137
  general form, E-136–37
  subject headings, E-137–38
Halsbury's Laws of Canada,
  E-135–36
  online edition, E-136
  print edition, E-135

Essay Collection, E-132–33

European Union Documents. *See* **International Documents**

Factum, E-4–6

Footnotes, E-6–9
combined, E-7
indication of in text, E-6
introductory signals, E-7–8
non-English sources, citation of, E-7
parenthetical information within, E-9
when to use, E-6
where to place, E-7
textual footnotes, E-6

Foreign Language
footnotes, E-18
quotations, E-18
source, E-18
writing in, E-18–19

Foreign Sources. *See* **Common Law Jurisdiction Sources; France**

France, Sources From, *see also* **Case/Legislation Comments; Encyclopedic Digests, E-134**
codes, E-197–98
debates, E-204–06
  1871 to present, E-204–05
  1787 to 1860, 7.5.3.1.1, E-204
Journal official, earlier versions of, E-205–06
jurisprudence, E-198–203
  annotations, reports and conclusions, E-203
  courts, E-198–200
    abbreviation of chambers, E-199–200
    abbreviations of names of, E-199
    Conseil constitutionnel, E-200
    Conseil d'Etat, E-200
    Cour de cassation, E-199
    Court of Appeal, E-199
    courts of first instance, E-198
  Gazette du Palais, E-201
  general form, E-198
  page and decision number, E-203
  parallel citation, E-203
  pinpoint citation, E-203
  reports, style and names, E-201–202
  section titles, E-202
  session, E-201
  style of cause, E-201
  year, E-201
non-parliamentary documents, E-208
Parliamentary documents, E-206–07
  rapports d'information (reports), E-207
  travaux et reunions parlementaires, E-206
periodicals, E-122
statutes and other legislative instruments, E-197

Gazettes
general form, E-41–2
jurisdictional abbreviations of, E-42
Orders in Council, E-42–43
  federal, E-43
  Privy Council abbreviation, E-43
  provincial and territorial, E-43
Proclamation, E-44
Royal instruction, E-44

Government Documents
intergovernmental conferences, public papers of, E-85
non-Parliamentary documents, E-80–85
  articles, E-82–83
  book-length publications, E-81–82
  bulletins, E-82–83
  general form, E-81
  manuals, E-81–82
  reports, E-81–82
  reports of inquiries and commissions, E-84
    multiple titles, under, E-84
    single title, under, E-84
  short publications, E-82–83
  tax information circulars, E-83
  tax interpretation bulletins, E-83
Parliamentary papers, E-77–80
  debates, E-77
  journals, E-78
  order papers, E-78
  reports published in debates, E-80
  reports published separately, E-80
  sessional papers, E-79
  votes and proceedings, E-79

Historical Legal Material, E-142–44
Canon law, E-143
Roman law, E-142
Talmudic law, E-143–44

***Ibid*, E-12**

***Infra*, E-13**

Intellectual Property, E-151–52
copyright, E-152
patents, E-151
trade-marks, E-151

International Cases, E-102–13
Canada-United States Free Trade Agreement Panels, E-111
Court of Justice of the European Communities, E-105
European Commission of Human Rights, E-105–06
  before 1999, E-105–06

1999 and later, E-106
European Court of First Instance, E-105
European Court of Human Rights,
    E-105–06
    before 1999, E-105–06
    1999 and later, E-106
General Agreement on Tariffs and Trade
    1947 Panel Reports, E-109–10
Inter-American Commission on Human
    Rights, E-108
Inter-American Court of Human Rights,
    E-107–08
    advisory opinions, E-107
    documents, E-107–08
    judgments, E-107
    oral arguments, E-107–08
    orders, E-107
    pleadings, E-107–08
International Court of Justice (1946–present),
    E-103–05
    advisory opinions, E-104
    documents, E-104–05
    judgments, E-104
    oral arguments, E-104–05
    orders, E-104
    pleadings, E-104–05
international arbitration cases, E-112
international criminal tribunals, E-108–09
international law cases decided before
    national courts, E-113
North American Free Trade Agreement
    Binational Panels, E-111–13
Permanent Court of International Justice
    (1922–1946), E-102–03
    advisory opinions, E-102–03
    documents, E-103
    judgments, E-102–03
    oral arguments, E-103
    orders, E-102–03
    pleadings, E-103
World Intellectual Property Organization
    arbitration cases, E-112
    Uniform Domain Name Dispute
        Resolution Policy, E-112
World Trade Organization Panel and
    Appellate Body Reports, E-110

International Documents
Council of Europe documents, E-98–99
European Union documents, E-96–98
    debates of European Parliament, E-97
    decisions, E-96–97
    directives, E-96–97
    general publications, E-98
    information and notices, E-98
    Official Journal of the European Union,
        E-98
    periodicals, E-98
    regulations, E-97
General Agreement on Tariffs and Trade
    documents, E-100–01
international agreements, E-89–92
Organization for Economic Co-operation
    and Development documents, E-101
Organization of American States docu-
    ments, E-99–100
treaties, E-89–92
    Australian treaty neutral citation, E-92
    First Nations treaties, E-102
United Nations documents, E-92–96
    abbreviations used, E-92
    annexes, E-95
    Charter of the United Nations, E-92
    decisions, E-94
    masthead documents, E-95
    meetings, E-93
    mimeographs, E-95
    official records, E-92–93
    periodicals, E-96
    reports, E-94
    resolutions, E-94
    sales publications, E-96
    supplements, E-94
    yearbooks, E-96
World Trade Organization documents,
    E-100–01

International Material
cases. *See* International Cases
documents. *See* International Documents
internet sites, E-113

Internet Sites, *see also* **Electronic Sources;
    International Material**

Interviews, E-150

In-text References, E-4–6

Jurisprudence, *see also* **Arbitration Cases; International Cases**
administrative bodies and tribunals, E-72–73
  online decisions, E-73
  printed report decisions, E-72
arguments, E-73–74
court, E-66–67
evidentiary documents, E-73–74
history of case, E-68–71
  leave to appeal, E-69–71
  prior, E-68
  prior and subsequent, E-69
  subsequent, E-68–69
interlocutory judgments, E-72
judge, E-67
jurisdiction, E-66–67
motions, E-72
neutral citation, E-57–59
  decision number, E-59
  general form, E-57–58
  Tribunal identifier, E-58–59
  year, E-58
online databases, E-64–66
  Azimut, E-66
  CanLII, E-65
  judgments with neutral citation, E-64
  Lexis, E-66
  other services, E-66
  published judgments, E-64
  Quicklaw, E-65
  service with own identifier, E-66
  unpublished judgments with no neutral citation, E-65–66
  Westlaw Canada, E-66
pinpoint, E-60–61
  cited reporter, E-60–61
  general form, E-60
printed reporter, E-61–64
  first page, E-64
  official reporters, E-62
  semi-official reporters, E-62–63
  series, E-63–64
  unofficial reporters, E-63

  year of reporter, E-61–62
sources
  availability of, E-49–50
  electronic services, E-64–66
  hierarchy of, E-49–50
  neutral citation available, E-50
  no source available, E-50
  official reporter, E-62
  unofficial reporter,
style of cause, E-51–56
  bankruptcies and receiverships, E-53
  companies and partnerships, E-52
  constitutional references, E-56
  Crown, E-53
  Crown corporations, E-54
  countries, E-52
  Ex Rel Rule, E-56
  federal units, E-52
  general form, E-51
  government entities, E-54
  municipal boards and bodies, E-55
  municipalities, E-52
  names of parties, E-51
  person represented by guardian/tutor, E-52
  procedural phrases, E-56
  provinces, E-52
  school boards, E-55
  social welfare agencies, E-55
  statute titles, E-53
  Sub Nom Rule, E-56
  undisclosed parties, E-55
  unions, E-55
  wills and estates, E-53
unreported decision without neutral citation, E-71–72
year of decision, E-57

Language. *See* **Foreign Language**

Legislation. *See* **Bills; Codes; Gazettes; Municipal Bylaws; Regulations; Rules Of Practice; Securities Commissions Rules; Statutes**

Letters, E-150

Magazines, E-147

Memoranda, E-5, E-150

Municipal By-laws, E-44

New Zealand, *see also* **Common Law Jurisdiction Sources**
debates, E-218–19
delegated legislation, E-215
jurisprudence, E-216–18
   courts, abbreviations, E-218
   general form, E-216
   Law Reports, abbreviations, E-216–17
   neutral citation, E-216
   reporter, E-216–17
parliamentary papers, E-219
regulations, E-215
statutes, E-215

News Releases, E-149

Newspapers, E-148–49
editorials, and letters to editor, E-149
general form, E-148

Newswires, E-148

Notes, E-141

Nunavut, E-39

Online Resources, *see also* **Electronic Sources; Encyclopedic Digests; Jurisprudence**
generally, E-14–15
Singapore, E-222
United Kingdom, E-168
United States, E-183

Order in Council. *See* **Gazettes**

Parliamentary Papers. *See* **Government Documents**

Periodicals, E-119–23
author, E-119-20
   joint authors, E-119–20
   single author, E-119
first page of article, E-122–23
   article published in parts, E-122–23
general form, E-121
issue, E-122

pinpoint, E-119
series, E-120–21
title of article, E-120
   France, E-122
title of journal, E-121–22
   France, E-122
year of publication, E-120
volume, E-120–21

Pinpoints, Generally, E-13–14

Prior References. *See* **Subsequent References**

Proclamation, E-44

Quotations, E-17–18
format of, E-17–18
positioning of, E-17
quotation of original source, E-15–16
source in another language, E-18

Quote of Original Source, E-15

Regulations
federal, E-36–37
   consolidated regulations, E-36–37
   revised regulations, E-36–37
   unrevised regulations, E-37
jurisdictional basis, E-36
provincial and territorial, E-37–41
   Alberta, E-37
   British Columbia, E-37
   Manitoba, E-37–38
   New Brunswick, E-38
   Newfoundland and Labrador, E-38
      revised, E-38
      unrevised, E-38–39
      revised, E-39
      unrevised, E-38
   Nova Scotia, E-39
   Nunavut, E-39
   Ontario, E-39
      revised, E-39
      unrevised, E-39
   Prince Edward Island, E-40
   Quebec, E-40
      current version, E-40
      historical versions, E-40
   Saskatchewan, E-40

revised, E-40
unrevised, E-40
Yukon, E-41

Remarks, E-141

Reprint of Original Source, E-15–16

Roman Law, E-142

Royal Instruction, E-44

Rules of Practice, E-150
book reviews, E-139–40
books. *See* Books
case/legislation comments. *See* Case/Legislation Comments
codes of professional conduct, E-138
comments, E-141
conference address and papers, E-146
course materials, E-146–47
dictionaries. *See* Dictionaries
electronic sources. *See* Electronic Sources
encyclopedias, E-134
encyclopedic digests. *See* Encyclopedic Digests
essay collection, E-132–33
historical legal materials. *See* Historical Legal Materials
intellectual property. *See* Intellectual Property
interviews, E-150
letters, E-150
magazines, E-147
memoranda, E-4–5, E-149
news releases, E-149
newspapers. *See* Newspapers
newswires, E-148–149
notes, E-141
periodicals. *See* Periodicals
remarks, E-141
theses and dissertations, E-145
unpublished manuscripts. *See* Unpublished Manuscripts
working papers, E-152

Securities Commissions, E-46

***Sic*, use of, E-18**

Singapore, *see also* Common Law Jurisdiction Sources
constitutional documents, E-220
jurisprudence, E-222
courts, abbreviations, E-223
general form, E-222
neutral citation, E-223
online databases, E-224
reporters, E-223
unreported decisions without neutral citation, E-224
notifications, E-223
orders, E-223
parliamentary debates, E-226
practice directions, E-226
amendments to, E-227
consolidated practice directions, E-227
Supreme Court Practice Directions, E-226
regulations, E-221–22
rules, E-221–22

Social Media. *See* Electronic Sources

Source
emphasis on citing, E-16
non-English, E-18
obscure original source, E-15–16
quote of original, E-16–17
reprint of original, E-15–16

South Africa, *see also* Common Law Jurisdiction Sources
bills, E-226
debates, E-228
discussion papers, E-229
issue papers, E-229
jurisprudence, E-226
courts, abbreviations, E-228
general form, E-226
neutral citation, E-226–27
reporters, abbreviations, E-227
reports, E-229
statutes, E-225
amendments, E-225
general form, E-222
repeals, E-222

Statutes, E-220–21

amendments, E-221
English statutes applicable, E-221
general form, E-220–21
repeals, E-221
Revised Edition, E-32
annual volumes, E-28
appendices, E-32–33
chapter, E-31
constitutional statutes. *See* Constitutional
Statutes
general form of, E-23
jurisdiction abbreviations, E-29–30
loose-leafs, E-28–29
pinpoint, E-31
point in time citation, E-24
re-enactments, E-32
repeals, E-32
revised statutes, E-28
session, E-30–31
sources, E-24–27
statutes within statutes, E-33
subsidiary legislation, E-221–22
revised, E-221–22
unrevised, E-222
supplement, E-30–31
title, E-27–28
year, E-30–31

Subsequent References
"above" and "below", use of, E-13
ibid, E-12
infra, E-13
pinpoints, E-13–14
short form, establishment of, E-9–11
cases, E-10–11
legislation, E-10
general rules, E-9–10
secondary materials, E-11
supra, E-12–13

Supra, **E-12**

Tables of Authorities, E-3–4

Talmudic Law, E-143–44

Treaties. *See* **International Documents**

United Kingdom, *see also* **Common Law**
   Jurisdiction Sources
bills, E-168
Northern Ireland, E-168
Scotland, E-168
United Kingdom, E-170
debates, parliamentary, E-177–78
before 1803, E-177–86
1803 and after, E-178
journals, E-179
jurisprudence, E-171–77
Appeal Courts, E-171–72
general form, E-171
High Court, E-175
judge, E-176
Law Reports, E-172–74
abbreviations, E-173
1875-1890, E-173
1865-1875, E-173
1537-1865, E-173
retroactive neutral citation, E-174
neutral citation, E-171, E-175
Northern Ireland, E-176
online databases, E-177
BAILII, E-177
service with no identifier (Justis), E-177
reprints, E-174–75
Scotland, E-175
yearbooks, E-174
non-parliamentary papers, E-180–81
parliamentary papers, E-179–80
regulations, E-169–70
Northern Ireland, E-169–70
Scotland, E-170
United Kingdom, E-168
Wales, E-170
statutes, E-166–67
general form, E-166
Northern Ireland, E-166–67
passed by Northern Ireland, E-166–67
passed by United Kingdom, E-166–67
Scotland, E-167
Wales, E-167

United Nations Documents. *See* **Interna-**
   tional Documents

United States, *see also* **Common Law Jurisdiction Sources**
bills, E-186–87
  federal, E-186
  state, E-187
committee hearings, E-194
  federal, E-194
  state, E-194
constitutions, federal and state, E-181–82
debates, congressional, E-193
documents, *see* reports and documents
jurisprudence, E-189–93
  abbreviations, E-190–91
  court, E-192
    federal, E-192
    state, E-192
  general form, E-189
  pinpoint, E-191
  neutral citation, E-189
  online databases, E-193
    Lexis, E-193
    Westlaw, E-193
  reporter and series, E-190–91
  style of cause, E-189
  year of decision, E-192
regulations, E-186–89
  administrative registers, E-188–89
  Code of Federal Regulations, E-188
  Federal Register, E-188–89

reports and documents, E-195–96
  federal, E-195
    abbreviation of numbers, E-195
    numbered documents and reports, E-195
    unnumbered documents and committee prints, E-196
  state, E-196
resolutions, E-186–87
  federal, E-186–87
  state, E-187
Restatements, E-185–86
statutes, federal and state, E-182–84
  codes, E-182–83
  order of preference resources, E-182
  session laws, E-184–85
  unofficial reporters of session laws, E-185
Uniform Acts, E-185–86
Uniform Codes, E-185–86

Unpublished Manuscripts, E-144–45
forthcoming manuscripts, E-144–45
general form, E-144
theses and dissertations, E-145

Web Logs. *See* **Electronic Sources**

Working Papers, E-152

Writing in Foreign Language. *See* **Foreign Language**

MOT DE LE RÉDACTEUR

La huitième édition du *Manuel canadien de la référence juridique* vise, de la même manière que ses prédécesseurs, à faciliter la communication efficace entre auteurs et lecteurs. Afin de servir cet objectif, chaque édition du *Manuel* a fondé ses règles en fonction des principes de logique, de clarté et d'accessibilité.

Cet objectif et ces principes ont cependant toujours été appréciés en contexte. Bien que la référence juridique se classe parmi les aspects les plus prosaïques de la rédaction juridique, celle-ci touche chaque constituant de la profession juridique et détient ainsi une variété de parties prenantes de la plus grande ampleur possible. Les usagers du *Manuel* trouveront dans ses pages le résultat d'un équilibrage entre, d'une part, l'objectif et les principes régissant le *Manuel* et, d'autre part, les conventions professionnelles, l'évolution de la rédaction juridique, et les commentaires soumis par nos usagers et nos conseillers.

L'esprit d'équilibre infuse le *Manuel* dans son intégrité, à compter de la première page. Même l'uniformité que le *Manuel* prétend établir est en réalité tempérée : les lecteurs s'apercevront que certaines cours qui adoptent le *Manuel* ont des directives spéciales qui prévalent sur certaines de ses règles. L'on ne peut pas s'attendre à ce que toutes les communautés juridiques dont les exigences sont adressées par le *Manuel* aient des besoins identiques. Comme le souligne le juge Laskin dans son avant-propos, chaque public a ses intérêts distincts. Que ce soit la rédaction d'un article, d'un mémoire, ou d'un jugement, la référence juridique communique différentes informations à différents lecteurs, et le *Manuel* tente de fournir des règles flexibles qui peuvent être modulées au besoin.

C'est une tâche complexe que de produire un standard de référence juridique unique et uniforme pour couvrir les multiplicités de parties prenantes, de communautés et de publics auxquels s'adresse le *Manuel*. Décrivant les circonstances entourant la conception du *Manuel*, l'avant-propos du juge Kasirer fait mention à la fois du droit commun et de la pluralité juridique. Il serait utile de faire le lien entre ces idées et le projet du *Manuel*. Les rédacteurs du *Manuel* ont essayé d'adresser les besoins d'une pluralité de voix participantes; malgré les différences de perspectives, celles-ci visent toutes un but commun, celui de trouver une méthode de communication d'informations juridiques qui soit claire et précise. Dans de telles circonstances, les règles établies collectivement devraient être interprétées non pas comme une loi rigide, mais plutôt — tel que l'indique le titre anglais de ce travail — comme un guide.

Cette édition est l'issu d'un travail ardu et rigoureux. Nous sommes profondément endettés envers Me Daniel Boyer (Vice-doyen des services aux usagers de la Bibliothèque de McGill et Bibliothécaire en chef de la Bibliothèque de droit Nahum Gelber), dont l'aide et les conseils ont été indispensables à la création de l'institution qu'est devenu le *Manuel*. Nous devons également de grands remerciements à l'Honorable Nicholas Kasirer (Juge de la Cour d'appel du Québec et Chercheur au Centre Paul-André Crépeau de droit privé et comparé), ainsi qu'à l'Honorable John I. Laskin (Juge de la Cour d'Appel d'Ontario), d'avoir généreusement pris le temps de partager leurs pensées à propos de la référence juridique et du *Manuel*.

Nous souhaitons remercier les membres du Sous-comité consultatif de référence juridique, Neil Campbell, Me Anne-Marie Lizotte, Ilana Ludwin (2012-2013) et Me Svetlana Samochkine (2013-2014), pour leurs précieux conseils sur les modifications et les ajouts suggérés, et pour leur orientation au cours du processus de publication; les rédacteurs composant le Comité de référence juridique des volumes 58 et 59, Lawrence David, Caitlin Morin, Thang Nguyen, Mark Phillips, Isabelle Rémillard, Michael Shortt, Sara Shearmur, William Stephenson, Nicolas Torti, Aaron Wenner, et Nancy Zagbayou, pour leur contribution au *Manuel* et leur révision diligente des versions préliminaires; ainsi que tous les libraires de droit et officiers de la cour qui nous ont fourni des commentaires et d'excellentes suggestions. J'adresse enfin mes sincères remerciements à la Rédactrice en chef, aux Rédacteurs en chefs adjoints et à l'administration du volume 59 de la *Revue de droit de McGill*, pour leur appui grandement apprécié.

Je souhaite remercier spécialement mon prédécesseur, Montano Cabezas, pour son inestimable contribution globale et son engagement à l'amélioration du *Manuel*, ainsi qu'à sa rigoureuse attention au détail au cours du processus de rédaction.

Par-dessus tout, je souhaite remercier ma femme, Nancy, pour sa force, sa grâce et son appui au cours de notre arrivée à la complétion du *Manuel*.

A. Max Jarvie
Rédacteur du Manuel de référence
Revue de droit de McGill, volume 59

Si vous avez des commentaires ou des suggestions, veuillez communiquer avec nous à l'adresse suivante :

Revue de droit de McGill
3644 rue Peel
Montréal, Québec H3A 1W9
Canada

Tel : 514 398-7397
Fax : 514 398-7360
http://lawjournal.mcgill.ca
journal.law@mcgill.ca

Préface par l'honorable Nicholas Kasirer

Le titre de cet important ouvrage ne fournit au lecteur qu'un indice imparfait des objectifs recherchés par ses rédacteurs : en fait, ce *Manuel* est bien plus qu'un simple guide aux lecteurs ; il vise à établir un standard — une « référence » pour reprendre le titre, qui soit « Uniform » selon le titre anglais — pour l'ensemble des citations juridiques au pays[1]. Il est justifié de voir la normalisation comme l'objectif non annoncé sur lequel repose cette grande odyssée de la méthodologie juridique à McGill. Déjà à sa huitième édition, le « Livre Rouge » n'est plus seulement perçu comme un « manuel de citations », mais également comme un « site de normativité » pour le droit canadien.

« Adopté »[2] par de nombreuses revues spécialisées, ainsi que par des tribunaux, étudiants, praticiens et universitaires, le *Manuel* s'est incontestablement mérité une place au sein de l'ordre juridique. Dès lors, dans quelle mesure « ordonner » joue-t-il un rôle dans ce succès? Certes, le *Manuel* a apporté un certain ordre au chaos du droit — à tout le moins pour ce qui est de la signification secondaire conférée par Jean Carbonnier, qui percevait dans l'ordre juridique « une simple nécessité d'hygiène sociale »[3]. Or, en dissipant quelque peu la confusion avec laquelle les juristes canadiens déployaient les autorités juridiques avant la parution de sa première édition, le *Manuel* a aussi, consciemment, imposé une discipline à ses lecteurs. En ce sens, le Livre Rouge de McGill semblerait avoir une ambition assurément normative[4]. À quel point cet ouvrage sur les sources du droit devrait-il être considéré comme une source de droit en lui-même ?

Il est difficile d'imaginer que les rédacteurs de la première édition, parue en 1986, n'aient pas nourri un espoir autre que le simple catalogage des règles d'usage pour le placement habile de crochets et de virgules dans les textes juridiques. Lorsque l'on se rappelle qu'ils étaient tous des étudiants de la Faculté à une époque où leurs professeurs étaient fortement engagés dans un examen critique portant sur la nature du droit et de ses sources véritables, on peut supposer que les rédacteurs espéraient également façonner le parcours du droit à leur manière. Certes, l'idée selon laquelle le droit trouvait expression en dehors des recueils de lois et de jurisprudence s'est manifestée dans les recherches savantes les plus prestigieuses du

---

[1]   Les ambitions normatives de cet ouvrage sont-elles abordées différemment dans les versions française et anglaise du Livre Rouge de McGill? Un « guide » est d'abord et avant tout un principe directeur ou un individu qui mène par l'exemple (généralement comportant quelque chose de plus qu'un simple catalogue); un « manuel » est simplement un livre d'instructions comme le « Chicago Manual of Style ». Bien qu'il soit possible de trouver un sens commun aux termes « guide » et « manuel », où se trouve le mot « uniforme » dans le titre français? Est-il sous-entendu dans le mot « référence »? Sur l'idée opportune que le français et l'anglais devraient être lus conjointement pour ne former qu'un seul texte en droit canadien, voir Roderick Macdonald, « Legal Bilingualism » (1997) 42:1 McGill LJ 119.

[2]   Les rédacteurs utilisent ce terme *soft* comme pour suggérer que le choix d'adhérer au *Manuel* n'a pas été imposé normativement — la coutume est-elle émergente? — mais plutôt par l'effet du libre choix. Voir la liste impressionnante de revues et de tribunaux ayant adopté le *Manuel*, ci-dessus aux pp E-iii–E-iv.

[3]   Jean Carbonnier, *Droit civil I : Introduction, Les personnes, La famille*, Paris, Presses Universitaires de France, 2004, au para 105.

[4]   Des exemples se trouvent notés à chaque page de cette nouvelle édition du *Manuel*. Voir par exemples les distinctions à apporter (et les règles à suivre) dans la différenciation entre « Voir par ex » et « Voir », « Voir aussi », « Voir notamment », « Voir généralement », « Voir toutefois » et l'englobant « *Contra* » (ci-dessous aux pp F-8–F-9).

moment à la Faculté : des réflexions sur ce qui constitue « *persuasive authority* » en droit[5]; sur la reconnaissance par le droit de la « normativité implicite et "inférentielle" »[6]; sur la vaste gamme d'artefacts juridiques pertinents pour découvrir les sources d'obligations[7]; sur les idées du *droit commun* en dehors du processus législatif[8]; sur les sources disparates qui doivent être examinées afin de tenir compte de la culture juridique[9], et plus encore. Faisant écho à travers cette première édition du *Manuel* est l'idée, pas si farfelue, qu'un groupe d'étudiants au sous-sol de la Faculté a eu une influence sur le phénomène du *law-in-the-making*. Aujourd'hui, les rédacteurs sont peut-être trop pudiques quant à leur rôle et prennent même soin de ne pas dicter une « hiérarchie des sources » aux lecteurs non avertis[10]. Cela dit, le *Manuel* est sans aucun doute un excellent exemple du phénomène que les civilistes nomment la « doctrine comme source de droit »[11].

De plus, le *Manuel* vise à façonner le comportement des juristes canadiens tout en étant soucieux qu'il le fait au travers du prisme transsystémique que McGill propose pour l'étude du droit. La perspective nuancée qu'adoptent les rédacteurs à l'égard de la langue en est un parfait exemple. Selon eux, peu importe que l'on écrive à Lyons ou Lyon, Londres ou London; ce qui importe réellement est que l'on choisisse d'écrire en anglais ou en français[12]. Il y a des exceptions de principe — le titre du *Code civil du Québec*, un latin toujours aussi transsystémique, ainsi qu'un détail dans l'intitulé de cause devant les tribunaux bilingues[13] — qu'ils exposent dans une prose limpide dans les deux langues. Les rédacteurs décrivent ce magnifique exploit linguistique avec beaucoup d'humilité : « Puisqu'il s'agit d'un ouvrage intrinsèquement canadien, les règles de ce Manuel s'appliquent à la rédaction de textes dans les deux langues officielles »[14]. Peu de gens au Canada sont aussi bien placés que les étudiants rédacteurs de McGill pour faire le tout avec autant de savoir-vivre.

Ailleurs, on retrouve quelques signes de l'influence qu'exerce l'épistémologie juridique propre à la Faculté de droit de McGill : les abréviations pour les *Institutes*,

---

[5]   H Patrick Glenn, « Persuasive Authority » » (1987) 32:2 McGill LJ 261.

[6]   Roderick Macdonald, « Pour la reconnaissance d'une normativité juridique implicite et "inférentielle" » (1986) 18 Sociologie et sociétés 47.

[7]   Voir Paul-André Crépeau, *Théorie générale de l'obligation juridique : Éléments d'une introduction*, Montréal, Université McGill et le Centre de recherche en droit privé et comparé, 1987.

[8]   Voir John EC Brierley, « Quebec's 'Common Laws' (droits communs) : How Many Are There? » dans Ernest Caparros, dir, *Mélanges Louis-Philippe Pigeon*, Montréal, Wilson & Lafleur, 1989, à la p 109.

[9]   Voir G Blaine Baker et al, *Sources in the Law Library of McGill University for a Reconstruction of the Legal Culture of Quebec, 1760-1890*, Montréal, Université McGill et le Montreal Business History Project, 1987.

[10] Lorsque les rédacteurs recommandent de suivre la « hiérarchie des sources » lorsqu'on fait référence à la jurisprudence, leur souci n'est pas de suivre la pyramide de Kelsen, mais bien de distinguer les sources faisant le plus « autorité », notamment les références neutres, par opposition à celles qui sont moins officielles comme les recueils non officiels (voir ci-dessous à la p F-49).

[11] Voir John EC Brierley et Roderick Macdonald, dir, *Quebec Civil Law*, Toronto, Emond Montgomery, 1993 au para 102.

[12] Les rédacteurs précisent la « règle » ainsi : « L'écriture en français exige le respect des règles de référence françaises, quelle que soit la langue dans laquelle la source est rédigée » et vice-versa (voir ci-dessous à la p F-7).

[13] Cette dernière exception est particulièrement nuancée : quand pouvons-nous utiliser « c » (pour « contre ») par opposition à « v » (pour « versus ») dans l'intitulé d'une cause? Les rédacteurs expliquent : « L'utilisation du c ou du v dans l'intitulé indique la langue dans laquelle la décision est rendue. Si la décision est rendue en anglais, utiliser le v. Si la décision est rendue en français, utiliser le c. Pour les décisions bilingues, utilisez c pour la rédaction d'un texte en français [et v si le texte est rédigé en anglais] » (ci-dessous à la p F-51).

[14] Voir à la p F-19, ci-dessous.

Digeste et *Codex* de Justinien ne se trouvent qu'à quelques pages de distance des *Halsbury's Laws of England*; il n'y a pas de confusion entre le statut du *Code civil* et du *Code criminel* dans la liste des textes promulgués[15]; et il y a un chapitre sur les « sources étrangères » qui chevauche, si naturellement dans ce parcours intellectuel nomade, le clivage entre la common law et le droit civil. Cette nouvelle édition du *Manuel* est parue dans l'air enivrant et l'espace infini d'une faculté de droit dominée par une approche de plus en plus éclatée à l'égard de la diversification des sources de droit, résolument comparative et pluraliste dans ses postulats. À tout le moins, le *Manuel* élargit la portée de ce qui peut et de ce qui doit être répertorié comme du droit au Canada, que ces sources soient décrites comme internationales, étrangères ou même microsystémiques. Alors que d'autres font l'éloge à juste titre, de l'accent que met McGill sur le pluralisme juridique comme « une description de ce qu'est le droit » [notre traduction][16], le *Manuel* reflète de manière concrète le fait que la Faculté de droit s'efforce à « naviguer le transsystémique » [notre traduction][17] depuis plus d'une décennie.

Le *Manuel* n'est donc pas qu'un simple ouvrage de livre référence établi aux fins d'un nouvel ordre juridique ou d'un lieu de polyjuralité imaginaire, mais bien l'expression d'un moyen d'appréhender le droit qui incarne — à l'honneur des rédacteurs — les plus hautes aspirations de recherche transsystémique, faisant ainsi la fierté de la Faculté de droit de l'Université McGill.

Nicholas Kasirer
Juge de la Cour d'appel du Québec
Chercheur au Centre Paul-André Crépeau de droit privé et comparé
Janvier 2014

---

[15] Voir aux pp F-23, F-34, ci-dessous.
[16] Sally Engle Merry, « McGill Convocation Address: Legal Pluralism in Practice » (2013) 59:1 McGill LJ 1 à la p 2.
[17] Shauna Van Praagh, « Navigating the Transsystemic: A Course Syllabus » (2005) 50:4 McGill LJ 701.

Préface par l'honorable John I. Laskin

Tous les quatre ans, et ce depuis 1986, la *Revue de droit de McGill* publie une nouvelle édition du *Manuel canadien de référence juridique*. Il me fait plaisir de rédiger une préface à cet effet, pour cette huitième édition du *Manuel*.

Le *Manuel* avait comme but d'établir un système de règles uniformes pour la référence juridique au Canada ainsi que de créer un outil de référence approuvé à l'échelle nationale. Cet objectif fut largement atteint. La majorité des revues de droit au Canada, des avocats et des universités, ainsi que de nombreux tribunaux ont adopté le *Manuel* comme le guide canadien officiel en ce qui a trait à la référence juridique.

En tant que l'un des nombreux juges qui délèguent régulièrement la vérification des sources et références à ses stagiaires juridiques, j'ai peut-être sous-estimé l'importance des références juridiques. Néanmoins, j'en suis venu à apprécier l'importance cruciale qu'elles ont dans le travail des tribunaux — tant pour les lecteurs que pour ceux qui rédigent.

Pour les lecteurs, les références juridiques remplissent deux principales fonctions. Tout d'abord, elles permettent aux lecteurs de trouver, facilement et rapidement, une version fiable de la source citée, que ce soit une décision judiciaire ou un article de revue, et, lorsqu'approprié ou nécessaire, de vérifier et de retracer les origines de cette source. Deuxièmement, la référence transmet d'importantes informations au sujet de la source. Pour la jurisprudence, par exemple, la référence fournit l'année de la décision, l'indication géographique du lieu oª le jugement fut décidé, et le niveau de la cour. Ces informations sont souvent nécessaires afin d'évaluer l'importance d'une affaire.

La seconde fonction qu'assurent les références juridiques a influencé ma propre rédaction. Il y a plusieurs années, j'ai expérimenté en inscrivant mes références juridiques en notes de bas de page dans mes jugements. Cet essai fut de courte durée. J'ai rapidement constaté que l'information véhiculée par les références juridiques était trop importante pour être laissée en notes de bas de page; elle méritait d'être insérée dans le corps du texte de mes motifs.

Ainsi, les références juridiques au sein des tribunaux sont importantes non seulement pour les lecteurs, mais également pour ceux qui rédigent : pour les juges lorsqu'ils écrivent leurs motifs, et particulièrement pour les avocats lorsqu'ils écrivent leurs mémoires pour les tribunaux.

En rédigeant des mémoires contenant des références exhaustives et précises, les avocats démontrent que leur travail est bien documenté. Ce faisant, ils renforcent leur crédibilité auprès des tribunaux. D'autre part, la plupart des juges regardent d'un mauvais œil la crédibilité des avocats qui, trop souvent, omettent de re-connaître une source, ou la reconnaissent, mais ne s'y réfèrent pas correctement.

Jusqu'à présent, j'ai discuté de l'importance générale des références juridiques. Je tiens également à dire quelques mots au sujet de cette huitième édition du *Manuel*. Les deux caractéristiques du *Manuel* que j'estime le plus sont sa clarté et son intelligibilité. Le *Manuel* expose les règles de référence en détail, mais le fait d'une manière qui les rend faciles à repérer. Il donne également des explications claires pour chaque règle, et il fournit de nombreux exemples afin de rendre les règles plus facilement applicables.

J'apprécie également la flexibilité que le *Manuel* permet dans l'application de ses règles. L'auteur a souvent la possibilité de donner davantage d'informations lorsque cela s'avérerait utile pour le lecteur. Lorsque cela est possible, la huitième édition élargit cette flexibilité pour certaines règles, et augmente ainsi leur utilité générale.

Les auteurs du *Manuel* — les rédacteurs passés et actuels de la *Revue de droit de McGill* — ont donné à tous ceux qui travaillent dans le domaine juridique — les juges, les avocats, les universitaires et les maisons d'édition juridiques — une riche et précieuse ressource. Pour la production et la mise à jour du *Manuel*, nous leur devons toute notre reconnaissance.

John Laskin
Cour d'appel de l'Ontario
Janvier 2014

TABLE DES MATIÈRES

F — MOT DE LE RÉDACTEUR... F-i

F — PRÉFACE PAR L'HONORABLE NICHOLAS KASIRER .... F-iii

F — PRÉFACE PAR L'HONORABLE JOHN I. LASKIN .... F-vii

F — 1 RÈGLES FONDAMENTALES F-3

F -1.1 Bibliographies F-3

F -1.2 Références dans le texte : note de service et factum................ F-5

    F -1.2.1 Note de service F-5

    F -1.2.2 Factum.. F-5

F -1.3 Règles concernant les notes de bas de page............................ F-6

    F -1.3.1 La création des notes de bas de page F-6

    F -1.3.2 L'indication des notes de bas de page dans le texte F-7

    F -1.3.3 L'emplacement des notes de bas de page F-7

    F -1.3.4 La combinaison des notes de bas de page.......................... F-7

    F -1.3.5 Les références aux sources non françaises F-7

    F -1.3.6 Formules introductives.. F-8

    F -1.3.7 Information entre parenthèses dans les notes de bas de page..... F-9

F -1.4 Références ultérieures et antérieures...................................... F-10

    F -1.4.1 Titre abrégé.. F-10

        F -1.4.1.1 Modèle de base... F-10

        F -1.4.1.2 Législation... F-10

        F -1.4.1.3 Jurisprudence... F-11

        F -1.4.1.4 Doctrine... F-12

    F -1.4.2 *Ibid*.. F-12

    F -1.4.3 *Supra* F-13

    F -1.4.4 *Infra* F-13

    F -1.4.5 Ci-dessus et ci-dessous F-14

F -1.5 Références précises F-14

F -1.6 Ressources électroniques.. F-15

F -1.7 Références aux sources citant ou reproduisant la source
originale F-16

    F -1.7.1 Source originale difficile à trouver.............................. F-16

    F -1.7.2 Emphase sur la source citante.................................. F-17

F -1.8 Règles générales concernant les citations F-18

    F -1.8.1 Emplacement des citations F-18

    F -1.8.2 Forme des citations F-18

    F -1.8.3 Citation d'une source dans une autre langue F-19

F -1.9 Rédaction d'un texte en langue étrangère F-19

F — 2 LÉGISLATION F-23

F -2.1 Lois F-23

F -2.1.1   Modèle de base F-23
F -2.1.2   Référence à un moment précis F-24
F -2.1.3   Sources F-24
F -2.1.4   Titre F-27
F -2.1.5   Lois révisé es et recueils annuels F-28
F -2.1.6   Recueils à feuilles mobiles F-28
F -2.1.7   Indication géographique F-29
F -2.1.8   Année, session et supplément F-30
F -2.1.9   Chapitre F-31
F -2.1.10 Référence précise F-31
F -2.1.11 Modifications, abrogations et remises en vigueur ... F-32
F -2.1.12 Annexes F-32
F -2.1.13 Loi contenue dans une autre loi F-33

F -2.2   Lois constitutionnelles F-33
         F -2.2.1   Référence précise F-34

F -2.3   Codes F-34

F -2.4   Projets de loi F-35

F -2.5   Règlements F-36
         F -2.5.1   Règlements fédéraux F-37
                    F -2.5.1.1   Règlements refondus F-37
                    F -2.5.1.2   Règlements non refondus F-37
         F -2.5.2   Règlements provinciaux et territoriaux F-37
                    F -2.5.2.1   Alberta, Colombie-Britannique F-38
                    F -2.5.2.2   Manitoba F-38
                    F -2.5.2.3   Nouveau-Brunswick F-38
                    F -2.5.2.4   Terre-Neuve-et-Labrador F-38
                                F -2.5.2.4.1   Non refondus F-39
                                F -2.5.2.4.2   Refondus F-39
                    F -2.5.2.5   Territoires du Nord-Ouest F-39
                                F -2.5.2.5.1   Non refondus F-39
                                F -2.5.2.5.2   Refondus F-39
                    F -2.5.2.6   Nouvelle-Écosse F-39
                    F -2.5.2.7   Nunavut F-40
                    F -2.5.2.8   Ontario F-40
                                F -2.5.2.8.1   Non refondus F-40
                                F -2.5.2.8.2   Refondus F-40
                    F -2.5.2.9   Île-du-Prince-Édouard F-40
                    F -2.5.2.10 Québec F-41
                                F -2.5.2.10.1 Version historique F-41
                                F -2.5.2.10.2 Version courant F-41
                    F -2.5.2.11 Saskatchewan F-41
                                F -2.5.2.11.1 Non refondus F-41
                                F -2.5.2.11.2 Refondus F-41
                    F -2.5.2.12 Yukon F-41

F -2.6   Autres informations publiées dans les Gazettes F-42
         F -2.6.1   Modèle le de base F-42
         F -2.6.2   Décrets F-43
                    F -2.6.2.1   Fédéral F-43
                    F -2.6.2.2   Provincial et territorial F-44

F -2.6.3 Proclamations et instructions royales F-44

F -2.7 Règlements municipaux F-45

F -2.8 Règles de pratique F-45

F -2.9 Commissions de valeurs mobilières F-46

F — 3 JURISPRUDENCE F-49

F -3.1 Sources F-49

F -3.2 Modèle le de base F-50
  F -3.2.1 Référence neutre disponible F-50
  F -3.2.2 Référence neutre non disponible F-51

F -3.3 Intitulé F-51
  F -3.3.1 Nom des parties F-52
  F -3.3.2 Personne représenté e par un tuteur F-52
  F -3.3.3 Noms corporatifs et de sociétés F-52
  F -3.3.4 Pays, unités fédérales, provinces et municipalités F-53
  F -3.3.5 Testaments et successions F-53
  F -3.3.6 Faillites et mises sous séquestre F-53
  F -3.3.7 Titres de lois F-53
  F -3.3.8 La Couronne F-54
  F -3.3.9 Entités gouvernementales F-54
  F -3.3.10 Sociétés d'État F-55
  F -3.3.11 Conseils et organismes municipaux F-55
  F -3.3.12 Conseils scolaires F-55
  F -3.3.13 Syndicats F-55
  F -3.3.14 Agences d'aide sociale F-55
  F -3.3.15 Noms de parties protégées F-56
  F -3.3.16 Intitulés différents pour une même cause : l'emploi de sub nom. F-56
  F -3.3.17 Tierce partie agissant pour une des parties : ex rel. F-56
  F -3.3.18 Expressions procédurales et renvois constitutionnels F-56

F -3.4 Année de la décision F-57

F -3.5 Référence neutre F-57
  F -3.5.1 Année F-58
  F -3.5.2 Identifiant du tribunal F-58
  F -3.5.3 Numéro de la décision F-59

F -3.6 Référence précise F-60
  F -3.6.1 Modèle de base F-60
  F -3.6.2 Recueil auquel les références sont faites F-61

F -3.7 Recueil imprimé F-61
  F -3.7.1 Année du recueil F-61
  F -3.7.2 Recueil F-62
    F -3.7.2.1 Recueils officiels F-62
    F -3.7.2.2 Recueils semi-officiels F-63
    F -3.7.2.3 Recueils non officiels F-63
  F -3.7.3 Série F-64
  F -3.7.4 Première page F-64

F -3.8 Services de base de données en ligne F-64

F -3.8.1 Jugements publiés et jugements possédant une référence neutre F-65

F -3.8.2 Jugements non publiés et ne possédant pas de référence neutre F-65

    F -3.8.2.1 CanLII... F-55

    F -3.8.2.2 Quicklaw... F-65

    F -3.8.2.3 Westlaw Canada... F-66

    F -3.8.2.4 Azimut... F-66

    F -3.8.2.5 Autres services.. F-66

F -3.9 Indication géographique et cour F-67

F -3.10 Juge F-67

F -3.11 Étapes successives d'une cause F-68

    F -3.11.1 Étapes antérieures F-68

    F -3.11.2 Étapes postérieures F-68

    F -3.11.3 Étapes antérieures et postérieures................. F-69

    F -3.11.4 Autorisation de pourvoi F-69

F -3.12 Jugements non publiés et sans référence neutre........ F-72

F -3.13 Jugements interlocutoires F-72

F -3.14 Organes et tribunaux administratifs........................ F-72

    F -3.14.1 Références aux recueils imprimés.................... F-72

    F -3.14.2 Décisions en ligne F-73

F -3.15 Plaidoiries et documents de preuve à l'audience F-74

F — 4 DOCUMENTS GOUVERNEMENTAUX...................F-77

F -4.1 Documents parlementaires F-77

    F -4.1.1 Débats législatifs... F-77

    F -4.1.2 Journaux.. F-78

    F -4.1.3 Feuilletons.. F-78

    F -4.1.4 Sessional Papers F-79

    F -4.1.5 Procès-verbaux F-79

    F -4.1.6 Rapports publiés dans un journal des débats....... F-80

    F -4.1.7 Rapports publiés séparément F-80

F -4.2 Documents non parlementaires F-81

    4.2.1 Modèle de base... F-81

        F -4.2.1.1 Rapports, manuels et autres publications volumineuses F-81

        F -4.2.1.2 Articles, bulletins et autres courtes publications F-83

    F -4.2.2 Bulletins d'interprétation (IT) en matière d'impôts et circulaires d'information F-84

    F -4.2.3 Rapports d'enquêtes et de commissions............... F-85

        F -4.2.3.1 Rapports portant le même titre...................... F-85

        F -4.2.3.2 Rapports portants des titres différents.................. F-85

    F -4.2.4 Documents de conférences intergouvernementales F-86

F — 5 DOCUMENTATION INTERNATIONALE F-89

F -5.1 Traités et documents internationaux F-89

F -5.1.1 Traités, documents des Nations Unies et autres accords
internationaux.. F-89
    F -5.1.1.1 Référence neutre des traités australiens................ F-92
F -5.1.2 Documents des Nations Unies.. F-92
    F -5.1.2.1 Charte des Nations Unies................................ F-92
    F -5.1.2.2 Documents officiels...................................... F-93
        F -5.1.2.2.1 Séances F-93
        F -5.1.2.2.2 Suppléments............................... F-94
        F -5.1.2.2.3 Annexes F-96
    F -5.1.2.3 Documents à en-tête de l'Organisation des Nations
Unies (Documents miméographiés)....................... F-97
    F -5.1.2.4 Périodiques F-97
    F -5.1.2.5 Annuaires F-97
    F -5.1.2.6 Publications de vente F-98
F -5.1.3 Documents de l'Union européenne.................................... F-98
    F -5.1.3.1 Règlements, directives et décisions..................... F-98
    F -5.1.3.2 Débats du Parlement européen.........................F-100
    F -5.1.3.3 Autres documents F-100
F -5.1.4 Documents du Conseil de l'Europe F-101
F -5.1.5 Documents de l'Organisation des États américains................F-102
F -5.1.6 Documents de l'Organisation mondiale du commerce (OMC) et de
l'Accord général sur les tarifs douaniers et le commerce (GATT) . F-103
F -5.1.7 Documents de l'Organisation de coopération et de
développement économiques (OCDE)...............................F-104
F -5.1.8 Traités avec les Premières nations...................................F-105

F -5.2 Jurisprudence F-106
F -5.2.1 Cour permanente de Justice internationale (1922–1946) F-106
    F -5.2.1.1 Jugements, ordonnances et avis consultatifs F-106
    F -5.2.1.2 Plaidoiries, exposés oraux et autres documents......F-107
F -5.2.2 Cour internationale de Justice (1946 à aujourd'hui)................F-107
    F -5.2.2.1 Jugements, ordonnances et avis consultatifs F-108
    F -5.2.2.2 Mémoires, plaidoiries et documents....................F-109
F -5.2.3 Cour de Justice des Communautés européennes et Tribunal
de première instance..F-109
F -5.2.4 Cour européenne des Droits de l'Homme et Commission
européenne des Droits de l'Homme...................................F-110
    F -5.2.4.1 Avant 1999...F-110
    F -5.2.4.2 À partir de 1999..F-110
F -5.2.5 Cour interaméricaine des Droits de l'Homme F-112
    F -5.2.5.1 Jugements, ordres et avis consultatifs................F-112
    F -5.2.5.2 Mémoires, plaidoiries et documents....................F-113
F -5.2.6 Commission interaméricaine des Droits de l'Homme F-113
F -5.2.7 Tribunaux de droit pénal international F-114
F -5.2.8 Groupes spéciaux de l'Accord général sur les tarifs douaniers
et le commerce (GATT) 1947 ....F-115
F -5.2.9 Rapports de Groupes spéciaux et de l'Organe d'appel de
l'Organisation mondiale du commerce (OMC) F-116
F -5.2.10 Rapports de Groupes spéciaux de l'Accord de libre-échange
canado-américain..F-117

F -5.2.11 Rapports de Groupes spéciaux de l'Accord de libre-échange nord-américain (ALÉNA) F-118

F -5.2.12 Décisions d'arbitrage international......................................F-119

F -5.2.13 Décisions d'arbitrage de l'Organisation mondiale de la propriété intellectuelle (OMPI)...F-119

    F -5.2.13.1 Principes directeurs régissant le règlement uniforme des litiges relatifs aux noms de domaine (UDRP)....F-119

F -5.2.14 Décisions de droit international prises devant des cours nationales F-120

F -5.3 Sites internet F-120

F — 6 DOCTRINE ET AUTRES DOCUMENTS F-127

F -6.1 Périodiques F-127

  F -6.1.1 Modèle de base...F-127

  F -6.1.2 Auteur...F-127

    F -6.1.2.1 Un seul auteur...F-127

    F -6.1.2.2 Coauteurs F-128

  F -6.1.3 Titre de l'article...F-128

  F -6.1.4 Année de publication...F-128

  F -6.1.5 Volume, numéro et série F-129

  F -6.1.6 Titre du périodique F-129

    F -6.1.6.1 France F-130

  F -6.1.7 Première page de l'article..F-131

    F -6.1.7.1 Articles publiés en parties...............................F-131

  F -6.1.8 Référence précise F-131

F -6.2 Monographies F-132

  F -6.2.1 Modèle de base...F-132

  F -6.2.2 Auteur...F-133

    F -6.2.2.1 Un seul auteur...F-133

    F -6.2.2.2 Coauteurs F-133

    F -6.2.2.3 Directeur d'un ouvrage collectif F-133

    F -6.2.2.4 Directeur ou correcteur d l'ouvrage d'un autre auteur F-134

      F -6.2.2.4.1 Le nom de l'auteur original fait partie du titre F-134

      F -6.2.2.4.2 Le nom de l'auteur original ne fait pas partie du titre F-134

    F -6.2.2.5 Traducteur..F-134

      F -6.2.2.5.1 Traduction professionnelle F-135

      F -6.2.2.5.2 Traduction de l'auteur du texte (vous) .F-135

  F -6.2.3 Titre F-135

    F -6.2.3.1 Procédures publiées d'une conférence ou d'un symposium..F-136

  F -6.2.4 Numéro de volume F-136

    F -6.2.4.1 Livres en français F-136

    F -6.2.4.2 Livres en anglais...F-137

      F -6.2.4.2.1 Volumes publiés sous différentes titres F-137

      F -6.2.4.2.2 Volume publiés sous un même titre....F-137

F -6.2.5 Édition...F-138
F -6.2.6 Ouvrage à feuilles mobiles..F-138
F -6.2.7 Lieu d'édition F-139
F -6.2.8 Mainson d'édition F-139
F -6.2.9 Année d'édition..F-140
F -6.2.10 Référence précise F-140

F -6.3 Articles publiés dans des ouvrages collectifs............................F-142

F -6.4 Dictionnaires et encyclopédies F-143
F -6.4.1 Dictionnaires généraux F-143
F -6.4.2 Dictionnaires spécialisés F-143
F -6.4.3 Encyclopédies F-144

F -6.5 Recueils encyclopédiques...F-144
F -6.5.1 Canadian Encyclopedic Digest..F-144
F -6.5.1.1 CED version imprimée...F-144
F -6.5.1.1 CED version électronique F-144
F -6.5.2 Halsbury's Laws of Canada...F-145
F -6.5.2.1 Halsbury's Laws of Canada version imprimée F-145
F -6.5.2.2 Halsbury's Laws of Canada version électronique.....F-145
F -6.5.3 Common Law..F-146
F -6.5.4 France F-146
F -6.5.4.1 Modèle de base...F-146
F -6.5.4.2 Rubriques F-147

F -6.6 Codes de déontologie F-148

F -6.7 Décisions d'arbitrage F-148
F -6.7.1 Décisions d'arbitrage publiées...F-148
F -6.7.2 Décisions d'arbitrage non publiées F-149

F -6.8 Recensions...F-149

F -6.9 Chroniques de jurisprudence et de législation F-150
F -6.9.1 France F-151
F -6.9.1.1 Notes...F-151
F -6.9.1.2 Chroniques publiées dans les recueils généraux.....F-151

F -6.10 Commentaires, remarques et notes F-152

F -6.11 Documents historiques légaux...F-152
F -6.11.1 Droit romain..F-152
F -6.11.2 Droit canonique F-153
F -6.11.3 Droit Talmudique..F-153

F -6.12 Manuscrits non publiés...F-154
F -6.12.1 Modèle de base..F-154
F -6.12.2 Manuscrits à paraître F-154
F -6.12.3 Thèses et dissertations F-155

F -6.13 Allocutions et textes présentés durant des conférences F-156

F -6.14 Recueils de cours...F-157

F -6.15 Périodiques F-157

F -6.16 Journaux, fils de presse et autres sources de nouvelles.............F-158
F -6.16.1 Éditoriaux et lettres à la rédaction....................................F-159

F -6.17 Communiqués de presse..F-160

F -6.18 Lettres et entrevues...F-161

F -6.19 Documents archivés F-162

F -6.20 Propriété intellectuelle...F-162
    F -6.20.1 Brevets...F-162
    F -6.20.2 Marques de commerce F-163
    F -6.20.3 Droits d'auteur..F-163

F -6.21 Documents de travail F-164

F -6.22 Sources électroniques..F-164
    F -6.22.1 Bases de données en ligne...F-165
    F -6.22.2 Revues en ligne (eJournals)..F-165
    F -6.22.3 Sites web..F-166
        F -6.22.3.1 Journaux web (blogues)..................................F-166
            F -6.22.3.1.1 Entrées F-166
            F -6.22.3.1.2 Commentaires............................F-167
        F -6.22.3.2 Réseaux sociaux...F-167
            F -6.22.3.2.1 Entrées Twitter (Tweets) F-167
            F -6.22.3.2.2 Entrées Facebook F-168
            F -6.22.3.2.3 Entrées Reddit F-168
        F -6.22.3.3 Vidéos et agrégateurs de vidéos en ligne..............F-169
    F -6.22.4 Autres supports numériques..F-169
    F -6.22.5 Identifiants numériques d'objets F-170

F — 7 SOURCES ÉTRANGÈRES...F-175

F -7.1 Jurisdictions de la Common Law F-175
    F -7.1.1 Forme générale F-175
    F -7.1.2 Intitulé, référence précise, titre abrégé, et histoire judiciaire F-175
    F -7.1.3 Année F-175
    F -7.1.4 Référence neutre, recueil imprimé, service électronique, ou
            décision non publiée F-176
    F -7.1.5 Juridiction et cour...F-176
    F -7.1.6 Juge F-177

F -7.2 Juridictions de droit civil F-177

F -7.3 Royaume-Uni...F-178
    F -7.3.1 Législation..F-178
        F -7.3.1.1 Lois..F-178
            F -7.3.1.1.1 Irlande du Nord.............................F-178
                F -7.3.1.1.1.1 Lois adoptées par le
                      Royaume-Uni F-178
                F -7.3.1.1.1.2 Lois adoptées par
                      l'Irlande du Nord F-178
            F -7.3.1.1.2 Écosse...F-179
            F -7.3.1.1.3 Pays de Galles F-179
        F -7.3.1.2 Projets de loi...F-180
            F -7.3.1.2.1 Royaume-Uni F-180
            F -7.3.1.2.2 Irlande du Nord.............................F-180
            F -7.3.1.2.3 Écosse...F-180

F -7.3.1.3　Règlements F-181
  F -7.3.1.3.1　Royaume-Uni F-181
  F -7.3.1.3.2　Règlements et ordres de l'Irlande du
    Nord F-181
  F -7.3.1.3.3　Écosse F-181
    F -7.3.1.3.3.1　Règlements adoptés par
      le Royaume-Uni F-182
    F -7.3.1.3.3.2　Règlements adoptés par
      l'Écosse....................F-182
  F -7.3.1.3.4　Pays de Galles F-182
F -7.3.2　Jurisprudence..F-182
 F -7.3.2.1　Modèle de base....................................F-182
 F -7.3.2.2　Référence neutre F-183
 F -7.3.2.3　Cours d'appel.....................................F-183
 F -7.3.2.4　High Court...F-183
 F -7.3.2.5　Recueils F-184
  F -7.3.2.5.1　Law Reports F-184
    F -7.3.2.5.1.1　Modèle d'une cause de
      1875 à 1890 ....F-185
    F -7.3.2.5.1.2　Modèle d'une cause de
      1865 à 1875 ....F-185
    F -7.3.2.5.1.3　Modèle d'une cause de
      1537 à 1865 ....F-185
    F -7.3.2.5.1.4　Références neutres
      rétroactives...............F-185
 F -7.3.2.6　Annuaires F-185
 F -7.3.2.7　Réimpressions......................................F-186
 F -7.3.2.8　Écosse, Irlande et Irlande du Nord....................F-186
  F -7.3.2.8.1　Référence neutre F-186
    F -7.3.2.8.1.1　Écosse....................F-187
    F -7.3.2.8.1.2　Irlande...................F-187
    F -7.3.2.8.1.3　Irlande du Nord..........F-187
 F -7.1.2.9　Juge F-188
 F -7.3.2.10　Bases de données en ligne.........................F-188
  F -7.3.2.10.1　BAILII F-188
  F -7.3.2.10.2　Service sans identifiant (Justis) F-188
F -7.3.3　Documents gouvernementaux................................F-188
 F -7.3.3.1　Débats F-189
  F -7.3.3.1.1　Avant 1803...............................F-189
  F -7.3.3.1.2　1803 à aujourd'hui........................F-189
 F -7.3.3.2　Journaux...F-190
 F -7.3.3.3　Documents parlementaires.........................F-190
 F -7.3.3.4　Documents non parlementaires F-191
F -7.4　États-Unis F-192
F -7.4.1　Législation..F-192
 F -7.4.1.1　Constitution fédérale et constitutions des États.......F-192
 F -7.4.1.2　Lois...F-193
  F -7.4.1.2.1　Codes....................................F-193
  F -7.4.1.2.2　Lois sessionnelles F-195

F -7.4.1.2.3   Recueil non officiel de lois
                   sessionnelles F-196
F -7.4.1.3   Uniform Codes, Uniform Acts et Restatements F-196
F -7.4.1.4   Projets de loi et résolutions F-197
       F -7.4.1.4.1   Projets de loi fédéraux F-197
       F -7.4.1.4.2   Résolutions fédérales F-197
       F -7.4.1.4.3   Résolutions et loi étatiques F-198
F -7.4.1.5   Règles et règlements F-198
       F -7.4.1.5.1   Code of Federal Regulations F-198
       F -7.4.1.5.2   Registre administratif.....................F-199
F -7.4.2   Jurisprudence...F-199
   F -7.4.2.1   Modèle de base F-199
   F -7.4.2.2   Intitulé...F-200
   F -7.4.2.3   Référence neutre F-200
   F -7.4.2.4   Recueil et série..F-200
   F -7.4.2.5   Référence précise F-201
   F -7.4.2.6   Cour F-202
       F -7.4.2.6.1   Cours fédérales F-202
       F -7.4.2.6.2   Cours d'États F-202
   F -7.4.2.7   Année de la décision.......................................F-202
   F -7.4.2.8   Bases de données en ligne..............................F-202
       F -7.4.2.8.1   Westlaw F-202
       F -7.4.2.8.2   Lexis..F-203
F -7.4.3   Documents gouvernementaux................................F-203
   F -7.4.3.1   Débats F-203
   F -7.4.3.2   Sessions de comités F-204
       F -7.4.3.2.1   Fédéral......................................F-204
       F -7.4.3.2.2   État F-204
   F -7.4.3.3   Rapports et documents....................................F-205
       F -7.4.3.3.1   Fédéral......................................F-205
               F -7.4.3.3.1.1 Documents et rapports
                                  numérotés.................F-205
               F -7.4.3.3.1.2 Documents non numérotés
                                  et Committee Prints F-206
       F -7.4.3.3.2   État F-206
F -7.5   France F-207
   F -7.5.1   Législation..F-207
       F -7.5.1.1   Lois et autres instruments législatifs F-207
       F -7.5.1.2   Codes F-207
   F -7.5.2   Jurisprudence..F-208
       F -7.5.2.1   Modèle de base F-208
       F -7.5.2.2   Cour F-208
           F -7.5.2.2.1   Tribunaux de première instance F-208
           F -7.5.2.2.2   Cour d'appel F-209
           F -7.5.2.2.3   Cour de cassation F-209
           F -7.5.2.2.4   Conseil d'État...............................F-210
           F -7.5.2.2.5   Conseil constitutionnel F-210
       F -7.5.2.3   Intitulé...F-211
       F -7.5.2.4   Année F-211
       F -7.5.2.5   Semestre F-211

F -7.5.2.6 Recueil..F-211
F -7.5.2.7 Partie du recueil..F-212
F -7.5.2.8 Page et numéro de la décision...........................F-213
F -7.5.2.9 Référence précise F-213
F -7.5.2.10 Référence parallèle..F-213
F -7.5.2.11 Notes, rapports et conclusions F-213
F -7.5.3 Documents gouvernementaux..F-213
F -7.5.3.1 Débats..F-214
F -7.5.3.1.1 De 1787 à 1860...........................F-214
F -7.5.3.1.2 De 1871 à aujourd'hui F-214
F -7.5.3.2 Anciens journaux officiels F-215
F -7.5.3.3 Documents parlementaires...............................F-216
F -7.5.3.3.1 Travaux et réunions parlementaires....F-216
F -7.5.3.3.2 Rapports d'information....................F-216
F -7.5.3.4 Documents non parlementaires F-217

F -7.6 Australie...F-217
F -7.6.1 Législation..F-217
F -7.6.1.1 Lois..F-217
F -7.6.1.2 Législation déléguée (règlements).....................F-218
F -7.6.2 Jurisprudence...F-219
F -7.6.2.1 Modèle de base..F-219
F -7.6.2.2 Référence neutre F-219
F -7.6.2.3 Recueil...F-220
F -7.6.2.3.1 Law Reports F-220
F -7.6.2.4 Cour..F-221
F -7.6.3 Documents gouvernementaux..F-221
F -7.6.3.1 Débats F-222
F -7.6.3.2 Rapports parlementaires F-222
F -7.6.3.3 Rapports non parlementaires..............................F-222
F -7.6.3.4 Documents des ministères.................................F-222

F -7.7 Nouvelle-Zélande F-223
F -7.7.1 Législation..F-223
F -7.7.1.1 Lois..F-223
F -7.7.1.2 Législation déléguée (règlements).......................F-223
F -7.7.2 Jurisprudence...F-224
F -7.7.2.1 Modèle de base..F-224
F -7.7.2.2 Référence neutre F-224
F -7.7.2.3 Recueil...F-224
F -7.7.2.3.1 Law Reports F-224
F -7.7.2.4 Cour..F-226
F -7.7.3 Documents gouvernementaux..F-226
F -7.7.3.1 Débats F-226
F -7.7.3.2 Documents parlementaires...............................F-227

F -7.8 Singapour..F-227
F -7.8.1 Législation..F-227
F -7.8.1.1 Documents constitutionnels...............................F-228
F -7.8.1.2 Lois..F-228
F -7.8.1.3 Modifications et abrogations F-229
F -7.8.1.4 Lois anglaises applicables à Singapour F-229

F -7.8.1.5 Législation auxiliaire (Règles, règlements, avis,
ordonnances) F-229
    F -7.8.1.5.1 Refondus F-229
    F -7.8.1.5.2 Non refondus F-230
F -7.8.2 Jurisprudence...F-230
  F -7.8.2.1 Modèle de base...F-230
  F -7.8.2.2 Référence neutre F-230
  F -7.8.2.3 Recueil...F-231
  F -7.8.2.4 Cours..F-231
  F -7.8.2.5 Décisions non publiées sans référence neutre........F-231
  F -7.8.2.6 Bases de données en ligne...............................F-232
F -7.8.3 Documents gouvernementaux..F-232
  F -7.8.3.1 Débats parlementaires...................................F-232
  F -7.8.3.2 Directives de pratique....................................F-232
    F -7.8.3.2.1 Directives de pratique consolidées F-232
    F -7.8.3.2.2 Modifications aux directives de
pratique F-232

F -7.9 Afrique du sud F-233
F -7.9.1 Législation..F-233
  F -7.9.1.1 Lois...F-233
  F -7.9.1.2 Modifications et abrogations F-233
  F -7.9.1.3 Projets de loi..F-233
F -7.9.2 Jurisprudence...F-233
  F -7.9.2.1 Modèle de base...F-233
  F -7.9.2.2 Référence neutre F-234
  F -7.9.2.3 Recueil...F-234
  F -7.9.2.4 Tribunal F-235
F -7.9.3 Documents gouvernementaux..F-236
  F -7.9.3.1 Débats F-236
  F -7.9.3.2 Rapports, documents de discussion et exposés......F-236

Index F-237

1 Règles fondamentales **F-3**

F -1.1 Bibliographies F-3

F -1.2 Références dans le texte : note de service et factum F-5
    F -1.2.1 Note de service F-5
    F -1.2.2 Factum F-5

F -1.3 Règles concernant les notes de bas de page F-6
    F -1.3.1 La création des notes de bas de page F-6
    F -1.3.2 L'indication des notes de bas de page dans le texte F-7
    F -1.3.3 L'emplacement des notes de bas de page F-7
    F -1.3.4 La combinaison des notes de bas de page F-7
    F -1.3.5 Les références aux sources non françaises F-7
    F -1.3.6 Formules introductives F-8
    F -1.3.7 Information entre parenthèses dans les notes de bas de page F-9

F -1.4 Références ultérieures et antérieures F-10
    F -1.4.1 Titre abrégé F-10
        F -1.4.1.1 Modèle de base F-10
        F -1.4.1.2 Législation F-10
        F -1.4.1.3 Jurisprudence F-11
        F -1.4.1.4 Doctrine F-12
    F -1.4.2 *Ibid.* F-12
    F -1.4.3 *Supra* F-13
    F -1.4.4 *Infra* F-13
    F -1.4.5 Ci-dessus et ci-dessous F-14

F -1.5 Références précises F-14

F -1.6 Ressources électroniques F-15

F -1.7 Références aux sources citant ou reproduisant la source originale F-16
    F -1.7.1 Source originale dificile à trouver F-16
    F -1.7.2 Emphase sur la source citante F-17

F -1.8 Règles générales concernant les citations F-18
    F -1.8.1 Emplacement des citations F-18
    F -1.8.2 Forme des citations F-18
    F -1.8.3 Citation d'une source dans une autre langue F-19

F -1.9 Rédaction d'un texte en langue étrangère F-19

1   RÈGLES FONDAMENTALES

Les règles établies dans ce *Manuel* s'appliquent seulement aux **notes de bas de page**, aux **références dans le texte** et aux **bibliographies**. Elles ne s'appliquent pas au corps du texte ou aux notes textuelles (par ex. des phrases et des clauses qui existent en dehors des limites de la citation); un guide de style devrait être utilisé pour ces derniers.

Utiliser les règles de la partie française pour écrire en français, et ce, même lorsque la source originale est dans une autre langue. N'utiliser les règles de la partie anglaise que pour écrire en anglais.

Lorsqu'un acronyme ou une abréviation est employée dans une phrase complète, suivre les règles grammaticales usuelles dans l'usage des **points**. Omettre ces points dans les notes de bas de page « mécaniques ».

Les **caractères gras en couleur** de ce *Manuel* mettent les exemples en évidence.

Si la règle impose des parenthèses **( )**, ne pas les remplacer par des crochets **[ ]** et vice-versa.

1.1   BIBLIOGRAPHIES

LÉGISLATION

Barristers and Solicitors Act, RSBC 1979, c 26.
Loi antiterroriste, LC 2001, c 41.
Loi de 1991 sur les sages-femmes, LO 1991, c 31.
Loi sur les sociétés de fiducie et les sociétés d'épargne, RLRQ c S-29.01.

JURISPRUDENCE

Delgamuukw c Colombie-Britannique, [1997] 3 RCS 1010, 153 DLR (4e) 193.
Kendle v Melsom, [1998] HCA 13.
Cass civ 1re, 26 juin 2001, (2001) D Jur 2593 (note V Avena-Robardet).
Létourneau c Laflèche Auto Ltée, [1986] RJQ 1956 (CS).
Nouvelle-Écosse (Workers' Compensation Board) c Martin, 2003 CSC 54, [2003] 2 RCS 504.

DOCTRINE : MONOGRAPHIES

Lafond, Pierre-Claude. *Précis de droit des biens*, Montréal, Thémis, 1999.
Médina, Annie. *Abus de biens sociaux : prévention, détection, poursuite*, Paris, Dalloz, 2001.
Nadeau, Alain-Robert. *Vie privée et droits fondamentaux*, Cowansville (Qc), Yvon Blais, 2000.
Tan, Cheng Han. *Matrimonial Law in Singapore and Malaysia*, Singapore, Butterworths Asia, 1994.

DOCTRINE : ARTICLES

Lamontagne, Denys-Claude. « L'imbrication du possessoire et du pétitoire », (1995) 55 R du B 661.
Lamontagne, Denys-Claude. « L'influence du droit public sur le droit immobilier », [1986] RDI 401.

> Turp, Daniel. « Le droit au Québec à l'autodétermination et à l'indépendance : la loi sur la *clarté* du Canada et la loi sur les *droits fondamentaux* du Québec en collision » dans Marie-Françoise Labouz, dir, *Intégrations et identités nord-américaines : vues de Montréal*, Bruxelles, Bruylant, 2001, 137.
> Wang Sheng Chang. « Combination of Arbitration with Conciliation and Remittance of Awards — with
>   Special Reference to the Asia-Oceana Region » (2002) 19 J Int Arb 51.

- Diviser les bibliographies et les listes d'autorités de textes juridiques en sections (par ex. **législation**, **jurisprudence** et **doctrine**). Si certaines sources ne correspondent pas à l'une de ces catégories, ajouter une section résiduelle (**autres sources**). Il peut être utile de diviser la section contenant la doctrine en sous-sections (par ex. **monographies**, **périodiques** et **ouvrages collectifs**). Il est également possible de diviser les sources entre **sources internes** et **sources étrangères**.

- Dans chaque section, classer les sources par **ordre alphabétique**. Classer la législation selon le titre de la loi, la jurisprudence selon l'intitulé et la doctrine selon le nom de famille de l'auteur.

- Pour la doctrine contenue dans une bibliographie, présenter le **nom de famille de l'auteur en premier** pour faciliter le classement par ordre alphabétique. Attention : l'ordre du prénom et du nom de famille change selon les traditions culturelles (avant, après ou entre les prénoms). Si le nom de famille apparaît en premier sur l'édition, omettre la virgule après ce nom (par ex. **Wang Sheng Chang**). Si le prénom apparaît en premier, mettre une virgule après le nom (par ex. **Smith, Graham JH**). Afin d'assurer l'exactitude de la forme et de respecter la source originale, présenter le nom de l'auteur tel qu'il apparaît dans la publication, en incluant les initiales, et ce, même si le nom d'un même auteur est différent dans une référence ultérieure.

- S'il y a une référence avec plus d'un auteur, écrire le prénom avant le nom de famille pour tous les auteurs excepté le premier (par ex. **Baudouin, Jean-Louis et Pierre-Gabriel Jobin**).

- S'il y a une référence à une œuvre par un seul auteur, ainsi qu'une œuvre par cet auteur et d'autres auteurs (par ex. **Baudouin** et **Baudouin et Jobin**), écrire celle avec un seul auteur d'abord.

- Chaque référence devrait avoir un **retrait** de 1/4 de pouce ou 0,63 cm (mettre en retrait toutes les lignes sauf la première).

- Suivre les règles des notes de bas de page du *Manuel* pour toute information d'une référence à la doctrine (excepté pour l'ordre des noms de l'auteur ou du directeur d'un ouvrage collectif).

1.2 RÉFÉRENCES DANS LE TEXTE : NOTE DE SERVICE ET FACTUM

La règle habituelle exige l'utilisation de notes en bas de page pour la rédaction de textes juridiques. Toutefois, dans certains types de documents, les références doivent être incluses **dans le corps même du texte**.

1.2.1 Note de service

En plus des conditions pour « méfait donnant ouverture à un droit d'action » indépendamment de la violation pour laquelle on poursuit, les dommages-intérêts punitifs seront accordés lorsque la conduite du défendeur est si « malveillante, opprimante et abusive qu'elle choque le sens de dignité de la cour » (***Hill c Église de scientologie de Toronto*, [1995] 2 RCS 1130 au para 196, 184 NR 1, juge Cory [*Hill*]**). Une telle conduite comprend la diffamation (***ibid***), l'omission de fournir des soins médicaux (***Robitaille v Vancouver Hockey Club*, [1981] 3 WWR 481, 124 DLR (3ᵉ) 228 (BCCA))**, et exceptionnellement les comportements abusifs des compagnies d'assurance (***Whiten c Pilot Insurance*, 2002 CSC 18, [2002] 1 SCR 595 [*Whiten*]**).
Puisque le premier mécanisme punitif est le droit criminel, la modération doit primer dans les recours aux dommages punitifs (***ibid* au para 69**). Il faut aussi noter qu'il ne peut y avoir responsabilité solidaire à l'égard de dommagesintérêts punitifs, car seul le responsable de la mauvaise conduite doit être condamné à les verser (***Hill* au para 195**).

- Inclure la référence immédiatement après le texte, entre parenthèses.
- La première fois qu'une référence apparaît, suivre les règles habituelles pour les notes de bas de page. Si la référence sera répétée par la suite, créer un titre abrégé après la première référence (voir *Hill*). Si la référence n'est pas répétée, ne pas créer de titre abrégé (voir *Robitaille*).
- À partir de la deuxième apparition d'une référence, utiliser uniquement le titre abrégé. Ajouter la référence précise (par ex. ***Hill* au para 195**).
- Utiliser *ibid* (section 1.4.2) pour indiquer la référence précédente immédiatement. Utiliser *supra* (section 1.4.3) pour indiquer que la référence a déjà été mentionnée plus tôt. **Ne pas utiliser *infra*** (section 1.4.4) dans une note de service.

1.2.2 Factum

5.   En plus des conditions pour « méfait donnant ouverture à un droit d'action » indépendamment de la violation pour laquelle on poursuit, les dommages-intérêts punitifs seront accordés lorsque la conduite du défendeur est si « malveillante, opprimante et abusive qu'elle choque le sens de dignité de la cour » (*Hill*). Une telle conduite comprend la diffamation (*Hill*), l'omission de fournir des soins médicaux (*Robitaille*), et exceptionnellement les comportements abusifs des compagnies d'assurance (*Whiten*).

> ***Hill c Église de scientologie de Toronto* [1995] 2 RCS 1130 au para 196, 186 NR 1, juge Cory [*Hill* avec renvois aux RCS].**
> ***Robitaille v Vancouver Hockey Club*, [1981] 3 WWR 481, 124 DLR (3ᵉ) 228 (BCCA) [*Robitaille*].**
> ***Whiten c Pilot Insurance*, 2002 CSC 18, [2002] 1 RCS 595 [*Whiten*].**

> 6.   Puisque le premier mécanisme punitif est le droit criminel, la modération doit primer dans les recours aux dommages punitifs (*Whiten*). Il faut aussi noter qu'il ne peut y avoir responsabilité solidaire à l'égard de dommagesintérêts punitifs, car seul le responsable de la mauvaise conduite doit être condamné à les verser (*Hill*).
>
>   ***Whiten, supra* para 5 au para 69.**
>   ***Hill, supra* para 5 au para 195.**

- Les paragraphes doivent être numérotés. Ces numéros commencent habituellement à la section « Faits ».

- Fournir un titre abrégé pour chaque source citée.

- Écrire le titre abrégé entre parenthèses immédiatement après le texte.

- Indiquer la référence complète **à la fin du paragraphe**. Mettre en retrait les marges de gauche et de droite et utiliser une plus petite police de caractères.

- Mettre les références **dans l'ordre de leur apparition dans le corps du texte**. Changer de ligne après chaque référence (ne pas mettre de point-virgule).

- Écrire le titre abrégé, utilisé dans le corps du texte, en italiques et entre crochets, après la première référence complète de chaque source.

- Suivre les règles habituelles pour l'utilisation du *supra* (section 1.4.3). Toutefois, au lieu de se référer au numéro d'une note de bas de page, l'indicatif suivant le *supra* se réfère au numéro du paragraphe dans lequel est apparue la source pour la première fois (par ex. ***Whiten, supra* para 5 au para 69**). **Ne pas utiliser *infra*** (section 1.4.4) **ni *ibid*** (section 1.4.2) dans un factum.

- À la fin du paragraphe, inclure les références précises s'appliquant à tout le paragraphe (par ex. ***Whiten c Pilot Insurance*, 2002 CSC 18, [2002] 1 RCS 595 aux para 69, 101, 110**).

1.3   RÈGLES CONCERNANT LES NOTES DE BAS DE PAGE

Les notes en bas de page des textes juridiques sont habituellement des notes discursives ou des notes de référence. Les **notes discursives** regroupent les commentaires pertinents, mais assez périphériques risquant ainsi de dévier le lecteur du sujet principal. Les **notes de référence** indiquent les sources desquelles proviennent les arguments ou les citations. L'information discursive et de référence peut être combinée dans une même note.

1.3.1   La création des notes de bas de page

- Créer des notes de bas de page dans les cas suivants : (1) à la première référence à la source en question ; (2) à chaque référence ou allusion à un passage particulier de la source ; et (3) à chaque citation ultérieure tirée de la source. Fournir la référence complète dans la première référence à la source uniquement.

1.3.2 L'indication des notes de bas de page dans le texte

▨ Indiquer les notes de bas de page par des numéros en chiffres arabes (par ex. **1, 2, 3**) en exposant. Ne pas utiliser de chiffres romains ou de caractères tels que *, † et ‡.

☐ De préférence, mettre le numéro de la note de bas de page à la fin d'une phrase, mais avant la ponctuation[1]. (Cet ordre diffère de celui exigé pour les textes anglais, dans lesquels le numéro suit la ponctuation.)

☐ Pour faire référence à un seul mot, placer le numéro de la note[2] immédiatement après le mot en question.

☐ Si le mot est suivi d'un signe de ponctuation[3], le numéro précède la ponctuation.

☐ S'il s'agit d'une citation placée « entre guillemets »[4], le numéro suit les guillemets et précède la ponctuation.

1.3.3 L'emplacement des notes de bas de page

▨ Les notes de bas de page figurent au bas de la page, sous le texte, et se trouvent autant que possible sur la même page que le texte auquel elles correspondent. Distinguer les notes de bas de page du texte par une **plus petite police de caractères** et par une séparation du texte à l'aide d'une **ligne horizontale**.

1.3.4 La combinaison des notes de bas de page

▨ Ne jamais mettre plus d'un numéro de note à un même endroit dans le texte. Combiner plutôt les références en une seule note de bas de page. Lorsque plusieurs références figurent dans une même note, elles sont séparées par un point-virgule et la note se termine par un point.

> [7] *Godbout c Longueuil (Ville de)*, [1997] 3 RCS 844 ; *Aubry c Vice-Versa*, [1998] 1 RCS 591.

▨ Si cela n'entraîne aucune confusion, il est possible de combiner les références à plusieurs documents en une note dont le numéro est placé à la fin du paragraphe. Éviter la combinaison s'il s'agit de citations provenant de sources différentes.

1.3.5 Les références aux sources non françaises

▨ L'écriture en français exige le respect des règles de référence françaises, quelle que soit la langue dans laquelle la source est rédigée.

> [1] David Kairys, dir, *The Politics of Law: A Progressive Critique*, 3ᵉ éd, New York, Basic Books, 1998 à la p. 76.
>
> [2] *Credit Union Act*, SNS 1994, c 4.

▨ Conserver le titre (incluant l'usage des majuscules et de la ponctuation) dans la langue d'origine, mais pour tout autre élément de la référence, respecter les règles françaises, particulièrement en ce qui a trait à l'usage de la ponctuation.

1.3.6   Formules introductives

> **Voir** *Spar Aerospace ltée c American Mobile Satellite Corp*, 2002 CSC 78, [2002] 4 RCS 205 [*Spar*] ; *Morguard Investments Ltd c De Savoye*, [1990] 3 RCS 1077, 76 DLR (4e) 256. **Voir toutefois** *Beals c Saldanha*, 2003 CSC 72, [2003] 3 RCS 416.

▨ Les formules introductives permettent d'expliquer le lien logique entre la source à laquelle se réfèrent la note et l'idée énoncée dans le texte.

▨ Chaque formule introductive se rapporte à **toutes les références de la même phrase**. Dans l'exemple ci-dessus, la formule voir introduit à la fois *Spar* et *Morguard*, car ces références sont séparées par un point-virgule.

▨ Mettre toutes les formules dans une police romaine, excepté *contra*, qui est en italique. Sans être exhaustive, la liste suivante présente quelques formules :

Spar	Il n'y a pas de formule introductive lorsque l'autorité en question **est citée dans le texte ou est explicitement mentionnée dans le texte**.
Voir *Spar*	L'autorité en question **appuie l'idée** exprimée dans le texte.
Voir notamment *Spar*	L'autorité en question est **la plus concluante parmi plusieurs références** qui soutiennent l'idée exprimée dans le texte. Utiliser cette formule lorsque seules les meilleures sources sont présentées.
Voir par ex *Spar*	L'autorité en question en est **une parmi plusieurs appuyant l'idée** exprimée dans le texte.
Voir généralement *Spar*	L'autorité en question fournit des **renseignements généraux** sur le sujet.
Voir aussi *Spar*	L'autorité en question **s'ajoute à d'autres** qui appuient l'idée exprimée dans le texte, mais elle **n'est pas la plus concluante et n'est pas entièrement à propos**.
En accord avec *Spar*	Comme avec la formule « voir aussi », l'autorité en question s'ajoute à d'autres qui appuient l'idée exprimée dans le texte. Toutefois, dans ce cas-ci, **l'autorité appuie directement l'idée exprimée dans le texte et a autant de poids que la première autorité**. Le terme « accord » est également utilisé pour indiquer que la loi d'une indication géographique correspond avec la loi d'une autre indication géographique.

Comparer *Spar*	L'autorité en question offre une **comparaison intéressante** servant à illustrer l'idée exprimée dans le texte.
Voir toutefois *Spar*	L'autorité en question est en **désaccord partiel** avec l'idée exprimée dans le texte, mais elle ne la contredit pas directement.
Contra Spar	L'autorité en question **contredit directement** l'idée exprimée dans le texte.

1.3.7   Information entre parenthèses dans les notes de bas de page

[1] *Roncarelli c Duplessis*, [1959] RSC 121,16 DLR (2e) 689, juge Rand **(une décision discrétionnaire « [must] be based on considerations pertinent to the object of the administration » à la p 140)** ; *Oakwood Development Ltd c St. François Xavier (Municipalité)*, [1985] 2 RCS 164, 20 DLR (4e) 641, juge Wilson [*Oakwood* avec renvois aux RCS] **(« [l]'omission d'un organe de décision administrative de tenir compte d'un élément très important constitue une erreur au même titre que la prise en considération inappropriée d'un facteur étranger à l'affaire » à la p 174)**.

[2] Voir *Protection de la jeunesse — 631*, [1993] RDF 535 **(le parent a obtenu l'accès au journal intime de son adolescent)** ; *Droit de la famille — 2206*, [1995] RJQ 1419 (CS) [*DDF 2206*] **(le parent a enregistré la conversation téléphonique entre l'enfant et son père)**.

[3] *R c Robillard* (2000), [2001] RJQ 1, 151 CCC (3e) 296 (CA) **(le juge de la Cour supérieure a erré en déclarant que la réception en preuve des communications non confidentielles était susceptible de déconsidérer l'administration de la justice)**, infirmant [1999] JQ n° 5583 (CS).

▨ Lorsque l'idée affirmée ou infirmée par une cause manque de clarté, il peut être utile de fournir **entre parenthèses** une **brève description d'une phrase ou moins**. Une citation courte de la cause peut également être incluse entre parenthèses, suivie de la référence précise (voir *Oakwood*).

▨ L'information entre parenthèses poursuit l'idée de la phrase précédente et débute par une minuscule. Si la citation débute par une majuscule, changer la première lettre par une minuscule entre crochets (voir *Oakwood*).

▨ L'information entre parenthèses concerne la référence précédente. Ainsi, l'information entre parenthèses doit être placée après la décision à laquelle l'information se réfère (voir *Robillard*).

1.4 RÉFÉRENCES ULTÉRIEURES ET ANTÉRIEURES

Lorsqu'une source apparaît plus d'une fois, **ne mentionner la référence complète que la première fois**. Les références ultérieures renvoient à cette première référence.

1.4.1 Titre abrégé

1.4.1.1 Modèle de base

▪ Ne pas créer de titre abrégé si la référence n'est mentionnée qu'une fois dans le texte.

▪ Si le titre d'une source est court (environ trois mots ou moins), le titre complet peut être utilisé dans toutes les références ultérieures (voir note 10). Si le titre d'une source est plus long, créer un titre abrégé et l'utiliser dans toutes les références ultérieures.

▪ Mettre le titre abrégé entre crochets à la fin de la référence, avant l'information entre parenthèses (voir *DDF* à la section 1.3.7) et les étapes successives de la cause (section 3.11). Ne pas mettre les crochets en italique.

▪ Placer les titres abrégés de législation et de jurisprudence en italique (par ex. *Charte*). Toutefois, les abréviations comme **CcQ** ne sont pas considérées des titres abrégés et ne

> [4] *Lamborghini (Canada) inc c Automobili Lamborghini SPA* (1996), [1997] RJQ 58 (CA) **[Lamborghini]**.
>
> [7] *R c W (R)*, [1992] 2 SCR 122 au para 1, 74 CCC (3e) 134.
>
> [10] *R c W (R)*, *supra* note 7 au para 3
>
> [21] *Lamborghini*, *supra* note 4 à la p 66.
>
> [41] Christine Gagnon, « Les effets de la publication de la déclaration de copropriété » dans *La copropriété divise*, 2e éd, Cowansville (Qc), Yvon Blais, 2007 **[Gagnon]**.
>
> [80] **Gagnon**, *supra* note 41 à la p 1.

doivent pas être placées en italique. Il est tout de même possible d'utiliser *Code* en tant que titre abrégé. Si un seul code est mentionné dans le texte, il n'est pas nécessaire d'inclure cette forme abrégée entre crochets après la première référence.

▪ Toutes les références ultérieures (***supra, ibid***) doivent être précédées du titre abrégé de la source pour guider le lecteur à la note de la référence complète (voir note 80).

1.4.1.2 Législation

> [1] **Code criminel**, LRC 1985, c C-46.
>
> [2] *Charte des droits et libertés de la personne*, RLRQ c C-12 **[Charte québécoise]**.
>
> [3] *Loi sur la Gendarmerie royale du Canada*, LRC 1985 (2e supp), c 8 **[Loi sur la GRC]**.
>
> [4] *Charte canadienne des droits et libertés*, partie I de la *Loi constitutionnelle de 1982*, constituant l'annexe B de la *Loi de 1982 sur le Canada* (R-U), 1982, c 11 **[Charte canadienne]**.

▪ Si une loi a un **titre abrégé officiel**, lui seul devrait être fourni dans la première référence. Si ce titre abrégé officiel est suffisamment court, il peut être utilisé pour les références ultérieures (par ex. *Code criminel*).

▪ Si une loi n'a **pas de titre abrégé officiel ou que**

celui-ci est trop long pour les références ultérieures, il peut être abrégé par un titre distinctif indiqué entre crochets à la fin de la référence.

Les abréviations bien connues peuvent également être utilisées (par ex. *Loi sur la GRC*).

1.4.1.3 Jurisprudence

Choisir **une partie distincte de l'intitulé ou le nom de l'une des parties** pour créer un titre abrégé (par ex. *PPL*). Il est possible d'utiliser d'autres éléments afin d'identifier la cause, tels qu'un intitulé plus connu provenant d'une cour inférieure (par ex. *Éric c Lola*), le nom d'un navire pour la jurisprudence maritime (par ex. *Wagon Mound No 2*), ou le nom d'un médicament pour les litiges en matière de brevets pharmaceutiques (par ex. *Viagra*). Afin d'éviter toute confusion lorsqu'il y a plusieurs causes portant le même nom, utiliser l'année de la décision [noter que la date doit être en caractères romains]. Afin de différencier les décisions d'une même cause émanant de différentes cours, utiliser les abréviations de l'Annexe B-2 (par ex. *Pappajohn* **CSC** ; *Pappajohn* **CA** [noter que l'abréviation de la cour doit être en caractères romains]).

Si la référence originale comporte une référence parallèle, indiquer le recueil utilisé pour les références précises subséquentes à l'aide de la mention **avec renvois aux**, suivie de l'abréviation du recueil (voir note 2).

Si une référence précise est indiquée dans la référence originale, cela sous-entend que toutes les références subséquentes seront effectuées à la même source. Ne pas inclure **avec renvois aux** dans ce cas (voir note 10).

Les références précises subséquentes doivent être effectuées à la même source (par ex. *Van der Peet* ci-dessus ne peut pas faire référence au DLR pour les références précises subséquentes). Ne pas indiquer **avec renvois aux** dans ce cas (voir note 10).

Pour les causes ayant une **référence neutre**, il n'est pas nécessaire d'indiquer à quel recueil les références ultérieures appartiennent puisque la référence précise se fait aux paragraphes. La numérotation des paragraphes est uniforme pour tous les recueils.

---

[1] *PPL Corp v Commissioner*, 569 US 1___, 133 S Ct 1897 (2013) **[PPL]**.

[2] *R c Van der Peet*, [1996] 2 RCS 507, 137 DLR (4e) 289 **[Van der Peet avec renvois aux RCS]**.

[5] *Québec (PG) c A*, 2013 CSC 5 **[Éric c Lola]**.

[7] *Van der Peet*, *supra* note 1 à la p 512.

[8] *Overseas Tankship (UK) Ltd v Miller Steamship Co*, [1967] 1 AC à la p 625, [1966] 2 All ER 709 **[Wagon Mound No 2]**.

[10] *R c Ruzic*, 2001 CSC 24 au para 2, [2001] 1 RCS 687 **[Ruzic]**.

[11] *Apotex c Pfizer*, 2009 CAF 8 **[Viagra]**.

[13] *Pappajohn c R* [1980] 2 RCS 120, 111 DLR (3e) 1 **[Pappajohn CSC]**.

[14] *R c Pappajohn*, (1979) 45 CCC (2e) 67, [1979] WWR 562 (BCCA) **[Pappajohn CA]**.

[15] *Ruzic*, *supra* note 10 au para 18.

Règles fondamentales

1.4.1.4 Doctrine

> [1] Aline Grenon, « La protection du consommateur et les sûretés mobilières au Québec et en Ontario : solutions distinctes ? » (2001) R du B can 917 **[Grenon, « Protection »]**.
>
> [2] Marie-Thérèse Chicha, *L'équité salariale : mise en œuvre et enjeux*, 2e éd, Cowansville (Qc), Yvon Blais, 2000.
>
> [3] Aline Grenon, « Le crédit-bail et la vente à tempérament dans le *Code civil du Québec* » (1994) 25 RGD 217 **[Grenon, « Crédit-bail »]**.
>
> [12] **Chicha**, *supra* note 2 à la p 183.
>
> [13] Louise Rolland, « La simulation dans le droit civil des obligations : le mensonge révélateur » dans Nicholas Kasirer, *Le faux en droit privé*, Montréal, Thémis, 2000 à la p 93.
>
> [14] **Grenon, « Protection »**, *supra* note 1 à la p 923.
>
> [86] Philippe Jestaz, « Faux et détournement d'institution en droit français de la famille » dans **Kasirer**, *supra* note 13 à la p 13.

◪ Pour faire référence à de la doctrine dans une référence ultérieure, indiquer le **nom de famille de l'auteur** (voir notes 2 et 12).

◪ Si **plusieurs ouvrages d'un même auteur** sont mentionnés, utiliser le nom de famille de l'auteur et un titre abrégé (voir notes 1, 3 et 14). Respecter la forme typographique du titre du document dans le titre abrégé, soit l'utilisation d'italique pour les livres ou l'utilisation des guillemets pour les articles.

◪ Pour faire référence à **un autre article d'un même ouvrage collectif**, écrire au long le nom de l'auteur et de l'article. Écrire ensuite la référence du premier article en mentionnant le nom du directeur de l'ouvrage collectif (voir note 86).

1.4.2   Ibid

> [1] Voir *Lapointe c Hôpital Le Gardeur*, [1992] 1 SCR 382, 90 DLR (4e) 27 [*Lapointe*].
>
> [2] *Ibid* à la p 2629. Voir aussi *Laferrière c Lawson*, [1991] 1 RCS 541 à la p 592, 78 DLR (4e) 609 [*Laferrière*] ; *Wilson c Rowswell*, [1970] RCS 865, 1 DLR (3e) 737 [*Wilson*].
>
> [5] *Laferrière*, **supra** note 2 à la p 595.
>
> [6] *Ibid*.
>
> [7] *Ibid* à la p 262.
>
> [8] *Laferrière, supra* note 2.
>
> [98] Voir aussi *Pelletier c Roberge*, [1991] RRA 726, 41 QAC 161 [*Pelletier*]. *Pelletier* emploie la théorie de la perte de chance en droit québécois (voir *ibid* à la p 737).
>
> [99] Voir toutefois la *Loi sur les compagnies*, RLRQ c C-38, art 77 [*LSC*].
>
> [100] Voir la *LSC*, *ibid*, art 79.

▨ *Ibid* est l'abréviation du mot latin *ibidem* qui signifie « au même endroit ».

▨ Utiliser *ibid* pour indiquer la **référence immédiatement précédente**. Ne pas indiquer le numéro de la note référée.

▨ Utiliser *ibid* **après une référence complète** (voir note 2), **après un *supra*** (voir note 6) ou même **après un autre *ibid*** (voir note 7). S'il y a plus d'une référence dans la note de bas de page précédente, utiliser *supra* au lieu de *ibid*.

▨ Quand *ibid* est utilisé sans référence précise, *ibid* indique la même référence précise que la note précédente (voir note 6).

▨ Utiliser *supra* pour indiquer la référence originale complète lorsque la source précédente contenait une référence précise (voir note 8).

▨ Pour faire référence à la source précédente dans une même note, utiliser *ibid* entre parenthèses (voir note 98).

1.4.3 *Supra*

▨ *Supra* est le mot latin pour « ci-dessus ».

▨ Utiliser *supra* et le titre abrégé pour indiquer la **référence précédente contenant la référence complète**. *Supra* indique toujours la référence originale complète et non un autre *supra* ou *ibid*.

▨ Si la source est identifiée clairement dans le corps du texte (par ex. si le texte indique « **la cour d'appel dans *Biorex*[1]** »), il n'est pas nécessaire de la répéter dans la note (voir note 58).

▨ Pour faire référence **à la fois à la note et au corps du texte accompagné par la note**, utiliser la formule suivante : *supra* **note # et texte correspondant** (voir note 59).

---

[1] *Canada (PG) c Biorex inc*, [1996] RDJ 548 (disponible sur QL) (CA) [*Biorex*] ; voir aussi *Loi sur les jeunes contrevenants*, LRC 1985, c R-1.

[56] *Biorex*, **supra** note 1 à la p 551.

[57] *Ibid* aux pp 552–54. Voir aussi *Loi sur les jeunes contrevenants*, **supra** note 1, art 5.

[58] **Supra** note 43 à la p 120.

[59] Voir aussi **supra note 24 et texte correspondant**.

▨ Pour faire référence **uniquement au texte** et non aux notes de bas de page, utiliser **ci-dessus** (section 1.4.5) et non *supra*.

1.4.4 *Infra*

▨ *Infra* est le mot latin pour « ci-dessous ».

▨ Utiliser *infra* pour indiquer une **note ultérieure**.

▨ L'utilisation d'*infra* est **fortement déconseillée**. Il est préférable de fournir la référence au complet dès la première référence.

▨ Ne pas utiliser *infra* uniquement pour faire référence à une source apparaissant dans une note ultérieure. *Infra* existe pour diriger le lecteur vers un commentaire général ou un grand groupe de références qui apparaissent dans une note ultérieure, et qui ne peuvent pas être reproduites aisément (par ex. « Pour des références générales et une discussion approfondie sur la matière, voir *infra*, note 58 »).

Pour faire référence uniquement au texte, utiliser **ci-dessous** (section 1.4.5) et non *infra*.

1.4.5 Ci-dessus et ci-dessous

Utiliser les expressions *ci-dessus* et *ci-dessous* pour référer le lecteur à une **partie du texte** plutôt qu'aux notes de bas de page.

Si le texte n'est pas divisé en parties ou en paragraphes facilement identifiables (par ex. en sous-titres ou en numéros de paragraphes) ou si la pagination

> [1] Voir la partie III-A, **ci-dessus**, pour l'analyse de cette question.
>
> [2] Voir la discussion plus approfondie de cette cause aux pp 164-70, **ci-dessous**.
>
> [3] Voir l'analyse de la décision dans l'arrêt *Oakes* au **texte correspondant à la note** 41.

finale du texte n'est pas définitive au moment de la rédaction, utiliser la formule *voir texte correspondant à la note #*.

1.5 RÉFÉRENCES PRÉCISES

	page	paragraphe	article	note de bas de page
singulier	*Ibid* à la p 512.	*Ibid* au para 6.	*Ibid*, art 1457.	*Ibid* à la p 512, n 139.
pluriel	*Ibid* aux pp 512—14.	*Ibid* aux para 6, 12.	*Ibid*, arts 1457—69.	*Ibid* à la p 512, nn 139, 142—46.

Cette section contient des indications générales sur les références précises. Pour des indications plus détaillées, voir la section « Référence précise » de chacune des sources (c'est-à-dire Législation, Jurisprudence, Doctrine, etc.).

Utiliser une référence précise pour faire référence à une portion spécifique du texte.

Séparer les **références précises non-consécutives** par une **virgule**, et les **références précises consécutives** par un **tiret court** (–) et non un **trait d'union** (-).

Retenir au moins les deux derniers chiffres après le tiret court.

Si le modèle d'indexation des pages contient des traits d'union (par ex. 70.1-3, 70.1-4 etc.) ou tout autre modèle pouvant rendre ambigüe la séquence numérique lorsqu'unie avec un tiret court, privilégier la formule **à** pour unir la séquence de pages (par ex. 70.1-3 à 70.1-5).

Bien qu'il soit généralement préférable de faire référence à un numéro ou à une étendue spécifique, pour faire référence à une **zone générale**, placer **et s** (l'abréviation de « et suivant ») immédiatement après le nombre de la première page de cette zone.

▨ Ne pas abréger les éléments non numérotés (par ex. Préambule, Annexe, Disposition Préliminaire, etc.) dans une référence précise.

1.6   RESSOURCES ÉLÉCTRONIQUES

Référence traditionnelle,	en ligne: \<URL\>.
Henry Samuel, "March for Girl Set Alight After Marriage Refusal" *The Daily Telegraph* (28 November 2005),	en ligne: \<www.telegraph.co.uk/news/world-news/europe/ france/1504225/March-for-girl-set-alight-after-marriage-refusal.html\> .
Theodore de Bruyn, *A Plan of Action for Canada to Reduce HIV/AIDS-related Stigma and Dis-crimination*,	en ligne: **Canadian HIV/AIDS Legal Network** \<www.aidslaw.ca/publications/interfaces/ downloadFile.php?ref=48\> .
"Defamation in the Internet Age" (1 June 2008) (balado) au 00h :04m :21s.	en ligne: **Osler, Hoskin & Harcourt LLP** \<www.osler.com/outlook/fall2008en/ linkit_001.html\> .
Ardani c Ministre de la Citoyenneté et de l'Immigration (30 mai 2005), VA4-01907,	en ligne : **Commission de l'immigration et du statut de réfugié du Canada** \<www.canlii.org/ fr/ca/cisr/doc/2005/2005canlii56963/ 2005canlii56963.html\> .
La commissaire de la concurrence c Canfor Corporation (30 mars 2004), CT-2004-002,	en ligne : **Tribunal de la concurrence** \<www.ct-tc.gc.ca/CMFiles/CT-2004-002_0001c_38LMA-4272004-1912.pdf\> .

▨ Exception faite des sources uniquement électroniques (par ex. blogs, balados, sites internet, etc.), l'ajout de l'adresse universelle (URL) n'est qu'un supplément à la référence traditionnelle.

▨ Les ressources électroniques sont généralement moins constantes que les sources imprimées. Certaines exceptions incluent la législation provinciale et fédérale en version électronique. Ainsi, opter pour les références traditionnelles avec ajout d'une source électronique. Faire référence à la source électronique seulement si celle-ci conserve des archives sur plusieurs années.

▨ Pour les références aux ressources électroniques, fournir la référence traditionnelle entière, suivie d'une virgule. Ajouter **en ligne:** puis l'URL entre chevrons (**\<\>**).

▨ Indiquer la référence précise à la suite de l'URL. Il est possible de faire référence à d'autres éléments que le numéro des pages (par ex. **(balado) au 00h :04m :21s**).

▨ Indiquer toute information additionnelle pouvant guider le lecteur avant l'URL (par ex. **Commission de l'immigration et du statut de réfugié du Canada, Tribunal de la concurrence**).

▨ Faire référence à l'URL complet de la source, en excluant le protocole http://. Inclure ce protocole seulement s'il s'agit d'une forme autre que http:// (par ex. **https://**).

☐ Inclure **www lorsque la source elle-même l'inclut**. Autrement, cette omission pourrait mener vers un autre document.

☐ Inclure l'URL lorsque celui-ci débute par une forme autre que www (par ex. **ftp.sccwrp.org; ilreports.blogspot.ca**).

▓ Éliminer toute partie superflue de l'URL, telle que les paramètres qui ne sont pas nécessaires pour retrouver le site en question. Il est conseillé de s'assurer de sa fonctionnalité au préalable en effectuant un essai dans un navigateur.

✓	en ligne: <dealbook.nytimes.com/2013/07/15/citigroup-profit-climbs-42-percent/>
✗	en ligne: <dealbook.nytimes.com/2013/07/15/citigroup-profit-climbs-42-percent/ ?partner=rss&emc=rss>

▓ Certains sites web ne mentionnent pas les noms d'auteurs ou des titres formels. Dans ces cas, exercer son meilleur jugement pour inclure l'information de base permettant de retracer la source, au lieu de la référence traditionnelle (voir l'exemple **Osler**).

▓ Faire référence à une **balado** (*podcast* en anglais) comme tout autre site internet, et ajouter (balado) après la référence traditionnelle (voir l'exemple **Osler**). S'il est fourni, écrire le nom de l'orateur au lieu de celui de l'auteur.

▓ Inclure un numéro de paragraphe comme référence précise si disponible. Si la pagination d'une source imprimée est reproduite dans la source électronique, il est possible de faire référence à ces numéros de page.

1.7 RÉFÉRENCES AUX SOURCES CITANT OU REPRODUISANT LA SOURCE ORIGINALE

Il est toujours préférable de faire référence à la source originale. Si une source originale se trouve en partie dans une autre source (la source citante), consulter la source originale afin de vérifier le contexte et l'exactitude de la citation.

1.7.1 Source orginale difficile à trouver

Tel que cité dans	*Papers Relating to the Commission appointed to enquire into the state and condition of the Indians of the North-West Coast of British Columbia*, British Columbia Sessional Papers, 1888 aux pp 432-33, **tel que cité dans** Hamar Foster, « Honouring the Queen's Flag: A Legal and Historical Perspective on the Nisga'a Treaty » (1998) 120 BC Studies 11 à la p 13.

▓ Lorsque la source originale est difficile à trouver ou a été détruite, il est possible de se référer à la source originale telle qu'elle se trouve dans la source citante, en fournissant le plus d'information possible sur la source primaire, suivi de **tel que cité dans** et de la référence à la source citante.

Reproduit(e) dans	George R au Gouverneur Arthur Phillip, Instruction royale, 25 avril 1787 (27 Geo III), **reproduite dans** *Historical Documents of New South Wales*, t 1, 2ᵉ partie, Sydney, Government Printer, 1892-1901 à la p 67.

 Dans certains cas, la version originale d'un document entièrement réimprimé dans un ouvrage collectif (par ex. les collections reproduisant les débats, les lettres, les traités ou les manuscrits) est uniquement disponible dans les archives. Dans ce cas, fournir le plus d'information possible sur le document original, suivi de **reproduit(e) dans** et de la référence à la source citante.

 Ne pas faire référence aux éditions reproduisant des extraits de sources originales facilement disponibles (par ex. des manuels).

✓	*Pacte international relatif aux droits civils et politiques*, 19 décembre 1966, 999 RTNU 171, RT Can 1976 n° 47.
✗	*Pacte international relatif aux droits civils et politiques*, 19 décembre 1966, 999 RTNU 171, RT Can 1976 n° 47, reproduit dans Hugh M Kindred et al, dir, *International Law Chiefly as Interpreted and Applied in Canada : Documentary Supplement*, np, Emond Montgomery, 2000 à la p 87.

1.7.2   Emphase sur la source citante

Citant	*Canada (Citoyenneté et Immigration) c Khosa*, 2009 CSC 12, [2009] 1 SCR 339 au para 38, **citant** PierreAndré Côté, *Interprétation des lois,* 3ᵉ éd, Cowansville (Qc), Yvon Blais, 1999, à la p 91 n 123.

Pour souligner le fait qu'une source citante utilise la source originale (par ex. lorsque la source citante est plus éminente ou a plus de crédibilité), inclure la référence de la source citante, suivi de **citant** et de la source originale.

1.8   RÈGLES GÉNÉRALES CONCERNANT LES CITATIONS

Ces règles s'appliquent tant au corps du texte qu'aux notes de bas de page.

1.8.1   Emplacement des citations

Il rejette cet argument au motif que, selon lui, il n'existe **« aucune contradiction entre le refus de permettre le paiement d'honoraires extrajudiciaires et le droit d'accorder des honoraires spéciaux »**[4].

La juge Dutil est également amenée à traiter de l'importance du fait que l'usine s'est établie à cet endroit avant les réclamants. À ce sujet, elle affirme que

> **[l]a preuve ne démontre pas que les résidents du quartier Villeneuve savaient, à leur arrivée, qu'ils s'exposaient à des inconvénients aussi importants que ceux qu'ils ont vécus. Ils pouvaient s'attendre à certains inconvénients du fait qu'ils étaient voisins d'une cimenterie, cependant, ils s'installaient dans un quartier résidentiel [. . .]**[5].

L'art. 32 C.c.Q. accorde à l'enfant un statut qui lui a longtemps été dénigré à travers l'histoire. Il se lit comme suit :

> **Tout enfant a droit à la protection, à la sécurité et à l'attention que ses parents ou les personnes qui en tiennent lieu peuvent lui donner.**

- Insérer les citations courtes (de **moins de quatre lignes**) dans le texte entre guillemets.

- Mettre les citations plus longues (de **quatre lignes ou plus**) en retrait des marges, à simple interligne et sans guillemets. Les dispositions législatives peuvent également être citées en retrait des marges, bien qu'elles aient moins de quatre lignes.

1.8.2   Forme des citations

« **[L]**'objection identitaire s'avère **[. . .]** bien fondée »[32], et représente ainsi un élément important du débat.

Donc, « **[c]**ette dichotomie découle tout naturellement de *l'impossibilité des juges de se dégager de leurs principes nationaux* » **[nos italiques]**[53].

« L'intérêt d'autrui, auquel l'exercice d'un pouvoir est subordonné, le distingue essentiellement du droit subjectif que son titulaire exerce librement. La poursuite de l'intérêt d'autrui intègre nécessairement au pouvoir un but, dont l'attributaire doit tenir compte dans son exercice » **[notes omises]**.

- L'orthographe, les majuscules et la ponctuation d'une citation **reproduisent la source originale** ; toute modification doit être clairement indiquée entre crochets.

- Si la phrase devient grammaticalement incorrecte, faire un ajustement entre crochets au début de la citation (par ex. changer une majuscule pour une minuscule ou vice-versa).

▨ Utiliser **l'ellipse entre crochets [. . .]** lorsque la citation est incomplète ou que la phrase citée se poursuit. Omettre les ellipses au début ou à la fin d'une citation, sauf dans les cas où la phrase est délibérément laissé grammaticalement incomplète.

✓	Il incombe au requérant de démontrer que « **[c]**ompte tenu des circonstances, il ne pouvait renverser le fardeau de la preuve ».
✗	Il incombe au requérant de démontrer que « **[. . .]** compte tenu des circonstances, il ne pouvait renverser le fardeau de la preuve ».

▨ Lorsque la source originale contient une faute, **inclure la correction entre crochets**. Ne pas utiliser **[*sic*]**, à moins d'avoir une raison particulière de vouloir signaler l'erreur.

▨ Pour mettre l'accent sur une partie d'une citation, la mettre en italique et ajouter **[nos italiques]** immédiatement après la citation. Si les italiques étaient déjà indiquées dans la version originale, ajouter **[italiques dans l'original]**. Lorsque le texte original contient des notes de bas de page et qu'elles ne sont pas reproduites dans la citation, ajouter **[notes omises]** après la citation. (Cette règle est contraire aux règles de la partie anglaise, selon lesquelles ces expressions sont placées à la fin de la référence et non à la fin de la citation).

1.8.3   Citation d'une source dans une autre langue

▨ Utiliser autant que possible la version française de la source lorsque le texte rédigé est en français et une version anglaise lorsqu'il est rédigé en anglais.

> Comme l'indique Robin, « les faits de l'espèce ne permettent pas de conclure à la mauvaise foi » **[notre traduction]**[79].

▨ Le Canada, le Québec, le Manitoba, le Nouveau-Brunswick, l'Ontario, les Territoires du Nord-Ouest et le Yukon adoptent leurs lois en français et en anglais. Cependant, il est possible qu'avant une certaine date, celles-ci n'existent qu'en version anglaise.

▨ Dans un texte juridique, il n'est pas nécessaire de traduire un passage tiré d'une source dans une autre langue. Toutefois, si cela facilite la compréhension, la référence doit clairement indiquer qui a traduit la citation. Pour une traduction professionnelle, voir la section 6.2.2.5.1. Pour une traduction de l'auteur (vous), indiquer **[notre traduction]** après la citation.

1.9   RÉDACTION D'UN TEXTE EN LANGUE ÉTRANGÈRE

Puisqu'il s'agit d'un ouvrage intrinsèquement canadien, les règles de ce *Manuel* s'appliquent à la rédaction de textes dans les deux langues officielles. Toutefois, il est possible d'adapter ces règles pour toute autre langue en s'inspirant de la section anglaise **ou** française, selon le degré de maîtrise de l'auteur. Les règles d'or sont l'**uniformité**, la **clarté** et la **facilité de retracer une source** pour le lecteur. Les indications suivantes ne sont que des exemples d'adaptation des règles.

Traduire les formules comme « voir », « en accord avec », « tel que cité dans », « nos italiques » ou « avec renvois aux », mais conserver les expressions latines dans la langue d'origine.

Conserver les règles de **forme** telles quelles, comme l'ordre des éléments et la structure du document.

Suivre les **règles de ponctuation** de la langue de rédaction. Consulter un ouvrage grammatical si nécessaire. S'assurer que la forme employée soit toujours constante, tant dans les notes de bas de page que dans le corps du texte.

Pour la **législation et la jurisprudence**, suivre le modèle de base canadien, ou adapter les règles des « Sources étrangères » (section 7). Utiliser l'acronyme du recueil et de la législature tel que présenté dans un document officiel de la loi. Inclure une indication géographique.

Pour les sources jurisprudentielles, suivre la hiérarchie des sources. Toujours garder en tête le public cible et s'assurer que l'information soit accessible aux lecteurs. Utiliser l'acronyme du recueil tel que présenté dans la source et toujours inclure l'indication géographique et la cour.

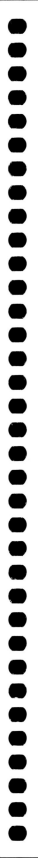

Législation

2   Législation...F-23

F -2.1   Lois F-23
    F -2.1.1   Modèle de base.. F-23
    F -2.1.2   Référence à un moment précis F-24
    F -2.1.3   Sources.. F-24
    F -2.1.4   Titre F-27
    F -2.1.5   Lois révisé es et recueils annuels F-28
    F -2.1.6   Recueils à feuilles mobiles...................................... F-28
    F -2.1.7   Indication géographique F-29
    F -2.1.8   Année, session et supplément F-30
    F -2.1.9   Chapitre.. F-31
    F -2.1.10 Référence précise F-31
    F -2.1.11 Modifications, abrogations et remises en vigueur F-32
    F -2.1.12 Annexes F-32
    F -2.1.13 Loi contenue dans une autre loi F-33

F -2.2   Lois constitutionnelles F-33
    F -2.2.1   Référence précise F-34

F -2.3   Codes F-34

F -2.4   Projets de loi.. F-35

F -2.5   Règlements F-36
    F -2.5.1   Règlements fédéraux F-37
        F -2.5.1.1   Règlements refondus F-37
        F -2.5.1.2   Règlements non refondus...................... F-37
    F -2.5.2   Règlements provinciaux et territoriaux...................... F-37
        F -2.5.2.1   Alberta, Colombie-Britannique................................ F-38
        F -2.5.2.2   Manitoba.. F-38
        F -2.5.2.3   Nouveau-Brunswick F-38
        F -2.5.2.4   Terre-Neuve-et-Labrador F-38
            F -2.5.2.4.1   Non refondus................... F-39
            F -2.5.2.4.2   Refondus........................ F-39
        F -2.5.2.5   Territoires du Nord-Ouest F-39
            F -2.5.2.5.1   Non refondus................... F-39
            F -2.5.2.5.2   Refondus........................ F-39
        F -2.5.2.6   Nouvelle-Écosse F-39
        F -2.5.2.7   Nunavut.. F-40
        F -2.5.2.8   Ontario.. F-40
            F -2.5.2.8.1   Non refondus................... F-40
            F -2.5.2.8.2   Refondus........................ F-40
        F -2.5.2.9   Île-du-Prince-Édouard............................ F-40
        F -2.5.2.10 Québec.. F-41
            F -2.5.2.10.1 Version historique F-41
            F -2.5.2.10.2 Version courant................................. F-41
        F -2.5.2.11 Saskatchewan F-41
            F -2.5.2.11.1 Non refondus................... F-41
            F -2.5.2.11.2 Refondus........................ F-41
        F -2.5.2.12 Yukon F-41

F -2.6   Autres informations publiées dans les Gazettes F-42

     F -2.6.1 Modèle le de base... F-42

     F -2.6.2 Décrets F-43

          F -2.6.2.1 Fédéral.. F-43

          F -2.6.2.2 Provincial et territorial... F-44

     F -2.6.3 Proclamations et instructions royales F-44

F -2.7   Règlements municipaux F-45

F -2.8   Règles de pratique F-45

F -2.9   Commissions de valeurs mobilières F-46

Législation

2 LÉGISLATION

2.1 LOIS

2.1.1 Modèle de base

Titre,	recueil	législa-ture	année,	chapi-tre,	autre élément d'indexa-tion,	(ses-sion ou supplé-ment),	référence précise.
Code criminel,	LR	C	1985,	c C-46,			art 745.
Loi de l'impôt sur le revenu,	LR	C	1985,	c 1		(5e supp),	art 18(1)(m)(-iv)(c).
Charte des droits et libertés de la personne,	RLR	Q		c C-12,			art 10.
Loi sur les valeurs mobilières,	RLR	Q		c V-1.1,			art 9.
Loi de 2002 sur le SkyDome (sta-tionnement d'au-tobus),	L	O	2002,	c 8,	annexe K,		art 2.
Loi sur les caisses d'en-traide économi-que,	LR	Q		c C-3,			art 1.

▪ Ne pas mettre d'espace entre le recueil et la législature (par ex. *Code Criminel,* **LRC** 1985; *Loi de 2002 sur le SkyDome (stationnement d'autobus),* **LO** 2002).

▪ Si la référence à une loi contient une session ou un supplément, omettre la virgule qui suivrait normalement l'élément qui précède; voir la *Loi de l'impôt sur le revenu.*

▪ Pour faire référence à la version la plus récente d'une loi québecoise présentement en vigueur, utiliser la désignation **RLRQ** (Recueil des lois et règlements du Québec). Utiliser **LRQ** et **LQ** seulement pour faire référence à des versions historiques.

▪ Pour les lois constitutionnelles, voir la section 2.2.

▪ Pour les projets de lois, voir la section 2.4.

2.1.2   Référence à un moment précis

Pour faire référence à une loi telle qu'elle parut à un moment précis lorsque la forme de référence standard est inadéquate, utiliser **telle que parue le [jour mois année]** ou **telle que parue en [mois année]** pour clarifier le moment auquel on se réfère.

> *Loi de l'impôt sur le revenu*, LRC 1985, c 1 (5e supp), art 20(1)(c) **telle que parue le 12 octobre 2012**.
>
> *Loi sur la santé publique*, LRQ c S-2.2, art 10 **telle que parue en décembre 2009**.

2.1.3   Sources

Chercher la législation dans les **versions électroniques officielles** de chaque juridiction. Si elles ne sont pas disponibles, faire référence aux **volumes imprimés de lois révisées**, **refondues** ou **réadoptées**, aux **recueils annuels**, ou aux **recueils à feuilles mobiles**. Consulter le tableau suivant pour connaître les sources à utiliser pour chacune des juridictions canadiennes.

Juridiction	Ordre des sources à citer
Canada	Faire référence à la **version électronique officielle** au <http://lois-laws.justice.gc.ca/fra/> . Ce site web contient des versions historiques de lois datant de 2001 jusqu'à présent. *Si la version officielle n'est pas disponible en ligne* : Utiliser les **lois révisées** si possible (dernière révision : 1985). Utiliser les **recueils annuels** imprimés si : ☐ une loi a été adoptée après la publication de la dernière révision ou ☐ l'article pertinent a été ajouté ou modifié depuis la date de révision.
Alberta	Faire référence à la **version électronique officielle** au <www.qp.alberta.ca/Laws_Online.cfm> . *Si la version officielle n'est pas disponible en ligne* : Utiliser les **lois révisées** si possible (dernière révision : 2000). Utiliser les **recueils annuels** imprimés si : ☐ une loi a été adoptée après la publication de la dernière révision ou ☐ l'article pertinent a été ajouté ou modifié depuis la date de révision.
Colombie Britanique	La Colombie-Britannique **n'a pas** actuellement de version électronique officielle (une base de données non officielle est toutefois dipsonible au <www.bclaws.ca>). Utiliser les **lois révisées** si possible (dernière révision : 2000). Utiliser les **recueils annuels** imprimés si :

Législation

	☐ une loi a été adoptée après la publication de la dernière révision ou ☐ l'article pertinent a été ajouté ou modifié depuis la date de révision.
Ile-du-Prince-Édouard	L'Île-du-Prince-Édouard **n'a pas** actuellement de version électronique officielle (une base de données non officielle est toutefois disponible au <www.gov.-pe.ca/ca/regulations/index.php3>). Utiliser les **lois révisées** si possible (dernière révision : 2000). Utiliser les **recueils annuels** imprimés si : ☐ une loi a été adoptée après la publication de la dernière révision ou ☐ l'article pertinent a été ajouté ou modifié depuis la date de révision.
Manitoba	Le Manitoba **n'a pas actuellement** de version électronique officielle (une base de données non officielle est toutefois disponible au <www.gov.mb.ca/laws>). Utiliser les **lois révisées** si possible (dernière révision : 1987).Utiliser les **recueils annuels** imprimés si : ☐ une loi a été adoptée après la publication de la dernière révision ou ☐ l'article pertinent a été ajouté ou modifié depuis la date de révision. Facultatif : faire référence à la *Codification permanente des lois du Manitoba* (CPLM) après les recueils annuels (section 2.1.5)
Nouveau-Brunswick	Faire référence à la **version électronique officielle** au <www2.gnb.ca/content/gnb/fr/ministeres/procureur_general/lois_et_reglements.html> . Ce site web contient la révision la plus récente (2011), les lois actuellement en vigueur, et les recueils annuels depuis l'an 2000. *Si la version officielle n'est pas disponible en ligne (avant 2000)* : Utiliser les **recueils annuels imprimés**.
Nouvelle-Écosse	Faire référence à la **version électronique officielle** au <www.assembly.nl.-ca/legislation/> pour les lois sanctionnées durant la deuxième session de 2003 ou plus tard. *Si la version officielle n'est pas disponible en ligne (avant 2003)* : Utiliser les **lois révisées** ou les **recueils à feuilles mobiles** si possible (dernière révision : 1989). Utiliser les **recueils annuels** imprimés si : ☐ une loi a été adoptée après la publication de la dernière révision, ou, ☐ l'article pertinent a été ajouté ou modifié depuis la date de révision.
Nunavut	Faire référence à la **version électronique officielle** au <www.justice.gov.nu.ca> pour les lois sanctionnées durant la deuxième session de 2003 ou plus tard. Ce site web contient des documents pdf de toutes les publications de l'Imprimeur du Territoire. → Pour les lois adoptées par les Territoires de Nord-Ouest spécifiquement à

Législation

	l'égard du Nunavut et avant le 1er Avril 1999, ajouter ceci à la suite de la référence standard: « telle qu'adoptée pour le Nunavut, conformément à la *Loi sur le Nunavut*, LC 1993, c 28 » (par ex. *Loi sur l'organisation judiciaire*, LTNu 1998, c 34, **telle qu'adoptée pour le Nunavut, conformément à la *Loi sur le Nunavut*, LC 1993, c 28**).
	→ Beaucoup de lois des Territoires du Nord-Ouest sont appliquées, *mutatis mutandi*, au Nunavut via l'article 29 de la loi fédérale *Loi sur le Nunavut*, LC 1993, c 28. Le cas échéant, ajouter la formule suivante à la suite de la référence standard : « telle que dupliquée pour le Nunavut par l'article 29 de la *Loi sur le Nunavut*, LC 1993 c 28 » (par ex. *Loi sur les langues officielles*, LRNT 1998, c O-1, telle que dupliquée pour le Nunavut par l'article 29 de la *Loi sur le Nunavut*, LC 1993 c 28.
Ontario	Faire référence à la **version éléctronique officielle** au <www.e-laws.gov.on.ca/> . Ce site web contient les versions historiques de lois depuis 1990 (date de la dernière révision). *Si la version officielle n'est pas disponible en ligne (avant 2000)* : Utiliser les **recueils annuels imprimés**.
Québec	Le Québec entretient le *Recueil des lois et règlements du Québec* (RLRQ), un **recueil officiel et une mise à jour** des lois en vigueur, au <www.publicationsduquebec.gouv.qc.ca/> . Les références faites à cette base de données utilisent la désignation RLRQ au lieu de LQ ou LRQ. Cette base de données est constamment mise à jour et n'est pas datée; ainsi, ne pas écrire de date pour faire référence au RLRQ. Une référence à un moment précis pourrait être appropriée dans certains cas (section 2.1.2). Les **versions historiques officielles** depuis 1969 sont disponibles en ligne au <www3.publicationsduquebec.gouv.qc.ca/loisreglements/ loisannuelles.fr.html> . Utiliser la désignation LQ ou LRQ (et non pas RLRQ) pour faire référence aux versions historiques . Actuellement, les années 1977-1995 ne sont que disponibles en français. *Si la version officielle n'est pas disponible en ligne* : Utiliser les **lois révisées** si possible (dernière révision : 2009). Utiliser les **recueils annuels** ou **recueils à feuilles mobiles** imprimés si : ☐ une loi a été adoptée après la publication de la dernière révision, ou, ☐ l'article pertinent a été ajouté ou modifié depuis la date de révision.
Saskatchewan	Le Saskatchewan **n'a pas** actuellement de version éléctronique officielle (une base de données non officielle est toutefois disponible au <www.qp.gov.sk.ca>). Utiliser les **lois révisées** si possible (dernière révision : 1978). Utiliser les **recueils annuels** imprimés si : ☐ une loi a été adoptée après la publication de la dernière révision, ou, ☐ l'article pertinent a été ajouté ou modifié depuis la date de révision.

Terre-Neuve et Labrador	Faire référence à la **version éléctronique officielle** au <www.assembly.nl.-ca/legislation> . Ce site web contient la révision la plus récente (1990), les lois actuellement en vigueur, et les recueils annuels depuis 1990. *Si la version officielle n'est pas disponible en ligne (avant 2000)* : Utiliser les **recueils annuels imprimés**.
Territoires du Nord-Ouest	Les Territoires du Nord-Ouest **n'ont pas** actuellement de version électronique officielle. Cependant, le site web <www.justice.gov.nt.ca/Legislation/AlphaSearch.shtml> contient des documents pdf des dernières lois mises à jour qui sont imprimées par l'Imprimeur du Territoire . Utiliser les **lois révisées** si possible (dernière révision : 1988). Utiliser les **recueils annuels** imprimés si : ☐ une loi a été adoptée après la publication de la dernière révision, ou, ☐ l'article pertinent a été ajouté ou modifié depuis la date de révision.
Yukon	Le Yukon **n'a pas** actuellement de version éléctronique officielle (une base de donnnées non officielle est toutefois disponible au <www.gov.yk.ca/legislation>). Utiliser les **lois révisées** si possible (dernière révision : 2002). Utiliser les **recueils annuels** imprimés si : ☐ une loi a été adoptée après la publication de la dernière révision ou ☐ l'article pertinent a été ajouté ou modifié depuis la date de révision.

2.1.4   Titre

▦   Indiquer le titre de la loi en italique et mettre une virgule non italique après le titre.

> *Loi de 2000 sur la cour d'appel*, LS 2000, c C-42.1, art 11.

▦   Utiliser le **titre abrégé officiel**, qui se trouve généralement dans la première section de la loi. S'il n'y a aucun titre abrégé, indiquer le

> *Health Care Protection Act*, SA 2000, c H-3.3.

titre qui se trouve au début de la loi. N'ajouter l'article défini (**le**, **la**) que s'il fait partie du titre (tel qu'indiqué dans le titre abrégé officiel ou au début de la loi).

▦   Si le titre de la loi est indiqué dans le corps du texte, ne pas le répéter dans la référence.

▦   Respecter l'usage des majuscules dans le titre de la loi.

▦   Si l'année fait partie du titre de la loi, elle doit être indiquée comme telle en italique (par ex. *Loi de 2000 sur la cour d'appel*). Inclure l'année après la législature même si l'année fait partie du titre.

N.B. Les lois sont adoptées en français et en anglais dans les juridictions suivantes : Canada, Manitoba, Nouveau-Brunswick, Ontario, Québec, Nunavut, les Territoires du

Nord-Ouest et Yukon. Toutefois, il est possible que des lois adoptées avant une certaine date n'existent qu'en anglais.

2.1.5   Lois révisées et recueils annuels

Lois révisées	*Code des droits de la personne*, **LR**O 1990, c H. 19. *Loi sur les compagnies*, **RLR**Q c C-38, art 29.
Recueils annuels	*Protected Areas of British Columbia Act,* **S**BC 2000, c 17.

▨ Abréger **Lois révisées**, **Lois refondues** et **Lois réadoptées** par **LR**. Abréger **Lois** et **Statuts** par **L** pour les références aux volumes annuels. Abréger **Statutes** par **S**.

▨ Utiliser **L** pour **Lois** (et non **O** pour **Ordonnances**) pour une référence à un recueil de lois des Territoires du Nord-Ouest ou du Yukon.

N.B. Lorsqu'une loi ne se trouve pas dans les recueils actuels de lois révisées, ne pas présumer que la loi n'existe pas ou qu'elle n'est plus pertinente. Par exemple, la *York University Act, 1965*, SO 1965, c 143, reste en vigueur malgré ne pas étant inclus dans une révision. Certaines provinces, comme l'Ontario, liste ces lois dans un table des lois non consolidées.

2.1.6   Recueils à feuilles mobiles

Manitoba	*Code des droits de la personne*, LM 1987-88, c 45, **CPLM c H175**, art 8.

▨ Les recueils à feuilles mobiles sont des consolidations de législation continuellement mises à jour. Ainsi, une référence à un recueil à feuilles mobiles ne contient pas de date et le recueil est présumé être la version la plus récente (si plus de précision est nécessaire, faire référence à un moment précis, section 2.1.2). Avec l'arrivée des consolidations en ligne, les recueils à feuilles mobiles sont de moins en moins utilisés.

▨ Seules les provinces du Manitoba et de la Nouvelle-Écosse publient une version officielle de recueils à feuilles mobiles. (Certaines juridictions, telles que l'Alberta, publient un recueil à feuilles mobiles non officiel).

▨ Les recueils à feuilles mobiles de la Nouvelle-Écosse peuvent aussi être retrouvés dans la version en ligne de la consolidation officielle de la province.

▨ Le Manitoba, qui n'a pas de base de données officielle en ligne, maintient un service de recueil à feuilles mobiles intitulé *la Codification permanente des lois du Manitoba* (CPLM); cependant, cette publication ne doit être utilisée qu'en tant que source parallèle optionelle, accompagnant une référence principale faite soit aux lois révisées, soit aux recueils annuels.

▨ Le Québec a cessé de produire les mises à jour des recueils à feuilles mobiles du RSQ en 2010 quand ce service a été remplacé par le Recueil des lois et règlements du Quebec.

◼ Ne pas mettre de virgule entre le recueil et le numéro de chapitre.

2.1.7 Indication géographique

◼ Inscrire l'indication géographique immédiatement après le recueil.

> *Loi sur les agences de voyages*, LRO 1990, c T.19.
> *Workers Compensation Act*, SPEI 1994, c 67.

Abréviations des indications géographiques dans les références législatives :

Canada	C
Alberta	A
Bas-Canada	B-C
Colombie-Britannique	BC
Haut-Canada	UC
Île-du-Prince-Édouard	PEI
Manitoba	M
Nouveau-Brunswick	N-B
Nouvelle-Écosse	NS
Nunavut (à partir du 1er avril 1999)	Nu
Ontario	O
Province du Canada	Prov C
Québec	Q
Saskatchewan	S
Terre-Neuve (Lois et règlements abrogés avant le 6 décembre 2001 / *Gazette* publiée avant le 21 décembre 2001)	N
Terre-Neuve-et-Labrador (Lois et règlements en vigueur à partir du 6 décembre 2001 / *Gazette* publiée à partir du 21 décembre 2001)	NL
Territoires du Nord-Ouest	TN-O
Yukon	Y

◼ Voir l'annexe A-1 pour les abréviations d'autres juridictions.

2.1.8   Année, session et supplément

Année	*Loi de 1998 sur l'adoption internationale*, LO **1998**, c 29.
Session qui s'étend sur plus d'une année	*Hospital Act*, LY 1989-90, c 13.
Plus d'une session dans une même année	*An Act to Amend the Labour Act*, SPEI **2000 (1ʳᵉ sess)**, c 7.
Supplément	*Loi sur les douanes*, LRC 1985, c 1 **(2ᵉ supp)**.
Année du règne	*An Act respecting the Civilization and Enfranchisement of certain Indians*, S Prov C 1859 **(22 Vict)**, c 9.

Écrire l'année après l'indication géographique, suivie d'une virgule. Si un numéro de session ou de supplément suit l'année, placer la virgule après l'indication de ce numéro ou de ce supplément.

Ne pas indiquer l'année pour le Recueil de lois et règlements du Québec (RLRQ) ou pour les recueils à feuilles mobiles du Manitoba **(CPLM)**, puisque ces sources sont continuellement mises à jour et ne contiennent pas de date de publication. S'il est nécessaire d'ajouter plus de précision, utiliser la référence à un moment précis dans le temps (section 2.1.2).

Lorsqu'une **session s'étend sur plus d'une année**, se référer à toutes les années sur lesquelles s'étend le recueil (par ex. **1980–81**).

Si un **recueil contient les lois de plusieurs sessions**, les chapitres sont numérotés indépendamment pour chaque session. Indiquer entre parenthèses le numéro de la session (**1ʳᵉ**, **2ᵉ**, **3ᵉ** ou **4ᵉ**), suivi de **sess** après l'année.

Faire référence au **supplément** pour les lois et modifications qui ont été adoptées pendant l'année d'une révision ou d'une refonte des lois, mais qui n'ont pas été comprises dans la refonte. Par exemple, le LRC 1985 n'a été mis en vigueur qu'à la fin de l'année 1988. Ainsi, les lois de 1985–1988 ont été réimprimées pour les mettre à niveau avec les lois nouvellement révisées (Premier supplément = lois de 1985; Deuxième supplément = lois de 1986; Troisième supplément = lois de 1987; Quatrième supplément = lois de 1988; Cinquième supplément = *Loi de l'impôt sur le revenu*). Indiquer entre parenthèses le numéro de supplément, suivi de **supp** après le chapitre.

Pour les lois fédérales adoptées avant 1867, ainsi que pour les lois provinciales adoptées avant que la province ne se joigne à la confédération, indiquer **l'année du règne** entre parenthèses, à la suite de l'année du calendrier.

Anne	Ann		George	Geo
Edward	Edw		Victoria	Vict
Elizabeth	Eliz		William	Will

2.1.9   Chapitre

▨ Abréger chapitre par **c**.

▨ Écrire la référence numérique ou alphanumérique du chapitre telle qu'indiquée dans le recueil, **incluant les traits d'union et les points**.

N.B. Entre 1934 et 1975–76, les lois des recueils annuels de Terre-Neuve sont désignées par un numéro. Abréger numéro par **nᵒ**.

> *Chester Trails Act*, RSNS 2001, **c 21**.
>
> *Loi sur les tribunaux judiciaires*, RLRQ **c T-16**.
>
> *Loi sur le cadastre*, RLRQ **c C-1**.
>
> *Landlord and Tenant (Residential Tenancies) Act, 1973*, SN 1973, **nᵒ 18**.

2.1.10   Référence précise

▨ Pour indiquer un article particulier d'une loi, écrire la référence précise après le chapitre et après une virgule.

▨ Abréger **article(s)** par **art** (et non **à l'art**) dans les notes de bas de page, mais jamais dans le corps du texte.

▨ Séparer les **articles consécutifs** par un tiret court et les articles **non consécutifs** par une virgule (voir note 1 et 2).

▨ Bien qu'il soit préférable de faire référence à des articles spécifiques, pour indiquer une **partie générale**, inscrire **et s** (abréviation de « et suivantes ») immédiatement après le numéro d'article (par ex. art **5 et s** »).

▨ À l'exception des alinéas non numérotés ou sans désignation alphabétique (voir note 3), les subdivisions plus précises que les articles (par ex. les paragraphes ou sous-paragraphes) sont aussi abrégées par **art** (voir note 2).

> [1] *Citizens' Representative Act*, SN 2001, C-141, **art 41, 46–48**.
>
> [2] *Dangerous Goods Transportation and Handling Act*, SA 1998, c D-3, **art 3(a)–(d), 6(1)(a), (b)**.
>
> [3] *Loi de 1999 sur les services gouvernementaux*, LC 1999, c 13, **art 2(1), al 4**.
>
> [4] *Loi sur les aspects civils de l'enlèvement international et interprovincial d'enfants*, RLRQ c A-2301, **préambule**.
>
> [5] *Loi sur l'assurance-emploi*, LC 1996, c 23, **annexe II**.

▨ Après le numéro de l'article, indiquer chaque alinéa numéroté ou désigné par une lettre entre parenthèses (**art 92(1)(a)**) et ce, même s'il n'y a pas de parenthèses dans la version officielle de la loi.

▨ Faire référence à un paragraphe non numéroté ou sans désignation alphabétique comme un alinéa, abrégé **al** (voir note 3). Ne pas mettre **al** entre parenthèses.

▨ Ne pas abréger **préambule** ni **annexe** (voir note 4 et 5).

Législation

2.1.11   Modifications, abrogations et remises en vigueur

Modification sous-entendue	*Loi sur les représentations théâtrales*, LRQ 1977, c R-25.
Modification mentionnée	*Loi sur les mesures d'urgence*, LM 1987, c 11, **modifiée par LM 1997, c 28**. *Municipal Government Act*, RSA 2000, c M-26, art 694(4), **modifiée par** *Municipal Government Amendment Act,* SA 2003, c 43, art 4.
Abrogation	*Loi sur les prestations familiales*, LRO 1990, c F2, **abrogée par** *Loi de 1997 sur la réforme de l'aide sociale*, **LO 1997, c 25, art 4(1)**.
Loi modifiant une loi antérieure	*Loi modifiant la Loi sur les normes du travail*, LTN-O 1999, c 18, **modifiant LRTN-O 1988, c L-1**.
Loi abrogeant une loi antérieure	*Loi sur la Société de développement autochtone de la Baie James*, RLRQ c S-91, **abrogeant** *Loi constituant la Société de développement autochtone de la Baie James*, **LQ 1978, c 96**.

▨ Il est sous-entendu que les références se rapportent à la **loi telle que modifiée à la date de publication** du texte de l'auteur.

▨ **Indiquer que la loi a été modifiée uniquement si cette mention est pertinente** à la question traitée dans le texte. Lorsqu'il y a une modification, faire référence d'abord à la loi originale, suivie de **modifiée par** et de la référence à la nouvelle loi.

▨ Dans le cas d'une loi qui a été **abrogée**, se référer à la loi abrogative en l'introduisant par la formule **abrogée par**.

▨ Indiquer **modifiant** lorsqu'une référence est faite à une **loi qui modifie une loi antérieure** et indiquer **abrogeant** lorsqu'il s'agit d'une loi qui abroge une loi antérieure.

▨ Indiquer le **titre de la deuxième loi** (qu'il s'agisse d'une loi modifiée ou abrogée, ou d'une loi modifiant ou abrogeant) uniquement s'il est différent du titre de la première loi ou s'il n'est pas compris dans le titre de celle-ci (voir par ex. ci-dessus, *Loi sur les mesures d'urgence* et *Loi modifiant la Loi sur les normes du travail*).

▨ Si une loi ou une partie d'une loi a été **abrogée et remplacée par une autre**, se référer à la loi originale en premier, suivie de **remise en vigueur par** et de la référence complète de la nouvelle partie. N'utiliser cette terminologie que lorsque les dispositions abrogées et remplacées se trouvent dans le même article.

2.1.12   Annexes

▨ Pour les lois paraissant dans une annexe, indiquer la révision ou le volume dont fait partie l'annexe, suivis d'une virgule et du numéro de l'annexe.

> *Déclaration canadienne des droits*, LC 1960, c 44, **reproduite dans LRC 1985, annexe III**.

▨ Toujours indiquer la référence officielle, suivie de **reproduite dans** pour introduire la référence à l'annexe.

▨ Écrire le numéro de l'annexe en chiffres romains.

2.1.13   Loi contenue dans une autre loi

> *Loi sur la Société d'expansion du Cap-Breton*, art 27, **constituant** la partie II de la *Loi organique de 1987 sur le Canada atlantique*, LC 1988, c 50.

▨ Faire référence au titre de la loi contenue dans la loi principale en premier lieu, suivi d'une virgule. Écrire ensuite la référence complète de la partie pertinente de la loi principale, introduite par **constituant**.

▨ Les références précises à la loi contenue sont indiquées avant la référence à la loi principale (voir l'emplacement de l'art 27 dans l'exemple).

2.2   LOIS CONSTITUTIONNELLES

Loi constitutionnelle de 1867	*Loi constitutionnelle de 1867* (R-U), 30 & 31 Vict, c 3, reproduite dans LRC 1985, annexe II, n° 5.
Loi de 1982 sur le Canada	*Loi de 1982 sur le Canada* (R-U), 1982, c 11.
Loi constitutionnelle de 1982	*Loi constitutionnelle de 1982*, constituant l'annexe B de la *Loi de 1982 sur le Canada* (R-U), 1982, c 11.
Charte	*Charte canadienne des droits et libertés*, partie I de la *Loi constitutionnelle de 1982*, constituant l'annexe B de la *Loi de 1982 sur le Canada* (R-U), 1982, c 11.
Autres lois constitutionnelles	*Acte de Québec de 1774* (R-U), 14 Geo III, c 83, art 3, reproduit dans LRC 1985, annexe II, n° 2.

▨ Beaucoup de lois constitutionnelles ont été adoptées sous des noms différents de ceux couramment utilisés ; il faut utiliser le **nouveau titre**. Consulter l'annexe de la *Loi constitutionnelle de 1982* pour trouver le nouveau titre de la loi. Si l'ancien titre est pertinent, l'indiquer entre parenthèses à la fin de la référence.

▨ La *Loi de 1982 sur le Canada* est une loi du Royaume-Uni. Sa référence doit donc se conformer aux règles concernant les lois du Royaume-Uni (section 7.3.1).

▨ Puisque la *Charte* n'a pas été promulguée indépendamment, faire référence à la partie I de la *Loi constitutionnelle de 1982*.

▨ Au besoin, inclure une référence à l'**annexe II des LRC 1985** après la référence officielle, puisque la plupart des lois constitutionnelles canadiennes s'y trouvent.

Législation

2.2.1   Référence précise

Loi constitutionnelle de 1867	*Loi constitutionnelle de 1867* (R-U), 30 & 31 Vict, c 3, **art 91**, reproduit dans LRC 1985, annexe II, n° 5.
Loi de 1982 sur le Canada	*Loi de 1982 sur le Canada* (R-U), 1982, c 11, **art 1**.
Loi constitutionnelle de 1982	*Loi constitutionnelle de 1982*, **art 35**, constituant l'annexe B de la *Loi de 1982 sur le Canada* (R-U), 1982, c 11.
Charte	*Charte canadienne des droits et libertés*, **art 7**, partie I de la *Loi constitutionnelle de 1982*, constituant l'annexe B de la *Loi de 1982 sur le Canada* (R-U), 1982, c 11.
Autres lois constitutionnelles	*Acte de Québec de 1774* (R-U), 14 Geo III, c 83, **art 3**, reproduit dans LRC 1985, ann II, n° 2.

Indiquer les références précises (section 2.1.10) aux articles de la *Charte* et de la *Loi constitutionnelle de 1982* immédiatement après le titre.

Indiquer les références précises aux autres lois constitutionnelles après le numéro du chapitre.

2.3   CODES

Code civil du Québec	Art 1457 **CcQ**
Code civil du Québec (1980)	Art 441 **CcQ (1980)**
Code civil du Bas Canada	Art 838 **CcBC**
Code de procédure civile	Art 20 **Cpc**
Code de procédure pénale	Art 104 **Cpp**

Ne pas fournir la référence complète pour désigner un code.

Pour un code mentionné ci-contre, utiliser le nom abrégé dès la première référence.

Pour un code canadien qui n'est pas dans la liste, écrire le nom du code au complet dans la première référence et créer une version abrégée si nécessaire. Si le titre ne comprend pas d'indication géographique, inclure cette information en caractères romains avant le titre abrégé (**art 1** *Code des professions* **[QC C prof]**).

Pour les codes étrangers, voir les règles appropriées à la section 7.

Faire référence à un paragraphe non numéroté ou sans désignation alphabétique comme à un alinéa, abrégé **al** (**art 1457, al 2 CcQ**).

Pour faire référence à une Disposition Préliminaire (ou autre section pareillement distincte) suivre les même principes que pour les articles (par ex. **Disposition Préliminaire, al 2 CcQ**).

▨ Pour faire référence aux **Commentaires du ministre** à propos du Code civil du Québec, voir la section 4.2.1.

N.B. Le **CcQ (1980)** se réfère à une série de dispositions concernant le droit de la famille promulguées en 1980 : la *Loi instituant un nouveau Code civil et portant réforme du droit de la famille*, LQ 1980, c 39. Ne pas confondre cette loi avec le *Code civil du Québec*, RLRQ c C-1991 (CcQ), en vigueur depuis le 1er janvier 1994 et remplaçant le *Code civil du Bas Canada* de 1866.

2.4 PROJETS DE LOI

	Numéro,	*titre,*	session,	législature,	indication géographique,	année,	référence précise	(renseignements supplémentaires) (facultatif).
Canada	PL C-7,	*Loi concernant l'Agence des services frontaliers du Canada,*	1re sess,	37e parl,		2005,	art 5(1)(e)	(adopté par la Chambre des communes le 13 juin 2005).
	PL S-1,	*Loi concernant les chemins de fer,*	2e sess,	40e lég,		2009,	art 1	(première lecture le 26 janvier 2009).
Provinces et territoires	PL 161,	*Loi concernant le cadre juridique de technologies de l'information,*	2e sess,	36e lég,	Québec,	2001		(sanctionné le 21 juin 2001), LQ 2001, c 32.

▨ Le numéro des projets de loi de la Chambre des communes est précédé par **C-**, et le numéro des projets de loi du Sénat par **S-**.

Législation

- Indiquer le **titre non abrégé** du projet de loi. Mettre le titre en italique et respecter l'usage des majuscules.
- Pour une référence à un projet de loi provincial, mentionner l'indication géographique.
- Ne pas indiquer l'année du règne.
- Diviser les projets de loi en **articles (art)**.
- Indiquer les renseignements supplémentaires (par ex. la date d'une des lectures ou l'étape franchie dans l'adoption du projet de loi) entre parenthèses à la fin de la référence, s'il y a lieu.
- Si possible, indiquer le numéro de chapitre de la future loi en tant que renseignement supplémentaire (par ex. **(sanctionnée le 21 juin 2001), LQ 2001, c 32)**).

2.5 RÈGLEMENTS

Indication géographique	Non refondus	Révisés, refondus ou réadoptés
Canada	DORS/2000-111, art 4	CRC, c 1180, art 3 (1978)
Alberta	Alta Reg 184/2001, art 2	–
Colombie-Britannique	BC Reg 362/2000, art 4	–
Île-du-Prince-Édouard	PEI Reg EC1999-598, art 3	–
Manitoba	Règl du Man 155/2001, art 3	Règl du Man 368/97R, art 2
Nouveau-Brunswick	Règl du N-B 2000-8, art 11	–
Nouvelle-Écosse	NS Reg 24/2000, art 8	–
Nunavut	Nu Reg 045-99, art 2	–
Ontario	Règl de l'Ont 426/00, art 2	RRO 1990, Reg 1015, art 3
Québec	D 1240-2000, 25 octobre 2000, GOQ 2000II6817, art 2	RLRQ c A-12, r 15, art 2.01
Saskatchewan	Sask Reg 67/2001, art 3	RRS, c C-502, Reg 21, OC 359/2000, art 6
Terre-Neuve	Nfld Reg 78/99, art 4	–
Terre-Neuve-et-Labrador	NLR 08/02, art 2	CNLR 1151/96, art 6
Territoires du Nord-Ouest	TN-O Reg 253-77, art 3	RRTN-O 1990, c E-27, art 16
Yukon	YD 2000/130, art 9	–

Législation

2.5.1   Règlements fédéraux

2.5.1.1 Règlements refondus

Titre,	CRC,	chapitre,	référence précise	(année) (facultatif).
Règlement sur le fil de fer barbelé,	CRC,	c 1180,	art 3	(1978).

▨ Abréger **Codification des règlements du Canada** par **CRC**.

▨ L'indication de l'année de la révision des règlements est facultative. À moins qu'une année ne soit spécifiée, il est sous-entendu que les références se réfèrent à la dernière révision. Pour plus de précision quant à la date de révision, il est possible de faire référence à un moment précis dans le temps (section 2.1.2).

2.5.1.2 Règlements non refondus

Titre (facultatif),	DORS/	année-numéro du règlement,	référence precise.
Règlement canadien sur la sûreté aérienne,	DORS/	2000-111,	art 4.

▨ Les règlements fédéraux promulgués après la codification se trouvent dans la **partie II de la** *Gazette du Canada*. Il n'est pas nécessaire de faire référence à la *Gazette*.

▨ Abréger **Décrets, ordonnances et règlements** par **DORS**.

▨ L'indication du titre du règlement est facultative.

▨ Pour faire référence aux règlements avant l'année 2000, utiliser les deux derniers chiffres de l'année (**98** et non **1998**).

2.5.2   Règlements provinciaux et territoriaux

▨ L'indication du titre du règlement au début de la référence (en italique et suivi d'une virgule) est facultative.

▨ Certaines jurisdictions utilisent tous les chiffres de l'année à partir de l'an 2000, alors que d'autres n'utilisent que les deux derniers chiffres.

N.B. L'Alberta, la Colombie-Britannique, l'Île-du-Prince-Édouard, le Nouveau-Brunswick, Terre-Neuve-et-Labrador, le Nunavut, la Nouvelle-Écosse et le Yukon ne publient pas de version révisée de leurs règlements.

2.5.2.1 Alberta, Colombie-Britannique

Indication géographique	Reg	numéro/année,	référence précise.
Alta	Reg	184/2001,	art 2.
BC	Reg	362/2000,	art 4.

▓ Faire référence aux règlements consolidés de l'Alberta et de la Colombie-Britannique de la même façon qu'aux règlements non révisés (section 2.5.1.2).

2.5.2.2 Manitoba

	Règl du	Indication géographique	numéro/année	référence precise.
Non réadopté	Règl du	Man	155/2001,	art 3.
Réadopté	Règl du	Man	468/88R,	art 2.

▓ La plupart des règlements manitobains ont été réadoptés en anglais et en français en **1987** et en **1988**.

▓ Pour les règlements manitobains réadoptés, ajouter un **R** immédiatement après les deux derniers chiffres de l'année.

2.5.2.3 Nouveau-Brunswick

Règl du	indication géographique	année-numéro,	référence précise.
Règl du	N-B	2000-8,	art 11.

▓ Les règlements du Nouveau-Brunswick ont été refondus en **1963**.

▓ Le recueil à feuilles mobiles des règlements du Nouveau-Brunswick n'est pas une refonte officielle.

2.5.2.4 Terre-Neuve-et-Labrador

▓ Toutes les références à « Newfoundland » ont été changées pour « Newfoundland and Labrador ». Pour les règlements qui ont été abrogés avant le 6 décembre 2001, indiquer seulement **Newfoundland**.

Législation

2.5.2.4.1 Non refondus

■ Pour les règlements abrogés avant le 6 décembre 2001, écrire **Nfld Reg**. Pour les autres règlements, écrire **NL**.

Indication géographique	R	numéro/deux derniers chiffres de l'année	référence précise.
NL	R	8/02,	art 2.

2.5.2.4.2 Refondus

■ Les règlements de Terre-Neuve-et-Labrador ont été refondus en 1996. Utiliser **CNLR** pour indiquer *Consolidated Newfoundland and Labrador Regulation*.

CNLR	numéro/ l'année de codification,	référence précise.
CNLR	1151/96,	art 6.

■ Pour les règlements qui ont été abrogés avant le 6 décembre 2001, faire référence à **CNR** pour indiquer *Consolidated Newfoundland Regulation*.

2.5.2.5 Territoires du Nord-Ouest

2.5.2.5.1 Non refondus

Règl des	indication géographique	numéro-deux derniers chiffres de l'année,	référence précise.
Règl des	TN-O	253-77,	art 3.

2.5.2.5.2 Refondus

RRTN-O	année de refonte,	chapitre,	référence précise.
RRTN-O	1990,	c E-27,	art 16.

2.5.2.6 Nouvelle-Écosse

Indication géographique	Reg	numéro/année,	référence précise.
NS	Reg	24/2000,	art 8.

Législation

2.5.2.7 Nunavut

Règl du	indication géographique	numéro-deux derniers chiffres de l'année,	référence précise.
Règl du	Nu	045-99,	art 2.

▦ Consulter la *Gazette du Nunavut* pour tous les règlements **à partir du 1er avril 1999**.

▦ Pour tous les règlements **avant le 1er avril 1999**, consulter les *Règlements révisés des Territoires du Nord-Ouest* (1990), ainsi que la *Gazette des Territoires du Nord-Ouest*, IIe partie.

▦ Aucune version révisée officielle des règlements du Nunavut n'a été publiée.

2.5.2.8 Ontario

2.5.2.8.1 Non refondus

Règl de	indication géographique	numéro/deux derniers chiffres de l'année,	référence précise.
Règl de	l'Ont	426/00,	art 2.

2.5.2.8.2 Refondus

RRO	année de refonte,	Reg	numéro,	référence précise.
RRO	1990,	Reg	1015,	art 3.

2.5.2.9 Île-du-Prince-Édouard

Indication géographique	Reg	ECannée-numéro,	référence précise.
PEI	Reg	EC1999-598,	art 3.

▦ Dans le numéro du règlement, **EC** est l'abréviation de *Executive Council*. Il n'y a pas d'espace entre **EC** et **année-numéro**.

2.5.2.10 Québec

2.5.2.10.1 Version historique

D	numéro-année,	référence à la *Gazette*,	référence précise.
D	1240-2000,	(2000) GOQ II, 6817,	art 2.

▢ Abréger **Décret** par **D**.

▢ Pour les références à la *Gazette officielle du Québec*, voir la section 2.6.1.

2.5.2.10.2 Version courante

RLRQ	chapitre,	numéro du règlement,	référence précise.
RLRQ	c A-12,	r 15,	art 2.01.

2.5.2.11 Saskatchewan

2.5.2.11.1 Non refondus

Indication géographique	Reg	numéro/année,	référence précise.
Sask	Reg	67/2001,	art 3.

2.5.2.11.2 Refondus

RRS	chapitre,	numéro,	référence précise.
RRS,	c C-50.2,	Reg 21,	art 6.

2.5.2.12 Yukon

Indication géographique	D	année/numéro,	référence précise.
Y	D	2000/130,	art 9.

▢ Abréger **Décret** par **D**.

2.6 AUTRES INFORMATIONS PUBLIÉES DANS LES *GAZETTES*

2.6.1 Modèle de base

Titre (information supplémentaire),	(année)	abréviation de la *Gazette*	partie de la *Gazette*,	page	(renseignements supplémentaires) (facultatif).
Ministerial Order 36/91,	(1991)	A Gaz	I,	1609.	
Avis (Banque du Canada),	(1995)	Gaz C	I,	4412.	
D309/2001,	(2001)	A Gaz	I,	1752	(*Provincial Parks Act*).

▓ Placer un espace entre l'abréviation de la *Gazette* et la partie de la *Gazette* (**A Gaz I**).

▓ Indiquer le titre du document s'il y a lieu. Si le document est numéroté, inclure le numéro avec le titre, tel qu'indiqué dans la *Gazette*. Inclure le numéro du texte réglementaire (**TR**) après l'abréviation s'il y en a un. Le nom de la personne ou de la partie concernée par un avis peut être inclus entre parenthèses après le titre (**Avis (Banque du Canada)**).

▓ Indiquer la partie de la *Gazette* après l'abréviation. Si la *Gazette* n'est pas publiée en plusieurs parties, indiquer la page immédiatement après le point suivant l'année (**GOQ, 74**).

▓ Inclure des renseignements supplémentaires nécessaires, comme le nom de la loi en vertu de laquelle un décret est promulgué (voir *Provincial Parks Act*).

Abréviations des *Gazettes* :

The Alberta Gazette	A Gaz
The British Columbia Gazette	BC Gaz
La Gazette de l'Ontario	Gaz O
Gazette des Territoires du Nord-Ouest	Gaz TN-O
Gazette du Canada	Gaz C
Gazette du Manitoba	Gaz M
Nouveau-Brunswick : *Gazette royale*	Gaz N-B
La Gazette du Yukon	Gaz Y
Gazette officielle du Québec	GOQ
The Newfoundland Gazette (avant le 21 décembre 2001)	N Gaz

Législation

The Newfoundland and Labrador Gazette (du 21 décembre 2001 à aujourd'hui)	NL Gaz
Nouvelle-Écosse : Royal Gazette	NS Gaz
Gazette du Nunavut	Gaz Nu
Île-du-Prince-Édouard : Royal Gazette	PEI Gaz
The Saskatchewan Gazette	S Gaz

N.B. La version PDF de la *Gazette du Canada* est officielle depuis le 1er avril 2003 sur le site <canadagazette.gc.ca>.

2.6.2 Décrets

Un décret est un instrument du pouvoir exécutif mettant en œuvre une décision du gouvernment (par ex. la création d'un règlement).

2.6.2.1 Fédéral

Titre (s'il y a lieu),	**CP année-numéro** ou **numéro du texte réglementaire,**	**référence à la** *Gazette,*	**(renseignements supplémentaires)** (facultatif).
	CP 1997-627,	(1997) Gaz C II, 1381.	
Décret refusant d'annuler ou de référer au CRTC une décision concernant CFJO-FM,	TR/97-51,	(1997) Gaz C II, 1523.	

▨ Inclure le titre en italique s'il y en a un.

▨ Abréger **Conseil Privé** par **CP**.

▨ Inscrire le numéro du texte réglementaire (**TR**), s'il y a lieu.

▨ Inclure des renseignements supplémentaires entre parenthèses à la fin de la référence (par ex. le titre de la loi en vertu de laquelle le décret a été promulgué) s'il y a lieu.

Législation

2.6.2.2 Provincial et territorial

Titre (s'il y a lieu),	numéro du décret,	référence à la Gazette	(renseignements supplémentaires) (facultatif).
	D 1989/19,	(1989) Gaz Y II, 57.	
Town of Paradise Order,	OC 99-529,	(1999) N Gaz II, 451	(Municipalities Act).
Règlement sur la levée de la suspension et sur l'application de l'article 411 de la Loi sur les normes du travail à l'égard de certains salariés,	D 570-93,	(1993) GOQ II, 3309.	

░ Inclure le titre en italique s'il y a lieu.

░ Pour **Order in Council**, utiliser l'abréviation telle qu'elle paraît dans la Gazette. Utiliser **D** pour **Décret**.

░ Fournir le numéro tel qu'il paraît dans la Gazette. Ce numéro comprend parfois l'année ou les deux derniers chiffres de l'année.

░ Inclure des renseignements supplémentaires entre parenthèses à la fin de la référence si nécessaire (par ex. le titre de la loi en vertu de laquelle le décret est promulgué).

2.6.3 Proclamations et instructions royales

Référence à la loi entrée en vigueur ou émetteur de la Proclamation ou de l'Instruction,	type de document,	date,	numéro du texte réglementaire,	référence.
Loi sur l'Agence spatiale canadienne, LC 1990, c 13,		entrée en vigueur le 14 décembre 1990,	TR/91-5,	(1991) Gaz C I, 74.
	Proclamation,	1er avril 1991,		(1991) S Gaz I, 1174.
George R,	Proclamation,	7 octobre 1763 (3 Geo III),		reproduite dans LRC 1985, ann II, n° 1.
George R au Gouverneur Arthur Phillip,	Instruction royale,	25 avril 1787 (27 Geo III),		reproduite dans Historical Documents of New South Wales, t 1, 2e partie, Sydney, Government Printer, 1892-1901 à la p 67.

◫ Inclure **Proclamation** et **Instruction royale** si le contexte l'exige.

◫ Indiquer la date, suivie de la *Gazette* ou autre référence.

◫ Pour les proclamations fédérales de 1972 à aujourd'hui, indiquer le numéro du texte réglementaire (**TR**).

2.7   RÈGLEMENTS MUNICIPAUX

	Ville,	Règlement ou Règlement refondu	numéro,	*titre*	(date),	référence precise.
Non re-fondus	Ville de Blainville,	Règlement	n° 955-43,	*Règlement de zonage*	(10 janvier 1994),	art 2366.
Refondus	Ville de Montréal,	Règlement refondu	c S-011,	*Règlement sur les Services de collecte,*		art 5.

◫ Indiquer le numéro du règlement municipal et le titre complet s'il n'existe pas de titre abrégé.

2.8   RÈGLES DE PRATIQUE

Indication géographique (s'il y a lieu),	organisme (s'il y a lieu),	*titre,*	numéro d'indexation (s'il y a lieu),	information d'indexation additionnelle (s'il y a lieu),	référence précise.
		Règles de la Cour suprême du Canada,			r 16.
Terre-Neuve-et-Labrador,		*Rules of the Supreme Court,*			r 16.01(2).
	Commission québécoise des libera-tions condi-tionnelles,	*Règles de pratique,*			r 10(4).
Alberta,		*Rules of Court,*	AR 124/2010,	vol 1,	r 10.50.

- Les règles de pratique (ou règles de procédure) balisent et régissent le fonctionnement des organes ou organismes judiciaires et administratifs.

- Écrire l'indication géographique et l'organisme à moins que l'information ne fasse partie du titre des règles.

- Ne pas écrire **Canada** pour les règles de la Cour suprême du Canada, ni pour les règles de la Cour fédérale.

- Abréger **règle** par **r**.

- Pour faire référence au *Code de procédure civile* et au *Code de procédure pénale* du Québec, voir la section 2.3.

2.9   COMMISSIONS DE VALEURS MOBILIÈRES

Titre,	commission	document	bulletin (s'il y a lieu)	(date),	référence précise.
Mutual Reliance Review System for Exemptive Relief Applications,	OSC	NP 12-201		(26 août 2005).	
Proposed Amendments to Multilateral Instrument 52-109 Certification of Disclosure in Issuers' Annual and Interim Filings and Companion Policy 52-109CP,	MSC	Notice 2005-19		(1 avril 2005).	
Règlement 62-104 sur les offres publiques d'achat et de rachat,	AMF	Consultation,	(2006) 3 : 20 BAMF : Valeurs mobilières 1		à la p 2.

- Pour les **instructions canadiennes**, les **normes canadiennes**, et d'autres documents de valeurs mobilières, faire référence aux **commissions de valeurs mobilières provinciales**.

- Abréger **Instruction canadienne** par **IC** et **Norme canadienne** par **NC**.

- Pour les **modifications**, les **règlements en consultation**, les **avis du personnel** et d'autres textes de commission, faire référence au **Bulletin de commission** ou à une autre publication similaire.

- Abréger *Bulletin de l'Autorité des marchés financiers : section Valeurs mobilières* par **BAMF : Valeurs mobilières**.

- Si des règlements ou des textes sont uniquement publiés en anglais, indiquer le nom de la commission et du document en anglais.

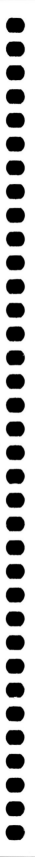

Jurisprudence

3   Jurisprudence **F-49**

F -3.1   Sources F-49

F -3.2   Modèle le de base.. F-50
    F -3.2.1   Référence neutre disponible................................... F-50
    F -3.2.2   Référence neutre non disponible F-51

F -3.3   Intitulé.. F-51
    F -3.3.1   Nom des parties F-52
    F -3.3.2   Personne représenté e par un tuteur F-52
    F -3.3.3   Noms corporatifs et de sociétés F-52
    F -3.3.4   Pays, unités fédérales, provinces et municipalités F-53
    F -3.3.5   Testaments et successions F-53
    F -3.3.6   Faillites et mises sous séquestre F-53
    F -3.3.7   Titres de lois.. F-53
    F -3.3.8   La Couronne.. F-54
    F -3.3.9   Entités gouvernementales....................................... F-54
    F -3.3.10 Sociétés d'État.. F-55
    F -3.3.11 Conseils et organismes municipaux........................ F-55
    F -3.3.12 Conseils scolaires F-55
    F -3.3.13 Syndicats... F-55
    F -3.3.14 Agences d'aide sociale F-55
    F -3.3.15 Noms de parties protégées F-56
    F -3.3.16 Intitulés différents pour une même cause : l'emploi de sub nom....... F-56
    F -3.3.17 Tierce partie agissant pour une des parties : ex rel.... F-56
    F -3.3.18 Expressions procédurales et renvois constitutionnels F-56

F -3.4   Année de la décision F-57

F -3.5   Référence neutre.. F-57
    F -3.5.1   Année... F-58
    F -3.5.2   Identifiant du tribunal... F-58
    F -3.5.3   Numéro de la décision... F-59

F -3.6   Référence précise F-60
    F -3.6.1   Modèle de base F-60
    F -3.6.2   Recueil auquel les références sont faites................. F-61

F -3.7   Recueil imprimé F-61
    F -3.7.1   Année du recueil.. F-61
    F -3.7.2   Recueil... F-62
        F -3.7.2.1   Recueils officiels F-62
        F -3.7.2.2   Recueils semi-officiels F-63
        F -3.7.2.3   Recueils non officiels........................... F-63
    F -3.7.3   Série... F-64
    F -3.7.4   Première page.. F-64

F -3.8   Services de base de données en ligne............................. F-64
    F -3.8.1   Jugements publiés et jugements possédant une référence neutre..... F-65
    F -3.8.2   Jugements non publiés et ne possédant pas de référence neutre..... F-65
        F -3.8.2.1   CanLII... F-55
        F -3.8.2.2   Quicklaw... F-65

F -3.8.2.3 Westlaw Canada F-66
F -3.8.2.4 Azimut F-66
F -3.8.2.5 Autres services F-66

F -3.9 Indication géographique et cour F-67

F -3.10 Juge F-67

F -3.11 Étapes successives d'une cause F-68
F -3.11.1 Étapes antérieures F-68
F -3.11.2 Étapes postérieures F-68
F -3.11.3 Étapes antérieures et postérieures F-69
F -3.11.4 Autorisation de pourvoi F-69

F -3.12 Jugements non publiés et sans référence neutre F-72

F -3.13 Jugements interlocutoires F-72

F -3.14 Organes et tribunaux administratifs F-72
F -3.14.1 Références aux recueils imprimés. F-72
F -3.14.2 Décisions en ligne F-73

F -3.15 Plaidoiries et documents de preuve à l'audience F-74

3   JURISPRUDENCE

3.1   SOURCES

Ordre hiérarchique des sources :

```
┌─────────────────────────────┐
│       Référence neutre       │
└─────────────────────────────┘
              ⇩
┌─────────────────────────────────────────┐
│ Recueil officiel pour les juridictions    │
│ nationales (par ex. RCS, CF ou RC de l'É);│
│ recueil semi-officiel pour les juridictions│
│ provinciales (par ex OR, RJQ)             │
└─────────────────────────────────────────┘
              ⇩
┌─────────────────────────────────────────────────┐
│ Autres sources (recueil non officiel, base de     │
│ données en ligne etc.)                            │
└─────────────────────────────────────────────────┘
```

 Il est fortement recommandé de citer **au moins deux** sources (« référence parallèle ») pour que l'information soit **bien identifiée** et **accessible**.

  ☐ En conjonction avec la hiérarchie des sources, la référence parallèle permet d'accentuer la pertinence d'un jugement s'il se trouve dans un recueil prestigieux ou spécifique à un domaine du droit (par ex. DLR, CCC, Admin LR, etc.)

 Avant de se référer aux sources moins officielles, s'assurer que les sources faisant le plus autorité ne sont pas disponibles (par ex. ne pas citer de recueil non-officiel avant de citer un recueil officiel).

  ☐ Toujours indiquer la référence neutre si elle existe.

  ☐ Après la référence neutre, faire référence aux recueils officiels (RCS, RCF ou RC de l'É) pour les juridictions nationales ou les recueils semi-officiels pour les juridictions provinciales.

  ☐ En dernier lieu, utiliser d'autres sources (recueil non officiel, service électronique, etc.).

Choisir les **autres sources** avec soin en gardant en tête le lectorat visé.

  ☐ Préférer les recueils imprimés **facilement disponibles**, **généraux** et couvrant un **vaste territoire** (section 3.7.2).

  ☐ Préférer les bases de données en ligne **facilement accessibles** (par ex. CanLII) aux services à abonnement.

Consulter le tableau ci-dessous pour les sources à citer selon les références disponibles.

Jurisprudence

Sources disponibles	Règle	Exemple
Référence neutre uniquement	Indiquer la référence neutre. Ne pas citer de service électronique.	*Burke c MNR*, **2008 CCI 680**.
Référence neutre et recueil(s) imprimé(s)	Inclure la référence neutre et ensuite faire référence au recueil faisant le plus autorité.	*R c Latimer*, **2001 CSC 1, [2001] 1 RCS 3**.
Recueil officiel et autre(s) recueil(s)	Indiquer le recueil officiel et utiliser le recueil faisant le plus autorité comme référence parallèle.	*Baker c Canada (Ministre de la Citoyenneté et de l'Immigration)*, **[1999] 2 RCS 817, 174 DLR (4ᵉ) 193**.
Recueil(s) imprimé(s) non officiel(s) et/ou service(s) électronique(s)	Faire référence aux deux sources les plus accessibles.	*Coldmatic Refrigeration of Canada Ltd v Leveltek Processing LLC* (2004), **70 OR (3ᵉ) 758** (CA).
Aucune source disponible	Suivre les règles pour les décisions non publiées (section 3.12).	*Commission des droits de la personne du Québec c Brasserie O'Keefe* (**13 septembre 1990), Montréal 500-05-005826-878** (CS).

3.2   MODÈLE DE BASE

3.2.1   Référence neutre disponible

Intitulé,	référence neutre	référence précise,	recueil,	juge (facultatif)	[titre abrégé].
Dunsmuir c Nouveau-Brunswick,	2008 CSC 9	au para 122,	[2008] 1 RCS 190,	juge Binnie	[*Dunsmuir*].
Stewart v Berezan,	2007 BCCA 150	aux para 11, 15,	64 BCLR (4ᵉ) 152,	juge Donald	[*Stewart*].

3.2.2 Référence neutre non disponible

Intitulé	(année de la décision) (si nécessaire),	recueil	référence précise,	référence parallèle,	(indication géographique et/ou cour) (si nécessaire)	juge (facultatif)	[titre abrégé].
R c S (RD),		[1997] 3 RCS 484	au para 16,	161 NSR (2e) 241,		juge Major, dissident	[*R c S*].
R c Caouette	(1998),	149 CCC (3e) 310,		1998 CanLII 12532	(QC CA)		[*Caouette*].

3.3 INTITULÉ

- L'intitulé est une version abrégée du titre d'une décision qui permet de s'y référer de manière informelle.

- **Lorsque l'intitulé est indiqué dans le recueil, utiliser cet intitulé tel quel**. Si la décision ne fournit pas d'intitulé, voir les sections 3.3.1 à 3.3.18.

- Ne pas répéter l'intitulé dans la note de bas de page s'il est déjà mentionné dans le texte.

- Mettre en italique le nom des parties et le *c* ou le *v* qui sépare le nom des parties.

- L'utilisation du *c* ou du *v* dans l'intitulé indique la langue dans laquelle la décision est rendue. Si la décision est rendue en anglais, utiliser le *v*. Si la décision est rendue en français, utiliser le *c*. Pour les décisions bilingues, utilisez le *c* pour la rédaction d'un texte en français.

- Quand l'intitulé comprend des termes qui apparaissent normalement en italique, il faut mettre ceux-ci en caractères romains (italique inversé). Ceci s'applique, par exemple, à un navire qui est poursuit in rem (par ex. *Porter v The* **Pinafore**). Comme indiqué ci-haut, cette règle ne s'applique pas aux *v* et *c*.

Décision rendue en français	*Traverse Trois-Pistoles Escoumins Ltée **c** Québec (Commission des transports)*
Décision rendue en anglais	*Pacific Developments Ltd **v** Calgary (Ville de)*
Décision bilingue	*Comité pour le traitement égal des actionnaires minoritaires de la Société Asbestos Ltée **c** Ontario (Commission des valeurs mobilières)*

3.3.1   Nom des parties

✓	**Blackburn-Moreault** c **Moreault** **Marcil** c **Hétu**
✗	Rolande Blackburn-Moreault c Henri Moreault Marcil c Hétu et Hurtubise

▨ N'utiliser que les noms de famille. Omettre les prénoms et les initiales.

▨ Lorsqu'il y a jonction de plusieurs instances, ne mentionner que la première instance.

▨ Éviter l'expression **et al** pour indiquer qu'il y a plusieurs parties.

▨ Mettre en majuscule la première lettre du nom de chaque partie, ainsi que la première lettre des noms propres. Ne pas mettre en majuscule les prépositions, les conjonctions et les autres mots faisant partie des expressions procédurales (par ex. *in re*, *ex rel*).

▨ Traduire en français les descriptions telles que **Ville de**, mais ne traduire ni les mots qui appartiennent au nom d'une partie (par ex. **Université**), ni les abréviations (par ex. **Ltée** ou **srl**).

▨ Ne pas inclure **Le**, **La**, **L'**, **Les** ou **The** s'il s'agit du premier mot du nom d'une partie, même s'il s'agit d'une raison sociale. Toutefois, indiquer l'article défini s'il fait partie du nom d'une chose poursuivie *in rem* (tel qu'un navire ou un avion, par ex. *Le Mihalis Angelos*).

3.3.2   Personne représentée par un tuteur

Dobson **(Tuteur à l'instance)** c Dobson

3.3.3   Noms corporatifs et de sociétés

▨ Il est important d'identifier les entités commerciales comme tel. Ainsi, toujours inclure **Ltd**, **Ltée**, **srl** ou **LLP**. Ne pas traduire ces expressions ou abréviations.

▨ Indiquer les prénoms et les initiales qui font partie de la raison sociale.

▨ Indiquer les noms de tous les partenaires d'une société.

✓	Pelletier c **Madawaska Co Ltée** **JJ Joubert Ltée** c Lapierre KPMG **srl** c Lachance Lemieux c **Société** Radio-Canada
✗	Pelletier c Madawaska Co Joubert Ltée c Lapierre Lemieux c Radio-Canada
Société	**Astier, Favrot** c Mendelsohn

▨ Lorsqu'une compagnie a un nom bilingue, utiliser le nom de la compagnie dans la langue de la décision de référence. Si la décision est bilingue, utiliser le nom dans la langue du texte rédigé.

Jurisprudence

3.3.4 Pays, unités fédérales, provinces et municipalités

Pays	✓	*États-Unis* c Shulman
	✗	*Les États-Unis d'Amérique* c Shulman
Province, État		*Québec (PG)* c Auger
Municipalités		*Laurentide Motels Ltd c **Beauport** (Ville de)*
		***Charlesbourg-Est (Municipalité de)** c Asselin*
		*Vigi Santé Ltée c Montréal **(Communauté urbaine de)***

▨ Indiquer **le nom français du pays habituellement utilisé** et non son nom officiel ou son abréviation.

▨ Omettre **Province de**, **État de**, **Peuple de** ou tout autre identificateur du genre.

▨ Placer les identificateurs, comme **Ville de**, **Communauté urbaine de**, **Comté de**, **District de** ou **Municipalité de** entre parenthèses après le nom du lieu.

3.3.5 Testaments et successions

▨ Ne pas indiquer le nom des exécuteurs testamentaires.

▨ Le terme **Re** doit précéder le nom

Nom de la succession	*Tremblay c **Trudel, succession***
Nom de la succession (lorsque ni le demandeur, ni le défendeur ne sont inclus dans l'intitulé)	***Re Succession Eurig***

de la succession. Cependant, toujours suivre l'intitulé indiqué par le recueil, même si le **Re** est placé différemment (par ex. *Succession Lipton (Re)*).

3.3.6 Faillites et mises sous séquestre

▨ Indiquer le nom du failli ou de la compagnie mise sous séquestre suivi de **syndic de**, **séquestre de** ou **liquidateur de** entre parenthèses.

*Chablis Textiles **(Syndic de)** c London Life Insurance*
*Lasalle Land Co **(Liquidateur de)** c Alepin*

3.3.7 Titres de lois

Si le nom de la loi indique clairement l'indication géographique	*Re Code canadien du travail*
Si l'indication géographique ne peut être déduite du nom de la loi	*Renvoi relatif à la Loi sur l'instruction publique (Québec)*

Jurisprudence

3.3.8   La Couronne

Utiliser **R** pour identifier la Couronne pour remplacer les expressions telles que **La Reine**, **Régina**, **La Couronne**, **La Reine du chef de** ou tout terme semblable qui sert à identifier la Couronne.	*R c Blondin*

3.3.9   Entités gouvernementales

Procureur général (PG)	*Schreiber c Canada **(PG)***	
Ministre du Revenu national (MRN)	*Savard c **MRN***	
Autres organismes gouvernementaux	*Chagnon c Québec **(Commission d'accès à l'information)***	
Ne pas répéter le nom de l'indication géographique	✓	*Banque Laurentienne du Canada c Canada **(Commission des droits de la personne)***
	✗	*Banque Laurentienne du Canada c Canada (Commission canadienne des droits de la personne)*
Ne pas inclure le nom d'un individu représentant un organisme gouvernemental	✓	*Canada **(Ministre de l'Emploi et de l'Immigration)** c Jiminez-Perez*
	✗	*Jean Boisvert (Directeur du centre d'Immigration Canada de Winnipeg) c Jiminez-Perez*

- **Identifier la juridiction** que l'entité gouvernementale représente.
- Utiliser le nom de l'indication géographique, suivi du nom de l'organisme gouvernemental (tel qu'une commission, un ministère ou un département) entre parenthèses.
- Abréger **Ministre du Revenu national** par **MRN** et **Sous-ministre du Revenu national** par **Sous-MRN**.
- Écrire l'abréviation **PG** pour désigner **Procureur général**.
- Pour faire référence à un **tribunal administratif fédéral ou provincial**, suivre les règles énoncées à la section 3.14.
- Ne pas inclure le nom d'un individu représentant un organisme gouvernemental.

Jurisprudence

3.3.10   Sociétés d'État

Westaim Corp c ***Monnaie*** ***royale canadienne***	Ne pas indiquer le nom de l'indication géographique avant le nom de la société d'État.

3.3.11   Conseils et organismes municipaux

Québec (PG) c Montréal (Communauté urbaine) ***Service de police***

☐   Indiquer le nom du conseil ou de l'organisme municipal après la juridiction (par ex. *Montréal (Communauté urbaine) Service de police*).

3.3.12   Conseils scolaires

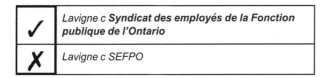 Omettre les termes tels que **Conseil scolaire** et **Conseil d'administration** ; n'indiquer que le nom de l'institution.

✓	*Ross c* ***District nº 15 du Nouveau-Brunswick***
✗	*Ross c Conseil scolaire du district nº 15 du Nouveau-Brunswick*

3.3.13   Syndicats

✓	*Lavigne c* ***Syndicat des employés de la Fonction*** ***publique de l'Ontario***
✗	*Lavigne c SEFPO*

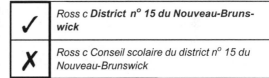 Ne pas abréger le nom des syndicats car de telles abréviations varient d'un cas à l'autre.

3.3.14   Agences d'aide sociale

Doe c ***Metropolitan Toronto Child and Family Services***
Manitoba ***(Directeur de la protection de l'enfance)*** *c Y*

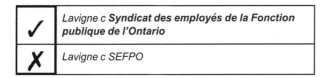 Inclure le nom de la communauté d'où provient l'agence, sauf si le nom de la communauté fait partie du nom de l'agence.

Jurisprudence

3.3.15   Noms de parties protégées

> *DP c S*
> *Droit de la famille - 1763*

■ Si les noms des parties ne sont pas divulgués, utiliser les initiales disponibles ou le titre et la description numérique fournis dans le recueil.

3.3.16   Intitulés différents pour une même cause : l'emploi de *sub nom*

> *Compagnie des chemins de fer nationaux du Canada c Canada (Commission des droits de la personne)*, [1987] 1 RCS 1114, (**sub nom** *Action Travail des Femmes c Canadian National Railways Co*) 40 DLR (4e) 193.

■ *Sub nom* est l'abréviation de *sub nomine*, soit « sous le nom » en latin.

■ Débuter toute référence par les noms des parties tels qu'ils paraissent dans le recueil le plus officiel (voir la hiérarchie des sources à la section 3.1).

■ Si un autre recueil fait référence aux mêmes parties sous des noms différents, indiquer **sub nom**, suivi de l'intitulé entre parenthèses immédiatement avant la référence en question.

3.3.17   Tierce partie agissant pour une des parties : *ex rel*

> *Ryel c Québec (PG) ex rel*
> *Société immobilière du*
> *Québec*

■ *Ex rel* est l'abréviation d'*ex relatione*, qui signifie « à cause de la relation ou de l'information » en latin.

■ Utiliser l'expression *ex rel* pour indiquer qu'une tierce partie agit au nom d'une autre partie.

3.3.18   Expressions procédurales et renvois constitutionnels

Constitutionnel	*Renvoi relatif à la Loi sur les armes à feu*
Autre	*Re* Denis **Ex parte** *Royal Dress Co : **Re** Hudson Fashion Shoppe Ltd*

■ L'expression **Renvoi relatif à** n'est utilisée que pour les renvois constitutionnels. Dans tous les autres cas, écrire **Re**.

■ Remplacer *In re*, **Dans l'affaire de** et *In the matter of* par **Re**.

■ Dans l'intitulé d'une décision, l'expression *ex parte* signifie que la partie nommée après la mention a demandé l'action.

3.4   ANNÉE DE LA DÉCISION

Lorsqu'une décision comporte une référence neutre, ne pas indiquer l'année entre parenthèses après l'intitulé. **Appliquer les règles suivantes s'il n'y a pas de référence neutre :**

L'année du recueil n'est pas mentionnée	Fournir l'année de la décision entre parenthèses	*R v Borden* **(1993),** 24 CR (4ᵉ) 184 (NSCA).
L'année du recueil et l'année de la décision sont différentes	Fournir les deux années	*Joyal c Hôpital du Christ-Roi* **(1996), [1997]** RJQ 38 (CA).
L'année du recueil et l'année de la décision est la même	Fournir l'année du recueil	*Cadbury Schweppes c Aliments FBI Ltée,* **[1999]** 1 RCS 142. ✗*Cadbury Schweppes c Aliments FBI Ltée* (1999), [1999] 1 RCS 142.

▪ Les **parenthèses** sont utilisées pour **l'année de la décision** et sont suivies d'une virgule.

▪ Les **crochets** sont utilisés pour **l'année du recueil** et sont précédées d'une virgule.

3.5   RÉFÉRENCE NEUTRE

Les références neutres émanent directement de la cour dans laquelle une décision est prise, et seule la désignation officielle doit être utilisée. Toutes les cours canadiennes et un nombre croissant de tribunaux administratifs ont adopté la référence neutre. Pour connaître leur date d'adoption, voir l'**annexe B-3**.

La référence neutre permet l'identification d'une cause indépendamment des recueils imprimés ou du service électronique dans lesquels elle est publiée.

Pour plus d'information, consulter la section 3.2.2 (« Référence neutre ») du document du Comité canadien de la référence intitulé *La préparation, la référence et la distribution des décisions canadiennes*, disponible sur <lexum.org/ccc-ccr/preparation/fr/>.

Jurisprudence

Intitulé,	référence neutre			renseignements facultatifs,		référence traditionnelle.
	année	identifiant du tribunal	numéro de la décision	numéro de paragraphe	note	
R c Law,	2002	CSC	10,			[2002] 1 RCS 227.
R v Senko,	2004	ABQB	60	au para 12,		352 AR 235.
Ordre des arpenteurs-géomètres du Québec c Tremblay	2001	QCTP	24		à la n 14,	
Effigi Inc c Canada (Procureur général),	2004	CF	1000	aux para 34–35, 40.		

- La référence est assignée par la cour et ne doit pas être modifiée.

- L'indication géographique et le niveau de la cour sont identifiés dans la référence neutre elle-même. Ne pas ajouter d'abréviation ou d'indication géographique additionnelle.

- Certains services de banques de données électroniques utilisent des codes de désignation qui ressemblent à la référence neutre (par ex. SCJ ou OJ de Quicklaw). N'utiliser ces désignations que pour citer une source provenant de ces banques de données, et non pas en lieu d'une référence neutre officielle.

- Dans un texte destiné à un lectorat étranger, ou lorsque référence est faite à de la jurisprudence étrangère, il pourrait être utile d'ajouter avant la référence neutre le code de pays de trois lettres établi par la norme internationale **ISO 3166-1 alpha-3** (par ex. *R c Law*, **CAN 2002 SCC 10**). D'autres exemples de code sont **GBR** pour le Royaume-Uni, **FRA** pour la France, **AUS** pour l'Australie, **NZL** pour la Nouvelle-Zélande, **SGP** pour le Singapour et **ZAF** pour l'Afrique du Sud.

3.5.1   Année

La référence neutre commence avec l'année à laquelle la décision a été rendue par la cour.

3.5.2   Identifiant du tribunal

Le code de désignation du tribunal est assigné par la cour et peut contenir jusqu'à huit caractères. Le code de désignation des provinces et territoires débute par un préfixe de deux caractères qui, à l'exception des Territoires du Nord-Ouest, correspond au code de l'indication géographique traditionnelle de deux lettres (celles-ci sont les mêmes en anglais et en français).

Alberta	AB
Colombie-Britannique	BC
Île-du-Prince-Édouard	PE
Manitoba	MB
Nouveau-Brunswick	NB
Nouvelle-Écosse	NS
Nunavut	NU
Ontario	ON
Québec	QC
Saskatchewan	SK
Terre-Neuve-et-Labrador	NL (NF avant 2002)
Territoires du Nord-Ouest	NWT or NT
Yukon	YK

Suivre ce préfixe de **l'acronyme habituel du tribunal ou de la cour**, mais omettre la réintroduction de toute lettre représentant l'indication géographique (par ex. le Tribunal des professions du Québec est **QCTP** et non **QCTPQ**).

Les tribunaux et les cours fédéraux ne suivent pas la règle du préfixe décrite ci-haut (par ex. Cour suprême du Canada = CSC, Cour d'appel fédérale = CAF, Cour fédérale = CF, Cour canadienne de l'impôt = CCI). Noter que la Cour fédérale portait l'abréviation CFPI de 2001 à 2003. Voir l'annexe **B-3** pour une liste complète d'abréviations pour les références neutres.

3.5.3   Numéro de la décision

Le numéro de séquence est assigné par la cour. Ce numéro revient à « 1 » le 1er janvier de chaque année.

Jurisprudence

3.6   RÉFÉRENCE PRÉCISE

3.6.1   Modèle de base

R c Latimer, 2001 CSC 1 **au para 27**, [2001] 1 RCS 3.

Bagagerie SA c Bagagerie Willy (1992), 45 CPR (3e) 503 **à la p 507** (CAF).

Québec (PG) c Germain, [1995] RJQ 2313 **à la p 2320 et s** (CA).

Canadien Pacifique c Bande indienne de Matsqui, [1995] 1 RCS 3 **aux para 40, 49**, 122 DLR (4e) 129.

Madden c Demers (1920), 29 BR 505 **aux pp 510–12**.

Ordre des arpenteurs-géomètres du Québec c Tremblay, 2001 QCTP 24 au para 18, **n 14**.

- Indiquer la référence précise **après la référence neutre**. S'il n'y a pas de référence neutre, indiquer la référence après la première page du jugement.

- **Toujours indiquer le paragraphe lorsqu'il y a une référence neutre** ou s'il y a une numérotation officielle des paragraphes (c'est-à-dire une numérotation établie par la cour et suivie uniformément par tous les recueils). S'il n'y a pas de référence neutre ou numérotation officielle des paragraphes, indiquer le numéro de page ou du paragraphe et identifier le recueil auquel les références sont faites (section 3.6.2). Lorsque les paragraphes sont numérotés, y faire référence en écrivant **au para** et pour plusieurs paragraphes, **aux para**. Pour se référer à une page, utiliser **à la p** et pour plusieurs pages, utiliser **aux pp**.

- Ne pas mettre de virgule avant la référence précise.

- Pour indiquer une **partie générale**, écrire **et s** (pour indiquer « et suivantes ») immédiatement après le numéro. Il est toutefois préférable de se référer aux pages ou aux paragraphes précis.

- Séparer **les pages ou paragraphes consécutifs** par un **tiret court**. Retenir au moins les deux derniers chiffres des nombres (par ex. **aux pp 32–35** et non **aux pp 32–5**).

- Séparer **les pages ou paragraphes non consécutifs** par une virgule (par ex **aux pp 40, 49**).

- Faire référence à une note de bas de page avec **n** (voir *Ordre des arpenteurs-géomètres*). Pour faciliter la référence, inclure le numéro du paragraphe correspondant, et séparer la référence au paragraphe de celle à la note de bas de page par une virgule.

3.6.2   Recueil auquel les références sont faites

R v Sharpe, **2007 BCCA 191**, 219 CCC (3e) 187 [*Sharpe*].

Delgamuukw v British Columbia (1991), 79 DLR (4e) 185, [1991] 3 WWR 97 (BCSC) [*Delgamuukw* **avec renvois aux DLR]** .

Université du Québec à Trois-Rivières c Larocque, [1993] 1 RCS 471 **à la p 473**, 101 DLR (4e) 494 [*Larocque*].

▨ Lorsqu'il n'y a pas de référence neutre, la numérotation de paragraphes peut varier d'un recueil à l'autre. Le lecteur doit être en mesure d'identifier le recueil qui est la source de la référence précise.

▨ La référence précise se fait autant que possible **au recueil imprimé le plus officiel, mentionné en premier lieu.** Pour des références subséquentes, utiliser le même recueil.

▨ Ne pas spécifier la source de la référence précise lorsqu'il y a une référence neutre (voir *Sharpe*). Dans ce cas, les numéros des paragraphes sont établis par la cour et non par l'éditeur individuel.

▨ Ne pas spécifier la source de la référence précise lorsqu'il y a une référence précise lors de la première mention d'un cas (voir *Laroque*). Cela sous-entend que les références subséquentes suivront le même modèle et feront référence au même recueil.

▨ Pour faire des références précises subséquentes, ajouter **avec renvois au(x)**, après le titre abrégé, suivi du nom du recueil (voir *Delgamuukw*).

3.7   RECUEIL IMPRIMÉ

3.7.1   Année du recueil

Recueil classé par année	un volume publié par année	*Hébert c Giguère* (2002), **[2003]** RJQ 89 (CS).
	plusieurs volumes publiés par année	*Renvoi relatif à la sécession du Québec*, **[1998] 2** RCS 217.
Recueil dont les volumes sont classés par série		*R v Borden* (1993), **24** CR (4e) 184 (NSCA).

▨ Les recueils sont publiés en volumes classés par année de parution (par ex. RCS ; RJQ) ou en volumes classés par série (par ex. DLR ; CCC).

☐ Si les volumes sont classés par **année de parution**, l'année est nécessaire à l'identification du volume. Fournir l'année du recueil entre crochets.

☐ Certains recueils classés par année de parution publient **plusieurs volumes à chaque année** (par ex. RCS). Indiquer l'année entre crochets, suivie du numéro du volume.

☐ Si les volumes sont classés par **série**, ne pas indiquer l'année pour identifier le volume (mais se rappeler d'inclure l'année dans l'intitulé si elle n'est pas par ailleurs indiqué dans la référence : voir la section 3.4).

Noter aussi que **certains recueils ont changé leur mode de classification des volumes**.

☐ Entre les années 1877 et 1923, les *Supreme Court Reports* ont été classés par volume (par ex. **27 CSC**). Entre 1923 et 1974, le recueil a été classé par année (par ex. **[1950] CSC**). Depuis 1975, plusieurs volumes sont publiés par année (par ex. **[1982] 2 CSC**).

☐ Avant 1974, les *Ontario Reports* étaient classés par année de parution (par ex. **[1973] OR**). À partir de 1974, ils ont été organisés par série (par ex. **20 OR**). Si les volumes sont classés par **série**, ne pas indiquer l'année pour identifier le volume.

3.7.2   Recueil

Indiquer l'abréviation du nom du recueil selon la liste des abréviations de recueils à l'**annexe C**.

> *Forbes c Desaulniers* (1991), [1992] **RL** 250 (CA).

3.7.2.1 Recueils officiels

Les recueils officiels s'appliquent aux juridictions fédérales et sont publiés par l'Imprimeur de la Reine.

S'il existe des différences entre deux versions du même jugement, la version publiée dans les recueils officiels a préséance.

Recueils officiels :

Recueils de la Cour suprême (1970 à aujourd'hui)	RCS
Canada Law Reports : Supreme Court of Canada (1923–1969)	
Canada Supreme Court Reports (1876–1922)	
Recueils des décisions la Cour fédérale (2003 à aujourd'hui)	RCF
Recueils de la Cour fédérale (1971–2002)	CF
Recueils de jurisprudence de la Cour de l'Échiquier (1923–1970)	RC de l'É
Exchequer Court of Canada Reports (1875–1922)	

3.7.2.2 Recueils semi-officiels

Les recueils semi-officiels sont publiés sous l'égide du barreau d'une province ou d'un territoire. Actuellement, seules les associations des barreaux du Nouveau-Brunswick,

Jurisprudence

de la Terre Neuve et Île du Prince Édouard, de la Nouvelle-Écosse, de l'Ontario et du Québec publient des recueils semi-officiels.

▦ Beaucoup de recueils non-officiels ont des noms qui s'apparentent à des recueils semi-officiels (par ex. *British Columbia Law Reports* (Carswell), *Manitoba Law Reports* (Maritime Law Book)). Malgré leurs noms, ces publications sont non-officiels puisqu'ils ne sont pas associés à une entité gouvernementale telle que l'Imprimeur de la Reine ou une association de barreau.

Recueils semi-officiels actuellement publiés :

Nouveau-Brunswick	*New Brunswick Reports* (2e) (1969 à aujourd'hui)	NBR (2e)
Nouvelle-Écosse	*Nova Scotia Reports* (2e) (1969 à aujourd'hui)	NSR (2e)
Ontario	*Ontario Reports* (3e) (1991 à aujourd'hui)	OR (3e)
Québec	*Recueils de jurisprudence du Québec* (1975 à aujourd'hui)	RJQ
Terre-Neuve et Île-du-Prince-Édouard	*Newfoundland & Prince Edward Island Reports* (1971 à aujourd'hui)	Nfld & PEIR

Pour une liste complète des recueils semi-officiels, courants et historiques, voir l'**annexe C-2**.

3.7.2.3 *Recueils non officiels*

▦ Pour choisir le recueil approprié, respecter les directives suivantes :

☐ les recueils **généraux** (par ex. les *Western Weekly Reports*) sont préférés aux recueils spécialisés (par ex. les *Canadian Criminal Cases*). Cependant, si un texte est destiné à un lectorat specialisé, il est possible de citer un recueil spécifique à leur domaine de droit (par ex. Recueil de jurisprudence en droit administratif, *Canadian Labour Law Reporter*) ;

☐ les recueils couvrant un **grand territoire géographique** (par ex. les *Dominion Law Reports*) sont préférés aux recueils couvrant un territoire géographique plus limité (par ex. les *Saskatchewan Reports*) ;

☐ les recueils **facilement disponibles** (par ex. les *Dominion Law Reports*) sont préférés aux recueils moins accessibles.

Voir la liste des recueils non officiels à l'**annexe C-3**.

Jurisprudence

3.7.3 Série

Numéro de série	✓	*Newell v Royal Bank of Canada* (1997), 156 NSR **(2ᵉ)** 347 (CA).
	✗	*Newell v Royal Bank of Canada* (1997), 156 NSR **(2ᵉ)** 347 (CA).
Nouvelle série		*Re Cameron* (1974), 18 CBR **(ns)** 99 (CS Qué).

▨ Si le recueil a été publié en plusieurs séries, indiquer la série entre parenthèses, entre l'abréviation du recueil et la première page du jugement.

▨ Remplacer **nouvelle série** ou *New Series* par **ns**.

▨ Indiquer le numéro de série en français (**(4ᵉ)** et non **(4th)**).

N.B. Certaines bases de données en ligne ne reconnaissent pas les numéros de série français lorsque la décision est publiée en anglais uniquement. Adapter la recherche en conséquence.

3.7.4 Première page

Ford c Québec (PG), [1988] 2 RCS **712**.	▨ Indiquer le numéro de la première page du jugement après le recueil.

3.8 SERVICES DE BASE DE DONNÉES EN LIGNE

▨ Avant de faire référence à un service de base de données en ligne (« le service »), s'assurer qu'il s'agit bien de la source la plus appropriée (section 3.1).

▨ Éviter de faire référence à un service auquel la majorité des lecteurs ne pourra pas accéder (par ex. éviter Azimut si l'auditoire ciblé n'est pas au Québec).

▨ Inclure le numéro de paragraphe comme référence précise. **Ne pas faire référence aux numéros de page** fournis par le service, puisque la numérotation peut changer d'un format électronique à un autre (par ex. pdf, txt, html).

▨ Utiliser les abréviations des noms des services à l'**annexe E**.

3.8.1 Jugements publiés et jugements possédant une référence neutre

Référence au recueil imprimé ou référence neutre,	identifiant fourni par le service	(abréviation du nom du service s'il n'est pas apparent dans la référence).
Desputeaux c Éditions Chouette (1987) Inc, [2001] RJQ 945,	AZ-50085400	(Azimut).
R v Wilkening, 2009 ABCA 9,	2009 CarswellAlta 11	(WL Can).
Caisse populaire de Maniwaki c Giroux, [1993] 1 RCS 282,	1993 CanLII 151.	

▨ Lorsqu'un jugement **est publié dans un recueil imprimé ou possède une référence neutre**, écrire la référence neutre ou le recueil imprimé, puis l'identifiant fourni par le service. Si le service ne fournit pas d'identifiant pour le jugement, écrire le nom du service entre parenthèses (suivant les abréviations listés à l'annexe E).

3.8.2 Jugements non publiés et ne possédant pas de référence neutre

3.8.2.1 CanLII

Intitulé,	identifiant fourni par le service	référence précise	(indication géographique et/ou cour) (si possible).
R v Veeve,	1999 CanLII 1451	au para 39	(Nu CJ).

▨ L'Institut canadien d'information juridique (CanLII) est un service gratuit et accessible à tous sur <canlii.org>. Favoriser CanLII au lieu des autres services pour s'assurer de la plus grande accessibilité pour le lecteur.

3.8.2.2 Quicklaw

Intitulé,	identifiant fourni par le service	(QL)	référence précise	(indication géographique et/ou cour) (si possible).
Fuentes v Canada (Minister of Citizenship and Immigration),	[1995] FCJ no 206	(QL)	au para 10	(FCTD).

Jurisprudence

▨ Trouver le code de désignation Quicklaw sous l'intitulé. Ne pas le confondre avec des recueils imprimés (par ex. **AJ** pour Alberta Judgments, **BCJ** pour British Columbia Judgments et **OJ** pour Ontario Judgments).

▨ S'assurer que le jugement n'a pas été publié ailleurs à l'aide de QuickCITE, une banque de données qui donne une liste de toutes les sources disponibles du jugement.

3.8.2.3 Westlaw Canada

Intitulé,	identifiant fourni par le service	référence précise	(indication géographique et/ou cour) (si possible)	(WL Can).
Underwood v Underwood,	1995 CarswellOnt 88		(Gen Div)	(WL Can).

▨ Si le seul code de désignation est celui fourni par Westlaw Canada, le jugement n'est pas publié ailleurs.

3.8.2.4 Azimut

Intitulé	(année),	identifiant fourni par le service	(Azimut)	référence précise	(indication géographique et/ou cour) (si possible)
Desputeaux c Éditions Chouette	(2001),	AZ-50085400	(Azimut)	au para 19	(CA Qc).

▨ Azimut est une banque de données créée par la Société québécoise d'information juridique (SOQUIJ). Si les lecteurs visés ne se trouvent pas uniquement au Québec, éviter de faire référence à Azimut.

3.8.2.5 Autres services

Faire référence aux services de base de données en ligne ayant à la fois une table des matières claire, des engins de recherche et des rédacteurs professionnels.

Intitulé	(année) (s'il y a lieu),	identifiant fourni par le service	(nom du service) (s'il y a lieu)	référence précise	(indication géographique et/ou cour) (si possible).
Abitibi-Consolidated Inc c Doughan		EYB 2008-139174	(REJB)	au para 23	(CS Qc).

▨ Ajouter l'année et le nom du service uniquement si le l'information n'est pas déjà fournie à l'intérieur du code de désignation.

Jurisprudence

░ Si l'abréviation du service ne se trouve pas dans l'**annexe E** du *Manuel*, utiliser le nom le plus communément utilisé. Par exemple, écrire **REJB** et non **Répertoire électronique de jurisprudence du Barreau**.

░ Si la base de données en ligne ne fournit pas d'identifiant, suivre le modèle figurant à l'article 7.3.2.10.2.

3.9   INDICATION GÉOGRAPHIQUE ET COUR

Beauchemin c Blainville (Ville de) (2001), 202 DLR (4ᵉ) 147 **(CS Qc)**.

Re McEachern (1996), 147 Nfld & PEIR 146 **(PEISC (TD)**.

Rempel v Reynolds (1991), 94 **Sask R** 299 **(QB)**.

Air Canada c Joyal, [1982] **CA** 39 **(Qc)**.

Miller c Monit International, 2001 **CSC** 13, [2001] 1 RCS 432.

░ Fournir l'indication géographique et le niveau de la cour :

☐ s'il n'y a **pas de référence neutre** (comportant l'indication géographique et la cour) ; **et**

☐ si ces **informations ne peuvent être déduites** du nom du recueil.

░ Fournir l'indication géographique et la cour entre parenthèses après le numéro de page ou la référence précise, ainsi qu'après toutes les références parallèles.

░ Utiliser les abréviations françaises des indications géographiques et des cours lorsque le lieu en question est bilingue (par ex. **BR Man** plutôt que **Man QB**) ; si la cour ne rend que des jugements en anglais, utiliser l'abréviation anglaise (par ex. **Sask QB**).

░ Ne pas ajouter d'espace entre les lettres majuscules des abréviations des cours. Toutefois, inclure un espace quand l'abréviation est formée de majuscules et de minuscules (par ex. **CQ** ; **BCCA** ; **Div gén Ont** ; **CQ crim & pén**).

Voir les abréviations des indications géographiques à l'**annexe A-1** et les abréviations des cours à l'**annexe B**.

3.10   JUGE

R c Sharpe, 2001 CSC 2, [2001] 1 RCS 45 au para 14, **juge en chef McLachlin**.

Gosselin c Québec (PG), [1999] RJQ 1033 (CA), **juge Robert, dissident**.

R c Wholesale Travel Group Inc, [1991] 3 RCS 154, **en banc**.

░ Indiquer le nom du juge à la fin de la référence s'il est pertinent. Ajouter **dissident(e)** précédé par une virgule s'il s'agit d'une dissidence.

░ Lorsque le banc entier a entendu la cause, il est possible d'utiliser le terme **en banc**.

3.11 ÉTAPES SUCCESSIVES D'UNE CAUSE

3.11.1 Étapes antérieures

Confirmant	*Law c Canada (Ministre de l'Emploi et de l'Immigration)*, [1999] 1 RCS 497, **confirmant** (1996), 135 DLR (4e) 293 (CFA).
Infirmant	*Wilson & Lafleur Ltée c Société québécoise d'information juridique*, [2000] RJQ 1086 (CA), **infirmant** [1998] RJQ 2489 (CS).

▣ Indiquer les étapes antérieures d'une cause à la fin de la référence si elles sont pertinentes.

▣ Séparer les décisions par une virgule.

▣ Les expressions **confirmant** et **infirmant** se rapportent à la première référence. Dans *Tsiaprailis*, la Cour suprême confirme la décision de la Cour d'appel qui avait infirmé la décision de la Cour canadienne de l'impôt.

> *Tsiaprailis c Canada*, 2005 CSC 8, 248 DLR (4e) 385, **confirmant** 2003 CAF 136 [2003] 4 CF 112, **infirmant [2012]** 1 CTC 2858, 2002 DTC 1563 (CCI [procédure générale]).

▣ Si la décision confirme ou infirme une décision antérieure pour des motifs autres que ceux discutés, utiliser **confirmant pour d'autres motifs** ou **infirmant pour d'autres motifs**.

▣ Si la décision confirme ou infirme une décision antérieure en partie seulement, utiliser **confirmant en partie** ou **infirmant en partie**.

3.11.2 Étapes postérieures

Décision confirmée	*Granovsky c Canada (Ministre de l'Emploi et de l'Immigration)*, [1998] 3 FC 175 (CA), **conf par** 2000 CSC 28, [2000] 1 RCS 703.
Décision infirmée	*Ontario English Catholic Teachers' Association c Ontario (PG)* (1998), 162 DLR (4e) 257 (Div gén Ont), **inf en partie par** (1999), 172 DLR (4e) 193 (CA Ont), **inf par** 2001 CSC 15, [2001] 1 RCS 470.

▣ Indiquer les étapes postérieures d'une cause si celle-ci a été jugée postérieurement par d'autres cours.

▣ Les étapes postérieures d'une cause figurent à la fin de la référence.

▣ Les différentes décisions sont séparées par des virgules.

▣ Utiliser **conf par** pour abréger **confirmé par** et **inf par** pour abréger **infirmé par**.

▣ Si la décision a été confirmée ou infirmée pour des motifs autres que ceux discutés, utiliser **conf pour d'autres motifs par** ou **inf pour d'autres motifs par**.

▣ Si la décision a été confirmée ou infirmée en partie seulement, utiliser **conf en partie par** ou **inf en partie par**.

Les expressions **conf par** et **inf par** se rapportent à la première référence. Ainsi, dans l'exemple *Ontario English Catholic Teachers' Association*, la Cour suprême a confirmé la décision de la Cour d'appel d'Ontario, selon laquelle la décision de la division générale de la Cour de justice de l'Ontario devait être infirmée. La Cour suprême n'a pas infirmé la décision de la Cour d'appel de l'Ontario.

3.11.3 Étapes antérieures et postérieures

Décision confirmée	*Ardoch Algonquin First Nation v Ontario* (1997), 148 DLR (4ᵉ) 126 (CA Ont), **infirmant** [1997] 1 CNLR 66 (Div gén Ont), **conf par** 2000 CSC 37, [2000] 1 RCS 950 [*Ardoch*].
Décision infirmée	*Canada c Canderel Ltée*, [1995] 2 CF 232 (CA), **infirmant** [1994] 1 CTC 2336 (CCI), **inf par** [1998] 1 RCS 147 [*Canderel Ltée*].

Suivre les règles pour les étapes antérieures et postérieures des sections ci-dessus.

Toute décision confirmative ou infirmative renvoie à la première référence :

□ Dans *Ardoch*, la Cour d'appel de l'Ontario a infirmé la décision de la Cour de justice de l'Ontario; cette infirmation a été confirmée par la Cour suprême du Canada.

□ Dans *Canderel Ltée*, la Cour fédérale d'appel a infirmé la décision de la Cour canadienne de l'impôt, mais sa propre décision a été infirmée par la Cour suprême du Canada (c'est-à-dire que la Cour suprême du Canada a confirmé la décision de la cour de l'impôt).

Indiquer les étapes antérieures avant les étapes postérieures.

3.11.4 Autorisation de pourvoi

	Référence à la décision dont l'autorisation de pourvoi est demandée,	cour,	référence au recueil ou numéro de greffe (date).
Pourvoi demandé	*White Resource Management Ltd v Durish* (1992), 131 AR 273 (CA),	autorisation de pourvoi à la CSC **demandée**.	
Pourvoi accordé	*Westec Aerospace v Raytheon Aircraft* (1999), 173 DLR (4ᵉ) 498 (BCCA),	autorisation de pourvoi à la CSC **accordée**,	[2000] 1 RCS xxii.
Pourvoi refusé	*Cie pharmaceutique Procter & Gamble Canada, Inc c Canada (Ministre de la Santé)*, 2004 CAF 393,	autorisation de pourvoi à la CSC **refusée**,	30714 (21 avril 2005).
Pourvoi de plein droit	*Whiten v Pilot Insurance* (1996), 132 DLR (4ᵉ) 568 (Div gén Ont),	**pourvoi de plein droit** à la CA.	

▨ Les décisions d'autorisation de pourvoi à la **Cour suprême du Canada** se trouvent sur CanLII, Lexum, Westlaw Canada et Quicklaw, ainsi qu'au début des RCS. Les décisions d'avant 2005 se trouvent uniquement aux début des RCS.

▨ Les décisions de **cours d'appel** concernant l'autorisation de pourvoi se trouvent parfois dans les recueils de jurisprudence et dans les services de base de données en ligne.

▨ Inclure la référence à la décision pour laquelle l'autorisation de pourvoi est demandée.

▨ Indiquer la cour devant laquelle la demande de pourvoi a été faite. Si possible, indiquer si le pourvoi a été autorisé ou refusé et faire référence à cette décision.

▨ Fournir une référence soit à un recueil imprimé (voir *Westec* Aerospace), soit au numéro de greffe suivi par la date entre parenthèses (voir *Procter & Gamble*).

▨ Certaines requêtes sont publiées. Dans ces cas, utiliser les règles de référence pour une décision standard, et ajouter le résuler (**autorisation de pourvoi à [la cour] autorisée, ou autorisation de pourvoi à [la cour] refusée;** voir *Gallagher*).

> *R v Gallagher*, 2013 ABCA 269, autorisation de pourvoi à Alta CA refusée.

Accès aux pourvois par juridiction		
Cour suprême	Les décisions d'autorisation de pourvoi sont disponibles sur CanLII, Lexum, Westlaw Canada, Quicklaw, ainsi qu'au début du RCS.	
Cour d'appel fédérale	Les décisions d'autorisation de pourvoi ne sont pas actuellement disponibles en ligne.	
Alberta	Certaines décisions d'autorisation de pourvoi ont une référence neutre et sont disponibles sur le site-web de la cour.	www.albertacourts.ab.ca
Colombie Britannique	Certaines décisions d'autorisation de pourvoi ont une référence neutre et sont disponibles sur le site-web de la cour.	www.courts.gov.bc.ca
Manitoba	Certaines décisions d'autorisation de pourvoi ont une référence neutre et sont disponibles sur CanLII.	
Nouveau-Brunswick	Certaines décisions d'autorisation de pourvoi datant depuis 2012 sont listés dans les Décisions sur les motions.	www.gnb.ca/cour/03COA1/motions-f.asp

Terre Neuve et Labrador	Les décisions d'autorisation de pourvoi ne sont pas actuellement disponibles en ligne.	
Territoires du Nord-Ouest	Certaines décisions d'autorisation de pourvoi ont une référence neutre et sont disponibles sur le sites-web du Département de Justice.	www.justice.gov.nt.ca/CourtLibrary/library_decisions_FR.shtml
Nouvelle-Écosse	Certaines décisions d'autorisation de pourvoi ont une référence neutre et sont disponibles sur le sites-web du Département de Justice.	decisions.courts.ns.ca/site/nsc/en/nav.-do
Nunavut	Certaines décisions d'autorisation de pourvoi ont une référence neutre et sont disponibles sur le sites-web de la cour.	www.justice.gov.nt.ca/CourtLibrary/library_decisions.shtml
Ontario	Les pourvois datant depuis 2002 se trouvent listés avec leur numéro de greffe.	www.ontariocourts.ca/coa/en/leave/
Île du Prince Édouard	Certaines décisions d'autorisation de pourvoi ont une référence neutre et sont disponibles sur le sites-web de la cour.	www.gov.pe.ca/courts/supreme/reasons.php3
Québec	Certaines décisions d'autorisation de pourvoi ont une référence neutre et sont disponibles sur une base de données en ligne de la province.	www.jugements.qc.ca/
Saskatche-wan	Certaines décisions d'autorisation de pourvoi ont une référence neutre et sont disponibles sur CanLII ou sur une base de données en ligne de la province (qui mène à CanLII).	www.lawsociety.sk.ca/library/public-resources/court-of-appeal-judgments.aspx
Yukon	Les décisions d'autorisation de pourvoi ne sont pas actuellement disponibles en ligne.	

NB: les informations concernant les sites-web des tribunaux est aussi généralement disponible via CanLII ou d'autres bases de données en ligne.

Jurisprudence

3.12 JUGEMENTS NON PUBLIÉS ET SANS RÉFÉRENCE NEUTRE

Intitulé	(date),	district judiciaire	numéro de greffe	référence à *Jurisprudence Express* (Québec) (s'il y a lieu)	(indication géographique et cour).
R c Crète	(18 avril 1991),	Ottawa	97/03674		(CP Ont).
Commission des normes du travail c Mercier	(13 novembre 2000),	Québec	200-22-010758-993,	JE 2000-2257	(CQ).

☐ Indiquer l'intitulé et la date de la décision entre parenthèses, suivis d'une virgule, du district judiciaire et du numéro de greffe, ainsi que de l'indication géographique et de la cour entre parenthèses.

☐ Pour les **causes provenant du Québec**, fournir la référence à *Jurisprudence Express* (**JE**) après le numéro de greffe si possible.

3.13 JUGEMENTS INTERLOCUTOIRES

Intitulé ou nom des parties	(date),	district judiciaire,	identifiant de la cour	numéro de dossier	type de document (par ex. requête en irrecevabilité).
Marris Handold v Tyson Blair	(23 avril 2011),	Montréal,	CA Qc	500-02-019902-944	(jugement interlocutoire).

3.14 ORGANES ET TRIBUNAUX ADMINISTRATIFS

3.14.1 Références aux recueils imprimés

Contradictoire	*Médecins (Ordre professionnel des) c Latulippe (CD Méd)*, [1997] DDOP 89 (TP).
Non contradictoire	*Re Citric Acid and Sodium Citrate* (1985), 10 CER 88 (Tribunal canadien des importations).

■ Fournir l'intitulé de la décision tel qu'il apparaît dans le recueil, et indiquer si le processus est contradictoire (séparer le nom des parties par *c*) ou non (mettre *Re* avant l'intitulé). Lorsqu'il n'y a pas d'intitulé, indiquer le numéro de la décision.

■ Indiquer l'abréviation employée par l'organe ou le tribunal administratif entre parenthèses à la fin de la référence s'il est impossible de le déduire du titre du recueil (utiliser le nom si aucune abréviation n'est trouvée).

■ Utiliser une abréviation courte pour les provinces et les territoires (par ex. la Commission des valeurs mobilières du Québec est abrégée **CVMQ**, la Commission des valeurs mobilières de l'Ontario est abrégée **CMVO** et la Newfoundland and Labrador Human Rights Commission est abrégée **NLHRC**). À noter que les abréviations d'un recueil imprimé peuvent être différentes de celle d'un organisme administratif (par ex. **OSC** ; **OSCB**).

3.14.2   Décisions en ligne

Intitulé	(date),	numéro de la décision (s'il y a lieu),	en ligne :	organe ou tribunal adminis- tratif	<URL>.
Réexamen de la décision de radiodiffusion 2008-222 conformément aux décrets CP 2008-1769 et CP 2008-1770	(11 août 2009),	CRTC 2009-481,	en ligne :	CRTC	<www.crtc.gc.ca/fra/archive/2009/2009-481.htm> .
La commissaire de la concurrence c Phone-time Inc	(5 novembre 2009),	CT-2009-017,	en ligne :	Tribunal de la concurrence	<www.ct-tc.gc.ca/CasesAffaires/AffairesDetails-fra.asp?CaseID=321> .
Autorité des marchés financiers c Jean-Yves Mulet	(9 septembre 2009),	2009-019,	en ligne :	BDRVM	<www.bdrvm.com> .

■ Indiquer la date précise de la décision entre parenthèses après l'intitulé, et suivie d'une virgule.

■ Indiquer le numéro de la décision (s'il y a lieu), suivi de **en ligne :** et de l'abréviation utilisée par le tribunal ou l'organe administratif. Utiliser une abréviation courte pour les provinces et les territoires (par ex. la Commission des valeurs mobilières du Québec est abrégée **CVMQ**, la Commission des valeurs mobilières de l'Ontario est abrégée **CVMO** et la *Newfoundland and Labrador Human Rights Commission* est abrégée **NLHRC**).

Jurisprudence

▨ Si possible, fournir un lien URL qui mène directement à la source citée. Toutefois, s'il y a des doutes quant à la stabilité du lien URL en question, fournir le lien de la page d'accueil seulement de sorte à éviter un lien mort (voir *Autorité des marchés financiers*).

3.15   PLAIDOIRIES ET DOCUMENTS DE PREUVE À L'AUDIENCE

Mémoire	*Renvoi relatif à la sécession du Québec*, [1998] 2 RCS 217 **(mémoire de l'appelant au para 16)**.
Plaidoiries orales	*Vriend c Alberta*, [1998] 1 RCS 493 **(plaidoirie orale de l'appelant)**.
Règlement hors cour	*Mulroney c Canada (PG)* **[Règlement hors cour]**, [1997] AQ n° 45 (CS) (QL).
Éléments de preuve	*R c Swain*, [1991] 1 RCS 933 **(preuve, recommandation du Dr Fleming de remettre l'appelant en libérté)**.

▨ Pour un **mémoire**, indiquer la référence complète de la cause. Ensuite, écrire entre parenthèses : **mémoire de**, le nom de la partie (**appelant** ou **intimé**) et le numéro de la page ou du paragraphe. Utiliser les références complètes pour les parties. Créer un titre abrégé lors de la première référence au document (par ex. **mémoire de l'appelant au para 16 [MA]**).

▨ Pour une **plaidoirie orale**, indiquer la référence complète de la décision, suivie de **plaidoirie orale de** et du nom de la partie, entre parenthèses.

▨ Pour un **règlement public hors cour**, fournir l'intitulé, suivi de **Règlement hors cour** entre crochets, et des autres éléments de la référence. Si le règlement a été annoncé dans un communiqué de presse, voir la section 6.17.

▨ Pour un **élément de preuve**, indiquer la référence complète de la décision, suivie de **preuve** et d'une brève description de l'élément entre parenthèses.

▨ Pour une **transcription**, suivre les règles des jugements non publiés à la section 3.12.

▨ Adapter la forme générale fournie ci-haut à d'autre types de documents, dont les témoignages, les dépositions, les affidavits, les assignations, les mémoranda, les transcriptions, les plumitifs, etc.

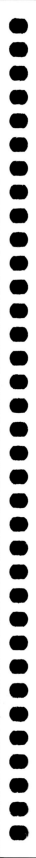

Documents
gouvernementaux

4 Documents gouvernementaux...F-77

F -4.1 Documents parlementaires F-77
    F -4.1.1 Débats législatifs... F-77
    F -4.1.2 Journaux.. F-78
    F -4.1.3 Feuilletons... F-78
    F -4.1.4 Sessional Papers F-79
    F -4.1.5 Procès-verbaux F-79
    F -4.1.6 Rapports publiés dans un journal des débats............................ F-80
    F -4.1.7 Rapports publiés séparément F-80

F -4.2 Documents non parlementaires.. F-81
    4.2.1   Modèle de base... F-81
        F -4.2.1.1 Rapports, manuels et autres publications volumineuses.... F-81
        F -4.2.1.2 Articles, bulletins et autres courtes publications F-83
    F -4.2.2 Bulletins d'interprétation (IT) en matière d'impôts et circulaires
           d'information F-84
    F -4.2.3 Rapports d'enquêtes et de commissions................................... F-85
        F -4.2.3.1 Rapports portant le même titre................................. F-85
        F -4.2.3.2 Rapports portants des titres différents....................... F-85
    F -4.2.4 Documents de conférences intergouvernementales F-86

4 DOCUMENTS GOUVERNEMENTAUX

4.1 DOCUMENTS PARLEMENTAIRES

Cette section s'applique aux documents publiés directement par un organe parlementaire. Pour tous les documents gouvernementaux fédéraux, n'ajouter l'indication géographique (**Canada**) que si des références à des documents internationaux dans le texte risquent de confondre le lecteur.

4.1.1 Débats législatifs

Indica-tion géo-graphi-que,	législa-ture,	*titre*,	numéro de la lég-islature et session,	volume et/ou numéro	(date)	référ-ence précise	(orateur) (s'il y a lieu).
		Débats de la Chambre des com-munes,	37ᵉ parl, 1ʳᵉ sess,	nᵒ 26	(9 mars 2009)	à la p 1457	(Linda Duncan).
		Débats du Sénat,	39ᵉ parl, 2ᵉ sess,	nᵒ 44	(1 avril 2008)	à la p 1017	(Noël A Kinsella).
Québec,	Assemblée nationale,	*Journal des débats*,	36ᵉ lég, 21ᵉ sess,	nᵒ 6	(24 mai 2001)	à la p 12	(M Mar-san).
Manitoba,	Legislative Assembly,	*Debates and Pro-ceedings*,	39ᵉ lég, 3ᵉ sess,	nᵒ 21	(7 avril 2008)	à la p 525	(Ms Os-wald).

- Écrire l'indication géographique (s'il s'agit d'une province) et la législature, à moins que ces informations ne fassent partie du titre du recueil des débats.

- Indiquer le titre du recueil des débats en italique.

- Si le recueil est divisé en volumes ou en numéros, indiquer ces précisions après la virgule (non italique) suivant le titre.

- Indiquer la date complète des débats entre parenthèses, suivie d'une référence précise.

- S'il y a lieu, indiquer l'orateur entre parenthèses à la fin de la référence.

- Si pertinent, indiquer le titre du projet de loi en discussion, entre guillemets, suivis par une virgule et le nombre de sa lecture, devant la juridiction, la législature, et le titre (par ex. **« Projet de loi C-8, Loi modifiant la loi sur le droit d'auteur, la loi sur les marques de commerce et d'autres lois en conséquence », 2ᵉ lecture,** *Débats de la Chambre des communes*, 41ᵉ parl, 2ᵉ sess, no 9 (28 octobre 2013) a la p 1504 (Hon Steven Blaney)).

4.1.2   Journaux

Indica-tion géo-graphi-que,	législa-ture,	*titre,*	numéro de la lég-islature et session,	volume ou numéro	(date)	référ-ence précise	(orateur) (s'il y a lieu).
	Sénat,	*Journaux du Sénat,*	40ᵉ lég, 2ᵉ sess,	nᵒ 40	(2 juin 2009).		
	Chambre des com-munes	*Journaux,*	40ᵉ lég, 2ᵉ sess,	nᵒ 36	(30 mars 2009)	à la p 333.	
Québec,		*Journaux de l'Assem-blée natio-nale du Québec,*	29ᵉ lég, 2ᵉ sess,	vol 106	(23 février 1971)	à la p 23.	
		Journaux de la Chambre d'Assem-blée du Bas-Cana-da,	8ᵉ parl, 2ᵉ sess,	vol 25	(16 janvier 1816)	à la p 15	(Thomas Dou-glass).

▪ Écrire l'indication géographique (s'il s'agit d'une province) et la législature, à moins que ces informations ne fassent partie du titre des journaux.

▪ Indiquer le titre du recueil des débats en italique.

▪ Si le recueil est divisé en volumes ou en numéros, indiquer ces précisions après la virgule non italique suivant le titre.

▪ Indiquer la date complète des débats entre parenthèses, suivie d'une référence précise.

▪ S'il y a lieu, indiquer l'orateur entre parenthèses à la fin de la référence.

4.1.3   Feuilletons

Indication géographique,	législature,	*titre du recueil,*	numéro de la législature et session,	numéro	(date)	référence précise.
	Chambre des Communes	*Feuilleton*	39ᵉ lég, 1ʳᵉ sess,	nᵒ 167	(8 juin 2007).	
Québec,	Assemblée nationale,	*Feuilleton et préavis*	38ᵉ lég, 1ʳᵉ sess,	nᵒ 79	(6 mai 2008).	

- Inscrire l'indication géographique s'il s'agit d'une province.
- Au fédéral, le *Feuilleton* et le *Feuilleton des avis* sont deux parties d'une seule publication. Indiquer le recueil pertinent comme titre du recueil.

4.1.4 *Sessional Papers*

Indica-tion géogra-phique,	législa-ture,	« titre du rapport »	par	auteur	dans	*titre du recueil,*	nu-méro	(an-née)	réfé-rence pré-cise.
	Parle-ment,	« Report of the Chief Inspector of Dominion Lands Agencies »	par	HG Cuttle	dans	*Ses-sional Papers,*	n° 25	(1920)	à la p 3.
Ontario,	Assem-blée lég-islative,	« Report on Workmen's Compensa-tion for Injuries »	par	James Mavor	dans	*Ses-sional Papers,*	n° 40	(1900)	à la p 6.

- Inscrire l'indication géographique s'il s'agit d'une province.
- Fournir le titre du rapport entre guillemets après la mention de la législature.
- S'il y a un auteur, indiquer son nom après le titre du rapport, suivi de **par**.
- Si le *Sessional Paper* est numéroté, indiquer le numéro après le titre du recueil et une virgule.
- Indiquer l'année et non la date complète entre parenthèses.

4.1.5 Procès-verbaux

Indication géogra-phique,	législature,	*titre du recueil,*	numéro de la législature et session	volume et/ou numéro	(date)	référence précise.
Québec,	Assemblée nationale,	*Procès-verbal,*	39e lég, 1re sess,	n° 48	(18 juin 2009)	à la p 517.
Ontario,	Assemblée législative,	*Procès-verbaux,*	38e lég, 2e sess,	n° 34	(14 décembre 2005).	

- Écrire l'indication géographique (s'il s'agit d'une province) et la législature, à moins que ces informations ne fassent partie du titre du recueil.

▥ Indiquer en italique le titre du recueil.

▥ Indiquer le numéro de la législature et de la session.

▥ Si le recueil est divisé en volumes ou en numéros, indiquer ces précisions après la virgule suivant la session.

4.1.6   Rapports publiés dans un journal des débats

Indication géographique,	législature,	organisme,	« titre du rapport »	dans	titre du recueil,	volume, numéro	(date)	référence precise.
Québec,	Assemblée nationale,	Commission permanente de l'Éducation,	« Étude détaillée du projet de loi n° 12 : Loi sur l'aide financière aux études »	dans	Journal des débats de la Commission permanente de l'Éducation,	vol 37, n° 11	(1er juin 2001)	à la p 1.

▥ Inscrire l'indication géographique s'il s'agit d'une province.

▥ Suivre les règles concernant les débats législatifs à la section 4.1.1 en y ajoutant le nom de l'organisme dont émane le rapport et le titre du rapport après le nom de la législature. Placer le titre du rapport entre guillemets.

▥ Fournir le numéro du rapport, s'il y en a un, après le titre du recueil et une virgule.

4.1.7   Rapports publiés séparément

Indication géographique,	législature,	organisme,	titre	(date)	référence précise	(président) (s'il y a lieu).
Québec	Assemblée nationale,	Commission de l'aménagement et de l'équipement,	La procédure d'évaluation des impacts sur l'environnement : Rapport final	(9 avril 2002)	à la p 10.	

▥ Inscrire l'indication géographique s'il s'agit d'une province.

▥ Après la législature et le nom de l'organisme, indiquer le titre du rapport en italique.

▥ Indiquer entre parenthèses la date complète telle que fournie par le rapport.

▨ Si le nom du président est indiqué sur la page couverture, ajouter cette information entre parenthèses (par ex. **(président : Rob Anders)**).

▨ Cette section s'applique aux rapports publiés directement par un organe parlementaire. Si le rapport est publié par tout autre organe, voir la section 4.2 sur les rapports non parlementaires.

4.2 DOCUMENTS NON PARLEMENTAIRES

Cette section s'applique à tout document gouvernemental qui n'est pas publié par un organisme législatif. Suivre les règles générales de la section 4.2.1, sauf si le document fait partie d'une catégorie specifique comprise dans les sections 4.2.2–4.2.4.

4.2.1 Modèle de base

En référence juridique, la plupart des documents gouvernementaux sont divisés en deux sous-catégories. Cependant, la catégorie dont fait partie un document importe moins que de fournir des informations complètes et précises au sujet d'une source.

4.2.1.1 Rapports, manuels et autres publications volumineuses

Indication géographique,	organisme,	*titre,*	renseignements additionnels (facultatif),	renseignements sur l'édition	référence précise.
Canada,	Commission royale sur la réforme électorale et le financement des partis,	*Pour une démocratie électorale renouvelée,*	t 4,	Ottawa, Groupe Communication, 1991	à la p 99.
	Office de la propriété intellectuelle,	*Recueil des pratiques du Bureau des brevets,*	mise à jour décembre 2010,	Ottawa, Industrie Canada, 1998	à la p 12.
	Statistique Canada,	*Statistiques sur les crimes déclarés par la police au Canada, 2011,*	par Shannon Brennan, no de catalogue 82-002-X,	Ottawa, Statistique Canada, 11 octobre 2012.	
Québec,	Ministère de la justice,	*Commentaires du ministre de la Justice : le Code civil du Québec,*	t 2,	Québec, Publications du Québec, 1993	à la p 5.
Québec,	Office de révision du Code civil,	*Rapport sur les obligations,*	par le Comité du droit des obligations,	Montréal, ORCC, 1975.	

Documents gouvernementaux

- Inclure l'indication géographique, à moins qu'elle ne fasse partie du nom de l'organisme ou du titre du document.

- Indiquer l'organisme responsable à moins qu'il ne fasse partie du titre.

- Si le document porte le nom d'un auteur spécifique au sein de l'organisme responsable, fournir le nom de l'auteur après le titre, séparé de ce dernier d'une virgule et précédé du mot « par ». Pour le reste de la référence, suivre les règles de la section 6.2.2.

- Après le titre du document et le nom de l'auteur spécifique (si nécessaire), fournir toute autre information qui pourrait aider les lecteurs à trouver une source (par ex. données provenant (ou tirées) d'un catalogue) ou à évaluer l'autorité d'une source (par ex. la date où la source a été mise à jour, ou une indication que la source est en examen ou a été annulée). Séparer chaque élément par une virgule. Si le document est divisé en plusieurs volumes, suivre les règles de la section 6.2.4.

- Si l'organisme responsable est également l'éditeur du document, il est possible de l'abréger ou de le remplacer par un acronyme dans la section « renseignements sur l'édition » (voir l'exemple de l'Office de révision du Code civil). Pour toute autre information sur l'édition, suivre les règles des sections 6.2.5–6.2.9.

- Si le type de document (par ex. **Étude**, **Document de travail** ou **Guide**) est indiqué sur la page titre, fournir ce renseignement entre parenthèses après le titre du document (par ex. Commission de la santé et de la sécurité du travail du Québec, *Planification des mesures d'urgence pour assurer la sécurité des travailleurs* (**Guide**), Québec, CSST, 1999 à la p 53).

- L'indication du nom du commissaire ou du président entre parenthèses après le titre est facultative.

- Présumer que les documents fédéraux sont publiés à Ottawa et que les documents provinciaux ou territoriaux sont publiés dans la capitale de la province ou du territoire, à moins que l'indication géographique ne soit précisée dans le titre lui-même.

4.2.1.2 *Articles, bulletins et autres courtes publications*

Indication géographique,	organisme,	*titre,*	renseignements additionnels (facultatif),	renseignements sur l'édition	référence précise.
	Service correctionnel du Canada,	*Activités de loisir,*	Directive du commissaire no 760,	Ottawa: CSC, 25 septembre 2008	au para 7.
	Agence canadienne des médicaments et des technologies de la santé,	*CEDAC Final Recommendation: Abacavir/ Lamivudine,*	par le Comité consultatif canadien d'expertise sur les médicaments,	Ottawa, ACMTS, 16 novembre 2005	aux para 2–4.
Nouvelle-Écosse,	Commission d'indemnisation des accidents du travail,	*Chronic Pain,*		Halifax, CIAT, avril 2008.	
Canada,	Ministère de la Défense Nationale,	*Programme de terminologie de la Défense,*	Directive et ordonnance administrative de la Défense no 6110-1, en examen,	Ottawa, MDN, 29 janvier 2010.	
	Statistique Canada,	*Les unions interculturelles,*	par Anne Milan et Brian Hamm, dans *Tendances sociales canadiennes*, no de catalogue No 11-008-X,	Ottawa, Statistique Canada, 2004.	

▨ Indiquer l'indication géographique, à moins qu'elle ne fasse partie du nom de l'organisme ou du titre du document.

▨ Indiquer l'organisme responsable à moins qu'il ne fasse partie du titre.

▨ Si le document porte le nom d'un auteur spécifique au sein de l'organisme responsable, fournir le nom de l'auteur après le titre, séparé de ce dernier d'une virgule et précédé du mot « par ». Pour le reste de la référence, suivre les règles de la section 6.2.2.

▨ Après le titre et l'auteur, le cas échéant, indiquer le type de document à moins que ce ne soit déjà évident dans le titre (par ex. **CEDAC** ci-dessus), ou que le type de document n'aide déjà les lecteurs à trouver ou à comprendre la source (par ex. le document

Chronic Pain est décrit comme un « Fact Sheet », mais cette information ne contribue pas à l'appréciation de la source par le lecteur).

▨ Après le type de document, fournir toute autre information qui pourrait aider les lecteurs à trouver une source (par ex. données provenant d'un catalogue) ou à évaluer l'autorité d'une source (par ex. la date où la source a été mise à jour, ou une indication que la source est en examen ou a été annulée). Séparer chaque élément par une virgule.

▨ Si l'organisme responsable est également l'éditeur du document, il est possible de l'abréger ou de le remplacer par un acronyme dans la section « renseignements sur l'édition » (voir l'exemple de l'Office de révision du Code civil). Pour toute autre information sur l'édition, suivre les règles des sections 6.2.5–6.2.9.

▨ Présumer que les documents fédéraux sont publiés à Ottawa et que les documents provinciaux ou territoriaux sont publiés dans la capitale de la province ou du territoire, à moins que l'indication géographique ne soit précisée dans le titre lui-même.

▨ Indiquer la date de publication la plus complète disponible sur la base des informations contenues dans le document de la source.

▨ L'indication du nom du commissaire ou du président entre parenthèses à la fin de la référence est facultative.

4.2.2   Bulletins d'interprétation (IT) en matière d'impôts et circulaires d'information (IC)

Ministère,	Bulletin d'interprétation	numéro du bulletin,	« titre »	(date)	référence précise.
Agence du revenu du Canada,	Bulletin d'interprétation	IT-459,	« Projet comportant un risque ou une affaire de caractère commercial »	(8 septembre 1980).	
Agence du revenu du Canada,	Bulletin d'interprétation	IT-525R,	« Artistes de la scène »	(17 août 1995).	
Agence du revenu du Canada,	Bulletin d'interprétation	IT-244R3,	« Dons de polices d'assurance-vie à des œuvres charitables »	(6 septembre 1991)	au para 4.

▨ Les **IT** sont des bulletins d'interprétation courants en matière d'impôt sur le revenu et sont publiés par l'Agence du revenu du Canada. Les **IC** sont des circulaires d'information et sont également publiés par l'Agence du revenu du Canada. Des documents similaires sont publiés dans les provinces.

▨ Faire suivre le numéro de bulletin d'un **R** s'il a été révisé. Le nombre de révisions est indiqué par le chiffre suivant le R (par ex. **R3**).

◼ Lorsque les bulletins d'interprétation en matière d'impôt sont divisés en paragraphes, faire référence au numéro de paragraphe.

4.2.3   Rapports d'enquêtes et de commissions

4.2.3.1 Rapports portant le même titre

Indication géogra-phique,	organisme,	titre,	renseigne-ments sur l'édition	volume	(prési-dent) (s'il y a lieu)	référ-ence précise.
Canada,	Commission d'enquête sur le programme de comman-dites et les ac-tivités publici-taires,	Qui est responsable ? Rapport factuel,	Ottawa, Travaux publics et Services gouverne-mentaux Canada, 2005			à la p 14.

◼ Inclure l'indication géographique, à moins qu'elle ne paraisse ailleurs dans la référence.

◼ Inclure le nom de l'organisme, à moins qu'il ne soit déjà mentionné dans le titre du rapport.

◼ Si un mot comme **livre** ou **cahier** paraît sur la page titre du document, utiliser cette terminologie plutôt que vol.

◼ Ne pas indiquer le numéro de volume dans les références ultérieures. Toutefois, pour faire référence à un autre volume du rapport dans une référence ultérieure, indiquer le numéro du volume pour éviter toute confusion (*Rapport sur le bilinguisme*, **livre 2**, *supra* **note 5**).

4.2.3.2 Rapports portant des titres différents

Référence au premier livre	;	référence au deuxième livre.
Rapport de la Commission d'enquête sur la situation de la langue française et sur les droits linguistiques au Québec : la langue de travail, **livre 1**, Québec, Éditeur officiel, 1972 aux pp 150, 300	;	*Rapport de la Commission d'enquête sur la situation de la langue française et sur les droits linguistiques au Québec : les droits linguistiques*, **livre 2**, Québec, Éditeur officiel, 1972 à la p 38.

◼ Pour faire référence à un rapport publié dans des volumes distincts portant des titres différents, indiquer la référence complète pour chaque division, séparées d'un point-virgule. Indiquer le titre du volume comme si c'était un sous-titre du document (précédé d'un deux-points).

◼ Indiquer le volume (ou le livre ou le cahier) après le titre abrégé (par ex. *Rapport sur la langue française*, **livre 2**, *supra* **note 4 à la p 38**) dans les références ultérieures.

Documents gouvernementaux

■ Pour le reste de la référence, suivre les règles de la section 4.2.3.1.

4.2.4   Documents de conférénces intergouvernementales

Conférence ou co- mité,	titre,	numéro du document,	lieu de la conférence,	date de tenue de la conférence.
Réunion fédérale-pro- vinciale-territoriale des ministres responsables de la justice,	*Groupe de travail féd- éral-provincial-territor- ial sur la provocation, Rapport intérimaire,*	Doc 830-600/ 020,	Montréal,	4–5 décem- bre 1997.
Conférence fédérale- provinciale des Pre- miers ministres,	*Compte rendu textuel de la Conférence féd- érale-provinciale des Premiers ministres sur les questions constitu- tionnelles intéressant les autochtones,*	Doc 800-18/ 004,	Ottawa,	8–9 mars 1984.

■ Indiquer le nom complet de la conférence ou du comité, suivi du titre du document et du numéro du document.

■ Indiquer le lieu et la date complète de la conférence.

5   Documentation internationale F-89

F -5.1 Traités et documents internationaux F-89
    F -5.1.1 Traités, documents des Nations Unies et autres accords
           internationaux.. F-89
           F -5.1.1.1 Référence neutre des traités australiens F-92
    F -5.1.2 Documents des Nations Unies F-92
           F -5.1.2.1 Charte des Nations Unies F-92
           F -5.1.2.2 Documents officiels F-93
                      F -5.1.2.2.1 Séances... F-93
                      F -5.1.2.2.2 Suppléments F-94
                      F -5.1.2.2.3 Annexes... F-96
            F -5.1.2.3 Documents à en-tête de l'Organisation des Nations
                      Unies (Documents miméographiés) F-97
           F -5.1.2.4 Périodiques F-97
           F -5.1.2.5 Annuaires F-97
           F -5.1.2.6 Publications de vente F-98
    F -5.1.3 Documents de l'Union européenne... F-98
           F -5.1.3.1 Règlements, directives et décisions......................... F-98
           F -5.1.3.2 Débats du Parlement européen...............................F-100
           F -5.1.3.3 Autres documents F-100
    F -5.1.4 Documents du Conseil de l'Europe F-101
    F -5.1.5 Documents de l'Organisation des États américains....................F-102
    F -5.1.6 Documents de l'Organisation mondiale du commerce (OMC) et de
           l'Accord général sur les tarifs douaniers et le commerce (GATT) F-103
    F -5.1.7 Documents de l'Organisation de coopération et de développement
           économiques (OCDE)..F-104
    F -5.1.8 Traités avec les Premières nations.......................................F-105

F -5.2 Jurisprudence F-106
    F -5.2.1 Cour permanente de Justice internationale (1922–1946) F-106
           F -5.2.1.1 Jugements, ordonnances et avis consultatifs F-106
           F -5.2.1.2 Plaidoiries, exposés oraux et autres documents............F-107
    F -5.2.2 Cour internationale de Justice (1946 à aujourd'hui)......................F-107
           F -5.2.2.1 Jugements, ordonnances et avis consultatifs F-108
           F -5.2.2.2 Mémoires, plaidoiries et documents.........................F-109
    F -5.2.3 Cour de Justice des Communautés européennes et Tribunal de
           première instance...F-109
    F -5.2.4 Cour européenne des Droits de l'Homme et Commission
           européenne des Droits de l'Homme.......................................F-110
           F -5.2.4.1 Avant 1999...F-110
           F -5.2.4.2 À partir de 1999...F-110
    F -5.2.5 Cour interaméricaine des Droits de l'Homme F-112
           F -5.2.5.1 Jugements, ordres et avis consultatifs......................F-112
           F -5.2.5.2 Mémoires, plaidoiries et documents........................F-113
    F -5.2.6 Commission interaméricaine des Droits de l'Homme F-113
    F -5.2.7 Tribunaux de droit pénal international F-114
    F -5.2.8 Groupes spéciaux de l'Accord général sur les tarifs douaniers et
           le commerce (GATT) 1947 ....F-115
    F -5.2.9 Rapports de Groupes spéciaux et de l'Organe d'appel de
           l'Organisation mondiale du commerce (OMC) F-116

F -5.2.10 Rapports de Groupes spéciaux de l'Accord de libre-échange
canado-américain F-117
F -5.2.11 Rapports de Groupes spéciaux de l'Accord de libre-échange
nord-américain (ALÉNA) F-118
F -5.2.12 Décisions d'arbitrage international F-119
F -5.2.13 Décisions d'arbitrage de l'Organisation mondiale de la propriété
intellectuelle (OMPI) F-119
F -5.2.13.1 Principes directeurs régissant le règlement uniforme
des litiges relatifs aux noms de domaine (UDRP) F-119
F -5.2.14 Décisions de droit international prises devant des cours
nationales F-120

F -5.3   Sites internet F-120

5   DOCUMENTATION INTERNATIONALE

5.1   TRAITÉS ET DOCUMENTS INTERNATIONAUX

5.1.1   Traités, documents des Nations Unies et autres accords internationaux

Titre,	parties (s'il y a lieu),	date de signature,	recueil de traités	référence précise,	(la date d'entrée en vigueur et informa-tion supplémentaire).
Traité sur l'ex-tradition,	Espagne et Costa Rica,	23 octobre 1997,	2025 RTNU 251		(entrée en vigueur : 30 juillet 1998).
Convention de sauvegarde des droits de l'homme et des libertés fonda-mentales,		4 novem-bre 1950,	213 RTNU 221	à la p 233	(entrée en vigueur : 3 septembre 1953) [Con-vention européenne des droits de l'homme].
Pacte interna-tional relatif aux droits civils et politiques,		19 décem-bre 1966,	999 RTNU 171	arts 9—14	(entrée en vigueur : 23 mars 1976, acces-sion du Canada 19 mai 1976) [PIDCP].
Accord de li-bre-échange nord-américain entre le gou-vernement du Canada, le gouvernement des États-Unis et le gouverne-ment du Mexi-que,		17 décem-bre 1992,	RT Can 1994 n° 2		(entrée en vigueur : 1er janvier 1994) [ALÉNA].
Accord général sur les tarifs douaniers et le commerce,		30 octobre 1947,	58 RTNU 187		(entrée en vigueur : 1er janvier 1948) [GATT de 1947].

Indiquer le titre complet du traité. Si le nom des signataires est inclus dans le titre, raccourcir le nom selon l'usage courant (par ex. **Royaume-Uni** et non **Royaume-Uni de Grande-Bretagne et d'Irlande du Nord**), mais sans l'abréger (par ex. **R-U**).

■ Indiquer la date de la première signature du traité ou de son ouverture à la signature.

■ Indiquer la date d'entrée en vigueur entre parenthèses à la fin de la référence.

■ Si le nom des parties à un traité bilatéral n'est pas indiqué dans le titre, écrire la version courte (mais non abrégée) du nom des parties après le titre, entre virgules. Inclure le nom des parties à un traité multilatéral à la fin de la référence, si nécessaire.

■ Écrire la référence du recueil de traités après la date.

■ Suite à la citation de la série des traités, il est facultatif de fournir une référence parallèle à des autres recueils de traités et de suivre l'ordre des recueils suivant : (1) *Recueil de traités des Nations Unies* [**RTNU**] ou *Recueil de traités de la Société des Nations* [**RTSN**] ; (2) recueils de traités officiels des États pertinents (par ex. *Recueil des traités du Canada* [**RT Can**], *United Kingdom Treaty Series* [**UKTS**]) ; (3) autres recueils de traités et accords internationaux.

■ Fournir une référence parallèle à *International Legal Materials* [**ILM**] si disponible.

■ Fournir des informations supplémentaires à la fin de la référence, après la date d'entrée en vigueur, si nécessaire (par ex. le nom des parties au traité, le nombre de ratifications et le statut de certains États).

Recueils de traités et accords internationaux et leurs abréviations :

Air and Aviation Treaties of the World	AATW
Australian Treaty Series	ATS
British and Foreign State Papers	UKFS
Canada Treaty Series	Can TS
Consolidated Treaty Series	Cons TS
Documents juridiques internationaux	DJI
European Treaty Series	Eur TS
International Legal Materials	ILM
Journal officiel	JO
League of Nations Treaty Series	LNTS
Organization of American States Treaty Series	OASTS
Recueil des traités d'alliance, de paix, de trêve, de neutralité, de commerce, de limites, d'échange, et plusieurs autres actes à la connaissance des relations étrangères des puissances et États de l'Europe	Rec TA
Recueil des traités de la Société des Nations	RTSN
Recueil des traités des Nations Unies	RTNU
Recueil des traités du Canada	RT Can
Recueil des traités et accords de la France	RTAF
Recueil général des traités de la France	Rec GTF
Série des traités et conventions européennes	STE
Treaties and other International Agreements of the United States of America 1776-1949	TI Agree (*anciennement USBS*)
United Kingdom Treaty Series	UKTS
United Nations Treaty Series	UNTS
United States Statutes at Large	US Stat
United States Treaties and Other International Acts Series	TIAS
United States Treaties and Other International Agreements	UST

5.1.1.1 Référence neutre des traités australiens

Le gouvernement australien de la Commonwealth a adopté sa propre méthode de référence neutre pour les traités, qui doit accompagner toute référence à un recueil imprimé. Introduire la référence neutre après le titre du traité et la date de signature. Indiquer l'année de publication entre crochets, suivie de l'identificateur du recueil et du numéro de document.

Identificateurs de recueils pour la référence neutre :

Australian Treaty Series	ATS
Australian Treaty National Interest Analysis	ATNIA
Australian Treaty not yet in force	ATNIF

Agreement on the Conservation of Albatrosses and Petrels, 19 juin 2001, **[2004] ATS 5**.

5.1.2 Documents des Nations Unies

Chaque document des Nations Unies ne contient pas toujours tous les éléments inclus dans les exemples ci-dessous. Adapter les références de manière à ce qu'elles fournissent l'information nécessaire à l'identification du document.

Abréviations du vocabulaire fréquemment utilisé dans les documents des Nations Unies :

Décision	déc	Recommandation	rec
Document	doc	Régulier	rég
Document officiels	doc off	Résolution	rés
Extraordinaire	extra	Session	sess
Miméographié	miméo	Spécial	spéc
Numéro	n°	Supplément	supp
Pléniaire	plén	Urgence	urg

5.1.2.1 Charte des Nations Unies

Une référence complète n'est pas nécessaire pour la *Charte des Nations Unies*. Il est possible de faire référence à la *Charte* de la façon suivante : ***Charte des Nations Unies*, 26 juin 1945, RT Can 1945 n° 7.**

5.1.2.2 Documents officiels

Les documents officiels publiés par les organes des Nations Unies se divisent en trois parties, soit les **séances**, les **suppléments** et les **annexes**. Faire référence aux documents officiels en inscrivant **Doc off** avant l'acronyme de l'organe qui en est responsable.

Abréviations officielles des principaux organes des Nations Unies :

Assemblée générale	AG
Conférence des Nations Unies sur le commerce et le développement	CNUCED
Conseil économique et social	CES
Conseil de sécurité	CS
Conseil de tutelle	CT
Conseil du commerce et du développement	CCED
Première commission, Deuxième commission, etc.	C1, C2, etc.

Fournir le nom complet des organes de l'ONU qui n'ont pas d'acronyme officiel.

5.1.2.2.1 Séances

Doc off et acronyme de l'organe responsable,	numéro de sess ou nombre d'années écoulées depuis la création de l'organe ou année civile,	numéro de séance,	numéro de document de l'ONU et (numéro de vente) (s'il y a lieu)	(année du document) (s'il y a lieu)	référence précise	[provisoire] (s'il y a lieu).
Doc off CCED CNUCED,	23e sess,	565e séance,	Doc NU TD/B/SR.565	(1981).		
Doc off CS NU,	53e année,	3849e séance,	Doc NU S/PV.3849	(1998)		[provisoire].
Doc off CES NU,	1984,	23e séance plén,	Doc NU E/1984/SR.23.			

▪ Indiquer **Doc off** pour **Documents officiels**, suivi de **l'abréviation de l'organe des Nations Unies** et de la mention **NU**, sauf si celle-ci fait déjà partie de l'acronyme de l'organe.

▪ Fournir le **numéro de session** après le nom de l'organe ou de la mention **NU**. Si le numéro n'est pas disponible, indiquer **le nombre d'années écoulées depuis la création de** l'organe. Si ni l'une ni l'autre des informations ne sont disponibles, indiquer **l'année civile**.

▦ Indiquer le **numéro de séance** après le numéro de session.

▦ Indiquer le **numéro de document** après le numéro de séance. Si un document a plusieurs numéros, indiquer chacun d'entre eux, séparés par des virgules. Indiquer le numéro de vente (s'il y a lieu) entre parenthèses après le numéro de document.

▦ Indiquer l'année civile du document entre parenthèses après le numéro de document si elle n'a pas été mentionnée précédemment dans la référence.

▦ Précéder toute référence précise d'une virgule.

▦ Indiquer qu'un document est provisoire en ajoutant **[provisoire]** à la fin de la référence.

5.1.2.2.2 Suppléments

Les résolutions, les décisions et les rapports de l'ONU paraissent dans des suppléments aux documents officiels.

	Auteur (s'il y a lieu),	*titre,*	Rés ou Déc et organe et no,	Doc off,	session ou année de l'organe ou année civile,	numéro de supp,	numéro de document de l'ONU	(année civile) (s'il y a lieu)	1re page et référence précise.
Résolution		*Déclaration universelle des droits de l'Homme,*	Rés AG 217A (III),	Doc off AG NU,	3e sess,	supp n° 13,	Doc NU A/810	(194-8)	71.
Décision		*Protection of the heritage of indigenous people,*	Déc CES 1998/ 277,	Doc off CES NU,	1998,	supp n° 1,	Doc NU E/1998/ 98		113 à la p 115.
Rapport		*Rapport du Secrétaire général Boutros-Ghali sur les travaux de l'Organisation,*		Doc off AG NU,	46e sess,	supp n° 1,	Doc NU A/46/1	(199-1).	
	Commission on Crime prevention and Criminal Justice,	*Report on the Ninth Session,*		Doc off CES NU,	2000,	supp n° 10,	Doc NU E/2000/ 30.		

▨ Pour les rapports, indiquer l'auteur avant le titre, s'il n'est pas déjà mentionné dans celui-ci.

▨ Indiquer le titre en italique.

▨ Pour faire référence à une décision ou une résolution, indiquer le numéro de décision ou de résolution après le titre.

Documentation internationale

■ Indiquer **Doc off** pour **Documents officiels**, suivi de **l'abréviation de l'organe des Nations Unies** et de la mention **NU**, si celle-ci ne fait pas partie de l'acronyme de l'organe. Pour les résolutions et les décisions, indiquer cette information après le numéro de résolution ou de décision. Pour les rapports, indiquer cette information immédiatement après le titre du rapport.

■ Indiquer le **numéro de session**. S'il n'est pas disponible, indiquer **le nombre d'années écoulées depuis la création de l'organe**. Si ni l'une ni l'autre information n'est disponible, indiquer **l'année civile**.

■ Après la session, faire référence au **numéro de supplément** et au **numéro de document**.

■ Indiquer l'année civile du document entre parenthèses après le numéro de document, si elle n'est pas déjà mentionnée dans la référence.

■ Placer ensuite le numéro de la première page du document et la référence précise, s'il y a lieu. Si aucune information n'est indiquée entre le numéro de document et le numéro de page, placer une virgule après le numéro de document afin d'éviter toute confusion.

5.1.2.2.3 Annexes

Titre,	Doc off et acronyme de l'organe responsable	numéro de sess ou année de l'organe ou année civile,	annexe, point numéro,	numéro de document de l'ONU	(année civile) (s'il y a lieu)	1re page et/ou référence précise.
Protectionism and Structural Adjustment,	Doc off CNUCED CCED,	32e sess,	annexe, point 6,	Doc NU TD/ B/1081	(1986)	23.
URSS : Projet de résolution,	Doc off CES NU,	3e année, 7e sess,	annexe, point 7,	Doc NU E/ 884/Rev.1	(1948)	29 au para 3.

■ Indiquer le titre en italique, suivi d'une référence aux documents officiels de l'organe responsable.

■ Si **le numéro de session** n'est pas disponible, indiquer **le nombre d'années écoulées depuis la création de l'organe**. Si ni l'une ni l'autre information n'est disponible, indiquer **l'année civile**.

■ Indiquer **l'annexe** et le point d'ordre du jour, suivis du numéro de document.

■ Si l'année civile n'a pas été précédemment indiquée, l'inscrire entre parenthèses après le numéro de document.

■ Placer ensuite le numéro de la première page du document si celui-ci fait partie d'une collection reliée, et une référence précise, s'il y a lieu. Si aucune information n'est indiquée entre le numéro de document et le numéro de page, placer une virgule après le numéro de document afin d'éviter toute confusion.

5.1.2.3 Documents à en-tête de l'Organisation des Nations Unies (Documents miméographiés)

Nom du corps,	Nom du sous-corps ou de la commission	Auteur (si applic-able),	*titre*,	Session, Réunion, Supplé-ment,	Doc NU No,	date	référ-ence précise	[titre abré-gé].
NUCS,	Commis-sion du désarme-ment,		*Questions about Arms Manufactur-ing in East-ern Iraq,*		Doc NU S/ CN.10/ L.666	July 1993.		

▨ La forme miméographique est officielle, mais ne devrait être citée que si le document n'est pas publié dans les documents officiels. Les documents miméographiés sont disponibles sur le site <documents.un.org/>.

▨ Il est improbable qu'un document indique tous les éléments listés ci-haut.

▨ L'élément le plus important est le **Doc NU No**, puisque ceci est le moyen de recherche en ligne le plus facile, suivi du nom du corps, du titre, et de la date. Les autres éléments sont moins essentiels, mais doivent être inclus s'ils se trouvent sur la page couverture.

5.1.2.4 Périodiques

▨ Pour faire référence à un **périodique publié par l'ONU**, suivre les règles de référence aux périodiques énoncées à la section 6.1. Si le titre n'indique pas que le

> « Emplois rémunérés dans les activités non agricoles » (1989) 63:9 Bulletin mensuel de statistiques 12 (NU, Département des affaires économiques et sociales internationales).

périodique est publié par les Nations Unies, ajouter **NU** et l'organe responsable de la publication entre parenthèses à la fin de la référence.

5.1.2.5 Annuaires

> « Report of the Commission to the General Assembly on the work of its thirty-ninth Session » (Doc NU A/42/10) dans *Yearbook of the International Law Commission 1987*, vol 2, partie 2, New York, NU, 1989 à la p 50 (Doc NUA/CN.4/SER.A/1987/Add.1).

▨ Pour les **articles d'annuaires des Nations Unies**, suivre les règles des ouvrages collectifs à la section 6.3. Si possible, inclure le numéro de document. Indiquer le nom de l'auteur et du directeur s'ils sont disponibles.

5.1.2.6 Publications de vente

NU, *Recommandations sur le transport des produits dangereux*, 9ᵉ éd, New York, NU, 1995 à la p 118.	▨ Faire référence aux **publications de vente** en utilisant les mêmes règles que pour les monographies (section 6.2).

5.1.3   Documents de l'Union européenne

Les règlements, les directives, les décisions, les débats et les autres documents sont publiés dans le ***Journal officiel de l'Union européenne*** (JO). Celui-ci remplace le *Journal officiel des Communautés européennes* depuis le 1ᵉʳ février 2003.

Le JO est publié chaque jour de travail dans les langues officielles de l'Union européenne. Il comprend deux séries (la série L pour **la législation** et la série C pour **l'information et les annonces**), ainsi qu'un supplément (la série S pour **les offres publiques** disponibles en format électronique depuis le 1ᵉʳ juillet 1998).

5.1.3.1 Règlements, directives et décisions

La législation des Communautés européennes comprend des règlements, des directives et des décisions qui sont publiés dans la **série L** (Législation) du *Journal officiel de l'Union européenne*.

	CE,	*titre,*	[année du journal]	JO,	série et numéro de volume/1ʳᵉ page	référence précise.
Règlements	CE,	*Règlement (CE) 218/2005 de la Commission du 10 février 2005 portant ouverture et mode de gestion d'un contingent tarifaire autonome pour l'ail à dater du 1ᵉʳ janvier 2005,*	[2005]	JO,	L 39/5	à la p 6.
Directives	CE,	*Directive 2004/ 79/CE de la Commission du 4 mars 2004 concernant la fixation des caractères et des conditions minimales pour l'examen des variétés de vigne,*	[2004]	JO,	L 71/22.	
Décisions	CE,	*Décision 98/85/ CE de la Commission du 16 janvier 1998 relative à certaines mesures de protection à l'égard des oiseaux vivants originaires de Hong Kong ou de la République populaire de Chine,*	[1998]	JO,	L 15/45	à la p 46.

▦ Indiquer **CE**, suivi du titre complet de l'instrument en italique.

▦ Le numéro de l'instrument est inclus dans le titre. **Le numéro des directives** et des décisions est composé des deux derniers chiffres de l'année et d'un numéro séquentiel (par ex. **98/85**).

░ Le numéro des règlements est composé, à l'inverse, d'un numéro séquentiel suivi des deux derniers chiffres de l'année (par ex. **1149/99**).

░ Pour faire référence au *Journal officiel de l'Union européenne*, indiquer **JO**, suivi de la série (**L**). Ajouter le numéro de volume et de la première page de l'instrument, séparés par une barre oblique (**/**).

5.1.3.2 Débats du Parlement européen

CE,	*titre ou date de la séance,*	[année]	JO	Annexe et numéro de volume/1re page	référence précise.
CE,	*Séance du mercredi 5 mai 1999,*	[1999]	JO	Annexe 4-539/144	à la p 152.

░ Les débats du Parlement européen sont publiés dans l'annexe au *Journal officiel de l'Union européenne* (**JO**).

░ Indiquer **CE** suivi du titre du document ou de la date de séance.

░ Indiquer ensuite l'année de publication de la séance entre crochets, suivi de **JO** ainsi que du numéro d'annexe et de la première page. Une barre oblique (**/**) sépare le numéro de volume de la première page (par ex. **2-356/1**).

5.1.3.3 Autres documents

Communications et informations	CE, *Note explicative relative à l'annexe III de l'accord UE-Mexique (décision n° 2/2000 du Conseil conjoint UE-Mexique),* [2004] JO C 40/2.
Publications générales	CE, Commission, *Communication de la Commission au Conseil et au Parlement européen*, Luxembourg, CE, 1995.
Périodiques	CE, *Commerce extérieur : statistiques mensuelles* (1994) n° 1 à la p 16.

░ Indiquer **CE** pour désigner les Communautés européennes en tant qu'organe responsable. Fournir des précisions sur l'auteur s'il y a lieu.

░ Faire référence au *Journal officiel de l'Union européenne : Communications et Informations* (**série C**) de la même manière que les autres sections du journal officiel.

░ Pour les **publications générales**, suivre les règles du chapitre 6.

░ Pour les **périodiques**, mettre le titre en italique, suivi de l'année et du numéro du périodique.

5.1.4   Documents du Conseil de l'Europe

Les documents émanant du Conseil de l'Europe se trouvent dans les publications officielles suivantes :

Publications officielles	Abréviations
Bulletin d'information sur les activités juridiques	Bull inf
Comptes rendus des débats	Débats
Documents de séance	Documents
Ordres du jour et procès-verbaux	Ordres
Textes adoptés par l'Assemblée	Textes adoptés

	Conseil de l'Europe,	organe,	informa-tion sur la session,	*titre* (s'il y a lieu),	publica-tion offi-cielle	(année)	référ-ence pre-cise.
Débats	Conseil de l'Europe,	AP,	2001 sess ordinaire (1re partie),		Débats, vol 1	(2001)	à la p 67.
Textes adoptés	Conseil de l'Europe,	AC,	21e sess, partie 3,		Textes adoptés, Rec 585	(1970)	à la p 1.
Ordres du jour et procès-verbaux	Conseil de l'Europe,	AC,	21e sess, partie 2,		Ordres, 10e séance	(1969)	à la p 20.
Docu-ments de séance	Conseil de l'Europe,	AP,	38e sess,	*Déclaration écrite n° 150 sur la pro-tection du site archéo-logique de Pompei,*	Docu-ments, vol 7, Doc 5700	(1987)	à la p 1.
Séries	Conseil de l'Europe,	Comité des Min-istres,		*Recomman-dation R(82)1,*	(1980) 12 Bull inf 58.		

░ Indiquer **Conseil de l'Europe**, suivi de l'organe responsable. Abréger **Assemblée parlementaire** par **AP** et **Assemblée consultative** par **AC**.

░ Fournir des renseignements sur la session, suivis du titre du document, s'il y a lieu.

░ Utiliser l'abréviation de la publication officielle.

░ Indiquer entre parenthèses l'année de publication après la référence à la publication officielle.

░ Pour les références aux périodiques (**Bull inf**), suivre les règles de la section 6.1.

5.1.5 Documents de l'Organisation des États américains

OÉA,	organe,	numéro de session (s'il y a lieu),	*titre,*	numéro de document	(année)	référence précise.
OÉA,	Assemblée générale,	2e sess,	*Draft Standards Regarding the Formulation of Reservations to Multilateral Treaties,*	Doc off OEA/ Ser.P/AG/ Doc.202	(1972).	
OÉA,	Commission interaméricaine des Droits de l'Homme,		*Draft of the Inter-American Declaration on the Rights of Indigenous Peoples,*	Doc off OEA/ Ser.L/V/II.90/ Doc.14, rev. 1	(1995)	à la p 1.

░ Les documents de l'OEA n'ont pas d'auteur. Indiquer l'organe responsable du document, à moins que le nom ne soit indiqué dans le titre du document.

░ Indiquer le numéro de session ou le numéro de séance après avoir indiqué l'organe responsable du document, s'il y a lieu.

░ Fournir le titre officiel du document.

░ Écrire **Doc off** (Documents officiels) devant le numéro du document commençant par **OEA**. Le numéro du document débute avec les trois lettres **OEA** (Organización de los Estados Americanos) et non pas OÉA ou OAS.

░ Indiquer l'année de publication du document entre parenthèses à la fin de la référence, suivie d'une référence précise, s'il y a lieu.

5.1.6 Documents de l'Organisation mondiale du commerce (OMC) et de l'*Accord général sur les tarifs douaniers et le commerce* (GATT)

	OMC ou GATT,	titre,	numéro de Déc, Rec ou Doc,	numéro de session,	IBDD	service électronique (s'il y a lieu).
Décisions et recommandations		*Accession of Guatemala,*	GATT PC Déc L/6824,	47e sess,	supp n° 38 IBDD (1991) 16.	
		Liberté de contrat en matière d'assurance,	GATT PC Rec du 27 mai 1959,	15e sess,	supp n° 8 IBDD (1960) 26.	
Rapports	GATT,	*Report of the Panel adopted by the Committee on Anti-Dumping Practices on 30 October 1995,*	GATT Doc ADP/137,		supp n° 42 IBDD (1995) 17.	
	OMC,	*Rapport du groupe de travail sur l'accession de la Bulgarie,*	OMC Doc WT/ACC/ BGR/5 (1996),			en ligne : OMC <docsonline. wto.org > .
Réunions	OMC, Conseil général,	*Compte rendu de la réunion* (tenue le 22 novembre 2000),	OMC Doc WT/GC/M/ 60,			en ligne : OMC <docsonline. wto.org > .

▨ **Les décisions et les recommandations n'ont pas d'auteur**. Indiquer le GATT, l'OMC et les organes plus précis comme responsables des rapports, à moins que le nom ne soit indiqué dans le titre du rapport.

▨ Indiquer le numéro de décision ou de recommandation. S'il n'y a pas de numéro, indiquer la date complète de la décision ou de la recommandation. **PC** désigne **Parties contractantes**, **Déc** désigne **Décision** et **Rec** désigne **Recommandation**.

▨ Si possible, se référer aux *Instruments de base et documents divers* (IBDD) du GATT. Indiquer l'année entre parenthèses et la première page du document.

Si un rapport est publié indépendamment, sans numéro de document, suivre les règles pour les monographies (section 6.2) (par ex. **GATT**, *Les marchés internationaux de la viande : 1990/91*, **Genève, GATT, 1991**).

5.1.7   Documents de l'Organisation de coopération et de développement économiques (OCDE)

	OCDE, organe (s'il y a lieu),	*titre,*	titre de la série,	numéro du document de travail,	numéro du document	(renseignements sur l'édition).
Série	OCDE,	*Japon (n° 34),*	Examens en matière de coopération pour le développement,			Paris, ODCE, 1999.
Documents de travail	OCDE, Département économique,	*Pour une croissance écologiquement durable en Australie,*		Document de travail n° 309,	n° de doc ECO/ WK-P(2001) 35	(2001).
Périodiques	OCDE,	*Données OCDE sur l'environ-ne-ment : Com-pendium 1995*				(1995).

Indiquer **OCDE** et l'organe particulier, suivi du titre en italique.

Si le document fait partie d'une série, fournir le titre de la série.

Si le document est un document de travail, fournir le numéro du document de travail (s'il y a lieu) ainsi que le numéro du document de l'OCDE. Noter que le numéro de document débute avec **OCDE** en français et en anglais.

Indiquer les renseignements sur l'édition. Si la seule information disponible est la date, mettre cette date entre parenthèses. Dans le cas d'un périodique, indiquer la date la plus précise possible.

5.1.8   Traités avec les Premières nations

Titre,	date (s'il n'ap-paraît pas dans le titre),	en ligne: <www.aadnc-aandc.gc.ca/chemin d'accès complet>	[titre abrégé].
Traité 3 conclu entre Sa Majesté la Reine et la tribu des Saulteux de la nation des Ojibeways et un point situé à l'angle Nord-Ouest du lac des Bois et adhésions à ce dernier,	3 octobre 1873,	en ligne: <www.aadnc-aandc .gc.ca/fra/ 1100100028675/ 1100100028679>	[Traité 3].
Traité No 8 conclu le 21 juin 1899,		en ligne: <www.aadnc-aandc.gc.ca/fra/ 1100100028805/ 1100100028807>	[Traité 8].

Inclure le titre complet du traité.

5.2 JURISPRUDENCE

Voir l'annexe A-5 pour une liste des abréviations des organismes internationaux et de leurs recueils.

5.2.1   Cour permanente de Justice internationale (1922–1946)

Faire référence aux lois et aux règles de la CPJI par titre, numéro de recueil et nom de l'édition, suivis de la première page ou du numéro de document (par ex. *Revised Rules of the Court* **(1926), CPJI 33 (sér D) n° 1)**.

5.2.1.1 Jugements, ordonnances et avis consultatifs

	Intitulé (nom des parties)	(année),	type de décision,	recueil	numéro de la décision	référence precise.
Jugements	*Affaire des zones franches de la Haute-Savoie et du pays de Gex (France c Suisse)*	(1932),		CPJI (sér A/B)	n° 46	à la p 167.
Avis consultatifs	*Trafic ferroviaire entre la Lituanie et la Pologne*	(1931),	Avis consultatif,	CPJI (sér A/B)	n° 41	à la p 3.
Ordonnan-ces	*Chemin de fer Pa-nevezys-Saldutis-kis (Estonie c Lituanie),*		Ordon-nance du 30 juin 1938,	CPJI (sér A/B)	n° 75	à la p 8.

- Fournir l'intitulé et le nom des parties entre parenthèses. Ne pas indiquer le nom des parties pour les avis consultatifs.

- Pour les jugements et les avis consultatifs, indiquer l'année de la décision entre parenthèses après l'intitulé.

- Préciser s'il s'agit d'une ordonnance ou d'un avis consultatif. Fournir la date complète lorsqu'il s'agit d'une ordonnance. Dans un tel cas, il n'est pas nécessaire de fournir l'année en parenthèses après l'intitulé.

- Faire référence à une série de la CPJI et indiquer le numéro de la décision. **Les jugements de la CPJI** sont publiés dans la *Série A : Recueil des arrêts* **(CPJI (Sér A))** et dans la *Série A/B : Arrêts, ordonnances et avis consultatifs* **(CPJI (Sér A/B))**. **Les ordonnances** et **les avis consultatifs** sont publiés dans la *Série B : Recueil des avis consultatifs* **(CPJI (Ser B))** et dans la *Série A/B : Arrêts, ordonnances et avis consultatifs* **(CPJI (Sér A/B))**.

5.2.1.2 *Plaidoiries, exposés oraux et autres documents*

Intitulé (nom des parties),	« titre du document précis »	(date du document),	recueil	numéro de décision,	1re page	référence precise.
Affaire franco-hellenique des phares (France c Grèce),	« Exposé oral de M le professeur Basdevant »	(5 février 1934),	CPJI (sér C)	n° 74,	222	à la p 227.
Affaire Pajzs, Csáky, Esterházy (Hongrie c Yougoslavie),	« Requête introductive d'instance »	(1er décembre 1935),	CPJI (sér C)	n° 79,	10	à la p 12.

░ Fournir l'intitulé suivi du nom des parties entre parenthèses.

░ Indiquer le titre officiel du document précis entre guillemets, suivi de la date complète entre parenthèses.

░ Faire référence à la série CPJI et indiquer le numéro de la décision. **Les plaidoiries, les exposés oraux** et **les autres documents avant 1931** sont publiés dans la *Série C : Actes et documents relatifs aux arrêts et aux avis consultatifs de la cour* (**CPJI (Sér C)**), et **les documents datant d'après 1931** dans la *Série C : Plaidoiries, exposés oraux et documents* (**CPJI (Sér. C)**). **Les documents de base**, **les annuaires** et **les indices** paraissent dans les séries D à F.

░ Mettre une virgule entre le numéro de décision et la première page du document.

5.2.2   Cour internationale de Justice (1946 à aujourd'hui)

Faire référence aux lois et aux règles de la CIJ par titre, numéro de recueil et nom de l'édition, suivis de la première page ou du numéro de document (par ex. *Travel and Subsistence Regulations of the International Court of Justice*, **[1947] CIJ Acts & Doc 94**).

5.2.2.1 Jugements, ordonnances et avis consultatifs

Les jugements, opinions et ordres de la CIJ qui ne sont pas encore publiés sont disponibles sur le site Internet de la CIJ <www.icj-cij.org>. Suivre les règles de la référence en ligne pour la jurisprudence (voir la section 5.3).

	Intitulé (nom des parties),	type de décision,	[année du re-cueil]	recueil	1re page	référence précise.
Jugements	Affaire relative au Timor oriental (Portugal c Australie),		[1995]	CIJ rec	90	à la p 103.
Ordonnances	Compétence en matière de pêcheries (Espagne c Canada),	Ordonnance du 8 mai 1996,	[1996]	CIJ rec	58.	
Avis consultatifs	Licéité de l'utilisation des armes nucléaires par un État dans un conflit armé,	Avis consultatif,	[1996]	CIJ rec	226	à la p 230.

- Indiquer l'intitulé officiel et le nom des parties entre parenthèses. Bien que le CIJ Rec sépare parfois le nom des parties par une barre oblique (*El Salvador/Honduras*), remplacer la barre oblique par un *c* (*Portugal c Australie*). Ne pas indiquer le nom des parties dans le cas d'un avis consultatif.

- Après l'intitulé, préciser s'il s'agit d'une ordonnance ou d'un avis consultatif. Fournir la date complète lorsqu'il s'agit d'une ordonnance.

- Faire référence au recueil de la CIJ et indiquer la première page de la décision. Les jugements, les ordonnances et les avis consultatifs de la Cour internationale de Justice sont publiés dans le recueil officiel de la cour : *Recueil des arrêts, avis consultatifs et ordonnances* (**CIJ Rec**).

5.2.2.2 Mémoires, plaidoiries et documents

Intitulé officiel (nom des parties),	« titre du document précis »	(date du document),	[année du recueil]	recueil et numéro de volume	1re page	référence précise.
Affaire du droit de passage sur le territoire indien (Portugal c Inde),	« Plaidoirie de Shri MC Setalvad »	(23 septembre 1957),	[1960]	CIJ Mémoires (vol 4)	14	à la p 23.
Compétence en matière de pêcheries (Espagne c Canada),	« Requête introductive d'instance par l'Espagne »	(28 mars 1995),		CIJ Mémoires	3.	

- Indiquer l'intitulé officiel suivi du nom des parties entre parenthèses.

- Fournir le titre officiel du document après l'intitulé, puis indiquer la date précise du document entre parenthèses.

- Faire référence au recueil et à la première page du document. La CIJ publie les mémoires et autres documents dans *Mémoires, plaidoiries et documents* (**CIJ Mémoires**). S'il y a lieu, inclure un numéro de volume avant l'indication de la première page en chiffres arabes (par ex. **1, 2, 3**) et entre parenthèses (par ex. **CIJ Mémoires (vol 4)**).

- Après 1981, les mémoires n'indiquent pas la date de publication du recueil. Les volumes sont identifiés à partir du titre de la décision à laquelle le document se rapporte. Les mémoires sont disponibles sur le site Internet de la CIJ : <www.icj-cij.org>.

5.2.3 Cour de Justice des Communautés européennes et Tribunal de première instance

	Intitulé,	numéro de décision,	[année du recueil]	recueil	1re page	référence précise,	référence parallèle.
CJE	Commission c Luxembourg,	C-26/99,	[1999]	ECR	I-8987	à la p I-8995.	
CJ (1re inst)	Kesko c Commission,	T-22/97,	[1999]	ECR	II-3775	à la p II-3822.	

- Indiquer l'intitulé en utilisant la forme abrégée du nom des institutions (par ex. **Conseil** et non **Conseil des Communautés européennes**).

Documentation internationale

■ Écrire le numéro de la décision. Un **C-** indique les décisions de la **Cour de Justice des Communautés européennes** (CJE) et un **T-** indique celles du **Tribunal de première instance** (CJ (1re inst)).

■ Faire référence au **Rec CE** et indiquer la première page de la décision. Les décisions de la CJE et les décisions de la CJ (1re inst) sont reproduites dans la publication officielle de la Cour, le *Recueil de la jurisprudence de la Cour et du Tribunal de première instance*, couramment appelé *Recueil de la Cour européenne* (Rec CE).

■ Les numéros de page sont précédés par **I-** s'il s'agit d'une **décision de la CJE** et par **II-** s'il s'agit du **Tribunal de première instance**.

■ Si possible, inclure une référence parallèle aux *Common Market Law Reports* (**CMLR**) ou au *Common Market Reporter* (**CMR**).

5.2.4   Cour européenne des Droits de l'Homme et Commission européenne des Droits de l'Homme

5.2.4.1 Avant 1999

Intitulé	(année de la décision),	numéro de volume	recueil	1re page et référence précise,	référence parallèle.
Kurt c Turquie	(1998),	74	CEDH (Sér A)	1152,	27 EHRR 373.
Spencer c Royaume-Uni	(1998),	92A	Comm Eur DHDR	56,	41 YB Eu. Conv H.R 72.

■ Indiquer l'intitulé suivi de l'année de la décision entre parenthèses.

■ Indiquer le numéro de volume du recueil suivi du nom du recueil et de la première page de la décision. Renvoyer aux publications officielles de la Cour et de la Commission : *Cour européenne des Droits de l'Homme, Série A : Arrêts et décisions* (**Cour Eur DH (Sér A)**) ; *Recueil de décisions de la Commission européenne des Droits de l'Homme* (**Comm Eur DH Rec** (de 1960 à 1974)) ; *Décisions et rapports de la Commission européenne des Droits de l'Homme* (**Comm Eur DH DR** (de 1975 à 1999)).

■ Si possible, fournir une référence parallèle à l'*Annuaire de la Convention européenne des Droits de l'Homme* (**Ann Conv Eur DH**) ou aux *European Human Rights Reports* (**EHRR**).

5.2.4.2 À partir de 1999

Le Protocole n° 11 de la *Convention de sauvegarde des Droits de l'Homme et des Libertés fondamentales*, en vigueur depuis le 1er novembre 1998, a remplacé l'ancienne cour et l'ancienne commission par une nouvelle cour permanente.

Intitulé,	numéro de demande,	[année]	numéro de volume	recueil	1re page,	référence parallèle.
Allard c Suède,	n° 35179/97,	[2003]	VII	CEDH	207,	39 EHRR 321.
Chypre c Turquie,	n° 25781/94,	[2001]	IV	CEDH	1,	35 EHRR 731.

▢ Indiquer **[GC]** entres crochets après l'intitulé et avant la virgule, si l'arrêt ou la décision ont été rendus par la Grande Chambre de la Cour.

▢ Indiquer entre parenthèses après l'intitulé et avant la virgule, s'il y a lieu : **(déc)** pour une **décision sur la recevabilité**, **(exceptions préliminaires)** pour un arrêt portant uniquement sur des **exceptions préliminaires**, **(satisfaction équitable)** pour un arrêt portant uniquement sur la **satisfaction équitable**, **(révision)** pour un arrêt de **révision**, **(interprétation)** pour un arrêt d'**interprétation**, **(radiation)** pour un arrêt **rayant l'affaire du rôle**, ou **(règlement amiable)** pour un arrêt sur un **règlement amiable**.

▢ S'il existe **plus d'un numéro de demande**, inclure uniquement le premier numéro.

▢ Pour les **décisions non publiées**, indiquer le numéro de demande, suivi de la date du jugement (par ex. *Roche c Royaume-Uni*, **n° 32555/96 (19 octobre 2005))**.

5.2.5   Cour interaméricaine des Droits de l'Homme

5.2.5.1 Jugements, ordres et avis consultatifs

	Intitulé (nom de l'État impliqué)	(année de la décision),	type de décision et numéro,	recueil	numéro de décision,	référence précise,	référence parallèle.
Jugements	Affaire Neira Alegría (Pérou)	(1996),		Inter-Am Ct HR (Sér C)	n° 29,	au para 55,	Annual Report of the Inter-American Court of Human Rights: 1996, OEA/ Ser.L/V/ III.19/doc.4 (1997) 179.
Avis con-sultatifs	Reports of the Inter-American Commission on Human Rights (Art 51 of the American Convention on Human Rights) (Chili)	(1997),	Avis consul-tatif OC-15/97,	Inter-Am Ct HR (Sér A),	n° 15,	au para 53,	Annual Report of the Inter-American Commission on Human Rights: 1997, OEA/Ser.L/ V/III.39/doc.5 (1998) 307.

Inscrire l'intitulé, suivi de l'année de la décision entre parenthèses. Si la cause implique un État individuel, indiquer le nom de celui-ci entre parenthèses avant l'année de la décision.

Mettre l'année de la décision entre parenthèses.

Indiquer si la décision est un **avis consultatif** et fournir le numéro de la décision.

Indiquer le recueil et le numéro de la décision. La Cour interaméricaine des Droits de l'Homme publie ses **décisions** dans *Inter-American Court of Human Rights Series C: Decisions and Judgments* (**Inter-Am Ct HR (Sér C)**) et ses **avis consultatifs** dans *Inter-American Court of Human Rights Series A: Judgments and Opinions* (**Inter-Am Ct HR (Sér A)**).

Si possible, fournir une référence parallèle au rapport annuel de la Cour, aux *International Legal Materials* (**ILM**) ou à l'*Inter-American Yearbook on Human Rights*.

5.2.5.2 Mémoires, plaidoiries et documents

Intitulé (nom de l'État impliqué),	type de décision et numéro,	« titre du document »	(date du document),	recueil et (série)	1re page,	référence précise.
Proposed Amendments to the Naturalization Provisions of the Constitution of Costa Rica,	Avis consultatif OC-4/84,	« Verbatim Record of Public Hearing »	(7 septembre 1983),	Inter-Am Ct HR (Sér B)	203.	

▨ Inscrire l'intitulé. Si l'information n'est pas déjà présente dans l'intitulé, indiquer le nom de l'État impliqué entre parenthèses.

▨ Indiquer si la décision est un **avis consultatif** et fournir le numéro de la décision.

▨ Inclure le titre entre guillemets suivi de la date du document entre parenthèses.

▨ Indiquer le recueil et la première page de la décision. La Cour interaméricaine des Droits de l'Homme publie les mémoires, les plaidoiries et d'autres documents dans *Inter-American Court of Human Rights Series B: Pleadings, Oral Arguments and Documents* (**Inter-Am Ct HR (Sér B)**).

5.2.6   Commission interaméricaine des Droits de l'Homme

Intitulé	(année du jugement),	Inter-Am Comm HR,	numéro de la décision,	référence précise,	rapport annuel,	numéro du document.
Sánchez c Mexico	(1992),	Inter-Am Comm HR,	No 27/92,		Annual Report of the Inter-American Commission on Human Rights : 1992–93,	OEA/Ser.L/ V/ II.83/ doc.14 104.

▨ Inscrire l'intitulé suivi de l'année de la décision entre parenthèses.

▨ Inscrire **Inter-Am Comm HR** suivi du numéro de la décision.

▨ Les décisions de la Commission interaméricaine des Droits de l'Homme sont publiées dans ses rapports annuels. Faire référence au recueil annuel de la Commission et indiquer son numéro de document. Le numéro de document des publications de l'Organisation des États américains débute toujours avec **OEA** (Organización de les Estados Americanos) et non OÉA, quelle que soit la langue du document.

5.2.7   Tribunaux de droit pénal international

Cette section s'applique aux documents provenant :

☐ de la Cour pénale internationale ;

☐ du Tribunal pénal international pour l'ex-Yougoslavie ;

☐ du Tribunal pénal international pour le Rwanda ;

☐ de la Cour spéciale pour la Sierra Leone ; et

☐ des Groupes d'enquête sur les crimes graves du Timor oriental.

Intitulé,	Numéro de l'affaire,	titre du document (version)	(date du document)	référence précise	(tribunal),	référence.
Le Procureur c Zdravko Mucic (Jugement Celebici),	IT-96-21-Abis,	Arrêt relatif à la sentence	(8 avril 2003)	au para 8	(Tribunal pénal international pour l'ex-Yougoslavie, Chambre d'appel),	(WL).
Le Procureur c Théoneste Bagosora,	ICTR-98-41-I,	Procès-verbal d'audience	(2 avril 2002)		(Tribunal pénal international pour le Rwanda, Chambre de première instance),	en ligne: TPIR <www.ictr.org >.
Deputy General Prosecutor for Serious Crimes v Sito Barros,	01/2004,	Jugement final	(12 mai 2005)	au para 12	(Groupes d'enquête sur les crimes graves (Timor-Leste)),	en ligne: Judicial System Monitoring Program <www.jsmp.minihub.org >.

▨ Indiquer le **prénom** de l'accusé dans l'intitulé, s'il y a lieu.

▨ S'il y a plus d'un accusé, indiquer uniquement le nom du premier accusé dans l'intitulé.

▨ Inclure les **désignations informelles** (par ex. *Jugement Celebici*), si désiré, entre parenthèses après le titre.

▨ Le titre du document indique sa fonction. Noter si le renvoi est la **version publique** du document ou la **version confidentielle** dont l'accès est limité au public.

▨ Suivre les directives fournies à la section 5.3 pour une référence à un site Internet. Certains sites Internet officiels des organismes judiciaires ne publient qu'une portion limitée des documents disponibles, alors que d'autres bases de données en ligne commerciaux offrent une sélection de documents plus étendue.

▨ Si le nom du site Internet est le même que celui du tribunal, indiquer uniquement les initiales pour identifier le site Internet (par ex. **TPIR**).

5.2.8 Groupes spéciaux de l'*Accord général sur les tarifs douaniers et le commerce* (GATT) 1947

Intitulé (plainte(s))	(année du docu-ment),	numéro de doc GATT,	numéro IBDD et (année)	1re page et référence précise,	référence parallèle.
République de Corée – Restrictions à l'importation de la viande de bœuf (Plainte de la Nouvelle-Zélande)	(1989),	GATT Doc L/6505,	Supp n° 36 IBDD (1990)	234,	en ligne : OMC <www.wto.org> .
États-Unis – Droits compensateurs sur la viande de porc fraîche, réfrigérée et congelée en provenance du Canada (Plainte du Canada)	(1991),	GATT Doc DS7/R,	Supp n° 38 IBDD (1990-91)	30,	en ligne : OMC <www.wto.org> .

▨ Fournir l'intitulé suivi du nom de l'État (ou des États) ayant déposé la plainte entre parenthèses.

▨ Indiquer la date de la décision entre parenthèses suivie d'une virgule et du numéro de document GATT.

▨ Se référer aux **IBDD** (*Instruments de base et documents divers*) du GATT en indiquant le numéro de volume suivi de **IBDD**, de l'année entre parenthèses et de la première page du document.

▨ Faire référence à la page et au paragraphe précis immédiatement après l'année.

▨ Fournir les références électroniques suivant les règles énoncées à la section 5.3.

5.2.9   Rapports de Groupes spéciaux et de l'Organe d'appel de l'Organisation mondiale du commerce (OMC)

	Intitulé (plainte(s))	(année de la dé-cision),	numéro du document de l'OMC	référ-ence précise	(type de rapport),	référence par-allèle.
Groupe spécial	États-Unis – Articles 301 à 310 de la Loi de 1974 sur le commerce ex-térieur (Plainte des commu-nautés eur-opéennes)	(1999),	OMC Doc WT/DS152/R	au n° 3.1	(Rapport du Groupe spécial),	en ligne : OMC <www.wto.org/french/docs_f/docs_f.htm>.
Organe d'appel	Inde – Protec-tion conférée par un brevet pour les pro-duits pharma-ceutiques et les produits chimi-ques pour l'agriculture (Plaintes des États-Unis)	(1997),	OMC Doc WT/DS50/AB/R		(Rapport de l'Or-gane d'appel),	en ligne : OMC <www.wto.org/french/docs_f/docs_f.htm>.

Fournir l'intitulé du rapport, suivi du nom de l'auteur ou des auteurs de la plainte. Si les plaintes sont étudiées dans **un seul rapport**, indiquer le nom de tous les États ayant déposé une plainte après l'intitulé du rapport. Si plusieurs États ont déposé des plaintes **traitées séparément**, indiquer le nom de l'État visé par le rapport. Si plus de trois États ont déposé la plainte, indiquer le nom d'un seul État, suivi de **et al**.

Après avoir indiqué l'année du rapport, fournir le numéro du document. Un rapport peut avoir plusieurs numéros de document (par ex. **WT/DS 8, 10, 11/AB/R**). Dans le numéro du document, les lettres **WT-DS** indiquent un **World Trade Dispute Settlement**, **AB** représente l'abréviation d'*Appellate Body* et **R** indique un **rapport**. Si un rapport est destiné à un État particulier parmi plusieurs ayant déposé une plainte, l'abréviation du nom de cet État apparaît dans le numéro de document (par ex. **OMC doc WT/DS27/R/USA**).

À la suite du numéro de document de l'OMC, indiquer entre parenthèses s'il s'agit d'un rapport d'un Groupe spécial ou d'un Organe d'appel.

Fournir les références électroniques selon les règles énoncées à la section 5.3.

5.2.10 Rapports de Groupes spéciaux de l'Accord de libre-échange canado-américain

	Intitulé	(année de la dé-cision),	numéro de docu-ment,	recueil	(Groupe spécial),	référence par-allèle.
Publiés	Re Framboises rouges du Cana-da	(1990),	USA-89-1904-01,	3 TCT 8175	(Groupe spéc c 19),	en ligne : Secré-tariat de l'ALÉNA <www.nafta-sec-alena.org> .
Non publiés	Re Porc frais, fri-gorifié et congélé du Canada	(1991),	ECC-91-1904-01 USA		(Comité cont. extr),	en ligne : Secré-tariat de l'ALÉNA <www.nafta-sec-alena.org> .

▪ À la suite de l'intitulé, indiquer l'année entre parenthèses et le numéro de document. Faire référence à un recueil imprimé si possible.

▪ Fournir des renseignements pour le chapitre sous lequel la plainte a été soumise. Abréger les divers groupes spéciaux de la façon suivante : **Groupe spéc ch 18** pour **Groupe spécial crée en vertu du chapitre 18**, **Groupe spéc ch 19** pour **Groupe spécial crée en vertu du chapitre 19** et **Comité pour cont extr** pour **Comité pour contestation extraordinaire**.

▪ Suivre les règles énoncées à la section 5.3 pour les références électroniques.

5.2.11   Rapports de Groupes spéciaux de l'Accord de libre-échange nord-américain (ALÉNA)

	Intitulé (nom des parties)	(année de la décision),	numéro du document	(groupe spécial),	référence parallèle.
Révision des décisions définitives d'organismes américains	*Re Certains produits de bois d'œuvre résineux du Canada (États-Unis c Canada)*	(2005),	ECC-2004-1904-01USA	(Comité cont extr),	en ligne : Secrétariat de l'ALÉNA <www.nafta-sec-alena.org>.
Révision des décisions définitives de l'organisme mexicain	*Re Polystyrène et cristale impacte en provenance des États-Unis d'Amérique (États-Unis c Mexique)*	(1995),	MEX-94-1904-03	(Groupe spéc c 19),	en ligne : Secrétariat de l'ALÉNA <www.nafta-sec-alena.org>.
Révision des mesures canadiennes	*Re Tarifs douaniers appliqués par le Canada sur certains produits agricoles en provenance des États-Unis d'Amérique (États-Unis c Canada)*	(1996),	CDA-95-2008-01	(Groupe arb c 20),	en ligne : Secrétariat de l'ALÉNA <www.nafta-sec-alena.org>.

▦ Après l'intitulé, indiquer le nom des parties entre parenthèses.

▦ Fournir l'année de la décision entre parenthèses. Inclure le numéro de document et faire référence à un recueil si possible.

▦ Fournir des renseignements sur le chapitre dans lequel la plainte a été soumise. Abréger le nom des groups spéciaux de la façon suivante : **Groupe spéc ch 19** pour **Groupe spécial binational Chapitre 19**, **Groupe Arb ch 20** pour **Groupe arbitral crée en vertu du chapitre 20**, et **Comité cont extr** pour **Comité pour contestation extraordinaire**.

▦ Suivre les règles énoncées à la section 5.3 pour les références électroniques.

5.2.12   Décisions d'arbitrage international

	Intitulé ou numéro de la décision	(année de la dé-cision),	recueil et référence précise	(cadre)	(arbitres) (fa-cultatif).
Nom des parties divulgué	*Southern Paci-fic Properties c Egypt*	(1992),	32 ILM 933 à la p 1008	(International Center for Settle-ment of Invest-ment Disputes)	(Arbitres : Dr Eduardo Jimé-nez de Arécha-ga, Mohamed Amin El Mahdi, Robert F. Pie-trowski Jr).
Parties anonymes	Déc n° 6248	(1990),	19 YB Comm Arb 124 à la p 129	(International Chamber of Commerce).	

▪ Fournir l'intitulé avec le nom des parties si elles sont divulguées. Si les parties sont anonymes, indiquer le numéro de la décision.

▪ Indiquer l'année de la décision entre parenthèses, suivie de la référence au recueil.

▪ Indiquer l'organisme qui a fourni le cadre ou le mécanisme d'arbitrage.

▪ Indiquer le nom des arbitres entre parenthèses à la fin de la référence (facultatif).

5.2.13   Décisions d'arbitrage de l'Organisation mondiale de la propriété intellectuelle (OMPI)

5.2.13.1   *Principes directeurs régissant le règlement uniforme des litiges relatifs aux noms de domaine (UDRP)*

Intitulé,	numéro du litige	\<nom de domaine\>	(Centre d'arbitrage et de médiation de l'OM-PI (UDRP)).
CareerBuilder, LLC v Names for sale,	D2005-0186	\<careersbuilder.com\>	(Centre d'arbitrage et de médiation de l'OMPI (UDRP)).

Margin

5.2.14   Décisions de droit international prises devant des cours nationales

Intitulé,	recueil du pays d'origine,	recueil international	(pays et juridiction).
Re Noble and Wolf,	[1949] 4 DLR 375,	[1948] Ann Dig ILC 302	(Can, CA Ont).
Lindon v Commonwealth of Australia (n° 2)	(1996), 136 ALR 251,	118 ILR 338	(Austl, HC).
Institute of Chartered Accountants in England and Wales v Commisioners of Customs and Excise,	[1999] 2 All ER 449,	[1999] 2 CMLR 1333	(R-U, HL).

Si une décision de portée internationale est rendue par une **cour nationale**, fournir une référence à un recueil du pays d'origine. Indiquer une référence à un recueil international tel que l'*Annual Digest and Reports of Public International Law Cases* (**Ann Dig ILC**), l'*International Law Reports* (**ILR**), les *Common Market Law Reports* (**CMLR**) ou le *Common Market Reporter* (**CMR**).

Indiquer le pays où la décision a été prise et préciser la cour qui a pris la décision.

5.3   SITES INTERNET

Référence traditionelle,	en ligne :	nom du site	<URL>.
US, Commission on Security and Cooperation in Europe, *Presidential Elections and Independence Referendums in the Baltic States, the Soviet Union and Successor States*, Washington (DC), The Commission, 1992 à la p 53,	en ligne :	Commission on Security and Coopera- tion in Europe	<www.csce.gov>.
Convention relative aux droits de l'enfant, 20 novembre 1998, 1577 RTNU 3,	en ligne :	Collection des traités des Nations Unies	<treaties.un.org>.

Fournir la référence traditionelle suivie d'une virgule. Écrire **en ligne :** et le nom du site Internet suivis de l'adresse universelle (URL).

Faire référence à l'adresse universelle de **la page d'accueil** du site Internet.

Plusieurs textes en ligne disparaissent après un certain temps. Faire référence à une source en ligne si cette source fournit des documents archivés remontant à quelques années.

▓ Inclure un numéro de paragraphe comme référence précise si possible. Si la numérotation de la page d'une source imprimée est reproduite dans une source électronique, faire référence à la numérotation utilisée par la source imprimée.

Doctrine et autres
documents

6 DOCTRINE ET AUTRES DOCUMENTS F-127

F -6.1 Périodiques F-127
    F -6.1.1 Modèle de base F-127
    F -6.1.2 Auteur F-127
        F -6.1.2.1 Un seul auteur F-127
        F -6.1.2.2 Coauteurs F-128
    F -6.1.3 Titre de l'article F-128
    F -6.1.4 Année de publication F-128
    F -6.1.5 Volume, numéro et série F-129
    F -6.1.6 Titre du périodique F-129
        F -6.1.6.1 France F-130
    F -6.1.7 Première page de l'article F-131
        F -6.1.7.1 Articles publiés en parties F-131
    F -6.1.8 Référence précise F-131

F -6.2 Monographies F-132
    F -6.2.1 Modèle de base F-132
    F -6.2.2 Auteur F-133
        F -6.2.2.1 Un seul auteur F-133
        F -6.2.2.2 Coauteurs F-133
        F -6.2.2.3 Directeur d'un ouvrage collectif F-133
        F -6.2.2.4 Directeur ou correcteur d l'ouvrage d'un autre auteur F-134
            F -6.2.2.4.1 Le nom de l'auteur original fait partie du titre F-134
            F -6.2.2.4.2 Le nom de l'auteur original ne fait pas partie du titre F-134
        F -6.2.2.5 Traducteur F-134
            F -6.2.2.5.1 Traduction professionnelle F-135
            F -6.2.2.5.2 Traduction de l'auteur du texte (vous) F-135
    F -6.2.3 Titre F-135
        F -6.2.3.1 Procédures publiées d'une conférence ou d'un symposium F-136
    F -6.2.4 Numéro de volume F-136
        F -6.2.4.1 Livres en français F-136
        F -6.2.4.2 Livres en anglais F-137
            F -6.2.4.2.1 Volumes publiés sous différentes titres F-137
            F -6.2.4.2.2 Volume publiés sous un même titre F-137
    F -6.2.5 Édition F-138
    F -6.2.6 Ouvrage à feuilles mobiles F-138
    F -6.2.7 Lieu d'édition F-139
    F -6.2.8 Mainson d'édition F-139
    F -6.2.9 Année d'édition F-140
    F -6.2.10 Référence précise F-140

F -6.3 Articles publiés dans des ouvrages collectifs F-142

F -6.4 Dictionnaires et encyclopédies F-143
    F -6.4.1 Dictionnaires généraux F-143
    F -6.4.2 Dictionnaires spécialisés F-143
    F -6.4.3 Encyclopédies F-144

F -6.5   Recueils encyclopédiques...F-144
    F -6.5.1 Canadian Encyclopedic Digest..................................F-144
        F -6.5.1.1 CED version imprimée...........................F-144
        F -6.5.1.1 CED version électronique F-144
    F -6.5.2 Halsbury's Laws of Canada....................................F-145
        F -6.5.2.1 Halsbury's Laws of Canada version imprimée F-145
        F -6.5.2.2 Halsbury's Laws of Canada version électronique...........F-145
    F -6.5.3 Common Law..F-146
    F -6.5.4 France F-146
        F -6.5.4.1 Modèle de base...................................F-146
        F -6.5.4.2 Rubriques F-147

F -6.6   Codes de déontologie F-148

F -6.7   Décisions d'arbitrage F-148
    F -6.7.1 Décisions d'arbitrage publiées............................F-148
    F -6.7.2 Décisions d'arbitrage non publiées F-149

F -6.8   Recensions...F-149

F -6.9   Chroniques de jurisprudence et de législation F-150
    F -6.9.1 France F-151
        F -6.9.1.1 Notes...F-151
        F -6.9.1.2 Chroniques publiées dans les recueils généraux...........F-151

F -6.10 Commentaires, remarques et notes F-152

F -6.11 Documents historiques légaux....................................F-152
    F -6.11.1 Droit romain..F-152
    F -6.11.2 Droit canonique F-153
    F -6.11.3 Droit Talmudique...F-153

F -6.12 Manuscrits non publiés..F-154
    F -6.12.1 Modèle de base F-154
    F -6.12.2 Manuscrits à paraître F-154
    F -6.12.3 Thèses et dissertations F-155

F -6.13 Allocutions et textes présentés durant des conférences F-156

F -6.14 Recueils de cours..F-157

F -6.15 Périodiques F-157

F -6.16 Journaux, fils de presse et autres sources de nouvelles..................F-158
    F -6.16.1 Éditoriaux et lettres à la rédaction........................F-159

F -6.17 Communiqués de presse..F-160

F -6.18 Lettres et entrevues...F-161

F -6.19 Documents archivés F-162

F -6.20 Propriété intellectuelle..F-162
    F -6.20.1 Brevets...F-162
    F -6.20.2 Marques de commerce F-163
    F -6.20.3 Droits d'auteur..F-163

F -6.21 Documents de travail F-164

F -6.22 Sources électroniques.. F-164
    F -6.22.1 Bases de données en ligne... F-165
    F -6.22.2 Revues en ligne (eJournals).. F-165
    F -6.22.3 Sites web... F-166
        F -6.22.3.1 Journaux web (blogues)..................................... F-166
            F -6.22.3.1.1 Entrées.. F-166
            F -6.22.3.1.2 Commentaires F-167
        F -6.22.3.2 Réseaux sociaux.. F-167
            F -6.22.3.2.1 Entrées Twitter (Tweets)....................... F-167
            F -6.22.3.2.2 Entrées Facebook.............................. F-168
            F -6.22.3.2.3 Entrées Reddit................................. F-168
        F -6.22.3.3 Vidéos et agrégateurs de vidéos en ligne................... F-169
    F -6.22.4 Autres supports numériques... F-169
    F -6.22.5 Identifiants numériques d'objets F-170

Doctrine et autres documents

6   DOCTRINE ET AUTRES DOCUMENTS

6.1   PÉRIODIQUES

6.1.1   Modèle de base

Auteur,	« titre de l'article »	(année)	vo-lume	:	nu-méro (s'il y a lieu)	abrévia-tion du périodi-que	pre-mière page	référ-ence pré-cise	(service électro-nique) (s'il y a lieu).
Marie-Claude Pré-mont,	« La fisca-lité locale au Québec : de la co-habitation au refuge fiscal »	(2001)	46	:	3	RD McGill	713	à la p 720	(QL).

6.1.2   Auteur

6.1.2.1 Un seul auteur

Frédéric Bachand, « L'efficacité en droit québécois d'une convention d'arbitrage ou d'élection de for invoquée à l'encontre d'un appel en garantie » (2004) 83:2 R du B 515.

L'honorable Louis LeBel, « La protection des droits fondamentaux et la responsabilité civile » (2004) 49:2 RD McGill 231.

▪ Indiquer le nom de l'auteur **tel qu'il paraît sur la page couverture**. Inclure tous les noms et initiales utilisés. Ne pas mettre d'espace entre les initiales. Ne pas inscrire un nom lorsque des initiales sont utilisées et ne pas inclure d'intiales lorsqu'un nom est utilisé.

▪ Si le nom de l'auteur sur la page de couverture est précédé d'un **titre honorifique** tel que **l'honorable**, **Rabbin**, **Professeur** ou **Lord**, inclure ce titre dans la référence. Inclure également les **suffixes** tels que **Jr** ou **IV**. Ne pas indiquer les diplômes ou autre références.

6.1.2.2 Coauteurs

> **Murielle Paradelle, Hélène Dumont et Anne-Marie Boisvert**, « Quelle justice pour quelle réconciliation ? : Le Tribunal pénal pour le Rwanda et le jugement du génocide » (2005) 50:2 RD McGill 359.
>
> **Armel Huet et al**, *Capitalisme et industries culturelles,* Grenoble, Presses Universitaires de Grenoble, 1978.

▨ Ne pas indiquer plus de trois auteurs.

  ☐ S'il y a **deux auteurs**, séparer les noms des auteurs par et.

  ☐ S'il y a **trois auteurs**, séparer les deux premiers noms par une virgule et écrire et avant le dernier nom.

  ☐ S'il y a **plus de trois auteurs**, indiquer le nom du premier auteur, suivi de **et al**.

▨ Pour les autres types de **collaborations,** suivre la formule utilisée sur la page titre.

6.1.3 Titre de l'article

> Ghislain Otis, **« Les sources des droits ancestraux des peuples autochtones »** (1999) 40:3 C de D 591.
>
> Darcy L MacPherson, **« Extending Corporate Criminal Liability?: Some Thoughts on Bill C-45 »** (2004) 30:3 Man LJ 253.

▨ Indiquer le titre de l'article **entre guillemets**.

▨ Ne pas mettre de virgule après le titre.

▨ Séparer un titre d'un sous-titre à l'aide de deux-points (:). Ne pas utiliser de tiret (—).

▨ Respecter les règles des **majuscules** et de la **ponctuation** de la langue du titre. Peu importe la langue du titre, utiliser des guillemets français avant et après le titre (par ex. **« Titre »**).

▨ Pour plus de détails concernant la langue et la ponctuation les titres, voir la section 6.2.3.

6.1.4 Année de publication

Le périodique est organisé par numéro de volume	Michel Poirier, « La convention d'emphytéose peut-elle être à titre gratuit ? » **(1998)** 58 R du B 401.
Le périodique est organisé par année de publication	Frédéric Pollaud-Dulian, « À propos de la sécurité juridique » **[2001]** RTD civ 487.

▨ Si le périodique **est divisé en volumes numérotés**, indiquer la date de publication **entre parenthèses**.

▨ Si le périodique **n'est pas divisé en volumes numérotés, mais en années**, indiquer l'année **entre crochets**.

6.1.5   Volume, numéro et série

Auteur, « titre de l'article » (année de publication)	volume	:	numéro	titre de la revue	série (s'il y a lieu)	première page de l'article
Cédric Milhat, « La représentation juridique de la mémoire. L'exemple français. » (2009)	43	:	1	RJT		51.
Damian Powell, « Coke in Context: Early Modern Legal Observation and Sir Edward Coke's *Reports* » (2000)	21	:	3	Health L Rev		34.
RRA Walker, « The English Property Legislation of 1922-6 » (1928)	10			J Comp Legis & Int'l L	(3e)	1.

▨ Placer le numéro du volume après l'année de publication, suivi d'un deux-points et du numéro de la revue. **Inclure le numéro**, peu importe si la pagination des numéros d'un volume est consécutive ou non.

▨ Indiquer le volume et le numéro en chiffres Arabes (par ex. 1,2,3), même si la revue utilise des chiffres Romains.

▨ Si une revue est aussi divisée en **séries**, indiquer le numéro de la série entre parenthèses après le titre de la revue.

6.1.6   Titre du périodique

▨ Abréger le titre du périodique selon la liste des abréviations prévue à l'**annexe D**.

▨ Si l'abréviation fournie dans l'**annexe D** risque de n'être reconnue que par les membres d'un domaine de pratique très spécialisé, écrire le titre de la revue en entier.

> Will Kymlicka, « Federalism and Secession: At Home and Abroad » (2000) 13 **Can JL & Jur** 207.
>
> André Cellard et Gérald Pelletier, « Le Code criminel canadien, 1892-1927 : étude des acteurs sociaux » (1998) 79 **Canadian Historical Review** 261.

▨ Si le périodique n'apparaît pas dans l'**annexe D**, appliquer les règles suivantes. Écrire au complet les mots qui n'apparaissent pas dans la liste ci-dessous.

☐ Annuaire = Ann

☐ Association = Assoc

☐ Barreau = B

☐ Bulletin = Bull

☐ Canada ou canadien(ne) = Can

☐ Droit = Dr

☐ Et = &

☐ Gazette = Gaz

☐ International = Intl

☐ Journal = J

☐ Légal = Lég

☐ Revue = R

☐ Université = U

Omettre les mots « de/du » et « le/la/les » dans les titres abrégés.

Placer un espace entre deux mots ayant des caractères minuscules, et entre une esperluette et les mots ou lettres qui l'encadrent (par ex. Actu & dr int). Ne pas mettre d'espace entre des lettres majuscules adjacentes (par ex. RTD civ).

Appliquer les abréviations de juridiction de l'annexe A pour les noms d'endroits. S'il n'y a pas de telle abréviation, écrire le nom du lieu au complet.

Lorsqu'un journal a un sous-titre, omettre le sous-titre et n'abréger que le titre principal.

Les titres de périodiques anglais qui n'apparaissent pas dans l'annexe D doivent être abrégés selon les règles de la section anglaise de ce Guide.

Ne pas mettre l'abréviation ou le titre du périodique en italique.

6.1.6.1 France

Auteur,	« titre »	renseignements sur l'édition.
Jean-Christophe Galloux,	« La loi du 6 mars 1998 relative à la sécurité et à la promotion d'activités sportives »	(1998) JCP I 1085.

Indiquer le nom et le titre d'articles publiés dans les recueils généraux de France de la manière énoncée aux sections 6.1.2 et 6.1.3. Voir aussi l'**annexe C-3** pour la liste de ces recueils.

Consulter la section 3.7 pour les références aux recueils.

Abréviations de recueils :

Actualité juridique de droit administratif	AJDA
Bulletin de la Cour de cassation, section civile	Bull civ
Gazette du Palais	Gaz Pal
Recueil des décisions du Conseil d'État ou *Recueil Lebon*	Rec
Recueil Dalloz et *Recueil Dalloz Sirey* (1945–présent)	D
Semaine juridique (1937–présent)	JCP

6.1.7   Première page de l'article

Marie-Josée Bernardi, « La diversité génétique humaine : éléments d'une politique » (2001) 35 RJT **327**.

▪ Indiquer la première page de l'article après le titre de la revue. **Ne pas écrire** « p » ou « à la p ».

▪ Pour les références précises, voir la section 6.1.8.

6.1.7.1 Articles publiés en parties

Publication dans différents volumes	RA Macdonald, « Enforcing Rights in Corporeal Moveables: Revendication and Its Surrogates » (1986) 31:4 RD McGill 573 **et** (1986) 32:1 RD McGill 1.
Publication dans différentes parties d'un même volume	Roderick A Macdonald, « L'image du Code civil et l'imagination du notaire » (1995) 74 R du B can **97 et 330**.

▪ Si les parties de l'article ont été publiées dans **plusieurs volumes**, indiquer l'auteur et le titre, suivis de la référence complète pour chaque partie, réunies par **et**.

▪ Si les parties de l'article ont été publiées dans **un même volume**, indiquer les premières pages de chaque partie, séparées par **et**.

6.1.8   Référence précise

Nicholas Kasirer, « Agapè et le devoir juridique de secours : qui est mon prochain ? » [2001] RIDC 575 **aux pp 579-80**.

Adrian J Bradbrook, Susan V MacCallum et Anthony P Moore, *Australian Real Property Law,* 2ᵉ éd, Sydney, Law Book Company, 1997 **au para 509**.

Louis Beaudoin et Madeleine Mailhot, *Expressions juridiques en un clin d'œil*, Cowansville (Qc), Yvon Blais, 1997 **à la p 55, n 1**.

▪ Indiquer la référence précise à la fin de la référence.

▨ Indiquer la page ou le paragraphe. Lorsque les paragraphes sont numérotés, y faire référence à l'aide de **au para**. Pour faire référence à une page, utiliser **à la p** et pour plusieurs pages, utiliser **aux pp**.

▨ Séparer les pages et les paragraphes **consécutifs** par un tiret court. Pour les nombres de deux chiffres et plus, conserver au moins les deux derniers chiffres (par ex. **158–60** ou **32–35**, mais jamais **32–5**).

▨ Utiliser une virgule pour séparer les pages et les paragraphes **non consécutifs** (par ex. **aux pp 21, 48**).

▨ Pour indiquer une **partie générale**, inscrire **et s** (abréviation de « et suivantes ») immédiatement après le numéro. Il est toutefois préférable de faire référence aux pages ou paragraphes précis.

▨ Pour faire référence à **une note de bas de page**, indiquer le numéro de la page où se trouve la note ainsi que le numéro de la note (par ex. **à la p 99, n 140**). Pour faire référence à **plusieurs notes**, indiquer le numéro de la page où se trouvent les notes ainsi que les numéros des notes (par ex. **à la p 142, nn 73–75**). Toutefois, si le numéro de la page n'est pas disponible, faire référence au numéro de la note uniquement (par ex. **n 140**).

▨ Utiliser le même format de chiffre que le texte (par ex. **5–6**; **v–vi**).

6.2 MONOGRAPHIES

6.2.1 Modèle de base

Auteur,	*titre,*	édi-tion,	autres élém-ents	lieu d'édition,	maison d'édition,	année d'édi-tion	référ-ence précise	(service électron-ique) (si utilisé).
Éric Ca-nal-For-gues,	*Le règle-ment des dif-férends à l'OMC,*	2ᵉ éd,		Bruxelles,	Bruylant,	2004	à la p 53.	
J An-thony VanDu-zer,	*The Law of Part-ner-ships and Cor-pora-tions,*			Toronto,	Irwin Law,	1997	ch 2 (B) (3)	(QL).

▨ D'autres éléments peuvent être indiqués, si nécessaire, dans la section « autres éléments » entre l'édition et le lieu d'édition. Leur ordre de présentation est le suivant : **nom du directeur d'un ouvrage collectif** (section 6.2.2.3) ; **nom du traducteur** (section 6.2.2.5) ;

numéro du volume (section 6.2.4) ; **titre du volume** ; **titre d'une collection et le numéro du volume dans cette collection** et **feuilles mobiles** (section 6.2.6).

6.2.2 Auteur

6.2.2.1 Un seul auteur

> **Sylvio Normand**, *Introduction au droit des biens*, Montréal, Wilson & Lafleur, 2000.
>
> **Jean-Pierre Baud**, *L'affaire de la main volée : une histoire juridique du corps*, Paris, Seuil, 1993 à la p 4.
>
> **Lucie Laflamme**, *Le partage consécutif à l'indivision*, Montréal, Wilson & Lafleur, 1999.
>
> **Lord Denning**, *What Next in the Law*, Londres, Butterworths, 1982.

Indiquer le nom de l'auteur **tel qu'il paraît sur la page couverture**. Inclure tous les noms et initiales utilisés. Ne pas mettre d'espace entre les initiales. Ne pas inscrire un nom lorsque des initiales sont utilisées et ne pas inclure d'intiales lorsqu'un nom est utilisé.

Si le nom de l'auteur sur la page de couverture est précédé d'un **titre honorifique** tel que **l'honorable**, **Rabbin**, **Professeur** ou **Lord**, inclure ce titre dans la référence. Inclure également les suffixes tels que **Jr** ou **IV**. Ne pas indiquer les diplômes ou autre références.

6.2.2.2 Coauteurs

> [1] **Jacques Bourdon, Jean-Marie Pontier et Jean-Claude Ricci**, *Droit des collectivités territoriales*, Paris, Presses Universitaires de France, 1987.
>
> [9] **Joel Bakan et al**, *Canadian Constitutional Law*, 3e éd, Toronto, Emond Montgomery, 2003.
>
> [10] **Pierre-Gabriel Jobin avec la collaboration de Nathalie Vézina**, *Baudouin et Jobin : Les obligations*, 6e éd, Cowansville (Qc), Yvon Blais, 2005.

Ne pas indiquer plus de trois auteurs. S'il y en a plus, indiquer le nom du premier auteur, suivi de **et al**.

Séparer le nom des deux derniers auteurs par **et**.

Pour les **autres types de collaborations** (par ex. **avec la collaboration de**), suivre la formule utilisée sur la page titre de la monographie (voir note 10 ci-haut).

6.2.2.3 Directeur d'un ouvrage collectif

Indiquer le nom du directeur avant le titre de l'ouvrage collectif, suivi de **dir** entre virgules.

> **Denis Ferland et Benoît Emery, dir**, *Précis de procédure civile du Québec*, 3e éd, Cowansville (Qc), Yvon Blais, 1997.

Doctrine et autres documents

Doctrine et autres documents

- **Indiquer jusqu'à trois directeurs**, séparant le nom des deux premiers par une virgule et celui des deux derniers par **et**.

- S'il y a **plus de trois directeurs**, indiquer seulement le nom du premier directeur suivi de **et al**.

- L'abréviation **dir** vaut autant pour le singulier que le pluriel.

- Si la référence concerne un **article en particulier** et non l'ouvrage en général, indiquer le nom de l'auteur et de l'article, suivi de **dans** avant le nom du directeur (voir la section 6.3).

6.2.2.4 Directeur ou correcteur de l'ouvrage d'un autre auteur

6.2.2.4.1 Le nom de l'auteur original fait partie du titre

Directeur,	dir,	*titre*,	édition (s'il y a lieu),	renseignements sur l'édition.
M Dupin,	dir,	*Oeuvres de Pothier*,	2e éd,	Paris, Pichon-Béchet, 1835.

- Si le nom de l'auteur fait partie du titre, faire référence au directeur, suivi de **dir** entre virgules.

6.2.2.4.2 Le nom de l'auteur original ne fait pas partie du titre

Auteur,	*titre*,	édition (s'il y a lieu)	par	directeur,	renseignements sur l'édition.
Aubry et Rau,	*Droit civil français*,	8e éd	par	André Ponsard et Ibrahim Fadlallah,	Paris, Librairies techniques, 1989.

- Si le nom de l'auteur ne fait pas partie du titre, mettre le nom du directeur après la mention de l'édition, et l'introduire avec **par**.

- S'il y a plusieurs éditions, indiquer le numéro (par ex. **8e éd par**).

- Indiquer le(s) nom(s) du ou des auteur(s) et du ou des directeur(s) tels qu'ils apparaissent dans la publication.

6.2.2.5 Traducteur

Traduire les textes en langues étrangères qui pourraient ne pas être connues des lecteurs. Le texte original d'une citation peut être inclus dans la note de bas de page.

6.2.2.5.1 Traduction professionnelle

Auteur,	*titre,*	traduit par	traducteur,	renseignements sur l'édition	[modifiée par l'auteur] (s'il y a lieu).
Jürgen Habermas,	*Droit et démocracie : entre faits et normes,*	traduit par	Rainer Rochlitz et Christian Bouchindhomme,	Paris, Gallimard, 1997.	

▨ Faire référence à une traduction professionnelle en indiquant le nom du traducteur avant les renseignements sur l'édition, introduit par **traduit par**.

▨ S'il est nécessaire de modifier la traduction d'un passage cité, introduire la modification par **[modifiée par l'auteur]** après les renseignements sur l'édition.

▨ Toujours inclure l'information sur le directeur ou le correcteur (section 6.2.2.4) avant l'information sur le traducteur (6.2.2.5).

6.2.2.5.2 Traduction de l'auteur du texte (vous)

Comme le dit Kronby : « la cour fut convaincue par la preuve de l'épouse » **[notre traduction]**[28].

▨ L'ajout **[notre traduction]** se réfère à l'auteur (vous) et non à l'auteur du texte cité.

▨ Dans la mesure du possible, traduire un passage tiré d'une source rédigée dans une autre langue que le français ou l'anglais.

▨ Insérer l'ajout **[notre traduction]** dans le corps même du texte, après les guillemets de la citation traduite et immédiatement avant l'appel de note.

6.2.3   Titre

[1] B Lefebvre, *La bonne foi dans la formation du contrat*, Montréal, Yvon Blais, 1998.

[2] AH Oosterhoff et EE Gillese, *Text, Commentary and Cases on Trusts*, 5e éd, Toronto, Carswell, 1998.

[3] Frédéric Garron, *La caducité du contrat : étude de droit privé*, Aix-en-Provence, Presses Universitaires d'Aix-Marseille, 2000.

[4] Michel Vepreaux, *La naissance du pouvoir réglementaire, 1789-1799*, Paris, Presses Universitaires de France, 1991.

[5] Jürgen Schwarze, *Europaïsches Varwaltungsrecht* [Droit administratif européen], 2e éd, Bruxelles, Bruylant, 2009.

[6] Waldo Ansaldi, dir, *La démocratie en Amérique latine : Un bateau de la dérive* (en espagnol), Buenos Aires, Fondo de Cultura Económica, 2007.

Doctrine et autres documents

▨ Indiquer le titre principal en entier et en italique. Suivre l'orthographe et la ponctuation du titre tel que publié avec les exceptions suivantes :

☐ précéder le sous-titre de deux-points (notes 3 et 6) ; et

☐ insérer une virgule avant une date comprise à la fin du titre, s'il y a lieu (note 4).

▨ Respecter les règles des majuscules et de la ponctuation de la langue du titre.

▨ Si le titre de l'ouvrage est dans une langue qui n'est pas le français, l'anglais ou une autre langue familière aux lecteurs, suivre **l'une** des règles suivantes :

☐ Inscrire le titre original suivi d'une traduction en français (note 5). Ne pas mettre la traduction en italique, mais entre crochets, sans ponctuation entre le titre original et la traduction. Si le titre original n'est pas en lettres latines (par ex. en chinois ou en hébreu), transcrire le titre en écriture romaine (par ex. **Menachem Elon,** *Ha-Mishpat Ha-Ivri* **[Droit juif]**).

☐ Traduire le titre en français et le mettre en italique suivi de l'indication de la langue originale du texte entre parenthèses (note 6). Ne pas ajouter de ponctuation entre la traduction du titre et les parenthèses.

6.2.3.1 Procédures publiées d'une conférence ou d'un symposium

▨ Traiter toute information concernant la conférence ou le symposium comme faisant partie du titre.

> Marie-France Bich, « Petits éléments pour une réflexion polémique sur la solidarité en droit du travail » dans *Droits de la personne : solidarité et bonne foi. Actes des Journées strasbourgeoises de l'Institut canadien d'études juridiques supérieures 2000 tenues du 2 au 8 juillet 2000 à Strasbourg*, Cowansville (Qc), Yvon Blais, 2000.

6.2.4 Numéro de volume

6.2.4.1 Livres en français

Auteur,	*titre,*	tome et/ou volume,	édition,	directeur (s'il y a lieu),	renseignements sur l'édition.
Jean Carbonnier,	*Droit civil : les obligations,*	t 4,	22e éd,		Paris, Presses Universitaires de France, 2000.
Henri Mazeaud et al,	*Leçons de droit civil,*	t 3, vol 1,	7e éd,	Yves Picod, dir,	Paris, Montchrestien, 1999.

▨ Les ouvrages français peuvent être divisés en tomes et subdivisés en volumes.

▨ Utiliser **t** pour **tome** et **vol** pour **volume**.

▨ Indiquer les numéros de tomes et de volumes en chiffres arabes (par ex. **1, 2, 3**).

▓ Faire suivre le titre par les indications du tome et du volume et les placer entre virgules.

▓ Ne pas répéter le numéro du tome et du volume dans les références suivantes, à moins qu'il n'y ait une référence à un tome ou un volume différent ailleurs dans le document citant (par ex. **Mazeaud et al, t 3, vol 2,** *supra* **note 10**).

6.2.4.2 Livres en anglais

6.2.4.2.1 Volumes publiés sous différents titres

Auteur,	*titre,*	volume,	renseignements sur l'édition	référence précise.
Anne F Bayefsky,	*Canada's Constitution Act 1982 & Amendments: A Documentary History,*	vol 2,	Toronto, McGraw-Hill, 1989	à la p 669.

▓ Indiquer le numéro du volume **avant** les renseignements sur l'édition.

▓ Indiquer le numéro du volume en chiffres arabes (par ex. **1, 2, 3**), même si l'éditeur utilise des chiffres romains.

▓ Ne pas répéter le numéro du volume dans les références suivantes, à moins qu'il y ait une référence à un volume différent ailleurs dans le document citant (par ex. **Bayefsky, vol 1,** *supra* **note 89**).

6.2.4.2.2 Volumes publiés sous un même titre

Auteur,	*titre,*	directeur (s'il y a lieu),	traduction (s'il y a lieu),	renseigne-ments sur l'édition,	volume	référen-ce pré-cise
Karl Marx,	*Capital: A Critical Ana-lysis of Capi-talist Produc-tion,*	Friedrich Engels, dir,	trad par Sa-muel Moore et Edward Aveling,	Londres, Swan Son-nenschein, 1908,	vol 1	à la p 15.

▓ Indiquer le numéro du volume **après** les renseignements sur l'édition.

▓ Indiquer le numéro du volume en chiffres arabes (par ex. **1, 2, 3**), même si l'éditeur utilise des chiffres romains.

▓ Ne pas répéter le numéro du volume dans les références suivantes, à moins qu'il y ait une référence à un volume différent ailleurs dans le document citant (par ex. **Marx, vol 2,** *supra* **note 4**).

Doctrine et autres documents

6.2.5   Édition

Germain Brière, *Le nouveau droit des successions*, **2ᵉ éd**, Montréal, Wilson & Lafleur, 1997.

Maurice Tancelin, *Des obligations : contrat et responsabilité*, **éd révisée**, Montréal, Wilson & Lafleur, 1986.

▨ Indiquer le numéro de l'édition (par ex. **2ᵉ éd**) après le titre.

▨ Abréger **édition** par **éd**.

▨ Lorsque l'ouvrage a été révisé mais qu'aucun numéro d'édition n'est précisé, indiquer **éd révisée** après le titre.

6.2.6   Ouvrage à feuilles mobiles

Auteur,	titre,	renseignements sur l'édition,	(feuilles mobiles numéro / date de la mise à jour / supplement),	référence précise.
Georges Audet et al,	*Le congédiement en droit québécois en matière de contrat individuel de travail,*	Cowansville (Qc), Yvon Blais, 1991	(feuilles mobiles mise à jour 18 :1),	ch 5 à la p 71.
Madeleine Lemieux,	*Tribunaux administratifs du Québec : Règles et législation annotées,*	Cowansville (Qc), Yvon Blais, 2002	(feuilles mobiles mise à jour 15),	ch R9 à la p 85.
Robert W Hillman	*Hillman on Lawyer Mobility : The Law and Ethics of Partner Withdrawals and Law Firm Breakups,*	2ᵉ éd, Austin, Wolters Kluwer, 1998	(feuilles mobiles supplement 2009),	ch 2 à la p 85.

▨ Les règles de cette section s'appliquent aux **ouvrages de doctrine** dont le contenu est **continuellement renouvelé**. Pour faire référence à la législation sous forme de recueils à feuilles mobiles, voir la section 2.1.5.

▨ Après les renseignements sur l'édition, mettre entre parethèses la phrase **feuilles mobiles** et le numéro de la mise à jour où du supplement.

▨ Si l'année de la révision n'est pas déjà indiquée dans le numéro de la mise à jour ou du supplément, il est possible de l'inclure dans la reference (par ex. JD Green, *The Law of Tort*, Toronto, Thomson Reuters, 2011 (feuilles mobiles **mises à jour en 2013**, version 20), ch 5 à la p 71).

▨ Utiliser la date d'édition qui paraît sur la page où sont indiquées les informations sur les droits d'auteur, même si cette date diffère de la date qui se trouve ailleurs dans le livre.

▨ Faire référence au chapitre en plus de la page si l'ouvrage est divisé en chapitres.

6.2.7   Lieu d'édition

▨ Indiquer le lieu d'édition si l'information est disponible. Le lieu d'édition peut servir à signaller au lecteur la juridiction pertinente à l'œuvre citée.

> J-L Aubert, *La responsabilité civile des notaires*, 3e éd, **Paris**, Defrénois, 1998.
>
> Andrée Lajoie, *Pouvoir disciplinaire et tests de dépistage de drogues en milieu de travail*, **Cowansville (Qc)**, Yvon Blais, 1995.

▨ Indiquer le lieu d'édition tel qu'il figure au recto ou au verso de la page titre. Utiliser la **version française** du nom de la ville si elle existe (par ex. écrire **Londres (R-U)** et non **London (UK)**).

▨ S'il y a **plus d'un lieu d'édition**, ne mentionner que le premier lieu.

▨ Si **aucun lieu d'édition n'est fourni**, omettre le lieu ainsi que la virgule qui s'y attache.

▨ Si des renseignements supplémentaires sont requis pour identifier le lieu d'édition (par ex. la province, l'état ou le pays), abréger ces renseignements entre parenthèses après le lieu d'édition (par ex. **Cowansville (Qc)**). Si deux villes peuvent être confondues, ajouter les renseignements supplémentaires nécessaires (par ex. **London (Ont)** et **Londres (R-U)**).

▨ Voir les abréviations couramment utilisées des provinces canadiennes de l'**annexe A-1** et les abréviations des états américains de l'**annexe A-2**.

6.2.8   Maison d'édition

✓	Mireille D Castelli et Dominique Goubau, *Précis de droit de la famille*, Sainte-Foy (Qc), **Presses de l'Université Laval**, 2000.
✓	Pierre-Claude Lafond, *Précis du droit des biens*, Montréal, **Thémis**, 1999.
✗	Pierre-Claude Lafond, *Précis du droit des biens*, Montréal, **Les Éditions Thémis inc**, 1999.

▨ Indiquer le nom de la maison d'édition **tel qu'il figure à la page titre**.

▨ Ne pas abréger le nom de la maison d'édition (par ex. **Presses de l'Université Laval** et non **PUL**).

▨ Omettre l'article défini (**le, la, les, l', *the***) si c'est le premier mot du nom de la maison d'édition.

▨ Omettre les expressions indiquant le statut corporatif (par ex. **ltée, inc**).

▨ Écrire « édition(s) », « *Publishing* » ou « *Publishers* » uniquement s'il s'agit d'une partie inséparable du nom (par ex. **Éditions de l'Homme**). Suivre cette même règle pour les autres langues (par ex. **Verlag**).

▓ Indiquer **Presses** en français et **Press** en anglais si c'est inclus dans le nom de la maison d'édition sur la page titre.

▓ S'il y a **plus d'un éditeur**, fournir les lieux d'édition et les noms des coéditeurs, suivis de l'année. Séparer les lieux d'édition l'un de l'autre par **et**. De même, sépararer les noms des coéditeurs par **et**. Voir l'exemple ci-dessous.

Premier lieu d'édition et	deuxième lieu d'édition	:	premier coéditeur et	deuxième coéditeur,	année.
Latzville (C-B) et	Montreal	:	Oolichan Books et	Institute for Research on Public Policy,	1992.

▓ Si un éditeur travaille pour une **organisation**, indiquer **pour** avant le nom de l'organisation (par ex. **Janet E Gans Epner pour la Commission on Women in the Profession**).

▓ Si **aucune maison d'édition** n'est indiquée, écrire **maison d'édition inconnue**.

6.2.9   Année d'édition

▓ Indiquer l'année de **l'édition actuelle**, et non celle de la première édition. En général, utiliser la date la plus récente indiquée sur l'édition, à moins que l'année de publication ne soit présentée de façon explicite.

> Jean Pineau, Danielle Burman et Serge Gaudet, *Théorie des obligations*, 4ᵉ éd, Montréal, Thémis, **2001**.

▓ Ne pas indiquer l'année d'impression.

▓ Si **aucune année** n'est indiquée, ommettre l'année.

6.2.10   Référence précise

Pierre-André Côté, *Interprétation des lois*, 3ᵉ éd, Montréal, Thémis, 1999 **à la p 307**.

Jean-Louis Baudouin, *La responsabilité civile délictuelle*, 4ᵉ éd, Cowansville (Qc), Yvon Blais, 1994 **aux pp 102–08, 121–25**.

Ronald Joseph Delisle et Don Stuart, *Learning Canadian Criminal Procedure*, 5ᵉ éd, Scarborough, Carswell, 1998, **ch 2 à la p 377 et s**.

Francis Delpérée, *Le droit constitutionnel de la Belgique*, Belgique, Bruxelles, Bruylant, 2000 au n° 257.

Isabelle Schulte-Tenckhoff, *La question des peuples autochtones*, Bruxelles, Bruylant, 1997 **à la p 56, n 61**.

▓ Indiquer la référence précise après l'information sur la publication.

Doctrine et autres documents

■ **Les références aux paragraphes sont préférables à celles aux pages**. Lorsque les paragraphes sont numérotés, indiquer **au para ou aux para**. Pour faire référence à une page, utiliser **à la p** et pour plusieurs pages, utiliser **aux pp**.

■ Séparer les pages et les paragraphes **consécutifs** par un tiret court, en conservant au moins les deux derniers chiffres (par ex. **158–60** ou **32–35**, mais jamais **32–5**).

■ Utiliser une virgule pour séparer les numéros **non consécutifs** (**aux pp 21, 48**).

■ Pour indiquer une **partie générale**, indiquer **et s** (abréviation de « et suivantes ») immédiatement après le numéro. De préférence, indiquer les pages et paragraphes précis.

■ Abréger **chapitre** et **chapitres** par **ch**.

■ Pour faire référence à une **note de bas de page**, indiquer le numéro de la page où se trouve la note ainsi que le numéro de la note (par ex. **à la p 99, n 140**). Au pluriel, **n** devient **nn**. Si le numéro de la page n'est pas disponible, indiquer le numéro de la note (par ex. **n 140**) seulement.

■ Pour les chiffres, utiliser le même format que dans le texte (par ex. **5–6**; **v–vi**).

6.3 ARTICLES PUBLIÉS DANS DES OUVRAGES COLLECTIFS

Auteur de l'article,	« titre de l'article »	dans	directeur (s'il y a lieu),	dir,	*titre de l'ouvrage,*	renseigne-ments sur l'édi-tion,	1re page de l'article	référence précise (s'il y a lieu).
Made-leine Cantin Cumyn,	« Le Code civil et la ges-tion des biens d'autrui »	dans	Jean-Louis Bau-douin et Patrice Deslau-riers,	dir,	*La re-sponsabil-ité civile des cour-tiers en va-leurs mobi-lières et des ges-tionnaires de fortune : aspects nouveaux,*	Montréal, Yvon Blais, 1999,	121	à la p 128.
Daniel Jutras,	« Le code et le min-istre, es-sai sur les com-men-taires »	dans			*Mélanges offerts à Paul-An-dré Cré-peau,*	Cowansville (Qc), Yvon Blais, 1997,	451	à la p 453.
Jocelyn Ma-clure,	« Intro-duc-tion »	dans	Jocelyn Maclure et Alain-G Gag-non,	dir,	*Passages : l'identité, diversité et citoyen-neté au Québec,*	Montréal, Québec Amérique, 2001,	xi.	

- Indiquer le nom de l'auteur et le titre de l'article suivis de la référence à l'ouvrage collectif.
- Indiquer le nom du directeur, suivi de **dir** entre virgules. Omettre l'identité du directeur si celle-ci n'est pas fournie.
- Indiquer le titre de l'ouvrage collectif en italique, suivi des renseignements sur l'édition.
- Lorsque d'autres éléments peuvent être ajoutés (section 6.2.1), les placer entre le titre de l'ouvrage et les renseignements sur l'édition.
- Indiquer la première page de l'article et la référence précise s'il y a lieu.

■ Si le texte n'est pas un article, utiliser comme titre d'article **Avant-propos**, **Préface**, **Introduction**, **Conclusion**, ou le titre donné à cette section en suivant les règles qui s'appliquent aux articles (voir l'exemple de Jocelyn Maclure).

■ Pour faire référence à deux ou plusieurs articles d'un même ouvrage collectif, utiliser le titre abrégé approprié (section 1.4.1.4) pour le second article ainsi que pour tous ceux qui suivent.

6.4   DICTIONNAIRES ET ENCYCLOPÉDIES

6.4.1   Dictionnaires généraux

Titre,	**édition** ou **année,**	*sub verbo*	**« mot cherché ».**
Le nouveau petit Robert,	1990,	*sub verbo*	« amphigourique ».
Black's Law Dictionary,	6e éd,	*sub verbo*	« promissory estoppel ».

■ Indiquer le titre du dictionnaire en italique.

■ Indiquer l'édition ou l'année.

■ Écrire *sub verbo*, signifiant « au mot » en latin.

6.4.2   Dictionnaires spécialisés

Directeur ou auteur,	**dir** (s'il y a lieu),	*titre,*	**édition** (s'il y a lieu),	**renseignements sur l'édition,**	*sub verbo*	**« mot cherché ».**
Gérard Cornu,	dir,	*Vocabulaire juridique,*	7e éd,	Paris, Presses Universitaires de France, 2005,	*sub verbo*	« minorité ».
Office québécois de la langue française		*Grand dictionnaire terminologique*			*sub verbo*	« hypothèque ».

■ Faire référence au dictionnaire de la même manière qu'à une monographie (section 6.2).

■ Écrire *sub verbo*, signifiant « au mot » en latin.

Doctrine et autres documents

6.4.3   Encyclopédies

Auteur (s'il y a lieu),	« titre de l'entrée »	dans	titre de l'encyclo- pédie,	édition (s'il y a lieu)	par	directeur	(renseignements sur l'édition).
Rev Edward Mewburn Walker,	"Constitu- tion of Athens"	dans	Encyclo- paedia Britannica,	11ᵉ éd	par	Hugh Chisholm	New York, Ency- clopaedia Britan- nica, 1911.

▨   Certaines encyclopédies reconnaissent explicitement les contributions d'auteurs. Inscrire le nom de ces auteurs lorsqu'ils sont disponibles.

6.5   RECUEILS ENCYCLOPÉDIQUES

6.5.1   *Canadian Encyclopedic Digest*

▨   Le *Canadian Encyclopedic Digest* (CED) est une encyclopédie publiée en feuilles mobiles donnant de l'information générale sur un sujet particulier du droit. Chacun des volumes est organisé par sujet (par ex. droit criminel, droit de la famille).

6.5.1.1 *CED version imprimée*

CED	(série	édition),	volume,	titre	section.
CED	(Ont	4ᵉ),	vol 1,	titre 2	à la s 10.

▨   Écrire **CED** plutôt que le nom au complet de l'encyclopédie au long.

▨   Indiquer la série sous forme abrégée : **Ontario CED (Ont)** et **Western CED (West)**.

6.5.1.2 *CED version électronique*

CED	édition	(en ligne),	sujet	(série) (s'il y a lieu),	« rubrique et sous- rubrique » (facultatif)	(code de la sous-rubrique CED) (facultatif)	section
CED	4ᵉ éd	(en ligne),	Actions	(Ont),	« Forms and Classes of Action : Penal Actions : General »	(II.5.(a))	à la s 3.
CED	4ᵉ éd	(en ligne),	Citizenship,		« Taking the Test and Oath of Citizenship : Oral Interview for Citizenship »	(III.(6))	à la s 57.

▨ Séparer les rubriques et sous-rubriques par un deux-points.

▨ Inscrire le code de la sous-rubrique tel qu'il apparaît dans le CED en ligne.

▨ Favoriser une référence à la version électronique. Si vous souhaitez faire référence à la version imprimée, suivre les règles de la section 6.5.1.1 en incluant la série. Westlaw fournit un lien vers les renseignements nécessaires pour une référence à la version imprimée, à partir de la version électronique du CED.

6.5.2   Halsbury's Laws of Canada

▨ *Halsbury's Laws of Canada* fournit des résumés d'un large éventail de sujets juridiques. Chaque volume est organisé par sujet (par ex. procédures criminelles, assurances).

▨ Les mises à jour sont faites par l'entremise de suppléments cumulatifs publiés annuellement.

6.5.2.1 Halsbury's Laws of Canada version imprimée

Halsbury's Laws of Canada,	volume,	*sujet,*	renseignements sur l'édition,	section	mise à jour (s'il y a lieu).
Halsbury's Laws of Canada,	vol 2,	*Business Corporations,*	Markham (Ont), LexisNexis Canada, 2013,	dans HBC-301 « Prescribed by statute »	(Supp Cum version 4).

▨ Lorsque la partie citée fut mise à jour par un supplément cumulatif, faire référence à ce supplément et à son numéro de version entre parenthèses et à la suite de la section, en utilisant la forme abrégée (**Supp Cum version** x).

6.5.2.2 Halsbury's Laws of Canada version électronique

Halsbury's Laws of Canada (en ligne),	*sujet,*	« rubrique et sous-rubrique » (facultatif)	(code de la sous-rubrique) (facultatif)	section	mise à jour (s'il y a lieu).
Halsbury's Laws of Canada (en ligne),	*Business Corporations,*	« Shareholder Remedies : The Oppression Remedy : Standing »	(XIII.2.(6))	dans HBC-301 « Prescribed by statute »	(Supp Cum version 4).

▨ Lorsque la partie citée fut mise à jour par un supplément cumulatif, faire référence à ce supplément et à son numéro de version entre parenthèses et à la suite de la section, en utilisant la forme abrégée (**Supp Cum version** x).

6.5.3   Common Law

Halsbury's Laws of England, 4ᵉ éd, vol 34, Londres, Butterworths, 1980 à la p 60, au para 71.

American Jurisprudence, 2ᵉ éd, vol 17A, Rochester (NY), Lawyer's Cooperative, 1991 au titre « Contracts », § 97.

- Suivre les règles pour les monographies à la section 6.2 **sans indiquer le nom de l'auteur**.
- **Faire référence à des paragraphes (para)**. Utiliser le symbole § pour les ouvrages américains.
- Indiquer le titre d'une partie entre guillemets, s'il y a lieu, après les renseignements sur l'édition et l'indication **au titre** (voir *American Jurisprudence*).

6.5.4   France

6.5.4.1 *Modèle de base*

Titre du répertoire,	édition (s'il y a lieu),	identification de la rubrique	par	auteur de la rubrique	référence précise.
Juris-classeur civil,		art 1354, fasc A	par	Roger Perrot.	
Encyclopédie juridique Dalloz : répertoire de droit commercial,	2ᵉ éd,	« Ventes commerciales »	par	Luc Bihl	au nº 256.

- Si possible, se rapporter au ***Juris-classeur civil***.
- Indiquer l'encyclopédie et le titre du répertoire non abrégé et en italique.
- Lorsque **plus d'une édition** a été publiée, indiquer le numéro de l'édition.

Abréviations des principaux répertoires :

Encyclopédie juridique Dalloz : Répertoire de droit administratif	*Rép admin*
Encyclopédie juridique Dalloz : Répertoire de droit civil	*Rép civ*
Encyclopédie juridique Dalloz : Répertoire de droit commercial	*Rép com*
Juris-classeur administratif	*J-cl admin*
Juris-classeur civil	*J-cl Civ*
Juris-classeur civil annexe	*J-cl civ annexe*
Juris-classeur commercial	*J-cl Com*
Juris-classeur commercial : Banque et crédit	*J-cl com Banque et crédit*
Juris-classeur répertoire notarial	*J-cl rép not*
Juris-classeur responsabilité civile	*J-cl resp civ*

6.5.4.2 Rubriques

Classées par ordre alphabétique	*Encyclopédie juridique Dalloz : Répertoire de droit civil*, « **Personnalité (droits de la)** », par D Tallon au n° 153. *Juris-classeur civil annexes*, « **Associations** », **fasc 1-A**, par Robert Brichet.
Classées selon les articles d'un code	*Juris-classeur civil*, app **art 3, fasc 4**, par Yves Luchaire. *Juris-classeur civil*, **art 1315–1326**, par Daniel Veaux.
Classées par volume	*Juris-classeur commercial : Banque et crédit*, **vol 2, fasc 32**, par Jean Stoufflet.

- **Classées par ordre alphabétique** : indiquer les mots-clés qui identifient la rubrique entre guillemets. Ajouter **fasc** et le numéro approprié après le nom de la rubrique, s'il y a lieu.

- **Classées selon les articles d'un code** : indiquer le numéro de l'article ou des articles sous lesquels la rubrique est classée. Utiliser la même forme que celle du répertoire. Ajouter **fasc** après le numéro d'article s'il y a lieu.

- **Classées par volume** : indiquer le numéro du volume où se trouve la rubrique. Ajouter **fasc** après le numéro d'article s'il y a lieu.

- Peu importe la méthode de classification des rubriques, toujours indiquer le numéro du fascicule après celui du volume.

- Ne pas indiquer la date de révision du fascicule.

Doctrine et autres documents

6.6 CODES DE DÉONTOLOGIE

Organisme,	titre du code,	renseignements sur l'édition,	référence précise.
L'Association du Barreau canadien,	Code de déontologie professionnelle,	Ottawa, ABC, 2006,	ch VI, r 1(a).
Association des infirmières et infirmiers du Canada,	Code de déontologie des infirmières et infirmiers,	Ottawa, AIIC, 2008,	préambule à la p 2.

- Si l'organisme et l'éditeur sont les mêmes, indiquer l'abréviation officielle de l'organisme dans les renseignements sur l'édition (par ex. **ABC** pour L'Association du Barreau canadien).

- Abréger **règle** par **r**.

- Certains codes de déontologie sont établis par la législation. Faire référence à ces codes comme à des lois ordinaires (section 2.1) (par ex. *Code des professions*, **RLRQ c C-26**).

6.7 DÉCISIONS D'ARBITRAGE

Pour des décisions d'**arbitrage international**, voir la section 5.2.12. Pour des décisions de l'**OMPI**, voir la section 5.2.13.

6.7.1 Décisions d'arbitrage publiées

Intitulé ou numéro de la décision	(année de la décision),	recueil	référence précise	(arbitres) (facultatif).
California State University v State Employers Trade Council — United	(2009),	126 Lab Arb (BNA) 613		(arbitre : Bonnie G Bogue).

- Indiquer l'intitulé ou le numéro de la décision, suivi de l'année de la décision entre parenthèses et une virgule.

- Si la décision est publiée dans un recueil écrit, faire référence au recueil d'arbitrage comme à tout recueil de jurisprudence (section 3.7).

- Ajouter **le nom de l'arbitre** entre parenthèses (facultatif).

6.7.2   Décisions d'arbitrage non publiées

Intitulé ou numéro de la décision	(année de la décision),	code de désignation fourni par le service	(service) (s'il y a lieu)	référence précise	(arbitres) (facultatif).
Winona School District ISD 861 Winona v Winona Education Association	(2006),	2006 WL 3876585	(WL Can)		(arbitre : Daniel J Jacobowski).

▨ Indiquer l'intitulé ou le numéro de la décision, suivi de l'année de la décision entre parenthèses et une virgule.

▨ Si la décision est publiée dans un service électronique, inclure le code de désignation fourni par le service. Ajouter l'abréviation du service entre parenthèses si elle n'est pas déjà mentionnée dans le code de désignation.

▨ Ajouter **le nom de l'arbitre** entre parenthèses (facultatif).

6.8   RECENSIONS

Auteur,	« titre de la recension » (s'il y a lieu),	recension de	*titre de l'ouvrage recensé*	de	auteur ou éditeur de l'ouvrage recensé	renseignements sur l'édition.
Bjarne Melkevik,		recension de	*Démocratie et procéduralisation du droit*	de	Philippe Coppens et Jacques Lenoble	(2001) 42 C de D 337.
Yves-Marie Morissette,		recension de	*L'administration de la preuve*	de	Léo Ducharme	(2001) 46 RD McGill 1179.

▨ Les recensions sont l'équivalent des *book reviews* en anglais.

▨ Si la recension porte un titre, indiquer celui-ci après le nom de l'auteur, suivi d'une virgule.

▨ Indiquer **recension de** avant le titre de l'ouvrage recensé.

▨ Introduire par **de** le nom de l'auteur après le titre de l'ouvrage recensé.

   ☐ Si le titre de la recension indique **à la fois le titre de l'ouvrage recensé et son auteur**, omettre ces informations dans le reste de la référence.

☐ Si le titre de la recension indique *soit* **le titre de l'ouvrage recensé,** *soit* **son auteur,** indiquer cette information après **recension de**, même si une partie de l'information sera répétée.

▨ Si l'ouvrage recensé possède un éditeur plutôt qu'un auteur, écrire **éd** après le nom de l'éditeur de l'ouvrage recensé et une virgule (par ex. **Ronald E Dimock, éd**).

6.9   CHRONIQUES DE JURISPRUDENCE ET DE LÉGISLATION

	Auteur,	« titre » (s'il y a lieu),	type de chronique	de	intitulé ou nom de la loi ou du projet de loi,	renseignements sur l'édition.
Commentaire d'arrêt	Léo Ducharme,	« La proclamation de l'existence en droit québécois de la règle de common law de l'engagement implicite de confidentialité : *Lac d'amiante*, une décision judiciaire erronée »,	commentaire	de	*Lac d'amiante du Québec ltée c 2858-0702 Québec inc,*	(2000) 79 R du B can 435.
Chronique de législation	Jean-Pierre Colpron,	« Les nouvelles règles visant à réduire les pertes en capital »,	chronique	de	l'art 1123 de la *Loi de l'impôt sur le revenu,*	(1996) 18 Rev de plan fisc & success 177.

▨ Indiquer le titre du commentaire d'arrêt ou de la chronique de législation entre guillemets, s'il y a lieu.

▨ Pour faire référence à **un commentaire d'arrêt**, mentionner **commentaire de** avant l'intitulé de l'arrêt. Toutefois, si le titre indique déjà le nom de l'arrêt, omettre ces informations du reste de la référence.

▨ Pour faire référence à **une chronique de législation**, la mention **chronique de** précède le titre de la loi. Toutefois, si le titre indique déjà le nom de la loi pertinente, omettre ces informations du reste de la référence.

6.9.1   France

6.9.1.1 Notes

Auteur,	note sous	nom du tribunal,	date de la décision,	(année de publication)	recueil	titre abrégé ou numéro de la partie	première page.
Danielle Corrignan-Carsin,	note sous	Cass soc,	10 mai 1999,	(1999)	JCP	II	1425.

▨ Après le nom de l'auteur et la mention **note sous**, faire référence à la décision et aux recueils pertinents de la même manière que l'on fait référence à la jurisprudence française (section 7.5.2).

▨ Ajouter un espace entre l'année de publication, le recueil et le titre abrégé ou le numéro de la partie (par ex. **(1999) JCP 11 1425**).

6.9.1.2 Chroniques publiées dans les recueils généraux

Auteur,	« titre »	(année de publication)	recueil	titre abrégé ou numéro de la partie.	première page	référence précise.
Bertrand Mathieu et Michel Verpeaux,	« Jurisprudence constitutionnelle »	(2000)	JCP	I	2178	à la p 2180.
Xavier Labbée,	« Esquisse d'une définition civiliste de l'espèce humaine »	(1999)	D	Chron	437	à la p 440.

▨ Ajouter un espace entre l'année de publication, le recueil et le titre abrégé ou le numéro de la partie (par ex. **(1999) D Chron 437 à la p 440**).

▨ Indiquer l'information concernant les recueils français selon les règles de la section 7.5.2.6.

6.10   COMMENTAIRES, REMARQUES ET NOTES

Auteur (s'il y a lieu),	« titre » (s'il y a lieu),	genre du texte,	renseignements sur l'édition.
Monroe Leigh,		Commentaire éditorial,	(1996) 90 : 2 AJIL 235.
	« What We Talk About When We Talk About Persons: The Language of Legal Fiction »,	Note,	(2001) 114 : 6 Harv L Rev 1745.

▨ Inscrire le genre du texte (**Commentaire éditorial**, **Note** ou **Remarque**) avant les renseignements sur l'édition.

6.11   DOCUMENTS HISTORIQUES LÉGAUX

6.11.1   Droit romain

Collection	Abréviation	Exemple
Lois des douze tables	XII Tab	XII Tab 8.2
Institutes de Gaius	G	G 3.220 (trad par Julien Reinach)
Code de Théodose	Cod Th	Cod Th 8.14.1
Institutes de Justinien	Inst	Inst 4.4 pr
Digeste de Justinien	Dig	Dig 47.10.1 (Ulpian)
Codex de Justinien	Cod	Cod 6.42.16
Nouvelles	Nov	Nov 22.3

▨ Faire référence à la **division traditionnelle** (généralement un livre, un titre ou une partie) et non au numéro de page de l'édition ou de la traduction. Ne pas ajouter d'espace entre les numéros des différentes parties.

▨ L'abréviation **pr**, précédée d'un espace, signifie « *principium* » ou « début » et fait référence au document non numéroté avant la première section d'un titre.

▨ Pour faire référence au *Digeste* **de Justinien**, indiquer (s'il y a lieu) l'auteur du passage entre parenthèses à la fin de la référence.

▨ Utiliser des chiffres arabes (par ex. **1, 2, 3**), suivis de points, pour indiquer les divisions, quelle que soit l'utilisation de l'édition ou de la traduction.

▨ L'édition ou la traduction utilisée peut être indiquée entre parenthèses à la fin de la référence (par ex. **(trad par Julien Reinach)**).

6.11.2   Droit canonique

Collection	Abréviation	Exemple
Decretum de Gratien	Decr (facultatif)	**1re partie** : D 50 c 11 **2e partie** : C 30 q 4 c 5 **2e partie, De poenitentia** : De poen D 1 c 75 **3e partie** : De cons D 1 c 5
Décrétales de Gregoire IX (*Liber extra*)	X	X 5.38.12
Décrétales de Boniface VIII (*Liber sextus*)	VI	VI 5.2.16
Constitutions de Clément V (*Clementinae*)	Clem	Clem 3.7.2
Extravagantes de Jean XXII (*Extravagantes Johannis XXII*)	Extrav Jo XII	Extrav Jo XII 14.2
Extravagantes communes (*Extravagantes communes*)	Extrav Com	Extrav Com 3.2.9
Codex Iuris Canonici (1917)	1917 Code	1917 Code c 88, § 2
Codex Iuris Canonici (1983)	1983 Code	1983 Code c 221, § 1

- Faire référence à la division traditionnelle et non au numéro de page de l'édition ou de la traduction utilisée.
- Indiquer l'édition ou la traduction utilisée entre parenthèses à la fin de la référence.

6.11.3   Droit Talmudique

Talmud,	*traité,*	référence précise.
Talmud de Babylone,	*Bava Metzia,*	11b.
Talmud de Jérusalem,	*Sanhédrin,*	Mish 1 Hal 5.

- Indiquer le Talmud de Babylone ou le Talmud de Jérusalem.
- Mettre le nom du traité en italique.
- Pour faire référence au Talmud de Babylone, indiquer la **pagination traditionnelle** (de l'édition Vilna) et non le numéro de page fourni par l'éditeur ou par le traducteur. Il est toujours sous-entendu que le texte provient de l'édition Vilna. Cependant, si une édition différente est utilisée (par ex. Warsaw), indiquer le nom de l'édition après la référence précise.

▓ Utiliser des chiffres arabes (par ex. **1, 2, 3**) pour le numéro de feuille et les lettres **a** et **b** pour indiquer le numéro de page.

▓ Pour faire référence à une **édition** ou à une **traduction particulière**, indiquer le nom de la maison d'édition entre parenthèses suivi d'une référence précise (sections 6.2.2.5.1 et 6.2.7 à 6.2.9).

▓ S'il y a une traduction, indiquer **[notre traduction]** ou **[traduction par l'auteur]** à la fin de la citation, après les guillemets et avant l'appel de note (section 6.2.2.5.2).

▓ Pour faire référence au **Talmud de Jérusalem**, fournir une référence précise correspondant au Mishna (**Mish**) et au Halacha (**Hal**) et non à la page. Indiquer une référence précise à une page si tous les renseignements sur l'édition peuvent être fournis entre parenthèses (sections 6.2.7 à 6.2.9).

6.12   MANUSCRITS NON PUBLIÉS

6.12.1   Modèle de base

Auteur,	*titre* ou « titre »,	date	[non publié,	archivé	lieu].
J Tremblay,	« Nouveaux développements en droit du travail »,	mai 1997	[non publié,	archivé	à la *Revue de droit de McGill*].

▓ Faire référence au titre du manuscrit selon son genre. Pour les articles, placer le titre entre guillemets. Pour les monographies, inscrire le titre en italique.

▓ Faire suivre le titre du manuscrit de sa date de création.

▓ Indiquer que le manuscrit n'a pas été publié en mettant **[non publié, archivé]**, ainsi que l'endroit où le manuscrit se trouve.

6.12.2   Manuscrits à paraître

Auteur,	*titre* ou « titre »,	renseignements sur l'édition	[à paraître en	date de publication prévue].
Gérard Notebaert,	« Faut-il réformer le système de l'arbitrage de griefs au Québec ? »	53 RD McGill	[à paraître en	2008].
Alain Supiot,	*Le Nouvel âge du droit social*,	Seuil	[à paraître en	octobre 2009].

▓ Faire référence au titre du manuscrit selon son genre. Pour les articles, placer le titre entre guillemets. Pour les monographies, inscrire le titre en italique.

▓ Inscrire les renseignements sur l'édition selon le genre du manuscrit, mais ne pas indiquer la date de publication.

☐ S'il s'agit d'une revue et que le numéro de la prochaine publication est connu, indiquer ce numéro.

▨ Indiquer que le manuscrit n'a pas encore été publié en ajoutant [**à paraître**] et la date de publication prévue si disponible.

6.12.3 Thèses et dissertations

Auteur,	*titre,*	diplôme,	institution,	année	renseigne-ments sur l'édition ou [non publié].
Louise Potvin,	*La personne et la protection de son image,*	thèse de doctorat en droit,	Université McGill,	1989	[non publiée].
C Morneau,	*L'éthique dans les entreprises multinationales : une étude développementale des codes d'éthique,*	mémoire de M Sc,	HEC Montréal,	2006	[non publié].

▨ Après avoir indiqué l'auteur et le titre du document, inscrire le diplôme dans le cadre duquel il a été écrit. Inclure la **discipline étudiée** (par ex. droit, science politique, économie), si l'on ne peut la déduire du diplôme ou du nom de l'institution.

▨ Après la mention de l'année, écrire [**non publié**].

▨ Si le manuscrit a été publié, faire référence à la source publiée et non à la thèse ou à la dissertation en soi. Suivre les règles appropriées du *Manuel* pour la source publiée.

▨ Faire référence aux thèses publiées sur support de microfiche (par ex. les *University Microfilms International*), de la même manière que les références aux thèses sur support papier.

6.13   ALLOCUTIONS ET TEXTES PRÉSENTÉS DURANT DES CONFÉRENCES

Conféren-cier,	« titre » ou allocution,	événement,	présen-té(e) à	lieu ou institu-tion,	date	renseigne-ments sur l'édi-tion ou [non publié(e)].
Son excel-lence John Ralston Saul,	allocution d'ouver-ture,	Conférence d'ouverture de la conférence du Conseil in-ternational d'études cana-diennes,	présen-tée à	l'Univer-sité d'Otta-wa,	18 mai 2000	[non publiée], en ligne : Le gou-verneur général du Canada <www.gg.ca> .
Le juge John H Gomery,	« The Pros and Cons of Commis-sion of In-quiry »	Série de confér-ences annuelles de la Revue de droit de McGill,	présen-tée à	la Fa-culté de droit de McGill,	15 février 2006	(2006) 51 RD McGill 783.

◼ Indiquer le titre de l'allocution, si possible. Si **aucun titre** n'est fourni, utiliser **allocution**.

◼ Inscrire l'événement dans le cadre duquel l'allocution a été prononcée ou le texte a été présenté.

◼ Indiquer le lieu ou l'institution où l'allocution a été faite.

◼ Inclure les renseignements sur l'édition.

◼ Pour faire référence à une **allocution non publiée**, inscrire **[non publié(e)]** à la fin de la référence (section 6.12.1).

   ☐ Si l'allocution non publiée est disponible en ligne, inscrire l'adresse électronique sous **renseignements sur l'édition** (section 6.22).

◼ Pour faire référence à une **allocution publiée dans une collection**, respecter les règles de référence des ouvrages collectifs (section 6.3).

Doctrine et autres documents

6.14   RECUEILS DE COURS

Professeur,	*titre,*	type de document (s'il y a lieu),	faculté,	date ou année	référence précise.
Lara Khoury et Geneviève Saumier,	*Coursepack: Extra-contractual Obligations/Torts,*		Faculté de droit, Université McGill,	2003	à la p 20.
Jean-Sébastien Brière,	*Droit des brevets,*	recueil de cours,	Faculté de droit, Université de Sherbrooke,	automne 2008	à la p 331.

▨ Indiquer le type de document s'il n'est pas déjà inclus dans le titre :

☐ Les **recueils de cours** sont des compilations de textes pour les fins d'un cours particulier. Il est préférable d'indiquer la référence originale.

☐ Les **notes de cours** sont rédigées par le professeur pour un cours en particulier. Elles ne possèdent pas de référence originale.

6.15   PÉRIODIQUES

Auteur (s'il y a lieu),	« titre de l'article »,	*titre du magazine*	volume : numéro ou n°	(date)	1re page de l'article	référence précise	source électronique (s'il y a lieu).
Jacques Julliard,	« Requiem pour un "peuple interdit" »,	*Le Nouvel Observateur*	n° 1740	(12 mars 1998)	47	à la p 12.	
Julie Latour,	« Garde partagée, avis partagés »,	*Magazine National [de l'Association du Barreau canadien]*		(mars 2001),			en ligne : <www.cba.org/abc/> .
Me Jean Lozeau et Me Paul Ryan,	« La faillite et la responsabilité fiscale des administrateurs et des tiers »,	*Le Monde Juridique*	12 : 6		17	à la p 19.	

▨ Indiquer le nom de l'auteur suivi du titre de l'article entre guillemets.

Doctrine et autres documents

- Indiquer le nom du magazine en italique. Placer tout autre renseignement (par ex. le lieu de publication) à la suite du nom du magazine, entre crochets et en italique.

- Indiquer le **volume et le numéro** en séparant ces informations par deux-points (par ex. **10 : 30**). S'il n'y a pas de volume, n'indiquer que le numéro (par ex. **n° 20**).

- Indiquer la **date complète** entre parenthèses. Si la revue indique une période, n'indiquer que la **première journée de cette période** (par ex. **22 novembre** et non **22-29 novembre**).

6.16 JOURNAUX, FILS DE PRESSE ET AUTRES SOURCES DE NOUVELLES

Auteur (s'il y a lieu),	« titre de l'article »,	*journal [lieu d'édition]* (si nécessaire)	(date)	page	source électronique (s'il y a lieu).
Michel Venne,	« Pour un accès gratuit aux lois sur Internet »,	*Le Devoir de Montréal*	(28 mai 1997)	A2.	
	« Un organisme d'aide juridique est menacé de fermeture par Québec »,	*La Presse canadienne*	(8 août 2001)		(QL).
Sylvia Zappi,	« La Cour de cassation refuse de faire bénéficier les enfants isolés étrangers du droit des mineurs »,	*Le Monde*	(11 novembre 2001),		en ligne : <www.le monde.fr/recherche > .
	« Défaite des fabricants de tabac aux Etats-Unis »,	*La Presse [de Montréal]*	(28 mai 1997)	B10.	
LesAvocatsᴾʳᵒ	« Vol à l'étalage : combien de temps dure la procédure ? »,		(24 septembre 2009),		en ligne : Avocat Droit Criminel Montréal <avocatcriminel.blog.ca > .

- Indiquer le nom de l'auteur, s'il y a lieu, suivi du titre de l'article entre guillemets.

- Indiquer le nom du journal, du fil de presse ou de toute autre source en italique.

- Tout autre renseignement, tel que le lieu de publication, se place à la suite du titre, entre crochets (par ex. *La Presse [de Montréal]*).

Journaux :

- Indiquer le numéro du cahier si les pages sont numérotées par cahier (par ex. **B10**).

- Pour les références précises, ne pas répéter le numéro de page si l'article ne paraît que sur une seule page.

Fils de Presse :

▨ Un fil de presse est un service d'information transmettant les toutes dernières nouvelles par satellite ou tout autre système électronique.

▨ Remplacer le nom du journal par le nom du fil de presse.

▨ Pour plus de renseignements sur la référence aux sources électroniques, voir la section 6.22.

6.16.1 Éditoriaux et lettres à la rédaction

Auteur (s'il y a lieu),	« titre de l'éditorial » (s'il y a lieu),	type de document,	*journal*	(date)	page	source électronique (s'il y a lieu).
Jean Barrué,		lettre à la rédaction,	*Le Monde diplomatique*	(avril 1997)	2.	
Marie-Andrée Chouinard,	« Coup dur »,	éditorial,	*Le Devoir*	(23 octobre 2009)	A8.	

▨ Indiquer **lettre à la rédaction** après le nom de l'auteur de la lettre.

▨ Indiquer **éditorial** après le titre d'un éditorial.

▨ Mettre en italique le nom du journal, de la revue ou de toute autre source. Placer à la suite du titre, entre crochets et en italique, tout autre renseignement tel que le lieu de publication (par ex. *La Presse [de Montréal]*).

Doctrine et autres documents

6.17   COMMUNIQUÉS DE PRESSE

Organisme responsable,	genre du document,	numéro (s'il y a lieu),	« titre » (facultatif)	(date)	source électronique (s'il y a lieu).
Organisation des Nations Unies,	communiqué,	CS/2284,	« Le conseil demande le retrait immédiat des troupes israéliennes des villes palestiniennes dont Ramallah et la coopération des parties avec l'Envoyé spécial de Washington »	(29 mars 2002),	en ligne : Recherche de communiqués de presse des Nations Unies <www.un.org/french/apps/pressreleases> .
Cabinet du premier ministre du Québec,	communiqué,		« Journée internationale des femmes : "Nouvelles réalités, solidarités nouvelles" »	(8 mars 2002),	en ligne : Site officiel du premier ministre du Québec <www.premier-ministre.gouv.qc.-ca/salle-de-presse> .
Comité permanent de l'accès à l'information, de la protection des renseignements personnels et de l'éthique,	communiqué,		« Dépôt du rapport concernant la réforme de la *Loi sur l'accès à l'information* »	(18 juin 2009),	en ligne : Parlement du Canada <www.parl.qc.ca> .

▨ Indiquer le genre du document tel qu'énoncé sur le document (par ex. **communiqué**).

▨ Indiquer le **numéro du document** immédiatement après le genre du document, s'il y a lieu.

▨ Si possible, fournir la **date du document** entre parenthèses à la fin de la référence, mais avant la source électronique.

6.18 LETTRES ET ENTREVUES

Lettre ou Entrevue	nom des personnes impliquées	(date)	renseignements supplémentaires (archives, sources électroniques ou imprimées).
Lettre de	B Diamond au Premier ministre R Lévesque	(30 novembre 1982).	
Entrevue de	Edward Beauvais par Douglas Sanderson	(29 mai 1948)	sur *This Week*, CBC Radio, Toronto, CBC Radio Archives.
Lettre de	PE Moore, Acting Superintendent of Medical Services, Indian Affairs Branch, à Ellen L Fairclough, Minister of Citizenship	[aucune date]	Hull, Affaires Indiennes et du Nord Canada (6-24-3, vol 2).

▨ Identifier une **lettre** ou une **entrevue** en indiquant **lettre de** ou **entrevue de**, suivi du nom des parties au début de la référence.

▨ Inclure le nom des parties, suivi de la date à laquelle la lettre a été rédigée. Si **aucune date n'est fournie**, inscrire **[aucune date]**.

▨ Si le titre d'une personne impliquée n'est pas mentionné dans le texte ou ne peut être déduit, fournir autant de renseignements que possible sur ce titre, précédés d'une virgule (par ex. **PE Moore, Acting Superintendent of Medical Services, Indian Affairs Branch**).

▨ Fournir le nom de l'intervieweur s'il n'est pas aussi l'auteur.

▨ Si la lettre ou l'entrevue est publiée, disponible en ligne ou archivée, inclure la référence.

Doctrine et autres documents

6.19 DOCUMENTS ARCHIVÉS

Titre du document et (autre information),	lieu des archives,	nom des archives,	(numéro de classification).
Lettres patentes du roi François 1er nommant Jacques Cartier capitaine général de l'expédition destinée au Canada (17 octobre 1540/Saint-Prix),	Ottawa,	Archives nationales du Canada	(MG 1-Série C11A).
Chief Andrew Paull à TA Crerar (22 juin 1944),	Ottawa,	Archives nationales du Canada	(RG 10, vol 6826, file 496-3-2, pt 1).

Si un document se trouve dans des archives locales, fournir le plus de renseignements possibles sur le document selon les règles de références traditionnelles, suivis de l'information des archives.

6.20 PROPRIÉTÉ INTELLECTUELLE

6.20.1 Brevets

« Titre de l'invention »,	Pays	Brevet n°	PCT Brevet n°	(date de dépôt),	référence précise.
« Épaulière pour violon »,	Can	Brevet n° 2414383,	PCT Brevet n° PCT/US2001/021243	(29 juin 2001),	rev 10.
« Parallel network processor array »,	É-U	Brevet n° 6854117		(31 octobre 2000),	fig 9.

Indiquer **le titre de l'invention** entre guillemets.

Indiquer **l'abréviation du pays** où le brevet a été émis ainsi que le numéro du brevet.

Si le brevet a été délivré par le biais du **Traité de coopération en matière de brevets** (PCT), utiliser le même modèle de référence (**PCT Brevet n°**).

Indiquer **la date de dépôt** entre parenthèses.

Si nécessaire, indiquer le numéro de brevet du pays et le numéro de brevet PCT séparés d'une virgule.

Faire référence à l'abrégé (**abrégé**), au numéro de revendication (**rev**) ou à une figure (**fig**) en référence précise.

S'il s'agit d'une **demande de brevet**, écrire **demande déposée le** avant la date de dépôt (par ex. **demande déposée le 30 août 2008**).

6.20.2   Marques de commerce

« Marque de commerce »,	propriétaire inscrit,	pays	n° d'enregistrement	(date d'enregistrement),	état.
« Kellogg's Cinnamon Mini Buns à la Cannelle »,	Kellogg Company,	Can	n° enr LMC424258	(4 mars 1994),	radiée.
« Lego »,	Lego Juris A/S,	USA	78882203	(3 juin 2008),	existante.

▦   Indiquer **la marque de commerce** entre guillemets.

▦   Indiquer **le propriétaire inscrit** et **l'abréviation du pays** où la marque de commerce a été enregistrée.

▦   Écrire **le numéro d'enregistrement**. Le format du numéro varie selon le pays.

▦   Indiquer **la date d'enregistrement** entre parenthèses.

▦   Écrire **l'état actuel** de la marque de commerce dans le régistre. Pour les marques de commerce des États-Unis, écrire **existante** pour *live* et **non existante** pour *dead*. Pour le Canada, écrire **enregistrée** ou **radiée**.

6.20.3   Droits d'auteur

« Titre de l'œuvre protégée »	(catégorie)	titulaire du droit d'auteur,	pays	n° d'enregistrement	(date d'enregistrement)	état.
« Twilight »	(musique)	Mary Chapin Carpenter,	É-U	Pau002997899	(20 décembre 2005).	
« Feel Happy »	(enregistrement sonore)	Warner Music Canada,	Can	1035760	(24 janvier 2006)	enregistré.
« Agrippa : Le livre noir »	(littéraire)	Éditions Michel Quintin,	Can	1056747	(11 mars 2003)	enregistré.

▦   Indiquer **le titre** de l'œuvre protégée entre guillemets.

▦   Au Canada, **la catégorie de l'œuvre** inclut les **œuvres littéraires, artistiques, dramatiques** et **musicales originales**; les **prestations d'interprètes, enregistrements sonores** et **signaux de communication**; ainsi que les **dispositifs mécaniques**.

Indiquer **le titulaire du droit d'auteur** et **l'abréviation du pays** où le droit d'auteur a été enregistré.

Écrire **le numéro d'enregistrement**. Le format du numéro varie selon le pays.

Indiquer **la date d'enregistrement** entre parenthèses.

Si disponible, écrire **l'état actuel** (**enregistré** ou **radié**) du droit d'auteur dans le régistre.

6.21   DOCUMENTS DE TRAVAIL

Auteur,	« titre »	(année)	institution	Document de travail	numéro/index.
Bernard Dafflon,	« L'économie politique et la gestion territoriale des services environnementaux »	(2013)	Agence Française de Développement	Document de travail	135.
Jacques Saint-Pierre,	« Finance, stratégie et gouvernance »	(2006)	Faculté des sciences de l'administration de l'Université Laval	Document de travail	No 2006-021.

Si le document de travail est disponible en ligne, indiquer son emplacement après le numéro/index (voir la section 1.6).

6.22   SOURCES ÉLECTRONIQUES

Exception faite des bases de données en ligne (section 6.22.1), cette section fournit des conseils pour les sources qui existent seulement ou principalement en ligne. Pour des conseils généraux sur comment citer aux sources en ligne qui sont en supplément de publications imprimées, voir la section 1.6. Pour des conseils spécifiques par rapport à certaines sources disponibles à la fois en ligne en publication traditionnelle, voir la section appropriée pour le genre de source (par ex. jurisprudence (3.8), encyclopédies (6.5), journaux (6.16)).

Quand une source est seulement disponible en ligne, soyez prudent de ne pas vous fier sur du contenu potentiellement éphémère (par ex. sites-web personnels hébergés par l'employeur, publications Facebook, fils de discussion Reddit).

6.22.1   Bases de données en ligne

Référence traditionelle	(service électronique ou base de données).
Denise Boulet, « Le traitement juridique du mineur suicidaire » (2002) 32 RDUS 317	(QL).
Joseph Eliot Magnet, *Constitutional Law of Canada: Cases, Notes and Materials*, 8e éd, Kingston (Ont), QL, 2001	(QL).

▦ Les bases de données en ligne rassemblent diverses sources d'information, tel que la jurisprudence, les lois, et des articles de revues. En citant à une source qui a une version autoritaire imprimée, fournir la référence traditionnelle complète, suivie du service électronique entre parenthèses.

▦ S'il n'y a pas d'éditeur ou si le texte n'est publié que sur un serveur électronique, identifier le service en ligne comme l'éditeur (par ex. **Kingston (Ont), QL, 2001**).

▦ Si possible, ne pas faire référence à un service électronique auquel la majorité des lecteurs ne pourra accéder. Par exemple, ne pas faire référence à Azimut lorsque l'auditoire ciblé n'est pas au Québec.

▦ Pour une liste des abréviations des bases de données en ligne, voir l'**annexe E**.

6.22.2   Revues en ligne (eJournals)

Référence traditionelle,	en ligne :	(année)	volume : numéro (s'il y a lieu)	revue	numéro de l'article	référence précise	<URL>.
Grant Yang, « Stop the Abuse of Gmail! »,	en ligne :	(2005)		Duke L & Tech Rev	14	au para 5	<www. law.-duke.edu/ journals/ dltr/> .
Kahikino Noa Dettweiler, « Racial Classification or Cultural Identification?: The Gathering Rights Jurisprudence of Two Twentieth Century Hawaiian Supreme Court Justices »,	en ligne :	(2005)	6 : 1	Asian Pac L & Pol'y J	5		<www. hawaii.edu/ aplpj> .

- Certaines revues ne sont publiées qu'en ligne et possèdent leur propre système de référence.

- Faire référence à ces revues en suivant ce système de classification interne. Indiquer l'adresse Internet à la fin de la référence.

6.22.3 Sites web

6.22.3.1 Journaux web (blogues)

6.22.3.1.1 Entrées

Auteur,	« Titre »	(date),	nom du blogue (blogue),	en ligne : <URL>.
Stéphane Bolle,	« Le nouveau code électoral du Cameroun »	(11 septembre 2013),	La Constitution en Afrique (blogue),	en ligne : <www.la-con-stitution-en-afrique.org/article-le-nouveau-code-electoral-du-cameroun-119993446.html>.
Pierre Fournier-Simard,	« Crowdfunding en ca-pital au Canada : dével-oppements récents (Partie 1) »	(8 août 2013),	Édilex (blo-gue),	en ligne : <www.edilex.com/blogue/crowd fundig-en-capital-au-canada-developpe ments-recents-partie-1#axzz2fACWjs7F>.

Doctrine et autres documents

6.22.3.1.2 Commentaires

Nom ou pseudonyme	(date et heure),	en ligne : <URL> (si possible),	commentaire sur	référence complète du blog (telle que ci-dessus).
ligulaire	(17 sept 2013 à 8h22),		commentaire sur	Patrick Lagacé, « Enlève ton hidjab quand t'es dans l'autobus » (17 septembre 2013) *Le blogue de Patrick Lagacé* (blogue) en ligne : <blogues.lapresse.ca/ lagace/2013/09/17/en-leve-ton-hidjab-quand-tes-dans-lautobus/> .
petes_PoV	(6 oct 2012 à 12:09pm),	en ligne : <news. slashdot.org/ comments.pl? sid = 3167773& cid = 41568655 > ,	commentaire sur	« Timothy, "Gas Prices Jump: California Hardest Hit » (6 octobre 2012) *Slashdot* (blogue).

Certains sites offrent un lien direct vers les commentaires individuels. Dans ces cas, faire référence à cet url au lieu de celui de l'entrée principale du blog.

6.22.3.2 *Réseaux sociaux*

6.22.3.2.1 Entrées Twitter (Tweets)

Nom,	« contenu complet du tweet »	(date et heure),	en ligne : <twitter.com/ piste_complète>.
Daniel Jutras,	« Unanimité des élus municipaux contre la Charte des valeurs QC. Pas de virage à droite sur l'ile de Montréal (y compris aux feux rouges). »	(12 septembre 2013 à 10h02),	en ligne : Twitter <twitter.-com/DeanJutras/status/ 378202075005333504> .

6.22.3.2.2 Entrées Facebook

Auteur,	« première phrase de l'entrée »	(date de l'entrée),	publié sur *une page de groupe ou un profil individuel,*	en ligne : <URL>.
La Presse,	« Le rapport de l'ONU sur l'attaque chimique du 21 août dernier en Syrie est maintenant disponible. »	(16 septembre 2013),	Publié sur *La Presse,*	en ligne : Facebook <www.facebook.com/ LaPresseFB/posts/ 10152216007003312>.

▓ Si la première phrase est trop longue, tronquer la phrase convenablement et ajouter des points de suspension avant le dernier guillemet (par ex. « **Again our mighty Senators are blowing our tax money . . .** »).

▓ Pour citer une page de groupe ou un profil individuel, remplacer la première phrase par le nom du groupe ou du profil individuel, suivi de la date de création du groupe ou profil si disponible.

6.22.3.2.3 Entrées Reddit

Auteur,	« première phrase de l'entrée »	(date de l'entrée),	publié sur *titre du fil,*	en ligne : <URL>.
pierluc,	« J'ai cru comprendre que ces coupures vont financer une bonification des prêts et bourses, par contre.»	(17 mars 2013),	publié sur *Crédit d'impôt pour les droits de scolarité passe de 20% à 8%. Impact pour les étudiants?,*	en ligne : Reddit <bb.reddit.com/r/ Quebec/comments/ 19gha8/crédit_dimpôt_ pour_les_droits_de_ scolarité_passe/c8ntjz1>.

▓ Si la première phrase est trop longue, tronquer la phrase convenablement et ajouter des points de suspension avant le dernier guillemet (par ex. « **You advocate in your book . . .** »).

Doctrine et autres documents

6.22.3.3 Vidéos et agrégateurs de vidéos en ligne

Titre du site web ou nom du compte,	« titre de la vidéo »	(date mise en ligne),	en ligne : <URL>	Reference précise hh:mm:ss.
CPAC,	« Audiences de la Cour suprême : La Cour suprême se penche sur le renvoi relatif à la nomination du juge Marc Nadon »	(15 janvier 2014),	en ligne : CPAC <www.cpac.ca/en/programs/supreme-court-hearings/episodes/29928389/>	au 02h:29m:30s.
Radio-Canada,	« Poursuite scolaire en Colombie-Brittannique »	(2 septembre 2013),	en ligne : YouTube <www.youtube.com/watch?v = EFTkzKQtWuM>	au 00h:02m:18s.
CPAC TV,	« Vancouver 2010 Jeux olympiques »	(11 février 2010),	en ligne : YouTube <www.youtube.com/watch?v = IDm7PW7K_TU> .	

▓ Les vidéos en ligne sont souvent copiées et mises sur d'autres comptes sans permission ou attribution. Toujours citer au site web original ou le compte qui a initialement mis la vidéo en ligne, si connu.

6.22.4   Autres supports numériques

Référence traditionnelle,	type de support numérique :	Titre du support si différent,	renseignements sur l'édition.
PW Hogg et ME Turpel, « Implementing Aboriginal Self-Government: Constitutional and Jurisdictional Issues »,	CD-ROM :	Pour sept générations : legs documentaire de la Commission royale sur les peuples autochtones,	Ottawa, Libraxus, 1997.
The Paper Chase, 1973,	DVD,		Beverly Hills (Cal), 20th Century Fox Home Entertainment, 2003.

▓ Fournir la référence traditionelle du document, suivie d'une virgule après.

Doctrine et autres documents

- Indiquer le type de support numérique (par ex. **CD-ROM**, **DVD**, **BluRay**, **MiniDisc**) après la virgule.

- Si le titre du support est différent, ajouter un deux-points et indiquer le titre du disque en italique, suivi d'une virgule.

- Fournir les renseignements sur l'édition du support numérique entre parenthèses en y incluant le lieu d'édition, l'éditeur et l'année d'édition.

6.22.5   Identifiants numériques d'objets

Citation traditionnelle,	DOI : <identifiant numérique d'objet>.
Anne Pineau, « Conjuguer relations tripartites et sous-traitance avec travail decent » (2013) 54:2 C de D 461,	DOI : <10.7202/1017621ar>.

- Un identifiant numérique d'objet (DOI) est un repère de ressource permanent et unique qui identifie un document en ligne sans égard à leur emplacement en ligne. Pour trouver un document qui a un DOI, entrer l'identifiant dans un outil de recherche qui reconnaît les DOI.

- Quand un DOI est disponible pour un document quelconque, ajouter facultativement le DOI à la fin de la citation traditionnelle.

- Certains périodiques ont créé des DOI pour leurs volumes et éditions. Préférer les DOI d'articles uniques où possible.

- Quand un DOI unique n'est pas disponible, citer au DOI du volume ou de l'édition en insérant le volume ou l'édition avant le DOI (par ex. **volume DOI : <10.7574/ cjicl.01.01.11>**).

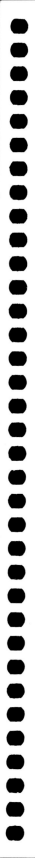

Sources étrangères

7 Sources étrangères F-175

F -7.1   Jurisdictions de la Common Law F-175
    F -7.1.1   Forme générale F-175
    F -7.1.2   Intitulé, référence précise, titre abrégé, et histoire judiciaire F-175
    F -7.1.3   Année F-175
    F -7.1.4   Référence neutre, recueil imprimé, service électronique, ou décision
                non publiée F-176
    F -7.1.5   Juridiction et cour F-176
    F -7.1.6   Juge F-177

F -7.2   Juridictions de droit civil F-177

F -7.3   Royaume-Uni F-178
    F -7.3.1   Législation F-178
        F -7.3.1.1   Lois F-178
                F -7.3.1.1.1   Irlande du Nord F-178
                        F -7.3.1.1.1.1 Lois adoptées par le
                                    Royaume-Uni F-178
                        F -7.3.1.1.1.2 Lois adoptées par l'Irlande
                                      du Nord F-178
                F -7.3.1.1.2   Écosse F-179
                F -7.3.1.1.3   Pays de Galles F-179
        F -7.3.1.2   Projets de loi F-180
                F -7.3.1.2.1   Royaume-Uni F-180
                F -7.3.1.2.2   Irlande du Nord F-180
                F -7.3.1.2.3   Écosse F-180
        F -7.3.1.3   Règlements F-181
                F -7.3.1.3.1   Royaume-Uni F-181
                F -7.3.1.3.2   Règlements et ordres de l'Irlande du Nord F-181
                F -7.3.1.3.3   Écosse F-181
                        F -7.3.1.3.3.1 Règlements adoptés par le
                                    Royaume-Uni F-182
                        F -7.3.1.3.3.2 Règlements adoptés par
                                      l'Écosse F-182
                F -7.3.1.3.4   Pays de Galles F-182
    F -7.3.2   Jurisprudence F-182
        F -7.3.2.1   Modèle de base F-182
        F -7.3.2.2   Référence neutre F-183
        F -7.3.2.3   Cours d'appel F-183
        F -7.3.2.4   High Court F-183
        F -7.3.2.5   Recueils F-184
                F -7.3.2.5.1   Law Reports F-184
                        F -7.3.2.5.1.1 Modèle d'une cause de
                                      1875 à 1890 ....F-185
                        F -7.3.2.5.1.2 Modèle d'une cause de
                                      1865 à 1875 ....F-185
                        F -7.3.2.5.1.3 Modèle d'une cause de
                                        1537 à 1865 ....F-185
                        F -7.3.2.5.1.4 Références neutres rétroactives . F-185
        F -7.3.2.6   Annuaires F-185
        F -7.3.2.7   Réimpressions F-186

F -7.3.2.8 Écosse, Irlande et Irlande du Nord............................F-186
    F -7.3.2.8.1 Référence neutre.................................F-186
        F -7.3.2.8.1.1 Écosse F-187
        F -7.3.2.8.1.2 Irlande...........................F-187
        F -7.3.2.8.1.3 Irlande du Nord F-187
F -7.1.2.9 Juge...F-188
F -7.3.2.10 Bases de données en ligne...................................F-188
    F -7.3.2.10.1 BAILII...F-188
    F -7.3.2.10.2 Service sans identifiant (Justis)...............F-188
F -7.3.3 Documents gouvernementaux......................................F-188
    F -7.3.3.1 Débats F-189
        F -7.3.3.1.1 Avant 1803 ....F-189
        F -7.3.3.1.2 1803 à aujourd'hui F-189
    F -7.3.3.2 Journaux..F-190
    F -7.3.3.3 Documents parlementaires.............................F-190
    F -7.3.3.4 Documents non parlementaires F-191

F -7.4 États-Unis F-192
  F -7.4.1 Législation...F-192
    F -7.4.1.1 Constitution fédérale et constitutions des États............F-192
    F -7.4.1.2 Lois..F-193
        F -7.4.1.2.1 Codes F-193
        F -7.4.1.2.2 Lois sessionnelles......................F-195
        F -7.4.1.2.3 Recueil non officiel de lois sessionnelles....F-196
    F -7.4.1.3 Uniform Codes, Uniform Acts et Restatements.............F-196
    F -7.4.1.4 Projets de loi et résolutions...........................F-197
        F -7.4.1.4.1 Projets de loi fédéraux F-197
        F -7.4.1.4.2 Résolutions fédérales...................F-197
        F -7.4.1.4.3 Résolutions et loi étatiques...............F-198
    F -7.4.1.5 Règles et règlements F-198
        F -7.4.1.5.1 Code of Federal Regulations...................F-198
        F -7.4.1.5.2 Registre administratif F-199
  F -7.4.2 Jurisprudence...F-199
    F -7.4.2.1 Modèle de base.....................................F-199
    F -7.4.2.2 Intitulé...F-200
    F -7.4.2.3 Référence neutre F-200
    F -7.4.2.4 Recueil et série.....................................F-200
    F -7.4.2.5 Référence précise F-201
    F -7.4.2.6 Cour...F-202
        F -7.4.2.6.1 Cours fédérales.........................F-202
        F -7.4.2.6.2 Cours d'États...........................F-202
    F -7.4.2.7 Année de la décision................................F-202
    F -7.4.2.8 Bases de données en ligne F-202
        F -7.4.2.8.1 Westlaw F-202
        F -7.4.2.8.2 Lexis F-203
  F -7.4.3 Documents gouvernementaux..................................F-203
    F -7.4.3.1 Débats F-203
    F -7.4.3.2 Sessions de comités F-204
        F -7.4.3.2.1 Fédéral F-204
        F -7.4.3.2.2 État....................................F-204
    F -7.4.3.3 Rapports et documents..............................F-205

F -7.4.3.3.1 Fédéral F-205
         F -7.4.3.3.1.1 Documents et rapports
                numérotés F-205
         F -7.4.3.3.1.2 Documents non numérotés et
                Committee Prints F-206
F -7.4.3.3.2 État..F-206

F -7.5 France F-207
  F -7.5.1 Législation...F-207
    F -7.5.1.1 Lois et autres instruments législatifs F-207
    F -7.5.1.2 Codes F-207
  F -7.5.2 Jurisprudence...F-208
    F -7.5.2.1 Modèle de base F-208
    F -7.5.2.2 Cour F-208
      F -7.5.2.2.1 Tribunaux de première instance..............F-208
      F -7.5.2.2.2 Cour d'appel....................................F-209
      F -7.5.2.2.3 Cour de cassation............................F-209
      F -7.5.2.2.4 Conseil d'État F-210
      F -7.5.2.2.5 Conseil constitutionnel F-210
    F -7.5.2.3 Intitulé...F-211
    F -7.5.2.4 Année F-211
    F -7.5.2.5 Semestre F-211
    F -7.5.2.6 Recueil..F-211
    F -7.5.2.7 Partie du recueil...F-212
    F -7.5.2.8 Page et numéro de la décision................................F-213
    F -7.5.2.9 Référence précise F-213
    F -7.5.2.10 Référence parallèle..F-213
    F -7.5.2.11 Notes, rapports et conclusions F-213
  F -7.5.3 Documents gouvernementaux.....................................F-213
    F -7.5.3.1 Débats F-214
      F -7.5.3.1.1 De 1787 à 1860 ....F-214
      F -7.5.3.1.2 De 1871 à aujourd'hui......................F-214
    F -7.5.3.2 Anciens journaux officiels F-215
    F -7.5.3.3 Documents parlementaires.....................................F-216
      F -7.5.3.3.1 Travaux et réunions parlementaires F-216
      F -7.5.3.3.2 Rapports d'information F-216
    F -7.5.3.4 Documents non parlementaires...............................F-217

F -7.6 Australie..F-217
  F -7.6.1 Législation...F-217
    F -7.6.1.1 Lois..F-217
    F -7.6.1.2 Législation déléguée (règlements)...........................F-218
  F -7.6.2 Jurisprudence...F-219
    F -7.6.2.1 Modèle de base F-219
    F -7.6.2.2 Référence neutre F-219
    F -7.6.2.3 Recueil..F-220
      F -7.6.2.3.1 Law Reports....................................F-220
    F -7.6.2.4 Cour F-221
  F -7.6.3 Documents gouvernementaux.....................................F-221
    F -7.6.3.1 Débats F-222
    F -7.6.3.2 Rapports parlementaires F-222
    F -7.6.3.3 Rapports non parlementaires..................................F-222

          F -7.6.3.4 Documents des ministères.....................................F-222

F -7.7 Nouvelle-Zélande F-223
     F -7.7.1 Législation..F-223
          F -7.7.1.1 Lois...F-223
          F -7.7.1.2 Législation déléguée (règlements)....................F-223
     F -7.7.2 Jurisprudence...F-224
          F -7.7.2.1 Modèle de base.....................................F-224
          F -7.7.2.2 Référence neutre F-224
          F -7.7.2.3 Recueil..F-224
               F -7.7.2.3.1 Law Reports....................F-224
          F -7.7.2.4 Cour..F-226
     F -7.7.3 Documents gouvernementaux................................F-226
          F -7.7.3.1 Débats F-226
          F -7.7.3.2 Documents parlementaires.........................F-227

F -7.8 Singapour...F-227
     F -7.8.1 Législation..F-227
          F -7.8.1.1 Documents constitutionnels.........................F-228
          F -7.8.1.2 Lois...F-228
          F -7.8.1.3 Modifications et abrogations F-229
          F -7.8.1.4 Lois anglaises applicables à Singapour F-229
          F -7.8.1.5 Législation auxiliaire (Règles, règlements, avis,
                     ordonnances)......................................F-229
               F -7.8.1.5.1 Refondus.......................F-229
               F -7.8.1.5.2 Non refondus...................F-230
     F -7.8.2 Jurisprudence...F-230
          F -7.8.2.1 Modèle de base.....................................F-230
          F -7.8.2.2 Référence neutre F-230
          F -7.8.2.3 Recueil..F-231
          F -7.8.2.4 Cours...F-231
          F -7.8.2.5 Décisions non publiées sans référence neutre.............F-231
          F -7.8.2.6 Bases de données en ligne.........................F-232
     F -7.8.3 Documents gouvernementaux................................F-232
          F -7.8.3.1 Débats parlementaires..............................F-232
          F -7.8.3.2 Directives de pratique..............................F-232
                F -7.8.3.2.1 Directives de pratique consolidées...........F-232
               F -7.8.3.2.2 Modifications aux directives de pratique F-232

F -7.9 Afrique du sud F-233
     F -7.9.1 Législation..F-233
          F -7.9.1.1 Lois...F-233
          F -7.9.1.2 Modifications et abrogations F-233
          F -7.9.1.3 Projets de loi.......................................F-233
     F -7.9.2 Jurisprudence...F-233
          F -7.9.2.1 Modèle de base.....................................F-233
          F -7.9.2.2 Référence neutre F-234
          F -7.9.2.3 Recueil..F-234
          F -7.9.2.4 Tribunal...F-235
     F -7.9.3 Documents gouvernementaux................................F-236
          F -7.9.3.1 Débats F-236
          F -7.9.3.2 Rapports, documents de discussion et exposés............F-236

Sources étrangères

7 SOURCES ÉTRANGÈRES

7.1.1 Forme générale

Pour faire référence à une source d'un pays de common law qui n'est pas traité dans ce chapitre, utiliser le modèle suivant comme guide.

Intitulé	(année de décision) (si nécéssaire),	citation neutre, recueil imprimé, etc.	réf. précise	réf. parallèle,	(cour, si nécessaire	juridic-tion)	[titre abrégé].
Singh v Punjab,		[1980] 2 Supreme Court Journal 475	à la p 524		(	Inde)	[*Singh*].
Hong Kong v Chan Hing Hung,		[1998] 4 Hong Kong Court 487	à la p 488C		(CFI	Hong Kong)	[*Chan*].
Alla Rahka v Mohamed Ahmed	(1956),	29 LRK 6			(	Kenya)	[*Alla Rahka*].
Campbell v MGN Ltd,		[2004] UKHL 22,		[2004] 2 AC 457	(	R-U)	[*MGN*].

7.1.2 Intitulé, référence précise, titre abrégé, et histoire judiciaire

▨ Utiliser les règles régissant la jurisprudence canadienne pour l'intitulé (section 3.3), les références précises (section 3.6), les recueils imprimés (section 3.7), et l'histoire judiciaire (section 3.11).

▨ Pour le titre abrégé, voir la section 1.4.1.

7.1.3 Année

▨ Généralement, ne que fournir l'année de la décision, ou bien l'omettre selon les règles de la section 3.4.

▨ Si nécessaire pour éviter l'ambiguïté (par ex. lorsqu'on fait référence à une décision non publiée), indiquer la date entière au lieu de l'année seule.

7.1.4   Référence neutre, recueil imprimé, service éléctronique, ou décision non publiée

	année et/ou volume	recueil impimé ou identifiant du tribunal	(série)	première page ou numéro de décision	(service électron-ique)	référence précise.
référence neutre	[2004]	UKHL		22.		
recueil imprimé	11	F Supp	(2e)	858		at 860.
service électronique	[1995]	FCJ		no 206	(QL).	

▦ Favoriser une référence neutre à un recueil imprimé. Suivre les conventions de référence neutre adoptées par le pays (par ex. le Royaume Uni place l'année entre crochets), mais sinon, suivre les règles régissant les décisions canadiennes (année, volume, recueil imprimé, série, page).

▦ Favoriser un recueil imprimé à une base de données en ligne. Suivre la section 3.7 pour les recueils imprimés.

▦ Pour les bases de données en ligne, utiliser les références fournies par le service. À moins que le service soit certainement connu du lecteur, le rajouter entre parenthèses.

▦ Pour les décisions non publiées qui n'ont aucun des élément ci-haut, suivre la convention adoptée par la juridiction, s'il y a lieu, ou bien fournir de l'information claire qui identifie le district judiciaire et le numéro de dossier (voir section 3.12). Indiquer la date entière, au lieu de l'année seulement, entre parenthèses à la suite de l'intitulé.

▦ Parmi les recueils imprimés, l'ordre décroissant de préférence est comme suit :

☐ recueils imprimés officiels;

☐ recueils imprimés semi-officiels; et

☐ recueils imprimés ayant la plus grande étendue géographique.

7.1.5   Juridiction et cour

Le nom de pays et celui de la cour sont écrits au complet, sauf pour les exceptions suivantes :

▦ Les abréviations certainement connues par le lecteur (par ex. É-U, R-U).

▦ Un nom distinctif et d'usage commun qui désigne un pays au lieu de son nom officiel (par ex. Pays-Bas au lieu du Royaume des Pays-Bas).

▦ Indiquer la cour et/ou la juridiction au sein du pays si ceux-ci ne sont pas évidents d'après le reste de la référence.

Sources étrangères

7.1.6   Juge

▓   Utiliser des abréviations de titres seulement si celles-ci sont certainement connues par le lecteur (par ex. l'on assume communément que JC désigne le juge en chef).

7.2   JURIDICTIONS DE DROIT CIVIL

Utiliser les directives suivantes pour faire référence à une source provenant d'une juridiction de droit civil qui n'est pas listé plus loin dans ce chapitre.

Cour et chambre,	ville,	date,	*intitulé* (si applicable),	(année de publication),	recueil imprimé ou périodique	section	page et/ ou numéro de décision	(annoté par l'auteur)	(pays).
Tribunal de Commerce,	Ostende,	12 octobre 1987		(1988),	Revue de Droit Commercial Belge		268	(annoté par Verougstraete)	(Belgique).
Corte Suprema de Justicia [Supreme Court],		15 novembre 1954,	*Suàrez, Alfredo c Perez Estella,*		190 Revista Gaceta Jurídica		145, No 124-2008		(Chili).
Interm People's Court,	Shanghai,	11 Mai 1988,	*China National Technical Importer/ Exporter v Industry Res*	(22 août 1988),	China Law & Practice		26		(Chine).
Mahkamat al-Tamiez [Cour de Cassation	Tamiez],	6 Mars 1974,			année 5, 1 Al-Nashra al-Qadaiah		161, No 1428		(Iraq).

▓   Inclure tout élément qui s'applique.

▓   Inclure entre crochets une traduction française du nom de la Cour ou du chambre, si ceci aidera le lecteur.

7.3 ROYAUME-UNI

Voir notamment le *Oxford Standard for Citation of Legal Authorities*.

7.3.1 Législation

7.3.1.1 Lois

▨ Mettre **(R-U)** après le titre de la loi pour indiquer son origine.

Avant 1963	*Statute of Westminster, 1931* (R-U), 22 & 23 Geo V, c 4, art 2.
1ᵉʳ janvier 1963 à aujourd'hui	*Terrorism Act 2000* (R-U), c 11, art 129.

▨ **Avant 1963** : Lorsque le titre comprend l'année, mettre une virgule avant l'année. Écrire l'année de règne en chiffres arabes (par ex. **1, 2, 3**) et le nombre suivant l'abréviation du monarque en chiffres romains (**Geo V**).

▨ **Du 1ᵉʳ janvier 1963 à aujourd'hui** : Lorsque le titre inclut l'année, ne pas mettre une virgule avant l'année. Lorsque le titre n'inclut pas l'année, l'indiquer après **(R-U)**, précédée d'une virgule.

7.3.1.1.1 Irlande du Nord

7.3.1.1.1.1 Lois adoptées par le Royaume-Uni

Avant 1963	*Public Health (Ireland) Act, 1878* (R-U), 41 & 42 Vict, c 52.
1ᵉʳ janvier 1963 à aujourd'hui	*Northern Ireland Act 1998* (R-U), 1998, c 47, art 5.

▨ Faire référence à la législation de l'Irlande du Nord adoptée par le Royaume-Uni de la même manière qu'à celle du Royaume-Uni.

7.3.1.1.1.2 Lois adoptées par l'Irlande du Nord

1921-1972	*Criminal Law Amendment (Northern Ireland) Act*, RSNI 1923, c 8.
	National Insurance Act, NI Pub Gen Acts 1946, c 23, art 7.
1999 à aujourd'hui	*Family Law Act (Northern Ireland) 2001* (IN), 2001, c 12.

▨ Abréger ***Northern Ireland Public General Acts*** par **NI Pub Gen Acts**.

▨ Abréger **Statutes Revised, Northern Ireland** par **RSNI**.

▨ Le Royaume-Uni a adopté les lois pour l'Irlande du Nord de 1972 à 1999. L'Assemblée de l'Irlande du Nord, établie le 19 novembre 1998, a obtenu le pouvoir d'adopter ses propres lois à partir du 2 décembre 1999. Pour les lois adoptées par l'Assemblée après

1999, écrire **(IN)** après le titre de la loi pour indiquer son origine. À noter que le Royaume-Uni peut encore adopter des lois qui s'appliquent en Irlande du Nord.

N.B. L'Assemblée de l'Irlande du Nord et l'exécutif ont été suspendus périodiquement. Durant de telles périodes, le **Secretary of State for Northern Ireland** et le **Northern Ireland Office** sont responsables des ministères de l'Irlande du Nord.

7.3.1.1.2 Écosse

Avant 1998, faire référence à la législation de l'Écosse de la même manière qu'à celle du Royaume-Uni.

Avant 1998	*Contract (Scotland) Act 1997* (R-U), 1997, c 34.
	Scotland Act 1998 (R-U), 1998, c 46, art 4.
1998 à aujourd'hui	*Standards in Scotland's Schools etc Act*, ASP 2000, c 6, art 2.

Les *Acts* adoptés par le Royaume-Uni s'appliquent à l'Écosse si ces lois se rapportent à une question réservée ou non transmise.

Abréger *Acts of Scottish Parliament* par **ASP** à partir du 19 novembre 1998.

7.3.1.1.3 Pays de Galles

Government of Wales Act 1998 (R-U), 1998, c 38, art 3.

Public Audit (Wales) Act 2013, ANAW 2013, c 3, art 4.

Pour la législation adoptée avant le 25 juillet 2006, suivre le même modèle de référence que pour la législation du Royaume-Uni.

En 2006, la *National Assembly for Wales* a acquis des pouvoirs législatifs limités concernant les domaines dévolus. Entre le 25 juillet 2006 et le 5 mai 2011, chaque loi a nécessité l'autorisation du Royaume-Uni avant d'être adoptée au Pays de Galles. Pour la législation datant de cette période, suivre le même modèle de référence que pour la législation du Royaume-Uni.

Depuis le 5 mai 2011, l'Assemblée détient l'autorité de passer ses propres lois pour les vingt Sujets décrits dans la *Government of Wales Act 2006* (R-U), c 32 art 7. Pour les **Acts of the National Assembly for Wales**, utiliser l'abréviation **ANAW**.

7.3.1.2 Projets de loi

7.3.1.2.1 Royaume-Uni

Numéro du projet de loi,	*titre*,	session,	année,	référence précise	(renseignements supplémentaires) (facultatif).
Bill 4,	*London Olympics Bill*,	sess 2005–2006,	2005		(1re lecture 1 juillet 2005).
Bill 40,	*Harbours Bill [HL]*,	sess 2005–2006,	2005,	art 2.	

■ Inclure **[HL]** (non italique) après le titre pour les projets de loi qui proviennent de la Chambre des Lords.

7.3.1.2.2 Irlande du Nord

Nu-méro,	*titre*,	session,	année,	référence précise	(renseignements supplémentaires) (facultatif).
NIA Bill 15/00,	*A Bill to amend the Game Preservation (Northern Ireland) Act 1928*,	sess 2001-2002,	2001,	art 2	(Committee Stage Extension 29 octobre 2001).
NIA Bill 17/07,	*Child Maintenance Bill*,	sess 2007-2008,	2008,	art 12.	

7.3.1.2.3 Écosse

Numéro,	*titre*,	session,	année,	référence précise	(renseignements supplémentaires) (facultatif).
SP Bill 42,	*Human Tissue (Scotland) Bill*,	2e sess,	2005,	art 6	(1re lecture 3 juin 2005).
SP Bill 17,	*Climate Change (Scotland) Bill*,	3e sess,	2008,	art 3(2)(b)	(1re étape du débat 6-7 mai 2009).

Sources étrangères

7.3.1.3 Règlements

7.3.1.3.1 Royaume-Uni

	Titre (facultatif)	SR & O ou SI	année/numéro.
Avant 1948	*Public Health (Prevention of Tuberculosis) Regulations 1925,*	SR & O	1927/757.
1948 à aujourd'hui	*The Welfare Food (Amendment) Regulations 2005,*	SI	2005/68844.

▨ L'indication du titre du règlement est facultative.

▨ Abréger *Statutory Rules & Orders* (avant 1948) par **SR & O** et *Statutory Instruments* (après 1948) par **SI**.

7.3.1.3.2 Règlements et ordres de l'Irlande du Nord

Titre (facultatif),	SR & O ou SI	année/numéro	(NI numéro).
The Proceeds of Crime (Northern Ireland) Order 1996,	SI	1996/1299	(NI 9).
The Tax Credits 2001 (Miscellaneous Amendments No 8) (Northern Ireland) Regulations,	SI	2001/3086.	
Cheese Regulations (NI) 1970,	SR & O	1970/14.	

▨ L'indication du titre du règlement est facultative.

▨ Les règlements et les ordres adoptés par le Royaume-Uni se trouvent dans les *Statutory Instruments* (**SI**).

▨ Abréger un règlement adopté par l'Assemblée de l'Irlande du Nord par **SR** (*Statutory Rule*).

▨ Les règlements de l'Irlande du Nord sont inclus dans les *Statutory Regulations and Orders* (abrégés **SR & O**) à partir de 1922.

▨ S'il y a un **numéro d'ordre de l'Irlande du Nord**, l'inclure après **année/numéro** pour indiquer que l'ordre a été promulgué par l'Assemblée de l'Irlande du Nord.

7.3.1.3.3 Écosse

Faire référence aux règlements de l'Écosse de la même manière qu'à ceux du Royaume-Uni (section 7.3.1.3.1).

7.3.1.3.3.1 Règlements adoptés par le Royaume-Uni

Titre (facultatif),	SR & O ou SI	année/numéro.
Employment Tribunals (Constitution and Rules of Procedure) (Scotland) Regulations 2001,	SI	2001/1170.
Local Government Pension Scheme Amendment (Scotland) Regulations 2009,	SI	2009/93.

7.3.1.3.3.2 Règlements adoptés par l'Écosse

Titre (facultatif),	Scot SI	année/numéro.
National Health Service (General Ophthalmic Services) (Scotland) Amendment Regulations 2001,	Scot SI	2001/62.
Plastic Materials and Articles in Contact with Food (Scotland) Regulations 2009,	Scot SI	2009/30.

▨   Abréger *Scottish Statutory Instruments* par **Scot SI**.

7.3.1.3.4 Pays de Galles

Titre (facultatif),	SR & O ou SI	année/numéro	(W numéro).
Children's Homes Amendment (Wales) Regulations 2001,	SI	2001/140	(W 6).

▨   Après **année/numéro**, inclure le numéro du règlement du Pays de Galles pour indiquer qu'il a été promulgué par l'Assemblée du Pays de Galles.

7.3.2   Jurisprudence

7.3.2.1 Modèle de base

Intitulé	(année de la décision),	référence neutre,	[année du recueil]	volume	recueil	page	(cour).
R v Woollin	(1998),		[1999]	1	AC	82	(HL (Eng)).
Campbell v MGN Ltd,		[2004] UKHL 22,	[2004]	2	AC	457.	

▨ Les *Law Reports* (voir section 7.3.2.5.1) ont préséance sur les *Weekly Law Reports* (WLR) et sur les *All England Law Reports* (All ER).

▨ Voir la liste des recueils de jurisprudence du Royaume-Uni et leurs abréviations à l'**annexe C**, et la liste des cours et de leurs abréviations à l'**annexe B**.

7.3.2.2 Référence neutre

▨ Plusieurs tribunaux du Royaume-Uni ont officiellement adopté un système de référence neutre. Suivre les règles de la référence neutre au Canada (section 3.5), à l'exception de l'année, qui est placée entre crochets.

▨ Pour les références neutres rétroactives, voir la section 7.3.2.5.1.4.

7.3.2.3 Cours d'appel

[1] *Campbell v MGN Limited*, [2004] UKHL 22.

[2] *Fraser v HM Advocate*, [2011] UKSC 24.

[3] *Copping v Surrey County Council*, [2005] EWCA Civ 1604 au para 15.

Supreme Court of the United Kingdom	[année] UKSC numéro
House of Lords	[année] UKHL numéro
Privy Council	[année] UKPC numéro
England and Wales Court of Appeal (Division civile)	[année] EWCA Civ numéro
England and Wales Court of Appeal (Division criminelle)	[année] EWCA Crim numéro

▨ Les références neutres pour les cours d'appel et de l'*Administrative Court* de la *High Court* sont officielles **depuis le 11 janvier 2001**.

▨ La *Supreme Court of the United Kingdom* a assumé les fonctions judiciaires de la *House of Lords* le 1er octobre 2009.

▨ Indiquer l'année de la décision entre crochets, suivie du code de désignation du tribunal et du numéro de la cause.

7.3.2.4 High Court

[Année]	cour	numéro	(division)	paragraphe.
[2005]	EWHC	1974	(Admlty)	au para 10.
[2005]	EWHC	2995	(Comm).	

▨ Les références neutres pour la *High Court* sont officielles **depuis le 14 janvier 2002**.

▨ Pour les causes plaidées devant la *High Court*, la division de cette cour est placée entre parenthèses après le numéro de la cause.

▨ N.B. La référence neutre pour les causes plaidées devant l'*Administrative Court* durant l'année 2001 s'écrit de la façon suivante : **[année] EWHC Admin numéro**. Ce format est semblable à celui de la Cour d'appel (section 7.3.2.3).

- Faire des références précises aux paragraphes. Utiliser **au para**.
- La *High Court* a trois divisions principales et plusieurs cours spécialisées.

Divisions et abréviations de la *High Court* :

Queen's Bench Division	QB
Administrative Court	Admin
Commercial Court	Comm
Admiralty Court	Admlty
Technology & Construction Court	TCC

Chancery Division	Ch
Patents Court	Pat
Companies Court	Comp

Family Division	Fam

7.3.2.5 Recueils

7.3.2.5.1 Law Reports

- Les *Law Reports* sont **organisés en séries**. Se référer à la série et non aux *Law Reports*.
- Il n'y a pas de recueil distinct pour la Cour d'appel. Inclure l'abréviation **CA** pour « *Court of Appeal* » à la fin de chaque référence à une décision rendue par cette cour.

Les *Law Reports* et leurs abréviations:

Appeal Cases (*House of Lords* et *Judicial Committee of the Privy Council*)	AC
Chancery (*Chancery Division* et decisions en appel de la *Court of Appeal*)	Ch
Queen's (King's) Bench (Division du Banc de la Reine (du Roi) et décisions de ces divisions en appel devant la *Court of Appeal*)	QB (KB)
Probate (1891–1971) (*Family Division*, *Probate*, *Divorce* et *Admiralty Division*, décisions en appel de ces divisions et *Ecclesiastical Courts*)	P
Family (1972 à aujourd'hui)	Fam
Industrial Courts Reports (1972–1974) and *Industrial Cases Reports* (1975 à aujourd'hui)	ICR
Law Reports Restrictive Practices (1957–1972) (*National Industrial Relations Court and Restrictive Practices Court*, décisions en appel de cette cour et les décisions de la *High Court* pertinentes aux relations industrielles)	LR RP

Sources étrangères

7.3.2.5.1.1 Modèle d'une cause de 1875 à 1890

▨ Indiquer **D**, l'abréviation de ***Division***, après l'abréviation du titre du recueil, afin de distinguer la collection des

Bird v Jones (1845), 7 **QBD** 742 (CA) [*Bird*].

recueils datant de 1875 à 1890 de la collection plus récente qui porte le même nom.

7.3.2.5.1.2 Modèle d'une cause de 1865 à 1875

Currie v Misa (1875), **LR 10 Ex** 153.

▨ Indiquer **LR**, l'abréviation de ***Law Reports***, avant le volume, afin de distinguer cette collection de recueils de la collection plus récente qui porte le même nom.

7.3.2.5.1.3 Modèle d'une cause de 1537 à 1865

▨ Avant 1865, les recueils n'ont été ni officiels ni

Lord Byron v Johnston (1816), 2 Mer 28, 35 ER 851 (Ch).

exhaustifs. Par contre, des avocats et des juges individuels ont publié des recueils de droit privé sous leur propre nom. Peu de lecteurs ont accès à ces recueils nommés (*nominate reporters*). Au lieu de citer un recueil nommé, il est préférable de fournir une référence aux *English Reports* (**ER**) ou au moins une référence parallèle.

▨ Les *English Reports* et les *All England Reports Reprints* sont des réimpressions. L'intégralité des *English Reports* est disponible au public sur le site-web CommonLII.

7.3.2.5.1.4 Références neutres rétroactives

▨ Plusieurs arrêts plus vieux, en particulier ceux de la *House of Lords* et du *Privy Council*, ont des références neutres

Thomas v Sorrell, **[1673] EWHC KB J85**, 124 ER 1098, Vaughan 330.

rétroactives. Traiter ces références neutres rétroactives comme des références neutres données par la Cour. Des références neutres rétroactives sont disponibles sur BAILII.

7.3.2.6 *Annuaires*

Intitulé	(année),	annuaire	trimestre	année du règne	monarque,	numéro du plaidoyer (*plea*),	numéro du feuillet (*folio*).
Doige's Case	(1422),	YB	Trin	20	Hen VI,	pl 4,	fol 34.

▨ Utiliser les abréviations de trimestres suivantes : **Mich** pour **Michaelmas**, **Hil** pour **Hilary**, **Pach** pour **Easter** et **Trin** pour **Trinity**.

▨ Indiquer l'année du règne en chiffres arabes.

▨ Indiquer le monarque en chiffres romains.

▓ Abréger **plea** par **pl**.

▓ Abréger **folio** par **fol**.

7.3.2.7 Réimpressions

Référence à l'annuaire,	reproduit dans,	traduit par (si applicable)	traducteur /directeur,	référence à la réimpression.
Randolph v Abbot of Hailes (1313-14), YB 6&7 Edw II (Eyre of Kent),	reproduit dans *Year-books of 6 Edward II* (1926),	traduit par	William Craddock, dir,	27 Selden Soc 32 à la p 33.

▓ Pour une réimpression, fournir autant de renseignements que possible sur la première édition de l'annuaire. Se référer à la source dans laquelle se trouve la réimpression.

7.3.2.8 Écosse, Irlande et Irlande du Nord

Écosse	*M'Courtney v HM Advocate*, [1977] JC 68 (HCJ **Scot**).
Irlande	*Hardman v Maffet* (1884), 13 **LR Ir** 499 (ChD).
Irlande du Nord	*R v Crooks*, [1999] **NI** 226 (CA).

▓ Lorsque le titre du recueil n'indique pas l'indication géographique, indiquer **Scot** pour *Scotland*, **Ir** pour *Ireland*, et **NI** pour *Northern Ireland*, entre parenthèses à la fin de la référence.

▓ Indiquer le nom de la cour, car chaque volume est divisé en parties selon la cour et chaque partie est paginée séparément.

▓ Voir l'**annexe B** pour les abréviations des tribunaux et l'**annexe C** pour celles des recueils.

7.3.2.8.1 Référence neutre

▓ Les règles concernant les références neutres sont les mêmes pour l'Écosse, l'Irlande et l'Irlande du Nord. Suivre les règles de la référence neutre au Canada (section 3.5), à l'exception de l'année, qui est placée entre crochets.

Sources étrangères

7.3.2.8.1.1 Écosse

Si la référence neutre ne contient pas d'indication géographique, indiquer **Scot** entre parenthèses à la fin de la référence.

Smith v Brown, [2005] HCJT 2 (Scot).	**High Court of Justiciary**	[année] HCJT numéro
Kinross v Dunsmuir, [2005] HCJAC 3 au para 12 (Scot).	**Court of Criminal Appeal**	[année] HCJAC numéro
McBride v MacDuff, [2005] CSOH 4 (Scot).	**Court of Session, Outer House**	[année] CSOH numéro
	Court of Session, Inner House	[année] CSIH numéro

7.3.2.8.1.2 Irlande

Finnigan v O'Dair, [2006] IEHC 4.	**High Court**	[année] IEHC numéro
Mackey v Mackey, [2005] IESC 2 au para 4.	**Supreme Court**	[année] IESC numéro
	Court of Criminal Appeal	[année] IECCA numéro

7.3.2.8.1.3 Irlande du Nord

McDonnell v Henry, [2005] NICA 17.	**Court of Appeal**	[année] NICA numéro
Barkley v Whiteside, [2004] NIQB 12 au para 12.	**Crown Court**	[année] NICC numéro
	County Court	[année] NICty numéro
	Magistrates Court	[année] NIMag numéro

High Court :

Queen's Bench Division	[année] NIQB numéro
Family Division	[année] NIFam numéro
Chancery Division	[année] NICh numéro

7.3.2.9 Juge

Lord Justice	LJ
Lord Justices	LJJ
Master of the Rolls	MR
Lord Chancellor	LC
Vice Chancellor	VC
Baron	B
Chief Baron	CB

7.3.2.10 Bases de données en ligne

7.3.2.10.1 BAILII

Intitué,	Identifiant donné par le service	(BAILII)	reference précise	(juridiction et/ou cour) (s'il y a lieu).
London Borough of Harrow v Johnstone,	[1997] UKHL 9	(BAILII)	au para 6.	

▓ Ne pas confondre l'identifiant BAILII avec une référence neutre. Ajouter (**BAILII**) après l'identificateur d'éviter toute confusion.

7.3.2.10.2 Service sans identifiant (Justis)

Intitulé	(année),	reference précise	(juridiction et/ou cour)	(disponible sur	nom du service éléctronique).
R v Woollin	(1998),	au para 23	(HL)	(disponible sur	Justis).

7.3.3   Documents gouvernementaux

Indiquer **R-U** au début de la référence.

7.3.3.1 Débats

7.3.3.1.1 Avant 1803

R-U,	chambre,	*Parliamentary History of England*,	volume,	colonne	(date)	(orateur) (facultatif).
R-U,	HC,	Parliamentary History of England,	vol 12,	col 1327	(27 mai 1774).	
R-U,	HL,	Parliamentary History of England,	vol 2,	col 791	(24 mai 1641).	

▓ Pour les débats d'avant 1803, se référer au recueil *Parliamentary History of England*.

▓ Abréger *House of Commons* par **HC** et *House of Lords* par **HL**.

▓ Indiquer l'orateur entre parenthèses à la fin de la référence si nécessaire.

7.3.3.1.2 1803 à aujourd'hui

R-U,	cham-bre,	*titre*,	série,	vo-lume,	co-lonne	référence précise	(date)	(orateur) (facultatif).
R-U,	HL,	*Parlia-mentary Debates*,	5ᵉ sér,	vol 442,	col 3	à la col 6	(3 mai 1983)	(Baroness Masham of Ilton).
R-U,	SP,	*Official Report*,	sess 1 (2000),	vol 7, n° 6,	col 634		(22 juin 2000)	(Peter Pea-cock).
R-U,	NIA,	*Official Report*				à la p 500	(24 octobre 2000).	
R-U,	NAW,	*Official Record*				à la p 27	(19 juillet 2001).	

▓ L'orateur peut être indiqué entre parenthèses à la fin de la référence.

▓ Après **R-U**, indiquer la chambre.

Sources étrangères

Abréviations des chambres :

House of Commons	HC
House of Lords	HL
National Assembly for Wales	NAW
Northern Ireland Assembly	NIA
Scottish Parliament	SP

7.3.3.2 Journaux

R-U,	journal,	volume	(date)	référence précise.
R-U,	Journal of the House of Commons,	vol 234	(9 décembre 1977)	à la p 95.
R-U,	Journal of the House of Lords,	vol 22	(10 janvier 1995)	à la p 89.

▨ Ne pas répéter le nom de la chambre, puisqu'il est indiqué dans le titre du journal.

7.3.3.3 Documents parlementaires

R-U,	chambre,	« titre »,	numéro sessionnel ou command number	dans Sessional Papers,	vol	(année)	1re page	référence précise	(président) (s'il y a lieu).
R-U,	HC,	« Report of the Committee on the Law Relating to Rights of Light »,	Cmnd 473	dans Sessional Papers,	vol 17	(1957-58)	955		(Président : Sir CE Harman).
R-U,	HC,	« Monopolies and Mergers Commission Report on the Supply in the UK of the Services of Administering Performing Rights and Film Synchronisation Rights »,	Cm 3147	dans Sessional Papers		(1995-96)	1.		

▨ Indiquer le titre tel qu'il apparaît à la page titre du rapport.

▨ Indiquer le numéro sessionnel ou le numéro du *Command Paper* après le titre.

▨ Se référer aux **Sessional Papers** de la *House of Commons* à moins que le document n'apparaisse que dans les *Sessional Papers* de la *House of Lords*.

▨ Écrire le numéro du volume (s'il y a lieu) après *Sessional Papers*.

▨ Inscrire le nom du président entre parenthèses à la fin de la référence si cette information est connue.

▨ **L'abréviation appropriée du *Command* est essentielle pour identifier le document.** Elle apparaît sur la première page de chaque *Command Paper* :

1833-1869	1re série (1-4222)	c
1870-1899	2e série (1-9550)	C
1900-1918	3e série (1-9239)	Cd
1919-1956	4e série (1-9889)	Cmd
1957-1986	5e série (1-9927)	Cmnd
1986 à aujourd'hui	6e série (1-)	Cm

▨ Indiquer la première page du document après la date.

▨ Utiliser la pagination interne du document pour les références précises.

7.3.3.4 Documents non parlementaires

R-U,	organisme,	*titre*,	(type de document) (s'il y a lieu)	auteur (s'il y a lieu),	renseignements sur l'édition.
R-U,	Royal Commission on Criminal Procedure,	*Police Interrogation: The Psychological Approach*,			Londres, Her Majesty's Stationery Office, 1980.
R-U,	Royal Commission on the Press,	*Studies on the Press*	(Working Paper n° 3)	par Oliver Boyd-Barret, Colin Seymour-Ure et Jeremy Turnstall,	Londres, Her Majesty's Stationery Office, 1978.
R-U,	Law Commission,	*Contempt of Court*	(Consultation Paper n° 209)		Londres, The Stationery Office, 2012.
R-U,		*Report of the Committee on Homosexual Offences and Prostitution*,			Londres, Her Majesty's Stationery Office, 1957.

▨ Suivre les règles des documents non parlementaires canadiens, à la section 4.2.

▓ Ne pas indiquer l'organisme s'il est déjà spécifié dans le titre (voir l'exemple *Report of the Committee on Homosexual Offences and Prostitution*).

▓ Beaucoup des fonctions officielles d'édition de *Her Majesty's Stationery Office* ont été assumées par *The Stationery Office* (TSO), une entreprise privée, en 1996.

7.4 ÉTATS-UNIS

▓ Tous les éléments de référence à la législation des États-Unis sont en anglais, à l'exception des mentions telles que « codifié à ».

▓ Voir *The Bluebook: A Uniform System of Citation*.

7.4.1 Législation

7.4.1.1 Constitution fédérale et constitutions des États

▓ Abréger **article** par **art**, **section** par § et **sections** par §§.

▓ Un paragraphe qui fait partie d'une section est une **clause**, abrégée **cl** (au singulier comme au pluriel).

▓ Abréger **amendement** par **amend**.

▓ Abréger **préambule** par **pmbl**.

> US Const art II, § 2, cl 1.
>
> US Const amend XVIII, § 1.
>
> Fla Const, Part V, § 3(b)(4).

▓ Indiquer les numéros d'article et de modification en chiffres romains majuscules. Les numéros de section et de clause sont indiqués en chiffres arabes.

Voir l'**annexe A-2** pour la liste des abréviations des états.

Sources étrangères

7.4.1.2 Lois

Ordre hiérarchique des sources :

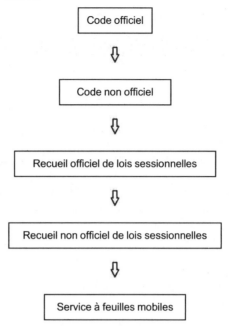

7.4.1.2.1 Codes

▪ Aux États-Unis, un code constitue le regroupement et la codification par sujet des lois générales et permanentes des États-Unis.

▪ Un **code officiel** est un code des lois des États-Unis organisé en moins de 50 titres et rédigé sous la surveillance d'une autorité gouvernementale appropriée (par ex. le département de la Justice fédérale).

▪ Le *United States Code* (**USC**) est le code officiel du gouvernement fédéral.

▪ Pour déterminer si un code étatique est officiel ou non, consulter le *Bluebook* ou la liste de codes étatiques disponible sur Findlaw (http://statelaws.findlaw.com/state-codes/).

▪ Un **code non officiel** est un code des lois des États-Unis préparé par une maison d'édition. Il existe deux codes non officiels pour les lois fédérales :

☐ le *United States Code Service* (**USCS**) et

☐ le *United States Code Annotated* (**USCA**).

	Titre (exceptionnel-lement),	partie du code (s'il y a lieu)	titre abrégé du code	numéro du titre (s'il y a lieu)	article	(éditeur	Supplé-ment (s'il y a lieu)	année).
Codes officiels	*Patient Protection and Affordable Care Act,*	42	USC		§ 18001			(2010).
			Minn Stat		§ 169947			(1990).
			IRC		§ 61			(1994).
Codes non officiels		18	USCA		§ 351	(West		1997).
			Pa Stat Ann	tit 63	§ 4253	(West	Supp	1986).
			Wis Stat Ann		§ 939645	(West	Supp	1992).

▪ Ne pas se référer au titre original d'une loi codifiée. **N'indiquer le titre que pour des raisons particulières** (par ex. si la loi est normalement connue sous ce nom). Mettre le titre en italique.

▪ Si le code est **classé** par titres, chapitres ou volumes distincts et numérotés, indiquer le numéro de cette division. Dans le cas du code fédéral, indiquer la division avant l'abréviation du code.

▪ Ne pas mettre le titre abrégé du code en italique. Pour une référence à l'*Internal Revenue Code*, il est possible de remplacer **26 USC** par **IRC**.

▪ À moins que le code ne soit publié par un éditeur officiel, indiquer le nom de l'éditeur avant l'année ou avant **Supp**, selon le cas.

▪ Pour indiquer un supplément inséré dans une pochette, écrire **Supp** avant la mention de l'année qui paraît sur la page titre du supplément.

▪ Indiquer l'année de publication du code entre parenthèses à la fin de la référence. Pour un **recueil relié**, fournir l'année qui paraît sur la reliure. Pour un **supplément**, fournir l'année qui figure sur la page titre du supplément.

Sources étrangères

7.4.1.2.2 Lois sessionnelles

Les lois sessionnelles sont les lois promulguées par une session du Congrès, reliées et organisées par ordre chronologique. Les lois sessionnelles font le suivi d'une loi.

Titre ou date de promulgation,	numéro de la loi ou du chapitre,	partie (s'il y a lieu),	référence au recueil des lois sessionnelles	première page de la loi	référence précise au recueil	(année) (si elle n'est pas dans le titre)	(référence au code) (facultatif).
The Deficit Reduction Act of 1984,	Pub L No 98-369,		98 Stat	494			(codifié tel que modifié au 26 USC § 1-9504 (1988)).
Coastal Zone Protection Act of 1996,	Pub L No 104-150,	§ 7(2),	110 Stat	1380	à la p 1382	(1997).	
Act of 25 April 1978,	c 515,	§ 3,	1978 Ala Acts	569	à la p 569.		

- Indiquer le titre de la loi en italique. Si la loi n'a pas de titre, l'identifier par la date de sa promulgation (**Act of 25 April 1978**). S'il n'y a pas de date de promulgation, identifier la loi par sa date de mise en vigueur (**Act effective [date]**).

- Indiquer le numéro de la loi (**public law number**), introduit par l'abréviation **Pub L No** ou par le numéro du chapitre précédé de **c**. Le numéro devant le trait d'union du *public law number* est le numéro de session; le numéro après le trait d'union est le numéro de référence.

- Pour se référer à une **partie particulière**, indiquer le numéro de la partie après le numéro de la loi ou le numéro du chapitre, selon le cas. Indiquer la référence précise au recueil.

- Le **recueil officiel** des lois fédérales est le *Statutes at Large*, abrégé **Stat**. L'abréviation du recueil est précédée par le numéro de volume et suivie par la première page de la loi. Pour déterminer si un recueil de lois sessionnelles étatiques est officiel ou non, consulter le *Bluebook*.

- Indiquer la **référence précise** au recueil de lois sessionnelles après la référence à la première page. Inclure une référence précise à la partie après le numéro de la loi ou du chapitre.

- Indiquer l'**année de publication** entre parenthèses à la fin de la référence, à moins que l'année ne fasse partie du titre de la loi. Si l'année du titre ne coïncide pas avec l'année de publication de la loi, les deux années doivent être indiquées. Voir l'exemple du *Coastal Zone Protection Act of 1996.*

Fournir les renseignements concernant la **codification de la loi** s'ils sont disponibles. Si une loi est divisée et classée sous plusieurs sections du code, fournir ce renseignement entre parenthèses à la fin de la référence (**(codifié tel que modifié dans plusieurs sections du 26 USC)** suivi du nom du code).

7.4.1.2.3 Recueil non officiel de lois sessionnelles

Titre,	numéro de la loi,	[volume]	recueil non officiel	référence précise,	référence au Statutes at Large.
Veteran's Benefits Improvements Act of 1996,	Pub L No 104-275,	[1996]	USCCAN	3762,	110 Stat 3322.

Le recueil de lois sessionnelles fédérales le plus important est le *United States Code Congressional and Administrative News*, abrégé **USCCAN**.

Pour citer l'USCCAN, indiquer la référence aux *Statutes at Large* (**Stat**), recueils officiels dans lequel paraîtra la loi.

7.4.1.3 Uniform Codes, Uniform Acts et Restatements

Titre	partie	(année d'adoption).
UCC	§ 2-012	(1995).
Uniform Adoption Act	§ 10	(1971).
Restatement of Contracts	§ 88	(1932).
Restatement (Second) of the Law of Property	§ 15	(1977).

Les *Uniform Codes* et *Uniform Acts* sont des propositions législatives publiées par la *National Conference of Commissioners of Uniform State Laws*, qui visent l'adoption par tous les congrès d'états, les districts et les protectorats. Les *Restatements* sont des rapports sur l'état de la *common law* américaine qui porte sur tel sujet ou telle interprétation des lois publiques publiées par le *American Law Institute*.

Indiquer le titre en italique, à moins qu'il ne s'agisse d'un code.

Ne pas mettre de virgule après le titre d'un code ou d'un *Restatement*.

Lorsqu'il existe plus d'un *Restatement*, indiquer son numéro entre parenthèses.

Indiquer l'année d'adoption, de promulgation ou de la plus récente modification entre parenthèses à la fin de la référence.

Sources étrangères

7.4.1.4 Projets de loi et résolutions

7.4.1.4.1 Projets de loi fédéraux

É-U,	Bill	chambre	numéro,	*titre,*	numéro du Congrès,	année,	référence précise	(état, si promulgué).
É-U,	Bill	HR	6,	*Higher Education Amendments of 1988,*	105e Cong,	1997		(promulgué).
É-U,	Bill	S	7,	*Educational Excellence for All Learners Act of 2001,*	107e Cong,	2001,	art 103.	

Abréger *House of Representatives* par **HR** et *Senate* par **S**.

7.4.1.4.2 Résolutions fédérales

É-U,	résolution	numéro,	*titre,*	numéro du Congrès,	année	(état, si promulgué).
É-U,	HR Con Res	6,	*Expressing the Sense of the Congress Regarding the Need to Pass Legislation to Increase Penalties on Perpetrators of Hate Crimes,*	107e Cong,	2001.	
É-U,	HR Res	31,	*Designating Minority Membership on Certain Standing Committees of the House,*	104e Cong,	1995	(promulgué).

Abréviations employées pour les résolutions :

House Concurrent Resolutions	HR Con Res
House Resolutions	HR Res
House Joint Resolutions	HRJ Res
Senate Concurrent Resolutions	S Con Res
Senate Resolutions	S Res
Senate Joint Resolutions	SJ Res

7.4.1.4.3 Résolutions et lois étatiques

É-U,	catégor-ie du Bill ou de la résolu-tion	nu-méro,	titre,	année ou numéro de la législa-ture,	numéro ou désigna-tion de la session législative,	état,	année,	référ-ence précise	(état, si promulgué).
É-U,	AB	31,	An Act to Add Section 51885 to the Educa-tion Code, Relating to Educational Technology,	1997-98,	Reg Sess,	Cal,	1996,	art 1.	
É-U,	SR	10,	Calling for the Establishment of a Delaware State Police Community Relations Task Force,	141e Gen Assem,	Reg Sess,	Del,	2001		(promulgué).

▨ En plus des *Regular Sessions* (**Reg Sess**), les législateurs étatiques peuvent tenir des ***First, Second* et *Third Extraordinary Sessions*.** Abréger ces expressions par **1st Extra Sess, 2d Extra Sess** et **3d Extra Sess.** Abréger *Special Sessions* par **Spec Sess.**

▨ Voir la liste des abréviations des états à l'**annexe A-2**.

7.4.1.5 Règles et règlements

7.4.1.5.1 Code of Federal Regulations

Le *Code of Federal Regulations* regroupe les règlements codifiés des États-Unis, classés selon les 50 mêmes titres que le *United States Code*.

Titre (exceptionellement),	volume	recueil	référence précise	(année).
EPA Effluent Limitations Guidelines,	40	CFR	§ 405.53	(1980).
	47	CFR	§ 73.609	(1994).

▨ Indiquer le titre de la règle ou du règlement s'il est mieux connu ainsi.

▨ Pour les règles et les règlements fédéraux, se référer à la compilation officielle du gouvernement, si possible.

▨ Le *Code of Federal Regulations*, abrégé **CFR**, est la compilation officielle du gouvernement fédéral.

N.B. Pour identifier les compilations étatiques officielles, voir le *Bluebook*.

7.4.1.5.2 Registre administratif

Les registres administratifs comprennent entre autres les règlements administratifs mis en application par les autorités gouvernementales.

Titre (s'il y a lieu),	volume	Fed Reg	première page	(année)	(information sur la codification	référence précise).
	44	Fed Reg	12437221	(1979)	(to be codified at 29 CFR	§ 552).
Outer Continental Shelf Air Regulations Consistency Update for California,	70	Fed Reg	19472	(2009)	(sera codifié au 40 CFR	§ 55).

▓ Lorsque des règles ou des règlements n'ont pas encore été codifiés, se référer aux registres administratifs.

▓ Au niveau fédéral, se référer au *Federal Register* (**Fed Reg**).

▓ Indiquer le numéro du volume, l'abréviation du registre, le numéro de page et l'année.

▓ Si possible, indiquer à quel endroit la règle ou le règlement paraîtra dans le CFR ou autre compilation officielle à la fin de la référence.

N.B. Pour identifier les registres administratifs étatiques, voir le *Bluebook*.

7.4.2 Jurisprudence

7.4.2.1 Modèle de base

Intitulé,	vol	recueil	(série)	première page	référence précise	(indication géographi- que et/ou cour	année)	(autre information) (s'il y a lieu).
People v Kevor- kian,	527	NW	(2d)	714		(Mich	1994).	
Roche Holding Ltd,	113	FTC		1086	aux pp 1087-90		(1990).	
Headquarters Space & Missile,	103	Lab Arb Rep (BNA)		1198			(1995)	(McCurdy, Arb).

▓ Les références aux décisions administratives et à l'arbitrage suivent le même modèle de référence que les autres jugements.

▓ Pour l'arbitrage, fournir le nom de l'arbitre suivi d'une virgule et **Arb** entre parenthèses à la fin de la référence.

7.4.2.2 Intitulé

✓	California v United States Larez v Los Angeles (City of)
✗	State of California v United States of America Larez v LA

- Indiquer l'intitulé selon les règles de la section 3.3.

- Pour un État ou un pays, utiliser le nom couramment utilisé plutôt que la forme descriptive ou l'abréviation.

- Si une des parties est une ville dont le nom pourrait être confondu avec celui d'un État, indiquer les renseignements permettant de l'identifier entre parenthèses : **New York (City of)** ou **Washington (DC)**.

7.4.2.3 Référence neutre

Il n'existe **aucun standard uniforme aux États-Unis pour les références neutres**, toutefois certaines juridictions ont adopté ces références. Pour plus de détails, voir le *Bluebook*.

7.4.2.4 Recueil et série

- Après l'intitulé, indiquer le numéro du volume, l'abréviation du recueil, le numéro de la série et la première page de l'arrêt. Il y a toujours un espace entre l'abréviation du recueil et le numéro de la série.

> *Lotus Development v Borland International*, 140 **F (3d)** 70 (1er Cir 1998) [*Lotus*].
>
> *Scott v Sanford*, 60 **US** (19 How) 393 (1857).

- **Avant 1875**, les *US Reports* sont aussi numérotés en ordre consécutif selon chaque éditeur. Indiquer ce numéro ainsi que le nom de l'éditeur entre parenthèses après **US**.

Abréviations d'éditeurs :

Wallace	Wall
Black	Black
Howard	How
Peters	Pet
Wheaton	Wheat
Cranch	Cranch
Dallas	Dal

Sources étrangères

Abréviations des principaux recueils :

Atlantic Reporter	A
California Reporter	Cal
Federal Reporter	F
Federal Supplement	F Supp
Lawyers' Edition	L Ed (2d)
New York Supplement	NYS
North Eastern Reporter	NE
North Western Reporter	NW
Pacific Reporter	P
South Eastern Reporter	SE
South Western Reporter	SW
Southern Reporter	So
Supreme Court Reporter	S Ct
United States Reports	US
United States Law Week	USLW

▢ Pour la Cour suprême des États-Unis, faire référence aux recueils dans l'ordre de préférence suivant : **US → S Ct → L Ed (2d) → USLW**.

▢ Pour les cours fédérales, se référer à **F** ou **F Supp**.

▢ Pour les cours d'États, renvoyer au recueil régional plutôt qu'au recueil de l'État.

▢ Pour une liste plus étoffée des recueils et de leurs abréviations, voir l'**annexe C-3**.

7.4.2.5 *Référence précise*

United States v McVeigh, 153 F (3d) 1166 **à la p 1170** (10ᵉ Cir 1998).
McVeigh, *supra* note 1 **à la p 1173**.

▢ Indiquer **à la p** avant la référence précise.

Sources étrangères

7.4.2.6 Cour

7.4.2.6.1 Cours fédérales

Cour suprême des États-Unis	*Roe v Wade*, 410 **US** 113 (1973). *AT&T v Iowa Utilities Board*, 66 USLW 3387 (**US** 17 novembre 1997).
Cours d'appel	*Microsystems v Microsoft*, 188 F3d 1115 (**9ᵉ Cir** 1999).
Cours de district	*Yniguez v Mofford*, 730 F Supp 309 (**D Ariz** 1990).

■ La **Cour suprême des États-Unis** ne nécessite pas d'abréviation, à moins de citer au *United States Law Week* (**USLW**). Pour citer à l'USLW, ajouter **US** ainsi que la date (jour, mois et année) entre parenthèses à la fin de la référence.

■ Abréger les cours d'appel de chaque circuit en précisant le numéro du circuit.

■ Utiliser **DC Cir** pour désigner la **Cour d'appel du circuit du *District of Columbia*** et **Fed Cir** pour désigner la **Cour du circuit fédéral**.

■ Pour les cours de district, fournir l'abréviation du nom du district.

7.4.2.6.2 Cours d'États

■ Indiquer le nom de la cour et l'indication géographique entre parenthèses, en utilisant les abréviations des **annexes A-2** et **B**.

■ Ne pas inclure le nom de l'État si celui-ci fait partie du titre du recueil.

■ Ne pas inclure le nom de la cour s'il s'agit du plus haut tribunal de l'État.

> *Peevyhouse v Garland Coal & Mining*, 382 P (2d) 109 (**Okla Sup Ct** 1963).
>
> *Truman v Thomas*, 165 **Cal** Rptr 308 (**Sup Ct** 1980).
>
> *Hinterlong v Baldwin*, 308 **Ill App** (3d) 441 (App Ct 1999).

7.4.2.7 Année de la décision

■ Fournir l'année de la décision entre parenthèses à la fin de la référence. S'il y a une abréviation d'un tribunal, inclure l'année au sein des mêmes parenthèses (**(App Ct 1999)**).

7.4.2.8 Bases de données en ligne

7.4.2.8.1 Westlaw

Intitulé,	identifiant donné par le service	reference précise	(juridiction et/ou cour) (s'il y a lieu).
Fincher v Baker,	1997 WL 675447	à la p 2	(Ala Civ App).

▨ Si le seul identifiant est celui fourni par Westlaw, la decision est non publiée.

7.4.2.8.2 Lexis

Intitulé,	identifiant donné par le service	reference précise	(juridiction et/ou cour) (s'il y a lieu).
Association for Molecular Pathology v Myriad Genetics,	2013 US Lexis 4540	at 5	(USSC).

▨ Si le seul identifiant est celui fourni par Lexis, la decision est non publiée.

7.4.3   Documents gouvernementaux

Indiquer **É-U** au début de la référence.

7.4.3.1 Débats

É-U,	Cong Rec,	édition,	tome,	partie,	référence précise	(date)	(orateur) (facultatif).
É-U,	Cong Rec,		t 125,	15,	à la p 18691	(1979).	
É-U,	Cong Rec,	daily ed,	t 143,	69,	à la p H3176	(22 May 1977)	(Rep Portman).

▨ Faire référence au *Congressional Record* (**Cong Rec**) pour les débats du Congrès qui ont eu lieu après 1873.

▨ Pour se référer aux débats plus anciens du Congrès, consulter le *Bluebook*.

▨ Utiliser **l'édition quotidienne** seulement si le débat ne se trouve pas encore dans l'édition reliée.

7.4.3.2 Sessions de comités

7.4.3.2.1 Fédéral

É-U,	*titre,*	numéro du Congrès,	renseignements sur l'édition	référence précise	(orateur) (facultatif).
É-U,	*Federal Property Campaign Fundraising Reform Act of 2000 : Hearing on HR 4845 Before the House Committee of the Judiciary,*	106ᵉ Cong,	2000	à la p 2-3.	
É-U,	*Assisted Suicide : Legal, Medical, Ethical and Social Issues : Hearing Before the Subcommittee on Health and Environment of the House Committee on Commerce,*	105ᵉ Cong,	Washington, DC, United States Government Printing Office, 1997	à la p 2	(Dr C Everett Koop).

▪ Toujours indiquer l'année de publication. Outre l'année, fournir le plus de renseignements possible sur l'édition.

7.4.3.2.2 État

É-U,	*titre,*	numéro du corps législatif ou année,	numéro ou désignation de la session législative,	État	(renseignements sur l'édition)	référence précise	(orateur) (facultatif).
É-U,	*Rico Litigation: Hearing on S 1197 Before the Senate Comm on Commerce and Econ Dev,*	41ᵉ légis,	1ʳᵉ sess rég 5,	Ariz	(1993)		(affirmé par Barry Wong, analyste politique).

▪ Voir la liste d'abréviations des États à l'**annexe A-2**.

▪ Toujours indiquer l'année de publication et fournir le plus de renseignements possible sur l'édition.

Sources étrangères

7.4.3.3 Rapports et documents

7.4.3.3.1 Fédéral

7.4.3.3.1.1 Documents et rapports numérotés

É-U,	organisme,	*titre*	(numéro),	renseignements sur l'édition	référence precise.
É-U,		*Secrecy: Report of the Commission on Protecting and Reducing Government Secrecy: Pursuant to Public Law 236, 103rd Congress*	(S Doc n° 105-2),	Washington, DC, US Government Printing Office, 1997	à la p 3.
É-U,	Senate Committee on the Budget, 111e Cong,	*Concurrent Resolution on the Budget FY 2010,*		Washington, DC, US Government Printing Office, 2009	à la p 213.

▨ Indiquer l'organisme responsable, à moins qu'il ne soit mentionné dans le titre.

▨ Toujours indiquer l'année de publication et fournir le plus de renseignements possible sur l'édition.

Abréviations des numéros :

Documents	Rapports
HR Doc n°	HR Rep n°
HR Misc Doc n°	HR Conf Rep n°
S Doc n°	S Rep n°
S Exec Doc n°	

7.4.3.3.1.2 Documents non numérotés et *Committee Prints*

É-U,	organisme,	*titre,*	Committee Print (si pertinent),	renseignements sur l'édition	référence precise.
É-U,	Staff of House Committee on Veterans' Affairs, 105th Cong,	*Persian Gulf Illnesses: An Overview,*	Committee Print,	1998	à la p 15.
É-U,	National Commission on Children,	*Beyond Rhetoric: A New American Agenda for Children and Families,*		Washington (DC), The Commission, 1991	à la p 41.

▨ Indiquer le numéro du congrès avec l'organisme si pertinent.

▨ Toujours indiquer l'année de publication et fournir le plus de renseignements possible sur l'édition.

7.4.3.3.2 État

	É-U,	organisme,	*titre*	(numéro) (si pertinent),	renseignements sur l'édition	référence precise.
Documents et rapports numérotés	É-U,	California Energy Commission	*Existing Renewable Resources Account,* vol 1	(500-01-014V1),	2001.	
Documents et rapports non numérotés	É-U,	Washington State Transport Commission,	*Washington's Transportation Plan 2003–2022,*		Washington State Department of Transportation, 2002.	

▨ Fournir le numéro du document, s'il y a lieu.

▨ Toujours indiquer l'année de publication et fournir le plus de renseignements possible sur l'édition.

7.5 FRANCE

7.5.1 Législation

7.5.1.1 Lois et autres instruments législatifs

Titre,	JO,	date de publication,	(NC) (s'il y a lieu),	page,	référence parallèle.
Loi n° 99-493 du 15 juin 1999,	JO,	16 juin 1999,		8759,	(1999) D Lég 3.7.
Ordonnance n° 2001-766 du 29 août 2001,	JO,	31 août 2001,		13946,	(2001) D Lég 2564.
Décret du 5 décembre 1978 portant classement d'un site pittoresque,	JO,	6 décembre 1978	(NC),	9250.	

▦ Inclure le titre si l'instrument législatif n'est pas numéroté. S'il est numéroté, l'inclusion du titre est facultative.

▦ Toujours faire référence au *Journal officiel de la République française* en premier lieu, abrégé **JO**, suivi de la date de publication et du numéro de page. Pour une liste des titres des anciens journaux officiels, voir la section 7.5.3.2. Pour les suppléments du JO, indiquer **(NC)** pour **numéro complémentaire** après la date de publication.

▦ Si possible, indiquer une référence parallèle à un recueil général français, selon les règles à la section 7.5.2.10.

7.5.1.2 Codes

Code civil des Français (1804–1807)	art 9 **CcF**
Code Napoléon (1807–1814)	art 9 **CN**
Code civil (1815–)	art 2203 **C civ**
Code pénal	art 113-10 **C pén**
Code de propriété intellectuelle	art 123(8) **CPI**
Nouveau Code de procédure civile	art 1435 **NC proc civ**
Code de procédure pénale	art 144(2) **C proc pén**

▪ Ne jamais fournir une référence complète pour se rapporter à un code.

▪ Pour faire référence aux codes mentionnés ci-dessus, utiliser le titre abrégé dès la première référence.

▪ Pour faire référence à un code qui n'est pas dans la liste, écrire le nom du code au complet dans la première référence et créer un abrégé si nécessaire (**art 1** *Code de la consommation* **[C conso]**).

7.5.2　Jurisprudence

Toujours indiquer **la pagination en haut** des pages de *La semaine juridique* et non celle du bas.

7.5.2.1　Modèle de base

	Tribunal ou chambre (s'il y a lieu)	**ville** (s'il y a lieu),	**date,**	*intitulé* (s'il y a lieu),	**(année du recueil)**	**recueil**	**partie du recueil** (s'il y a lieu)	**page** et/ou **numéro de la décision**	**(note)** (s'il y a lieu).
Cour de cassation	Cass civ 2e,		14 juin 2001,		(2001)	D	Jur	3075	(annotation Didier Cholet).
Cour d'appel	CA	Paris,	12 janvier 2000,		(2000)	JCP	II	10433	(annotation Philippe Pierre).
Cour de première instance	Trib gr inst	Mans,	7 septembre 1999,		(2000)	JCP	II	10258	(annotation Colette Saujot).

7.5.2.2　Cour

7.5.2.2.1　Tribunaux de première instance

Tribunal	**ville,**	**date,**	*intitulé* (s'il y a lieu),	**(année de publication du recueil**	**semestre)** (s'il y a lieu)	**recueil**	**partie du recueil**	**page**	**(note)** (s'il y a lieu).
Trib admin	Nantes,	27 novembre 1981,	*Mme Robin,*	(1981)		Rec		544.	
Trib gr inst	Paris,	10 septembre 1998,		(1999	1er sem)	Gaz Pal	Jur	37.	

▪ Indiquer la ville où le tribunal siège après le nom du tribunal.

Abréviations des tribunaux :

Tribunal administratif	Trib admin
Tribunal civil ou Tribunal de première instance (Tribunal civil de droit commun avant 1958)	Trib civ
Tribunal commercial	Trib com
Tribunal correctionnel	Trib corr
Tribunal de grande instance (Tribunal civil de droit commun après 1958)	Trib gr inst
Tribunal d'instance (Tribunal civil de droit commun pour les petites créances après 1958)	Trib inst

Pour une liste plus complète des cours et tribunaux, voir l'**annexe B-2**.

7.5.2.2.2 Cour d'appel

CA	ville,	date,	intitulé (s'il y a lieu),	(année de publication	semestre) (s'il y a lieu)	recueil	partie du recueil	page,	numéro de décision,	(annotation).
CA	Orléans,	23 octobre 1997,		(1999	1er sem)	Gaz Pal	Jur	217	n° 94/002561	(annotation Benoît de Roquefeuil).
CA	Paris,	21 mai 2008,	K c E et Sté nationale de télévision France 2,	(2008)		JCP	Jur	390	n° 06/07678.	

7.5.2.2.3 Cour de cassation

Chambre,	date,	(année de publication)	recueil	section,	page,	numéro de décision (s'il y a lieu).
Cass civ 1re,	30 mars 1999,	(1999)	Bull civ	I,	77,	n° 118.
Cass crim,	24 février 2009,	(2009)	D Jur		951,	n° 08-87.409.

Abréviations des cours et des chambres :

Chambre civile	Cass civ 1re
	Cass civ 2^{e}
	Cass civ 3^{e}
Chambre commerciale	Cass com
Chambre sociale	Cass soc
Chambre criminelle	Cass crim
Chambre des requêtes	Cass req
Chambres réunies (avant 1967)	Cass Ch réun
Assemblée plénière (après 1967)	Cass Ass plén
Chambre mixte	Cass mixte

7.5.2.2.4 Conseil d'État

Cour,	date,	intitulé,	année de publication	recueil	page.
CE,	27 janvier 1984,	Ordre des avocats de la Polynésie française,	(1984)	Rec	20.

▪ Abréger *Conseil d'État* par **CE**.

7.5.2.2.5 Conseil constitutionnel

Cour,	date,	intitulé,	(année de publication)	recueil	page,	numéro de la decision.
Cons const,	25 juin 1986,	Privatisations,	(1986)	Rec	61,	86-207 DC.
Cons sonst,	19 juin 2008,		(2008)	JCP Jur	449,	2008-564 DC.

▪ Abréger **Conseil constitutionnel** par **Cons const**.
▪ Indiquer le numéro de la décision à la fin de la référence.

7.5.2.3 Intitulé

Cass com, 22 janvier 1991, *Ouest Abri*, (1991) D Jur 175.

▨ **L'intitulé des causes françaises n'est habituellement pas indiqué, sauf** :

☐ pour se référer à une décision d'un tribunal administratif ou du Conseil d'État (mais pas dans tous les cas) ;

☐ pour se référer à un jugement non publié ou à un jugement résumé dans la partie « Sommaire » d'un recueil ;

☐ pour éviter la confusion (par ex. lorsqu'un tribunal a rendu deux décisions un même jour) ;

☐ lorsque la cause est mieux connue sous le nom des parties que selon les renseignements habituels.

▨ Mettre l'intitulé en italique, entre virgules, après la date à laquelle la décision a été rendue.

7.5.2.4 Année

Paris, 5 février 1999, (**1999** 2e sem) Gaz Pal Jur 452.

▨ Indiquer l'année de publication du volume avant l'abréviation du recueil.

7.5.2.5 Semestre

▨ Pour se référer à la *Gazette du Palais* (**Gaz Pal**), indiquer le numéro du semestre après l'année de publication, dans la parenthèse.

7.5.2.6 Recueil

Cour,	date,	(année de publication du recueil	semes-tre) (s'il y a lieu).	recueil	partie du recueil	page et/ou numéro de décision.
Cass civ 3e,	23 juin 1999,	(2000)		JCP	II	10333.
Cass soc,	3 février 1998,	(1998	1er sem)	Gaz Pal	Jur	176.

▨ Placer un seul espace entre chaque élément : (**1998 1re sem) Gaz Pal Jur 176**.

Liste des recueils les plus courants :

Recueil Dalloz et *Recueil Dalloz Sirey* (de 1945 à aujourd'hui)	D
Gazette du Palais	Gaz Pal
Bulletin de la Cour de cassation, section civile	Bull civ
Semaine Juridique (de 1937 à aujourd'hui)	JCP
Recueil des décisions du Conseil d'État ou Recueil Lebon	RCE ou Rec
Actualité juridique de droit administratif	AJDA

Voir l'**annexe C-3** pour une liste plus complète des abréviations des titres des recueils.

7.5.2.7 Partie du recueil

▪ Lorsque la partie du recueil est numérotée, indiquer le numéro de la partie en chiffres romains après l'année de publication.

▪ Lorsque la partie du recueil n'est pas numérotée, indiquer l'abréviation du titre de la partie.

▪ Ne pas inclure la partie du recueil dans le cas du ***Recueil Lebon*** (**Rec**) ou de l'***Actualité juridique de droit administratif*** (**AJDA**).

Abréviation des titres des parties des recueils :

Assemblée plénière	Ass plén
Chambre mixte	Ch mixte
Chambres des requêtes	Req
Chambres réunies	Ch réun
Chroniques	Chron
Doctrine	Doctr
Informations rapides	Inf
Jurisprudence	Jur
Legislation, Lois et décrets, Textes de lois, etc.	Lég
Panorama de jurisprudence	Pan
Sommaire	Somm

Sources étrangères

7.5.2.8 Page et numéro de la décision

Semaine juridique	Ass plén, 6 novembre 1998, (1999) JCP II **10000 bis**.
Bulletin de la Cour de cassation	Cass civ 2e, 7 juin 2001, (2001) Bull civ II **75, n° 110**.

- Indiquer la première page de la décision après la partie du recueil ou son année de publication.
- Pour la *Semaine juridique*, indiquer le numéro de la décision (par ex. **10000 bis**).
- Pour les *Bulletin de la Cour de cassation*, mentionner le numéro de page et le numéro de la décision, séparés par une virgule et un espace.

7.5.2.9 Référence précise

Trib gr inst Narbonne, 12 mars 1999, (1999 1re sem) Gaz Pal Jur 405 **à la p 406**.

- Étant donné la brièveté de la plupart des jugements, les références précises sont rarement utilisées. Le cas échéant, indiquer la référence précise après le numéro de la première page, précédée de **à la p**.

7.5.2.10 Référence parallèle

Première référence,	référence parallèle.
Cass civ 1re, 26 mai 1999, (1999) Bull civ I 115, n° 175,	**(1999) JCP II 10112.**
Cass crim, 21 janvier 2009, (2009) Bull crim 74, n° 08-83.492,	**(2009) D Jur 374.**

7.5.2.11 Notes, rapports et conclusions

Cass civ 1re, 6 juillet 1999, (1999) JCP II 10217 **(note Thierry Garé)**.

- Si la décision est suivie d'une note, d'un rapport ou d'une conclusion, ajouter cette information à la fin de la référence.
- Inscrire, entre parenthèses, l'information suivante : **note**, **rapport** ou **conclusion**, suivi du nom de l'auteur.

7.5.3 Documents gouvernementaux

Indiquer **France** au début de chaque référence à des documents gouvernementaux.

7.5.3.1 Débats

7.5.3.1.1 De 1787 à 1860

France,	Archives parlementaires,	série,	tome,	date,	référence précise	(orateur) (facultatif).
France,	Archives parlementaires,	1re série,	t 83,	5 janvier 1794,	s 3.	

▨ Abréger *Archives parlementaires : Recueil complet des débats législatifs et politiques des chambres françaises* par **Archives parlementaires**.

▨ Indiquer la série après le titre. La première série couvre les années 1787—1799, alors que la deuxième série couvre les années 1800—1860.

▨ Les références précises se font aux **sections** et non pas aux articles.

▨ Le nom de l'orateur peut être ajouté, entre parenthèses à la fin de la référence.

7.5.3.1.2 De 1871 à aujourd'hui

France,	journal,	chambre,	Débats parlementaires,	division,	numéro et date,	référence précise	(orateur) (facultatif).
France,	JO,	Assemblée nationale,	Débats parlementaires,	Compte rendu intégral,	1re séance du 23 janvier 2001,	à la p 635	(Gilbert Maurel).
France,	JO,	Sénat,	Débats parlementaires,	Compte rendu intégral,	séance du 3 avril 2001.		

▨ À partir de 1871, les débats parlementaires sont publiés dans le *Journal officiel de la République française*, abrégé *JO*.

☐ Indiquer la chambre, suivie de **Débats parlementaires.**

☐ 1871–1880 : omettre la chambre et **Débats parlementaires.**

☐ 1943–1945; 1945–1946; 1947–1958 : indiquer seulement **Débats de [nom de la chambre]**.

Nom des chambres selon les époques :

1881–1940	Chambre des députés	1880–1940	Sénat
1943–1945	Assemblée consultative provisoire		
1945–1946	Assemblée constituante		
1947–1958	Assemblée de l'Union française	1946–1958	Conseil de la République
1958 à aujourd'hui	Assemblée nationale	1958 à aujourd'hui	Sénat

Sources étrangères

La division ne doit être indiquée qu'à partir de 1980 pour l'Assemblée nationale et à partir de 1983 pour le Sénat. Dans le cas de l'Assemblée nationale, les débats parlementaires se scindent en deux : **Compte rendu intégral** et **Questions écrites remises à la Présidence de l'Assemblée nationale et réponses des ministres.** Il existe également deux divisions pour le Sénat : **Compte rendu intégral** et **Questions remises à la Présidence du Sénat et réponses des ministres aux questions écrites.**

Terminer par le numéro (s'il y a lieu) et la date de la séance, puis par la référence précise à la page consultée.

Si nécessaire, ajouter le nom de l'orateur entre parenthèses à la fin de la référence.

7.5.3.2 Anciens journaux officiels

France,	*titre*,	année ou date de publication,	tome ou volume	référence précise.
France,	*Journal officiel de l'Empire français*,	1868,	t 1	à la p 14.
France,	*Gazette nationale, ou le Moniteur universel*,	1er juillet 1791,	t 9	à la p 3.

Les débats parlementaires, les documents parlementaires et les documents non parlementaires **précédant l'année 1871** sont généralement publiés à l'intérieur d'anciennes versions du *Journal officiel de la République française.*

1787–1810	*Gazette nationale, ou le Moniteur universel*
1811–1848	*Moniteur universel*
1848–1852	*Moniteur universel, Journal officiel de la République*
1852–1870	*Journal officiel de l'Empire français*

Le mode de référence peut varier selon l'organisation du journal. Généralement, la référence devrait au moins inclure le titre du journal, l'année de référence ou la date de publication, le tome ou le volume (s'il y a lieu), ainsi que le numéro de la page consultée.

7.5.3.3 Documents parlementaires

7.5.3.3.1 Travaux et réunions parlementaires

France,	chambre,	organisme,	« titre des travaux »,	Compte rendu ou *Bulletin*	(date)	(président) (facultatif).
France,	Assemblée nationale,	Délégation aux droits des femmes,	« Auditions sur le suivi de l'application des lois relatives à l'IVG et à la contraception »,	Compte rendu n° 4	(6 novembre 2001)	(présidente : Martine Lignières-Cassou).
France,	Sénat,	Commission des affaires culturelles,	« Auditions de M Jack Lang, ministre de l'éducation nationale »,	*Bulletin* du 11 juin 2001	(13 juin 2001)	(président : Adrien Gouteyron).

▦ Indiquer le titre des travaux, puis le numéro du compte rendu ou du bulletin correspondant. Les **Comptes rendus** sont utilisés pour les travaux de l'Assemblée nationale, alors que les *Bulletins* sont utilisés pour les travaux du Sénat. Contrairement au terme **Compte rendu**, le terme *Bulletin* est en italique.

▦ Terminer par la date, le président des travaux (facultatif), et la référence précise.

7.5.3.3.2 Rapports d'information

France,	chambre,	organisme (s'il y a lieu),	*titre du rapport,*	par auteur(s),	numéro du rapport	(date)	référence précise.
France,	Sénat,	Délégation pour l'Union européenne,	*Le projet de traité établissant une Constitution pour l'Europe,*	par Hubert Haenel,	rapport n° 3	(1er octobre 2003)	à la p 4.
France,	Assemblée nationale,		*Rapport d'information déposé en application de l'article 145 du Règlement par la mission d'information commune sur le prix des carburants dans les départements d'outre-mer,*	par Jacques Le Guen et Jérôme Cahuzac,	rapport n° 1885	(23 juillet 2009)	à la p 63.

Sources étrangères

7.5.3.4 Documents non parlementaires

France,	organisme,	titre,	numéro, tome ou volume,	renseignements sur l'édition	référence précise	(renseigne- ments additionnels) (facultatif).
France,		Commission d'enquête sur la sécurité du transport maritime des produits dangereux ou polluants,	Rapport n° 2535, t 1			(5 juillet 2000 ; président : Daniel Paul).
France,	Conseil économique et social,	La conjoncture économique et sociale en 2005,		Avis et rapports du Conseil économique et social, JO, n° 2005-09	à la p I-4	(1er juin 2005 ; rapport présenté par Luc Guyau).
France,	Ministère de la justice,	Bulletin officiel,	n° 82		à la p 3	(1er avril–30 juin 2001).

▨ La référence aux documents non parlementaires de France suit le même modèle de référence que les documents non parlementaires canadiens à la section 4.2.

7.6 AUSTRALIE

7.6.1 Législation

7.6.1.1 Lois

Titre	(indication géographique),	référence précise.
Corporations Act 2001	(Cth).	
Electricity Reform Act 2001	(NT).	
Marine Pollution Act 1987	(NSW),	art 53(1)(d).

▨ Écrire le titre abrégé officiel de la loi en italique. Inclure l'année dans le titre.

▨ Indiquer l'abréviation de l'indication géographique immédiatement après le titre, entre parenthèses.

Abréviations des indications géographiques :

Commonwealth	Cth
Territoire de la capitale australienne	ACT
Nouvelle-Galles-du Sud	NSW
Territoire du Nord	NT
Queensland	Qld
Australie méridionale	SA
Tasmanie	Tas
Victoria	Vic
Australie occidentale	WA

Compilations statutaires :

Acts of Parliament of the Commonwealth of Australia	*Queensland Statutes*
Laws of the Australian Capital Territory, Acts	*South Australia Statutes*
Statutes of New South Wales	*Tasmanian Statutes*
Northern Territory of Australia Laws	*Acts of the Victorian Parliament*
Laws of the Northern Territory of Australia	*Victorian Statutes*
Queensland Acts	*Statutes of Western Australia*

7.6.1.2 Législation déléguée (règlements)

Titre	(indication géographique),	référence precise.
Admiralty Rules 2002	(Cth),	art 5(b).
Income Tax Regulations (Amendment) 1996	(Cth).	
Education Regulation 2005	(ACT),	art 5.

La référence aux règlements et aux règles suit le modèle des lois (section 7.6.1.1).

Compilations des règlements :

Commonwealth Statutory Rules
Laws of the Australian Capital Territory, Subordinate Legislation
New South Wales Rules, Regulations, and By-Laws
Queensland Subordinate Legislation
Tasmanian Statutory Rules
Victorian Statutory Rules, Regulations, and By-Laws
Western Australia Subsidiary Legislation

7.6.2   Jurisprudence

7.6.2.1 Modèle de base

Intitulé	(année),	référence neutre	[année du recueil]	volume	recueil	page	(indication géo-graphique et/ou cour) (s'il y a lieu).
Neilson v Overseas Projects Corporation of Victoria Ltd,		[2005] HCA 54.					
Macleod v Australian Securities and Investment Commission,		[2002] HCA 37,		211	CLR	287.	
Standard Portland Cement Company Pty Ltd v Good	(1983),			57	ALJR	151	(PC).
Thwaites v Ryan	(1983),		[1984]		VR	65	(SC).

▨ Donner l'année du recueil seulement si l'année du jugement en est différente.

7.6.2.2 Référence neutre

▨ Plusieurs tribunaux australiens ont adopté un système de référence neutre. Suivre les règles de la référence neutre au Canada (section 3.5), à l'exception de l'année, qui est placée entre crochets.

[année]	cour	numéro	paragraphe.
[2005]	HCA	54	au para 26.

7.6.2.3 *Recueil*

7.6.2.3.1 Law Reports

Abréviations des recueils des *Law Reports* :

Commonwealth Law Reports (de 1903 à aujourd'hui) : Officiel	CLR
Australian Law Reports (de 1973 à aujourd'hui)	ALR
Federal Court Reports (de 1984 à aujourd'hui) : Officiel	FCR
Australian Law Journal Reports (de 1958 à aujourd'hui)	ALJR
Federal Law Reports (de 1956 à aujourd'hui)	FLR
New South Wales Law Reports (de 1971 à aujourd'hui) : Officiel	NSWLR
Queensland State Reports (de 1902–1957) : Officiel	Qd SR
Queensland Reports (de 1958 à aujourd'hui) : Officiel	Qd R
South Australia State Reports (de 1922 à aujourd'hui) : Officiel	SASR
Tasmanian Law Reports (1896–1940) : Officiel	Tas LR
Tasmanian State Reports (1941–1978)	Tas SR
Tasmanian Reports (de 1979 à aujourd'hui) : Officiel	Tas R
Victorian Law Reports (1875–1956)	VLR
Victorian Reports (de 1957 à aujourd'hui) : Officiel	VR
Western Australia Law Reports (1899–1959)	WALR
Western Australia Law Reports (de 1960 à aujourd'hui) : Officiel	WAR
Australian Capital Territory Reports (de 1973 à aujourd'hui)	ACTR
Northern Territory Reports (de 1978 à aujourd'hui)	NTR
Northern Territory Law Reports (de 1992 à aujourd'hui)	NTLR

- Pour les décisions du ***Privy Council*** (PC) et de la ***High Court of Australia*** (HCA), faire référence aux **CLR** et au **ALR** dans cet ordre de préférence.

- Pour les autres décisions de cours générales, renvoyer de préférence au **FCR**.

- Pour les états et territoires australiens, privilégier le recueil étatique ou territorial officiel.

7.6.2.4 *Cour*

Abréviations des cours :

Cour	Abréviation
Privy Council (Australia)	PC
High Court of Australia	HCA
Federal Court of Australia	FCA
Supreme Court of Queensland — Court of Appeal	QCA
Supreme Court of Queensland	QSC
Supreme Court of the Australian Capital Territory	ACTSC
Supreme Court of New South Wales	NSWSC
Supreme Court of New South Wales — Court of Appeal	NSWCA
Supreme Court of Tasmania	TASSC
Supreme Court of Victoria — Court of Appeal	VSCA
Supreme Court of Victoria	VSC
Supreme Court of Southern Australia	SASC
District Court of Southern Australia	SADC
Supreme Court of Western Australia	WASC
Supreme Court of Western Australia — Court of Appeal	WASCA
Supreme Court of the Northern Territory	NTSC

▦ Si l'indication géographique des tribunaux étatiques et territoriaux est évidente, n'indiquer que l'instance de la cour.

7.6.3   Documents gouvernementaux

Indiquer **Austl** au début de la référence.

7.6.3.1 Débats

Austl,	indication géographique,	chambre,	*Parliamentary Debates*	(date)	référence précise	(orateur) (facultatif).
Austl,	Commonwealth,	House of Representatives,	*Parliamentary Debates*	(17 septembre 2001)	à la p 30739	(M Howard, premier ministre).
Austl,	Victoria,	Legislative Assembly,	*Parliamentary Debates*	(23 octobre 1968)	à la p 1197.	

■ Après **Austl**, inscrire l'indication géographique. Voir l'**annexe A-3** pour les abréviations australiennes.

■ Toujours utiliser les *Parliamentary Debates* en tant que recueil.

7.6.3.2 Rapports parlementaires

Austl,	indication géographique,	*titre,*	numéro	(année)	référence précise.
Austl,	Commonwealth,	*Department of Foreign Affairs Annual Report 1975,*	Parl Paper n° 142	(1976)	à la p 5.

■ Écrire **Parl Paper n°** avant le numéro.

7.6.3.3 Rapports non parlementaires

Austl,	indication géographique,	organisme,	*titre*	(type de document)	par auteur(s) (s'il y a lieu),	renseignements sur l'édition	référence précise.
Austl,	Commonwealth,	Royal Commission into Aboriginal Deaths in Custody,	*Report of the Inquiry into the Death of Stanley John Gollan*		par Commissioner Elliott Johnston, QC,	Canberra, Australian Government Publishing Service, 1990	à la p 31.
Austl,	Commonwealth,	Law Reform Commission,	*Annual Report 1998*	(Rapport n° 49),		Canberra, Australian Government Publishing Service, 1988.	

7.6.3.4 Documents des ministères

Auteur,	indication géographique,	*titre,*	service du document,	numéro	(date)	référence précise.
Paul Keating,	Commonwealth (Austl),	*Opening of the Global Cultural Diversity Conference,*	Ministerial Document Service,	n° 172/ 94-95	(27 avril 1995)	à la p 5977.

▨ Si des renseignements supplémentaires sont nécessaires pour identifier précisément l'indication géographique à l'intérieur de l'Australie, fournir l'indication géographique suivie de **Austl** entre parenthèses et avant la virgule précédant le titre.

7.7 NOUVELLE-ZÉLANDE

7.7.1 Législation

7.7.1.1 Lois

Titre	(N-Z),	année/numéro,	volume RS	première page.
Abolition of the Death Penalty Act 1989	(N-Z),	1989/119,	41 RS	1.
Kiwifruit Industry Restructuring Act 1999	(N-Z),	1999/95.		

▨ Fournir le numéro du volume, suivi de **RS** (l'abréviation de *Reprint Series*).

7.7.1.2 Législation déléguée (règlements)

Titre	(N-Z),	année/numéro ou *Gazette* année,	page de la *Gazette*	vol RS	première page.
Kiwifruit Export Regulations 1999	(N-Z),	1999/310.			
Ticketing of Meat Notice 1979	(N-Z),	*Gazette* 1979,	2030.		
High Court Amendment Rules (No 2) 1987	(N-Z),	1987/169,		40 RS	904.

▨ Fournir le numéro du volume, suivi de **RS** (l'abréviation de *Reprint Series*).

7.7.2 Jurisprudence

7.7.2.1 Modèle de base

Intitulé	(année de la décision),	référence neutre	[année du recueil]	volume	recueil	page	(indication géographique et/ou cour) (s'il y a lieu).
R v Clarke,		[2005] NZSC 60.					
Pfizer v Commissioner of Patents,			[2005]	1	NZLR	362	(HC).

7.7.2.2 Référence neutre

▊ La Cour suprême de Nouvelle-Zélande a officiellement adopté un système de référence neutre pour les jugements qui ont été rendus en 2005

[Année]	cour	numéro	paragraphe.
[2005]	NZSC	46	au para 4.

ou après. Suivre les règles de la référence neutre au Canada (section 3.5), à l'exception de l'année, qui est placée entre crochets.

7.7.2.3 Recueil

7.7.2.3.1 Law Reports

▊ Les *Law Reports* sont divisés en séries. **Faire référence aux séries plutôt qu'aux *Law Reports*.**

▊ Puisqu'il n'y a pas de recueil particulier pour le ***Judicial Committee of the Privy Council*** (après 1932), la ***Court of Appeal*** ou la ***High Court***, inclure **PC**, **CA**, ou **HC** à la fin de chaque référence à une décision d'une de ces cours.

Abréviations des séries des *Law Reports* :

New Zealand Law Reports (1883 à aujourd'hui) (Privy Council, Supreme Court of New Zealand, Court of Appeal, High Court)	NZLR
New Zealand Privy Council Cases (1840–1932)	NZPCC
Gazette Law Reports (1898–1953) (Court of Appeal, Supreme Court (High Court), Court of Arbitration)	GLR
District Court Reports (1980 à aujourd'hui)	NZDCR
Magistrates' Court Decisions (1939–1979)	MCD
Magistrates' Court Reports (1906–1953)	MCR
Book of Awards (1894–1991) (Arbitration Court, Court of Appeal)	BA
Employment Reports of New Zealand (1991 à aujourd'hui) (Court of Appeal, Labour Court, Aircrew Industrial Tribunal)	ERNZ
New Zealand Industrial Law Reports (1987–1990) (Labour Court, Court of Appeal, Aircrew Industrial Tribunal)	NZILR
Judgments of the Arbitration Court of New Zealand (1979–1986) (Arbitration Court, Court of Appeal)	NZAC
New Zealand Family Law Reports (1981 à aujourd'hui) (Privy Council, Court of Appeal, High Court, Family Court, Youth Court, District Court)	NZFLR
Criminal Reports of New Zealand (1993 à aujourd'hui) (Court of Appeal, High Court)	CRNZ

7.7.2.4 *Cour*

Privy Council (Nouvelle-Zélande)	PC
New Zealand Supreme Court — établie en 2004	NZSC
New Zealand Court of Appeal	NZCA
New Zealand High Court	NZHC
District Court of New Zealand	DCNZ
Magistrates' Court of New Zealand	Mag Ct NZ
Coroners Court	Cor Ct
New Zealand Employment Court	NZ Empl Ct
Environment Court	Env Ct
Family Court of New Zealand	Fam Ct NZ
*Maori Land Court	Te Kooti Whenua Maori*	Maori Land Ct
Maori Appellate Court	Maori AC
New Zealand Youth Court	NZYC
*Waitangi Tribunal	Te Rōpū Whakamana i te Tiriti o Waitangi*	Waitangi Trib

N.B. Le *Supreme Court Act 2003* a crée la Cour suprême de Nouvelle-Zélande et a aboli les appels au *Privy Council*.

7.7.3   Documents gouvernementaux

Indiquer **N-Z** au début de la référence.

7.7.3.1 *Débats*

N-Z,	*Hansard,*	étape : sujet	(numéro de la question)	date	(orateur) (facultatif).
N-Z,	*Hansard,*	Questions to Ministers : Biosecurity Risk-Motor Vehicle and Equipment Imports	(nº 3)	1er mars 2000	(Ian Ewen-Street).

Hansard fournit le type d'étape : *Questions to Ministers* ; *Debate-General* ; *Report of [nom] Committee* ou *Miscellaneous*.

▨ Indiquer le titre du débat en tant que sujet (**Labour, Associate Minister–Accountability**). Ne pas répéter l'information si l'étape et le sujet sont les mêmes.

7.7.3.2 Documents parlementaires

N-Z,	« titre »,	date,	session	(président) (facultatif)	préfixe et numéro.
N-Z,	« Report of the Government Administration Committee, Inquiry into New Zealand's Adoption Laws »,	août 2001,	46ᵉ parlement	(présidente : Dianne Yates)	
N-Z,	« Report of the Game Bird Habitat Trust Board for the year ended 31 August 1999 »,	février 2000,			C.22.

▨ Ne pas mettre d'espace entre le préfixe et le numéro. La lettre qui précède le numéro (le préfixe) indique le sujet sur lequel porte le rapport.

Sujet	Préfixe
Affaires politiques et étrangères	A
Finance et revenu	B
Environnement	C
Énergie et travaux	D
Bien-être et justice	E
Communications	F
Général	G
Commissions, Royal Commissions	H

7.8 SINGAPOUR

7.8.1 Législation

N.B. Si aucune autre information n'indique que le document législatif provient du Singapour, écrire **Rev Ed Sing**.

7.8.1.1 Documents constitutionnels

▓ Faire référence aux modifications constitutionnelles de la même manière qu'à toute autre forme de législation.

▓ Abréger *Revised Edition* par **Rev Ed**.

> *Constitution of the Republic of Singapore* (1999 Rev Ed), art 12(1).
>
> *Independence of Singapore Agreement 1965* (1985 Rev Ed).
>
> *Republic of Singapore Independence Act* (1985 Rev Ed), n° 9 de 1965, art 2.

7.8.1.2 Lois

Lois incluses dans l'édition refondue	*Penal Code* (Cap 224, 1985 Rev Ed Sing), art 34.
Lois qui n'ont pas encore un chapitre assigné dans l'édition refondue	*United Nations Act 2001* (n° 44 de 2001, Sing), art 2.

▓ Abréger *l'édition refondue des lois de la République de Singapour* par **Rev Ed Sing**.

▓ Abréger chapitre par **Cap**. Pour les lois récentes qui n'ont pas un chapitre assigné dans l'édition refondue, utiliser le numéro de la loi tel qu'indiqué dans l'exemple ci-dessus. Ne pas confondre le numéro de la loi avec le numéro du supplément de la loi (*Acts Supplement*), un numéro attribué à chaque supplément de la *Government Gazette* publiant les amendements subséquents de la loi.

▓ Pour la législation **précédant le 15 août 1945**, ajouter les abréviations suivantes après le titre de la loi :

☐ pour la législation promulguée de la **période de *Straits Settlements*** (du 1ᵉʳ avril 1867 au 15 février 1942), utiliser **SS**.

☐ pour la législation promulguée sous l'administration militaire japonaise lors de l'occupation de Singapour (du 15 février 1942 au 15 août 1945), utiliser **JMA** pour *Japanese Military Administration*.

▓ Pour la législation promulguée **après le 15 août 1945**, utiliser **Sing** pour se référer à la législation promulguée pendant les périodes suivantes :

☐ Administration militaire britannique (*British Military Administration*) ;

☐ Colonie de Singapour (*Colony of Singapore*) ;

☐ État de Singapour (*State of Singapore*) avant et pendant la fédération avec la Malaisie ; et

☐ République de Singapour (*Republic of Singapore*).

Sources étrangères

7.8.1.3 *Modifications et abrogations*

Penal Code (Cap 224, 1985 Rev Ed Sing), art 73, **mod par** *Penal Code (Amendment) Act*, n° 18 de 1998, art 2.

Control of Imports and Exports Act (Cap 56, 1985 Rev Ed Sing), **mod par** *Regulation of Imports and Exports Act 1995* (No 24 of 1995, Sing).

Pour plus de détails, voir la section 2.1.11.

7.8.1.4 *Lois anglaises applicables à Singapour*

Misrepresentation Act (Cap 390, 1994 Rev Ed Sing), art 2.

Hire-Purchase Act (Cap 125, 1999 Rev Ed Sing), art 5.

Faire référence aux lois anglaises applicables à Singapour en vertu du *Application of English Law Act* (Cap 7A, 1994 Rev Ed Sing) en utilisant l'édition refondue de Singapour de la même manière que les lois promulguées par Singapour.

7.8.1.5 *Législation auxiliaire (Règles, règlements, avis, ordonnances)*

7.8.1.5.1 Refondus

Titre	(Cap, type de législation et le numéro, Rev Ed),	référence précise.
Housing and Development Conveyancing Fees Rules	(Cap 129, R 2, 1999 Rev Ed Sing),	r 2.
Telecommunications (Class Licenses) Regulations	(Cap 323, Reg 3, 2000 Rev Ed Sing),	Reg 10.

Pour la législation auxiliaire refondue, le numéro **Cap** est le numéro du chapitre de la loi habilitante.

Utiliser **R** pour indiquer *Rule*, **Reg** pour *Regulation*, **N** pour *Notification* et **O** pour *Order*.

Indiquer l'année de l'édition refondue de la législation auxiliaire.

Abréger **Revised Edition** par **Rev Ed**.

Pour la référence précise, utiliser **r** pour indiquer *rule*, **reg** pour *regulation* **o** pour *order* et **n** pour *notification*.

N.B. Le type de la référence précise peut être différent de celui de la législation auxiliaire (par ex. une règle peut contenir des ordonnances).

7.8.1.5.2 Non refondus

Titre	(S numéro/année Sing),	référence précise.
United Nations (Anti-Terrorism Measures) Regulations 2001	(S 561/2001 Sing),	reg 3.
Monetary Authority of Singapore (Merchant Banks — Annual Fees) Notification 2005	(S 405/2005 Sing),	n 2(2).
Payment and Settlement Systems (finality and Netting) (Designated System) Order 2002	(S 620/2002 Sing),	o 3(a).

7.8.2   Jurisprudence

7.8.2.1 Modèle de base

Intitulé	(année de la décision),	référence neutre,	[année du recueil]	volume	recueil	page	(indication géographique et/ou cour) (s'il y a lieu).
Er Joo Nguang v Public Prosecutor,			[2000]	2	SLR	645	(HC).
Firstlink Energy Pte Ltd v Creanovate Pte Ltd,		[2006] SGHC 19.					
Re Ong Yew Teck	(1960),			26	MLJ	67	(Sing HC).

▨ **Toujours indiquer le nom au complet des parties** afin d'identifier la pluralité des pratiques culturelles gouvernantes à Singapour.

▨ Inclure l'abréviation Sing, sauf si la référence est au *Singapore Law Reports*.

7.8.2.2 Référence neutre

▨ Les tribunaux du Singapour ont officiellement adopté un système de référence neutre. Suivre les règles de la référence neutre au Canada (section 3.5), à l'exception de l'année, qui est placée entre crochets.

[année]	cour	numéro	paragraphe.
[2005]	SGCA	55	[11].

▨ Indiquer les numéros de paragraphe entre crochets (par ex. **[11]**).

La Cour suprême a établi que les références aux Singapore Law Reports ont priorité sur la référence neutre.

7.8.2.3 Recueil

Abréviations des principaux recueils :

Singapore Law Reports	SLR
Singapore Law Reports (Reissue) (1965–2002)	SLR (R)
Malayan Law Journal	MLJ
Criminal Law Aid Scheme News	CLASN
Straits Settlements Law Reports	SSLR

Les *Singapore Law Reports (Reissue)* entre les années 1965 et 2002 ont modifié les résumés précédents et numéroté les paragraphes. Ils sont tout aussi officiels que les *Singapore Law Reports.*

7.8.2.4 Cours

Abréviations des cours :

Cour	Abréviation	Désignation
Court of Appeal	CA	SGCA
High Court	HC	SGHC
District Court	Dist Ct	SGDC
Magistrates' Court	Mag Ct	SGMC

Les cours de première instance n'ont pas de subdivisions.

7.8.2.5 Décisions non publiées sans référence neutre

Intitulé	(date),	numéro de la décision	(indication géographique et/ou cour) (s'il y a lieu).
Public Prosecutor v Loh Chai Huat	(31 mai 2001),	DAC No 36923 de 2000	(Sing Dist Ct).

7.8.2.6 Bases de données en ligne

Intitulé	(date),	Identifiant de la base de don-nées indiqué par le service	(Lawnet)	référence précise	(indication géo-graphique et/ou cour) (s'il y a lieu).
Beryl Claire Clarke and Others v Silkair (Singapore) Pte Ltd	(2001),	Suit Nos 1746, 1748-1752 de 1999	(Lawnet)	at para 10	(Sing HC).

7.8.3   Documents gouvernementaux

7.8.3.1 Débats parlementaires

Parliamentary Debates Singapore: Official Report,	volume	colonne	(date)	(nom de l'orateur) (facultatif).
Parliamentary Debates Singapore: Official Report,	vol 73	à la col 2436	(15 octobre 2001)	(Professeur S Jayakumar).
Parliamentary Debates Singapore: Official Report,	vol 80	à la col 2293	(13 février 2006)	(Professeur Ivan Png Paak Liang).

7.8.3.2 Directives de pratique

Les directives de pratique sont publiées par la Cour suprême pour réglementer les litiges. Jusqu'en 1994, elles étaient publiées sous forme de documents distincts. Depuis, elles ont été consolidées dans un document intitulé *Supreme Court Practice Directions*.

7.8.3.2.1 Directives de pratique consolidées

Sing,	*The Supreme Court Practice Directions*	(année)	partie	article.
Sing,	*The Supreme Court Practice Directions*	(2007)	partie XV	art 123(1).

7.8.3.2.2 Modifications aux directives de pratique

Sing,	DP de la Cour suprême	numéro	de l'an-née,	article.
Sing,	DP de la Cour suprême	n° 1	de 2008,	art 7.

Indiquer **directives de pratique** par **DP**.

7.9 AFRIQUE DU SUD

7.9.1 Législation

7.9.1.1 Lois

Titre,	(S Afr),	numéro	de l'année,	référence précise.
Constitution of the Republic of South Africa 1996,		n° 108	de 1996.	
Consumer Protection Act	(S Afr),	n° 68	de 2008,	art 33.

7.9.1.2 Modifications et abrogations

Constitution of the Republic of South Africa, n° 108 de 1996 **mod par** Constitution of the Republic of South Africa Amendment Act, n° 3 de 1999.

▨ Pour plus de détails, voir la section 2.1.11.

7.9.1.3 Projets de loi

Numéro,	titre,	(S Afr),	session,	parlement,	année,	référence précise.
B30-2005,	Precious Metals Bill	(S Afr),	3e sess,	3e Parl,	2005.	
B26-2005,	Nursing Bill	(S Afr),	3e sess,	3e Parl,	2005,	art 17.

7.9.2 Jurisprudence

7.9.2.1 Modèle de base

Intitulé	(année de la dé-cision),	[année du re-cueil]	vo-lume	recueil	page,	référence précise	(indication géo-graphique et/ou cour) (s'il y a lieu).
Oosthuizen v Stanley,		[1938]		AD	322		(S Afr SC).
Messina Associated Carriers v Kleinhaus,		[2001]	3	S Afr LR	868		(SCA).

Se référer aux *South African Law Reports* ou aux *Butterworths Constitutional Law Reports* autant que possible.

7.9.2.2 Référence neutre

Certains tribunaux d'Afrique du Sud ont officiellement adopté un système de référence neutre. Suivre les règles de la référence neutre au Canada (section 3.5), à l'exception de l'année, qui est placée entre crochets.

[année]	cour	numéro	paragraphe.
[2006]	ZACC	25	au para 1.

7.9.2.3 Recueil

Abréviations des principaux recueils :

All South African Law Reports	All SA
Butterworths Constitutional Law Reports	B Const LR
South African Law Reports, Appellate Division (1910–1946)	S Afr LR, AD
South African Law Reports (1947 à aujourd'hui)	S Afr LR

Pour une liste plus complète des recueils, voir l'**annexe C-3**.

7.9.2.4 Tribunal

Abréviations des tribunaux :

Bophuthatswana High Court	Boph HC
Cape Provincial Division	Cape Prov Div
Ciskei High Court	Ciskei HC
Constitutional Court of South Africa	S Afr Const Ct
Durban and Coast Local Division	D&C Local Div
Eastern Cape Division	E Cape Div
Labour Court of South Africa	S Afr Labour Ct
Labour Court of Appeal of South Africa	S Afr Labour CA
Land Claims Court of South Africa	S Afr Land Claims Ct
Natal Provincial Division	Natal Prov Div
Northern Cape Division	N Cape Div
Orange Free State Provincial Division	OFS Prov Div
South-Eastern Cape Division	SE Cape Div
Supreme Court of Appeal of South Africa	S Afr SC
Transkei High Court	Transkei HC
Transvaal Provincial Division	Transv Prov Div
Venda High Court	Venda HC
Witwatersrand Local Division	Wit Local Div

7.9.3   Documents gouvernementaux

7.9.3.1 Débats

S Afr,	*Hansard,*	chambre,	date,	référence précise	(orateur) (facultatif).
S Afr,	*Hansard,*	Assemblée nationale,	9 février 2009,	à la p 1	(MJ Ellis).

7.9.3.2 Rapports, documents de discussion et exposés

Titre,	commission (s'il y a lieu),	numéro de projet (s'il y a lieu)	(date)	référence précise.
Truth and Reconciliation Commission of South Africa Report			(29 octobre 1998)	au ch 1, para 91.
Report on Trafficking in Persons,	South African Law Reform Commission,	projet n° 131	(août 2008)	à la p 23.
Domestic Violence,	South African Law Reform Commission,	projet n° 100	(30 mai 1997)	à la p 14.

▦ Inclure le nom de la commission si elle n'est pas mentionnée dans le titre.

INDEX

Accord

Accord de libre-échange canado-américain, rapports de Groupes spéciaux, F-117

Accord de libre-échange nord-américain (ALÉNA), rapports de Groupes spéciaux, F-118

Accord general sur les tariffs douaniers et le commerce (GATT) 1947, rapports de Groupes spéciaux, F-115

Accord général sur les tariff douaniers et le commerce (GATT), F-103

Traités et accords internationaux, F-89

Accord de libre-échange canado-américain, rapports de Groupes spéciaux, F-117

Accord de libre-échange nord-américain (ALÉNA), rapports de Groupes spéciaux, F-118

Accord general sur les tarifs douaniers et le commerce (GATT), F-103

Afrique du Sud, F-233

abrogations, F-233

documents gouvernementaux, F-236
   débats, F-236
   discussion, documents de, F-236
   exposés, F-236
   rapports, F-236

jurisprudence, F-233
   modèle de base, F-233
   recueil, F-234
   référence neutre, F-234
   tribunal, F-235

lois, F-235

modifications, F-233

projets de loi, F-233

Allocutions et textes présents durant des conférences, F-156

Annexes, F-32, F-96

annexe II des LRC 1985, F-32

Arbitrage

arbitrage international, décisions, F-119

Canada
   décisions non publiées, F-149
   décisions publiées, F-148

États-Unis, décisions, F-199

Nouvelle-Zélande, cours d'arbitrage,

Organisation mondiale de la propriété intellectuelle (OMPI), décisions, F-119

Archives

documents archivés, F-162

documents uniquement disponibles dans les archives, F-16

France, débats législatifs et politiques, F-214
   Archives parlementaires, F-214

Manuscrits non publiés et archives, F-154

Arrêtés *voir* **Jurisprudence canadienne**

Articles

d'un périodique, F-127
   année de publication, F-128
   auteur, F-127
   modèle de base, F-127
   numéro, F-129
   première page, F-131
   référence précise, F-131
   série, F-129
   titre de l'article, F-128
   titre du périodique, F-129
   volume, F-129

Australie, F-217

documents gouvernementaux, F-221
   débats, F-222
   documents des ministères, F-222
   rapports non parlementaires, F-222
   rapports parlementaires, F-222

jurisprudence, F-219
   cour, F-221
   modèle de base, F-219
   recueil (*Law Reports*), F-220
   référence neutre, F-219

législation, F-217
   lois, F-217
   législation déléguée (règlements), F-218

référence neutre des traités, F-92

Auteur *voir* **Monographies**

Azimut, F-66

BAILII, F-188

Bibliographies, F-3

Bulletin d'interprétation, F-84

Canonique, F-153

CD-ROM, F-169

Charte
Canada, F-33
Nations Unies, F-92

Chroniques
jurisprudence, de, F-150
législation, de, F-150

Citations,
d'une source dans une autre langue, F-19
emplacement, F-18
forme, F-18

Code civil *voir* **Codes**

Code de conduit *voir* **Codes—déontologie, codes de**

Codes
Canada
civil, F-24
déontologie, codes de, F-148
désignation du tribunal, F-58
droit canonique, F-153
États-Unis
Uniform Codes, F-196
ISO 3166-1 alpha-3 (code de pays), F-57
services électroniques, F-164

Commentaires, F-167
de décisions, F-152
du ministre, F-35, F-152
France
annotations, F-208
modèle de base, F-208

Commission européenne des droits de l'homme, F-110

Commission interaméricaine des droits de l'homme, F-113

Commissions, F-85

Communautés européennes
Cour de justice des Communautés européennes, F-109
débats du Parlement européen, F-100
Journal officiel de l'Union européenne, F-100
règlements, directives et decisions, F-98

Conférences
allocutions et textes, 6.13, F-156
Conférence des Nations Unies sur le commerce et le développement, F-93
conférence ou symposium, procédures publiées, F-136
documents de conférences intergouvernementales, F-86

Conseil de l'Europe, F-101

Cour européenne des droits de l'homme, F-110

Cour internationale de justice, F-107
jugements, ordonnances et avis consultatifs, F-108
mémoires, plaidoiries et documents, F-109

Couronne, F-54

Cours (éducation)
notes de cours, F-157
recueils de cours, F-157

Débats
Afrique du Sud, F-236
Australie, F-157
Canada
débats législatifs, F-77
rapports publiés dans un journal des débats, F-80
Conseil de l'Europe, F-101
États-Unis, F-203
France, F-214
Nouvelle-Zélande, F-226

Parlement européen, F-100
Royaume-Uni, F-189
Singapour, F-232

Décisions *voir* **Jurisprudence**

Déontologie, codes de, F-148

Dictionnaires, F-143
encyclopédies, F-144
généraux, F-143
spécialisés, F-143

Digital, support *voir* **Sources électroniques**

Dissertations, F-155

Doctrine et autres documents, F-89
documents internationaux, F-89
    Accord général sur les tarifs douaniers et
      le commerce, F-103
    Conseil de l'Europe, F-101
    documents des Nations Unies, F-92
      annexes, F-96
      annuaires, F-97
      Charte des Nations Unies, F-92
      documents officiels, F-93
      miméographiés, documents, F-97
      périodiques, F-97
      publications de vente, F-98
      séances, F-93
      suppléments, F-94
    Organisation de coopération et de
      développement économiques, F-104
    Organisation des États américains, F-102
    Organisation mondiale du commerce,
      F-103
    traités et autres accords internationaux,
      F-90
    Union européenne, F-98
      autres documents, F-100
      débats du Parlement européen, F-100
      décisions, F-98
      directives, F-98
      règlements, F-98
jurisprudence, F-106
    Accord de libre-échange canado-amér-
      icain, grouprs spéciaux, F-117

    Accord de libre-échange nord-américain,
      groupes spéciaux, F-118
    Accord général sur les tarifs douaniers et
      le commerce, groupes spéciaux,
      arbitrage international, décisions, F-119
    Commission européenne des droits de
      l'homme, F-110
    Commission interaméricaine des droits
      de l'homme, F-113
    Cour de justice des Communautés
      européennes, F-109
    Cour européenne des droits de l'homme,
      F-110
    Cour interaméricaine des droits de
      l'homme, F-112
    Cour permanente de Justice interna-
      tional, F-106, F-107
    décisions de droit international prises
      devant des cours nationales, F-120
    Organe d'appel de l'Organisation
      mondiale du commerce, groupes
      spéciaux, F-116
    Organisation mondiale de la propriété
      intellectuelle, décisions d'arbitrage,
      F-119
    Tribunaux de droit pénal international,
      F-114
sites Internet, F-120

Documents gouvernementaux canadiens,
  F-77
documents parlementaires, F-77
    débats législatifs, F-77
    feuilletons, F-78
    journaux, F-78
    procès-verbaux, F-79
    rapports publiés dans un journal des
      débats, F-80
    rapports publiés séparément, F-80
    Sessional Papers, F-79
documents non parlementaires, F-81
    auteurs ou éditeur particulier,
    bulletins d'interprétation, F-84
    conférences intergouvernementales,
      documents de, F-86
    modèle de base, F-81

rapports d'enquêtes et de commissions, F-85

DVD, F-169

eJournals *voir* **Revues en ligne**

Encyclopédies, F-144
Canadian Encyclopedic Digest, F-144
common law, F-146
France, F-146

Enquêtes, rapports, F-85

Entrevues, F-161

Étapes successives d'une cause, F-68
antérieures et postérieures, F-69
antérieures, F-68
authorisation de pourvoi, F-69
postérieures, F-68

États-Unis, F-192
constitution, fédérale et des états, F-192
documents gouvernementaux, F-203
    débats, F-203
    rapports et documents, F-205
        état, F-206
        fédéral, F-205
    sessions de comités, 7.4.3.2, F-204
        état, F-204
        fédéral, F-204
jurisprudence, F-199
    année de la décision, F-202
    base de données en ligne, F-202
        Lexis, F-203
        Westlaw, F-202
    cour, F-202
        fédérale, F-202
        d'état, F-202
    intitulé, F-200
    modèle de base, F-199
    recueil et série, F-200
    référence neutre, F-200
    référence précise, F-201
législation, F-192
    codes, F-193
    constitutions des états, F-192
    constitution fédérale, F-192

lois, F-193
lois sessionnelles, F-195
recueil non officiel des lois sessionnelles, F-196
projets de loi et résolutions, F-197
    états, F-198
    projets de loi fédéraux, F-197
    resolutions fédérales, F-197
règles et règlements, F-198
    Code of Federal Regulations, F-198
    registre administratif, F-199
Uniform Codes, Uniform Acts et *Restatements*, F-196

Ex rel, F-56

Factum, F-5
plaidoiries et documents de preuve à l'audience, F-74
références dans le texte, F-5

Feuilles mobiles, F-28, F-138
législation canadienne, F-28
monographies, F-132
statuts (É-U), F-193

Fils de presse, F-158

Formules introductives, F-8

France, F-146, F-151, F-207
chroniques publiées dans les recueils généraux, F-151
codes,
documents gouvernementaux, F-213
    anciens journaux officiels, F-215
    débats, F-214
    documents non parlementaires, F-217
    documents parlementaires, F-216
        travaux et réunions parlementaires, F-216
        rapports d'information, F-216
jurisprudence, F-208
    année, F-211
    conclusions, F-213
    cour, F-208
        Conseil constitutionnel, F-210
        Conseil d'État, F-210
        Cour d'appel, F-209

Cour de cassation, F-209
    tribunaux de première instance, F-208
intitulé, F-211
modèle de base, F-208
notes, F-213
numéro de la décision, F-213
page, F-213
partie du recueil, F-212
rapports, F-213
recueil, F-211
référence parallèle, F-213
référence précise, F-213
semestre, F-211
législation, F-207
codes, F-207
modèle de base, F-146
notes, F-151
rubriques, F-147
sources *voir aussi* chroniques de jurisprudence et de legislation; Canadian, F-150

GATT *voir* **Accord general sur les tariffs douaniers et le commerce, F-103**

Gazettes, F-42
abréviations, F-42
décrets, F-43
    fédéral, F-43
    provincial et territorial, F-44
instructions royales, F-44
modèle de base, F-42
proclamations, F-44

Historiques, documents légaux, F-152
droit canonique, F-153
droit romain, F-152
droit Talmudique, F-153

Ibid, 1.4.2, **F-12**

Infra, **F-13**

Institut canadien d'information juridique (CanLII), F-65

Intitulé *voir aussi* **Jurisprudence canadienne**

Journaux, F-158
    éditoriaux, F-159
    lettres à la redaction, F-159

Juge, F-67
Royaume-Uni, F-177

Jugements non publiés, F-65; F-72

Jurisprudence, F-10; F-6; F-49;F-106; F-150; F-182; F-199; F-208; F-219; F-224; F-230; F-233
voir aussi **Arbitrage; Documentation internationale**
année de la décision, F-57
bases de données en ligne, F-64
    jugements non publiés, F-65
        autres, F-66
        Azimut, F-66
        BAILII, F-188
        CanLII, F-65
        Lexis, F-66; F-203
        Quicklaw, F-65
        WestlawNext Canada, F-66
        Westlaw, F-202
    jugements publiés, F-65
cause, étapes successives d'une, F-68
    antérieures, F-68
    autorisation de pourvoi, F-69
    postérieures, F-68
documents à l'audience, F-74
étapes successive d'une cause, F-68
juge, F-67
jugements interlocutoires, F-72
jugements non publiés, F-72
indication géographique, F-67
intitulé, F-51
    agences d'aide sociale, F-55
    Couronne, F-54
    Entités gouvernementales, F-54
    expressions procédurales, F-56
    ex rel, F-56
    faillites et mises sous séquestre, F-53
    intitulés different pour une même cause, F-56
    municipaux, conseils et organismes, F-55
    nom des parties, F-52
    noms corporatifs et de sociétés, F-52
    noms de parties protégées, F-56
    pays, unités fédérales, provinces et municipalités, F-53

personne représentée par un tuteur, F-52
renvois constitutionnels, F-56
scolaires, conseils, F-55
sociétés d'État, F-55
sub nom, F-56
syndicats, F-55
testaments et successions, F-53
tierce partie agissant pour une des
parties, F-56
titres de lois, F-53
modèle de base, F-50
référence neutre disponible, F-50
référence neutre non disponible, F-51
organes et tribunaux administratifs, F-72
décisions en ligne, F-73
références aux recueils imprimés, F-72
plaidoiries, F-74
recueil imprimé, F-61
année du recueil, F-61
non officiel, F-63
officiel, F-62
première page, F-64
semi-officiel, F-62
série, F-64
référence neutre, F-57
année, F-58
identifiant du tribunal, F-58
numéro de la décision, F-59
référence précise, F-60
modèle de base, F-60
recueil auquel les rérences sont faites, F-61
sources, F-49

Jurisprudence canadienne, F-49

administratifs, organes et tribunaux, F-72
décisions en ligne, F-73
recueils imprimés, F-72
année de la décision, F-57
étapes successives d'une cause, F-68
antérieures et postérieures, F-69
antérieures, F-68
authorisation de pourvoi, F-69
postérieures, F-68
jugements interlocutoires, F-72
jugements non publiés et sans référence
neutre, F-12
indication géographique et cour, F-67

intitulé, F-51
agences d'aide sociale, F-55
Couronne, F-54
entités gouvernementales, F-54
expressions procédurales,
faillites et mises sous séquestre, F-53
intitulés différents pour une même cause,
municipaux, conseils et organismes, F-55
nom des parties, F-52
noms corporatifs et de sociétés, F-52
noms de parties protégées, F-56
pays, unités fédérales, provinces et
muncipalités, F-53
personne représentée par un tuteur, F-52
renvois constitutionnels, F-56
scolaires, conseils, F-55
sociétés d'État, F-55
syndicats, F-55
testaments et successions, F-53
tierce partie agissant pour une des
parties, F-56
titre de lois, F-53
juge, F-67
jugements non publiés et sans référence
neutre, F-72
modèle de base, F-50
plaidoiries et documents à l'audience, F-74
recueil auquel les references sont faites, F-61
recueils imprimés, F-72
référence neutre, F-50; F-51
référence précise, F-31; F-34; F-60
services électroniques, F-50; F-73
non publiés et sans référence, F-49
neutre, F-49
autres services, F-66
Azimut, F-66
CanLII, F-65
Lexis, F-66
Quicklaw, F-65
WestlawNext Canada, F-66
publiés et avec référence neutre, F-49
sources, F-49
hiérarchie des sources, F-49

Langue

rédaction d'un texte en langue étrangère, F-19
citations, F-19

notes de bas de page, F-20
source, F-19

Législation canadienne, F-10; F-23
arrêté, F-45
codes, F-34
valeurs mobilières, commission de, F-46
Gazettes, F-42
    décret, F-43
      fédéral, F-43
      provincial et territorial, F-44
    modèle de base, F-42
    proclamations et Instructions royales, F-44
lois, F-23
    abrogations, F-32
    année, F-30
    annexes, F-32
    chapitre, F-31
    constitutionnelles, F-33
    indication géographique, F-29
    loi contenue dans une autre loi, F-33
    lois révisées et recueils annuels, F-28
    modèle de base, F-23
    modications, F-32
    recueils à feuilles mobiles, F-28
    référence précise, F-24; F-31; F-34
    remises en vigueur, F-34
    session, F-30
    sources, F-24
    supplément, F-30
    titre, F-27
    version électronique officielle, F-15
Nunavut, F-40
projets de loi, F-35
règlements municipaux, F-45
règlements, F-36
    règlements fédéraux, F-37
    règlements provinciaux et territoriaux, F-37
      Alberta, F-38
      Colombie-Britannique, F-38
      Île-du-Prince-Édouard, F-40
      Manitoba, F-38
      Nouveau-Brunswick, F-38
      Nouvelle-Écosse, F-39
      Nunavut, F-40
      Ontario, F-40
      Québec, F-41
      Saskatchewan, F-41
      Terre-Neuve-et-Labrador, F-38
      Territoires du Nord-Ouest, F-39
      Yukon, F-41, F-45
règles de pratique, F-45

Lettres
lettres à la rédaction, F-159

Lexis, F-66; F-203

Lois constitutionnelles, F-33
Canada, F-33
États-Unis, fédéral et des états, F-192
référence précise, F-34
Singapour, F-228
sources, F-34

Lois sessionnelles (É-U), F-193

Manuscrits, F-154
à paraître, F-154
dissertations, F-155
modèle de base, F-154
thèses, F-155

Mémoire, F-109; F-113

Monographies, F-132
année d'édition, F-138
auteur, F-133
    coauteurs, F-133
    directeur d'un ouvrage collectif, F-133
    directeur ou correcteur de l'ouvrage d'un autre auteur, F-134
      nom de l'auteur fait partie du titre, F-134
      nom de l'auteur ne fait pas partie du titre, F-134
    traducteur, F-134
      traduction de l'auteur, F-135
      traduction professionnelle, F-135
    un seul auteur, F-133
conférence ou symposium, F-136
directeur d'ouvrage *voir* auteur, F-133
édition, F-138
feuilles mobiles, F-138
lieu d'édition, F-139

maison d'édition, F-139
modèle de base, F-132
référence précise, F-140
titre, F-135
    procédures publiées de conférences ou
        symposia, F-136
traducteur *voir* auteur
volume, numéro de, F-136
    livres en anglais, F-137
        volumes portants des titres différents,
        F-137
        volumes portant le même titre, F-137
    livres en français, F-136

Municipalités, F-53
arrêtés, F-45
intitulé, F-53
règlements municipaux, F-45

Nations Unies, F-89
annuaires, F-97
Charte des Nations Unies, F-92
documents officiels, F-93
    séances, F-93
    suppléments, F-94
    annexes, F-96
miméographies, documents, F-97
périodiques, F-97
publications de vente, F-98

Non françaises, sources, F-7

Non parlementaires, documents, F-81
Australie, F-222
Canada, F-81
    bulletins d'interprétation, F-84
    conférences intergourvernementales, F-86
    modèle de base, F-81
    rapports d'enquêtes et de commissions,
        F-85
France, F-215
Royaume-Uni, F-191

Note de service, F-5; F-213

Notes de bas de page, F-6
combinaison, F-7
création, F-6
emplacement, F-7

formules introductives, F-8
indication dans le texte, F-7
où utiliser, F-6
parenthèses, information entre, F-9
quand utiliser, F-6
références aux sources non françaises, F-7

Nouvelle-Zélande, F-223
documents gouvernementaux, F-226
    débats, F-226
    documents parlementaires, F-227
jurisprudence, F-224
    modèle de base, F-224
    référence neutre, F-224
    recueil, F-224
    cour, F-226
législation, F-223
    législation déléguée (règlements), F-223
    lois, F-223

Nouvelles, sources de, F-158

Nunavut, F-35; F-40

**Organes et tribunaux administratifs *voir*
    aussi Jurisprudence**
décisions en ligne, F-73
références aux recueils imprimés, F-72

**Organisation mondiale de la propriété
    intellectuelle (OMPI), F-119**

**Organisation mondiale du commerce
    (OMC)**
documents, F-103
rapports de groupes spéciaux, F-116

Périodiques, F-157

Proclamations, F-44

Projets de loi
Afrique du Sud, F-233
Canada, fédéral et provincial, F-35
Écosse, F-180
États-Unis, fédéral et des états, F-197; F-197
Irlande du Nord, F-180
Royaume-Uni, F-180; F-180

Propriété intellectuelle, F-119; F-162
brevets, F-162

droits d'auteur, F-163
marques de commerce, F-163

Québec
codes, F-34; F-41
feuilles mobiles, F-28; F-30
règlements, F-24

Quicklaw (QL), F-65

Rapports annuels, F-28

Recensions (*book reviews*), F-149

Recueil *voir aussi* Jurisprudence canadienne
Année, F-61
non officiel, F-63
officiel, F-62
première page, F-64
semi-officiel, F-62
séries, F-64

Recueils encyclopédiques, F-144
Canadian Encyclopedic Digests, F-144
    version électronique, F-144
    version imprimée, F-144
common law, F-146
France, F-146
    abréviations, F-146
    modèle de base, F-146
    rubriques, F-147
Halsbury's Laws of Canada, F-145
    version électronique, F-145
    version imprimée, F-145

Référence neutre *voir aussi* Jurisprudence canadienne
Afrique du Sud, F-234
Australie
    jurisprudence, F-219
    traités, F-92
États-Unis, F-200
étrangères, sources, F-176
jurisprudence canadienne, F-50; F-57
    année, F-58
    identifiant du tribunal, F-58
    numéro de la décision, F-59
    services électroniques,

jugements non publiés sans reference
    neutre, F-65
jugements publiés avec référence
    neutre, F-65
Nouvelle-Zélande, F-224
Royaume-Uni, F-183
    Écosse, F-187
    Irlande du Nord, F-187
    Irlande, F-187
    modèle de base, F-186
Singapour, F-230; F-231

Références
« ci-dessous », F-14; F-14
« ci-dessus », F-14
ibid, F-12
infra, F-13
source originale, F-16
supra, F-13
titre abrégé, F-10
    doctrine, F-12
    jurisprudence, F-11
    législation, F-10
    modèle de base, 1.4.1.1, F-10

Règlements *voir aussi* Législation
Afrique du Sud, F-233
Australie, F-217
Canada, F-36
    règlements non refondus, F-37
    règlements refondus, F-37
    municipaux, F-45
    provincinciaux et territoriaux, F-37
États-Unis, F-192
France, F-207
hors cour, F-74
Nouvelle-Zélande, F-223
Royaume-Uni, F-178
Singapour, F-227
Union européenne, F-98

Règles de pratique, F-45

Règles de procedure *voir* Règles de pratique

Réimpressions
Nouvelle-Zélande
    Reprint Series, F-223

Royaume-Uni, F-186

Remarques, F-152

Renvois
avec renvois aux, F-20
constitutionnels, F-56

Restatements (É-U), F-196

Revues en ligne, F-164

Romain, droit, F-152

Royales, proclamation et instructions, F-44

Royaume-Uni, F-178
jurisprudence, F-182
lois, F-178
    Écosse, F-179
    Irlande du Nord, F-178
    Pays Galles, F-179
projets de loi, F-180
    Écosse, F-180
    Irlande du Nord, F-180
    Royaume-Uni, F-180
règlements, F-181
    Écosse, F-181
    Irlande du Nord, F-181
    Pays de Galles, F-182
    Royaume-Uni, F-181

Sic, quand utiliser, F-18

Sierra Leone, Cour spéciale, F-114

Singapour, F-227
avis *voir* législation auxiliaire
documents gouvernementaux, F-232
    débats parlementaires, F-232
    directives de pratique, F-232
jurisprudence, F-230
    bases de données en ligne, F-232
    cours, F-231
    décisions non publiées sans référence
        neutre, F-231
    modèle de base, F-230
    recueil, F-231
    référence neutre, F-230
législation, F-227
    abrogations, F-229

documents constitutionnels, F-228
    législation auxiliaire, F-229
        non refondus, F-230
        refondus, F-229
    lois, F-228
    lois anglaises applicables à Singapour,
        F-229
    modifications, F-229
ordonnances *voir* legislation auxiliaire
règles *voir* législation auxiliaire
règlements *voir* législation auxiliaire

Sites Internet *voir* Sources électroniques

Sources des juridictions de droit civil, F-177

**Sources des juridictions de la common law,
    F-175**
Afrique du Sud *voir* Afrique du Sud
année, F-175
Australie *voir* Australie
cas historique, F-175
citation neutre, F-176
chroniques publiées, F-150
décisions non publiées, F-176
États-Unis *voir* États-Unis
forme abrégé, F-175
forme générale, F-175
intitulé, F-175
juge, F-177
juridiction et cour, F-176
modèle de base, F-175
Nouvelle-Zélande *voir* Nouvelle-Zélande
référence précise, F-175
Royaume-Uni *voir* Royaume-Uni
service électronique, F-176
Singapour *voir* Singapour

Sources électroniques, F-15; F-164
autres, F-169
balado, F-15
bases de données en ligne, F-165
blogues, F-166
    commentaires, F-167
    entrées, F-166
CD-ROM, F-169
documents internationaux, F-15
DVD, F-169

identifiants numériques d'objets, F-170
journaux web (blogues), F-166
   commentaires, F-167
   entrées, F-166
jurisprudence, F-165
   décisions en ligne, F-165
   non publiée et sans référence neutre, F-65
      autres services, F-66
      Azimut, F-66
      BAILII, F-188
      CanLII, F-65
      Lexis, F-66; F-203
      Quicklaw, F-65
      WestlawNext Canada, F-66
      Westlaw, F-202
législation canadienne, F-24
réseaux sociaux, F-167
   Facebook, F-168
   Reddit, F-168
   twitter, F-167
revues en ligne, F-165
services électroniques, F-164
sites Internet, F-166
sources secondaires, F-127
videos, F-169

Sources étrangères *voir* **Juridictions de la common law; France**

Statuts *voir* **Législation**

Sub nom, **F-56**

Symposium, F-136

Talmud, F-153

Thèses, F-155

Timor oriental, Groupes d'enquête sur les crimes graves, F-114

Titre abrégé, F-10
doctrine, F-12
jurisprudence, F-11
législation, F-10
modèle de base, F-10

Titre d'un arrêt *voir* **Intitulé**

Traduction
de l'auteur du texte, F-135
langue étrangère, rédaction d'un texte en, F-19
professionnelle, F-135
titre de doctrine, F-135

Traités et accords internationaux, F-89
modèle de base, F-89
abréviations, F-89

Tribunal de première instance (CE), F-109

Tribunaux de droit pénal international, F-114

Uniform Codes et *Uniform Acts* (É-U), F-196

Union européenne *voir* **Communautés européennes**

Valeurs mobilières, commission de, F-46

WestlawNext Canada, F-66

Westlaw, F-202

APPENDICES

ANNEXES

TABLE OF CONTENTS / TABLE DES MATIÈRES

A. Jurisdiction abbreviations - *Abréviations de juridictions*.....A-5

    (A-1)   Abbreviations for Canada - *Abréviations canadiennes* A-5

    (A-2)   Abbreviations for the United States - *Abréviations américaines*........... A-7

    (A-3)   Abbreviations for Australia - *Abréviations australiennes* A-8

    (A-4)   Other Jurisdictional Abbreviations - *Abréviations d'autres juridictions*... A-8

    (A-5)   Abbreviations of International Organizations - *Abréviations d'organismes internationaux*... A-9

B. Courts and Tribunals - *Cours et tribunaux* A-13

    (B-1)   General Rules - *Règles générales* A-13

    (B-2)   Abbreviations - *Abréviations*... A-15

    (B-3)   Neutral citation - *Référence neutre*.. A-25

C. Caselaw Reporters - *Recueils de jurisprudence* A-31

    (C-1)   Canadian Official Reporters - *Recueils officiels canadiens* A-31

    (C-2)   Canadian Semi-Official Reporters - *Recueils canadiens semi-officiels*.. A-31

    (C-3)   Other Reporters - *Autres recueils*.. A-33

D. Periodicals and Yearbooks - *Périodiques et annuaires* A-75

    Abbreviations - *Abréviations* A-75

E. Online Databases - *Bases de données en ligne*................. A-115

    Abbreviations - *Abréviations* A-115

APPENDIX A / ANNEX A

A. JURISDICTION ABBREVIATIONS ~ ABRÉVIATIONS DE JURIDICTIONS

(A-1) Abbreviations for Canada ~ Abréviations canadiennes

Jurisdiction	Statutes and Gazettes	Regulations	Courts and Journals	Neutral Citation	Law Reporters
Alberta	A	Alta	Alta	AB	A or Alta
British Columbia / Colombie-Britannique	BC	BC	BC	BC	BC
Canada	C	C	C or Can	–	C or Can
Lower Canada / Bas-Canada	LC	LC	LC	–	LC
Manitoba	M	Man	Man	MB	Man
New Brunswick / Nouveau-Brunswick	NB	NB	NB	NB	NB
Newfoundland[1] Terre-Neuve[2]	N	Nfld	Nfld	NF	Nfld
Newfoundland & Labrador[3] / Terre-Neuve-et-Labrador[4]	NL	NL	NL	NL (NF — before 19 March 2002 / avant le 19 mars 2002)	Nfld
Northwest Territories / Territoires du Nord-Ouest	NWT	NWT	NWT	NWT	NWT
Nova Scotia / Nouvelle-Écosse	NS	NS	NS	NS	NS
Nunavut	Nu	Nu	Nu	NU	Nu
Ontario	O	O	Ont	ON	O
Prince Edward Island / Île-du-Prince-Édouard	PEI	PEI	PEI	PE	PEI
Province of Canada	Prov C	Prov C	Prov C	–	–
Quebec / Québec	Q	Q	Q (Journals) or Qc (Courts)	QC	Q
Saskatchewan	S	S	Sask	SK	Sask
Upper Canada / Haut-Canada	UC	UC	UC	–	UC
Yukon	Y	Y	Y	YK	Y

[1] **Gazette**: before 21 December 2001 / **Regulations**: before 13 December 2001 / **Most other purposes including statutes**: before 6 December 2001.

[2] **Gazette**: avant le 21 décembre 2001 / **Règlements**: avant le 13 décembre 2001 / **Pour le reste (incluant les lois)** : avant le 6 décembre 2001.

[3] **Gazette**: 21 December 2001 and after / **Regulations**: 13 December 2001 and after / **Most other purposes including statutes**: 6 December 2001 and after.

[4] **Gazette**: depuis le 21 décembre 2001 / **Règlements** : depuis le 13 décembre 2001 / **Pour le reste (incluant les lois)** : depuis le 6 décembre 2001.

Appendices / Annexes

Commonly used Canadian Province Abbreviations / Abréviations couramment utilisées des provinces canadiennes :

The following is a list of commonly used Canadian province abbreviations. Use them when referring to provinces in documents that are not mentioned in the previous table (e.g. "F Allard et al, eds, *Private Law Dictionary of Obligations and Bilingual Lexicons*, (Cowansville, **Que**: Yvon Blais, 2003)").

Voici une liste des abréviations couramment utilisées des provinces canadiennes. Utiliser cette liste pour faire référence à des documents qui ne sont pas mentionnés dans le tableau précédent (par ex. « Louis Beaudoin et Madeleine Mailhot, *Expressions juridiques en un clin d'œil*, Cowansville (**Qc**), Yvon Blais, 1997 »).

Province / Territory	Abbreviation
Alberta	Alta
British Columbia	BC
Manitoba	Man
New Brunswick	NB
Newfoundland and Labrador	NL
Northwest Territories	NWT
Nova Scotia	NS
Nunavut	NU
Ontario	Ont
Prince Edward Island	PEI
Quebec	Que
Saskatchewan	Sask
Yukon	YT

Province/Territoire	Abréviation
Alberta	Alb
Colombie-Britannique	C-B
Manitoba	Man
Nouveau-Brunswick	N-B
Terre-Neuve-et-Labrador	T-N-L
Territoires du Nord-Ouest	TN-O
Nouvelle-Écosse	N-É
Nunavut	NU
Ontario	Ont
Île-du-Prince-Édouard	Î-P-É
Québec	Qc
Saskatchewan	Sask
Yukon	Yn

(A-2) Abbreviations for the United States ~ Abréviations américaines

Alabama	Ala		Minnesota	Minn
Alaska	Alaska		Mississippi	Miss
Arizona	Ariz		Missouri	Mo
Arkansas	Ark		Montana	Mont
California	Cal		Nebraska	Neb
Californie	Cal		Nevada	Nev
Caroline du Nord	NC		New Hampshire	NH
Caroline du Sud	SC		New Jersey	NJ
Colorado	Colo		New Mexico	N Mex
Connecticut	Conn		New York	NY
Dakota du Nord	N Dak		North Carolina	NC
Dakota du Sud	S Dak		North Dakota	N Dak
Delaware	Del		Nouveau Mexique	N Mex
District de Columbie	DC		Ohio	Ohio
District of Colombia	DC		Oklahoma	Okla
États-Unis	É-U		Oregon	Or
Florida	Fla		Pennsylvania	Pa
Floride	Fla		Pennsylvanie	Pa
Georgia	Ga		Rhode Island	RI
Géorgie	Ga		South Carolina	SC
Hawaii	Hawaii		South Dakota	S Dak
Idaho	Idaho		Tennessee	Tenn
Illinois	Ill		Texas	Tex
Indiana	Ind		United States	US
Iowa	Iowa		Utah	Utah
Kansas	Kan		Vermont	Vt
Kentucky	Ky		Virginia	Va
Louisiana	La		Virginie	Va
Louisiane	La		Virginie occidentale	W Va
Maine	Me		Washington	Wash
Maryland	Md		West Virginia	W Va
Massachussetts	Mass		Wisconsin	Wis
Michigan	Mich		Wyoming	Wyo

Appendices / Annexes

(A-3) Abbreviations for Australia ~ Abréviations australiennes

Jurisdiction / Juridiction	Legislation and Courts / Législation et cours	Neutral citation / Référence neutre
Australia	Austl	–
Commonwealth	Cth	–
Australian Capital Territory / Territoire de la capitale australienne	ACT	–
New South Wales / Nouvelle-Galles du Sud	NSW	NSW
Northern Territory / Territoire du Nord	NT	NT
Queensland	Qld	Q
South Australia / Australie méridionale	SA	SA
Tasmania / Tasmanie	Tas	TAS
Victoria	Vic	V
Western Australia / Australie occidentale	WA	WA

(A-4) Other Jurisdictional Abbreviations ~ Abréviations d'autres juridictions

Afrique du sud	Afr du sud
Écosse	Écosse
Étas-Unis	É-U
European Union	EU
France	France
Ireland	I
Irelande du nord	IN

New Zealand	NZ
Northern Ireland	NI
Nouvelle-Zélande	N-Z
Royaume-Uni	R-U
Scotland	Scot
Singapore / Singapour	Sing
South Africa	S Afr
Union européenne	UE
United Kingdom	UK
United States	US

(A-5) Abbreviations of International Organizations ~ Abréviations d'organismes internationaux

Abbreviation / Abréviation	Organization / Organisme
AC	Assemblée consultative (Conseil de l'Europe)
AG	Assemblée générale (NU)
AIEA	Agence internationale de l'énergie atomique (NU)
AP	Assemblée parlementaire (Conseil de l'Europe)
APEC	Asia Pacific Economic Cooperation
AU	African Union
Bur	Bureau (NU)
C1	Première Commission (NU)
C2	Deuxième Commission (NU)
C3	Troisième Commission (NU)
CA	Consultative Assembly (Council of Europe)
CIJ	Cour internationale de Justice

CJ (1re inst)	Tribunal de première instance (CE)
CJE	Cour de justice des Communautés européennes
CCED	Conseil du commerce et du dévoloppement (NU)
CDH	Commission des droits de l'homme (NU)
CE	Communautés européennes
CES	Conseil économique et social (NU)
CNUCED	Conférence des Nations Unies sur le commerce et le développement
CNUDCI	Commission des Nations Unies pour le droit commercial international
Comm Eur DH	Commission européenne des Droits de l'Homme
Comm Interam DH	Commission interaméricaine des Droits de l'Homme
Conseil de l'Europe	Conseil de l'Europe
Council of Europe	Council of Europe
Cour Eur DH	Cour européenne des Droits de l'Homme
Cour Interam DH	Cour interaméricaine des Droits de l'Homme
CPJI	Cour permanente de justice internationale
CS	Conseil de sécurité (NU)
CT	Conseil de tutelle (NU)
EC	European Communities
ECFI	European Court of First Instance
ECJ	Court of Justice of the European Communities
ESC	Economic and Social Council (UN)
EU	European Union
Eur Comm HR	European Commission of Human Rights
Eur Ct HR	European Court of Human Rights
FMI	Fonds monétaire international (NU)
GA	General Assembly (GA)
GATT	Accord général sur les tarifs douaniers et le commerce

	General Agreement on Tariffs and Trade
GC	General Committee (UN)
HCDH	Haut-Commissariat aux droits de l'homme (NU)
HCR	Haut-Commissariat des Nations Unies pour les réfugiés
HRC	Human Rights Committee (UN)
IAEA	International Atomic Energy Agency (UN)
ICAO	International Civil Aviation Organization (NU)
ICJ	International Court of Justice
ICTR	International Criminal Tribunal for Rwanda (UN)
ICTY	International Criminal Tribunal for the Former Yugoslavia (UN)
ILO	International Labor Organization (UN)
IMF	International Monetary Fund (UN)
Inter-Am Comm HR	Inter-American Commission on Human Rights
Inter-Am Ct HR	Inter-American Court of Human Rights
NATO	North Atlantic Treaty Organization
NU	Nations Unies
NUCED	Conférence des Nations Unies sur le commerce et le développement
OACI	Organisation de l'aviation civile internationale (NU)
OAS	Organization of American States
OÉA	Organisation des États américains
OIT	Organisation internationale du Travail
OMC	Organisation mondiale du commerce
OMPI	Organisation mondiale de la propriété intellectuelle
OTAN	Organisation du Traité de l'Atlantique Nord
PA	Parliamentary Assembly (Council of Europe)
PCIJ	Permanent Court of International Justice
SC	Security Council

Appendices / Annexes

TC	Trusteeship Council
TDB	Trade and Development Board (UN)
TPIR	Tribunal pénal international pour le Rwanda (NU)
TPIY	Tribunal pénal international pour l'ex-Yougoslavie (NU)
UA	Union africaine
UE	Union européenne
UN	United Nations
OHCHR	United Nations High Commissioner for Human Rights, Office of the (UN)
UNHCR	United Nations High Commissioner for Refugees
UNCITRAL	United Nations Commission on International Trade Law
UNCTAD	United Nations Conference on Trade and Development
WBO	Banque mondiale World Bank Organization
WIPO	World Intellectual Property Organization
WTO	World Trade Organization

APPENDIX B / ANNEX B

B. COURTS AND TRIBUNALS ~ COURS ET TRIBUNAUX

(B-1) General Rules ~ Règles générales

This appendix contains a list of abbrevations of courts and tribunals, both current and historical. Place the jurisdictional abbreviation before or after the court abbreviation according to the rules below.

- Identify a **court** unless it is obvious from the reporter (**SCR**). See section 3. 9.

- Identify the **jurisdiction** unless it is obvious from the name of the court or the reporter (**TAQ**).

  - ☐ For English abbreviations, the abbreviation for the province, territory, or state normally precedes the abbreviation for the court (**NBCA**; **Ont Gen Div**; **Qc Sup Ct**).

  - ☐ For French abbreviations, provide the abbreviation for the province after the abbreviation of the court for Ontario, New Brunswick and Quebec (**Div gén Ont**; **CA NB**; **CS Qc**), otherwise follow the English rule.

- Identify the **country** if the province, territory or state is unfamiliar to the majority of readers and is not found in this *Guide*. Generally, courts located in a province, territory, or state are only identified using the abbreviation of that province, territory, or state. For example, it would be incorrect to write "NSWCA Austl" or "NSCA Can" because it is redundant.

  - ☐ Generally, federal, national, and unitary courts are identified by their country unless the country is obvious either from the reporter or from the abbreviation of the court itself. (The jurisdiction is obvious from the court's abbreviation when the name of the jurisdiction is contained in the abbreviation or when no other court shares the abbreviation.)

  - ☐ When citing from the Citizenship Appeals Court of Canada, the Court Martial Appeal Court, or the Exchequer Court of Canada, include the abbreviation **Can** (**Cit AC Can**). For any other Canadian federal court, the jurisdiction is obvious and **Can** should not be included.

  - ☐ In most cases, the jurisdiction of French courts is obvious from the court abbreviation and the abbreviation **Fr** should not be included.

  - ☐ The country abbreviation normally follows the court abbreviation (**Dist Ct Sing**, **DCNZ**), but there are exceptions, especially if the name of the jurisdiction is part of the name of the court (**NZCA**). For Singapore, include the abbreviation **Sing** unless the citation is to the *Singapore Law Reports*.

- In **court acronyms**, there is no space in an abbreviation consisting solely of upper case letters. Leave a space when an abbreviation consists of both upper case letters and lower case letters (**BCCA**; **Ont Div Ct**; **NS Co Ct**; **Alta QB**).

▨ Include the abbreviation of the **federal or provincial administrative agency or tribunal** in parentheses at the end of the citation if it is not evident from the title of the cited reporter. If an abbreviation cannot be found, use the full name. Use the abbreviation as it is provided by the administrative body. For further information, see section 3.14.

NB: In English, the abbreviation for "Supreme Court of Canada" is SCC, and the abbreviation for Superior Court is **Sup Ct**. In French, "Cour supreme du Canada" is abbreviated **CSC** and "Cour supérieure" is abbreviated **CS**. Also, note that the American abbreviations are **Super Ct** for "Superior Court" and **Sup Ct** for a state Supreme Court.

Cette annexe comprend une liste des abréviations des cours et des tribunaux, à la fois actuels et historiques. Mettre l'abréviation des indications géographiques avant ou après l'abréviation des cours en respectant les règles ci-dessous.

▨ Identifier **la cour**, à moins que le recueil n'indique l'information (**RCS**). Voir section 3.9.

▨ Identifier **la juridiction**, à moins que cette information ne puisse être déduite du nom de la cour ou du recueil (**TAQ**).

☐ Pour les abréviations en anglais, l'abréviation de la province, du territoire ou de l'État précède normalement l'abréviation de la cour (**NBCA** ; **Ont Gen Div** ; **Qc Sup Ct**).

☐ Pour les abréviations en français, fournir l'abréviation de la province après l'abréviation de la cour pour l'Ontario, le Nouveau-Brunswick et le Québec (**Div gén Ont** ; **CA NB** ; **CS Qc**). Dans tous les autres cas, respecter la règle d'abréviation en anglais.

▨ Identifier **le pays** si l'abréviation de la province, du territoire ou de l'État risque de ne pas être connue des lecteurs ou n'est pas fournie dans ce *Manuel*. Généralement, les cours siégeant dans une province, un territoire ou un État sont déjà identifiées par l'abréviation de la province, du territoire ou de l'État. Par exemple, il serait redondant d'écrire « NSWCA Austl » ou « NSCA Can ».

☐ Les cours fédérale, nationale et unitaire sont identifiées par le nom du pays, à moins que celui-ci ne puisse être déduit du recueil ou de l'abréviation de la cour.

☐ Lorsqu'on renvoie à la Cour d'appel de citoyenneté, la Cour d'appel de la cour martiale du Canada, ou la Cour de l'Échiquier, il faut inclure l'abréviation **Can** (**CA cit Can**). Pour toute autre cour fédérale, l'indication géographique **Can** est évidente et ne doit pas être incluse.

☐ Dans la plupart des cas, la juridiction des cours en français est évidente et l'abréviation **Fr** ne doit pas être incluse.

☐ L'abréviation du pays suit l'abréviation de la cour (**Dist Ct Sing** ; **DCNZ**), sauf si le nom de la juridiction fait partie du nom de la cour (par ex. **NZCA**). Pour le Singapour, inclure l'abréviation **Sing** à moins que la référence ne provienne des *Singapore Law Reports*.

▨   Pour les **acronymes des cours**, il n'y a pas d'espace entre les lettres majuscules des abréviations. Toutefois, il y a un espace quand l'abréviation est formée de minuscules et/ou de majuscules (**CQ ; BCCA ; Div gén Ont ; CQ crim & pén**).

▨   Indiquer l'abréviation de **l'organe ou du tribunal administratif** entre parenthèses à la fin de la référence, s'il est impossible de le déduire du titre du recueil (utiliser le nom au complet si aucune abréviation n'est trouvée). Utiliser l'abréviation utilisée par l'organe administratif. Pour plus d'informations, voir la section 3.14.

N.B. En anglais, l'abréviation de « Supreme Court of Canada » est SCC et l'abréviation des cours supérieures est **Sup Ct**. En français, ces abréviations sont inversées : « Cour suprême du Canada » devient **CSC** et « Cour supérieure » devient **CS**. De plus, noter que les abréviations américaines sont **Super Ct** pour « Superior Court » et **Sup Ct** pour la Cour suprême des États.

(B-2) Abbreviations ~ Abréviations

Court or Tribunal / Cour ou tribunal	Abbreviation / Abréviation
Frequent abbreviations / Abréviations principales	
Cour d'appel	CA
Court of Appeal	CA
Court of Justice	Ct J
Cour provinciale	CP
Cour supérieure	CS
Cour Suprême du Canada	CSC
Federal Court of Appeal	FCA
High Court	HC
Provincial Court	Prov Ct
Superior Court	Sup Ct
Traffic Court	Traffic Ct
Youth Court	Youth Ct
Canadian Courts / Cours canadiennes	
Coroners Court	Cor Ct
Cour canadienne de l'impôt	CCI

Appendices / Annexes

Cour d'appel	CA
Cour d'appel fédérale	CAF
Cour de comté	Cc
Cour de l'Ontario, division générale	Div gén Ont
Cour des divorces et des causes matrimoniales	C div & causes mat
Cour des juges de la Cour de comté siégeant au criminel	C j Cc crim
Cour des petites créances	C pet cré
Cour des successions	C succ
Cour divisionnaire	C div
Cour du Banc de la Reine	BR
Cour du Banc de la Reine (Division de la famille)	BR (div fam)
Cour du Banc de la Reine (Division de première instance)	BR (1re inst)
Cour du Québec	CQ
Cour du Québec, Chambre de la jeunesse	CQ jeun
Cour du Québec, Chambre civile	CQ civ
Cour du Québec, Chambre civile (Division des petites créances)	CQ civ (div pet cré)
Cour du Québec, Chambre criminelle et pénale	CQ crim & pén
Cour fédérale, première instance	CF (1re inst)
Cour municipale	CM
Cour provinciale	CP
Cour provinciale (Division civile)	CP Div civ
Cour provinciale (Division criminelle)	CP Div crim
Cour provinciale (Division de la famille)	CP Div fam
Cour supérieure	CS
Cour supérieure (Chambre administrative)	CS adm
Cour supérieure (Chambre civile)	CS civ
Cour supérieure (Chambre criminelle et pénale)	CS crim & pén

Cour supérieure (Chambre de la famille)	CS fam
Cour supérieure (Division des petites créances)	CS pét cré
Cour supérieure (Chambre de la faillite et de l'insolvabilité)	CS fail & ins
Cour suprême (Division de la famille)	C supr fam
Cour suprême (Division d'appel)	C supr A
Cour suprême (Division du Banc de la Reine)	C supr BR
Cour suprême du Canada	CSC
Court Martial Appeal Court	Ct Martial App Ct
Cour d'appel de la cour martiale	CACM
Court of Appeal	CA
Court of Appeal in Equity	CA Eq
Court of Justice (General Division)	Ct J (Gen Div)
Court of Justice (General Division, Small Claims Court)	Ct J (Gen Div Sm Cl Ct)
Court of Justice (General Division, Family Court)	Ct J (Gen Div Fam Ct)
Court of Justice (Provincial Division)	Ct J (Prov Div)
Court of Justice (Provincial Division, Youth Court)	Ct J (Prov Div Youth Ct)
Court of Quebec	CQ
Court of Quebec (Civil Division)	CQ (Civ Div)
Court of Quebec (Civil Division, Small Claims)	CQ (Civ Div Sm Cl)
Court of Quebec (Criminal & Penal Division)	CQ (Crim & Pen Div)
Court of Quebec (Youth Division)	CQ (Youth Div)
Court of Queen's Bench	QB
Court of Queen's Bench (Family Division)	QB (Fam Div)
Court of Queen's Bench (Trial Division)	QB (TD)
Divisional Court	Div Ct
Divorce and Matrimonial Causes Court	Div & Mat Causes Ct
Federal Court of Appeal	FCA

Federal Court (Trial Division)	FCTD
High Court of Justice	H Ct J
Municipal Court	Mun Ct
Probate Court	Prob Ct
Provincial Court (Civil Division)	Prov Ct (Civ Div)
Provincial Court (Civil Division, Small Claims Court)	Prov Ct (Civ Div Sm Cl Ct)
Provincial Court (Criminal Division)	Prov Ct (Crim Div)
Provincial Court (Family Court)	Prov Ct (Fam Ct)
Provincial Court (Family Division)	Prov Ct (Fam Div)
Provincial Court (Juvenile Division)	Prov Ct (Juv Div)
Provincial Court (Small Claims Division)	Prov Ct (Sm Cl Div)
Provincial Court (Youth Court)	Prov Ct (Youth Ct)
Provincial Court (Youth Division)	Prov Ct (Youth Div)
Provincial Offences Court	Prov Off Ct
Small Claims Court	Sm Cl Ct
Superior Court (Canada)	Sup Ct
Superior Court (Administrative Division)	Sup Ct (Adm Div)
Superior Court (Bankruptcy and Insolvency Division)	Sup Ct (Bank & Ins Div)
Superior Court (Civil Division)	Sup Ct (Civ Div)
Superior Court (Criminal and Penal Division)	Sup Ct (Crim & Pen Div)
Superior Court (Family Division)	Sup Ct (Fam Div)
Superior Court (Small Claims Division)	Sup Ct (Sm Cl Div)
Supreme Court of Canada	SCC
Supreme Court (Appellate Division) (Can provincial / Can Provinciale)	SC (AD)
Supreme Court (Family Division)	SC (Fam Div)
Supreme Court (Queen's Bench Division)	SC (QB Div)
Supreme Court (Trial Division)	SC (TD)

Tax Court of Canada	TCC
Tax Review Board	T Rev B
Territorial Court	Terr Ct
Territorial Court (Youth Court)	Terr Ct Youth Ct

UK Courts / Cours du Royaume-Uni

Chancery Court	Ch
Court of Justice (Scotland / Écosse)	Ct Just
Court of Sessions (Scotland / Écosse)	Ct Sess
High Court of Admiralty	HC Adm
High Court of Justice	HCJ
High Court: Chancery Division (UK / R-U)	ChD
High Court: Family Division (UK / R-U)	FamD
High Court: Queen's Bench Division (UK / R-U)	QBD
House of Lords (England / Angleterre)	HL (Eng)
House of Lords (Scotland / Écosse)	HL (Scot)
Judicial Committee of the Privy Council (Commonwealth)	PC
Stipendiary Magistrates' Court	Stip Mag Ct

United States Courts / Cours américaines

Administrative Court	Admin Ct
Admiralty [Court, Division]	Adm
Alderman's Court	Alder Ct
Appeals Court	App Ct
Appellate Court	App Ct
Appellate Division	App Div
Bankruptcy Appellate Panel	BAP
Bankruptcy [Court, Judge]	Bankr

Appendices / Annexes

Board of Tax Appeals (US / É-U)	BTA
Borough Court	[name] Bor Ct
Chancery [Court, Division]	Ch
Children's Court	Child Ct
Circuit Court	Cir Ct
Circuit Court of Appeals (federal, US / fédéral, É-U)	Cir
Circuit Court of Appeals (state)	Cir Ct App
Circuit Court and Family Court	Cir Ct & Fam Ct
Citizenship Appeals Court (US / É-U)	Cit AC
City Court	[name] City Ct
City and Parish Courts	City & Parish Ct
Civil Appeals	Civ App
Civil Court	Civ Ct
Civil Court of Record	Civ Ct Rec
Civil District Court	Civ Dist Ct
Claims Court	Cl Ct
Commerce Court	Comm Ct
Common Pleas	CP
Commonwealth Court	Commw Ct
Conciliation Court	Concil Ct
Constitutional County Court	Const County Ct
County Court	Co Ct
County Court at Law	County Ct at Law
County Court Judges' Criminal Court	Co Ct J Crim Ct
County Judge's Court	County J Ct
County Recorder's Court	County Rec Ct
Court of Appeals (federal)	Cir

Appendices / Annexes

Court of Appeal[s] (state)	Ct App
Court of Chancery	Ct Ch
Court of Civil Appeals	Ct Civ App
Court of Claims	Ct Cl
Court of Common Pleas	Ct Com Pl
Court of Criminal Appeals	Ct Crim App
Court of Customs and Patent Appeals	CCPA
Court of Customs Appeals	Ct Cust App
Court of Errors	Ct Err
Court of Errors and Appeals	Ct Err & App
Court of Federal Claims	Ct Fed Cl
Court of First Instance	Ct First Inst
Court of [General, Special] Sessions	Ct [Gen, Spec] Sess
Court of International Trade	Ct Intl Trade
Court of Review	Ct Rev
Court of Special Appeals	Ct Spec App
Court of Tax Review	Ct T Rev
Criminal Appeals	Crim App
Criminal District Court	Crim Dist Ct
Customs Court	Cust Ct
District Court (US Federal / É-U fédéral)	D
District Court (US states / États des É-U)	Dist Ct
District Court of Appeal[s]	Dist Ct App
District Justice Court	Dist Just Ct
Domestic Relations Court	Dom Rel Ct
Emergency Court of Appeal[s]	Emer Ct App
Environmental Court	Env Ct

Equity [Court, Division]	Eq
Family Court	Fam Ct
General Sessions Court	Gen Sess Ct
High Court	High Ct
Housing Court	Housing Ct
Intermediate Court of Appeals	Intermed Ct App
Justice Court	J Ct
Justice of the Peace's Court	JP Ct
Juvenile Court	Juv Ct
Juvenile Delinquents' Court	Juv Del Ct
Juvenile and Family Court	Juv & Fam Ct
Land Court	Land Ct
Law Court	Law Ct
Magistrate Court	Magis Ct
Magistrate Division	Magis Div
Mayor's Court	Mayor's Ct
Municipal Court	[name] Mun Ct
Municipal Court not of Record	Mun Ct not Rec
Municipal Criminal Court of Record	Mun Crim Ct Rec
Orphans' Court	Orphans' Ct
Parish Court	[name] Parish Ct
Police Justice's Court	Police J Ct
Prerogative Court	Prerog Ct
Probate Court	Prob Ct
Recorder's Court	Rec Ct
Small Claims Court	Small Cl Ct
State Court	State Ct

Appendices / Annexes

Superior Court (US / É-U)	Super Ct
Supreme Court (federal)	US
Supreme Court (state, US / État, É-U)	Sup Ct
Supreme Court, Appellate Division (state, US / État, É-U)	Sup Ct App Div
Supreme Court of Appeals	Sup Ct App
Supreme Court of Errors	Sup Ct Err
Supreme Court of the United States	USSC
Supreme Judicial Court	Sup Jud Ct
Surrogate Court	Surr Ct
Tax Appeal Court	Tax App Ct
Tax Court	TC
Teen Court	Teen Ct
Town Court	Town Ct
Traffic Court	Traffic Ct
Tribal Court	[name] Tribal Ct
Unified Family Court	Unif Fam Ct
Water Court	Water Ct
Workers' Compensation Court	Workers' Comp Ct
Youth Court	Youth Ct

French Courts / Cours françaises

Conseil constitutionnel (France)	Cons const
Conseil d'État (France)	Cons d'État
Cour de cassation : Assemblée plénière (France)	Cass Ass plén
Cour de cassation : Chambre commerciale (France)	Cass com
Cour de cassation : Chambre criminelle (France)	Cass crim
Cour de cassation : Chambre des requêtes (France)	Cass req
Cour de cassation : Chambre mixte (France)	Cass Ch mixte

Cour de cassation : Chambre sociale (France)	Cass soc
Cour de cassation : Chambres réunies (France)	Cass Ch réun
Cour de cassation : Première chambre civile (France)	Cass civ 1^e
Cour de cassation : Deuxième chambre civile (France)	Cass civ 2^e
Cour de cassation : Troisième chambre civile (France)	Cass civ 3^e
Cour de magistrat	C mag
Cour de révision	C rév
Haute Cour de justice	HCJ
Justice de Paix (*before 1958 / avant 1958*) (France)	JP
Australian & New Zealand Courts / Cours d'Australie et de Nouvelle-Zélande	
District Court of New Zealand	DCNZ
Environment Court	Env Ct
Family Court	Fam Ct
Federal Court of Australia	FCA
High Court of Australia	HCA
Labour Court	Lab Ct
Magistrates' Court	Mag Ct
Magistrates' Court of New Zealand	Mag Ct NZ
New Zealand Court of Appeal	NZCA
New Zealand High Court	NZHC
New Zealand Employment Court	NZ Empl Ct
New Zealand Youth Court	NZYC
Singapore Courts / Cours de Singapour	
Court of Appeal	SGCA
High Court	SGHC
District Court	SGDC

Magistrates' Court	SGMC
South Africa Courts / Cours d'Afrique du Sud	
Constitutional Court of South Africa	S Afr Const Ct
Electoral Court of South Africa	S Afr Electoral Ct
High Court of South Africa	S Afr HC
Labour Court of South Africa	S Afr Labour Ct
Labour Court of Appeal of South Africa	S Afr Labour CA
Land Claims Court of South Africa	S Afr Land Claims Ct
Supreme Court of Appeal of South Africa	S Afr SC

(B-3) Neutral citation ~ Référence neutre

Below are the **dates of implementation** and the **abbreviations** of the neutral citation in Canadian courts. Before these dates, the neutral citation was not officially used and must not be cited for any given court.

Jurisdiction	Name of the court	Abbreviation	Implementation
Canada	Supreme Court of Canada	SCC	January 2000
	Federal Court	FC	February 2001
	Federal Court of Appeal	FCA	February 2001
	Tax Court of Canada	TCC	January 2003
	Court Martial Appeal Court of Canada	CMAC	October 2001
	Competition Tribunal of Canada	Comp Trib	January 2001
	Canadian Human Rights Tribunal	CHRT	January 2003
	Public Service Labour Relations Board	PSLRB	January 2000
Alberta	Court of Appeal	ABCA	January 1998
	Court of Queen's Bench	ABQB	January 1998
	Provincial Court	ABPC	January 1998
	Alberta Securities Commission	ABASC	June 2004

British Colum-bia	Court of Appeal	BCCA	January 1999
	Supreme Court of British Columbia	BCSC	January 2000
	Provincial Court of British Columbia	BCPC	February 1999
	British Columbia Human Rights Tribunal	BCHRT	January 2000
	British Columbia Securities Commission	BCSECCOM	January 2000
Manitoba	Court of Appeal	MBCA	March 2000
	Court of Queen's Bench of Manitoba	MBQB	April 2000
	Provincial Court of Manitoba	MBPC	January 2007
New Brunswick	Court of Appeal of New Brunswick	NBCA	May 2001
	Court of Queen's Bench of New Brunswick	NBQB	January 2002
	Provincial Court	NBPC	December 2002
Newfoundland and Labrador	Supreme Court of Newfoundland and Labrador, Court of Appeal	NFCA / NLCA	January 2001—2004 / January 2005
	Supreme Court of Newfoundland and Labrador, Trial Division	NLSCTD / NLTD	July 2003—2005 / 2005
Northwest Territories	Court of Appeal for the Northwest Territories	NWTCA	December 1999
	Supreme Court of the Northwest Territories	NWTSC	October 1999
	Territorial Court of the Northwest Territories	NWTTC	October 1999
Nova Scotia	Nova Scotia Court of Appeal	NSCA	September 1999
	Supreme Court of Nova Scotia	NSSC	December 2000
	Supreme Court of Nova Scotia, Family Division	NSSF	January 2001
	Provincial Court of Nova Scotia	NSPC	March 2001
	Nova Scotia Utility and Review Board	NSUARB	January 1997
	Nova Scotia Barristers' Society Hearing Panel	NSBS	January 2004
Nunavut	Nunavut Court of Justice	NUCJ	January 2001

	Court of Appeal of Nunavut	NUCA	May 2006
Ontario	Ontario Court of Appeal	ONCA	January 2007
	Ontario Superior Court	ONSC	January 2010
	Ontario Court of Justice	ONCJ	January 2004
	Workplace Safety and Insurance Appeals Tribunal	ONWSIAT	January 2000
	Law Society Appeal Panel	ONLSAP	February 2004
	Law Society Hearing Panel	ONLSHP	January 2004
Prince Edward Island	Supreme Court, Appeal Division	PESCAD	January 2000
	Supreme Court, Trial Division	PESCTD	January 2000
Quebec	Court of Appeal of Québec	QCCA	January 2005
	Superior Court of Québec	QCCS	January 2006
	Court of Québec	QCCP	January 2006
	Tribunal des professions du Québec	QCTP	January 1999
	Conseil de la magistrature du Québec	CMQC	November 2000
	Commission des relations du travail	QCCRT	November 2002
Saskatchewan	Court of Appeal for Saskatchewan	SKCA	January 2000
	Court of Queen's Bench	SKQB	January 1999
	Provincial Court	SKPC	January 2002
	Automobile Injury Appeal Commission	SKAIA	July 2003
Yukon	Court of Appeal	YKCA	March 2000
	Supreme Court of the Yukon Territory	YKSC	March 2000
	Territorial Court of Yukon	YKTC	December 1999
	Small Claims Court	YKSM	May 2004
	Youth Court	YKYC	January 2001

Le tableau ci-dessous expose les **dates d'entrée en vigueur** et les **abréviations** de la référence neutre pour les cours canadiennes. Avant ces dates, la référence neutre n'était pas officiellement en vigueur et ne peut être citée pour une cour.

Juridiction	Nom de la cour	Abréviation	En vigueur
Canada	Cour suprême du Canada	CSC	janvier 2000
	Cour fédérale	CF	février 2001
	Cour d'appel fédérale	CAF	février 2001
	Cour canadienne de l'impôt	CCI	janvier 2003
	Cour d'appel de la cour martiale du Canada	CAMC	octobre 2001
	Tribunal de la concurrence du Canada	Trib conc	janvier 2001
	Tribunal canadien des droits de la personne	TCDP	janvier 2003
	Commission des relations de travail dans la fonction publique	PSLRB	janvier 2000
Alberta	Court of Appeal	ABCA	janvier 1998
	Court of Queen's Bench	ABQB	janvier 1998
	Provincial Court	ABPC	janvier 1998
	Alberta Securities Commission	ABASC	juin 2004
Colombie-Britannique	Court of Appeal	BCCA	janvier 1999
	Supreme Court of British Columbia	BCSC	janvier 2000
	Provincial Court of British Columbia	BCPC	février 1999
	British Columbia Human Rights Tribunal	BCHRT	janvier 2000
	British Columbia Securities Commission	BCSECCOM	janvier 2000
Île-du-Prince-Édouard	Supreme Court, Appeal Division	PESCAD	janvier 2000
	Supreme Court, Trial Division	PESCTD	janvier 2000
Manitoba	Cour d'appel	MBCA	mars 2000
	Cour du Banc de la Reine du Manitoba	MBQB	avril 2000
	Cour provinciale du Manitoba	MBPC	janvier 2007
Nouveau-Brunswick	Cour d'appel du Nouveau-Brunswick	NBCA	mai 2001
	Cour du banc de la Reine du Nouveau-	NBQB	janvier 2002

	Brunswick		
	Cour provinciale	NBPC	décembre 2002
Nouvelle-Écosse	Nova Scotia Court of Appeal	NSCA	septembre 1999
	Supreme Court of Nova Scotia	NSSC	décembre 2000
	Supreme Court of Nova Scotia, Family Division	NSSF	janvier 2001
	Provincial Court of Nova Scotia	NSPC	mars 2001
	Nova Scotia Utility and Review Board	NSUARB	janvier 1997
	Nova Scotia Barristers' Society Hearing Panel	NSBS	janvier 2004
Nunavut	Cour de justice du Nunavut	NUCJ	janvier 2001
	Cour d'appel du Nunavut	NUCA	mai 2006
Ontario	Cour d'appel de l'Ontario	ONCA	janvier 2007
	Cour supérieure de l'Ontario	ONSC	janvier 2010
	Cour de justice de l'Ontario	ONCJ	janvier 2004
	Tribunal d'appel de la sécurité professionnelle et de l'assurance contre les accidents de travail	ONWSIAT	janvier 2000
	Comité d'appel du Barreau	ONLSAP	février 2004
	Comité d'audition du Barreau	ONLSHP	janvier 2004
Québec	Court of Appeal of Québec Cour d'appel du Québec	QCCA	janvier 2005
	Cour supérieure du Québec	QCCS	janvier 2006
	Cour du Québec	QCCP	janvier 2006
	Tribunal des professions du Québec	QCTP	janvier 1999
	Conseil de la magistrature du Québec	CMQC	novembre 2000
	Commission des relations du travail	QCCRT	novembre 2002
Saskatchewan	Court of Appeal for Saskatchewan	SKCA	janvier 2000
	Court of Queen's Bench	SKQB	janvier 1999

	Provincial Court	SKPC	janvier 2002
	Automobile Injury Appeal Commission	SKAIA	juillet 2003
Terre-Neuve-et-Labrador	Supreme Court of Newfoundland and Labrador, Court of Appeal	NFCA NLCA	janvier 2001—2004 janvier 2005
	Supreme Court of Newfoundland and Labrador, Trial Division	NLSCTD NLTD	juillet 2003—2005 2005
Territoires du Nord-Ouest	Cour d'appel des territoires du Nord-Ouest	NWTCA	décembre 1999
	Cour suprême des territoires du Nord-Ouest	NWTSC	octobre 1999
	Cour territoriale des territoires du Nord-Ouest	NWTTC	octobre 1999
Yukon	Cour d'appel	YKCA	mars 2000
	Cour suprême du territoire du Yukon	YKSC	mars 2000
	Cour territoriale du Yukon	YKTC	décembre 1999
	Cour des petites créances	YKSM	mai 2004
	Tribunal pour adolescents	YKYC	janvier 2001

APPENDIX C / ANNEX C

C. CASELAW REPORTERS ~ RECUEILS DE JURISPRUDENCE

(C-1) Canadian Official Reporters ~ Recueils officiels canadiens

Always cite to these reporters after the neutral citation (if available). Official reporters are published by the Queen's Printer. Whenever there is a discrepancy between two different versions of the same case, the version in the following reporters will be given precedence.

Only two reporters are still published today: the **Federal Court Reports** and the **Canada Supreme Court Reports**.

Ex CR	Canada Law Reports: Exchequer Court of Canada (1923–1970) Reports of the Exchequer Court of Canada (1875–1922)
FCR	Federal Court Reports (1971 – present)
SCR	Canada Supreme Court Reports (1970 – present) Canada Law Reports: Supreme Court of Canada (1923–1969) Canada Supreme Court Reports (1876–1922)

Toujours faire référence aux recueils officiels après la référence neutre (si elle existe). Les recueils officiels sont publiés par l'Imprimeur de la Reine. En cas de disparité entre un recueil officiel et un autre recueil, la version du recueil officiel a préséance.

Seuls deux recueils sont toujours publiés de nos jours : les **Recueils des arrêts de la Cour fédérale du Canada** et les **Recueils des arrêts de la Cour suprême du Canada**.

CF	Recueils des arrêts de la Cour fédérale du Canada (1971 – aujourd'hui)
RC de l'É	Recueils des arrêts de la Cour de l'Échiquier (1875–1922) Rapports judiciaires du Canada : Cour de l'Échiquier (1923–1970)
RCS	Recueils des arrêts de la Cour suprême du Canada (1877–1922) Rapports judiciaires du Canada : Cour suprême (1923–1969) Recueils des arrêts de la Cour suprême du Canada (1970 – aujourd'hui)

(C-2) Canadian Semi-Official Reporters ~ Recueils canadiens semi-officiels

The following reporters are published under the auspices of the local Law Society. Always cite to these reporters before any other, except the SCR, FC, or Ex CR.

Les recueils suivants sont publiés sous l'égide du barreau de la province ou du territoire en question. Faire référence à ces recueils après les CF, les RC de l'É et les RCS.

Alta LR	Alberta Law Reports (only between 1908–1932 / seulement entre 1908–1932)
AR	Alberta Reports (1976–1986 [volume 67]) / 1976 à 1986 [volume 67]) *NB: Unofficial after 1986 / NB non officiel après 1986*
BCLR	British Columbia Law Reports (1867–1947)
BR	Recueils de jurisprudence du Québec : Cour du Banc de la Reine/du Roi (1942–1969) Rapports judiciaires officiels de Québec : Cour du Banc de la Reine/du Roi (1892–1941)
CA	Recueils de jurisprudence du Québec : Cour d'appel (1970–1985)
CBES	Recueils de jurisprudence du Québec : Cour du bien-être social (1975–1985)
CP	Recueils de jurisprudence du Québec : Cour provinciale (1975–1987)
CS	Recueils de jurisprudence du Québec : Cour supérieure (1967–1985 / 1967 à 1985) Rapports judiciaires officiels de Québec : Cour supérieure (1892–1966)
CSP	Recueils de jurisprudence du Québec : Cour des Sessions de la paix (1975–1983 / 1975 à 1983)
Man R	Manitoba Reports (1883–1961) *NB: 2d series unofficial / NB 2e série non officielle*
NBR	New Brunswick Reports (2d) (1969–present / 1969 à aujourd'hui)
Nfld & PEIR	Newfoundland & Prince Edward Island Reports (1971–present / 1971 à aujourd'hui)
NSR	Nova Scotia Reports (2d) (1969–present / 1969 à aujourd'hui) Nova Scotia Reports (1965–1969) *NB: Not official from 1834–1929 / NB non officiel de 1834 à 1929*
NWTR	Northwest Territories Reports (1983–1998)
OAR	Ontario Appeal Reporters (1883–1899 vols 7–25)
OLR	Ontario Law Reports (1900–1931)
OR	Ontario Reports (2d) (1973–present / 1973 à aujourd'hui) Ontario Reports (1931–1973) *NB: Unofficial from 1882–1900 / NB non officiel de 1882 à 1900*
OWN	Ontario Weekly Notes (1909–1962)

RJQ	Recueils de jurisprudence du Québec (1975–present / 1975 à aujourd'hui)
Sask LR	Saskatchewan Law Reports (1907–1931)
Terr LR	Territories Law Reports (1885–1907)
TJ	Recueils de jurisprudence du Québec : Tribunal de la jeunesse (1975–present / 1975 à aujourd'hui)
YR	Yukon Reports (1986–1989)

(C-3) Other Reporters ~ Autres recueils

- For a more detailed list of Law Reports, consult the latest edition of *Bieber's Dictionary of Legal Abbreviations*.

- If an English reporter is reprinted in whole or in part in the *English Reports*, the applicable volume(s) are indicated.

- For the most part, selected reporters with recent jurisprudence have been included from all countries represented in this *Guide*, while selected reporters with both historical and recent jurisprudence have been included for Canada and the UK.

- French *Cahiers de droit* and yearbooks containing both doctrine and jurisprudence may be found in Appendix D.

- Because reporters may cover a large time period during which many names have existed for a jurisdiction, the jurisdiction listed in the jurisdiction column is always the most recent name for the jurisdiction covered by the reporter.

- This list only contains printed reporters. Decisions of many courts and administrative bodies are now available online. Follow the rules in Chapter 3 when citing decisions obtained online.

- Pour une liste plus détaillée des *Law Reports*, consulter la dernière édition du *Bieber's Dictionary of Legal Abbreviations*.

- Si un recueil anglais est reproduit entièrement ou en partie dans les *English Reports*, indiquer le volume approprié.

- La plupart des recueils de jurisprudence récents sont disponibles dans ce *Manuel*. Les recueils qui contiennent de la jurisprudence plus ancienne ne sont indiqués que pour le Canada et le Royaume-Uni.

- Pour les *Cahiers de droit* et les annuaires français de la doctrine et de la jurisprudence, voir l'annexe D.

- Puisque les recueils peuvent couvrir une longue période de temps durant laquelle le nom de la juridiction a pu changer, la liste ci-dessous représente le nom le plus récent de la juridiction.

Seuls les recueils imprimés sont inclus dans cette liste. Les décisions de plusieurs cours et organes administratifs sont maintenant diponibles en ligne.

Abbreviation / Abréviation	Title of Reporter / Titre du recueil	Jurisdiction / Indication géographique	Dates
A	Atlantic Reporter	US / É-U	1855-1938
A (2d)	Atlantic Reporter (Second Series)	US / É-U	1938-2010
A (3d)	Atlantic Reporter (Third Series)	US / É-U	2010-
A & N	Alcock and Napier's Reports	I	1831-1833
A Crim R	Australian Criminal Reports	Austl	1980-
Act	Acton's Prize Cases (ER vol 12)	US / É-U	1809-1811
A Intl LC	American International Law Cases	US / É-U	1783-1978
A Intl LC (2d)	American International Law Cases (Second Series)		1979-1989
A Intl LC (3d)	American International Law Cases (Third Series)		1990-2004
A Intl LC (4th)	American International Law Cases (Fourth Series)		2006-
ANWTYTR	Alberta, Northwest Territories & Yukon Tax Reporter	Can	1973-
AALR	Australian Argus Law Reports	Austl	1960-1973
AAR	Administrative Appeals Reports	Austl	1984-
AAS	Arbitrage — Santé et services sociaux	Can (QC)	1983-
ABC	Australian Bankruptcy Cases	Austl	1928-1964
ABD	Canada, Public Service Commission, Appeals and Investigation Branch, Appeal Board Decisions	Can	1979-1999
AC	Law Reports, Appeal Cases	UK / R-U	1890-
ACA	Australian Corporate Affairs Reporter	Austl	1971-1982
ACLC	Australian Company Law Cases	Austl	1971-
ACLP	Australian Company Law and Practice	Austl	1981-1991
ACLR	Australian Company Law Reports	Austl	1974-1989
ACLR	Australian Construction Law Reporter	Austl	1982-1997
ACSR	Australian Corporations and Securities Reports	Austl	1989-
ACTR	Australian Capital Territory Reports	Austl (ACT)	1973-
ACWS	All Canada Weekly Summaries	Can	1970-1979
ACWS (2d)	All Canada Weekly Summaries (Second Series)	Can	1980-1986
ACWS (3d)	All Canada Weekly Summaries (Third Series)	Can	1986-
AD	South African Law Reports, Appellate Division	S Afr du sud	1910-1946
Adam	Adam's Justiciary Cases	Scot	1893-1916
Add	Addams's Reports (ER vol 162)	UK / R-U	1822-1826

ADIL	Annual Digest and Reports of Public International Law Cases	Intl	1919-1949
Admin LR	Administrative Law Reports	Can	1983-1991
Admin LR (2d)	Administrative Law Reports (Second Series)	Can	1992-1998
Admin LR (3d)	Administrative Law Reports (Third Series)	Can	1998-2003
Admin LR (4th)	Administrative Law Reports (Fourth Series)	Can	2003-2010
Admin LR (5th)	Administrative Law Reports (Fifth Series)	Can	2010-
Ad & El	Adolphus & Ellis's Reports (ER vols 110-113)	US / É-U	1834-1842
ADR	Australian De Facto Relationships Law	Austl	1985-
AEBR	Australian Business & Assets Planning Reporter	Austl	1986-
AEBCN	Australian Business & Estate Planning Case Notes	Austl	1979-1981
AEUB	Alberta Energy and Utilities Board Decisions	Can (AB)	1995-
Afr LR (Comm)	African Law Reports: Commercial	Afr	1964-1980
Afr LR (Mal)	African Law Reports: Malawi Series	E Afr de l'est	1923-1972
Afr LR (SL)	African Law Reports: Sierra Leone Series	W Afr de l'ouest	1920-1936 1957-1960 1964-1966 1972-1973
AFTR	Australian Federal Tax Reporter	Austl	1969-
AILR	Australian Indigenous Law Reporter	Austl	1996-
AIA	Affaires d'immigration en appel	Can	1967-1970
AIA (ns)	Affaires d'immigration en appel (nouvelle série)	Can	1969-1977
AIN	Australian Industrial and Intellectual Property Cases	Austl	1982-
AJDA	Actualité juridique, droit administratif	France	1955-
AJDI	Actualité juridique, droit immobilier	France	1997-
AJDQ	Annuaire de jurisprudence et de doctrine du Québec	Can (QC)	1989-
AJPI	Actualité juridique, propriété immobilière	France	1955-1997
AJQ	Annuaire de jurisprudence du Québec	Can (QC)	1937-1988
Al	Aleyn's Select Cases (ER vol 82)	UK / R-U	1646-1649
Ala	Alabama Reports	US / É-U	1840-1946
Ala (NS)	Alabama Reports (New Series)	US / É-U	1846-1975
Alaska Fed	Alaska Federal Reports	US / É-U	1869-1937
Alaska R	Alaska Reports	US / É-U	1884-1958
ALD	Administrative Law Decisions	Austl	1976-
ALJR	Australian Law Journal Reports	Austl	1958-
All ER	All England Reports	UK / R-U	1936-

All ER (Comm)	All England Law Reports (Commercial Cases)	UK / R-U	1999-
All ER (EC)	All England Law Reports (European Cases)	UK / R-U	1995-
All ER Rep	All England Reports Reprints	UK / R-U	1558-1935
All ER Rep Ext	All England Reprints Extension Volumes	UK / R-U	1861-1935
ALLR	Australian Labour Law Reporter	Austl	1977-
ALMD	Australian Legal Monthly Digest	Austl	1967-
Alta BAA	Alberta Board of Arbitration, Arbitrations under the Alberta Labour Act	Can (AB)	1980-
Alta BAAA	Alberta Board of Adjudication, Adjudications and Arbitrations under the Public Service Employee Relations Act	Can (AB)	1980-1986
Alta BIR	Alberta Board of Industrial Relations Decisions	Can (AB)	1961-1982
Alta ERCB	Alberta Energy Resources Conservation Board (Decisions Reports)	Can (AB)	1995-
Alta HRCR	Alberta Human Rights Commission, Reports of Boards of Inquiry	Can (AB)	1972-1982
Alta LR	Alberta Law Reports	Can (AB)	1908-1933
Alta LR (2d)	Alberta Law Reports (Second Series)	Can (AB)	1976-1992
Alta LR (3d)	Alberta Law Reports (Third Series)	Can (AB)	1992-2002
Alta LR (4th)	Alberta Law Reports (Fourth Series)	Can (AB)	2002-2009
Alta LR (5th)	Alberta Law Reports (Fifth Series)	Can (AB)	2009-
Alta LRBD	Alberta Labour Relations Board Decisions	Can (AB)	1982-1986
Alta LRBR	Alberta Labour Relations Board Reports	Can (AB)	1986-
Alta OGCB	Alberta Oil and Gas Conservation Board Decisions	Can (AB)	1957-1971
Alta PSERB	Alberta Public Service Employee Relations Board Decisions	Can (AB)	1981-1986
Alta PSGAB	Alberta Public Services Grievance Appeal Board Adjudications and Arbitrations	Can (AB)	1980-1985
Alta PUB	Alberta Public Utilities Board Decisions	Can (AB)	1976-1995
ALR	Administrative Law Reports in the British Journal of Administrative Law	UK / R-U	1954-1957
ALR	American Law Reports	US / É-U	1919-1948
ALR (2d)	American Law Reports (Second Series)	US / É-U	1948-1965
ALR (3d)	American Law Reports (Third Series)	US / É-U	1965-1980
ALR (4th)	American Law Reports (Fourth Series)	US / É-U	1980-1991
ALR (5th)	American Law Reports (Fifth Series)	US / É-U	1992-
ALR	Argus Law Reports	Austl	1895-1959
ALR	Australian Law Reports	Austl	1973-

Amb	Ambler's Reports, Chancery (ER vol 27)	UK / R-U	1716-1783
AMC	American Maritime Cases	US / É-U	1923-
And	Anderson's Common Law Conveyancing and Equity (ER vol 123)	UK / R-U	1534-1605
Andr	Andrews' Reports (ER vol 95)	UK / R-U	1738-1739
Ann Conv Eur DH	Annuaire de la Convention européenne des droits de l'Homme	EU / UE	1958-
Anst	Anstruther's Reports (ER vol 145)	UK / R-U	1792-1797
App Cas	Appeal Cases	UK / R-U	1875-1890
App Div	New York Appellate Division Reports	UK / R-U	1896-1956
App Div (2d)	New York Appellate Division Reports (Second Series)	US / É-U	1956-2003
App Div (3d)	New York Appellate Division Reports (Third Series)	US / É-U	2003-
APR	Atlantic Provinces Reports	Can	1975-
Arb Serv Rep	Arbitration Services Reporter	Can	1977-
Ariz	Arizona Reports	US / É-U	1866-
Ark	Arkansas Reports	US / É-U	1837-
Ark App	Arkansas Appellate Reports	US / É-U	1981-
Arn	Arnold's Reports	UK / R-U	1838-1839
Arn & H	Arnold and Hodges's Reports	UK / R-U	1840-1841
AR	Alberta Reports	Can (AB)	1976-
ASLC	Australian Securities Law Cases	Austl	1971-
ASC Sum	Alberta Securities Commission Summaries	Can (AB)	1975-
Asp MLC	Aspinall's Maritime Law Cases	UK / R-U	1870-1940
ATB	Canada Air Transport Board Decisions	Can	1944-1967
ATC	Australian Tax Cases	Austl	1969-
Atk	Atkyns's Reports, Chancery (ER vol 26)	UK / R-U	1736-1755
Av Cas	Aviation Cases	US / É-U	1822-
Av L Rep	Aviation Law Reporter	US / É-U	1947-
AWLD	Alberta Weekly Law Digest	Can (AB)	1982-
B & Ad	Barnewall & Adolphus's Reports, King's Bench (ER vols 109-110)	UK / R-U	1830-1834
B & Ald	Barnewall & Alderson's Reports, King's Bench (ER vol 106)	UK / R-U	1817-1822
B & CR	Reports of Bankruptcy and Companies Winding-Up Cases	UK / R-U	1918-1941
B & Cress	Barnewall & Cresswell's Reports, King's Bench (ER vols 107-109)	UK / R-U	1822-1830

B & S	Best & Smith's Reports (ER vols 121-122)	UK / R-U	1861-1865
BA	Book of Awards (Arbtration Court, Court of Appeal)	NZ / N-Z	1894-1991
Ball & B	Ball and Beatty's Reports	I	1807-1814
Barn C	Barnardiston's Chancery Reports (ER vol 27)	UK / R-U	1740-1741
Barn KB	Barnardiston's King's Bench Reports (ER vol 94)	UK / R-U	1726-1735
Barnes	Barnes's Notes (ER vol 94)	UK / R-U	1732-1760
Batt	Batty's Reports	I	1825-1826
BC En Comm'n Dec	British Columbia Energy Commission Decisions	Can (BC)	1977-1980
BCHRC Dec	British Columbia Human Rights Commission Decisions	Can (BC)	1975-1982
BCSCW Summ	British Columbia Securities Commission Weekly Summary	Can (BC)	1987-
BC Util Comm'n	British Columbia Utilities Commission Decisions	Can (BC)	1980-
BCAC	British Columbia Appeal Cases	Can (BC)	1991-
BCD	Bulletin des contributions directes, de la taxe sur la valeur ajoutée et des impôts indirects	France	1961-1974
BCLR	British Columbia Law Reports	Can (BC)	1977-1986
BCLR (2d)	British Columbia Law Reports (Second Series)	Can (BC)	1986-1995
BCLR (3d)	British Columbia Law Reports (Third Series)	Can (BC)	1995-2001
BCLR (4th)	British Columbia Law Reports (Fourth Series)	Can (BC)	2002-2007
BCLR (5th)	British Columbia Law Reports (Fifth Series)	Can (BC)	2007-
BCLRB Dec	British Columbia Labour Relations Board Decisions	Can (BC)	1979-
B Const LR	Butterworths Constitutional Law Reports	S Afr du sud	1994-
BCLR	British Columbia Law Reports	Can (BC)	1867-1947
BCWCR	British Columbia Workers' Compensation Reporter	Can (BC)	1973-2005
BDM	Bulletin de droit municipal	Can (QC)	1994-
Bd Rwy Comm'rs Can	Board of Railway Commissioners for Canada — Judgments, Orders, Regulations, and Rulings	Can	1911-1938
Bd Trans Comm'rs Can	Board of Transport Commissioners for Canada — Judgments, Orders, Regulations, and Rulings	Can	1938-1967
Beat	Beatty's Reports	I	1813-1830
Beaubien	Beaubien	Can (QC)	1905-1906
Beav	Beavan's Reports (ER vols 48-55)	UK / R-U	1838-1866
Bel	Bellewe's Reports (ER vol 72)	UK / R-U	1378-1400
Bell	Bell's Reports (ER vol 169)	UK / R-U	1858-1860
Ben & D	Benloe & Dalison's Reports (ER vol 123)	UK / R-U	1486-1580
Benl	Benloe's Reports (ER vol 73)	UK / R-U	1531-1628

BILC	British International Law Cases	UK / R-U	1964-1973
Bing	Bingham's Reports (ER vols 130-131)	UK / R-U	1822-1834
Bing NC	Bingham's New Cases (ER vols 131-133)	UK / R-U	1834-1840
BISD	Basic Instruments and Selected Documents	GATT	1952-
Bla H	H Blackstone Reports	UK / R-U	1788-1796
Bla W	W Blackstone Reports	UK / R-U	1746-1779
BLE	Bulletin du libre-échange	Can	1990-1996
Bli	Bligh's Reports, House of Lords (ER vol 4)	UK / R-U	1819-1821
Bli NS	Bligh's Repors (New Series) (ER vols 4-6)	UK / R-U	1826-1837
BLR	Business Law Reports	Can	1977-1990
BLR (2d)	Business Law Reports (Second Series)	Can	1991-1999
BLR (3d)	Business Law Reports (Third Series)	Can	2000-2005
BLR (4th)	Business Law Reports (Fourth Series)	Can	2005-2012
BLR (5th)	Business Law Reports (Fifth Series)	Can	2012-
Bos & Pul	Bosanquet & Puller's Reports (ER vols 126-127)	UK / R-U	1796-1804
Bos & Pul NR	Bosanquet & Puller's New Reports (ER vol 127)	UK / R-U	1804-1807
BR	Recueils de jurisprudence du Québec : Cour du Banc de la Reine / du Roi	Can (QC)	1892-1941
BR	Rapports judiciaires officiels de Québec : Cour du Banc de la Reine / du Roi	Can (QC)	1942-1969
BREF	Décisions du Bureau de révision de l'évaluation foncière	Can (QC)	1980-1998
Bridg	Sir John Bridgman's Reports	UK / R-U	1613-1621
Bridg Conv	Sir Orlando Bridgman's Conveyances	UK / R-U	1600-1667
Bridg J	Sir J Bridgman's Reports (ER vol 123)	UK / R-U	1613-1621
Bridg O	Sir O Bridgman's Reports (ER vol 124)	UK / R-U	1660-1667
Bro CC	Brown's Chancery Cases (by Belt) (ER vols 28-29)	UK / R-U	1778-1794
Bro PC	Brown's Parliamentary Cases (ER vols 1-3)	UK / R-U	1702-1800
Brod & Bing	Broderip & Bingham's Reports (ER vol 129)	UK / R-U	1819-1822
Brooke NC	Brooke's New Cases (ER vol 73)	UK / R-U	1515-1558
Brown & Lush	Browning & Lushington's Admiralty Reports (ER vol 167)	UK / R-U	1863-1865
Brownl	Brownlow & Goldesborough's Reports (ER vol 123)	UK / R-U	1569-1624
Bull CVMQ	Bulletin — Commission des valeurs mobilières du Québec	Can (QC)	1970-
Bull civ	Bulletin des arrêts de la cour de cassation, Chambres civiles	France	1798-

Appendices / Annexes

Bull Concl fisc	Bulletin des conclusions fiscales	France	1992-
Bull Crim	Bulletin des arrêts de la cour de cassation, Chambre criminelle	France	1798-
Bull OSC	Bulletin of the Ontario Securities Commission	Can (ON)	1981-
Bulst	Bulstrode's Reports, King's Bench (ER vols 80-81)	UK / R-U	1609-1626
Bunb	Bunbury's Reports, Exchequer (ER vol 145)	UK / R-U	1713-1741
Burr	Burrow's Reports (ER vols 97-98)	UK / R-U	1756-1772
Burrell	Burrell's Reports (ER vol 167)	UK / R-U	1584-1839
C & J	Crompton & Jervis's Reports (ER vols 148-149)	UK / R-U	1830-1832
C & M	Crompton & Meeson's Reports (ER vol 149)	UK / R-U	1832-1834
C & S	Clarke and Scully's Drainage Cases	Can (ON)	1898-1903
CA	Recueils de jurisprudence du Québec : Cour d'appel	Can (QC)	1970-1985
CAC	Canada Citizenship Appeal Court, Reasons for Judgment	Can	1975-1977
CACM	Recueil des arrêts de la Cour d'appel des cours martiales du Canada	Can	1957-
CAEC	Commission d'appel des enregistrements commerciaux, Sommaires des décisions	Can (ON)	1971-1997
CAI	Décisions de la Commission d'accès à l'information	Can (QC)	1984-
Cal	California Reports	US / É-U	1850-1934
Cal (2d)	California Reports (Second Series)	US / É-U	1934-1969
Cal (3d)	California Reports (Third Series)	US / É-U	1969-1991
Cal (4th)	California Reports (Fourth Series)	US / É-U	1991-
CALP	Décisions de la Commission d'appel en matière de lésions professionnelles	Can (QC)	1986-1998
CALR	Criminal Appeals Law Reporter	Can	1993-
Calth	Calthrop's Reports (ER vol 80)	UK / R-U	1609-1618
Cam	Cameron's Privy Council Decisions	Can	1832-1929
Cameron PC	Cameron's Constitutional Decisions of the Privy Council	Can	1867-1915
Cameron SC	Cameron's Supreme Court Cases	Can	1880-1900
Camp	Campbell's Reports (ER vols 170-171)	UK / R-U	1807-1816
Cape SCR	Supreme Court Reports (Cape)	S Afr du sud	1880-1910
CAQ	Causes en appel au Québec	Can (QC)	1986-1995
CAR	Commonwealth Arbitration Reports	Austl	1905-
Car & K	Carrington & Kirwan Reports (ER vols 174-175)	UK / R-U	1843-1853
Car & M	Carrington & Marshman Reports (ER vol 174)	UK / R-U	1840-1842

Car & P	Carrington & Payne (ER vols 171-173)	UK / R-U	1823-1841
Carey	Carey's Manitoba Reports	Can (MB)	1875
Cart BNA	Cartwright's Cases on the British North America Act, 1867	Can	1882-1897
Carter	Carter's Reports, Common Pleas (ER vol 124)	UK / R-U	1664-1676
Carth	Carthew's Reports, King's Bench (ER vol 90)	UK / R-U	1686-1701
Cary	Cary's Chancery Reports (ER vol 21)	UK / R-U	1557-1604
CAS	Décisions de la Commission des affaires sociales	Can (QC)	1975-1997
Cas t Hard	Cases temp Hardwicke (ER vol 95)	UK / R-U	1733-1738
Cas t Talb	Cases temp Talbot (ER vol 25)	UK / R-U	1733-1738
CB	Common Bench Reports (ER vols 135-139)	UK / R-U	1845-1856
CB (NS)	Common Bench Reports (New Series) (ER vols 140-144)	UK / R-U	1856-1866
CBES	Recueils de jurisprudence du Québec : Cour du bien-être social	Can (QC)	1975-1977
CBR	Copyright Board Reports	Can	1990-1994
CBR	Canadian Bankruptcy Reports	Can	1920-1960
CBR (NS)	Canadian Bankruptcy Reports (New Series)	Can	1960-1990
CBR (3d)	Canadian Bankruptcy Reports (Third Series)	Can	1991-1998
CBR (4th)	Canadian Bankruptcy Reports (Fourth Series)	Can	1998-2004
CBR (5th)	Canadian Bankruptcy Reports (Fifth Series)	Can	2004-
CCC	Cahiers du Conseil constitutionnel	France	1996-2011
CCC (Nouv)	Nouveaux Cahiers du Conseil constitutionnel	France	2011-
CCC	Canadian Criminal Cases	Can	1898-1962
CCC (NS)	Canadian Criminal Cases (New Series)	Can	1963-1970
CCC (2d)	Canadian Criminal Cases (Second Series)	Can	1971-1983
CCC (3d)	Canadian Criminal Cases (Third Series)	Can	1983-
CCEL	Canadian Cases on Employment Law	Can	1983-1994
CCEL (2d)	Canadian Cases on Employment Law (Second Series)	Can	1994-2000
CCEL (3d)	Canadian Cases on Employment Law (Third Series)	Can	2000-2003
CCEL (4th)	Canadian Cases on Employment Law (Fourth Series)	Can	2003-
CCL	Canadian Current Law	Can	1948-1990
CCL	Canadian Current Law: Jurisprudence / sommaires de la jurisprudence	Can	1991
CCL	Canadian Current Law: Case Law Digests / sommaires de la jurisprudence	Can	1992-1996

CCL	Canadian Current Law: Case Digests / sommaires de la jurisprudence	Can	1996-
CCL Législation	Canadian Current Law: Annuaire de la législation	Can	1989-
CCL Legislation	Canadian Current Law: Legislation Annual	Can	1989-
CCLI	Canadian Cases on the Law of Insurance	Can	1983-1991
CCLI (2d)	Canadian Cases on the Law of Insurance (Second Series)	Can	1991-1998
CCLI (3d)	Canadian Cases on the Law of Insurance (Third Series)	Can	1998-2003
CCLI (4th)	Canadian Cases on the Law of Insurance (Fourth Series)	Can	2003-2012
CCLI (5th)	Canadian Cases on the Law of Insurance (Fifth Series)	Can	2012-
CCLR	Canadian Computer Law Reporter	Can	1983-1992
CCLS	Canadian Cases on the Law of Securities	Can	1993-1998
CCLT	Canadian Cases on the Law of Torts	Can	1976-1990
CCLT (2d)	Canadian Cases on the Law of Torts (Second Series)	Can	1990-2000
CCLT (3d)	Canadian Cases on the Law of Torts (Third Series)	Can	2000-
CCPB	Canadian Cases on Pensions and Benefits	Can	1994-
CCRI	Conseil canadien des relations industrielles, motifs de décision	Can	1999-
CCRTD	Conseil canadien des relations du travail, décisions	Can	1949-1974
CCRTDI	Conseil canadien des relations du travail, décisions et informations	Can	1974-1998
CDB-C	Collection de décisions du Bas-Canada	Can (QC)	1847-1891
CE	Commissaires enquêteurs	Can (QC)	1970-1982
CEB	Canadian Employment Benefits and Pension Guide Reports	Can	1995-
CEDH	Cour européenne des Droits de l'Homme	EU / UE	1960-
CEDH (Sér A)	Publications de la Cour européenne des Droits de l'Homme : Série A : Arrêts et décisions (autre titre / other title: Recueil des arrêts et décisions de la cour européenne des droits de l'homme)	EU / UE	1960-1999
CEDH (Sér B)	Publications de la Cour européenne des Droits de l'Homme : Série B : Mémoires, plaidoiries et documents	EU / UE	1961-1999
CEGSB	Crown Employees Grievance Settlement Board Decisions	Can (ON)	1976-1997
CELR	Canadian Environmental Law Reports	Can	1978-1985
CELR (NS)	Canadian Environmental Law Reports (New Series)	Can	1986-2003

Appendix C / Annex C A-43

Abbr	Title	Juris	Years
CELR (3d)	Canadian Environmental Law Reports (Third Series)	Can	2003-
CER	Canadian Customs and Excise Reports	Can	1980-1989
CF	Recueils des arrêts de la Cour fédérale du Canada	Can	1971-
CFLC	Canadian Family Law Cases	Can	1959-1977
CFP	Recueil des décisions des comités d'appel de la fonction publique	Can (QC)	1980-1989
Ch	Law Reports, Chancery	UK / R-U	1890-
Ch App	Law Reports, Chancery Appeal Cases	UK / R-U	1865-1875
Ch CR	Chancery Chambers Reports	Can (ON)	1857-1872
Ch Ca	Cases in Chancery (ER vol 22)	UK / R-U	1660-1698
Ch D	Law Reports, Chancery Division	UK / R-U	1875-1890
Ch R	Chancery Reports (ER vol 21)	UK / R-U	1625-1710
Chan Cas	Chancery Cases (ER vol 22)	UK / R-U	1615-1710
Chit	Chitty's Practice Reports, King's Bench	UK / R-U	1770-1822
Choyce Ca	Choyce Cases in Chancery (ER vol 21)	UK / R-U	1557-1606
CHRR	Canadian Human Rights Reporter	Can	1980-
CICB	Criminal Injuries Compensation Board Decisions	Can (ON)	1971-1989
CIJ Mémoires	Cour internationale de justice : Mémoires, plaidoiries et documents	Intl	1946-
CIJ Rec	Cour internationale de justice : Recueil des arrêts, avis consultatifs et ordonnances	Intl	1946-
CIPOO (M)	Commissaire à l'information et à la protection de la vie privée, Ontario, Ordres, Séries M	Can (ON)	1988-1998
CIPOO (P)	Commissaire à l'information et à la protection de la vie privée, Ontario, Ordres, Séries P	Can (ON)	1992-1998
CIPOS	Commissaire à l'information et à la protection de la vie privée, Ontario, Sommaires	Can (ON)	1990-1992
CIPR	Canadian Intellectual Property Reports	Can	1984-1990
CIRB	Canada Industrial Relations Board, Reasons for Decision	Can	1999-
CJCE	Recueil de la jurisprudence de la cour et du tribunal de première instance, Cour de justice des communautés européennes	EU / UE	1954-
Cl & F	Clark & Finnelly's Reports, House of Lords (ER vols 6-8)	UK / R-U	1831-1846
CLAS	Canadian Labour Arbitration Summaries	Can	1986-
CLD	Commercial Law Digest	Can	1987-1990
CLL	Canadian Current Law: Canadian Legal Literature	Can	1991-
CLLC	Canadian Labour Law Cases	Can	1944-

Appendices / Annexes

CLLR	Canadian Labour Law Reporter	Can	1982-
CLP	Décisions de la Commission des lésions professionnelles	Can (QC)	1998-
CLR	Commonwealth Law Reports	Austl	1903-
CLR	Construction Law Reports	Can	1983-1992
CLR (2d)	Construction Law Reports (Second Series)	Can	1992-2000
CLR (3d)	Construction Law Reports (Third Series)	Can	2000-2011
CLR (4th)	Construction Law Reports (Fourth Series)	Can	2011-
CLRBD	Canada Labour Relations Board Decisions	Can	1949-1974
CLRBR	Canadian Labour Relations Board Reports	Can	1974-1982
CLRBR (NS)	Canadian Labour Relations Board Reports (New Series)	Can	1983-1989
CLRBR (2d)	Canadian Labour Relations Board Reports (Second Series)	Can	1989-
CM & R	Crompton, Meeson & Roscoe's Reports (ER vols 149-150)	UK / R-U	1834-1835
CMAR	Canada Court Martial Appeal Reports	Can	1957-
CMQ	Commission municipale du Québec	Can (QC)	1982-
CMR	Common Market Law Reports	EU / UE	1962-1988
CMR	Common Market Reporter	EU / UE	1988-1997
CNLC	Canadian Native Law Cases	Can	1763-1978
CNLR	Canadian Native Law Reporter	Can	1979-
Coll	Collyer's Reports (ER vol 63)	UK / R-U	1844-1846
Colles	Colles's Reports, House of Lords (ER vol 1)	UK / R-U	1697-1713
COHSC	Canadian Occupational Health and Safety Cases	Can	1989-1993
Com	Comyns's Reports (ER vol 92)	UK / R-U	1695-1740
Comb	Comberbach's Reports (ER vol 90)	UK / R-U	1685-1699
Comm Eur DHDR	Décisions et rapports de la Commission européenne des Droits de l'Homme	EU / UE	1975-1999
Comm LR	Commercial Law Reports	Can	1903-1905
Comp Trib dec	Competition Tribunal, decisions	Can	1986-?
Conc Bd Rpts	Conciliation Board Reports	Can	1966-1974
Cons sup N-F	Inventaire des jugements et délibérations du Conseil supérieur de la Nouvelle-France	Can / US	1717-1760
Cook Adm	Cook's Vice-Admiralty Reports	Can (QC)	1873-1874
Cooke CP	Cooke's Reports (Common Pleas) (ER vol 125)	UK / R-U	1706-1747
Coop Ch Ch	Cooper's Chancery Chambers Reports	Can (ON)	1866

Appendices / Annexes

Coop Pr Ca	Cooper's Practice Cases, Chancery (ER vol 47)	UK / R-U	1822-1838
Coop t Br	Cooper, temp Brougham's Reports, Chancery (ER vol 47)	UK / R-U	1833-1834
Coop t Cott	Cooper, temp Cottenham's Reports, Chancery (ER vol 47)	UK / R-U	1846-1848
Coop G	Cooper's Cases in Chancery (ER vol 35)	UK / R-U	1792-1815
Co Rep	Coke's Reports, King's Bench (ER vols 76-77)	UK / R-U	1572-1616
Cowp	Cowper's Reports (ER vol 98)	UK / R-U	1774-1778
Cox	Cox's Equity Reports (ER vols 29-30)	UK / R-U	1783-1796
CP	Recueils de jurisprudence du Québec : Cour provinciale	Can (QC)	1975-1985
CPC	Carswell's Practice Cases	Can	1976-1985
CPC (2d)	Carswell's Practice Cases (Second Series)	Can	1985-1992
CPC (3rd)	Carswell's Practice Cases (Third Series)	Can	1992-1997
CPC (4th)	Carswell's Practice Cases (Fourth Series)	Can	1997-2001
CPC (5th)	Carswell's Practice Cases (Fifth Series)	Can	2001-2004
CPC (6th)	Carswell's Practice Cases (Sixth Series)	Can	2004-2011
CPC (7th)	Carswell's Practice Cases (Seventh Series)	Can	2011-
CPC (Olmstead)	Canadian Constitutional Decisions of the Judicial Committee of the Privy Council (Olmstead)	Can	1873-1954
CPC (Plaxton)	Canadian Constitutional Decisions of the Judicial Committee of the Privy Council (Plaxton)	Can	1930-1939
CPD	Law Reports, Common Pleas Division	UK / R-U	1875-1880
CPDR	Cape Provincial Division Reports	S Afr du sud	1910-1946
CPJI (Sér A)	Publications de la Cour permanente de justice internationale : Série A : Recueil des arrêts	Intl	1922-1930
CPJI (Sér B)	Publications de la Cour permamente de justice internationale : Série B : Recueil des avis consultatifs	Intl	1922-1930
CPJI (Sér A/B)	Publications de la Cour permamente de justice internationale : Série A/B : Arrêts, ordonnances et avis consultatifs	Intl	1931-1940
CPJI (Sér C)	Publications de la Cour permanente de justice internationale : Série C : Plaidoiries, exposés oraux et documents	Intl	1922-1940
CPR	Canadian Patent Reporter	Can	1941-1971
CPR (2d)	Canadian Patent Reporter (Second Series)	Can	1971-1984
CPR (3d)	Canadian Patent Reporter (Third Series)	Can	1985-1999
CPR (4th)	Canadian Patent Reporter (Fourth Series)	Can	1999-
CPRB	Procurement Review Board of Canada, Decisions	Can	1990-?

CPTA	Décisions de la Commission de protection du territoire agricole	Can (QC)	1984-1987
CR	Criminal Reports	Can	1946-1967
CR (NS)	Criminal Reports (New Series)	Can	1967-1978
CR (3rd)	Criminal Reports (Third Series)	Can	1978-1991
CR (4th)	Criminal Reports (Fourth Series)	Can	1991-1996
CR (5th)	Criminal Reports (Fifth Series)	Can	1997-2002
CR (6th)	Criminal Reports (Sixth Series)	Can	2002-
CRAC	Canadian Reports: Appeal Cases: appeals allowed or refused by the Judicial Committee of the Privy Council	Can	1828-1913
CRAT	Commercial Registration Appeal Tribunal — Summaries of Decisions	Can (ON)	1971-1979
CRC	Canadian Railway Cases	Can	1902-1939
CRD	Charter of Rights Decisions	Can	1982-
CRMPC	Commission de révision des marchés publics du Canada, décisions	Can	1990-?
CRNZ	Criminal Reports of New Zealand	NZ / N-Z	1983-
CRR	Canadian Rights Reporter	Can	1982-1991
CRR (2d)	Canadian Rights Reporter (Second Series)	Can	1991-
CRRBDI	Canada Labour Relations Board Decisions and Information	Can	1974-1998
CRT	Canadian Radio-Television and Telecommunications decisions and policy statements	Can	1975-1985
CRTC	Canadian Railway and Transport Cases	Can	1940-1966
CS	Rapports judiciaires de Québec : Cour supérieure	Can (QC)	1892-1966
CS	Recueils de jurisprudence du Québec : Cour supérieure	Can (QC)	1967-1985
CSD	Canadian Sentencing Digest	Can	1980-1994
CSP	Recueils de jurisprudence du Québec : Cour des Sessions de la paix	Can (QC)	1975-1985
CT	Jurisprudence en droit du travail : Décisions des commissaires du travail	Can (QC)	1969-1981
CT Cases	Canadian Transport Cases	Can	1966-1977
CTAB	Canada Tax Appeal Board Cases	Can	1949-1966
CTAB (NS)	Canada Tax Appeal Board Cases (New Series)	Can	1967-1971
CTBR	Canada Tariff Board Reports	Can	1937-1988
CTC	Canada Tax Cases	Can	1917-1971
CTC (NS)	Canada Tax Cases (New Series)	Can	1972-

Appendices / Annexes

CTC	Canadian Transport Cases	Can	1966-1977
CTCR	Canadian Transport Commission Reports	Can	1978-1986
CSST	Jurisprudence en santé et sécurité du travail	Can (QC)	1981-
CSTR	Canadian Sales Tax Reports	Can	1968-1994
CTR	Canadian Tax Reporter	Can	1972-
CTR	Cape Times Reports	S Afr du sud	1891-1910
CTR	Commission du tarif registre	Can	1981-1988
CTR	De Boo Commodity Tax Reports	Can	1987-1989
CTST	Canada Trade and Sales Tax Cases	Can	1989-1991
CTTT	Décisions du Commissaire du travail et du Tribunal du travail	Can (QC)	1982-1993
CTTTCRAA	Décisions du Commissaire du travail, du Tribunal du travail et de la Commission de reconnaissance des associations d'artistes	Can (QC)	1994-1997
Cun	Cunningham's Reports (ER vol 94)	UK / R-U	1734-1736
Curt	Curteis's Reports (ER vol 163)	UK / R-U	1834-1844
D	Recueil Dalloz / Recueil le Dalloz	France	1945-1965, 1997-
DA	Recueil analytique de jurisprudence et de législation (Dalloz)	France	1941-1944
Dan	Daniell's Reports (ER vol 159)	UK / R-U	1817-1820
Davis	Davis's Reports (Ireland) (ER vol 80)	I	1604-1612
DC	Recueil critique Dalloz	France	1941-1945
DCA	Canada, Commission de la fonction publique du Canada, décisions du comité d'appel	Can	1979-1999
DCA	Décisions de la cour d'appel / Queen's Bench Reports (Dorion)	Can (QC)	1880-1886
DCDRT	Décisions sur des conflits de droit dans les relations du travail	Can (QC)	1964-1970
DCL	Décisions de la Commission des loyers	Can (QC)	1975-1981
DCR	New Zealand District Court Reports	NZ / N-Z	1980-
DCRM	Commission de révision des marchés publics du Canada, décisions	Can	1990-?
DDCP	Décisions disciplinaires concernant les corporations professionnelles	Can (QC)	1974-
DDOP	Décisions disciplinaires concernant les ordres pro-fessionnels	Can (QC)	1995-
Dea & Sw	Deane & Swabey's Reports (ER vol 164)	UK / R-U	1855-1857
Dears	Dearsly's Crown Cases (ER vol 169)	UK / R-U	1852-1856

Dears & B	Dearsly and Bell's Crown Cases (ER vol 169)	UK / R-U	1856-1858
Déc B-C	Décisions des Tribunaux du Bas-Canada	Can (QC)	1851-1867
Déc trib Mont	Précis des décisions des tribunaux du district de Montréal	Can (QC)	1853-1854
De G & J	De Gex & Jones's Reports (ER vols 44-45)	UK / R-U	1857-1859
De G & Sm	De Gex & Smale's Reports (ER vols 63-64)	UK / R-U	1846-1849
De G F & J	De Gex, Fisher & Jones's Reports (ER vol 45)	UK / R-U	1859-1862
De G J & S	De Gex, Jones & Smith's Reports (ER vol 46)	UK / R-U	1863-1865
De G M & G	De Gex, Macnaghten & Gordon's Reports (ER vols 42-44)	UK / R-U	1851-1857
DELD	Dismissal and Employment Law Digest	Can	1986-
DELEA	Digest of Environmental Law and Environmental Assessment	Can	1992-
Den	Denison's Crown Cases (ER vols 1-2)	UK / R-U	1844-1852
Dés OAL	Décisions des orateurs de l'Assemblée législative de la province de Québec (Desjardins)	Can (QC)	1867-1901
DFQE	Droit fiscal québécois express	Can (QC)	1977-
DH	Recueil hebdomadaire Dalloz	France	1924-1940
Dick	Dickens's Reports (ER vol 21)	UK / R-U	1559-1798
DJC	Documentation juridique au Canada	Can	1991-
DJG	Dalloz jurisprudence général	France	1845-1923
DLQ	Droits et libertés au Québec	Can (QC)	1986-1987
DLR	Dominion Law Reports	Can	1912-1955
DLR (2d)	Dominion Law Reports (Second Series)	Can	1956-1968
DLR (3d)	Dominion Law Reports (Third Series)	Can	1969-1984
DLR (4th)	Dominion Law Reports (Fourth Series)	Can	1984-
DOAL	Décisions des orateurs, assemblée législative	Can (NB)	1923-1982
Dods	Dodson's Reports (ER vol 165)	UK / R-U	1811-1822
Donn	Donnelly's Reports (ER vol 47)	UK / R-U	1836-1837
Doug	Douglas's Reports (ER vol 99)	UK / R-U	1778-1785
Dow	Dow's Reports (ER vol 3)	UK / R-U	1812-1818
Dow & Cl	Dow & Clark's Reports (ER vol 6)	UK / R-U	1827-1832
Dowl & Ry	Dowling & Ryland's Reports (ER vol 171)	UK / R-U	1821-1827
DP	Recueil périodique et critique de jurisprudence (Dalloz)	France	1924-1940
Drap	Draper's King's Bench Reports	Can (ON)	1829-1831
Drew	Drewry's Reports (ER vols 61-62)	UK / R-U	1851-1859

Appendices / Annexes

Drew & Sm	Drewry & Smale's Reports (ER vol 62)	UK / R-U	1860-1865
DRL	Décisions de la Régie du logement	Can (QC)	1975-1981
DS / D	Recueil Dalloz et Sirey	France	1965-1996
DTC	Dominion Tax Cases	Can	1920-
DTE	Droit du travail express	Can (QC)	1982-
Dy	Dyer's Reports, King's Bench (ER vol 73)	UK / R-U	1513-1582
E & A	Grant's Upper Canada Error and Appeal Reports	Can (ON)	1846-1866
E Afr CAR	Eastern Africa Court of Appeals Reports	Afr	1934-1956
E Afr LR	Eastern Africa Law Reports	Afr	1957-1967
East	East's Reports (ER vols 102-104)	UK / R-U	1800-1812
ECHR	European Court of Human Rights	EU / UE	1960-
ECHR (Ser A)	Publications of the European Court of Human Rights: Series A: Judgments and Decisions	EU / UE	1960-1999
ECHR (Ser B)	Publications of the European Court of Human Rights: Series B Pleadings, Oral Arguments and Documents	EU / UE	1961-1999
ECR	European Court Reports: Reports of Cases before the Court	EU / UE	1954-
Eden	Eden's Reports, Chancery (ER vol 28)	UK / R-U	1757-1766
Edw	Edwards's Admiralty Reports (ER vol 165)	UK / R-U	1808-1812
E Distr LDR	Eastern Districts' Local Division Reports	S Afr du sud	1911-1946
E Distr R	Eastern Districts' Reports	S Afr du sud	1880-1910
EHRR	European Human Rights Reports	EU / UE	1979-
El & Bl	Ellis & Blackburn's Reports (ER vols 118-120)	UK / R-U	1852-1858
El & El	Ellis & Ellis's Reports, King's Bench (ER vols 120-121)	UK / R-U	1858-1861
El Bl & El	Ellis, Blackburn & Ellis's Reports (ER vol 120)	UK / R-U	1858
ELLR	Employment and Labour Law Reporter	Can	1991-
ELR	Eastern Law Reporter	Can	1906-1915
ELR	Environmental Law Reporter of New South Wales	Austl	1981-
EMLR	Entertainment and Media Law Reports	UK / R-U	1993-
Eq Ca Abr	Equity Cases Abridged, Chancery (ER vols 21-22)	UK / R-U	1667-1744
ER	English Reports	UK / R-U	1210-1865
ERNZ	Employment Reports of New Zealand	NZ / N-Z	1991-
Esp	Espinasse's Reports	UK / R-U	1793-1807
ETR	Estates and Trusts Reports	Can	1977-1994
ETR (2d)	Estates and Trusts Reports (Second Series)	Can	1994-2003
ETR (3d)	Estates and Trusts Reports (Third Series)	Can	2003-

Appendices / Annexes

EULR	European Union Law Reporter	EU / UE	1997-
Eur Comm'n HRCD	Collection of Decisions of the European Commission of Human Rights	EU / UE	1960-1974
Eur Comm'n HRDR	European Commission of Human Rights: Decisions and Reports	EU / UE	1975-1999
Ex CR	Exchequer Court of Canada Reports	Can	1875-1922
Ex CR	Canada Law Reports: Exchequer Court	Can	1923-1970
Ex D	Law Reports, Exchequer Division	UK / R-U	1875-1890
Exch Rep	Exchequer Reports	UK / R-U	1847-1856
F	Session Cases (Fraser) (Fifth Series)	Scot / Écosse	1898-1906
F	Federal Reporter	US / É-U	1880-1924
F (2d)	Federal Reporter (Second Series)	US / É-U	1925-1993
F (3d)	Federal Reporter (Third Series)	US / É-U	1993-
F & F	Foster and Finalson's Reports (ER vol 168)	UK / R-U	1856-1867
Fam	Law Reports, Family Division	UK / R-U	1972-
Fam LR	Family Law Reports	Austl	1975-
Farm Products App Trib Dec	Farm Products Appeal Tribunal Decisions	Can (ON)	1990-1996?
F Cas	Federal Cases	US / É-U	1789-1880
FC	Federal Court Reports	Can	1971-
FCAD	Federal Court of Appeal Decisions	Can	1981-1999
FLD	Family Law Digest	Can	1968-1982
FCR	Federal Court Reports	Austl	1984-
FLR	Federal Law Reports	Austl	1956-
FLRAC	Family Law Reform Act Cases	Can (ON)	1978-1985
FLRR	Family Law Reform Reporter	Can	1978-1987
Fitz-G	Fitz-Gibbons' Reports (ER vol 94)	UK / R-U	1727-1732
Foord	Foord's Reports	S Afr	1880
Forrest	Forrest's Reports (ER vol 145)	UK / R-U	1800-1801
Fort	Fortescue's Reports (ER vol 92)	UK / R-U	1695-1738
Fost	Foster's Reports (ER vol 168)	UK / R-U	1743-1761
Fox Pat C	Fox's Patent, Trade mark, Design, and Copyright Cases	Can	1940-1971
FPR	Fisheries Pollution Reports	Can	1980
F Supp	Federal Supplement	US / É-U	1933-1998
F Supp (2d)	Federal Supplement (Second Series)	US / É-U	1998-

FTLR	Financial Times Law Reports	UK / R-U	1981-1998
FTLR	Free Trade Law Reports	Can	1989-1991
FTR	Federal Trial Reports	Can	1986-
FTU	Free Trade Update	Can	1990-1996
Gaz LR	Gazette Law Reports	NZ / N-Z	1898-1952
Gaz Pal	Gazette du Palais	France	1886-
Ghana LR	Ghana Law Reports (West Africa)	W Afr	1959-1966, 1971-1978
Giff	Giffard's Reports (ER vols 65-66)	UK / R-U	1858-1865
Gilb Cas	Gilbert's Cases in Law & Equity (ER vol 93)	UK / R-U	1713-1715
Gilb Rep	Gilbert's Reports, Chancery (ER vol 25)	UK / R-U	1705-1727
GLR	Gazette Law Reports	NZ / N-Z	1898-1953
Godbolt	Godbolt's Reports (ER vol 78)	UK / R-U	1575-1638
Good Pat	Goodeve's Abstract of Patent Cases	UK / R-U	1785-1883
Gould	Gouldsborough's Reports (ER vol 75)	UK / R-U	1586-1602
Gow	Gow's Reports (ER vol 171)	UK / R-U	1818-1820
Gr	Grant's Upper Canada Chancery Reports	Can (ON)	1849-1882
Greg R	Gregorowski's Reports (Orange Free State)	S Afr du sud	1883-1887
Griq WR	Griqualand West Reports (Cape of Good Hope)	S Afr du sud	1882-1910
GSTR	Canadian Goods and Services Tax Reporter / Reports / Monitor	Can	1989-
GTC	Canadian GST & Commodity Tax Cases	Can	1993-
H & C	Hurlstone & Coltman's Reports (ER vols 158-159)	UK / R-U	1862-1866
H & M	Hemming & Miller's Reports (ER vol 71)	UK / R-U	1862-1865
H & N	Hurlstone & Norman's Reports (ER vols 156-158)	UK / R-U	1856-1862
H & Tw	Hall & Twells' Reports (ER vol 47)	UK / R-U	1849-1850
H & W	Haszard & Warburton's Reports	Can (PEI)	1850-1882
Hag Adm	Haggard's Admiralty Reports (ER vol 166)	UK / R-U	1822-1838
Hag Con	Haggard's Consistory Reports (ER vol 161)	UK / R-U	1752-1821
Hag Ecc	Haggard's Ecclesiastical Reports (ER vol 162)	UK / R-U	1827-1833
Hague Ct Rep	Hague Court Reports (1916)	Intl	1899-1915
Hague Ct Rep (2d)	Hague Court Reports (Second Series) (1932)	Intl	1916-1925
Hardr	Hardres' Reports (ER vol 145)	UK / R-U	1655-1669
Hare	Hare's Reports (ER vols 66-68)	UK / R-U	1841-1853
Harr & Hodg	Harrison and Hodgins Municipal Report	Can (ON)	1845-1851

Appendices / Annexes

Hay & M	Hay & Marriott's Reports (ER vol 165)	UK / R-U	1776-1779
Her Tr Nor	Heresy Trials in the Diocese of Norwich	UK / R-U	1428-1431
Het	Hetley's Reports (ER vol 124)	UK / R-U	1627-1632
HL Cas	Clark's House of Lords Cases (ER vols 9-11)	UK / R-U	1847-1866
HL Cas	House of Lords Cases	UK / R-U	1847-1866
Hob	Hobart's Reports (ER vol 80)	UK / R-U	1603-1625
Hodg	Hodgins Election Cases	Can (ON)	1871-1878
Hodges	Hodges' Reports	UK / R-U	1835-1837
Holt	Holt's Reports (ER vol 171)	UK / R-U	1815-1817
Holt, Eq	Holt's Equity Reports (ER vol 71)	UK / R-U	1845
Holt, KB	Holt's King's Bench Cases (ER vol 90)	UK / R-U	1688-1711
Hut	Hutton's Reports (ER vol 123)	UK / R-U	1612-1639
IAA	Industrial Arbitration Awards	NZ / N-Z	1901-
IAR	Industrial Arbitration Reports	Austl (NSW)	1902-
IBDD	Instruments de base et documents divers	GATT	1952-
ICC	Indian Claims Commission Decisions	US / É-U	1948-1978
I Ch R	Irish Chancery Reports	I	1852-1867
ICJ Pleadings	International Court of Justice: Pleadings, Oral Arguments, Documents	Intl	1946-
ICJ Rep	International Court of Justice: Reports of Judgments, Advisory Opinions, and Orders	Intl	1946-
ICLR	Irish Common Law Reports	I	1852-1867
ICR	Industrial Cases Reports	UK / R-U	1972-
ICR	Industrial Court Reports	UK / R-U	1972-1974
ICSID	International Centre for Settlement of Investment Disputes (World Bank)	Intl	1966-
ILR	Insurance Law Reporter	Can	1934-1950
ILR	Canadian Insurance Law Reporter	Can	1951-
ILR	International Law Reports	Intl	1950-
ILR	Irish Law Reports	I	1838-1850
ILRM	Irish Law Reports Monthly	I	1981-
ILTR	Irish Law Times Reports	I	1867-
IMA	Institute of Municipal Assessors of Ontario, Court Decisions	Can (ON)	1974-1986
Imm ABD	Immigration Appeal Board Decisions	Can	1977-1988
Imm AC	Immigration Appeal Cases	Can	1968-1970

Imm AC (2d)	Immigration Appeal Cases (Second Series)	Can	1969-1977
Imm LR	Immigration Law Reporter	Can	1985-1987
Imm LR (2d)	Immigration Law Reporter (Second Series)	Can	1987-1999
Imm LR (3d)	Immigration Law Reporter (Third Series)	Can	1999-2012
Imm LR (4th)	Immigration Law Reporter (Fourth Series)	Can	2012
Inter-Am Ct HR (Ser A)	Inter-American Court of Human Rights, Series A: Judgments and Opinions	Intl	1982-
Inter-Am Ct HR (Ser B)	Inter-American Court of Human Rights, Series B: Pleadings, Oral Arguments, and Documents	Intl	1983-
Inter-Am Ct HR (Ser C)	Inter-American Court of Human Rights, Series C: Decisions and Judgments	Intl	1987-
IR	Irish Law Reports	I	1892-
IR Eq	Irish Reports, Equity Series	I	1867-1878
IRCL	Irish Reports, Common Law Series	I	1867-1878
J & H	Johnson & Hemming's Reports (ER vol 70)	UK / R-U	1860-1862
Jac	Jacob's Reports (ER vol 37)	UK / R-U	1821-1822
Jac & W	Jacob & Walker's Reports (ER vol 37)	UK / R-U	1819-1821
J-cl Admin	Juris-classeur Administratif	France	
J-cl BC	Juris-classeur Banque et crédit	France	
J-cl Brev	Juris-classeur Brevets d'invention	France	
J-cl C-C	Juris-classeur Concurrence-consommation	France	
J-cl C-D	Juris-classeur Contrats-distribution	France	
J-cl Civ	Juris-classeur Civil	France	Publication
J-cl Civ Annexe	Juris-classeur Civil annexe	France	créée en
J-cl Coll terr	Juris-classeur Collectivités territoriales	France	1907
J-cl Com gén	Juris-classeur Commercial général	France	Mises à
J-cl Constr	Juris-classeur Construction	France	jour
J-cl Coprop	Juris-classeur Copropriété	France	trimestrielles
J-cl Div	Juris-classeur Divorce	France	
J-cl Dr comp	Juris-classeur Droit comparé	France	
J-cl Dr de l'enfant	Juris-classeur Droit de l'enfant	France	
J-cl Dr Intl	Juris-classeur Droit International	France	
J-cl Env	Juris-classeur Environnement	France	
J-cl Eur	Juris-classeur Europe	France	
J-cl F com	Juris-classeur Fonds de commerce	France	
J-cl Fisc	Juris-classeur Fiscal	France	

Appendices / Annexes

J-cl Fisc imm	Juris-classeur Fiscalité immobilière	France	
J-cl Fisc intl	Juris-classeur Fiscal international	France	
J-cl Foncier	Juris-classeur Foncier	France	
J-cl Impôt	Juris-classeur Impôt sur la fortune	France	
J-cl MDM	Juris-classeur Marques, dessins et modèles	France	
J-cl Not Form	Juris-classeur Notarial formulaire	France	
J-cl Pén	Juris-classeur Pénal	France	
J-cl Proc	Juris-classeur Procédure	France	Publication
J-cl Proc coll	Juris-classeur Procédures collectives	France	founded
J-cl Proc fisc	Juris-classeur Procédures fiscales	France	in 1907
J-cl Proc pén	Juris-classeur Procédure pénale	France	Quarterly
J-cl Prop litt art	Juris-classeur Propriété littéraire et artistique	France	updates
J-cl Rép prat Dr priv	Juris-classeur Répertoire pratique de droit privé	France	
J-cl Resp civ Ass	Juris-classeur Responsabilité civile et Assurances	France	
J-cl Séc Soc	Juris-classeur sécurité sociale	France	
J-cl Sociétés	Juris-classeur Sociétés	France	
J-cl Trav	Juris-classeur Travail	France	
JCP	Semaine Juridique	France	1937-
JE	Jurisprudence Express	Can (QC)	1977-
Jenk	Jenkins's Reports (ER vol 145)	UK / R-U	1220-1623
JL	Jurisprudence logement	Can (QC)	1982-
JL	Jurisprudence Logement	Can (QC)	1982-
JM	Décisions du juge des mines du Québec	Can (QC)	1967-1972
JM	Justice municipale	Can (QC)	1981-
Johns	Johnson's Reports (ER vol 70)	UK / R-U	1859
Jones T	Jones, T, Reports (ER vol 84)	UK / R-U	1667-1685
Jones W	Jones, W, Reports (ER vol 82)	UK / R-U	1620-1641
Jug et dél NF	Jugements et délibrérations du Conseil souverain de la Nouvelle-France	Can (QC)	1663-1704
Jug et dél Q	Jugements et délibrérations du Conseil supérieur de Québec	Can (QC)	1705-1716
K & J	Kay & Johnson's Reports (ER vols 69-70)	UK / R-U	1854-1858
Kay	Kay's Reports (ER vol 69)	UK / R-U	1853-1854
KB	Law Reports, King's Bench	UK / R-U	1901-1951
Keble	Keble's Reports (ER vols 83-84)	UK / R-U	1661-1679

Keen	Keen's Reports (ER vol 48)	UK / R-U	1836-1838
Keilway	Keilway's Reports (ER vol 72)	UK / R-U	1496-1531
Kel J / Kel	Kelyng, Sir John's Reports (ER vol 84)	UK / R-U	1662-1669
Kel W	Kelynge, William's Reports (ER vol 25)	UK / R-U	1730-1732
Keny	Kenyon's Reports (ER vol 96)	UK / R-U	1753-1759
Kenya LR	Kenya Law Reports	Kenya	1897-1956
KLR	Kenya Law Reports	Afr	1897-1956
Kn	Knapp's Privy Council Appeal Cases (ER vol 12)	UK / R-U	1829-1836
LAC	Labour Arbitration Cases	Can (ON)	1948-1972
LAC (2d)	Labour Arbitration Cases (Second Series)	Can (ON)	1973-1981
LAC (3d)	Labour Arbitration Cases (Third Series)	Can (ON)	1982-1989
LAC (4th)	Labour Arbitration Cases (Fourth Series)	Can (ON)	1989-
Lane	Lane's Reports (ER vol 145)	UK / R-U	1605-1611
Lap Sp Dec	Laperrière's Speakers' Decisions	Can	1841-1872
LAR	Labor Arbitration Reports	US / É-U	1946-
Latch	Latch's Reports, King's Bench (ER vol 82)	UK / R-U	1625-1628
LC Jur	Lower Canada Jurist	Can (QC)	1847-1891
LCBD	Land Compensation Board Decisions	Can (ON)	1971-1983
LCR	Land Compensation Reports	Can	1969-
LCR	Lower Canada Reports	Can (QC)	1851-1867
Leach	Leach's Cases on Crown Law (ER vol 168)	UK / R-U	1730-1815
L Ed	United States Supreme Court, Lawyers' Edition	US / É-U	1790-1955
L Ed (2d)	United States Supreme Court, Lawyers' Edition (Second Series)	US / É-U	1956-
Lee	Lee's Ecclesiastical Reports (ER vol 161)	UK / R-U	1752-1758
Leo	Leonard's Reports (ER vol 74)	UK / R-U	1540-1615
Lev	Levinz's Reports (ER vol 83)	UK / R-U	1660-1697
Lewin	Lewin's Crown Cases on the Northern Circuit (ER vol 168)	UK / R-U	1822-1838
Le & Ca	Leigh & Cave's Reports (ER vol 169)	UK / R-U	1861-1865
Ley	Ley's Reports (ER vol 80)	UK / R-U	1608-1629
Lilly	Lilly's Assize Cases	UK / R-U	1688-1693
Lit	Littleton's Reports (ER vol 120)	UK / R-U	1626-1632
Ll LR	Lloyd's List Law Reports	UK / R-U	1919-1950
Lloyd's Rep	Lloyd's Law Reports	UK / R-U	1968-

Lloyd's Rep	Lloyd's List Law Reports	UK / R-U	1951-1967
Lloyd's Rep Med	Lloyd's Law Reports (Medical)	UK / R-U	1998-
LN	Legal News	Can (QC)	1878-1897
LR A & E	Law Reports, Admiralty and Ecclesiastical Cases (ER vols 1-4)	UK / R-U	1865-1875
LR A & E	Law Reports, Admiralty and Ecclesiastical Cases	UK / R-U	1865-1875
LR CCR	Law Reports, Crown Cases Reserved	UK / R-U	1865-1875
LR CP	Law Reports, Common Pleas	UK / R-U	1865-1875
LR Ch App	Law Reports, Chancery Appeals	UK / R-U	1865-1875
LR Eq	Law Reports, Equity Cases	UK / R-U	1865-1875
LR Ex	Law Reports, Exchequer	UK / R-U	1865-1875
LRHL	Law Reports, English and Irish Appeals	I / UK / R-U	1865-1875
LR Ir	Law Reports, Ireland	I	1878-1893
LR P & D	Law Reports, Probate and Divorce	UK / R-U	1865-1875
LR QB	Law Reports, Queen's Bench	UK / R-U	1865-1875
LR RP	Law Reports, Restrictive Practices	UK / R-U	1957-1972
LR Sc & Div	Law Reports, House of Lords Scotch and Divorce Appeal Cases	UK / R-U	1866-1875
LRPC	Law Reports, Privy Council	UK / R-U	1865-1875
Lush	Lushington's Reports (ER vol 167)	UK / R-U	1859-1862
Lut	Lutwyche's Reports (ER vol 125)	UK / R-U	1682-1704
M & M	Moody & Malkin (ER vol 173)	UK / R-U	1826-1830
M & Rob	Moody & Robinson (ER vol 174)	UK / R-U	1831-1844
M & S	Maule & Selwyn's Reports (ER vol 105)	UK / R-U	1813-1817
M & W	Meeson & Welsby's Reports (ER vols 150-153)	UK / R-U	1836-1847
Mac & G	M'Naghten & Gordon's Reports (ER vols 41-42)	UK / R-U	1849-1851
Macl & R	Maclean & Robinson's Reports (ER vol 9)	UK / R-U	1839
MACMLC	Digest of the Selected Judgements of the Maori Appellate Court and Maori Land Court	NZ / N-Z	1858-1968
Madd	Maddock's Reports (ER vol 56)	UK / R-U	1815-1822
Man & G	Manning & Granger's Reports (ER vols 133-135)	UK / R-U	1840-1844
Man LR	Manitoba Law Reports (Queen's Bench)	Can (MB)	1884-1890
Man MTBD	Manitoba Motor Transport Board Decisions	Can (MB)	1936-
Man R	Manitoba Reports	Can (MB)	1883-1961
Man R (2d)	Manitoba Reports (Second Series)	Can (MB)	1979-
Man R temp Wood	Manitoba Reports temp Wood (ed Armour)	Can (MB)	1875-1882

Appendices / Annexes

Maori L Rev	Maori Law Review	NZ / N-Z	1993-
March, NR	March's New Cases (ER vol 82)	UK / R-U	1639-1642
MC	Malayan Cases	Sing	1939-?
MCC	Mining Commissioner's Cases	Can (ON)	1906-1979
MCD	Magistrates' Court Decisions	NZ /N-Z	1939-1979
M'Cle	M'Cleland's Reports (ER vol 148)	UK / R-U	1824
M'Cle & Yo	M'Cleland & Younge's Reports (ER vol 148)	UK / R-U	1824-1825
MCR	Montreal Condensed Reports	Can (QC)	1853-1854
MCR	Précis des décisions des tribunaux du district de Montréal	Can (QC)	1853-1854
MCR	Magistrates' Court Reports	NZ / N-Z	1939-1979
Mer	Merivale's Reports (ER vols 35-36)	UK / R-U	1815-1817
MHRC Dec	Manitoba Human Rights Commission Decisions	Can (MB)	1971-1982
MLB Dec	Manitoba Labour Board Decisions	Can (MB)	1985-
MLR (KB)	Montreal Law Reports, King's Bench	Can (QC)	1885-1891
MLR (QB)	Montreal Law Reports, Queen's Bench	Can (QC)	1885-1891
MLR (SC)	Montreal Law Reports, Superior Court	Can (QC)	1885-1891
MMC	Martin's Mining Cases	Can (BC)	1853-1908
Mod	Modern Reports (ER vols 86-88)	UK / R-U	1669-1732
Mont Cond Rep	Montreal Condensed Reports	Can (QC)	1853-1854
Moo Ind App	Moore's Reports, Indian Appeals, Privy Council (ER vols 18-20)	UK / R-U	1836-1872
Moo KB	Moore's Reports, King's Bench (ER vol 72)	UK / R-U	1519-1621
Moo PC	Moore's Reports, Privy Council (ER vols 12-15)	UK / R-U	1836-1862
Moo PCNS	Moore's Reports, Privy Council, (New Series) (ER vols 15-17)	UK / R-U	1862-1873
Mood	Moody's Reports (ER vols 168-169)	UK / R-U	1824-1837
Mos	Mosely's Reports (ER vol 25)	UK / R-U	1726-1731
MPLR	Municipal and Planning Law Reports	Can	1976-1990
MPLR (2d)	Municipal and Planning Law Reports (Second Series)	Can	1991-1999
MPLR (3d)	Municipal and Planning Law Reports (Third Series)	Can	1999-2004
MPLR (4th)	Municipal and Planning Law Reports (Fourth Series)	Can	2004-2012
MPLR (5th)	Municipal and Planning Law Reports (Fifth Series)	Can	2012-
MPR	Maritime Provinces Reports	Can	1929-1968
MVR	Motor Vehicle Reports	Can	1979-1988
MVR (2d)	Motor Vehicle Reports (Second Series)	Can	1988-1994

MVR (3d)	Motor Vehicle Reports (Third Series)	Can	1994-2000
MVR (4th)	Motor Vehicle Reports (Fourth Series)	Can	2000-2004
MVR (5th)	Motor Vehicle Reports (Fifth Series)	Can	2004-2011
MVR (6th)	Motor Vehicle Reports (Sixth Series)	Can	2011-
My & Cr	Mylne & Craig's Reports (ER vols 40-41)	UK / R-U	1835-1840
My & K	Mylne & Keen's Reports (ER vols 39-40)	UK / R-U	1832-1835
NACD	Native Appeal Court Selected Decisions (Natal and Transvaal)	S Afr du sud	1930-1948
NACR	Native Appeal Court Reports	S Afr du sud	1951-
NB Eq	New Brunswick Equity Reports (Trueman)	Can (NB)	1894-1911
NB Eq Cas	New Brunswick Equity Cases (Trueman)	Can (NB)	1876-1893
NBESTD	New Brunswick Employment Standards Tribunal Decisions	Can (NB)	1986-1993
NBHRC Dec	New Brunswick Human Rights Commission Decisions	Can (NB)	1974-1982
NBLEBD	New Brunswick Labour and Employment Board Decisions	Can (NB)	1994-
NBLLC	New Brunswick Labour Law Cases	Can (NB)	1965-1979
NBPPABD	New Brunswick Provincial Planning Appeal Board Decisions	Can (NB)	1973-1983
NBR	New Brunswick Reports	Can (NB)	1825-1928
NBR (2d)	New Brunswick Reports (Second Series)	Can (NB)	1969-
NE	Northeastern Reporter	US / É-U	1885-1936
NE (2d)	Northeastern Reporter (Second Series)	US / É-U	1936-
NEBD	National Energy Board, Reasons for Decision	Can	1970-
Nels	Nelson's Reports, Chancery (ER vol 21)	UK / R-U	1625-1693
Nfld & PEIR	Newfoundland and Prince Edward Island Reports	Can (NF/PEI)	1971-
Nfld LR	Newfoundland Law Reports	Can (NF)	1817-1949
Nfld Sel Cas	Newfoundland Selected Cases	Can (NF)	1817-1928
NHRC Dec	Newfoundland Human Rights Commission Decisions	Can (NF)	1971-1977
NI	Northern Ireland Law Reports	NI / IN	1925-
NLR	Nigeria Law Reports	Nigeria	1881-1955
NLR	Nyasaland Law Reports (Malawi)	Malawi	1922-1952
NLR (OS)	Natal Law Reports (Old Series)	S Afr du sud	1867-1872
NLR (NS)	Natal Law Reports (New Series)	S Afr du sud	1879-1932
Noy	Noy's Reports (ER vol 74)	UK / R-U	1559-1649
NPDR	Natal Provincial Division Reports	S Afr du sud	1933-1946

NR	National Reporter	Can	1973-
NSHRC Dec	Nova Scotia Human Rights Commissions Decisions	Can (NS)	1972-1980
NSBCPU Dec	Nova Scotia Board of Commissioners of Public Utilities Decisions	Can (NS)	1923-1973
NSCGA Dec	Nova Scotia Compendium of Grievance Arbitration Decisions	Can (NS)	1978-2000
NSR	Nova Scotia Reports	Can	1834-1929, 1965-1969
NSR (2d)	Nova Scotia Reports (Second Series)	Can (NS)	1969-
NSRUD	Nova Scotia Reported and Unreported Decisions	Can (NS)	1979-1988
NSWSCR	New South Wales Supreme Court Reports	Austl (NSW)	1862-1976
NSW St R	New South Wales State Reports	Austl (NSW)	1901-1970
NSWLR	New South Wales Law Reports	Austl (NSW)	1880-1900, 1971-
NSWR	New South Wales Reports	Austl (NSW)	1960-1970
NSWWN	New South Wales Weekly Notes	Austl (NSW)	1884-1970
NTAR	National Transportation Agency of Canada Reports	Can	1988-1995
NTJ	Northern Territory Judgments	Austl (NT)	1951-1976
NTLR	Northern Territory Law Reports	Austl (NT)	1992-
NTR	Northern Territory Reports	Austl (NT)	1978-
NW	Northwestern Reporter	US / É-U	1879-1942
NW (2d)	Northwestern Reporter (Second Series)	US / É-U	1942-
NWTR	Northwest Territories Reports	Can (NWT)	1983-1998
NWTSCR	Northwest Territories Supreme Court Reports	Can (NWT)	1889-1900
NY	New York Reports	US / É-U	1885-1955
NY (2d)	New York Reports (Second Series)	US / É-U	1956-2004
NYS (2d)	New York Supplement (Second Series)	US / É-U	1956-2004
NY (3d)	New York Reports (Third Series)	US / É-U	2004-
NZAC	Judgments of the Arbitration Court of New Zealand	NZ /N-Z	1979-1986
NZAR	New Zealand Administrative Reports	NZ / N-Z	1976-
NZBLC	New Zealand Business Law Cases	NZ / N-Z	1984-
NZFLR	New Zealand Family Law Reports	NZ / N-Z	1981-
NZILR	New Zealand Industral Law Reports	NZ / N-Z	1987-1990
NZIPR	New Zealand Intellectual Property Reports	NZ / N-Z	1967-1987
NZLR	New Zealand Law Reports	NZ / N-Z	1883-
NZPCC	New Zealand Privy Council Cases	NZ / N-Z	1840-1932

NZTC	New Zealand Tax Cases	NZ / N-Z	1973-
OAC	Ontario Appeal Cases	Can (ON)	1984-
OAR	Ontario Appeal Reports	Can (ON)	1876-1900
OELD	Ontario Environmental Law Digest	Can (ON)	1996-1999
OFLR	Ontario Family Law Reporter	Can (ON)	1987-
OHRCBI	Ontario Human Rights Commission, Board of Inquiry	Can (ON)	1963-1996
OHRC Dec	Ontario Human Rights Commission Decisions	Can (ON)	1956-1995?
OHRC Transcr	Ontario Human Rights Commission, Trancripts of Selected Hearings	Can (ON)	1968-1973
OIC Arb	Ontario Insurance Commission, Arbitration Cases	Can (ON)	1995-
Olmsted PC	Olmsted's Privy Council Decisions	Can	1867-1954
OLR	Ontario Law Reports	Can (ON)	1900-1931
OLRB Rep	Ontario Labour Relations Board Reports	Can (ON)	1944-
OMB Dec	Ontario Municipal Board Decisions	Can (ON)	1953-1994
OMB Index	Ontario Municipal Board Index to Applications Disposed of	Can (ON)	1969-1992
OMBR	Ontario Municipal Board Reports	Can (ON)	1973-
ONED	Office national de l'énergie, décisions	Can	1970-
Ont D Crim	Ontario Decisions — Criminal	Can (ON)	1997-1999
Ont D Crim Conv	Ontario Decisions — Criminal Convictions Cases	Can (ON)	1980-1996
Ont D Crim Sent	Ontario Decisions — Criminal Sentence Cases	Can (ON)	1984-1996
Ont Elec	Ontario Election Cases	Can (ON)	1884-1900
Ont En Bd Dec	Ontario Energy Board Decisions	Can (ON)	1961-
Ont Envtl Assessment Bd Dec	Ontario Environmental Assessment Board Decisions	Can (ON)	1980-
Ont Health Disciplines Bd Dec	Ontario Health Disciplines Board Decisions	Can (ON)	1980-
Ont Pol R	Ontario Police Reports	Can (ON)	1980-
OPR	Ontario Practice Reports	Can (ON)	1848-1901
OR	Ontario Reports	Can (ON)	1882-1900 1931-1973
OR (2d)	Ontario Reports (Second Series)	Can (ON)	1973-1990
OR (3d)	Ontario Reports (Third Series)	Can (ON)	1991-
Orange Free State Prov Div R	Orange Free State Provincial Division Reports	S Afr du sud	1910-1946
OSC Bull	Ontario Securities Commission Bulletin	Can (ON)	1949-
OSCWS	Ontario Securities Commission Weekly Summary	Can (ON)	1967-1980

OWCAT Dec	Ontario Workers' Compensation Appeals Tribunal Decisions	Can (ON)	1986-1989
Ow	Owen's Reports (ER vol 74)	UK / R-U	1556-1615
OWN	Ontario Weekly Notes	Can (ON)	1909-1962
OWR	Ontario Weekly Reporter	Can (ON)	1902-1916
P	Law Reports, Probate, Divorce, and Admiralty Division	UK / R-U	1891-1971
P	Pacific Reporter	US / É-U	1883-1931
P (2d)	Pacific Reporter (Second Series)	US / É-U	1931-2000
P (3d)	Pacific Reporter (Third Series)	US / É-U	2000-
P Wms	Peere Williams's Reports (ER vol 24)	UK / R-U	1695-1735
Palm	Palmer's Reports (ER vol 81)	UK / R-U	1619-1629
Park	Parker's Reports (ER vol 145)	UK / R-U	1743-1767
Patr Elec Cas	Patrick's Election Cases (Upper Canada / Canada West)	Can (ON)	1824-1849
PCIJ (Ser A)	Publications of the Permanent Court of International Justice: Series A, Collection of Judgments	EU / UE	1922-1930
PCIJ (Ser B)	Publications of the Permanent Court of International Justice: Series B, Collection of Advisory Opinions	EU / UE	1922-1930
PCIJ (Ser A/B)	Publications of the Permanent Court of International Justice: Series A/B, Judgments, Orders and Advisory Opinions	EU / UE	1931-1940
PCIJ (Ser C)	Publications of the Permanent Court of International Justice, Series C, Pleadings, Oral Statements and Documents	EU / UE	1922-1940
PD	Law Reports, Probate, Divorce, and Admiralty Division	UK / R-U	1875-1890
Peake	Peake's Reports (ER vol 170)	UK / R-U	1790-1812
Peake Add Cas	Peake's Reports (Additional Cases) (ER vol 170)	UK / R-U	1790-1912
PEI	Prince Edward Island Supreme Court Reports	Can (PEI)	1850-1882
PER	Pay Equity Reports	Can (ON)	1990-
Per CS	Extraits ou précédents des arrêts tirés des registres du Conseil supérieur de Québec (Perrault)	Can (QC)	1727-1759
Perr P	Extraits ou précédents des arrêts tirés des registres de la prévosté de Québec (Perrault)	Can (QC)	1753-1854
Peters	Peters' Prince Edward Island Reports	Can (PEI)	1850-1872
PFP	Pandectes françaises périodiques	France	1791-1844
Ph	Phillips' Reports (ER vol 41)	UK / R-U	1841-1849
Phill Ecc	Phillimore's Ecclesiastical Reports (ER vol 161)	UK / R-U	1809-1821

Appendices / Annexes

Pl Com	Plowden's Commentaries (ER vol 75)	UK / R-U	1550-1580
PNGCB Alta	Petroleum and Natural Gas Conservation Board of Alberta	Can (AB)	1938-1957
Pollex	Pollexfen's Reports (ER vol 86)	UK / R-U	1669-1685
Pop	Popham's Reports (ER vol 79)	UK / R-U	1592-1627
PPR	Planning and Property Reports	Can (ON)	1960-1963
PPSAC	Personal Property Security Act Cases	Can	1977-1990
PPSAC (2d)	Personal Property Security Act Cases (Second Series)	Can	1991-2000
PPSAC (3d)	Personal Property Security Act Cases (Third Series)	Can	2001-
PRBC	Procurement Review Board of Canada Decisions	Can	1990-1994
PRBR	Pension Review Board Reports	Can	1972-1986
Prec Ch	Precedents in Chancery (T Finch) (ER vol 24)	UK / R-U	1689-1722
Price	Price's Reports (ER vols 145-147)	UK / R-U	1814-1824
Pyke	Pyke's Reports	Can (QC)	1809-1810
QAC	Québec Appeal Cases	Can (QC)	1986-1995
QB	Queen's Bench Reports (ER vols 113-118)	UK / R-U	1841-1852
QBD	Law Reports, Queen's Bench Division	UK / R-U	1875-1890
Qc Comm dp déc	Québec Commission des droits de la personne, décisions des tribunaux	Can (QC)	1977-1981
Qld Lawyer Reps	Queensland Lawyer Reports	Austl (Qld)	1973-
QLR	Quebec Law Reports	Can (QC)	1875-1891
QPR	Québec Practice Reports	Can (QC)	1896-1944
QR	Queensland Reports	Austl (Qld)	1958-
Q St R	Queensland State Reports	Austl (Qld)	1902-1957
RAC	Ramsay, Appeal Cases	Can (QC)	1873-1886
RAT	Recueil d'arrêts sur les transports	Can	1966-1977
Raym Ld	Raymond, Lord Reports (ER vols 91-92)	UK / R-U	1694-1732
Raym T	Raymond, Sir T Reports (ER vol 83)	UK / R-U	1660-1684
RCCT	Recueil des décisions de la Commission canadienne des transports	Can	1978-1986
RCDA	Recueil des décisions de la Commission du droit d'auteur	Can	1990-1994
RCDA	Recueil de jurisprudence canadienne en droit des assurances	Can	1983-1991
RCDA (2e)	Recueil de jurisprudence canadienne en droit des assurances (deuxième série)	Can	1991-1998

RCDA (3ᵉ)	Recueil de jurisprudence canadienne en droit des assurances (troisième série)	Can	1998-2003
RCDA (4ᵉ)	Recueil de jurisprudence canadienne en droit des assurances (quatrième série)	Can	2003-2012
RCDA (5ᵉ)	Recueil de jurisprudence canadienne en droit des assurances (cinquième série)	Can	2012-
RCDE	Recueil de jurisprudence canadienne en droit de l'environnement	Can	1978-1985
RCDE (ns)	Recueil de jurisprudence canadienne en droit de l'environnement (nouvelle série)	Can	1986-2003
RCDE (ns)	Recueil de jurisprudence canadienne en droit de l'environnement (troisième série)	Can	2003-
RC de l'É	Recueil des arrêts de la Cour de l'Échiquier	Can	1875-1922
RC de l'É	Rapports judiciaires du Canada : Cour de l'Échiquier	Can	1823-1970
RCDF	Recueil de jurisprudence canadienne en droit de la faillite		1920-1960
RCDF (2ᵉ)	Recueil de jurisprudence canadienne en droit de la faillite (deuxième série)	Can	1960-1990
RCDF (3ᵉ)	Recueil de jurisprudence canadienne en droit de la faillite (troisième série)	Can	1991-1998
RCDF (4ᵉ)	Recueil de jurisprudence canadienne en droit de la faillite (quatrième série)	Can	1998-
RCDSST	Recueil de jurisprudence canadienne en droit de la santé et de sécurité au travail	Can	1989-1993
RCDT	Recueil de jurisprudence canadienne en droit du travail	Can	1983-1994
RCDT (2ᵉ)	Recueil de jurisprudence canadienne en droit du travail (deuxième série)	Can	1994-2000
RCDT (3ᵉ)	Recueil de jurisprudence canadienne en droit du travail (troisième série)	Can	2000-
RCDVM	Recueil de jurisprudence canadienne en droit des valeurs mobilières	Can	1993-1998
RCE / Rec / Recueil Lebon	Recueil des arrêts du Conseil d'Etat statuant au contentieux et du Tribunal des conflits, des arrêts des cours administratives d'appel et des jugements des tribunaux administratifs	France	1821-
RCRAS	Recueil de jurisprudence canadienne en matière de retraite et d'avantages sociaux	Can	1994-
RCRC	Recueil de jurisprudence canadienne en responsabilité civile	Can	1976-1990
RCRC (2ᵉ)	Recueil de jurisprudence canadienne en responsabilité civile (deuxième série)	Can	1990-2000
RCRC (3ᵉ)	Recueil de jurisprudence canadienne en respons-	Can	2000-2003

	abilité civile (troisième série)		
RCRC (4e)	Recueil de jurisprudence canadienne en respons-abilité civile (quatrième série)	Can	2003-
RCRP	Recueil des arrêts du Conseil de révision des pensions	Can	1972-1986
RCS	Rapports judiciaires du Canada : cour suprême	Can	1923-1969
RCS	Recueils des arrêts de la Cour suprême du Canada	Can	1877-1922, 1970-
RCT	Rapports de la Commission du tarif	Can	1937-1988
RDCC	Recueil des décisions du Conseil constitutionnel	France	1959-
RDCFQ	Recueil des décisions, Commission de la fonction publique et Comité d'appel de la fonction publique	Can (QC)	1990-
RDF	Recueil de droit de la famille	Can	1986-
RDFQ	Recueil de droit fiscal québécois	Can (QC)	1977-
RDI	Recueil de droit immobilier	Can (QC)	1986-
RDJ	Revue de droit judiciaire	Can (QC)	1983-1996
RDJC	Recueil de droit judiciaire de Carswell	Can	1976-1985
RDJC (2e)	Recueil de droit judiciaire de Carswell (deuxième série)	Can	1985-1992
RDJC (3e)	Recueil de droit judiciaire de Carswell (troisième série)	Can	1992-1997
RDJC (4e)	Recueil de droit judiciaire de Carswell (quatrième série)	Can	1997-2001
RDJC (5e)	Recueil de droit judiciaire de Carswell (cinquième série)	Can	2001-2004
RDJC (6e)	Recueil de droit judiciaire de Carswell (sixième série)	Can	2004-011
RDJC (7e)	Recueil de droit judiciaire de Carswell (septième série)	Can	2011-
RDP	Revue de droit pénal	Can (QC)	1978-1983
RDT	Revue de droit du travail	Can (QC)	1963-1976
RECJ	Records of the Early Courts of Justice of Upper Canada	Can (ON)	1789-1984
RED	Ritchie's Equity Decisions	Can (NB)	1872-1882
Rép admin	Encyclopédie juridique Dalloz : Répertoire de con-tentieux administratif	France	1951-
Rep Ch	Reports in Chancery (ER vol 21)	UK / R-U	1615-1710
Rép civ	Encyclopédie juridique Dalloz : Répertoire de droit civil	France	1951-
Rép com	Encyclopédie juridique Dalloz : Répertoire de droit commercial	France	1951-

Rép commun	Encyclopédie juridique Dalloz : Répertoire de droit communautaire	France	1957-
Rép pén & proc pén	Encyclopédie juridique Dalloz : Répertoire de droit pénal et de procédure pénale	France	1951-
Rép proc civ	Encyclopédie juridique Dalloz : Répertoire de procédure civile	France	1951-
Rép soc	Encyclopédie juridique Dalloz : Répertoire des sociétés	France	1951-
Rep t Finch	Reports, temp Finch (Nelson's folio Reports) (ER vol 23)	UK / R-U	1673-1681
Rép tr	Encyclopédie juridique Dalloz : Répertoire de droit du travail	France	1951-
Rev serv arb	Revue des services d'arbitrage	Can	1977-
RFL	Reports of Family Law	Can	1971-1978
RFL (2d)	Reports of Family Law (Second Series)	Can	1978-1986
RFL (3d)	Reports of Family Law (Third Series)	Can	1986-1994
RFL (4th)	Reports of Family Law (Fourth Series)	Can	1994-2000
RFL (5th)	Reports of Family Law (Fifth Series)	Can	2000-2004
RFL (6th)	Reports of Family Law (Sixth Series)	Can	2004-2011
RFL (7th)	Reports of Family Law (Seventh Series)	Can	2011
Rhod & NL R	Rhodesia & Nyasaland Law Reports	E Afr	1956-1963
Rhod LR	Rhodesian Law Reports	Zimb	1964-1979
Ridg t Hard	Ridgeway, temp Hardwicke's Reports (ER vol 27)	UK / R-U	1733-1745
RIAA	Report of International Arbitral Awards	Intl	1948-
Ritch Eq Rep	Ritchie's Equity Reports	Can (NS)	1873-1882
RJ imm	Recueil de jurisprudence en droit de l'immigration	Can	1985-1987
RJ imm (2e)	Recueil de jurisprudence en droit de l'immigration (deuxième série)	Can	1987-1999
RJ imm (3e)	Recueil de jurisprudence en droit de l'immigration (troisième série)	Can	1999-2012
RJ imm (4e)	Recueil de jurisprudence en droit de l'immigration (quatrième série)	Can	2012
RJC	Revue de jurisprudence commerciale	France	1957-
RJC	Recueil de jurisprudence en droit criminel	Can	1946-1967
RJC (ns)	Recueil de jurisprudence en droit criminel (nouvelle série)	Can	1967-1978
RJC (3e)	Recueil de jurisprudence en droit criminel (troisième série)	Can	1978-1991
RJC (4e)	Recueil de jurisprudence en droit criminel (quatrième	Can	1991-1996

Appendices / Annexes

	série)		
RJC (5e)	Recueil de jurisprudence en droit criminel (cinquième série)	Can	1997-2002
RJC (6e)	Recueil de jurisprudence en droit criminel (sixième série)	Can	2002
RJDA	Recueil de jurisprudence en droit des affaires	Can	1977-1990
RJDA (2e)	Recueil de jurisprudence en droit des affaires (deuxième série)	Can	1991-2000
RJDA (3e)	Recueil de jurisprudence en droit des affaires (troisième série)	Can	2000-2005
RJDA (4e)	Recueil de jurisprudence en droit des affaires (quatrième série)	Can	2005-2012
RJDA (5e)	Recueil de jurisprudence en droit des affaires (cinqième série)	Can	2012-
RJDC	Recueil de jurisprudence en droit de la construction	Can	1983-1992
RJDC (2e)	Recueil de jurisprudence en droit de la construction (deuxième série)	Can	1992-2000
RJDC (3e)	Recueil de jurisprudence en droit de la construction (troisième série)	Can	2000-2011
RJDC (4e)	Recueil de jurisprudence en droit de la construction (quatrième série)	Can	2011-
RJDI	Recueil de jurisprudence en droit immobilier	Can	1977-1989
RJDI (2e)	Recueil de jurisprudence en droit immobilier (deuxième série)	Can	1989-1996
RJDI (3e)	Recueil de jurisprudence en droit immobilier (troisième série)	Can	1996-2002
RJDI (4e)	Recueil de jurisprudence en droit immobilier (quatrième série)	Can	2002-2011
RJDI (5e)	Recueil de jurisprudence en droit immobilier (cinqième série)	Can	2011-
RJDM	Recueil de jurisprudence en droit municipal	Can	1976-1990
RJDM (2e)	Recueil de jurisprudence en droit municipal (deuxième série)	Can	1991-1999
RJDM (3e)	Recueil de jurisprudence en droit municipal (troisième série)	Can	1999-2001
RJDM (4e)	Recueil de jurisprudence en droit municipal (quatrième série)	Can	2004-2012
RJDM (5e)	Recueil de jurisprudence en droit municipal (cinquième série)	Can	2012-
RJDT	Recueil de jurisprudence en droit du travail	Can (QC)	1998-
RJF	Revue de jurisprudence fiscale	France	1975-

RJF	Recueil de jurisprudence en droit de la famille	Can	1971-1978
RJF (2e)	Recueil de jurisprudence en droit de la famille (deuxième série)	Can	1978-1986
RJF (3e)	Recueil de jurisprudence en droit de la famille (troisième série)	Can	1986-1994
RJF (4e)	Recueil de jurisprudence en droit de la famille (quatrième série)	Can	1994-2000
RJF (5e)	Recueil de jurisprudence en droit de la famille (cinquième série)	Can	2000-2004
RJF (6e)	Recueil de jurisprudence en droit de la famille (sixième série)	Can	2004-2011
RJF (7e)	Recueil de jurisprudence en droit de la famille (septième série)	Can	2011-
RJO (3e)	Recueil de jurisprudence de l'Ontario (troisième série) (1882-1991 : voir *Ontario Reports*)	Can (ON)	1991-
RJQ	Recueils de jurisprudence du Québec	Can (QC)	1875-1891, 1975-
RJS	Revue de jurisprudence sociale	France	1989-
RL	Revue légale	Can (QC)	1869-1892, 1943-
RL (ns)	Revue légale (nouvelle série)	Can (QC)	1895-1943
RNB (2d)	Recueil des arrêts du Nouveau Brunswick (deuxième série) (1825-1928 : voir *New Brunswick Reports*)	Can (NB)	1969-
Rob / Rob Chr	Robinson, C's Reports (ER vol 165)	UK / R-U	1798-1808
Rob Ecc	Robertson's Ecclesiastical Reports (ER vol 163)	UK / R-U	1844-1853
Rolle	Rolle's Reports (ER vol 81)	UK / R-U	1614-1625
RONTC	Recueil des décisions de l'office national des transports du Canada	Can	1988-
Roscoe	Roscoe's Reports	S Afr du sud	1861-1878
RPC	Reports of Patent Cases	UK / R-U	1884-1955
RPC	Reports of Patent, Design and Trademark Cases	UK / R-U	1957-
RPEI	Reports of cases determined in the Supreme Court, Court of Chancery, and Court of Vice-Admiralty of Prince Edward Island	Can (PEI)	1850-1872
RPQ	Rapports de pratique de Québec	Can (QC)	1897-1982
RPR	Real Property Reports	Can	1977-1989
RPR (2d)	Real Property Reports (Second Series)	Can	1989-1996
RPR (3d)	Real Property Reports (Third Series)	Can	1996-
RPTA	Recueil en matière de protection du territoire agricole	Can (QC)	1990-
RR	Revised Reports	UK / R-U	1785-1865

RRA	Recueil en responsabilité et assurance	Can (QC)	1986-
RS	Recueil Sirey	France	1955-1965
RSA	Recueil de sentences arbitrales	Intl	1948-
RSA	Recueil de sentences arbitrales	Can (QC)	1981-1983
RSE	Recueil des sentences de l'éducation	Can (QC)	1974-
RSF	Recueil de jurisprudence en droit des successions et des fiducies	Can	1977-1994
RSF (2e)	Recueil de jurisprudence en droit des successions et des fiducies (deuxième série)	Can	1994-2003
RSF (3e)	Recueil de jurisprudence en droit des successions et des fiducies (troisième série)	Can	2003-
RSP	Recueil des ordonnances de la régie des services publics	Can (QC)	1973-1978
RTC	Décisions et énoncés de politique sur la radiodiffusion et les télécommunications canadiennes	Can	1975-1985
Russ	Russell's Reports (ER vol 38)	UK / R-U	1823-1829
Russ & M	Russell & Mylne's Reports (ER vol 39)	UK / R-U	1829-1831
Russ & Ry	Russell & Ryan's Crown Cases (ER vol 168)	UK / R-U	1799-1823
Russ ER	Russell's Election Reports	Can (NS)	1874
SAFP	Sentences arbitrales de la fonction publique	Can (QC)	1983-
S Afr LR	South African Law Reports	S Afr du sud	1947-
SAG	Sentences arbitrales de griefs	Can (QC)	1970-1981
Salk	Salkeld's Reports (ER vol 91)	UK / R-U	1689-1712
SALR	South Australia Law Reports	Austl	1865-
Sarbah	Sarbah's Fanti Law Reports	Ghana	1845-1903
SARB Dec	Social Assistance Review Board Selected Decisions	Can (ON)	1975-1986
SARB Sum	Social Assistance Review Board Summaries of Decisions	Can (ON)	1988-1994
Sask C Comp B	Saskatchewan Crimes Compensation Board, Awards	Can (SK)	1968-1992
Sask Human Rights Comm'n Dec	Saskatchewan Human Rights Commission Decisions	Can (SK)	1973-1981
Sask LR	Saskatchewan Law Reports	Can (SK)	1907-1931
Sask LRBD	Saskatchewan Labour Relations Board Decisions	Can (SK)	1945-1977
Sask LRBDC	Saskatchewan Labour Relations Board, Decisions and Court Cases	Can (SK)	1945-1964
Sask LRBR	Saskatchewan Labour Relations Board, Report of Meetings	Can (SK)	1967-1973
Sask R	Saskatchewan Reports	Can	1980-

Sask SC Bull	Saskatchewan Securities Commission Monthly Bulletin	Can (SK)	1984-
SASR	South Australia State Reports	Austl (SA)	1921-
Sav	Savile's Reports (ER vol 123)	UK / R-U	1580-1594
Say	Sayer's Reports (ER vol 96)	UK / R-U	1751-1756
SCC Cam	Canada Supreme Court Cases (Cameron) (Published / publié 1918)	Can	1887-1890
SCC Cam (2d)	Canada Supreme Court Reports (Cameron) (Published / publié 1925)	Can	1876-1922
SCC Coutl	Canada Supreme Court Cases (Coutlée)	Can	1875-1907
SCCB	Supreme Court of Canada Bulletin of Proceedings	Can	1970-
SCCD	Supreme Court of Canada Decisions	Can	1978-
SCCR	Supreme Court of Canada Reports Service	Can	1971-
Scot LR	Scottish Law Reporter	Scot / Écosse	1865-1924
SCR	Canada Law Reports: Supreme Court of Canada	Can	1923-1969
SCR	Canada Supreme Court Reports	Can	1877-1922, 1970-
S Ct	Supreme Court Reporter	US / É-U	1882-
SE	South Eastern Reporter	US / É-U	1887-1939
SE (2d)	South Eastern Reporter (Second Series)	US / É-U	1939-1988
Searle	Searle's Reports	S Afr du sud	1850-1867
SEC Dec	Securities and Exchange Commission Decisions	US / É-U	1934-
Sel Ca t King	Select Cases, temp King (ER vol 25)	UK / R-U	1724-1733
Sem Jur	Semaine Juridique	France	1927-1936
Sess Cas	Session Cases	UK / R-U	1710-1748
Sess Cas	Session Cases	Scot / Écosse	1906-
Sess Cas S	Session Cases (Shaw & Balantine)	Scot / Écosse	1821-1838
Sess Cas D	Session Cases (Second Series) (Dunlop)	Scot / Écosse	1838-1862
Sess Cas F	Session Cases (Fifth Series) (Fraser)	Scot / Écosse	1898-1906
Sess Cas M	Session Cases (Third Series) (Macpherson)	Scot / Écosse	1862-1873
Sess Cas R	Session Cases (Fourth Series) (Rettie)	Scot / Écosse	1873-1898
Show KB	Shower's Reports, King's Bench (ER vol 89)	UK / R-U	1678-1695
Show PC	Shower's Reports, Privy Council (ER vol 1)	UK / R-U	1694-1699
Sid	Siderfin's Reports, King's Bench (ER vol 82)	UK / R-U	1657-1670
Sim	Simons's Reports (ER vols 57-60)	UK / R-U	1826-1852
Sim (NS)	Simons's New Reports (ER vol 61)	UK / R-U	1850-1852

Appendices / Annexes

Sim & St	Simons & Stuart's Reports (ER vol 57)	UK / R-U	1822-1826
SLLR	Sierra Leone Law Reports	W Afr	1960-1963
SLT	Scots Law Times	Scot / Écosse	1893-
SLR	Singapore Law Reports	Sing	1946-
SLR (R)	Singapore Law Reports (Reissue)	Sing	1965-2002
Skin	Skinner's Reports (ER vol 90)	UK / R-U	1681-1698
Sm & G	Smale & Giffard's Reports (ER vol 65)	UK / R-U	1852-1857
Sm & S	Smith and Sager's Drainage Cases	Can (ON)	1901-1913
SNB & B	Sarawak, North Borneo and Brunei Supreme Court Reports	Malay	1952-1963
So	Southern Reporter	US / É-U	1887-1941
So (2d)	Southern Reporter (Second Series)	US / É-U	1941-2009
So (3d)	Southern Reporter (Third Series)	US / É-U	2009-
SOLR	Sexual Offences Law Reporter	Can	1994-
Sp Ecc & Ad	Spinks's Ecclesiastical & Admiralty Reports (ER vol 164)	UK / R-U	1853-1855
Sp PC	Spinks' Prize Court Cases (ER vol 164)	UK / R-U	1854-1856
SRLA	Speakers' Rulings, Legislative Assembly	Can (NB)	1923-1982
SSC	Sarawak Supreme Court Reports	Malay	1928-1953
SSLR	Straits Settlements Law Reports	Sing	1893-1942
Stark	Starkie's Reports (ER vol 171)	UK / R-U	1814-1820
St-MSD	Saint-Maurice's Speakers' Decisions	Can (QC)	1868-1885
Stewart	Stewart's Vice-Admiralty Reports	Can (NS)	1803-1813
Stockton	Stockton's Vice-Admiralty Reports	Can (NB)	1879-1891
Str	Strange's Reports (ER vol 93)	UK / R-U	1716-1749
STR	Canadian Sales Tax Reporter	Can	1968-1989
Stu Adm	Stuart's Vice-Admiralty Reports (Lower Canada)	Can (QC)	1836-1874
Stu KB	Stuart's Reports (Lower Canada)	Can (QC)	1810-1835
Sty	Style's Reports (ER vol 82)	UK / R-U	1646-1655
Sudan LR	Sudan Law Reports	Sudan	1956-1971
SW	South Western Reporter	US / É-U	1887-1928
SW (2d)	South Western Reporter (Second Series)	US / É-U	1928-1999
SW (3d)	South Western Reporter (Third Series)	US / ÉU	1999-
Sw & Tr	Swabey & Tristram's Reports (ER vol 164)	UK / R-U	1858-1865
Swab	Swabey's Reports (ER vol 166)	UK / R-U	1855-1859

Swans	Swanston's Reports (ER vol 36)	UK / R-U	1818-1819
TA	Décisions du Tribunal d'arbitrage	Can (QC)	1982-1997
Talb	Talbot's Cases temp (ER vol 25)	UK / R-U	1733-1738
Taml	Tamlyn's Reports (ER vol 48)	UK / R-U	1829-1830
TAAT	Tribunal d'appel des accidents du travail	Can (ON)	1985-1997
TAQ	Décisions du Tribunal administratif du Québec	Can (QC)	1998-
Tas LR	Tasmanian Law Reports	Austl (Tas)	1896-1940
Tas R	Tasmania Reports	Austl (Tas)	1979-
Tas SR	Tasmania State Reports	Austl (Tas)	1941-1978
Taun	Taunton's Reports (ER vols 127-129)	UK / R-U	1807-1819
Tax ABC	Tax Appeal Board Cases	Can	1949-1966
Tax ABC (NS)	Tax Appeal Board Cases (New Series)	Can	1967-1972
TBR	Tariff Board Reports	Can	1937-1988
TBRD	Taxation Board of Review Decisions	Austl	1939-1949
TBRD (NS)	Taxation Board Review Decisions (New Series)	Austl	1950-1968
TCD	Tribunal de la concurrence, décisions	Can	1986-
TCT	Canadian Trade and Commodity Tax Cases	Can	1989-1992
TE	Recueils de jurisprudence du tribunal de l'expropria-tion	Can (QC)	1972-1986
Terr LR	Territories Law Reports	Can (NWT)	1885-1907
TJ	Recueils de jurisprudence du Québec : Tribunal de la jeunesse	Can (QC)	1978-1985
TLLR	Tenant and Landlord Law Repors	Can (ON)	1983-1988
TLR	Times Law Reports	UK / R-U	1884-1952
TMR	Trademark Reporter	US / É-U	1911-
Toth	Tothill's Reports (ER vol 21)	UK / R-U	1559-1646
TPEI	Tucker's Select Cases of Prince Edward Island	Can (PEI)	1817-1828
TR	Term Reports (ER vols 99-101)	UK / R-U	1785-1800
TSPAAT	Tribunal d'appel de la sécurité professionnelle et de l'assurance contre les accidents du travail	Can (ON)	1998-
TT	Tribunal du travail	Can (QC)	1970-1981
TTC	Hunter's Torrens Title Cases	Austl, Can, NZ N-Z, UK R-U	1865-1893
TTR	Trade and Tariff Reports	Can	1990-1996
TTR (2d)	Trade and Tarrif Reports (Second Series)	Can	1996-
Turn & R	Turner & Russell's Reports, Chancery (ER vol 37)	UK / R-U	1822-1824

UC Ch	Grant's Upper Canada Chancery Reports	Can (ON)	1849-1882
UC Chamb Rep	Upper Canada Chambers Reports	Can (ON)	1846-1852
UCCP	Upper Canada Common Pleas Reports	Can (ON)	1850-1882
UCE & A	Upper Canada Error and Appeal Reports (Grant)	Can (ON)	1846-1866
UCKB	Upper Canada King's Bench Report (Old Series)	Can (ON)	1831-1844
UCQB	Upper Canada Queen's Bench Reports (New Series)	Can (ON)	1842-1882
UCQB (OS)	Upper Canada Queen's Bench Reports (Old Series)	Can (ON)	1831-1838
Uganda LR	Uganda Law Reports	Uganda	1904-1973
US	United States Reports	US / É-U	1754-
US App DC	United States Court of Appeals Reports	US / É-U	1941-
USLW	United States Law Week	US / É-U	1933-
Vaugh	Vaughan's Reports (ER vol 124)	UK / R-U	1665-1674
Vent	Ventris' Reports (ER vol 86)	UK / R-U	1666-1688
Vern	Vernon's Reports (ER vol 23)	UK / R-U	1680-1719
Ves & Bea	Vesey & Beames' Reports (ER vol 35)	UK / R-U	1812-1814
Ves Jr	Vesey Junior's Reports (ER vols 30-34)	UK / R-U	1789-1817
Ves Sr	Vesey Senior's Reports (ER vols 27-28)	UK / R-U	1746-1755
VLR	Victorian Law Reports	Austl (Vic)	1886-1956
VR	Victorian Reports	Austl (Vic)	1870-1872, 1957-
WAC	Western Appeal Cases	Can	1991-
WALR	Western Australia Law Reports	Austl (WA)	1899-1959
WAR	Western Australia Reports	Austl (WA)	1960-1990
WAR (NS)	Western Australia Reports (New Series)	Austl (WA)	1990-
WCAT Dec	Workers' Compensation Appeal Tribunal Decisions	Can (NF)	1987-
WCATR	Workers' Compensation Appeals Tribunal Reporter	Can (ON)	1986-1997
WCB	Weekly Criminal Bulletin	Can	1976-1986
WCB (2d)	Weekly Criminal Bulletin (Second Series)	Can	1986-
WDCP	Weekly Digest of Civil Procedure	Can	1985-1989
WDCP (2d)	Weekly Digest of Civil Procedure (Second Series)	Can	1990-1997
WDFL	Weekly Digest of Family Law	Can	1982-
Welsb H & G	Welsby, Hurlstone & Gordon's Exchequer Reports (ER vols 154-156)	UK / R-U	1847-1856
West, t Hard	West, temp Hardwicke Reports (ER vol 25)	UK / R-U	1736-1739
West	West's Reports (ER vol 9)	UK / R-U	1839-1841

West's Alaska (2d)	West's Alaska Digest (Second Series)	US / É-U	1869-
Wight	Wightwick's Reports (ER vol 145)	UK / R-U	1810-1811
Will Woll & H	Willmore, Wollaston & Hodges's Reports	UK / R-U	1838-1839
Willes	Willes's Reports (ER vol 125)	UK / R-U	1737-1760
Wilm	Wilmot's Reports (ER vol 97)	UK / R-U	1757-1770
Wils Ch	Wilson's Reports, Chancery (ER vol 37)	UK / R-U	1818-1819
Wils Ex	Wilson's Reports, Exchequer (ER vol 159)	UK / R-U	1805-1817
Wils KB	Wilson's Reports, King's Bench (ER vol 95)	UK / R-U	1742-1774
Winch	Winch's Reports (ER vol 124)	UK / R-U	1621-1625
WLAC	Western Labour Arbitration Cases	Can	1966-1985
WLR	Weekly Law Reports	UK / R-U	1953-
WLR	Western Law Reporter	Can	1905-1917
WLRBD	Canadian Wartime Labour Relations Board Decisions	Can	1944-1948
WLTR	Western Law Times and Reports	Can	1890-1896
Wms Saund	Williams' & Saunders's Reports (ER vol 85)	UK / R-U	1666-1673
W Rob	W Robinson's Reports (ER vol 166)	UK / R-U	1838-1850
WSIATR	Workplace Safety and Insurance Appeals Tribunal Reporter	Can (ON)	1998-
W W & A'B	Wyatt, Webb & A'Beckett's Reports (Supreme Court of Victoria)	Austl	1866-1871
WWR	Western Weekly Reports	Can	1911-1950, 1971-
WWR (NS)	Western Weekly Reports (New Series)	Can	1951-1970
YAD	Young's Admiralty Decisions	Can (NS)	1864-1880
Y & C Ex	Younge & Collyer's Reports (ER vol 160)	UK / R-U	1834-1842
Y & C CC	Younge & Collyer's Chancery Cases (ER vols 62-63)	UK / R-U	1841-1843
Y & J	Younge & Jervis's Reports (ER vol 148)	UK / R-U	1826-1830
YB Eur Conv HR	Yearbook of the European Convention on Human Rights	EU / UE	1955-
YR	Yukon Reports	Can	1986-1989
Yel	Yelverton's Reports (ER vol 80)	UK / R-U	1603-1613
You	Younge's Reports (ER vol 159)	UK / R-U	1830-1832

APPENDIX D / ANNEX D

D. PERIODICALS AND YEARBOOKS ~ PÉRIODIQUES ET ANNUAIRES

Abbreviations ~ Abréviations

Name of Periodical or Yearbook / Nom du périodique ou de l'annuaire	Abbreviation / Abréviations
Actualités du droit	Actu du dr
Actualités juridiques, droit administratif	Actu jur dr admin
Actualité et droit international	Actu & dr int
Adelaide Law Review	Adel L Rev
Adelphia Law Journal	Adelphia LJ
Administrative and Regulatory Law News	Admin & Reg L News
Administrative Law Journal of the American University (formerly / anciennement Administrative Law Journal)	Admin LJ Am U
Administrative Law Review	Admin L Rev
Advocate (Vancouver)	Advocate
Advocate (Idaho)	Advocate (Idaho)
Advocates' Quarterly	Adv Q
Advocates' Journal	Adv J
African-American Law and Policy Report	Afr-Am L & Pol'y Rep
Air Force Law Review	AFL Rev
Air & Space Law	Air & Space L
Air & Space Lawyer	Air & Space Lawyer
Akron Law Review	Akron L Rev
Akron Tax Journal	Akron Tax J
Alabama Law Review	Ala L Rev
Alaska Law Review	Alaska L Rev
Albany Law Environmental Outlook	Alb L Envtl Outlook
Albany Law Journal of Science & Technology	Alb LJ Sci & Tech
Albany Law Review	Alb L Rev
Alberta Law Quarterly	Alta L Q
Alberta Law Review	Alta L Rev
Alternatives Journal	Alt J
American Association of Law Libraries Spectrum	AALL Spec

Appendices / Annexes

American Bankruptcy Institute Journal	Am Bankr Inst J
American Bankruptcy Institute Law Review	Am Bankr Inst L Rev
American Bankruptcy Law Journal	Am Bank LJ
American Bar Association Antitrust Law Journal	ABA Antitrust LJ
American Bar Association Criminal Justice	ABA Criminal Justice
American Bar Association Entertainment & Sports Lawyer	ABA Ent & Sports Lawyer
American Bar Association Family Advocate	ABA Fam Advocate
American Bar Association Family Law Quarterly	ABA Fam LQ
American Bar Association Journal	ABA J
American Bar Association Law Practice Management	ABA LPM
American Bar Association Section of Intellectual Property Law	ABAIPL
American Bar Association Tort and Insurance Law Journal	ABA Tort & Ins LJ
American Business Law Journal	Am Bus LJ
American Criminal Law Review	Am Crim L Rev
American Indian Law Review	Am Indian L Rev
American Intellectual Property Law Association Quarterly Journal	AIPLA QJ
American Journal of Comparative Law	Am J Comp L
American Journal of Criminal Law	Am J Crim L
American Journal of International Arbitration	Am J Intl Arb
American Journal of International Law	AJIL / Am J Intl L
American Journal of Jurisprudence	Am J Juris
American Journal of Law & Medicine	Am J L & Med
American Journal of Legal History	Am J Leg Hist
American Journal of Tax Policy	Am J Tax Pol'y
American Journal of Trial Advocacy	Am J Trial Advoc
American Law and Economics Review	Am L & Econ Rev
American Review of International Arbitration	Am Rev Intl Arb
American University International Law Review (*formerly / anciennement American University Journal of International Law & Policy*)	Am U Intl L Rev
American University Journal of Gender, Social Policy and the Law (*formerly / anciennement American University Journal of Gender and the Law*)	Am UJ Gender Soc Pol'y & L
American University Journal of International Law and Policy	Am U J Intl L & Pol'y
American University Law Review	Am U L Rev
Analyse de politiques (*Canadian Public Policy*)	Analyse de pol
Anglo-American Law Review	Anglo-Am L Rev

Animal Law	Animal L
Annales de droit aérien et spacial	Ann dr aér & spat
Annales de droit de Louvain	Ann dr Louv
Annales de la propriété industrielle artistique et littéraire	Ann pr ind art & lit
Annales de l'Université des sciences sociales de Toulouse	Ann de l'UssT
Annals of Air and Space Law	Ann Air & Sp L
Annals of Health Law	Ann Health L
Annuaire canadien de droit international	ACDI
Annuaire canadien des droits de la personne	ACDP
Annuaire de la Convention européenne des droits de l'Homme	Ann Conv eur DH
Annuaire de droit aérien et spatial	Ann dr aér & spat
Annuaire de droit maritime et aérien	Ann dr marit & aér
Annuaire de droit maritime et aéro-spatial	Ann dr marit & aéro-spat
Annuaire des collectivités locales	Ann coll loc
Annuaire français de droit international	AFDI
Annuaire français des droits de l'Homme	Ann fr DH
Annuaire français du transport aérien	Ann fr transp aér
Annuaire de la Haye de droit international	Ann Haye dr int
Annuaire de l'Institut de droit international	Ann inst dr int
Annuaire international de justice constitutionnelle	Ann int j const
Annuaire de la Société des Nations	Ann SN
Annuaire de la Société française de droit aérien et spatial	Ann S fr dr aér & spat
Annuaire de législation étrangère	Ann lég étrang
Annuaire de législation française	Ann lég fr
Annuaire de philosophie de droit	Ann phil dr
Annuaire des Nations Unies	Ann NU
Annuaire suisse de droit international	Ann suisse dr int
Annual Survey of American Law	Ann Surv Am L
Annual Survey of Australian Law	Ann Surv Austl L
Annual Survey of Commonwealth Law	Ann Surv Commonwealth L
Annual Survey of English Law	Ann Surv Engl L
Annual Survey of International & Comparative Law	Ann Surv Intl & Comp L
Annual Survey of South African Law	Ann Surv S Afr L
Antitrust Law and Economics Review	Antitrust L & Econ Rev
Antitrust Law Journal	Antitrust LJ

Appendices / Annexes

Appeal: Review of Current Law and Law Reform	Appeal
Arab Law Quarterly	Arab LQ
Arbitration International	Arb Intl
Arizona Journal of International and Comparative Law	Ariz J Intl & Comp L
Arizona Law Review	Ariz L Rev
Arizona State Law Journal	Ariz St LJ
Arkansas Law Review	Ark L Rev
Art, Antiquity, and the Law	Art Ant & L
Artificial Intelligence and Law	AI & L
Asian Law Journal	Asian LJ
Asia-Pacific Journal of Environmental Law	Asia Pac J Envtl L
Asia-Pacific Journal of Human Rights and the Law	Asia Pac J HR & L
Asia-Pacific Journal of International Law	Asia Pac J Intl L
Asia-Pacific Law Review	Asia Pac L Rev
Asian-Pacific American Law Journal (formerly / anciennement Asian American Pacific Islands Law Journal)	Asian Pac Am LJ
Asian-Pacific Law & Policy Journal	Asian Pac L & Pol'y J
Auckland University Law Review	Auckland UL Rev
Australian and New Zealand Journal of Criminology	Austl & NZ J Crim
Australian Bar Review	Austl Bar Rev
Australian Business Law Review	Austl Bus L Rev
Australian Competition and Consumer Law Journal	Austl Competition & Cons LJ
Austalian Insurance Law Journal	Austl Ins LJ
Australian Journal of Contract Law	Austl J Contract L
Australian Journal of Corporate Law	Austl J Corp L
Australian Journal of Family Law	Austl J Fam L
Australian Journal of Human Rights	Austl J H R
Australian Journal of Labour Law	Austl J Lab L
Australian Journal of Legal History	Austl J Leg Hist
Australian Law Journal	Austl LJ
Australian Property Law Journal	Austl Prop LJ
Australian Torts Law Journal	Austl Torts LJ
Austrian Journal of Public and International Law	Aus J Pub & Intl L
Austrian Review of International and European Law	Aus Rev Intl & Eur L
Baltimore Law Review	Baltimore L Rev

Banking and Finance Law Review	BFLR
Banking Law Journal	Banking LJ
Banking and Financial Services Policy Report: A Journal on Trends in Regulation and Supervision (*formerly / anciennement Banking Policy Report*)	Banking & Fin Serv Pol'y Rep
Banque et droit	B & dr
Baylor Law Review	Baylor L Rev
Behavioural Sciences and the Law	Behav Sci & L
Bench and Bar	B Bar
Berkeley Journal of African-American Law and Policy (*formerly / ancienne-ment African-American Law and Policy Report)*	Berkeley J Afr-Am L & Pol'y
Berkeley Journal of Employment and Labour Law	BJELL
Berkeley Journal of Health Care Law	Berkeley J Health Care L
Berkeley Journal of International Law	BJIL
Berkeley Technology Law Journal	BTLJ
Berkeley Journal of Gender Law and Justice (*formerly / anciennement Berkeley Women's Law Journal*)	Berkeley Women's LJ / Berkeley J Gender L & Just
Berkeley Women's Law Journal	Berkeley Women's LJ
Biotechnology Law Report	Biotech L Rep
Boston Bar Journal	Boston Bar J
Boston College Environmental Affairs Law Review	Boston College Envtl Aff L Rev
Boston College International and Comparative Law Review	Boston College Intl & Comp L Rev
Boston College Law Review	Boston College L Rev
Boston College Journal of Law & Social Justice (*formerly / anciennement Boston College Third World Law Journal*)	Boston College JL & Soc Just
Boston College Third World Law Journal	Boston College Third World LJ
Boston University International Law Journal	BU ILJ
Boston University Journal of Science and Technology Law	BUJ Sci & Tech L
Boston University Journal of Tax Law	BUJ Tax L
Boston University Law Review	BUL Rev
Boston University Public Interest Law Journal	BU PILJ
Brandeis Law Journal	Brandeis LJ
Brigham Young University Education and Law Journal	BYU Educ & LJ
Brigham Young University Law Review	BYUL Rev
British Columbia Law Notes	BCLN
British Institute of International and Comparative Law	Brit Inst Intl & Comp L
British Journal of Criminology	Brit J Crim

British Medical Journal	Brit Med J
British Tax Review	Brit Tax Rev
British Yearbook of International Law	Brit YB Intl L
Brooklyn Journal of International Law	Brook J Intl L
Brooklyn Law Review	Brook L Rev
Buffalo Criminal Law Review	Buff Crim L Rev
Buffalo Environmental Law Journal	Buff Envtl LJ
Buffalo Human Rights Law Review	Buff HRL Rev
Buffalo Law Review	Buff L Rev
Buffalo Public Interest Law Journal	Buff Pub Int LJ
Buffalo Women's Law Journal	Buff Women's LJ
Bulletin canadien VIH-SIDA et droit	Bull can VIH-SIDA & D
Bulletin of International Legal Developments (*formerly / anciennement Bulletin of Legal Developments*)	Bull Intl Leg Dev
Business Law Review	Bus L Rev
Business Lawyer	Bus Lawyer
BYU Journal of Public Law	BYUJ Pub L
Cahiers de droit	C de D
Cahiers de droit de l'entreprise	C de D entr
Cahiers de droit européen	C de D eur
Cahiers de l'Institut québécois d'administration judiciaire	CIQAJ
Cahiers de propriété intellectuelle	CPI
California Bankruptcy Journal	Cal Bankr J
California Criminal Law Review	Cal Crim L Rev
California Law Review	Cal L Rev
California Regulatory Law Reporter	Cal Reg L Rep
California State Bar Journal	Cal St Bar J
California Western International Law Journal	Cal W Int' LJ
California Western Law Review	Cal WL Rev
Cambridge Law Journal	Cambridge LJ
Cambridge Yearbook of European Legal Studies	Cambridge YB Eur Leg Stud
Campbell Law Review	Campbell L Rev
Canada Law Journal	Can LJ
Canada-United States Law Journal	Can-USLJ
Canadian Bar Association Papers	CBA Papers

Canadian Bar Association Year Book	CBAYB
Canadian Bar Journal	Can Bar J
Canadian Bar Review	Can Bar Rev
Canadian Bioethics Report	Can Bioethics R
Canadian Business Law Journal	Can Bus LJ
Canadian Business Review	Can Bus Rev
Canadian Class Action Review	Can Class Action Rev
Canadian Communications Law Review	Can Comm L Rev
Canadian Community Law Journal	Can Community LJ
Canadian Competition Law Review (*formerly / anciennement Canadian Competition Policy Record*)	Can Competition L Rev
Canadian Competition Policy Record	Can Competition Pol'y Rec
Canadian Competition Record (*formerly / anciennement Canadian Competition Policy Record*)	Can Competition Rec
Canadian Council on International Law (Proceedings)	Can Council Intl L Proc
Canadian Criminal Law Review	Can Crim L Rev
Canadian Criminology Forum	Can Crim Forum
Canadian Current Tax	Can Curr Tax
Canadian Environmental Law News	Can Envtl L News
Canadian Family Law Quarterly	Can Fam LQ
Canadian HIV/AIDS Policy and Law Review	Can HIV/AIDS Pol'y & L Rev
Canadian Human Rights Advocate	Can HR Advoc
Canadian Human Rights Yearbook	Can Hum Rts YB
Canadian Intellectual Property Review	CIPR
Canadian International Lawyer	Can Intl Lawyer
Canadian Journal of Administrative Law and Practice	Can J Admin L & Prac
Canadian Journal of Criminology and Criminal Justice (*formerly / anciennement Canadian Journal of Corrections, Canadian Journal of Criminology and Criminal Justice and Corrections*)	Can J Corr
Canadian Journal of Criminology	Can J Crim
Canadian Journal of Criminology and Corrections	Can J Crim & Corr
Canadian Journal of Family Law	Can J Fam L
Canadian Journal of Insurance Law	Can J Ins L
Canadian Journal of International Business Law and Policy	Can J Intl Bus L & Pol'y
Canadian Journal of Law and Jurisprudence	Can JL & Jur
Canadian Journal of Law and Society	CJLS

Appendices / Annexes

Canadian Journal of Law and Technology	CJLT
Canadian Journal of Women and the Law	CJWL
Canadian Labour and Employment Law Journal	CLELJ
Canadian Law Library Review (*formerly / anciennement Canadian Law Libraries*)	Can L Libr Rev
Canadian Law Review	Can L Rev
Canadian Law Times	Can LT
Canadian Lawyer	Can Lawyer
Canadian Legal Studies	Can Legal Stud
Canadian Medical Association Journal	CMAJ
Canadian Municipal Journal	Can Mun J
Canadian Native Law Bulletin	Can NL Bull
Canadian Public Policy	Can Pub Pol'y
Canadian Tax Foundation (Conference Report / Rapport de conférence)	Can Tax Found
Canadian Tax Highlights	Can Tax Highlights
Canadian Tax Journal	Can Tax J
Canadian Tax News	Can Tax N
Canadian Taxation: A Journal of Tax Policy	Can Tax'n
Canadian Yearbook of International Law	Can YB Intl Law
Capital University Law Review	Capital UL Rev
Cardozo Arts and Entertainment Law Journal	Cardozo Arts & Ent LJ
Cardozo Electronic Law Bulletin	Cardozo EL Bull
Cardozo Journal of International and Comparative Law (*formerly / anciennement New Europe Law Review*)	Cardozo J Intl & Comp L
Cardozo Journal of Law and Gender (*formerly / anciennement Cardozo Women's Law Journal*)	Cardozo J L & Gender
Cardozo Law Review	Cardozo L Rev
Cardozo Studies in Law and Literature	Cardozo Stud L & Lit
Caribbean Law Review	Caribbean L Rev
Carolina Law Journal	Carolina LJ
Case Western Reserve Journal of International Law	Case W Res J Intl L
Case Western Reserve Law Review	Case W Res L Rev
Catholic University Law Review	Cath U L Rev
Chapman Law Review	Chapman L Rev
Chicago Journal of International Law	Chicago J Intl L
Chicago-Kent Law Review	Chicagio-Kent L Rev

Chicano-Latino Law Review *(formerly / anciennement Chicano Law Review)*	Chicano-Latino L Rev
Chicago Lawyer	Chicago Lawyer
Children's Legal Rights Journal	Child Leg Rts J
China Law Reporter	China L Rep
Chinese Yearbook of International Law and Affairs	Chinese YB Intl L & Aff
Chitty's Law Journal	Chitty's LJ
Civil Liberties Review	Civ Lib Rev
Civil Justice Quarterly	CJQ
Cleveland State Law Review	Clev St L Rev
Cleveland-Marshall Law Review	Clev-Marshall L Rev
Clinical Law Review	Clinical L Rev
Coastal Management	Coastal Mgmt
Colorado Journal of International Environmental Law & Policy	Colo J Intl Envtl L & Pol'y
Colorado Lawyer	Colo Lawyer
Columbia Business Law Review	Colum Bus L Rev
Columbia Human Rights Law Review	Colum HRLR
Columbia Journal of Asian Law *(formerly / anciennement Journal of Chinese Law)*	Colum J Asian Law
Columbia Journal of East European Law	Colum J E Eur L
Columbia Journal of Environmental Law	Colum J Envtl L
Columbia Journal of European Law	Colum J Eur L
Columbia Journal of Gender and Law	Colum J Gender & L
Columbia Journal of Law and Social Problems	Colum JL & Soc Probs
Columbia Journal of Transnational Law	Colum J Transnat'l L
Columbia Law Review	Colum L Rev
Columbia Science and Technology Law Review	Colum Sci & Tech L Rev
Columbia Journal of Law and the Arts	Colum J L & Arts
Commercial Law Journal	Com LJ
Commercial Leasing Law and Strategy	Com Leasing L & Strategy
Common Law World Review	Comm L World Rev
Common Market Law Review	CML Rev
Commonwealth Law Bulletin	Commonwealth L Bull
Commonwealth Legal Education	Commonwealth Leg Educ
Communication Law & Policy	Comm L & Pol'y
Communications Lawyer	Comm Lawyer

Comparative and International Law Journal of Southern Africa	Comp & Intl LJS Afr
Comparative Juridical Review	Comp Jurid Rev
Comparative Labor Law and Policy Journal *(formerly / anciennement Comparative Labor Law Journal)*	Comp Lab L & Pol'y J
Computer Law and Security Report	Computer L & Sec Report
Computer Law Review and Technology Journal	Computer L Rev & Tech J
Computer Lawyer	Computer Lawyer
Congressional Digest	Cong Dig
Connecticut Bar Journal	Conn Bar J
Connecticut Insurance Law Journal	Conn Ins LJ
Connecticut Journal of International Law	Conn J Intl L
Connecticut Law Review	Conn L Rev
Connecticut Public Interest Law Journal	Conn Pub Int LJ
Connecticut Probate Law Journal	Conn Prob LJ
Constitutional Commentary	Const Commentary
Constitutional Forum Constitutionnel	Const Forum Const
Consumer Finance Law Quarterly Report	Cons Fin LQ Rep
Construction Law Journal	Construction LJ
Construction Lawyer	Construction Lawyer
Copyright Bulletin	Copyright Bull
Cooley Law Review	Cooley L Rev
Cornell International Law Journal	Cornell Intl LJ
Cornell Journal of Law & Public Policy	Cornell JL & Pub Pol'y
Cornell Law Review	Cornell L Rev
Corporate Taxation	Corp Tax'n
Cours de perfectionnement du notariat	CP du N
Creighton Law Review	Creighton L Rev
Crime, Law and Social Change	Crime L & Soc Change
Criminal Law Forum	Crim LF
Criminal Law Quarterly	Crim LQ
Criminal Law Review	Crim L Rev
Criminologie	Criminol
Critical Criminology	Crit Criminol
Croatian Arbitration Yearbook	Croatian Arb YB
Croatian Critical Law Review	Croat Crit L Rev

Appendices / Annexes

Cumberland Law Review	Cumb L Rev
Current Law Yearbook	Current LYB
Current Legal Problems	Current Leg Probs
Currents: International Trade Law Journal	Currents: Intl Trade LJ
Dalhousie Journal of Legal Studies	Dal J Leg Stud
Dalhousie Law Journal	Dal LJ
Defense Counsel Journal	Def Couns J
Delaware Journal of Corporate Law	Del J Corp L
Delaware Law Review	Del L Rev
Denver Journal of International Law & Policy	Denv J Intl L & Pol'y
Denver University Law Review (formerly / anciennement Denver Law Journal)	Denv UL Rev
Department of State Bulletin	Dep't St Bull
DePaul Business & Commercial Law Journal (formerly / anciennement DePaul Business Law Journal)	DePaul Bus & Comm LJ
DePaul Journal of Health Care Law	DePaul J Health Care L
DePaul Law Review	DePaul L Rev
DePaul-LCA Journal of Art and Entertainment Law and Policy	DePaul-LCA J Art & Ent L & Pol'y
Dickinson Journal of Environmental Law & Policy	Dick J Envtl L & Pol'y
Dickinson Journal of International Law	Dick J Intl L
Dickinson Law Review	Dick L Rev
Dispute Resolution Journal (formerly / anciennement Arbitration Journal)	Disp Resol J
District of Columbia Law Review	DCL Rev
Drake Journal of Agricultural Law	Drake J Agric L
Drake Law Review	Drake L Rev
Droit africain du travail	DAT
Droit des sociétés	Dr soc
Droit et cultures	Dr et cult
Droit et patrimoine	Dr et pat
Droit et société	Dr et soc
Droit européen des transports	Dr eur transp
Droit maritime français	Dr marit fr
Droit social	Dr social
Duke Environmental Law & Policy Forum	Duke Envtl L & Pol'y F
Duke Journal of Comparative & International Law	Duke J Comp & Intl L

Duke Journal of Gender Law & Policy	Duke J Gender L & Pol'y
Duke Law Journal	Duke LJ
Duke Law and Technology Review	Duke L & Tech Rev
Duquesne Business Law Journal	Duq Bus LJ
Duquesne Law Review	Duq L Rev
East European Business Law	E Eur Bus L
East European Constitutional Review	E Eur Const Rev
East European Human Rights Review	E Eur HR Rev
Ecology Law Quarterly	Ecology LQ
Edinburgh Law Review	Ed L Rev
Education & Law Journal	Educ & LJ
Elder Law Journal	Elder LJ
Election Law Journal	Election LJ
Electronic Journal of Comparative Law	Electronic J Comp L
Emory Bankruptcy Developments Journal	Emory Bankr Dev J
Emory International Law Review (formerly / anciennement Emory Journal of International Dispute Resolution)	Emory Intl L Rev
Emory Law Journal	Emory LJ
Employee Rights & Employment Policy Journal	Employee Rts & Employment Pol'y J
Energy Law Journal	Energy LJ
Entertainment & Sports Lawyer	Ent & Sports Lawyer
Entertainment Law & Finance	Ent L & Fin
Environmental Law	Envtl L
Environmental Law and Management	Envtl L & Mgmt
Environmental Law and Policy Journal	Envtl L & Pol'y J
Environmental Law Journal	Envtl LJ
Environmental Lawyer	Envtl Lawyer
Environmental Policy and Law	Envtl Pol'y & L
Environs: Environmental Law and Policy Journal	Environs
Estates and Trusts Journal (formerly / anciennement Estates and Trusts Quarterly)	Est & Tr J
Estates, Trusts and Pensions Journal (formerly / anciennement Estates and Trusts Journal)	Est Tr & Pensions J
Estates and Trusts Quarterly	E & TQ
Estates Trusts & Pensions Journal	ETPJ

Études internationales	Études int
European Business Law Review	Eur Bus L Rev
European Competition Law Review	Eur Competition L Rev
European Environmental Law Review	Eur Envtl L Rev
European Human Rights Law Review	Eur HRL Rev
European Intellectual Property Review	Eur IP Rev
European Journal of Health Law	Eur J Health L
European Journal of Law & Economics	Eur J L & Econ
European Journal of Law Reform	Eur J L Reform
European Journal of International Law	Eur J Intl L
European Journal for Education Law and Policy	Eur J Educ L & Pol'y
European Journal of Migration and Law	Eur J Migr & L
European Journal of Social Security	Eur J Soc Sec
European Journal of Criminal Policy & Research	Eur J Crim Pol'y & Research
European Journal of Crime, Criminal Law, and Criminal Justice	Eur J Crime, Crim L & Crim J
European Law Journal	Eur LJ
European Law Review	Eur L Rev
European Legal Forum	Eur Leg F
European Review of Private Law	Eur R Priv L
European Transport Law	Eur Transp L
Family Court Review *(formerly / anciennement Family & Conciliation Courts Review)*	Fam Ct Rev
Family Law Quarterly	Fam LQ
Family Law Review	Fam L Rev
Federal Bar News and Journal	Fed B News & J
Federal Circuit Bar Journal	Fed Cir BJ
Federal Communications Law Journal	Fed Comm LJ
Federal Courts Law Review	Fed Cts L Rev
Feminist Legal Studies	Fem Leg Stud
Florida Bar Journal	Fla BJ
Florida Coastal Law Review	Fla Coastal L Rev
Florida Journal of International Law	Fla J Intl L
Florida Law Review *(formerly / anciennement University of Florida Law Review)*	Fla L Rev
Florida State Journal of Transnational Law & Policy	Fla St J Transnat'l L & Pol'y

Appendices / Annexes

Florida State University Journal of Land Use & Environmental Law	Fla St UJ Land Use & Envtl L
Florida State University Law Review	Fla St UL Rev
Florida Tax Review	Fla Tax Rev
Food & Drug Law Journal	Food & Drug LJ
Fordham Environmental Law Review	Fordham Envtl LJ
Fordham Finance, Securities & Tax Law Forum	Fordham Fin Sec & Tax LF
Fordham Intellectual Property, Media & Entertainment Law Journal	Fordham IP Media & Ent LJ
Fordham International Law Journal	Fordham Intl LJ
Fordham Journal of Corporate and Finance Law (*formerly / anciennement Fordham Finance, Securities and Tax Law Forum*)	Fordham J Corp & Fin L
Fordham Law Review	Fordham L Rev
Fordham Urban Law Journal	Fordham Urb LJ
International Law FORUM du droit international	FORUM
George Mason Law Review	Geo Mason L Rev
George Mason University Civil Rights Law Journal	Geo Mason U Civ Rts LJ
George Washington International Law Review (*formerly / anciennement George Washington Journal of International Law and Economics*)	Geo Wash Intl L Rev
George Washington Law Review	Geo Wash L Rev
Georgetown Immigration Law Journal	Geo Immigr LJ
Georgetown International Environmental Law Review	Geo Intl Envtl L Rev
Georgetown Journal of Gender and the Law	Geo J Gender & L
Georgetown Journal of International Law	Geo J Intl L
Georgetown Journal of Legal Ethics	Geo J Leg Ethics
Georgetown Journal on Poverty Law & Policy (*formerly / anciennement Georgetown Journal on Fighting Poverty*)	Geo J on Poverty L & Pol'y
Georgetown Law Journal	Geo LJ
Georgetown Public Policy Review	Geo Pub Pol'y Rev
Georgia Journal of International and Comparative Law	Ga J Intl & Comp L
Georgia Law Review	Ga L Rev
Georgia State University Law Review	Ga St U L Rev
Global Business Law Review	Global Bus L Rev
Golden Gate University Law Review	Golden Gate UL Rev
Gonzaga Law Review	Gonz L Rev
Great Plains Natural Resources Journal	Great Plains Nat Resources J
Griffith Law Review	Griffith L Rev
Hague Yearbook of International Law	Hague YB Intl L

Hamline Journal of Public Law and Policy	Hamline J Pub L & Pol'y
Hamline Law Review	Hamline L Rev
Harvard BlackLetter Law Journal	Harv BlackLetter LJ
Harvard Civil Rights-Civil Liberties Law Review	Harv CR-CLL Rev
Harvard Environmental Law Review	Harv Envtl L Rev
Harvard Human Rights Journal *(formerly / anciennement Harvard Human Rights Yearbook)*	Harv Hum Rts J
Harvard International Law Journal	Harv Intl LJ
Harvard Journal of Law and Gender	Harv JL & Gender
Harvard Journal of Law and Public Policy	Harv JL & Pub Pol'y
Harvard Journal of Law & Technology	Harv JL & Tech
Harvard Journal on Legislation	Harv J on Legis
Harvard Law Review	Harv L Rev
Harvard Negotiation Law Review	Harv Negot L Rev
Harvard Women's Law Journal	Harv Women's LJ
Hastings Communications & Entertainment Law Journal	Hastings Comm & Ent LJ
Hastings Constitutional Law Quarterly	Hastings Const LQ
Hastings International and Comparative Law Review	Hastings Intl & Comp L Rev
Hastings Law Journal	Hastings LJ
Hastings West-Northwest Journal of Environmental Law and Policy	Hastings W-Nw J Envtl L & Pol'y
Hastings Women's Law Journal	Hastings Women's LJ
Hawaii Bar Journal	Haw Bar J
Hawaiil Law Review	Haw L Rev
Health and Human Rights	Health & Hum Rts
Health Law in Canada	Health L Can
Health Law Journal	Health LJ
Heidelberg Journal of International Law	Heidelberg J Intl L
High Technology Law Journal	High Tech LJ
Hitotsubashi Journal of Law and Politics	HJLP
Hofstra Labor & Employment Law Journal	Hofstra Lab & Empl LJ
Hofstra Law Review	Hofstra L Rev
Hofstra Property Law Journal	Hofstra Prop LJ
Holdsworth Law Review	Hold LR
Hong Kong Law Journal	Hong Kong LJ
Houston Journal of International Law	Hous J Intl L

Appendices / Annexes

Houston Law Review	Hous L Rev
Howard Journal of Criminal Justice	How J Crim Justice
Howard Law Journal	How LJ
Howard Scroll: The Social Justice Law Review	How Scroll
Human Rights Internet Reporter	HRIR
Human Rights Law Journal	HRLJ
Human Rights in Development	Hum Rts Dev
Human Rights Journal	Hum Rts J
Human Rights Quarterly	Hum Rts Q
Human Rights Tribune	Hum Rts Trib
ICSID Review	ICSID Rev
Idaho Law Review	Idaho L Rev
IDEA: The Journal of Law and Technology	IDEA
Illinois Bar Journal	Ill BJ
Illinois Law Quarterly	Ill LQ
ILSA Journal of International & Comparative Law	ILSA J Intl & Comp L
Immigration and Nationality Law Review	Immig & Nat'lity L Rev
Indiana International and Comparative Law Review	Ind Intl & Comp L Rev
Indiana Journal of Global Legal Studies	Ind J Global Leg Stud
Indiana Law Journal	Ind LJ
Indiana Law Review	Ind L Rev
Indigenous Law Journal	Indigenous LJ
Industrial Law Journal	Indus LJ
Industrial Relations Law Journal	Indus Rel LJ
Industrial & Labor Relations Review	Indus & Lab Rel Rev
Information Bulletin on Legal Affairs (Council of Europe)	Inf Bull
Information and Communications Technology Law	Inf & Comm Tech L
Insolvency Bulletin	Insol Bull
Intellectual and Comparative Law Quarterly	ICLQ
Intellectual Property Journal	IPJ
Intellectual Property Law Bulletin	IPL Bull
Intellectual Property Law Newsletter	IPL News
Intellectual Property & Technlology Forum	IP & Tech F
Intellectual Property & Technology Law Review	IP & Tech L Rev
International Arbitration Law Review	Intl Arb L Rev

International Business Law Journal	IBLJ
International Business Lawyer	Intl Bus Lawyer
International Commercial Litigation	Intl Com Lit
International Commission of Jurists Review	Intl Commission Jur Rev
International Community Law Review (*formerly / anciennement International Law FORUM du droit international*)	Intl Community L Rev
International Company and Commercial Law Review	Intl Co & Com L Rev
International and Comparative Corporate Law Journal	Intl & Comp Corp LJ
International and Comparative Law Quarterly (*formerly / anciennement British Institute of International and Comparative Law*)	ICLQ
International and Comparative Law Review	Intl & Comp L Rev
International Criminal Law Review	Intl Crim L Rev
International Financial Law Review	Intl Fin L Rev
International Insights	Intl Insights
International Insurance Law Review	Intl Ins L Rev
International Journal	Intl J
International Journal for Jurisprudence and Legal Philosophy	Intl J Juris & Leg Phil
International Journal for the Semiotics of Law	Intl J Sem L
International Journal of Children's Rights	Intl J Child Rts
International Journal of Communications Law & Policy	Intl J Comm L & Pol'y
International Journal of Comparative Labour Law and Industrial Relations	Intl J Comp Lab L & Ind Rel
International Journal of Conflict Management	Intl J Confl Mgmt
International Journal of Cultural Property	Intl J Cult Prop
International Journal of Franchising and Distribution Law	Intl J Franch & Distrib L
International Journal of Human Rights	Intl JHR
International Journal of Offender Therapy and Comparative Criminology	Intl J Off Ther & Comp Crim
International Journal of Law Policy and the Family	Intl JL Pol'y & Fam
International Journal of Law and Information Technology	Intl JL & IT
International Journal of Law and Psychiatry	Intl J L & Psychiatry
International Journal of Legal Information	Intl J Leg Info
International Journal of Marine and Coastal Law	Intl J Mar & Coast L
International Journal of the Sociology of Law	Intl J Soc L
International Journal of Refugee Law	Intl J Refugee L
International Journal of the Sociology of Law	Intl J Soc L
International Lawyer	Intl Lawyer

Appendices / Annexes

International Legal Materials	ILM
International Legal Perspectives	Intl Leg Persp
International Legal Practitioner	Intl Leg Practitioner
International Legal Theory	Intl Leg Theory
International Maritime and Commercial Law Yearbook	Intl Mar & Com L YB
International Review of Criminal Policy	Intl Rev Crim Pol'y
International Review of Industrial Property and Copyright Law	Intl Rev Ind Prop & C'right L
International Review of Law Computers & Technology	Intl Rev L Comp & Tech
International Review of Law & Economics	Intl Rev L & Econ
International Review of the Red Cross	Intl Rev Red Cross
International Tax and Business Lawyer	Intl Tax & Bus Lawyer
International Trade Law and Practice	Intl Trade L & Pract
International Trade Law & Regulation	Intl Trade L Reg
International Trade Law Quarterly	ITLQ
Iowa Law Review	Iowa L Rev
Irish Jurist	Ir Jur
Islamic Law & Society	Islamic L & Soc
Israel Law Review	Israel LR
Issues in Law & Medicine	Issues L & Med
Jersey Law Review	Jersey L Rev
Jewish Law Report	Jewish LR
John Marshall Journal of Computer and Information Law	John Marshall J Computer & Info L
John Marshall Law Quarterly	John Marshall LQ
John Marshall Law Review	John Marshall L Rev
Journal des juges provinciaux	J juges prov
Journal des notaires et des avocats	J not et av
Journal des tribunaux	J Tribun
Journal de droit européen	JDE
Journal du Barreau	J du B
Journal du droit des jeunes	J dr jeunes
Journal du droit international	JDI
Journal of Affordable Housing and Community Development Law	J Aff Housing & Community Dev L
Journal of African Law	J Afr L
Journal of Agricultural Law	J Agric L
Journal of Air Law	J Air L

Journal of Air Law and Commerce	J Air L & Com
Journal of Animal Law	J Animal L
Journal of Animal Law and Ethics	J Animal L & Ethics
Journal of Appellate Practice & Process	J App Pr & Pro
Journal of Art & Entertainment Law	J Art & Ent L
Journal of BioLaw & Business	J BioLaw & Bus
Journal of Business Law	J Bus L
Journal of Catholic Legal Studies (*formerly / anciennement The Catholic Lawyer*)	J Cath Leg Stud
Journal of Chinese Law	J Chinese L
Journal of College and University Law	JC & UL
Journal of Commonwealth Law and Legal Education	J Commonwealth L & Leg Educ
Journal of Comparative Business and Capital Market Law	J Comp Bus & Cap Mkt L
Journal of Conflict and Security Law (*formerly / anciennement Journal of Armed Conflict Law*)	J Confl & Sec L
Journal of Conflict Resolution	J Confl Resolution
Journal of Constitutional Law in Eastern and Central Europe	J Const LE & Cent Eur
Journal of Contemporary Health Law & Policy	J Contemp Health L & Pol'y
Journal of Contemporary Law	J Contemp L
Journal of Contemporary Legal Issues	J Contemp Leg Issues
Journal of Corporate Taxation	J Corp Tax'n
Journal of Corporation Law	J Corp L
Journal of Criminal Justice Education	J Crim J Educ
Journal of Criminal Law	J Crim L
Journal of Criminal Law & Criminology	J Crim L & Criminology
Journal of Dispute Resolution	J Disp Resol
Journal of Empirical Legal Studies	J Empirical Leg Stud
Journal of Energy Law & Policy	J Energy L & Pol'y
Journal of Energy, Natural Resources & Environmental Law	J Energy Nat Resources & Envtl L
Journal of Environmental Law	J Envtl L
Journal of Environmental Law & Practice	J Envtl L & Prac
Journal of Environmental Law & Litigation	J Envtl L & Litig
Journal of European Integration	J Eur Integration
Journal of Family Law	J Fam L
Journal of Gender, Race & Justice	J Gender Race & Just

Journal of Health and Hospital Law	J Health & Hosp L
Journal of Health Care Law and Policy	J Health Care L & Pol'y
Journal of Health Politics, Policy and Law	J Health Pol Pol'y & L
Journal of the History of International Law	J Hist Intl L
Journal of the Indian Law Institute	J Indian L Inst
Journal of Information, Law and Technology	J Inf L & Tech
Journal of Intellectual Property	J Intell Prop
Journal of Intellectual Property Law	J Intell Prop L
Journal of International Arbitration	J Intl Arb
Journal of International Banking Law and Regulation	J Intl Banking L & Reg
Journal of International Economic Law	J Intl Econ L
Journal of International Financial Markets, Institutions and Money	J Intl Fin Markets Inst & Money
Journal of International Law & Business	J Intl L & Bus
Journal of International Legal Studies	J Intl Leg Stud
Journal of International Taxation	J Intl Tax
Journal of International Wildlife Law and Policy	J Intl Wildlife L & Pol'y
Journal of Juvenile Law	J Juvenile L
Journal of Land Use and Environmental Law	J Land Use & Envtl L
Journal of Land, Resources and Environmental Law (*formerly / anciennement Journal of Energy, Natural Resources and Environmental Law*)	J Land Resources & Envtl L
Journal of Law and Commerce	JL & Com
Journal of Law and Economics	JL & Econ
Journal of Law, Economics and Organization	JL Econ & Org
Journal of Law and Education	JL & Educ
Journal of Law and Equality	JL & Equality
Journal of Law and Family Studies	JL & Fam Stud
Journal of Law and Health	JL & Health
Journal of Law, Information & Science	J L Info & Sci
Journal of Law and Policy	JL & Pol'y
Journal of Law and Politics	JL & Pol
Journal of Law and Religion	JL & Religion
Journal of Law and Social Policy	J L & Soc Pol'y
Journal of Law and Society	JL & Soc'y
Journal of Law in Society	JL in Soc'y
Journal of Law, Medicine and Ethics	JL Med & Ethics

Journal of Legal Advocacy and Practice	J Leg Advoc & Prac
Journal of Legal Economics	J Leg Econ
Journal of Legal Education	J Leg Educ
Journal of Legal History	J Leg Hist
Journal of Legal Medicine	J Leg Med
Journal of Legal Pluralism and Unofficial Law (formerly / anciennement Journal of Legal Pluralism)	J Leg Pluralism & Unofficial L
Journal of Legal Studies	J Leg Stud
Journal of Legislation	J Legis
Journal of Legislation and Public Policy	J Legis & Pub Pol'y
Journal of Maritime Law & Commerce	J Mar L & Com
Journal of Medicine and Law	J Med & L
Journal of Mineral Law & Policy	J Min L & Pol'y
Journal of Multistate Taxation and Incentives	J Multistate Tax'n & Incentives
Journal of Natural Resources & Environmental Law (formerly / anciennement Journal of Mineral Law & Policy)	J Nat Resources & Envtl L
Journal of Parliamentary and Political Law	JPPL
Journal of Personal Injury Law	J Pers Inj L
Journal of Pharmacy and Law	J Pharmacy & L
Journal of Planning and Environmental Law	J Plan & Envtl L
Journal of Politics and Law	J Politics & L
Journal of Private International Law	J Priv Intl L
Journal of Products Liability	J Prod Liab
Journal of Proprietary Rights	J Proprietary Rts
Journal of Public Policy, Administration and the Law	J Pub Pol'y Admin & L
Journal of Science & Technology Law	J Sci & Tech L
Journal of Small & Emerging Business Law	J Small & Emerging Bus L
Journal of Social Welfare Law	J Soc Welfare L
Journal of Social Welfare and Family Law (formerly / anciennement Journal of Social Welfare Law)	J Soc Welfare & Fam L
Journal of South Pacific Law	J South Pac L
Journal of Southern Legal History	J South Leg Hist
Journal of Space Law	J Space L
Journal of Taxation	J Tax'n
Journal of Technology Law & Policy	J Tech L & Pol'y
Journal of the Institute for the Study of Legal Ethics	J Inst for Study Leg Ethics

Appendices / Annexes

Journal of the Law Society of Scotland	JL Soc Scotland
Journal of the Legal Profession	J Leg Prof
Journal of the Patent & Trademark Office Society	J Pat & Trademark Off Soc'y
Journal of the Suffolk Academy of Law	J Suffolk Academy L
Journal of Transnational Law & Policy	J Transnat'l L & Pol'y
Journal of World Trade	J World Trade
Journal of World Trade Law, Economics and Policy	J World Trade L Econ & Pol'y
Juridical Review	Jurid Rev
Kansas Journal of Law & Public Policy	Kan JL & Pub Pol'y
Kansas Law Review	Kan L Rev
Kentucky Children's Rights Journal	Ky Children's Rts J
Kentucky Law Journal	Ky LJ
Korean Journal of International and Comparative Law	Korean J Intl & Comp L
La Raza Law Journal	La Raza LJ
Labor Law Journal	Lab LJ
Labor Lawyer	Lab Lawyer
Land and Water Law Review	Land & Water L Rev
Law and Business Review of the Americas (*formerly / anciennement NAFTA Law and Business Review of the Americas*)	L & Bus Rev Americas
Law and Contemporary Problems	Law & Contemp Probs
Law and Inequality	Law & Ineq
Law and History Review	L & Hist Rev
Law and Philosophy	Law & Phil
Law & Policy	Law & Pol'y
Law and Policy in International Business	Law & Pol'y Intl Bus
Law and Politics Book Review	Law & Pol Book Rev
Law and Practice of International Courts and Tribunals	Law & Prac Intl Cts & Trib
Law and Psychology Review	Law & Psychol Rev
Law and Sexuality: A Review of Lesbian and Gay Legal Issues	Law & Sexuality
Law and Social Inquiry	Law & Soc Inquiry
Law and Society Review	Law & Soc'y Rev
Law Librarian	Law Libr'n
Law Library Journal	Law Libr J
Law Office Management and Administration Report	Law Off Mgmt & Admin Rep
Law Office Technology Review	Law Off Tech Rev

Law Practice Management (formerly / anciennement Legal Economics)	Law Prac Mgmt
Law Quarterly Review	Law Q Rev
Law Review of Michigan State University Detroit College of Law	Law Rev Mich St U Det CL
Law Society Gazette (Law Society of Upper Canada)	L Soc'y Gaz
Law Society's Gazette and Guardian Gazette	L Soc'y Gaz & Guardian Gaz
Law, Technology and Insurance	Law Tech & Ins
Lawyers Journal (formerly / anciennement Pittsburgh Legal Journal)	Lawyers J
Legal Ethics (formerly / anciennement Ethics)	Leg Ethics
Legal History (formerly / anciennement Australian Journal of Legal History)	LH
Legal History Review	Leg Hist Rev
Legal Information Management	Leg Info Mgmt
Legal Issues of Economic / European Integration	LIEI
Legal Medical Quarterly	L Med Q
Legal Reference Services Quarterly	Leg Ref Serv Q
Legal Studies	LS
Legal Theory	Leg Theory
Leiden Journal of International Law	Leiden J Intl L
Lex Electronica : Revue du droit des technologies de l'information	Lex Electronica
Lloyd's Maritime and Commercial Law Quarterly	LMCLQ
Los Angeles Lawyer	LA Lawyer
Louisiana Bar Journal	La BJ
Louisiana Law Review	La L Rev
Lower Canada Jurist	LC Jurist
Lower Canada Law Journal	LCLJ
Loyola Consumer Protection Journal	Loy Con Prot J
Loyola Law Review (New Orleans)	Loy L Rev
Loyola of Los Angeles Entertainment Law Journal	Loy LA Ent LR
Loyola of Los Angeles International & Comparative Law Journal	Loy LA Intl & Comp LJ
Loyola of Los Angeles Law Review	Loy LA L Rev
Loyola Poverty Law Journal	Loy Poverty LJ
Loyola University of Chicago Law Journal	Loy U Chicago LJ
Maastricht Journal of European and Comparative Law	MJECL
Macquarie Jornal of International and Comparative Environmental Law	Macq J Intl & Comp Envtl L
Maine Law Review	Me L Rev

Malaya Law Review	Mal L Rev
Malayan Law Journal	MLJ
Manitoba Bar News	Man Bar N
Manitoba Law Journal	Man LJ
Maori Law Review	Maori L Rev
Marquette Intellectual Property Law Review	Marq Intell Prop L Rev
Marquette Law Review	Marq L Rev
Marquette Sports Law Review	Marq Sports L Rev
Maryland Journal of Contemporary Legal Issues	Md J Contemp Leg Issues
Maryland Journal of International Law (*formerly / anciennement Maryland Journal of International Law and Trade*)	Md J Intl L
Maryland Law Review	Md L Rev
Massachusetts Law Review	Mass L Rev
McGeorge Law Review *(formerly / anciennement Pacific Law Journal)*	McGeorge L Rev
McGill International Journal of Sustainable Development Law and Policy	JSDLP
McGill Journal of Law and Health (*formerly / anciennement McGill Health Law Publication*)	McGill JL & Health
McGill Law Journal	McGill LJ
Media Law & Policy	Media L & Pol'y
Medicine, Science and the Law	Med Sci Law
Medical Law Review	Med L Rev
Medicine & Law	Med & L
Medico-Legal Journal	Med Leg J
Melbourne University Law Review	Melbourne UL Rev
Mercer Law Review	Mercer L Rev
Michigan Bar Journal	Mich Bar J
Michigan Business Law Journal	Mich Bus LJ
Michigan Journal of Gender & Law	Mich J Gender & L
Michigan Journal of International Law	Mich J Intl L
Michigan Journal of Law Reform	Mich JL Reform
Michigan Journal of Race & Law	Mich J Race & L
Michigan Law & Policy Review	Mich L & Pol'y Rev
Michigan Law Journal	Mich LJ
Michigan Law Review	Mich L Rev
Michigan State University — DCL Journal of International Law and Practice (*formerly / anciennement Michigan State University — DCL Journal of*	MSU-DCL J Intl L & Prac

Appendices / Annexes

International Law)	
Michigan Telecommunications & Technology Law Review	Mich Telecomm & Tech L Rev
Military Law Review	Mil L Rev
Minnesota Journal of International Law (*formerly / anciennement Minnesota Journal of Global Trade*)	Minn J Intl L
Minnesota Journal of Law, Science, and Technology (*formerly / anciennement Minnesota Intellectual Property Review*)	Minn J L Sci & Tech
Minnesota Law Review	Minn L Rev
Mississippi College Law Review	Miss CL Rev
Mississippi Law Journal	Miss LJ
Mississippi Law Review	Miss L Rev
Missouri Environmental Law and Policy Review	Mo Envtl L & Pol'y Rev
Missouri Law Review	Mo L Rev
Modern Law Review	Mod L Rev
Monash University Law Review	Monash UL Rev
Monde Juridique	Monde Jur
Money Laundering Law Report	Money Laundering L Rep
Montana Law Review	Mont L Rev
Montana Lawyer	Mont Lawyer
Monthly Labor Review	Monthly Lab Rev
Murdoch University Electronic Journal of Law	Murdoch UEJL
NAFTA Law & Business Review of the Americas	NAFTA L & Bus Rev Am
National Banking Law Review	Nat'l Banking L Rev
National Black Law Journal	Nat'l Black LJ
National Insolvency Review	Nat'l Insolv Rev
National Institute of Justice Journal	Nat'l Inst Just J
National Journal of Constitutional Law	NJCL
National Journal of Sexual Orientation Law	Nat'l J Sex Orient L
National Law Journal	Nat'l LJ
National Law Review	Nat'l L Rev
National Real Property Law Review	Nat'l Real PLR
National Tax Journal	Nat'l Tax J
Natural Resources & Environment	Nat Resources & Env't
Natural Resources Journal	Nat Resources J
Naval Law Review	Naval L Rev

Nebraska Law Review	Neb L Rev
Neptunus: Maritime and Oceanic Law Review	Neptunus
Netherlands International Law Review	Nethl Intl L Rev
Netherlands Quarterly of Human Rights	Nethl QHR
New England International and Comparative Law Annual	New Eng J of Intl & Comp L Ann
New England Journal of International and Comparative Law (*formerly / anciennement New England International and Comparative Law Annual*)	New Eng J of Intl & Comp L
New England Journal of Medicine	New Eng J Med
New England Journal on Criminal & Civil Confinement	New Eng J Crim & Civ Confinement
New England Law Review	New Eng L Rev
New Europe Law Review	New Eur L Rev
New Jersey Lawyer	NJ Lawyer
New Law Journal	New LJ
New Mexico Law Review	NML Rev
New York City Law Review	NY City L Rev
New York International Law Review	NY Intl L Rev
New York Law Journal	NYLJ
New York Law Review	NYL Rev
New York Law School Journal of Human Rights	NYL Sch J Hum Rts
New York Law School Law Review	NYL Sch L Rev
New York State Bar Journal	NY St BJ
New York University Clinical Law Review	NYU Clin L Rev
New York University East European Constitutional Review	E Eur Const Rev
New York University Environmental Law Journal	NYU Envtl LJ
New York University International Journal of Constitutional Law	NYU Intl J Cont L
New York University Journal of International Law & Politics	NYUJ Intl L & Pol
New York University Journal of Legislation & Public Policy	NYUJ Legis & Pub Pol'y
New York University Law Review	NYUL Rev
New York University Review of Law & Social Change	NYU Rev L & Soc Change
New Zealand Law Journal	NZLJ
New Zealand Law Review	NZLR
New Zealand Universities Law Review	NZULR
Non-Profit Law Yearbook	Non-Profit L Yearbook
Non-State Actors and International Law	Non-State Actors & Intl L
Nordic Journal of International Law	Nordic J Intl L

North Carolina Central Law Review (*formerly / anciennement North Carolina Central Law Journal*)	NC Cent L Rev
North Carolina Journal of International Law & Commercial Regulation	NCJ Intl L & Com Reg
North Carolina Law Review	NCL Rev
North Dakota Law Review	NDL Rev
Northern Illinois University Law Review	N Ill UL Rev
Northern Ireland Legal Quarterly	N Ir Leg Q
Northern Kentucky Law Review	N Ky L Rev
Northwestern Journal of International Law & Business	Nw J Intl L & Bus
Northwestern University Law Review	Nw UL Rev
Notre Dame Journal of International and Comparative Law	Notre Dame J Intl & Comp L
Notre Dame Journal of Law Ethics and Public Policy	Notre Dame JL Ethics & Pub Pol'y
Notre Dame Law Review	Notre Dame L Rev
Nova Law Review	Nova L Rev
Ocean & Coastal Law Journal (*formerly / anciennement Territorial Sea Journal*)	Ocean & Coastal LJ
Ocean Development & International Law	Ocean Dev & Intl L
OECD Journal of Competition Law and Policy	OECD J Competition L & Pol'y
Ohio Northern University Law Review	Ohio NUL Rev
Ohio State Journal on Dispute Resolution	Ohio St J Disp Resol
Ohio State Law Journal	Ohio St LJ
Oklahoma City University Law Review	Okla City UL Rev
Oklahoma Law Review	Okla L Rev
Oregon Law Review	Or L Rev
Osaka University Law Review	Osaka UL Rev
Osgoode Hall Law Journal	Osgoode Hall LJ
Otago Law Review	Otago L Rev
Ottawa Law Review	Ottawa L Rev
Oxford Journal of Legal Studies	Oxford J Leg Stud
Oxford University Commonwealth Law Journal	OUCLJ
Pace Environmental Law Review	Pace Envtl L Rev
Pace International Law Review (*formerly / anciennement Pace Yearbook of International Law*)	Pace Intl L Rev Pace YB Intl L
Pace Law Review	Pace L Rev
Pacific Law Journal	Pac LJ
Pacific Rim Law and Policy Journal	Pac Rim L & Pol'y J

Pastwo i Prawo	Panstwo i Prawo
Patent Law Annual	Pat L Ann
Penn State Law Review	Penn St L Rev
Pepperdine Law Review	Pepp L Rev
Philippine Law Journal	Philippine LJ
Pittsburgh Legal Journal	Pittsburgh Leg J
Polish Contemporary Law	Polish Contemp L
Polish Yearbook of International Law	Polish YB Intl L
Potomac Law Review	Potomac L Rev
Probate and Property	Prob & Prop
Probate Law Journal	Prob LJ
Products Liability Law Journal	Prod Liab LJ
Provincial Judges Journal	Prov Judges J
Psychology, Public Policy & Law	Psychol Pub Pol'y & L
Public Contract Law Journal	Pub Cont LJ
Public Interest Law Review	Pub Int L Rev
Public Land Law Review	Pub Land L Rev
Public Land & Resources Law Review	Pub Land & Resources L Rev
Queen's Law Journal	Queen's LJ
Quinnipiac Health Law Journal	Quinnipiac Health LJ
Quinnipiac Law Review (*formerly / anciennement Bridgeport Law Review*)	Quinnipac L Rev
Quinnipiac Probate Law Journal (*formerly / anciennement Connecticut Probate Law Journal*)	Quinnipiac Prob LJ
Real Estate Law Journal	Real Est LJ
Real Property, Probate & Trust Journal	Real Prop Prob & Tr J
Recueil des Cours	Rec des Cours
Regent University Law Review	Regent UL Rev
Relations Industrielles (Industrial Relations)	RI
Responsabilité civile et assurances	Resp civ et assur
Restitution Law Review	RLR
Review of Central and East European Law	Rev Cent & E Eur L
Review of Constitutional Studies	Rev Const Stud
Review of European Community and International Environmental Law	RECIEL
Review of Banking and Financial Law (*formerly / anciennement Annual Review of Banking Law*)	Rev Banking & Fin L

Review of Litigation	Rev Litig
Revue administrative	Rev admin
Revue algérienne des sciences juridiques, économiques et politiques	Rev ASJEP
Revue belge de droit constitutionnel	RBDC
Revue belge de droit international	Rev b dr Intern
Revue canadienne des bibliothèques de droit	Rev can bibl dr
Revue canadienne de criminologie et de justice pénale	Rev can dr crim
Revue canadienne de droit communautaire	Rev can dr commun
Revue canadienne de droit de commerce	Rev can dr comm
Revue canadienne du droit de la concurrence	Rev Can dr con
Revue canadienne de droit familial	Rev Can dr fam
Revue canadienne de droit international	RCDI
Revue canadienne de droit pénal	RCDP
Revue canadienne droit et société	RCDS
Revue canadienne de propriété intellectuelle	RCPI
Revue canadienne du droit d'auteur	RCDA
Revue critique	Rev crit
Revue critique de droit international privé	Rev crit dr int privé
Revue critique de jurisprudence belge	RCJB
Revue critique de législation et de jurisprudence du Canada	RCLJ
Revue de la common law en français	RCLF
Revue de droit de l'ULB	Rev dr ULB
Revue de droit d'Ottawa	RD Ottawa
Revue de droit de l'Université de Sherbrooke	RDUS
Revue de droit de l'Université du Nouveau-Brunswick	RD UN-B
Revue de droit de McGill	RD McGill
Revue de droit des affaires internationales	RDAI
Revue de droit immobilier	RD imm
Revue de droit international de sciences diplomatiques et politiques	RDISDP
Revue de droit international et de droit comparé	Rev DI & DC
Revue de droit parlementaire et politique	RDPP
Revue de droit et santé de McGill (*anciennement / formerly Publication en droit de la santé de McGill*)	RD & santé McGill
Revue de droit social	RDS
Revue de droit uniforme	Rev dr unif

Revue de jurisprudence	R de J
Revue de l'arbitrage	Rev arb
Revue de législation et de jurisprudence	R de L
Revue de planification fiscale et financière (*anciennement / formerly Revue de planification fiscale et successorale*)	RPFF
Revue du Barreau	R du B
Revue du Barreau canadien	R du B can
Revue d'études constitutionnelles	R études const
Revue d'études juridiques	REJ
Revue d'histoire du droit	Rev hist dr
Revue d'histoire du droit international	Rev hist dr int
Revue d'intégration européenne	RIE
Revue du droit	R du D
Revue du droit de l'Union Européenne	RDUE
Revue du droit public et de la science politique en France et à l'étranger	RDP
Revue du Notariat	R du N
Revue de la Recherche Juridique	RRJ
Revue des Juristes de l'Ontario	Rev juristes de l'Ont
Revue des sociétés	Rev sociétés
Revue égyptienne de droit international	Rev EDI
Revue européenne de droit privé	RED privé
Revue européenne de droit public	RED public
Revue européenne de philosophie et de droit	REPD
Revue Femmes et Droit	RFD
Revue française de droit administratif	Rev fr dr admin
Revue française de droit aérien et spatial	Rev fr dr aérien
Revue française de droit constitutionnel	Rev fr dr constl
Revue générale de droit	RGD
Revue générale de droit international public	RGDIP
Revue générale du droit des assurances	RGDA
Revue hellénique de droit international	RHDI
Revue historique de droit français et étranger	RHD
Revue interdisciplinaire d'études juridiques	RIEJ
Revue internationale de droit comparé	RIDC
Revue internationale de droit économique	RIDE

Revue internationale de droit pénal	Rev IDP
Revue internationale de droit et politique de développement durable de McGill	RDPDD
Revue internationale de la Croix-Rouge	RICR
Revue internationale de la propriété industrielle et artistique	RIPIA
Revue internationale de politique criminelle	Rev IPC
Revue internationale du droit d'auteur	RIDA
Revue internationale de sémiotique juridique	RISJ
Revue juridique de l'environnement	RJE
Revue juridique des étudiants et étudiantes de l'Université Laval	RJEUL
Revue juridique La femme et le droit	Rev jur femme dr
Revue juridique Thémis	RJT
Revue juridique Thémis de l'Université de l'Université de Montréal (anciennement / formerly Revue juridique Thémis)	RJTUM
Revue nationale de droit constitutionnel	RNDC
Revue québécoise de droit international	RQDI
Revue suisse de droit international et de droit européen	RSDIE
Revue suisse de jurisprudence	RSJ
Revue trimestrielle de droit civil	RTD civ
Revue trimestrielle de droit commercial et de droit économique	RTDcom
Revue trimestrielle de droit européen	RTD eur
Revue universelle des droits de l'homme	RUDH
Richmond Journal of Global Law & Business	Rich J Global L & Bus
Richmond Journal of Law & Technology	Rich JL & Tech
Richmond Journal of Law and the Public Interest	Rich JL & Pub Int
Roger Williams University Law Review	Roger Williams U L Rev
Rutgers Computer & Technology Law Journal	Rutgers Computer & Tech LJ
Rutgers-Camden Law Journal	Rutgers-Camden LJ
Rutgers Journal of Law and Religion	Rutgers JL & Religion
Rutgers Law Journal (formerly / anciennement Rutgers-Camden Law Journal)	Rutgers LJ
Rutgers Law Review	Rutgers L Rev
Rutgers Race and the Law Review	Rutgers Race & L Rev
Saint John's Journal of Legal Commentary	St John's J Leg Comment
Saint John's Law Review	St John's L Rev
Saint Louis University Law Journal	Saint Louis ULJ

Appendices / Annexes

Saint Louis University Public Law Review	St Louis U Pub L Rev
Saint Louis-Warsaw Transatlantic Law Journal	St Louis-Warsaw Transatlantic LJ
Saint Mary's Law Journal	St Mary's LJ
Saint Thomas Law Review	St Thomas L Rev
San Diego Law Review	San Diego L Rev
San Joaquin Agricultural Law Review	San Joaquin Agric L Rev
Santa Clara Computer & High Technology Law Journal	Santa Clara Comp & High Tech LJ
Santa Clara Law Review	Santa Clara L Rev
Saskatchewan Bar Review	Sask Bar Rev
Saskatchewan Law Review	Sask L Rev
Scandinavian Studies in Law	Scand Stud L
Scottish Current Law Yearbook	Scot Curr LYB
Seattle University Law Review *(formerly / anciennement University of Puget Sound Law Review)*	Seattle UL Rev
Securities Regulation Law Journal	Sec Reg LJ
Seton Hall Constitutional Law Journal	Seton Hall Const LJ
Seton Hall Journal of Sports and Entertainment Law	Seton Hall J Sports & Ent L
Seton Hall Law Review	Seton Hall L Rev
Seton Hall Legislative Journal	Seton Hall Legis J
Sherbrooke Law Review	Sherbrooke L Rev
Singapore Academy of Law Annual Review	SAL Ann Rev
Singapore Academy of Law Journal	Sing Ac LJ
Singapore Journal of International and Comparative Law	Sing JICL
Singapore Journal of Legal Studies	Sing JLS
Singapore Law Review	Sing L Rev
Singapore Year Book of International Law	SYBIL
SMU Law Review	SMU L Rev
Social and Legal Studies	Soc & Leg Stud
South African Journal on Human Rights	SAJHR
South African Law Journal	SALJ
South African Yearbook of International Law	SAYBIL
South Carolina Environmental Law Journal	SC Envtl LJ
South Carolina Law Review	SCL Rev
South Dakota Law Review	SDL Rev
South Texas Law Review *(formerly / anciennement South Texas Law*	S Tex L Rev

Journal)	
Southern California Interdisciplinary Law Journal	S Cal Interdisciplinary LJ
Southern California Law Review	S Cal L Rev
Southern California Review of Law and Women's Studies	S Cal Rev L & Women's Stud
Southern California Sports & Entertainment Law Journal	S Cal Sports & Ent LJ
Southern Illinois University Law Journal	S Ill ULJ
Southern University Law Review	SUL Rev
Southwestern Journal of International Law *(formerly / anciennement Southwestern Journal of Law and Trade in the Americas)*	Sw J Intl L
Southwestern Law Review	Sw L Rev
Space Policy	Space Pol'y
Special Lectures of the Law Society of Upper Canada	Spec Lect LSUC
Sports Lawyers Journal	Sports Lawyer J
Stanford Environmental Law Journal	Stan Envtl LJ
Stanford Journal of Animal Law and Policy	Stan J Animal L & Pol'y
Stanford Journal of International Law	Stan J Intl L
Stanford Journal of Law, Business & Finance	Stan JL Bus & Fin
Stanford Journal of Legal Studies	Stan J Legal Stud
Stanford Law & Policy Review	Stan L & Pol'y Rev
Stanford Law Review	Stan L Rev
Stanford Technology Law Review	Stan Tech L Rev
Statute Law Review	Stat L Rev
Stetson Law Review	Stetson L Rev
Suffolk Journal of Trial and Appellate Advocacy	Suffolk J Trial & Appellate Advoc
Suffolk Transnational Law Review *(formerly / anciennement Suffolk Transnational Law Journal)*	Suffolk Transnat'l L Rev
Suffolk University Law Review	Suffolk UL Rev
Supreme Court Economic Review	Sup Ct Econ Rev
Supreme Court Review	Sup Ct Rev
Supreme Court Economic Review	Sup Ct Econ Rev
Supreme Court Law Review	SCLR
Sydney Law Review	Sydney L Rev
Syracuse Journal of International Law & Commerce	Syracuse J Intl L & Com
Syracuse Law Review	Syracuse L Rev
Syracuse University Law and Technology Journal	Syracuse UL & TJ

Tax Law Review	Tax L Rev
Telecommunications & Space Journal	Telecom & Space J
Temple Environmental Law & Technology Journal	Temp Envtl L & Tech J
Temple International & Comparative Law Journal	Temp Intl & Comp LJ
Temple Law Review (formerly / anciennement Temple Law Quarterly)	Temp L Rev
Temple Political & Civil Rights Law Review	Temp Pol & Civ Rts L Rev
Tennessee Law Review	Tenn L Rev
Texas Bar Journal	Tex BJ
Texas Journal on Civil Liberties and Civil Rights	Tex J on CL & CR
Texas Hispanic Journal of Law and Policy (formerly / anciennement Hispanic Law Journal)	Tex Hispanic J L & Pol'y
Texas Intellectual Property Law Journal	Tex Intell Prop LJ
Texas International Law Journal	Tex Intl LJ
Texas Journal of Business Law	Tex J Bus L
Texas Journal of Women & the Law	Tex J Women & L
Texas Law Review	Tex L Rev
Texas Review of Law & Politics	Tex Rev L & Pol
Texas Wesleyan Law Review	Tex Wesleyan L Rev
Texas Tech Law Review	Tex Tech L Rev
Theoretical Inquiries in Law	Theor Inq L
Third World Legal Studies	Third World Legal Stud
Thomas Jefferson Law Review	Thomas Jefferson L Rev
Thomas M Cooley Journal of Practical & Clinical Law	TM Cooley J Prac & Clinical L
Thomas M Cooley Law Review	TM Cooley L Rev
Thurgood Marshall Law Review	T Marshall L Rev
Tilburg Law Review	Tilburg L Rev
Toledo Journal of Great Lakes' Law, Science & Policy	Tol J Great Lakes' L Sci & Pol'y
Tolley's Communications Law	Tolley's Comm L
Tort Trial and Insurance Practice Law Journal (**formerly / anciennement Tort & Insurance Law Journal**)	Tort Trial & Ins Prac LJ
Touro Environmental Law Journal	Touro Envtl LJ
Touro International Law Review	Touro Intl L Rev
Touro Law Review	Touro L Rev
Trade Law Topics	Trade L Topics
Transnational Law & Contemporary Problems	Transnat'l L & Contemp Probs

Transportation Law Journal	Transp LJ
Travaux de l'Association Henri Capitant des amis de la culture juridique française	Travaux de l'assoc Henri Capitant
Tribal Law Journal	Tribal LJ
Tribune des droits humaine	Trib dr hum
Trust Law International	Trust L Intl
Trusts & Estates	Trusts & Est
Tulane Environmental Law Journal	Tul Envtl LJ
Tulane European & Civil Law Forum	Tul Eur & Civ LF
Tulane Journal of International & Comparative Law	Tul J Intl & Comp L
Tulane Journal of Law and Sexuality	Tul JL & Sexuality
Tulane Law Review	Tul L Rev
Tulane Maritime Law Journal	Tul Mar LJ
Tulsa Journal of Comparative & International Law	Tulsa J Comp & Intl L
Tulsa Law Journal	Tulsa LJ
UC Davis Journal of International Law & Policy	UC Davis J Intl L & Pol'y
UC Davis Law Review	UC Davis L Rev
UCLA Asian Pacific American Law Journal	UCLA Asian Pac Am LJ
UCLA Journal of Law and Technology	UCLA JL & T
UCLA Entertainment Law Review	UCLA Ent L Rev
UCLA Journal of Environmental Law & Policy	UCLA J Envtl L & Pol'y
UCLA Journal of International Law and Foreign Affairs	UCLA J Intl L & Foreign Aff
UCLA Law Review	UCLA L Rev
UCLA Pacific Basin Law Journal	UCLA Pac Basin LJ
UCLA Women's Law Journal	UCLA Women's LJ
UMKC Law Review	UMKC L Rev
UNCTAD Law Review: Journal on Law, Trade and Development	UNCTAD L Rev
Uniform Commercial Code Law Journal	Unif Comm Code L J
Uniform Law Conference of Canada (Proceedings)	Unif L Conf Proc
Uniform Law Review	Unif L Rev
United States-Mexico Law Journal	US-Mex LJ
University of Arkansas at Little Rock Law Review	U Ark Little Rock L Rev
University of Baltimore Intellectual Property Law Journal	U Balt Intell Prop LJ
University of Baltimore Journal of Environmental Law	U Balt J Envtl L
University of Baltimore Law Forum	U Balt LF

University of Baltimore Law Review	U Balt L Rev
University of British Columbia Law Review	UBC L Rev
University of California at Davis Law Review	UC Davis L Rev
University of Chicago Law Review	U Chicago L Rev
University of Chicago Law School Roundtable	U Chicago L Sch Roundtable
University of Chicago Legal Forum	U Chicago Legal F
University of Cincinnati Law Review	U Cin L Rev
University of Colorado Law Review	U Colo L Rev
University of Dayton Law Review	U Dayton L Rev
University of Detroit Mercy Law Review	U Det Mercy L Rev
University of Florida Journal of Law & Public Policy	U Fla JL & Pub Pol'y
University of Ghana Law Journal	UGLJ
University of Hawaii Law Review	U Haw L Rev
University of Illinois Law Review	U Ill L Rev
University of Kansas Law Review	U Kan L Rev
University of Louisville Law Review (*formerly /anciennement Brandeis Law Journal*)	U Louisville L Rev
University of Malaya Law Review	U Mal L Rev
University of Memphis Law Review	U Mem L Rev
University of Miami Business Law Review	U Miami Bus L Rev
University of Miami Entertainment & Sports Law Review	U Miami Ent & Sports L Rev
University of Miami Inter-American Law Review	U Miami Inter-Am L Rev
University of Miami International & Comparative Law Review *(formerly / anciennement University of Miami Yearbook of International Law)*	U Miami Intl & Comp L Rev
University of Miami Law Review	U Miami L Rev
University of Michigan Journal of Law Reform	U Mich JL Ref
University of New Brunswick Law Journal	UNBLJ
University of New South Wales Law Journal	UNSWLJ
University of Pennsylvania Journal of Constitutional Law	U Pa J Const L
University of Pennsylvania Journal of International Law (*formerly / anciennement **University of Pennsylvania Journal of International Economic Law**)*	U Pa J Intl L
University of Pennsylvania Journal of Labor and Employment Law	U Pa J Lab & Employment L
University of Pennsylvania Law Review	U Pa L Rev
University of Pittsburgh Law Review	U Pitt L Rev
University of Queensland Law Jounal	UQLJ

University of Richmond Law Review	U Rich L Rev
University of San Francisco Law Review	USF L Rev
University of San Francisco Journal of Law and Social Challenges	USF JL & Soc Challenges
University of San Francisco Maritime Law Journal	USF Mar LJ
University of Tasmania Law Review	U Tasm L Rev
University of the District of Columbia Law Review *(formerly / anciennement District of Columbia Law Review)*	UDC L Rev
University of Toledo Law Review	U Tol L Rev
University of Toronto Faculty of Law Review	UT Fac L Rev
University of Toronto Law Journal	UTLJ
University of Western Australia Law Review	UWA L Rev
University of Western Ontario Law Review	UWO L Rev
Upper Canada Law Journal	UCLJ
Utah Bar Journal	Utah BJ
Valparaiso University Law Review	Val U L Rev
Vanderbilt Journal of Entertainment Law & Practice	Vand J Ent L & Prac
Vanderbilt Journal of Transnational Law	Vand J Transnat'l L
Vanderbilt Law Review	Vand L Rev
Vermont Bar Journal	Vt BJ
Vermont Journal of Environmental Law *(formerly / anciennement Res Communes: Vermont's Journal of the Environment)*	VJEL
Victoria University of Wellington Law Review	VUWLR
Vietnam Law & Legal Forum	Vietnam L & Legal Forum
Villanova Environmental Law Journal	Vill Envtl LJ
Villanova Law Review	Vill L Rev
Villanova Sports and Entertainment Law Journal	Vill Sports & Ent LJ
Virginia Environmental Law Journal	Va Envtl LJ
Virginia Journal of International Law	Va J Intl L
Virginia Journal of Law & Technology	Va JL & Tech
Virginia Journal of Social Policy & Law	Va J Soc Pol'y & L
Virginia Journal of Sports and the Law	Va J Sports & L
Virginia Law Review	Va L Rev
Virginia Tax Review	Va Tax Rev
Waikato Law Review: Taumauri	Waikato L Rev
Wake Forest Law Review	Wake Forest L Rev

Appendices / Annexes

Waseda Bulletin of Comparative Law	Waseda Bull Comp L
Washburn Law Journal	Washburn LJ
Washington & Lee Race & Ethnic Ancestry Law Journal *(formerly / anciennement Race & Ethnic Ancestry Law Journal)*	Wash & Lee Race & Ethnic Ancestry LJ
Washington & Lee Law Review	Wash & Lee L Rev
Washington Law Review	Wash L Rev
Washington University Journal of Law & Policy	Wash UJL & Pol'y
Washington University Journal of Urban and Contemporary Law	Wash UJ Urb & Contemp L
Washington University Law Quarterly	Wash ULQ
Wayne Law Review	Wayne L Rev
Web Journal of Current Legal Issues	Web JCLI
West Virginia Journal of Law & Technology	W Va J L & T
West Virginia Law Review	W Va L Rev
West Virginia Lawyer	W Va Law
Western Law Review (San Francisco)	West L Rev
Western Law Review (Canada)	West LR
Western Ontario Law Review	West Ont L Rev
Western New England Law Review	W New Eng L Rev
Western State University Law Review	W St U L Rev
Widener Journal of Public Law	Widener J Pub L
Widener Law Symposium Journal	Widener L Symp J
Willamette Journal of International Law & Dispute Resolution	Willamette J Intl & Disp Resol
Willamette Law Review	Willamette L Rev
William & Mary Bill of Rights Journal	Wm & Mary Bill Rts J
William & Mary Environmental Law & Policy Review	Wm & Mary Envtl L & Pol'y Rev
William & Mary Journal of Women and the Law	Wm & Mary J Women & L
William & Mary Law Review	Wm & Mary L Rev
William Mitchell Law Review	Wm Mitchell L Rev
Windsor Review of Legal and Social Issues	Windsor Rev Legal Soc Issues
Windsor Yearbook of Access to Justice	Windsor YB Access Just
Wisconsin Environmental Law Journal	Wis Envtl LJ
Wisconsin International Law Journal	Wis Intl LJ
Wisconsin Law Review	Wis L Rev
Wisconsin Women's Law Journal	Wis Women's LJ
Women's Rights Law Reporter	Women's Rts L Rep

World Arbitration and Mediation Report	World Arb & Mediation Rep
World Arbitration and Mediation Review (*formerly / anciennement World Arbitration and Mediation Report*)	World Arb & Mediation Rev
World Trade and Arbitration Materials	WTAM
Wyoming Law Review (*formerly / anciennement Land and Water Law Review*)	Wyo L Rev
Yale Human Rights and Development Law Journal	Yale Human Rts & Dev LJ
Yale Journal of International Law	Yale J Intl L
Yale Journal of Law & Feminism	Yale JL & Feminism
Yale Journal of Law & the Humanities	Yale JL & Human
Yale Journal on Regulation	Yale J Reg
Yale Law & Policy Review	Yale L & Pol'y Rev
Yale Law Journal	Yale LJ
Yearbook: Commercial Arbitration	YB Comm Arb
Yearbook of Air and Space Law	YB Air & Sp L
Yearbook of Copyright and Media Law	YB Copyright & Media L
Yearbook of European Law	YB Eur L
Yearbook of European Environment Law	YB Eur Env L
Yearbook of International Law	YB Intl L
Yearbook of International Environmental Law	YB Intl Env L
Yearbook of International Humanitarian Law	YB Intl Human L
Yearbook of Maritime Law	YB Marit L
Yearbook of the Canadian Bar Association	YB CBA
Yearbook of the European Convention on Human Rights	YB Eur Conv HR
Yearbook of the Institute of International Law	YB Inst Intl L
Yearbook of the International Court of Justice	YBICJ
Yearbook of the United Nations	YBUN
Yearbook on Human Rights	YBHR

APPENDIX E / ANNEX E

E. ONLINE DATABASES ~ BASES DE DONNÉES EN LIGNE

Abreviations ~ Abréviations

Australasian Legal Information Institute	AustLII
Azimut (produced by / produit par SOQUIJ)	Azimut
British and Irish Legal Information Institute	BAILII
Butterworths Services	Butterworths
Canadian Legal Information Institute / Institut canadien d'information juridique	CanLII
Commonwealth Legal Information Institute	CommonLII
Hong Kong Legal Information Institute	HKLII
Justis	Justis
KluwerArbitration	Kluwer
Lawnet (Singapore)	Lawnet
Legal Information Institute	LII
Legifrance	Legifrance
LexisNexis	Lexis
LexUM	LexUM
New Zealand Legal Information Institute	NZLII
Pacific Islands Legal Information Institute	PacLII
Qualisult Systems	Qualisult
Quicklaw	QL
Répertoire électronique de jurisprudence du Barreau	REJB
Southern African Legal Information Institute	SAFLII
Taxnet Pro	Taxnet Pro
Westlaw (US)	WL
Westlaw Canada	WL Can

Appendices / Annexes

Westlaw International	WL Int
Westlaw (UK)	WL UK
Westlaw Next	WLNext
Westlaw Next Canada	WLNext Can
World Legal Information Institute	WorldLII